D1406873

LANGUAGE ARTS IN THE ELEMENTARY SCHOOL: READINGS

THE LIPPINCOTT CURRICULUM AND INSTRUCTION SERIES

Under the Editorship of

ALEXANDER FRAZIER

The Ohio State University

LANGUAGE ARTS IN THE ELEMENTARY SCHOOL: READINGS

Edited by

Hal D. Funk

University of North Carolina at Greensboro

DeWayne Triplett

Northern Illinois University at De Kalb

J. B. LIPPINCOTT COMPANY

Philadelphia

New York

Toronto

For Pat and Helen

ISBN—0-397-47211-0
Library of Congress Catalogue Card Number: 75-155876
Printed in the United States of America

Cover design by Jeanette Renich
Interior design by Mixed Media

Contents

Preface

The quality of language arts instruction in the elementary school determines, to a great extent, the success of each student's future educational endeavors. Learning language, however, involves more than perfecting the acts of listening, speaking, reading, and writing. Language is the medium of thought, communication, and feeling. It enables one to learn, to interact, and to develop self-awareness. Thus, it would be impossible to overemphasize the necessity for each elementary school teacher to understand our evolving English language and to be able to guide children's linguistic learning.

This anthology brings together selected articles concerning some of the more relevant aspects of language arts instruction in the elementary school. In addition to the inclusion of topics on methodology, the editors have attempted to give specific emphasis to philosophical and curricular issues which are fundamental to a pedagogically sound language arts program. With respect to the latter considerations, articles are included which discuss (1) the objectives of language arts instruction, (2) the background of our language heritage, (3) the cultural influences on children's language, and (4) the evaluation of language arts learnings. Because of space limitations some areas of the language arts curriculum are not covered as thoroughly as might be desired. However, the scope of the selections is broad, and almost every aspect of the language arts program is touched upon except reading instruction.

Essentially, the readings in this book were chosen to meet the needs of preservice and in-service teachers and curriculum developers who wish to keep abreast of contemporary trends in the elementary school language arts. This anthology may be used as an introductory language arts methods textbook or as a supplementary textbook for a graduate course or seminar. Since many of the articles emphasize practical suggestions and solutions to instructional problems, the readings in this volume could also be used in a general methods course.

The editors have attempted to select articles for each section that are well-written, of current interest, and which also make a valuable contribution to the language arts field. Most of the articles have been written by recognized authorities in the field of education. An introduction giving an overview of the content has been written for each section of the book in an effort to establish the relevance of that particular area to the total language arts program. A comprehensive bibliography is also provided at the end of each section to enable the reader to pursue each of these areas in greater depth.

Each division of the book focuses on the fundamental ideas that contribute to the development of a unified program in the language arts. Part I is concerned with an overview of the elementary school language arts program, its objectives, both general and behavioral, and how they may serve as the basis for an integrated program involving various modes of pupil inquiry. Part II is designed to impart a general orientation and sense of the magnitude of the historical and theoretical dimensions of language study, while Part III centers around children's linguistic competence and the need for teachers to consider language diversity when teaching basic skills of literacy. Part IV emphasizes the relationships of listening and speaking and elaborates on ways they may be taught. Part V endeavors to relate the material discussed in prior sections to the development of various modes of written expression. The concluding section of the book, Part VI, includes a series of articles which suggest means for evaluating language arts teaching.

The editors are indebted to the many authors and publishers who granted permission to use the material presented in this book.

PART ONE
Curriculum Perspectives in the Language Arts

A.
Overview

As man enters each new year and each new decade, he is disposed to reflect upon the past and to speculate about the future. In so doing he may evaluate his progress and redefine his goals. A clearer prediction for the future often results when historic benchmarks are assessed for their effect on contemporary thought. The decade of the sixties hosted several linguistic happenings that may portend the state of English language arts in the seventies.

One event which influenced the thinking and actions of educators in almost every discipline was the September 1959 Woods Hole Conference on Cape Cod which was attended by thirty-five science scholars. As an outgrowth of their deliberations, Jerome S. Bruner published *The Process of Education* in 1960, and he elaborated further upon his philosophy of education in his 1966 book, *Toward a Theory of Instruction.* His writings emphasize the structure of knowledge and its relationship to cognitive processes in teaching and learning. He advanced the idea of the "inquiry" or "discovery" method, explaining how it might be interpreted in a developmental pattern referred to as the spiral curriculum. It is not clear at this point what impact these concepts have had on people's problem-solving abilities, but there is considerable evidence of their application in books and curricular materials prepared by public schools and Curriculum Study Centers throughout the country.

A second event, the Anglo-American Seminar on the Teaching of English held at Dartmouth College in 1966, generated considerable discussion and writing in the United States and England. Several publications focussed on the concerns of this conference; among them are Herbert J. Muller's *The Uses of English* (New York: Holt, Rinehart and Winston, 1967), and John Dixon's *Growth Through English* (Reading, England: NATE, 1967), plus a number of National Council of Teachers of English publications. These writings emphasize the British educational philosophy that stresses the central importance of each child's self-perception—his interests, experiences, feelings—all of which may form the basis for further insights into himself and others. Some core components of a typical learner-centered program include pupil talk, dramatization, role-playing, and personal writing.

A third development, planning educational programs for the culturally different, is actually the product of several influences. A primary force is the Center for Applied Linguistics which has disseminated research results and writing over the entire range of regional and social dialects. In response to the demands of American ethnic groups who are seeking their own cultural identity, authors of textbooks and language programs are beginning to use research into minority group dialects and neglected ethnic literature. Examples of these concerns are reflected in the report of the 1965 NCTE Task Force on Teaching English to the disadvantaged, *Language Programs for the Disadvantaged.* Further awareness of racial groups was evidenced by the NCTE Board of Directors and Executive Committee in 1969 when they established a Task Force on Racism and Bias in the Teaching of English.

The preceding events influenced language programs of the sixties, giving them greater scope and character. But will they continue to shape English language programs in the seventies? In the overview that follows, an eminent scholar prophesies a revolution in the teaching of our language and proceeds to tell us how it will be taught 203 years following the American Revolution.

1.

English Language Programs for the Seventies

J. N. Hook

Come with me, please, into the year 1979, the two hundred and third anniversary of the American Revolution. We shall visit certain classrooms designed to effect another kind of revolution, a revolution in the teaching of the English language—the language of George Washington, of Chaucer, Shakespeare, Milton, of Lincoln and Churchill and Kennedy, the first or second language of almost a billion of the earth's inhabitants in 1979.

In the 1950's and 1960's it became increasingly apparent to Earthlings that for mutual ease of communication it was highly desirable for most or all to share a common tongue. Once Latin had served this purpose for the well-educated of the so-called civilized world, meaning, in the semantics of that time, in main the countries of Western Europe. A scholar could travel in England, Germany, France, Italy, Greece, parts of Middle Europe, and Scandinavia, and be understood by fellow-scholars in all those countries because he and they both knew Latin. He could not, however, speak with the peasants or the other unschooled ones. Some internationally minded businessmen also used Latin as a medium for conducting their affairs. Gradually, though, the use of Latin declined. In the days of Spanish power and then of French power, pockets of Spanish and French speakers came into existence almost around the globe. And then explorers from some islands just west of the European mainland began probing the far corners of the earth. Many of them settled abroad—in North America, in parts of South America, in Africa, in parts of Asia, in Australia. Their language, English, became the official tongue in many of these lands. And people in other lands found it useful for them to learn it, too. By the early 1960's perhaps as many as a third of the world's inhabitants had at least a smattering of English. In Scandinavian countries, every child studied it, because English was the language of trade, and Scandinavia was dependent on trade. In Russia it was more widely studied than any other foreign language. Japan had eighty thousand teachers of English, four-fifths as many as taught it in the secondary schools of the United States. In India, even after independence, English was a standard school subject. In Peru and Columbia public address systems broadcast English lessons to people sitting on benches in the town square. English lessons appeared in hundreds of daily papers around the world. English was one of the official languages of the United Nations. And in 1966, William Benton,

Reprinted from *Illinois English Bulletin* 57:1-13 (October 1969), by permission of author and publisher.

United States ambassador to UNESCO, recommended that English be designated the semi-official second language of the world, despite the outraged protests of Charles DeGaulle of France, who believed that French should be chosen.

Through the early 1960's the United States government had become increasingly aware that language could be a force for international understanding and had begun expending money on teaching English abroad. It set up libraries in foreign countries; some of them were pillaged and burned, but others remained. It sent teachers abroad to teach other teachers some of the best ways to give instruction in English; they went to Africa, to Asia, to South America, to the islands of the Pacific. Its soldiers picked up a few words of the languages of the countries in which they were stationed, and the natives of those countries learned still more English. The Center for Applied Linguistics encouraged scholarly research in the learning and teaching of English while it helped Americans to learn how to learn a foreign language. The United States Information Agency sponsored series of English textbooks for study abroad, and provided leadership so that emerging nations of Africa or developing nations of Asia and South America could master this tool of international communication and trade. Even Russia helped in the teaching of English; she prepared her own English textbooks for use abroad, with built-in lessons in opposition to "American imperialism."

By 1979 the work of some fifteen or more years has begun to show results. An American or British traveler can go almost anywhere in the world and be confident that he can order a meal or talk about the weather and be understood. Only in the remote vastnesses of China or central Africa might he find no one with whom to converse.

The method used in teaching English to the hundreds of millions in foreign countries emphasizes the oral language. This is the natural way to learn a language. The infant obviously does not learn his native language by studying its grammar and reading it. His mother does not say to him, "A noun is the name of a person, place, or thing." Instead, she says, "Ball. See the ball. Do you want the ball? This is a ball. I'll roll the ball to you. Roll the ball to me." After a while, the infant says, "Baw," and he's on his way. Soon he, too—through imitation first of words and then of the sentence patterns he hears—will be saying, "Roll the ball." Later, as he grows older, his sentences become more complex. By the time he reaches school age, he is using most of the sentence forms that adults use, yet he has not encountered a grammatical term and probably has not read more than a few words.

The teaching of English in foreign countries has influenced the teaching of English in the United States in 1979. Language is basically a spoken thing. Even the word *language* goes back to the Latin word for *tongue*, not to the Latin word for *pen*. But during most of our educational history, after the first or second grade, we ceased emphasizing the spoken language and stressed the written and printed forms. Study of grammar, the description of the language, is abstract. Dora V. Smith has pointed out that the technical study of grammar is as abstruse a subject as the calculus in mathematics. But in years gone by, even elementary school youngsters have had to parse and diagram sentences. Now, though, in 1979, the emphasis has changed. In the grades, children practice orally the patterns that are least familiar or most difficult for them. They play with sentences, seeing which parts fit together, which are moveable, which incapable of being shifted from one place to another. They supplement oral practice, in the lower grades, by "rolling readers," developed in part by Priscilla Tyler. These are small cubes, with a single word printed on each face. The child rolls the cubes in a certain order, a sentence results. He reads the sentence, rolls again, a different sentence comes up. But he finds that if he changes the order in which he rolls the cubes, there is no sentence—just nonsense. The seven-year old thus learns a basic fact about the English language: Word order is important. It is the guiding principle of the whole language. In earlier instruction, often based on the teaching of Latin, word order was not stressed. For that reason, a number of problems in sentence structure remained with children for the rest of their lives. Dangling modifiers, squinting modifiers, and countless other kinds of incoherence result from lack of a clear understanding of the significance of word order.

Matters of usage, in 1979, are also approached largely through oral practice. The child whose parents say "Me and him was walkin' along," the experience of many years has shown us, is not likely to be converted to "He and I were walking along" by grammatical analysis of the pronouns and the verb. But when, through games and oral repetition, the child has heard many times "He and I were walking along," that sentence comes to seem natural to the child; he begins using it and other sentences like it in school; eventually it becomes part of his language. At home he may still conform to the usage of his parents, because conformity is important to him. He feels the need to belong in his environment, and language conformity is essential to belonging.

This brings us to another facet of the English language teaching of the 1970's. In earlier times, when a child said "ain't" or "Me and him was walkin' along," his teacher told him that his language was wrong. "There's no such word as *ain't*," many teachers said. The child, in his infinite wisdom, knew better; of course there was such a word as *ain't*; he heard it every day; he could even find it in the dictionary. And why should the teacher say that it was wrong to say "Me and him was walkin' along?" His parents said things like that. His friends said them. Why should the teacher say that his parents were wrong? What made the teacher's language always right and his own language and that of his world wrong?

The schools of the 1970's, in contrast, do not make much use of the words *right* and *wrong*. The teacher's do talk a lot about dialects. They say that everyone speaks a dialect. In fact, every person speaks at least a little differently from every other person. He has his own personal dialect, or idolect. Dialects vary according to regions of a county. They vary also in smaller regions. Chicago has its own speech peculiarities; so has Philadelphia and New York and Minneapolis. Rural Minnesota has some speech oddities infrequently heard in the Twin Cities. In England, when one travels from one shire to another, he notices considerable change in dialect. In Yorkshire, different parts of the shire have very different speech habits. So dialects vary with place. Dialects vary also with time. Middle English differs in many ways from Modern English; the double negative, now largely frowned upon in formal English, was a perfectly acceptable construction in Chaucer's day. Old English is almost as different from Modern English as if it were a foreign language. Even eighteenth-century English varied in many ways from Modern English. In pronunciation for instance, one usually heard *tay* for *tea*, *jine* for *join*, *Lunnon* for *London*, *goold* for *gold*. In syntax, the eighteenth century seldom used the passive voice; one did not say, "The house is being built." Instead, it was "The house is building."

So students are shown that dialects differ according to geography and according to time. They differ also in other ways. We shift dialects depending upon where we are and whom we are talking with. The language we use at a ball game is not the same as that we use on a more formal occasion. And we use somewhat different language in talking to a child than we use in talking to a grandmother, a still different one in talking to a grandfather, and others when we are talking with a lawyer or a bank president or a possible employer.

Dialects vary also in prestige, we teach our children. In the courts of kings in centuries gone by, the language of the king and his courtiers was the most prestigious. It is said that the lisped Spanish *c,* such as in *Barcelona,* is due to a speech defect of a Spanish king; his courtiers wanted to talk as the king did, and other people imitated the courtiers, so Spaniards even today say *Barcelona.* In the United States, too, some dialect forms are more prestigious than others. *Ain't* isn't wrong, but it happens that in the twentieth century it is frowned upon by most users of the prestige dialect. "Me and him was walkin' along" happens now not to be prestigious, though it is perfectly clear. The etiquette of the prestige dialect demands that as a rule we refer to the other person before we refer to ourselves; it also says that *him* and *me* are used in some parts of a sentence but not in other parts. It also says that in some circumstances we use one form of *be (was)*; in other circumstances we use another form *(were).*

The prestige dialect is no more "right" than any other, but there are many times when we should be able to use it. We let our students realize that this dialect will be demanded if they go to college, that many employers insist upon it, that front doors open to its users, and that users of nonprestigious dialects may have to go to the back of the house. We do not try to eradicate the children's nonprestigious dialect forms. We do not say that their parents who use those forms are in the wrong, but we do try to make it possible for them to know the prestigious ones, to practice using them, and hopefully to switch as easily to these forms as they switch dialects when they go to a ball game or talk with someone not their own age.

Teachers in the 1970's teach grammar, too. The developments here have been very interesting. For years teachers taught what has come to be called traditional grammar. This was essentially a grammar based upon Latin, despite the fact that English is a Teutonic language, not a Romance language. It had strengths and weaknesses. Its strength was that it was a relatively complete system, developed over many years, and capable of describing—after a fashion—almost any sentence in the language. Its weaknesses were that its classifications were sometimes faulty, as when schoolbooks placed words like *very* and words like *suddenly* into the same category, adverbs, even though those words are used in quite unlike ways; second, the inadequacy of many of the definitions, much as "A sentence is a group of words expressing a complete thought" (a sentence is not necessarily a group of words, and nobody knows what a complete thought is); third, its lack of attention to language as basically spoken; and fourth, its failure to recognize the kernel sentences from which all others are formed.

The structuralist grammarians emphasized the oral language. They discovered elaborate principles of phonology, including the supersegmentals of stress, pitch, and juncture that contribute so much to our making ourselves understood when we speak. They consistently stressed form rather than meaning; whereas the traditionalist defined a noun, for example, in terms of its meaning, the structuralist defined it in terms of the form changes and the structures, the environments, that are characteristic of the noun. They paid much less attention to syntax than to morphology. This, together with their lack of emphasis on meaning, was their greatest weakness.

The generative or transformational grammarian, in contrast, emphasized syntax. He found that basically the English sentence is a simple statement, a kernel. Through a number of changes that can be precisely described (changes called transformations), negative structures, questions, and other variations are possible, but all are built upon a relatively small number of kernels. The transformationalists have described sentence structure in such precise mathematical terms that now, in the 1970's, they have made machine translation not only possible but also readable and idiomatic, and they have programmed computers that can "write" complex explanations at unbelievable speeds or even compose formula stories and write poetry. Unfortunately for teaching purposes, transformational grammar has become so complex that only graduate mathematicians and linguistic specialists can understand it, and none of them all of it.

So the schools have had to form their own grammar, and the task is still going on. Our school grammar in 1979 is a blend of traditional, structural, and transformational. Traditional has supplied much of the terminology; structural has presented the oral elements—especially pitch, stress, and juncture—and has clarified morphology; transformational has provided most of the syntax.

Some false conceptions about the reasons for teaching grammar have been eliminated. Teachers used to believe that if students could cerebrally comprehend grammar, they would inevitably write and speak "better." Despite many studies that revealed that grammatical understanding was no guarantee of "good" usage, teachers kept on doggedly, sure in their own minds that the researchers must be wrong. We now regard grammar as basically a cultural study. Language is one of man's greatest possessions, and any person who claims to be educated should know how it works. Beyond that, some still believe, grammatical knowledge may help some students to become more at home with some of the less usual sentence forms, and to improve their own writing on the more sophisticated levels. Also, a detailed knowledge of grammar contributes to ease in reading poetry or other difficult literature.

So in 1979 we still teach grammar, but not for exactly the same reasons that we once did.

The boundaries between grammar and rhetoric have meanwhile become somewhat blurred, thanks to the research of such men as Kellogg Hunt and Francis Christensen. Hunt, in 1962 to 1964, examined sentences written by fourth graders, eighth graders, twelfth graders, and professional writers. Differences in the sentences written by these various groups were not mainly in length. Fourth-graders, who tend to string ideas together with *and* or *so*, wrote sentences about as long as those of older students and professional writers. The difference lies in the degree of compactness of sentences. A twelfth-grader or a professional writer crams more ideas, more information, into a sentence of twenty words than does the fourth-grader. He has mastered such subordinating devices as the phrase and the dependent clause and the appositive; he often reduces a whole sentence to a phrase or even a single word. The fourth-grader writes, "I saw a dog, and it was big and brown." The twelfth-grader or often even the eighth-grader writes, "I saw a big, brown dog." As a result of the work of Hunt and others, in our teaching we now place much more emphasis on a combination of independent elements, on subordination, on compactness of expression. Our students therefore often write sentences that are rhetorically more effective than most students wrote in the sixties.

Francis Christensen in the sixties pointed out that in our stress upon the basic parts of a sentence—subject, verb, and complement—we often overlooked or minimized the importance of modifiers. These modifiers, he pointed out, are often what give a sentence its life. They determine the tone, the style, often the meaning. He illustrated by taking a passage from a professional writer like Walter Van Tilburg Clark, stripping it to its essentials, eliminating the subordinate elements and most of the descriptive terms. The style became dull, choppy, lifeless. The reinsertion of the modifiers brought it back to life. Many, perhaps most, of our students used to write stripped-down sentences. Teachers now, in the seventies, try to help them to see the details that should be added and to insert those details in rhetorically effective sentences.

Classroom methods have also changed greatly in the past decade or so. Though the closed-in classroom—one teacher facing thirty or so students at the same hour day after day—is still with us, it is by no means the universal that it once was. The emphasis has been increasingly placed upon giving each student what he needs most at a particular time. In the old days, if five students in a class of thirty did not understand the use of the semicolon we gave instruction in the semicolon to everybody, even though five-sixths of our students were wasting their time. Today, upon identifying the five students who need work on the semicolon, we place before them a piece of programmed material that in a few minutes teaches them the semicolon inductively and gives them practice in its use. Meanwhile the other twenty-five are working on other programmed materials—either more or less sophisticated—that they as individuals need. Programming does not work well with everything; in literature, for example, it is useful mainly in teaching certain literary items such as meter or metaphor. A program often gets in the way of appreciation, and hence has limited use in the teaching of literature. But it can be used extensively in the teaching of some facets of language. Grammar can be programmed. Usage can be improved through programming, especially when the program is supplemented by oral work. Punctuation can be taught by programming, and the programming can be reinforced by oral work stressing juncture. Spelling, though still a problem, can be programmed, and instruction via programmed spelling can be made much more individual than in the conventional method of giving everybody the same list on Monday and a test on Friday. Vocabulary can be strengthened by programming. One eighth-grade class in Manhasset, New York, for instance, through a program came to be quickly at home with useful but fairly difficult words such as *composure* or *juxtaposed.*

Besides programming, schools are using other relatively new devices. Thanks to federal help, most classrooms are much better equipped in the 1970's than they used to be. Record players, tape recorders, television sets, film and filmstrip projectors, and opaque and overhead projectors are standard equipment in most schools. Almost every English classroom has a room library, with many of the books changed frequently; the room has a dictionary for every child and single copies of other useful reference books. The biggest problem that some teachers face is that of choosing from the wealth of films, slides, transparencies, programmed instructional materials, books, and other materials that have become available. As a result, many school systems now employ media specialists whose principal function is to screen possibly useful material and tentatively recommend certain items for the more careful consideration of the teachers in the various departments.

Some of the more advanced schools in 1979 have installed computer-controlled learning rooms. A learning room is a small cubicle, just large enough for one student, and equipped with ear-phones, a small TV-like screen, and a microfilm reader. The student enters the room and dials the call number of material he or his teacher believes he should use. What happens next depends upon the nature of the material. The computer center electronically takes the necessary steps. If a film is to be viewed, it appears on the screen. If the material is a lecture or lecturette, the sound comes through the earphones. If it is programmed instruction, the screen may once more be used, or else the microfilm reader. If it is a book, the pages appear on either the screen or the reader, and the student "turns the pages" by pressing a button.

Team teaching is also used in many of our schools. The experiments of the sixties, though not uniformly successful, did show that some material may be effectively presented in large groups, that some things necessitate small group discussion and practice, and that some may be most effectively studied by individuals. Today we know more about what fits best into each type of instruction. Team teaching is not more economical than other instruction, but it does have the value that it can take advantage of special faculty strengths. Thus a teacher who is especially well grounded in the English language may play a leading role there, perhaps conducting the large-group sessions and planning the discussion groups and individual work in language. Other experts take the lead in other parts of the total English program.

As I said before, the stress in 1979 is on helping each individual student where he most needs help. Wide adoption of nongraded school plans has helped to facilitate this development. We have long known, for example, that thirty twelve-year-olds will have almost thirty different degrees of readiness for various parts of our instruction. Yet in the past all students had to move in the same lockstep fashion through every grade. In the nongraded school, though the system provides tremendous problems in scheduling, a student's age or his year in school does not determine what he studies. Instead, the stage he has reached in his own educational development is the major determinant. He is placed with other students who have reached about the same level, regardless of their chronological age, and, as I have said, a considerable share of this time is spent in individual work.

Two of the most important parts of the language program in 1979 I have not yet mentioned. One of these is the history of the language; the other is lexicology.

The English language has a fascinating history, and its relationships with other of the world's languages are also interesting. In the elementary schools in the seventies, when children are studying about other countries, something is usually said about the languages of those countries. If they are related to English, the relationships are pointed out. Thus the other Teutonic languages—particularly German and the Scandinavian languages—are called sister languages. The Romance languages—Italian, French, Spanish, Portugese, and Rumanian—are among the cousins of English. More distant cousins include Greek, Russian and other Slavic languages, Iranian, and even some of the languages of India. Older children may draw trees of language to illustrate how all the branches I have named, and still more, have grown from a single root. And since English has borrowed heavily from many languages—not just the Latin and Greek and French of which we are likely to think first—students in junior or senior high school may study some of those borrowings and perhaps draw a river to represent the English language, with tributaries of other languages feeding in—first Celtic, then Latin, then Danish, then French, then more Latin and some Greek, then Italian and Spanish, and finally a large number of smaller tributaries representing many other of the world's nations. The source of the river, of course—the Lake Itasca of English—lies in Northern Teutonic, the north part of Germany and the Scandinavian countries from which the Angles, Saxons, and Jutes emigrated to the British Isles. Such study is not wasteful of time. It adds some words to students' vocabularies, it is a reflection of historical developments, and it shows some of the interchange that has long gone on between speakers of English and speakers of other languages. It is an important contribution to the culture and to the human awareness of the young people.

The history of the English language, in addition to revealing borrowings from abroad, has other cultural and intellectual values. One is that it helps to account for the existence of dialects, about which I talked earlier. Another is that it demonstrates the fact that language is constantly changing. Nothing can be done to halt the forces of change. As long as users of a language exist, it will change, because the users are themselves undergoing change, having new experiences, developing new ideas, using new tools, finding new means of entertainment. The history of the language also reveals and explains many of the characteristics of the language, such as why so many of our short, everyday words are among the oldest, why most musical terms are Italian, why homonyms exist, how a word has changed its meaning over the years, how fashions in slang change almost as rapidly as fashions in dress, how people and places got their names, or how sentence patterns have evolved through the centuries. This kind of information makes students more aware of what they are doing when they speak or write; it makes them more meticulous in their use of language and more appreciative as consumers of language, for example, as readers of literature.

The last feature of English language instruction that I wish to discuss is lexicology. This term was seldom used ten years ago, in 1969. It is used now to refer to all facets of the study of words: semantics, vocabulary development, derivation, application, dictionary-making, and stylistic effects dependent on selection of words. Thus it is much broader than lexicography, a term with which it was once confused.

Many children and youth can be fascinated by words. The interesting stories of word origins appeal to them—for example, *abundance; unda* in that word is Latin for ocean or waves; *abundance* pertains to plenty, and nothing on earth is more plentiful than the waves of the ocean. The child who adds *abundance* to his vocabulary, or reinforces its meaning for himself, also adds *abundant, abundantly,* and possibly *undulant, undulate, undulation, inundate,* and even *redundant.* In our classes the teachers and students talk often about words. They experiment with them in sentences, noting the effects of using this word or that. They talk about why a professional writer choses this word instead of another. Interest in words is constant, not just something that appears in an isolated unit now and then.

Dictionary-making, or lexicography, is another facet of lexicology. Much of the furor over the Third Edition of Webster's, in the early sixties, was caused by popular ignorance of lexicography. Our students now learn that dictionaries are intended to describe, not regulate. They learn also how lexicographers work, how they determine a word's meaning and the other information they present. Students prepare their own definitions; they compile their own dictionaries of teen-age slang or other specialized topics. They thus become knowledgeable about dictionaries and simultaneously increase their knowledge of words.

The study of semantics has been revived in the seventies. It was a popular subject in the late forties and early fifties, and then became much less so. Basically, semantics shows the ways by which language can move men. It distinguishes reportorial language from the language of emotion. It explores connotations and not just denotations. Its study is important for the student as a user of language and as a reader of literature. Teachers of the sixties, we now believe, were mistaken to reduce their emphasis on semantics.

In summary, the English language program of the seventies differs from that of earlier decades in being richer. All through the nineteenth century and the first seven decades of the twentieth—with the exception of the classes of a few unusual teachers—the language program was an impoverished one. It consisted mainly of grammar and usage, with only incidental attention to the other aspects. It ignored the richness inherent in the language. It repeated grammatical analysis and usage rules *ad nauseam*. In many schools the language program used to be essentially a negative one, whose chief purpose was to tell students what they should not do. Our language programs in the seventies, in contrast, are affirmative. They offer students a rich diet of information about dialect, history of the language, lexicology, usage, and grammar. They engage students in constructive tasks, not just in the correction of error.

At the beginning I said that English in the seventies is being used increasingly around the world, that it is the major language of international communication. As the several hundred million native speakers of English learn more about it and use it with increasing effectiveness, they serve not only themselves but also the cause of increasing understanding among the peoples of the globe.

B. Objectives

There are at least three basic reasons for defining objectives of instruction; they are (1) to aid in curriculum development, (2) to encourage pupil achievement, and (3) to implement the process of program evaluation. In the last few years there has been increased emphasis on developing criteria for measuring the effectiveness of instructional programs. This impetus to providing objectives has come from a demand for accountability by the U.S. Office of Education, which has insisted that specified performance criteria become, whenever possible, an integral part of proposals for federal money. Additional impetus to defining educational objectives has come from a demand for guaranteed performance made by major industries negotiating with many of the largest school systems. The unprecedented interest in formulating broad objectives which has been elicited by these two developments may be applied to specific classroom situations.

Selected objectives to be met in the language arts at each of three stages between age four and maturity are hypothesized in the first contribution in this section. Because the writers believe that perception usually precedes expression, they have organized their objectives for learning a target language in an audiolingual progression: perceiving, listening, speaking, reading, writing. The objectives presented in the second selection are directed at learners with high verbal ability in nongraded schools. By formulating abstract objectives (attitudes, skills, concepts, and applications) the writers provide feasible guidelines for a school aiming at complete individualization.

Few persons deny that clearly formulated goals would clarify the educational process. Certainly, both educators and learners would benefit by knowing whether concrete behavioral objectives had been achieved. However, the thought processes involved in many creative usages of language are so subjective that they cannot be measured. Recognizing the limitations that set behavioral objectives can put on attaining "humanistic goals" in education, the National Council of Teachers of English, at their annual meeting in 1969, passed a resolution imploring teachers to preserve humanistic aims " . . . regardless of whether or not there exist instruments at the present time for measuring the desired changes in pupil behavior." In defense of the inquiring mind, the third contributor maintains that any behavioral objectives in the language arts must be directed toward three humanistic goals: imagination, power, and understanding. The fourth and final selection serves as a summary statement in challenging educators who would implement specific types of objectives to define more articulately how these objectives will achieve the "ultimate goal in children's language learning, the development of power in their use of language."

2.

Selected Objectives in the English Language Arts (Pre-K Through 12)

Mary Endres, Pose Lamb and Arnold Lazarus

However indispensable goals may be if everything else is not to be wasted or misguided, selecting a list of them in the English language arts is of course presumptuous and foolhardy unless one stipulates that the purpose of this inventory is to elicit dialogue. Please regard all these objectives as tentative, dear Reader, as parts of hypotheses to be tested, accepted, rejected, modified.

Ultimately objectives are best specified for individual children. The authors realize that they cannot know most of the individual children. Such information is even elusive for the more directly involved teachers, administrators, and parents, though they can indeed supply more relevant, more specific adaptations. Nevertheless, we submit the objectives we believe foundational to the effective functioning of human beings (regardless of skin color, ethos, or ethnic culture), and we invite rebuttal.

The three developmental stages that we have settled on are (1) early childhood (age 4 to approximately 7); (2) middle childhood (age 8 to approximately 12); and (3) adolescence (age 13 to maturity). There is nothing sacred about these arbitrary divisions, of course, though there is everything sacred about the individuals in them. We decided to begin with age 4 because of the strong interest in "preschool" learning and in the increasing numbers of children enrolled in "Headstart," day-care, and nursery schools. Although we do not specify by age a terminus to adolescence, we trust that this period ends when high school ends. But we are well aware of the reality that for some college students and other adults adolescence never ends and maturity never begins.

Because perception usually precedes expression—"intake" before "output"—we have organized our objectives in the audiolingual sequence now established for learning a target language: perceiving, listening, speaking, reading, writing. Though we are not sure how realistic anyone has been in his claims for a "sequential and developmental" program in the language arts, we can claim at least one dimension of the developmental in our organization. In the context of the taxonomy by Bloom, Krathwohl, and others, our objectives proceed from those of the consumer-assimilative to those of the producer-creative.

After the objectives the coding attempts to designate emphases according to age group. A series of dots (.......) signals that the objective receives little emphasis; a crosshatching (xxxxxxx) signals that the objective receives some emphasis; a line (__________) signals that the objective receives strong emphasis; white space suggests that the objective may be "not applicable here."

Whether in maturity or on the road to maturity, control of language can work a magic, as we all know. Surely, watching a human being grow in the imaginative and responsible uses of the language arts remains one of the teacher's supreme joys.

1. Perceiving

		Early Childhood — Middle Childhood — Adolescence
1.1	To develop an awareness of self—physically, emotionally, socially; to perceive oneself as an individual person	______________________________________
1.2	To associate graphemic and phonetic associations with pictorial representations of referent objects	____________ xxxxxxxxxxxxx
1.3	To perceive such sensuous appeals as those emanating from color, design, artifacts, photography, painting, sculpture, music, dance, drama, poetry, stories . . .	______________________________________
1.4	To perceive the advantages of taking criticism graciously	______________________________________
1.5	To perceive certain characteristics of the mass media—for example, the immediate and the graphic; perspective; opportunities for vicarious travel in time and space; to become aware of what one medium can do that another cannot do	xxxxxxxxxxxxxxxxx__________________
1.6	To perceive that a communication is a transaction that requires at least (1) sender, (2) message, and (3) receiver	..........xxxxxxx______________________
1.7	To perceive when the sender is (1) informing, or (2) entertaining, or (3) convincing, or (4) persuading—i.e., moving to action, or (5) inspiring—i.e., elevating the receiver's feelings, or (6) expressing his own feelings, or (7) doing a combination of the above	..........xxxxxxxxxxxxx______________

	Objective	Early Childhood — Middle Childhood — Adolescence
1.8	To realize that the sender's primary intention is usually not the most apparent to the receiver (sometimes not even to the sender himself); to recognize primary and secondary intentions	...............xxxxxxxx________________
1.9	To understand that a large part of the message is the medium and manner in which it is transmitted; that not only *what* is said but also *the way it is said* (tone of voice, gestures, musical accompaniment, photograhic background) influences the receiver's thoughts and actions	xxxxxxxxxxxxxxxx________________
1.10	To recognize differences between selective representations (art) and the non-selective (reports, candid shots)	xxxxxxxxxxxxxxxx________________
1.11	To perceive motivations behind emotional appeals on billboards, radio, television, etc.; to be able to identify rationalizations and double-talk	...............xxxxxxxxxxxxx________
1.12	To develop sensitivity to the freedoms concomitant with independence of thought; to be open to a variety of views before deciding what one accepts or rejects	xxxxxxxxxxxxx____________________

2. Listening

	Objective	Early Childhood — Middle Childhood — Adolescence
2.1	To enjoy listening to sounds around us; songs of birds, children's voices, whirr of toys, tones of musical instruments, bells, sounds of animals, rustle of leaves, etc.	____________________________________
2.2	To enjoy listening to jingles, nursery rhymes, stories, and personal experiences	____________________________________
2.3	To enjoy hearing legends, myths, and folklore	xxxxxxxxxxxx______________________

		Early Childhood · Middle Childhood · Adolescence
2.4	To become aware of how interesting words can be—words which rhyme, which are fun to say, which describe, which are "big"	————————xxxxxxxxxxxx
2.5	To listen to others' ideas with an open mind and to extend to others the courtesies in listening which one expects when speaking	xxxxx————————————
2.6	To acquire facts accurately and with reasonable ease when they are communicated through speech	..................................xxxxx———
2.7	To acquire skills of critical listening: i.e., listening for ideas and supporting data; to avoid being swayed by propaganda	xxxxxxxxxxxx———
2.8	To select from listening experiences the ideas which are of significance to the problem at hand, and to tune out the extraneous	xxxxxxxxxx—————
2.9	To change one's own behavior (decision-making, acquisition of concepts, attitudes towards individuals or groups) as a result of effective listening	...................xxxxxxxxxxxx———
2.10	To develop ability to select the level of listening (marginal, appreciative, attentive, critical) appropriate to a given situation and to flexibly apply these different skills implied by the levels involved	xxxxxxxxx———
2.11	To react sensitively to poetry and prose; to develop aesthetic taste	————————————————
2.12	To be silent occasionally and to know when to be silent; to realize the values of listening rather than speaking	xxxxxxxx———
2.13	To be able to decode manner or mode as well as content of a message (e.g., humor, sarcasm, romance, tragedy, etc.)	.......xxxxxxxxxxxxx————

	Objective	Early Childhood / Middle Childhood / Adolescence
2.14	To be able to identify the language devices used by an advertiser in making his appeals—e.g., slogans, jingles, repetition, tone of voice, loaded words, analogy, association of images and status symbols, etc.	........................xxxxxxxxxx________
2.15	To develop critical taste—e.g., to prefer the authentic and the imaginative over the sterotyped and contrived in movies, TV, and other media	........................xxxxxxxxxxxxx____
2.16	To cultivate a balanced media diet; to develop criteria for tuning in or tuning out	________________________________

3. Speaking

	Objective	Early Childhood / Middle Childhood / Adolescence
3.1	From the beginning to be talking before trying to read (Compare #4.13)	__________xxxxxxx
3.2	To speak spontaneously and easily with others; to speak freely when there is something significant to be said	________________________________
3.3	To enunciate clearly distinguishable phonemes; to project and modulate appropriately	____________xxxxxxxxxxxxxxxxxx
3.4	To express observations, experiences, and feelings	________________________________
3.5	To take part in an informal exchange of ideas with others; to consult with others in formulating plans	........xxxxx______________
3.6	To question as a way of learning	________________________________
3.7	To express one's self or to express one's interpretations in play acting, story telling, poetry reading, ballad singing	xxxxxxxxxxxxxx________________
3.8	To make effective use of pitch, stress, facial expression, and	

		Early Childhood / Middle Childhood / Adolescence
	gesture in order to make one's speech more interesting	.........xxxxx __________
3.9	To acquire the ability to present facts, ideas, and concepts in an organized manner	.........xxxxx __________
3.10	To apply the conventions of general American-English usage, put to use whatever functional variety of language is appropiate to the occasion	xxxxxxxxxxxxxxxxx ____________

4. Reading

		Early Childhood / Middle Childhood / Adolescence
4.1	To enjoy looking at picture books	____________ ....
4.2	To understand that a printed word represents not only spoken sounds but also lexical meaning	.............xxxxxxxxxxxxx __________
4.3	To be aware of similarities and differences in reading and speaking (Reading is "talk written down" but the author follows certain restrictive conventions and lacks the meaning-aids of pitch, stress, gesture, and facial expression available to speakers.)	.......xxxx ________
4.4	To recognize the nature of meanings of what is read; to make of reading a question-asking, problem-solving process; to realize that language SUGGESTS more than it says	.........xxxxxxxx __________
4.5	To read orally with evidence that one identifies with and understands the material, character motivation, emotional content, etc.	..........xxxxxxxxxxxx ___
4.6	To expand one's recognition-vocabulary in quantity and quality	.......xxxxxxxx ______________
4.7	To acquire and apply correctly word-analysis skills necessary for decoding unfamiliar words	......xxxx ________________

	Objective	Early Childhood / Middle Childhood / Adolescence
4.8	To read (silently) with ease, fluency, and appropriate speed	.....xxxxxxxxx________
4.9	To value the literary tradition of one's culture; to be able to identify folklore and allusions	......................_____________________
4.10	To develop (i.e., appropriately change) one's beliefs, attitudes, and concepts on the basis of rich and varied reading experiences	.................xxxxxxxx________
4.11	To read habitually and to cherish reading—to see its value as a leisure-time activity	.....xxxxxx________________
4.12	To tranfer skills developed in one field of reading to related fields	............................xxxxxxxx______
4.13	Once able to read, to be reading a lot before talking too much (Compare #3.1)	____________
4.14	To apply, in reading, certain techniques of critical listening; to distinguish between report and propaganda; between less slanted and more slanted news	.................xxxxxxx___________
4.15	To be able to identify a statement of fact, a statement of opinion, and the elements of a mixture	.................xxxxxxxxxxxxx __
4.16	To gain skills in critically comparing editorials	xxxxxxxxxx __
4.17	To gain skills in critically comparing reports of a news item in at least two different newspapers, examining emphases created by (1) amounts of space allotted, (2) positions within the newspaper—i.e., front page, middle, back page, etc. (3) omissions	xxxxxxxxxxxxxx __
4.18	To examine assumptions and implications of advertisements; to examine whether the sign or symbol associated with a product really says anything about the product itself	..........___________________________

5. Writing

	Early Childhood	Middle Childhood	Adolescence
5.1 To produce written signs and symbols with a sense of exploration and discovery	xxxxxxx____________________		
5.2 To take pride in producing neat legible manuscript and cursive writing	xxxxxxx____________________		
5.3 To accept responsibility for spelling correctly in order to communicate more effectively; to make use of the various aids to spelling, including one's own mnemonics; to consult the dictionary; to spell correctly in whatever subject		xxxxxx______________	
5.4 To improve the quality and precision of one's written vocabulary		xxxxxxxxx______	
5.5 To grow in the ability to use conventions in both formal and informal letters (communications)		xxxxxxx____________	
5.6 To develop increasing objectivity in revising one's written work		________________	
5.7 To develop an awareness of writing-styles and to improve one's own writing as a result of continuous exposure to literature	.........xxxxxxx____________		
5.8 To be able to encode manner(s) appropriate to message(s); to contribute creatively to class posters, newspapers, skits, etc.	................xxxxxx__________		
5.9 To enjoy writing prose and verse; to enjoy writing various genres and modes (haiku, free verse, stories, fables, skits, friendly letters, etc.)	......xxxxxxx____________		

3.

Objectives for Language Arts in Nongraded Schools

Sidney Drumheller

This writer is convinced that a non-graded program must have an individualized orientation. A system where a classroom teacher uses a variety of groupings in each subject and these groups use conventional materials in a lock-step fashion, remains a graded system.

The vitality of the nongraded school lies in that key concept, "individualized instruction." To be successful, the entire school must first commit itself to this. It may be necessary, due to lack of funds and materials, to compromise procedures somewhat by using groups. But these groups would have as their central characteristic the constant attention of the teacher to individual differences, and the justification of procedures on that basis. The traditional lock-step orientation dissolves when a school is committed to an ungraded system.

Upon analysis, only two clearly-defined patterns for curriculum organization emerge, which are poles of a continuum—these being the subject-centered approach that has controlled educational practices for 2,000 years, and the child-centered approach which has been discussed for a half century but has made

Subject. . . . . Child
Centered (Lock Step) Centered (Individualized)

few inroads in actual practice. Other approaches tend to fall somewhere along the continuum, and are defended as an ideal compromise between the extremes. The lock-step point of view is as essential to the traditional approach as the child-centered, individualized view is to the ungraded approach. One would be hard pressed, however, to find a teacher advocating either extreme in its pure form.

An ungraded school must have teachers committed to practice at the childcentered—individualized pole yet willing to postpone, for the sake of a smooth running system, the realization of this dream until adequate materials are available. This contradition is what makes the defining of precise objectives for the language arts program so difficult. There are clearly three areas where objectives must be developed—

From *Elementary English* 46:119-125 (February 1969).

1. Objectives defining desirable communications-related behaviors expected of the learners.
2. Objectives defining desirable individualized instruction oriented teacher behaviors, and
3. Objectives defining the "system" which organizes the schoolwide program into an organic functioning whole. (This system must run smoothly on an austerity budget with a limited amount of materials.)

Pupil Objectives

The major global language arts objectives have been plotted on the following chart.

One must differentiate between terminal and transitional objectives. The following chart is concerned with the terminal. If we were to tailor a language-arts program to an individual, we would consider his past experiences, learning styles, abilities, etc., and select individualized transitional objectives and routes.

CHART I.

As a result of his elementary school experiences the child will send and receive communications using each of the following media with a facility appropriate to his background of experiences, abilities, and age:

	Reading	Writing	Listening	Speaking
By Manipulating the Symbols				
By Communicating Information				
By Contriving and Interpreting Persuasive Communications				
By Producing and Receiving Aesthetic Communications				
By Producing and Receiving Social Communications				
By Producing and Receiving Business and Consumer Communications				

For instance, Guilford argues that we store our learnings roughly in four forms—images, symbols, words, and gross body movements. Each individual, however, uses his unique combination of these, and so the teacher, to facilitate learning, should identify the learner's profile. If we wanted to teach two beginning readers—one essentially verbal and the other neuro-muscular—we might use the Scott Foresman basal reader with its rule orientation system for the former, and "Words in Color" with its conditioning orientation for the latter. The end (terminal) objectives are the same, but the means (transitional) objectives are different.

It is obvious that reading has much in common with speaking, writing, and listening, and so materials in all four areas can and should have a common core of transitional objectives. For learners with certain style patterns, the rule system in reading might be modified so that it applies equally well to related media. This would make it almost imperative that a single publisher develop a complete set of learning materials for learners with certain characteristics and label them as such.

Chart II (A, B, C, and D) pp. 28, 29, 30, 31, 32, 33) presents an extensive list of language arts objectives, both terminal and transitional, which might be appropriate for a highly verbal learner. The row labeled Application describes the major categories on Chart I. The Concepts, Skills and Attitudes appearing in the remaining rows identify more specific responses likely to be essential in the performance of the application response at the appropriate time. There would certainly be a more extensive list of objectives defining the focuses of a comprehensive collection of daily lesson materials for an elementary school language-arts program. Most of these objectives would fall under one of those on the chart.

This chart should be useful as a guide in selecting published materials for an ungraded program for highly verbal learners to insure its comprehensiveness. Another chart would have to be developed for low-verbal learners.

Teacher Objectives

Teaching in an individualized setting requires techniques and skills somewhat alien to those needed in the "taught to the tune of the hickory stick" classroom. Let us examine a few of these.

The teacher must be able to identify learner characteristics which are related to the student's learning abilities, learning styles, and past experiences. This means that she must be able to administer and interpret test scores and cumulative record data, and make inferences from personal observations which are objective and accurate.

The teacher must be able to recognize the pressures which society is presently placing, and will eventually place, on the child. These pressures identify what he needs to know to live up to society's expectations and be accepted in it.

The teacher must be able to select terminal and transitional language arts objectives appropriate to the individual child. These objectives must consider both the uniqueness of the learner and the society into which he is merging.

The teacher must be able to choose learning materials appropriate to both the learner and the avowed objectives. This implies a much more sophisticated understanding of the relationship between the learner and the learning materials than had formerly been common among teachers.

The teacher must be able to appraise the progress of individual learners and provide guidance where remedial help is indicated. This implies a much more thorough understanding of strategies used in individualized materials than had been needed when a whole class was using the same program.

The transformation of a teacher from one pole to another of the above mentioned continuum can be likened to the trials and tribulations of a student learning a foreign language. Initially he has to think in the old language translating his every move. It is hoped that sooner or later he will find himself thinking and emoting in the new language. This does not always occur. Some never make the transition.

If the movement to initiate an ungraded program came from the teachers, the transition is likely to be more swift and complete than if initiated by the administrator. In either event, however, a thoroughgoing training program for teachers is essential.

System Objectives

"System" refers to the structure rationale, and those procedures which unify the program into an organic whole, yielding functional learners who exhibit the behavior specified in the avowed objectives of the school. The specifications outlined below must be met by an ungraded system.

The average classroom teacher should be able to comfortably plan, conduct and evaluate the learning activities of her class in a 40-45 hour week. If the teacher has to spend more time than this there is something wrong with the system. Either more materials and personnel are needed or some individualization has to go.

All classroom learning activities should be planned around the learning characteristics of the individual students. They can still be taught in groups as long as they do not lose their individuality.

The quality of the learner's performance, on application-focused objectives, should be the major criterion used to evaluate progress, with the standard based on a reasonable performance expected of a student with similar characteristics.

Prescribed guidelines should be available to insure that crucial objectives will be mastered at appropriate stages of development, based upon the abilities and backgrounds of the individual learner.

There should be frequently scheduled opportunities for student-teacher conferences, where each learner can get prompt attention with learning problems.

There should be materials, and activities scheduled, to provide for the educational needs of the learners so they don't have to wait for materials, or suffer boredom through over-exposure to a single program.

These guidelines should define a structure capable of providing a system flexible enough to serve the nongraded school throughout its transition toward complete individualization.

CHART II, A.

Attitudes	*Listening Attitudes:* The learner will: Use the appropriate concepts and skills in his daily performance of developmental tasks.
Specific Skills	*Skills related to Informative Communications:* The learner will: Identify main ideas, sequences of ideas, and details, and make two point outlines when appropriate. Systematically identify and use appropriate references in pursuit of information. *Skills related to Persuasive and Editorially Biased Communications:* The learner will: Identify the speaker's intent and mood, and attitude toward the subject. Discriminate between relevant and irrelevant ideas. Discriminate between fact and fiction. Draw inferences using cause-effect relationships. Compare two or more speeches for relative reliability on facts, bias, currency. *Recreational and Aesthetic Skills:* The learner will: Identify a variety of listening areas which interest him. Specify procedures he can take to find interesting listening in each area (above). Identify times in his schedule when he can get recreational materials and use them.

General Skills	Learner will: Produce the 40 basic English sounds when presented with the spoken letter or digraph. Recall and interpret sentences immediately after he has heard them. Identify relationships between ideas he has heard. Discriminate facts from fiction and from opinion in his listening. Summarize what he has heard.
Concepts	Concepts: the learner will describe: the importance of communications to the self the importance of communications to society the importance of communications to society's institutions the impact of scientific advancement on the media we use to communicate the ways in which the motives of man effect the communications they send and receive the techniques of deception in communications the difference between the free and controlled association of ideas and how a good communication requires both.
Application	*LISTENING:* The learner will translate, interpret, and extrapolate from formal and informal oral statements in the form of: *INFORMATIVE COMMUNICATIONS:* with a degree of proficiency appropriate to his developmental level and seek out such communications when life-problems require it *PERSUASIVE COMMUNICATIONS:* with a degree of proficiency appropriate to his developmental level *EDITORIALLY BIASED COMMUNICATIONS:* with a degree of proficiency appropriate to his developmental level *RECREATIONAL AND AESTHETIC COMMUNICATIONS:* with a degree of proficiency appropriate to his developmental level and seek out such communications when life-problems require it (self realization concerns)

CHART II, B.

Attitudes	*Reading Attitudes:* The learner will: Use the appropriate concepts and skills in his daily performance of developmental tasks.
Specific Skills	*Skills related to Informative Communications:* The learner will: Identify main ideas, sequences of ideas, and details, and make two point outlines when appropriate. Systematically identify and use appropriate references in pursuit of information.

	Skills related to Persuasive and Editorially Biased Communications: The learner will: Identify the author's intent and mood and attitude toward the subject. Discriminate between relevant and irrelevant ideas. Discriminate between fact and fiction. Draw inferences, using cause-effect relationships. Compare two or more sources of information for relative reliability on facts, bias, currency. *Recreational and Aesthetic Skills:* The learner will: Identify a variety of reading areas which interest him. Specify procedures he can take to find interesting books in each area (above). Identify times in his schedule when he can get recreational materials and use them.
General Skills	Learner will: Produce the 40 basic English sounds when presented with the printed letter or digraph. Read words using phonics, context clues, and recalled sight words. Recall and interpret sentences immediately after he has read them. Identify relationships between ideas he has read. Discriminate facts from fiction and from opinion in his reading. Summarize what he has read.
Concepts	Concepts: the learner will describe: the importance of communications to the self the importance of communications to society the importance of communications to society's institutions the impact of scientific advancement on the media we use to communicate the ways in which the motives of man effect the communications they send and receive the techniques of deception in communications the difference between the free and controlled association of ideas and how a good communication requires both.
Application	*READING:* The learner will translate, interpret, and extrapolate from formal and informal written statements in the form of: *INFORMATIVE COMMUNICATIONS:* with a degree of proficiency appropriate to his developmental level and seek out such communications when life-problems require it *PERSUASIVE COMMUNICATIONS:* with a degree of proficiency appropriate to his developmental level

	EDITORIALLY BIASED COMMUNICATIONS: with a degree of proficiency appropriate to his developmental level *RECREATIONAL AND AESTHETIC COMMUNICATIONS:* with a degree of proficiency appropriate to his developmental level and seek out such communications when life-problems require it (self realization concerns)

CHART II, C.

Attitudes	*Speaking Attitudes:* The learner will: Use the appropriate skills and concepts in his daily speaking encounters.
Specific Skills	*Skills related to Informative Communications:* The learner will: Communicate his desires in a socially acceptable manner, to appropriate persons when in need of assistance or information. Communicate appropriate responses to requests from others for information. *Skills related to Persuasive Communications:* The learner will: (Within a moral or ethical framework) convince others to modify their behavior to incorporate his needs or the needs of the larger society. *Skills related to Social Communications:* The learner will: When the occasion arises, engage in social conversation with both peers and adults in a manner which is mutually satisfying to the participants.
General Skills	The learner will perform the following skills in a manner appropriate to his developmental level. Skills in: accurately producing language sounds pronouncing and using words effectively phrasing ideas organizing communications producing effective voice quality effective delivery
Concepts	Concepts: The learner will describe: the importance of communications to the self the importance of communications to society the importance of communications to society's institutions the impact of scientific advancement on the media we use to communicate the ways in which the motives of man effect the communications they send and receive

	the techniques of deception in communications the difference between the free and controlled association of ideas and how a good communication requires both.
Application	*SPEAKING:* The learner will translate, interpret and extrapolate his own experiences and observations in: *INFORMATIVE SPOKEN COMMUNICATIONS:* which communicate with a degree of proficiency appropriate to his developmental level in a culturally appropriate manner commensurate with his developmental level *PERSUASIVE SPOKEN COMMUNICATIONS:* which persuade with a degree of proficiency appropriate to his developmental level in a culturally appropriate manner commensurate with his developmental level *SOCIAL SPOKEN COMMUNICATIONS:* which communicate with a degree of proficiency appropriate to his developmental level in a manner which is self-enhancing in a manner which enhances the speaker's social stimulus value in the eyes of the recipients

CHART II, D.

Attitudes	Writing Attitudes: The learner will: Use the appropriate skills and concepts in his daily writing encounters.
Specific Skills	*Skills related to Informative Communications:* The learner will: Communicate his desires in a socially acceptable manner, to appropriate persons when in need of assistance or information. Communicate appropriate responses to requests from others for information. *Skills related to Persuasive Communications:* The learner will: (Within a moral or ethical framework) convince others to modify their behavior to incorporate his needs or the needs of the larger society. *Skills related to Social Communications:* The learner will: When the occasion arises, correspond with friends in a manner which is mutually satisfying to the participants. *Recreational and Aesthetic Skills:* The learner will: Use all of the above writing media in a manner which is self enhancing. Identify and use for creative purposes oral media which are suitable to his abilities and provide for creative expression.

General Skills	The learner will perform the following skills in a manner appropriate to his developmental level. Skills in: Producing legible letters and words rapidly Producing appropriate words Phrasing communications Organizing communications Editing products for public consumption which are free from errors in: spelling format irrelevancies facts redundancies punctuation grammar
Concepts	Concepts: The learner will describe: the importance of communications to the self the importance of communications to society the importance of communications to society's institutions the impact of scientific advancement on the media we use to communicate the ways in which the motives of man effect the communications they send and receive the techniques of deception in communications the difference between the free and controlled association of ideas and how a good communication requires both.
Application	*WRITING:* The learner will translate, interpret and extrapolate his own experiences and observations in writing through: *INFORMATIVE COMMUNICATIONS:* which communicate with a degree of proficiency appropriate to his developmental level in a culturally appropriate manner commensurate with his developmental level *PERSUASIVE COMMUNICATIONS:* which persuade with a degree of proficiency appropriate to his developmental level in a culturally appropriate manner commensurate with his developmental level *SOCIAL COMMUNICATIONS:* which communicate with a degree of proficiency appropriate to his developmental level in a manner which is self-enhancing in a manner which enhances the speaker's social stimulus value in the eyes of the recipients *CREATIVE EXPRESSIONS:* in a manner which is self-enhancing and possibly in a manner which is educational.

4.

The Monkey on the Bicycle: Behavioral Objectives and the Teaching of English

Hans P. Guth

Author's Note: Many are the movements—or "trends"—that sweep over the teaching of English. Some, like courses in rock lyrics, add a touch of color to the passing scene. Some, like semantics or transformational grammar, survive after the original disciples have discovered new prophets and add something lasting to our efforts to help students understand and master language. Some, like the liberal or "permissive" movement in usage, or our growing recognition of America's cultural and linguistic pluralism, in slow but profound ways change our conception of who we are and what we do.

All of these movements have a common element: They gained momentum because they speak to English teachers as people with a common commitment—to our language and its role in our culture. But English teachers also have to reckon with movements of a different kind: these come to us, for better or for worse, from the outside. They import into our subject assumptions not our own. They are part of more general developments that we are often powerless to resist. Such was "progressive education," now remembered mainly in the anti-liberal polemics of education's rear guard mythologists. Such was the subject-matter panic of the post-Sputnik age. And such, finally, is the current movement toward behavioral objectives, which asks English teachers to identify specific behavioral goals, to design steps leading efficiently toward these goals, and to demonstrate results by measuring observable differences in student performance after teaching has taken place. This movement has powerful support from cost-conscious public officials, business-oriented administrators, and a marketwise communications industry.

No one who knows English teachers will be surprised to find that many of them regard the behavioral objectives movement with open hostility. It asks them for "data" at a time when many of them are in search of "soul." It asks them to make their students "perform" when many of them are concerned with "reaching" the student. It asks them to administer tailor-made "learning se-

---

From the *English Journal* 59:785-797 (September 1970).

quences" at a time when many are concerned with liberating the student's locked-in creative and human potential. The cynic, in this situation, will feel that nothing is less likely to result from the familiar triangle of conservative administrator, liberal teacher, and radical student than increased "efficiency." No doubt, in the long run, the pent-up frustrations of the teacher and the sheer rebelliousness of today's students will defeat the manufacturers of learning modules and performance tests.

In the meantime, however, teachers want to teach. They want to teach English. To make this possible, they will have to define more articulately and more forcefully than in the past what it is that English teachers do. They will have to explain why the goal of English is something larger and more obscure than a skill that can be measured at so many words typed a minute, or so many pages read with "comprehension" in a quarter of an hour. The following talk, first delivered at the NCTE convention in Washington, D.C., November 1969 was an attempt to help towards such a definition and explanation.

I might sound a little hoarse today, because some of us have already been arguing about behavioral objectives this week, and I've already been lectured about not getting too irrational and extremist about this topic. So today I'll try to be rational.

I'd like to start out with a broad generalization on this matter of defining the objectives of English. It seems to me that there are two large groups in the profession who have a position on this subject. First, there are those that I'm going to call the "vocal minority," and I mean "vocal" in the sense that they do verbalize freely about the matter of objectives. When they do a unit on place names, it is preceded by seven stated goals. They publish forty-eight approved objectives for the teaching of literature and things of this sort. On the other hand, there are the people that I am going to call the "inarticulate majority" the group to which I belong, because when I am asked to define the objectives of English, I always feel somewhat uneasy. All I really want to do is take my ditto sheet with the sample sentences from Stephen Crane, or the poem by Robert Frost. I want to go into the classroom, close the door softly behind me, and do my thing.

For instance, I take a ditto sheet into the classroom that has some sentences in pidgin English that I collected in Hawaii last summer. I present those sentences that I collected, and we talk about them. In class, I don't particularly theorize or argue. I simply take these along and read a few of them. They go like this:

My car went broke down. You can give me ride?

Yesterday she like go leech one ride from Dennis, but Dennis no like give her one.

Hurry up! We going home. You no like go or what?

He been work too hard.

Ugly dat one!

"Daddy, where you?" "I stay here."

Now suppose the assistant principal sitting in the back of the room came up to me afterward and said, "What are you doing this for? What's the point of taking this kind of thing in?" I suppose if backed into a corner, I would try to get at some of the things that I've tried to do with this ditto sheet. For example, one thing this exercise does is to help make students aware of language as language. Everyone uses language all the time, never really thinking about it or becoming aware of it. To the student, language is much the way water is to the fish in the sea. And contrast is a great educating agent. When we see something done differently, when it doesn't fit the mode, when we look at some of these pidgin sentences and they sound like English but not quite, we say, "Now what's the difference between this and the way we say it?" And then all of a sudden we become aware of some of the things that make our language work.

Let us look at some of these expressions, such as "My car *went* broke down" and "I'm going to tell mommy you *went* do that." If we get enough of those, we realize that *went* here doesn't have anything to do with *go*. It simply expresses past tense. "You went do that" means "You did that." The *went* is a past signal. It's an "auxiliary" to help form the past tense. And as we're going through, we soon find a future signal in this pidgin dialect. The word *going* is used as a future signal. And in a statement like "I *been* go shopping," *been* is used as the "perfect" auxiliary. If we do this for awhile, the student soon says, "Well, this thing has a system. In fact, it has a grammar. It's not mistakes; it's not as though the persons who speak it make it up as they go along. They follow certain rules." And, after the students have studied the sentences, they have learned something very essential about language: it has a system; it can be investigated; even something as unstable as this pidgin dialect has certain built-in rules.

Another thing I'm trying to get at is that the students using this kind of dialect are people, not just with parents from Korea and China, but from the Philippines, Samoa, mainland USA, and what not. Yet these people are living together in the islands, and they have to communicate in English. I want my students to realize one important fact that stares us in the face once we think about it: Many Americans—not just in Hawaii, but all over the country—are bilingual. And even if they aren't bilingual, somewhere in their background they have some contact with some kind of language other than English. They have some aunt, or grandmother, or friend, or somebody who, in fact, probably speaks a sort of working pidgin still, after twenty years or fifteen years or thirty years in this country. And this puts quite a different perspective on American English as a *common medium*, as something that people from many different backgrounds had to adopt or are still adopting as a means of communication. And we realize then that American English is one of the things that hold our country together. In our diversity of backgrounds and interests it provides the common medium.

Another thing I am trying to get at through these sentences is that language is basically intended to be responded to positively, to be fascinating. We don't go through these pidgin sentences in order to say, "Look at these ignorant people out there in the Pacific who can't even speak their own language properly." That's not the point of the assignment. The point of the assignment is to say, "Look at this use of language. Marvel at it. Be fascinated by it. Be entertained." This is something where we say, "Look at this kind of thing. Study it. Learn something from it."

Now, the trouble with trying to list these worthy objectives, the trouble with trying to formalize these worthy goals, is two or threefold. First of all, it's a lot to ask of these eight little sentences. It's a lot to ask to get all of these things out of this one sheet. In fact, even as I state these goals, we realize that these are not the objectives for this particular assignment. These are the *long-range goals* that we English teachers always work toward. These are the kinds of things that are implied in everything we do. For instance, fostering a positive interest in language, and showing that we approach language as a marvelous, flexible instrument, and that we are interested in what language can do—we do that all the time, even when we are off duty. For instance, we are somewhere in the lounge with a group of English teachers, and we still demonstrate that language is fascinating, language is something we can play on and play with. Just the other day, for example, I was listening to some talk between two English teachers. In California these days evolution versus Genesis is again a big topic. These teachers were talking about the Monkey Trial—the Scopes Trial, and one fellow said to the other, "You know, my father was at the Scopes Trial in Tennessee." So the other one looks at him and says, "As a witness—or as an exhibit?"

The second problem we have with these so-called objectives is that we write all of them down in our lesson plans—this is what we want to do—and then half of it comes off in class, and the other half doesn't. In other words, these things that I described are *opportunities.* If we have a good class hour, some of these things will come out, we hope. Some of this will come through. But we wouldn't want to be judged by results that say, "You've done Items 1 and 3, but did you slip up on Item 2!"

Finally, and most importantly, the whole thing is too *verbal.* It's so easy to state these goals that make us feel good and make us sound good, but it's so easy for these words just to be words. We are confronted in this country now with a whole generation that is suspicious of big words, brave words uttered by people over thirty. In fact, the assistant vice-principle, if he is still listening to me, by now is saying, "Hans, you are quite a talker, aren't you? In fact, now I realize why on campus they call you 'Talk-talk Guth.' "

If we talk about objectives at all in the teaching of English, we must be careful to make sure that these aims—these objectives—are not just words, that we talk not just about what people *say*, but especially what they are going to *do* in their classrooms—that we don't just talk about what people *think* about English, but also very much about what they *feel*; that we don't talk just in terms of official aims, but that we very much talk in terms of hidden premises, tacit assumptions, habits, customs, preferences, likes and dislikes. And in the short time I have left, I would like to verbalize perhaps the two or three most basic long-range goals of English, asking not just: "What is the goal officially?" but: "What kind of ditto sheet did *you* take into the classroom? And what short story did *you* assign for Monday morning? And what piece of student writing are you carrying around so that you can pin it up on the bulletin board?"

My first ditto sheet today has on it a poem, because my basic definition of an English teacher is a person who takes a poem to class or assigns a short story, or a play—in other words, someone who exposes students to imaginative literature. And I don't mean by literature necessarily a classic. I don't mean anything elitist; I don't mean anything college-level. My little girl is in the first grade, and she comes home these days humming little tunes, reciting little verses. And I say, "There's a language arts teacher at work somewhere! Someone is doing the job that she is being paid for." So literature here is a very broad area that includes all the creative, imaginative dimension of language—from the nursery rhyme to the play by Shakespeare. The following poem from the *New Yorker* (April 2, 1960) is a dialog between the seed and the flower. I hope it will illustrate for us the first basic long-range goal of English instruction.

THE OPENING

by Jon Swan

Seed said to Flower:
You are too rich and wide.

You spend too soon and loosely
That grave and spacious beauty
I keep secret, inside.
You will die of your pride.

Flower said to Seed: Each opens, gladly
Or in defeat. Clenched close,
You hold a hidden rose
That will break you to be
Free of your dark modesty.*

And if you say, "What's your objective in reading that poem?," I say, "I want to hear the silence deepen in the room as I read. I want to see the eyes glisten in the room. I want someone to say in the back row, 'That was nice.' " And you'll say, "Aren't you going to analyze it? Aren't you going to ask seven questions about this poem?" I say, "Yes, of course. For one thing, we want it to sink in. We want to be able to go back over it again, and we want to talk about it, and make sure the experience comes through." One intriguing thing about the poem is that the pattern is like a pendulum swinging, "Seed said to flower . . . flower said to seed." And we want to talk a little about the symbolism, because another intriguing thing about the poem is that the symbolism is so basic, that so many things in life are like the seed. Something is there that could grow, if it could only develop. In fact this whole matter of teaching English can be reduced to the metaphor of the student's potential: If we're lucky, we'll make it unfold; we'll make it broaden out. And if we're not so lucky, we will help stunt it; we will help repress it.

The first long-range goal in the teaching of English is making the student branch out emotionally and intellectually and opening something up through imaginative experience. And the important point about that is that this is not behavior in the overt sense. This deals with *internal experience*. And even though there are these external symptoms of the glistening eyes and of going to the bookshop afterwards and saying, "Do you have that collection of poems by Dylan Thomas?," those are just the symptoms. We don't teach literature just to produce the symptoms. I don't teach literature to teach the students how to make purring noises when I read Thomas to them.

Let me go on to the next ditto sheet that illustrates another basic goal of English. I have already hinted at the fact that in California we are again in one of these censorship quarrels, where the textbook authors are busy going through their books changing all the *damns* to *darns*, and changing all the *My Gods*, to *My Gosh*, and changing all the *Hell no's* to *Hell yes*. In fact, one of the authors now concludes his letters "Gosh Bless." And it's a futile and degrading thing. We encounter a four-letter word, and we try to explain that this word in context is not really obscene. And we don't really know how to handle this matter successfully. Ultimately, this is a matter of how well we ourselves use language. Here you stand: you are an English teacher. You are supposed to make language work for you and be persuasive and eloquent and have the public accept your version of the thing. But we realize that this is very difficult. We seem ourselves defeated in what is actually our second major assignment as teachers: to work in this area of using language for a purpose, as an instrument in human relations, in organizations, in politics. This is our second goal—one that we English teachers often neglect, because our first love often is literature, and we don't always get around to this realization that language is around us everyday and in everyday prosaic situations. One thing we should try to do for the student is to say, "Well, here is language. You can make it work *for* you, rather than *against* you."

As an example of someone who knows how to make language work for him, I often assign an essay by a Canadian humorist Stephen Leacock, who wrote about this matter of good and bad language. Leacock went into this whole matter of profanity in literature, and he explained that there were three or four ways of handling it, none of them satisfactory. He for instance pointed out that in some of the old-fashioned novels the writer will say, "Well, such and such said something with a terrible oath. . . ," to get around the matter of stating the oath. It goes something like this then in the actual novel:

> "Har, har," shouted the pirate with a foul oath. "They are in our power," "They certainly are," shouted the second pirate with an oath fouler than the first. "I'll say so," said the third pirate with an oath fouler still, a lot fouler. The fourth pirate remained silent. He couldn't make it.

Or some authors then fall back on making up their own sort of fancy and imaginary profanity, and then you get the passage that goes:

> "Odds piddlekins," cried Sir Gonderer, "By my halidome, thou art but a foul caitiff. Let me not or I'll have at you." "Nay, by the belly of St. Mark," answered the Seneschal, "I fear thee not. Have one on me" (or words to that effect).

The third possibility, Leacock said, was to use asterisks, dashes, and colons. But he said that once you try it out, you find it's feeble. It doesn't sound right. You can't swear right: "'Three asterisks,' shouted the pirate. 'Four,' shouted the next. 'I'll make it six,' yelled a third, adding a stroke and a colon."

What intrigues me about this essay by Leacock is that in this matter we are often the patsy. We are on the receiving end. We get the phone calls and the arguments from irate parents. And we are defeated by this. But this man, who has the gift of words—who has the gift of language, can handle it. And much of what we do when we teach figurative language and the rhetoric of the sentence and vocabulary and whatnot—all directly and indirectly contributes to building up this sort of confidence in the fact that language does work, that it is possible to communicate, that it is possible to get a given subject under control and to use words for a purpose.

Let us assume that in writing objectives for English we ask: "What is the secret of this man's power over words? What is there about his use of language that English teachers can work toward, or aim at?" The answer would be: Leacock's writing shows three or four features that are crucial in successful language use but that test-makers and measurement psychologists find very hard to handle. First, the author effectively *chooses* from a wide range of available resources. He could have handled censorship seriously, but he chose to handle it humorously. He could have attacked the ineptitude of censors directly, but he chose to attack it by implication. What he comes up with is totally *unexpected* and yet entirely suitable. This is what we mean by mastery: effective, free-ranging choice. Second, Leacock has the master's sense of his audience. He anticipates how we will respond to his hilarious incongruities, how we will be drawn along by his mock-solemn exposition while revelling in its glorious absurdity. This is again basic: Everyone who wants to speak and write successfully has to have at least a rudimentary sense of how a human being thinks, emotes, frowns, chuckles, and generally responds to verbal stimuli. The beginner is painfully acquiring the ability to anticipate such reactions; the master responds to shades and nuances. Third, there is a gusto, a sheer exuberance in Leacock's writing that says: "I *enjoyed* writing this." We don't expect a man to become an accomplished mechanic if he hates cars. We don't expect a student to do well in band if he hates music. A writer or speaker is making progress if he begins to get a personal satifaction out of what he is doing. To be successful in English as a subject, the student must begin to respond to some of its intrinsic rewards. This feeling of intrinsic satisfaction is palpably present in every successful English classroom—though no vocabulary count, or formula of syntactic density, or reading ease formula can translate it into quantitative curves and scores.

These are the three key ingredients of effective language use: effective free choice, sensitivity to audience response, and intrinsic satisfaction. These cannot be measured statistically, except in indirect, peripheral, and debatable ways. Only the most naive would set out to teach them once and for all in fifteen spaced lessons. They are not the result of any one unit, or set of units. They result from the sum total of a person's exposure to and experience with language. They are nurtured over the years by English teachers who provide the greatest possible range of opportunity and experiment, of involvement in and exposure to the use of living language. They hinge on two essential functions of the teacher: to provide for his students an ever-patient and ever-ready guinea pig audience, and to provide at least an approximate model for the accomplished, satisfying use of the riches of the mother tongue.

My microphone cord is going to be yanked in a few minutes, so I'm going to say just one or two words about the third long-range objective of the teaching of English. I mentioned the fact that sooner or later we ditto a little piece of student writing, or we pin something up on the board, or some of us even tape a little exchange that happened in the classroom, because, again, part of the definition of the teacher of English is that he is the person who says to the student, "Speak it to me," or "Write it to me." As one teacher said in the *English Journal*, "Dearly Beloved, say something to me. Would you please say something to me?" And when we look at these oral and written compositions that we get from our students, what do we look for?

I brought as Exhibit C a little exchange that someone recorded in a fourth-grade class, from an article called "Poetry in an Elementary Classroom." Apparently the person had taken in a Robert Frost poem, the one about the horse and the man in the woods on a winter evening, the dark lonely woods, covered with snow, the man lingering there and the horse wanting to go home to the stable. So at the end of this the teacher turned to the group and said, "Now what is the basic difference between the horse in this poem and the man?" And one student says, "Well, the horse has four legs, and the man has two." And the teacher says, "Good." And then someone else says, "One of them is happy and the other one is sad." And the teacher says, "Fine." And then another student says, "The man knows he's going to die and the horse doesn't." And the teacher doesn't say anything. He lets it sink in. And the point about that response by the student is that it is *true.* It is significant. It's worth taking in. It's worth pondering. And when composition ceases to be a skill that's taught, and becomes expression—communication—in the true sense, then we read it not as an exercise, but then we read because we want to see what the student has to say.

This perception of relations is what we aim at when we say that we want our students to think. Thinking establishes relations within the content of the student's experience. That content builds up slowly, and from a hundred sources, many of them not funded by the school board. A good teacher tries to broaden the students' experience. But he is not so foolish as to take a bow when the student's experience quotient goes up from 68 to 92.

Summing up these three goals of English, I think we can label them roughly: first, *imagination*, the area of extending feeling and thinking on the part of the student; second, *power*, the ability to use language, for a purpose—the power of words, the power of language as a medium; third, *understanding*, the ability to relate a piece of poetry to your own experience, to relate one piece of poetry to another and talk about a common theme or something of that sort. I call these humanistic goals, because they all have to do with the basic goals of humanistic education, which are to develop more fully and to bring out more fully whatever human potential there is in the student.

Where does this leave then people with the tests and the measurement items, the learning modules, the clearly defined, limited objectives? They come to us, and they say, "Here, you do six units of this or that, and in the statistics the performance rate goes up 25 per cent, and that is so much per dollar per pupil." All this kind of talk reminds me of the monkey we see on the Ed Sullivan show. Ed Sullivan once in a while has three trained chimpanzees who ride the bicycle. They do three laps and the audience goes wild, because the Ed Sullivan audience just loves to see a monkey do his three laps on the bicycle. In terms of overt behavior and measurable results, and of something we can demonstrate to the taxpayer, those monkeys are a tremendous success. When they started out being educated, they knew nothing about riding a bicycle. And now that they've been trained, they ride that bicycle and they do the three laps. But when you watch the monkey a little more closely, you realize that the monkey's heart is not really in it. And all the while that he's on that bicycle, his mind is somewhere else. His attention wanders. And you realize there's more to this monkey than Ed Sullivan will ever understand. There is a great unused potential for monkey business, and for monkeyshines. So my suggestion is—and I try to word it as rationally and calmly as I can—when the measurement people come to us with their instrument, my answer is: "Don't make a monkey out of me. I refuse to get on your bicycle."

5. Language Learning Goals

Mildred A. Dawson

What are the goals for children's language learning? Development of children's power in their use of language is the ultimate goal in learning language. Teachers may disagree on ways they seek this common goal of building power in expressing ideas through language.

No single emphasis in teaching can help develop power in the use of a language as complex as English. Variety and balance are essential. Among the more important procedures in building language power are the following:

• *Provide for a rich and varied intake of ideas.* It is only as a child can draw on a plentiful supply of ideas that he can speak or write with clarity and conviction or can listen and read with understanding. The teacher is concerned not only with children's speaking and writing, but also with experiences in which they observe, manipulate, read, listen or otherwise acquire information and viewpoints. Any teacher may, on occasion, relate facts and read orally in order to extend and enrich ideas; he should also provide many activities in which children actively seek out and acquire information. Power in language is dependent on an abundant intake of ideas as a prerequisite for speaking and writing effectively.

• *Make sure that there are occasions for oral and written language in which children are actually sharing ideas, in which the speakers have something to say that their listeners wish to hear, in which what is written provides news or desired information for classmates.* For instance, children may relate individual experiences or stories which they alone know. They may report on information found after several pupils have been searching for it; a child may come up with an explanation of a phenomenon that has mystified the class.

Language is social in nature and should be used in school to accomplish group purposes as children plan together, strive for a joint decision or a group judgment, or work at establishing rapport. Therefore language work should be on topics of mutual concern to class members and their talking and writing should be part of the process for sharing these ideas and viewpoints. Children are likely to speak with force, conviction and directness when actually conveying a message.

From *Childhood Education* 41:132-133 (November 1965). Reprinted by permission of Mildred A. Dawson and the Association for Childhood Education International, 3615 Wisconsin Avenue, N.W., Washington, D.C.

• *Give multiple opportunities for speaking and writing with the purpose of sharing ideas with an audience.* It is only as children have frequent opportunity to speak before their fellows and to write down ideas to be shared that they gain fluency and ease. Of course, mere exercises in speaking and writing will not suffice. There should be topics of intrinsic importance to children, for which frequent exchange of ideas takes place.

• For many children these multiple opportunities to speak and write with purpose do not guarantee the acquisition of skills involved in using language powerfully. *Children may need some direct teaching of skills concentrating on specific skills.* For instance, they may work at devising beginning sentences of stories that will evoke immediate interest and launch quickly into the action; they may learn how to make outlines for reports; there may be exercises to improve enunciation and/or voice quality, which pupils usually enjoy when they have come to realize that they lack force or clarity in presentation and that special help will improve skill.

Power in the use of language, then, is likely to result if there has been a sufficient intake of ideas, if there are enough opportunities to talk and write with purpose, and if there is direct teaching of requisite skills when children are aware of a need for learning a new skill or for improving one that has been poorly used.

Delving into Word Derivation

More than power is desirable, however. It is not enough for pupils to grow in skill and force. They should, in addition, gain enthusiasm for their mother tongue, acquire an interest in the nature of language, and learn how it works. Children will benefit from a rudimentary knowledge of linguistics. Language becomes fascinating to them when they are introduced to the history and derivation of words they speak so glibly; for instance, they may take delight in learning that *escape* originally referred to a prisoner who got away by slipping out of the cape held by his captors or that *curfew* is a descendant of a French word, *couvrefeu,* a signal that their own colonists were to cover their fires for the night. Also, by listening to their own tape-recorded speech and oral reading, children can become aware of the structure of the language they speak—grouping of words within sentences in thought units, pauses and junctures between these sentences—parts, inflections of voice that emphasize key words and ideas, behavior of the voice at the end of a statement or a question. The word order that is a peculiar and distinctive characteristic of the English language becomes evident as older children examine their sentences and become aware of the nature and work of the different kinds of words—nouns and their determiners, verbs, adjectives and adverbs.

With knowledge of the nature and workings of language come interest in it and respect for it. Experts in linguistics are showing us how a child's knowledge of language can aid in teaching silent reading; how oral reading can become more expressive when child readers understand sentence patterns of English and note the intonations and junctures of the voice in speaking sentences; how working with typical sentence patterns and putting words together to make such patterns are probably much more helpful in improving children's use of language than the analytic, sentence-dissecting approach of traditional grammar.

Uses of Language

Furthermore, children benefit from a study of the uses of language; that is, they can observe and sense increasingly how language is used in the world around them. They might be asked, how do advertisers use language to lure the public into purchasing specific products? Children might be asked to observe television programs for a week with the purpose of identifying different ways language is used to get favorable attitudes and increase sales. Or, how do politicians use language to discredit the opposition and to promote their own causes? How do tone of voice, facial expression, choice of words combine to create a prejudiced effect? After critically observing television productions, children may progress to an analysis of how they themselves use language to persuade, to convince, to repel, to curry favor. How do they "work" their parents to get what they want?

Conversely, children may note how others use language to make it beautiful. How do radio and television commentators and news reporters enunciate the ends of their words? Which voices often heard on these media do children prefer and why? Which recordings of a story are best liked? What in the rendition of this story makes it a favorite? Language can be made truly interesting to children when their attention is directed to ways in which others try to make their language more pleasing, more beautiful; learning what is or is not effective, what is a desirable model of language or one to be avoided will help to add to their own power in speaking, writing, listening and reading.

C.
Organizing for Instruction

The widespread adoption of the graded McGuffey *Readers* during the middle of the 1800s and the opening, in 1848, of the Quincy Grammar School marked the origin of mechanistic elementary school organization. The public, which at the time desired to adopt education standards, responded positively to the concepts underlying these two complementary movements; the lock-step, graded system developed from these. This is the system which exists in one form or another in many of our schools today.

From the inception of the system, educational critics deplored its unitary, prescriptive nature. And almost immediately innovations designed to meet the individual needs and interests of students and teachers were introduced. The study of child development which has taken place in recent decades has resulted in a more "child centered" curriculum. It allows the individual learner to achieve at a rate and through an approach which will meet his individual needs and interests.

If this approach is to be taken, objectives must be stated for each child individually. The recent concern with individualization and continuous progress has led to a reappraisal of the content of the curriculum.

Language unifies the various disciplines of science, math, and social studies; the challenge that teachers in the language arts should assume is that of relating language arts to the total program. How to focus on the language arts as a discipline, while relating language skills to other disciplines is a perplexing problem. The first two selections in this section present ideas on how the curriculum might be structured to accomplish these goals. The first article reviews the elements of language study and sets forth a schema which puts the study of the language arts into proper perspective while permitting a variety of both independent and group learning experiences. The structural components of language which are recommended in the second article as organizing concepts in curriculum design are the substantive, behavioral, and enabling elements, each of which is increasingly complex.

While these two models suggest how the content of language arts might be interpreted in the elementary school, the articles which follow elaborate upon ways in which both those teaching in teams in an open school and those teaching alone in a self-contained classroom may adapt learning tasks to individual differences. To individualize instruction the teacher must "individualize his teaching behavior." Once this objective has been attained, such contemporary teaching-learning theories as those of language experience, continuous progress, and individually prescribed instruction may become a reality. In the concluding articles in this section the writers have clarified the empirical aspects of individualization.

6.

Structure and the Elementary School Language Program

Patricia A. Lane

In the past few years scholarly groups have made many efforts to investigate the underlying structure of disciplines taught as school subjects. Mathematicians have developed programs based on structured knowledge for all grades from kindergarten through twelfth grade. Physicists and biologists have introduced new programs for high schools and have influenced elementary-school curriculum builders in developing science programs that support later courses.

In English, most of the study, by groups such as those involved in Project English, has been directed toward the incorporation of modern concepts of linguistics in the high-school English program. The elementary-school English program, unlike the mathematics and science programs, has been almost untouched by the work done at the high-school level. Those involved in building the curriculum for elementary schools must decide whether, and how, the concept of *structure* should influence the language program. Otherwise, the elementary-school language program may acquire a structure that is imposed from the top down or a structure developed only by those interested in the scholarly disciplines of linguistics or literature.

Our current attempts to clarify structure in elementary-school subjects are not the first struggles educators have had with this problem. More than a quarter of a century ago, Washburne and his contemporaries tried to discover how the curriculum could be restructured. The two considerations that guided these investigators were social utility and optimum grade placement of the topics to be studied. Through exploratory studies, and through somewhat less than rigorous experimental research, concerned educators tried to identify elements of the subjects that seemed to be most necessary in the daily lives of children and adults. After these elements, or topics, had been tentatively identified, broad studies were made to discover the grade at which the material could be learned most efficiently. Emphasis was placed not only on the earliest age at which certain concepts and skills could be introduced, but on the age at which the learning could occur with the least expenditure of time and effort and still be sequentially placed in the structure of the total program. In the elementary-school language program, this overemphasis on the product rather than on the

Reprinted from *Elementary School Journal* 68:147-156 (December 1967), by permission of Patricia A. Lane and The University of Chicago Press.

process of expression resulted in undue attention to correctness instead of growth in the effective expression of worthwhile ideas.

Children's Needs

Later investigators looked for structure in terms of the needs children demonstrated at various stages of their physical, intellectual, social, and emotional growth. Theirs, too, was a legitimate effort to consider the concept of readiness for learning and the priority of some learnings over others.

In the 1970's we are still confronted with the problem of considering the appropriate structure for the curriculum of the elementary school. There is some question whether we have succeeded in organizing curriculum experiences that provide the greatest opportunities for children to gain the knowledge, the skills, and the abilities deemed essential for complete participation in society.

As I considered the question of structure in the elementary-school language program, it seemed impossible to identify one kind of structure through which we could achieve the aims of education generally and of the language program in particular. Some scholarly commentators would expect this difficulty in the identification of a single structure, for they would say that the subject of elementary-school language is not a discipline, but a broad field of study.[1] However, it seems to me that even if we considered only one of the "disciplines," such as literature, on which the language program is based, it would still be necessary to work through more than one kind of structure to achieve the aims of the program. Therefore, I would like to present for your consideration one way in which we might look at structure and its implications for curriculum organization and teaching.

Three kinds of structure inherent in the elementary-school language program can be identified. These three structural components of language thread through the elementary-school program. They are parallel to one another, but highly interrelated. Each component develops in a sequential pattern of increasing complexity in the content or in the processes of learning, or both. However, it is only through the integration of the structural components at each stage of development that the aims of the language program can be fulfilled.

The Substantive Component

Consider first the substantive component of structure in elementary-school language. To me, this component consists of the ideas through which the child learns to know himself and the world about him. The language program has specific responsibility for considering the ideas found in literature and the ideas that develop through verbal self-expression. The language program shares with the rest of the school program a responsibility for presenting the ideas on which the knowledge of other disciplines, or subjects, is based. Growth in appreciation of historical concepts, scientific principles, and the aesthetic qualities of music and art is enhanced by the ability to use language effectively as a medium for exploring these disciplines. Learning based on the structural elements of the substantive component is directly related to the aim of developing an articulate person who speaks or writes when he has something to say, a worthwhile idea to express. A structure that reveals the complexity and the maturity of ideas in the elementary-school language program can be identified.

The Behavioral Component

A second element of structure in elementary-school language is the behavioral component. We can state in operational form the levels at which ideas—

the substance—can be understood, appreciated, or manipulated. There are many classifications and descriptions of the ways in which learning may be achieved. Bloom and others, in a classification of educational goals, identify six types of cognitive processes arranged in increasing order of complexity: knowledge, comprehension, application, analysis, synthesis, and evaluation.[2] This classification does not suggest that the higher-level cognitive processes are to be developed in the upper grades and the lower-level processes in the lower grades. The classification does imply that at each grade level, or for each individual, there should be an increase in the maturity of the behavioral processes through which content can be approached. Growth in the behavioral component of language leads to the development of independent learners who continue to be scholars, who have the ability to solve problems and to formulate opinions based on objective information.

The Enabling Component

Thus far, I have stated the need to consider both the ideas that can be found in literature and the other disciplines, and the ways in which we want children to work with these ideas. This leaves, for our consideration, the medium through which the processes can be brought to bear on the ideas. This medium I would like to call the enabling component of structure. To enable a child to analyze an idea, to identify its significant aspects, or to evaluate it, there must be knowledge of the structure of the language itself and competence in the use of language through listening, speaking, reading, and writing. In other words, we must provide for learning in both the science and the arts of language. Through learning of this kind, the aim of effective language expression can be achieved. In this enabling component we develop discipline in the use of language that frees children to concentrate on ideas through the various cognitive and affective processes.

Integrating the Components

The importance of integrating learning in the three structural components has already been stated. One or two examples will illustrate how the integration of the separate components might be achieved. The process of problem-solving is much emphasized as a style of learning. One initial stage in problem-solving can be described behaviorally as the ability to formulate hypotheses. The level at which we expect children to operate in formulating hypotheses will, of course, vary from child to child, and from grade to grade.

Working with Hypotheses

Worthwhile ideas—the substantive element—that form the basis for experience in formulating hypotheses may be selected from one or more of the content areas. In literature, children could investigate the motivation of a character in one of the many tradebooks of superior quality. Consider the little girl who is the main character in Kate Seredy's book *The Good Master*.[3] In this story, we come to know Kate, the brattish cousin of a young Hungarian boy, and her thoughtless, attention-getting behavior. Children could be led to speculate about the reasons for Kate's actions and the change in her disposition when she comes in contact with her uncle, the good master. The field of social studies offers many opportunities for experiences in formulating and testing hypotheses. Pupils might suggest and substantiate reasons for the various routes of exploration taken by early explorers. Farley Mowat's recent book, *Westviking*,[4] which describes the Norse discoveries of North America, is an excellent, though controversial, example of exploring history through hypotheses.

After a decision has been made on a method of inquiry into selected content, experience must be provided in the science and in the arts that will enable the child to use language as a medium of learning. A knowledge of appropriate linguistic structures is necessary to think about and to express hypothetical ideas. This approach does not mean that the syntactic structures must be labeled and examined. The child knows, much as a preschool child "knows" the grammar of his language, the ways in which hypotheses are expressed. The child who has experience in recognizing, both aurally and visually, the characteristic form of hypotheses is more likely to think about problems in terms of hypotheses. He should also have the linguistic knowledge that would encourage him to make tentative statements that can later be tested for validity. Walter Loban's longitudinal study of the language of children in the elementary school has produced an interesting finding on growth in ability to make tentative statements. As part of his study, he used the methods of the linguist to investigate the language of two groups of children: one with high verbal facility and one with low verbal facility. He reported: "Those subjects most proficient with language are the ones who most frequently use language to express tentativeness. Supposition, hypotheses, and conditional statements occur much less frequently in the spoken language of those lacking skill in language.[5] It is probable that in our teaching we have asked children to formulate hypotheses without providing experience in the verbal medium that would facilitate this process. A third facet of linguistic knowledge related to this stage of problem-solving would enable children to move from the vague to the precise in the vocabulary used to express their ideas. A knowledge of the structures of modification would enhance natural growth in the use of language and hasten development in this phase of behavior.

In the enabling component of language, there are also the language arts, which foster growth in the ability to formulate hypotheses. Listening and reading experiences give the child the opportunity to generate hypotheses about problems and to develop an awareness of problems or gaps in information. This kind of awareness is said to be one of the characteristics of the creative thinker. Through listening and reading, linguistic models for formulating hypotheses can be provided. Through speaking activities, such as discussion, the child can develop fluency and control in clarifying his thinking and in generating hypothetical statements. Through the impact of the reaction of his teacher and his peers, the child learns to modify his thinking or perhaps to hold fast to his ideas if he can provide logical support for them. Finally, after receiving opportunities to explore his ideas orally, he learns to write down his thoughts, using appropriate and effective language.

Synthesizing Findings

A second example of the interrelationship of the three structural components of the language program can be taken from a later stage of the problem-solving process. The behavioral element may be described as the ability to synthesize findings in order to communicate the results to others. The substantive element would be ideas obtained from several sources in any field of study. These ideas would be of two kinds: those that are directly related to the problem and those that serve as models for the creative process of problem-solving.

Through the science and the arts of language, we again provide the medium that enables the child to implement the behavioral process. Let me identify briefly some of the factors that might be important in the synthesis of ideas for presentation. Direct knowledge of at least three types of linguistic structures could be developed at this stage. These are the expression of parallel ideas through appropriate structure and position in the communication unit; the language of comparisons; and the structures of subordination that provide for accurate representation of the relationships among ideas. In addition to direct knowledge of syntax, it is desirable that the child develop the linguistic sophistication that enables him to express his ideas effectively through the achievement of flexibility within sentence patterns. Loban identified flexibility within basic sentence patterns as a characteristic of high language-proficiency. Important also are the attitudes toward language which allow for the choice of a standard of language usage that is appropriate to the form in which the ideas are presented.

A number of supportive language-arts experiences may be described briefly. Through discussion, by the class as a whole or by small "research" groups, facts gained by listening and reading can be subjected to tests of validity. Several sources of information can be compared to help in the selection of accurate and relevant facts to be reported. Through discussion, children might explore several ways of stating ideas in order to select the most effective method of presentation. At this stage of the problem-solving experience, skills such as outlining can be taught or reinforced. Many other learning activities could be listed here. They would all illustrate the need for planning that shows awareness of the relationships among the behavioral, enabling, and substantive components of structure in the language program.

Structure in the Behavioral Component

In addition to the interlocking structure across the three structural components, there is what might be called a vertical or spiral structure within each component. The structure within the behavior component can be illustrated by the way in which the levels of educational objectives in the cognitive domain (as shown in the taxonomy developed by Bloom and his colleagues) operate in one aspect of the language program—critical listening.

At the lowest level of cognition—knowledge—the critical listener acquires information in several ways. He identifies main ideas and supporting details. He differentiates fact from opinion, and fact and opinion from hypotheses. At the second level of cognition—comprehension—he tries to identify the bias and the purpose of the speaker to judge their influence on what is said. He tries to determine the authenticity of the material presented, to make inferences on the basis of implied information, and to generalize on the basis of the facts. At the level of application, the listener may appraise the facts in the light of his previous learning and experience. He may try to predict outcomes at various stages of the presentation, verifying or rejecting his predictions as he gets more information. In an analysis of an oral presentation, the person who listens critically tries to determine the validity of the sources of the speaker's information. He tries to structure the presentation and to determine the organization of the speaker's argument, in order to see the relationship between facts and ideas. At the fifth level of operation, the listener tries to synthesize the facts he hears. This synthesis may consist of ordering facts in a new and more meaningful pattern or determining the relevancy of facts to the purpose for listening. In evaluation, which Bloom and his associates identify as the highest level of cognition, the listener may make judgments about the value or suitability of the presentation, check the conclusions drawn by the speaker against the facts that have been presented, or note the items he would like to check against other sources.

Many of these thought-processes occur while the child listens to an oral presentation. Ralph Nichols, in his study of listening, found that a listener can listen at a speed much greater than a speaker can deliver his ideas.[6] How this time differential is used often makes a major difference between the poor listener and the good listener.

The various levels of cognition can be achieved, to some extent, at each grade level. The child in Grade 1 who listens to one of his friend's experiences in "Show and Tell" can reach the higher levels of cognition. We would expect the sixth-grader, listening to a speaker tell about life in another land, to operate in greater depth at all cognitive levels. Through the experiences that have been classified as the enabling elements, opportunities must be provided to elicit such responses.

Structure in the Substantive Component

To illustrate structure within the substantive component, let me select the "discipline" of literature. Examples from children's literature can be cited that indicate progressive complexity of ideas presented through the medium of each literary form. In fantasy, the young child enjoys the suspense of an original Norse folk tale such as *The Three Billy Goats Gruff.* He can appreciate the spine-chilling elements of the story secure in the knowledge that there is a clear separation of the real and the fanciful. At a later stage in his understanding of the fanciful story, the child reads E.B. White's *Charlotte's Web.*[7] In this story, the fanciful comes much closer to the child's world, and greater maturity of thought is required to differentiate reality and fancy. The story of Charlotte the spider, and of Wilbur the pig, is interpreted by a little girl who understands animal language. Most little girls shed a tear or two as the grim facts of the life cycle of the spider are revealed through this fanciful tale, but they come back to read the story again and again. A still more advanced level of understanding is found in an appreciation of the wonderful grotesqueness of the creatures and their activities in Carroll's *Alice's Adventures in Wonderland.* The child moves into the realm of the improbable and the impossible through much more complex language forms.

One more illustration, from another type of literature, may be sufficient to illustrate substantive structure. Authors in all ages have used the lives of our animal friends as a medium for comment on the ways of man. In these stories, of the "talking beast" variety, we see ourselves as others see us. In the English folk tale of *The Three Little Pigs* there is a clear illustration, almost moralistic, of the value of long-range goals and of the ways in which men differ in their approach to these goals. The theme and the plot are obvious; the characters are uncomplicated; and the style is simple and straightforward. A more advanced commentary on the ways of men is given in Robert Lawson's *Rabbit Hill.*[8] The elements of theme, plot, and characterization are more complex, and they are presented in a style that requires more maturity on the part of the reader. *Wind in the Willows* by Kenneth Grahame requires an even higher level of understanding.[9] The literal reader could read this book and miss entirely the subtleties of the theme. He might lose the plot because of the richness of language and the finely drawn characterization.

The structure that is apparent in literature can also be found in the other elements of the substantive component. An adequate language program will enable children to explore the ideas of literature and other fields through a carefully planned sequence of experiences.

Structure in the Enabling Component

In the area of the language program that has been labeled *the enabling component,* we find structure of two major kinds. First, there is the structure of the language arts, and its related skills and abilities. These skills and abilities are the developmental experiences in listening, speaking, reading, and writing. The importance of providing for competence in reading and writing through competence in listening and speaking, at each level of readiness, should be emphasized. One illustration of the sequential pattern of language experiences may indicate how this area of the curriculum could be structured. Consider the various levels of complexity in oral presentations and the comparable experiences in written expression. In each case, the task of learning to write is simplified and reinforced by previous experience in a similarly structured type of oral composition.

A number of activities illustrate complementary experiences in speaking and writing. On the one hand, we have conversation; and on the other, the writing of a friendly letter. Among the essential elements of conversation are a variety of topics, a concern for the social amenities, and a recognition of an appropriate level of language usage. A friendly letter is based on the same elements. Therefore, experience in conversation should enhance the ability to write friendly letters.

Discussion, a form of oral composition that is more difficult than conversation, may be paired with written reports that follow group experiences. Here, a central theme should be carried through to completion. The speaker is concerned that other participants understand his ideas. He may have to rephrase his ideas if he is to influence his peers. Also, in discussion the speaker is held to more rigorous standards of language usage than in casual conversation. Experience in the oral form should facilitate the writing of group reports.

Participation in a symposium or a panel is comparable to the writing of an organized argument to support a point of view. In a symposium or panel, usually, several ideas or approaches to a problem are presented. Panel members interact informally as they discuss the various points of view, and at the end of the presentation a summary, or concluding statement, is presented. In addition, panel members have the responsibility implied by their designation as "experts" on the topic under discussion. A similar process occurs in presenting an argument in writing. Curriculum experiences in the elementary-school program should be structured to complement the natural growth in language.

The second type of structure in the enabling component is the structure of the language itself. The linguists have, through scientific investigation, described the structure of the English language as it exists today. Our task is to determine how these linguistic findings may be used in the construction of an elementary-school language curriculum. The greatest contributions of linguistic structure may be the insights that educators gain into the natural process of language development and the clear indication that there should be greater stress on speech as the first form of language. The typical methods of the linguists may be more important than structure per se. The linguists have stressed the phylogenetic and the ontogenetic processes of moving through speech to writing, the inductive process for discovering structure in language, and the separation of description and evaluation of language. The search for structure has produced some remarkable insights into "the grammar which we have built into our heads!"

A simple paradigm from transformational grammar can be used to illustrate the inherent system of language. Noam Chomsky, in his book *Syntactic Structures*, has described the structure of the verb in English syntax.[10] His description of the verb is a simple, concise statement of the few, definite rewrite rules that allow us to generate all verbal structures. Such a powerful description should make the analysis of children's language, and the structuring of this part of the language curriculum, quite simple. At some point, yet to be determined, children might be taught the structure of the verb as it is described by transformational grammar.

This design for the structure of the language program is presented for your consideration. If the design is a valid one, there are two major implications for curriculum-building and elementary-school teaching. We must organize the experiences of the curriculum to capitalize on the interrelationships of the substantive, the behavioral, and the enabling components of structure. Further, we must provide learning opportunities that require increasing depth and maturity of thought and behavior within each structural component.

7.

Organizing for Language Learning

Miriam E. Wilt

"Certainly something special is called for to see a concept of over-all structure in English."[11] That "something special" is the concern of every curriculum coordinator, every elementary principal, and every classroom teacher. The writer can do no more than try to think through with the reader the possible causes of our present encapsulation and the possible ways to break through the lock-step of traditional patterns. Thinking together may help us move toward more flexible organizational models—models which may result in freeing our thinking about language learning.

On the verbal level, at least, language arts—or reading, writing, spelling, grammar, handwriting, and other language skills—has been replaced by a much broader complex of learnings and, at the same time, by narrower labeling, i.e., English Language Education. English Language Education includes language, literature, and composition. Inherent in the goals of these three aspects of the program are not only the skills, mechanics, and tools but also the knowledge, attitudes, feelings and understandings of the body of content itself. Thus, specifically, not only can the learner write reasonably legibly, but he can express himself well; he can not only pronounce the words he sees, but he can understand to some degree what the writer is saying. Finally, he can not only produce the sounds of his language and arrange those sounds into meaningful units, but he also knows on a conscious level what language is all about. Acceptance of this latter concept demands bold rethinking of the instructional patterns in our schools.

Change is inevitable. Too many pupils, too few teachers, too much knowledge, too finite results are plaguing us. The old patterns did not fail as some people are prone to reiterate whenever change is imminent, but they simply cannot operate in a world of population and knowledge explosion. Gone is the comfortable world of one teacher who knew enough to teach the basic skills at a leisurely pace to twenty-five youngsters during their elementary school years. In its place, we have a world of automation and specialization, package deals and world understanding, space exploration and atomic energy.

Before any school district can reorganize the instructional program, a basic question must be answered. Is the elementary school merely an apprenticeship school where the skills and tools of the trade (education) are mastered? Or is it a place where control of the tools, skills, and mechanics should be mastered as quickly as possible *when* and *as* they are needed so that the process of education (leading out) can proceed? Actually, one might answer *both,* but this is probably what has been done all along, and as the structure of our society has changed, often the tail, number one, has wagged the dog, number two.

If we are not to accept the "status quo" idea that what was good enough for grandmother is good enough for us, we must shake ourselves loose from the traditional patterns—from the famous treadmill of three ability reading groups, spelling lessons, usage drills, handwriting classes, and on ad infinitum through a day of pigeonholed classes in assorted sizes and shapes. Accepting the triangular approach of language, literature, and composition, we must see the tools, skills, and mastery of conventions not as the curriculum, but as what they are—a means to an end. The end is knowledge about and understanding of: our language, both historically and structurally; our heritage of literature, both the old and the new; and composition—the written or spoken expression of our beliefs, our sensory reactions, our feelings, and our thoughts. Something of what the above body of knowledge means can be taught to anybody at any age.

Teaching English in the elementary school can no longer consist of bits and pieces pasted together like a collage that hopefully will produce meaning and unity. These bits must start in context, be separated for expediency of learning, and be brought back into context. Language is more than a servant of other disciplines; it is itself a discipline, as well as the vehicle of all learning in every other discipline. In science, the humanities, and the arts, learning flourishes in direct proportion to students' capacity and ability to listen and speak, to read and write. The ability to manipulate symbols is the ability to learn. Whether the student is in his carrel or is one in a group of hundreds, symboling is the essence of his thinking, his problem solving, and his aesthetizing. Helping him to acquire this ability is a challenge to all elementary teachers of English. The *how* and *when* is our critical concern.

In thinking about the organization of the elementary school for language learning, it seemed not only relatively easy to ignore content and method, but necessary to do so because other articles have already met that requirement. However, this writer finds it impossible to speak of one without the other. In order to develop the points to be made, it will be necessary to show the organizational plans in their context. Contextual references will be as brief as possible, but at best there will be some unavoidable overlap.

Language

Organization must be based on some basic concepts or beliefs about what is to be attempted. Arbitrarily, language has been chosen as the first phase of the total program to be considered.

Teachers must know certain irrefutable facts about the language skill children bring with them when they come to school. Briefly, then from Wilson:

> . . . he is certainly a complicated and accurate linguistic machine. . . . When he enters school, then, a child alreadys knows, in an operational sense, that language has pattern, that language is arbitrary, that language changes, and that language has variety. He knows that it contains methods for changing a word from singular to plural, for increasing intensity, for changing tense, and for changing one kind of word into another kind of word. Although he lacks a

> technical vocabulary, he knows a good deal about syntax, about usage, about inflection, about comparison, and about derivational processes.[12]

And this is our starting point. All children will not know the same things in the same degree, but if any are to capitalize on what they already know, we must not separate them entirely—like cream from milk—into groups where the other children know no more and no less than they do. Language learning takes place best in a situation in which the child is a teacher of those at a lower level on the curve and a learner from those above him. Talking, listening, thinking, testing, feeling, he will grow. This supports the idea of placing children in multiple-age groups. In a school so organized, pupils spend time with children older and younger than themselves. Sometimes all ages will be represented, sometimes only one age; sometimes there will be only girls, sometimes only boys. Flexible grouping will bring children in contact with many different adults and with children of a wide age range.

An intrinsic part of this all-school grouping is the establishment of groups as needs arise to learn and practice certain skills. This does not assume the day to day progression through textual material, but the teaching of those necessary skills when and as they are needed by specific individuals. The rigid ability groupings of yesterday should never again shackle children in chain gangs that prevent them from ever breaking free scholastically to operate on a level at which they can be challenged and be creative. The elementary school of the future will not put ceilings on children, nor will it prevent their going back to the roots of their needs.

> . . . it is not the tools and the techniques of linguistic science that should be brought into the classroom; but, in some way, the substance of the knowledge and understanding won by linguistic science must be thoroughly assimilated and then used to shed new light upon the problems that arise wherever language is concerned.[13]
>
> Learning in literature and the humanities as well as in other disciplines depends on adequate command of language skills. Apart from academic learning, the child's image of himself and his relationships with others are enhanced, warped, or stunted, depending on the strength of this same command. There can be no question about the importance of helping children grow in their control over language.[14]

The teacher fortified by this kind of knowledge finds his way in an organizational pattern that provides instruction and learning in a variety of situations—all the way from the one-to-one relationship of individualized instruction to activities that are designed for hundreds of children. Varied and flexible groupings—including multiple and single age groups, multiple and single ability groups, multiple and single interest groups (the possibilities are numerous)—will become a part of his stock in trade. As of the moment, the writer feels that home groups should probably be composed of roughly the sixes to nines and the nines to twelves.

Literature

"Children become familiar with a basic imagery long before they go to school."[15] In the intimacy of his mother's lap, the child may well have his beginnings in literature. It is highly questionable whether it is desirable to delay literature or literary criticism until a child can read. "Allegory, imagery, and theme are a part of literature for all ages, and thus inherent in all reading. . . . Something of what these words mean can be taught to anybody at any age."[16] To talk about these matters to very young students should present no real difficulty.

While literature does not need to be read personally to be understood and enjoyed, it is highly desirable that each child learn the mechanics of reading to the very highest level of his ability. The critical, interpretive, aesthetic, and functional fact-gathering skills of reading must be considered elsewhere in the program; however, visual word recognition is mandatory to the use of reading for other purposes. Whether one subscribes to the pure linguistic approach of Bloomfield, to the modified approaches of Smith, Fries, and LeFevre, or to some other method of teaching reading is not our concern here. What is our concern is the organization of a school day, week or year in which these tools of the trade are mastered as quickly and as expeditiously as possible so that valuable learning time is not wasted in senseless drills and exercises that contribute nothing but busy work to eager young minds.

Again, our problem is not the *what* or the *how*, but rather an organization that gives full measure of attention to a literature program in the elementary school as well as an adequate, but not a disproportionate, amount of time to necessary skills.

Literature that relates to the other disciplines, yes; but literature, too, for its own sake. For discussion of literature, it would seem that with the usual exceptions, the basic home groups of sixes to nines and nines to twelves would be practical. But even here with excellent video and audio tapes, live performances, records, poetry readings, and other experiences, the age ranges would often be wider. Certainly, the sizes of the groups would vary through interest and need.

Reading itself is individual and certainly can never be a group process. Discussion of what is read and listening to others read is something else again, but a child and a book is a child with an author all to himself. Time must be planned into the program for reading—time for children to read when adult or other help is available when needed—but *time* they must have. In many cases, the habit of reading must be inculcated into the child in the school since the days of reading as a home leisure activity have almost passed away. Knowing how to read is not enough. The test of a good program is not whether children *can* read but whether they *do* read. Libraries are absolutely essential to the English language program. A school might very well survive without textbooks, but it could never survive without books. Shakespeare and the Bible have started many children off on the road to education. Careful sequential teaching of reading may be more easily implemented, but too often the reading program has controlled the whole curriculum in the elementary schools rather than serving its real function. Reading skill is truly only a means to read what the learner needs and wants to read.

Composition

How better can this discussion be started than with the words of Schlegel: "Read, read. Throw your grammars in the fire."

Written and spoken compositon have suffered near atrophy in the elementary schools since the advent of workbooks, practice sheets, and objective tests. Ridiculous as it may sound, a methods in teaching English book that the writer studied as a teacher education student, early in the rush toward mechanized learning, suggested that second graders could be expected to write a two sentence composition; fourth graders, four; sixth graders, six. Pity the poor child who said, "I have to talk so I know what I think." Prevented from saying it by schools that never provide enough time for audio-lingual activities and only able to write two sentences, how was she ever to find out what she thought?

Children who have teachers who understand the way the language works and who help them at the appropriate times to understand what they already use almost intuitively; children who have teachers who help them quickly grasp the conventions of written English; children who have teachers who have some knowledge of traditional, structural, and transformational grammar—these will be children who enrich and sharpen their own expression and learn to use spoken and written language as a valuable tool and as a personal outlet.

Joseph Royce, in his provocative book *The Encapsulated Man*, suggests that there are four paths to knowledge: thinking, based on rationalism; feeling, based on intuition; sensing, based on empiricism; and believing, based on authoritarianism.[17] He shows how man suffers encapsulation by being satisfied with less than all four approaches to knowledge and how even when all four are employed, there is still a barrier to reality. Since language, both spoken and written, is the symboling system in the quest for knowledge, the importance for children to use language not only in impression—reading and listening—but also in expression—speaking and writing—cannot be refuted. The point to be made is that through the language education program, young learners can be helped to more critical analysis of the world in which they live. The strong tendency to conform and accept can be attacked at the root of its forming.

What has this to do with composition? As with literature, and even more so, education of self-expression begins at the parent's knee. As the child searches for reality, he gathers empirical evidence, responds to his feelings, accepts the authority of his environment, and thinks his way logically to his conclusions. He really discovers what he thinks when he tries to put the experience into vocal symbols. This God-given ability to reason is frequently delayed because of having no one listen to him or encourage him.

Schools could, but seldom do, start the child immediately on this kind of discovery. The natural outgrowth of self-discovery is speech and written language. Long before the child has mastered the mechanics of spelling and handwriting, he can be encouraged to write (by dictation) about his discoveries and his imageries. It is perfectly obvious that this very important way to learn will demand a completely different set-up than one teacher to twenty-five six-year-olds. For written language activities, the wide age-level distribution is necessary. Nines, tens, and elevens can be helpful, useful scribes while the younger child learns to write independently.

The kinds of journals that are kept all through the early years in many European schools might be given a second look as possible means of helping children learn to write and as a record of what has been learned as well as a record of other kinds of thinking, feeling, and believing. If children write soon, write often, and write with increasing vigor and strength of expression, the howls of dismay from our college and secondary teachers that children can't write just might tend to disappear.

Organizing for Learning

So much for the English language syndrome and some hints about reorganization. What kind of an over-all pattern can be visualized?

In capsule form, the curriculum will include the humanities, the arts, and the natural and social sciences. Language will be a discipline in and of itself as well as a service department for all other disciplines. It is conceivable that two groups of twenty-five children each, one of sixes to nines, the other nines to twelves, would be a school family. For a thousand-pupil school, this would mean twenty paired groups. For the home base the groups would be completely heterogeneous within the normal range. The paired groups would be housed in adjoining rooms with a movable partition if possible. No matter how large or small the school, the pattern could be maintained. The home teacher would be a regularly certified elementary teacher with a major competence in one of the disciplines. This placement of pupils and teachers is not unique, but from here out the flexibility within the school is the major area of concern. Hopefully though not absolutely necessary, there would be some consultant service available for special subject areas.

One of the first advantages of this plan is the fact that a child's placement could be changed at any time for whatever good reason without the trauma that now attends moving a child from one grade or teacher to another. In any day, one child might have individual instruction with an adult, help from a tutor, small group work with people his own age, small group work with children with similiar interests, small group work with children whose needs are the same as his, work with large groups of children relatively the same age, and work with large groups of all ages. Conceivably, also, he would have time to be alone to explore his own interests, to read, work with art materials, do independent study, use programmed material, listen to tapes or records, experiment with science.

Looking at the variety of learning experiences, the prospect of making some sort of a schedule seems well-nigh impossible. No day, week, month, or year could possibly be expanded to include all these things, one is quick to think. Not so, and the first thing to go must be:

> Then suddenly there strikes a clanging and a clattering. It is the *bell*. The great Lord of the school that arranges when one starts thinking and one stops.[18]

No more forty-five minutes and then the mad rush to another room, another teacher, another discipline. Departmentalization, team teaching, nongraded groups have all broken down under the tyranny of a bell. The solution lies in careful daily, weekly, monthly, and yearly planning—always open ended and subject to change. With the day roughly divided into the three disciplinary areas—the humanities, the arts, the sciences—and one block for skills, teachers operating in their learning laboratories as specialists or generalists meet children in groups of varied sizes and often varied ages. The key to the puzzle is in scheduling each child in each of the four areas once a day. With as many centers operating as there are groups of children plus other specialized centers, children can move from one learning center to another without breaking the continuity of their learning. This will not mean that at such and such a time fourth grade reading will be going on, but that at any time of the day the children can find the help they need or be part of a learning experience geared to their maturity or interests. It is probable that one block of each day, the homeroom teacher will be the general skills teacher with his own group and the rest of the time will be involved in his special interest, which could be any area from literature to science, or as a special skills teacher. It also seems desirable that the homeroom teacher be responsible for planning the programs of only the twenty-five children for whom he is responsible.

Complex as it looks on paper, the simplicity of the plan is its great virtue. Team teaching, video tapes, films, language laboratories, libraries, programed learning, individualized instruction, all fall naturally into this type of organization. No one needs to get lost because every teacher, every child will be playing different roles at different times. When the six-year-old steps proudly into the kindergarden to read a story from a book, or one he has written himself, to the fives, he becomes a teacher; when the twelve-year-old tells him, *he* is assuming the teacher role. When he discusses with his peers or works with a teacher or another student he may be the learner. As he writes his reflections on some phenomenon, records his conclusions from an experiment, lists the facts he knows about something, or writes a tall tale, he is using language, and all day he has been developing language power.

Every year there will be seven or eight new children to replace the seven or eight that move up. There will always be a strong nucleus to weld the group together. Everyone will feel responsible for the newcomers rather than one teacher having to fit twenty-five six-year-olds into last year's boots. Every new nine-year-old in a group will have people who care enough to help him with the mysteries about to unfold. Every child will have an audience, and perhaps this is what every child needs. Someone to listen to him, someone to guide him, someone to challenge him, someone to cheer him. He will hear and read great literature, learn about language, observe it unfold in himself and those around him. He will find legitimate places to practice his skills whether they be in oral reading or in syntax; he will discuss with older children and younger children; he will experience the joy of learning through experimentation, reading, thinking, believing and feeling.

Conclusion

Perhaps it is time to take a long backward look. An attempt was made to take a look at the teaching of English in the elementary school as it is today. While teaching reading, spelling, handwriting, grammar, usage, and rhetoric is still important, these subjects are viewed as a means to an end rather than ends in themselves. With our sights focused on language, literature, and composition, we need to find a new framework into which we can fit a new kind of language program. The kind of program described here can work. Elements of this sort of program are already being field tested. Nobody except the persons involved can know just how this kind of rethinking will evolve in practice. One thing of which the writer feels certain is that each of the innovations in education has been and will be misused and misnamed. Each working group will need to develop its own implementation, and what the organizational labels are will not matter at all.

Education that is truly education leads out, not in. A program that stops with cognitive learning cannot really be said to educate. The thresholds of knowledge in every discipline are as far reaching as the vision of the educators involved. If teachers think of "intake" without "output," they will be satisfied to go on in traditional patterns that prepare people *for* learning but do not help them to learn. The barriers between scientists, philosophers, humanists, and artists must be broken down by the great leveler, language. Language education, then, first as a discipline and second as a service to all areas of learning, is the fundamental premise on which a new model can and must be constructed. Two questions one might ask. What kind of a man would you be? What kind of a man would you educate?

> . . . such a man, the man who is engaged in a lifetime quest away from encapsulation, moving in the direction of the broadest and deepest possible reality image, has the key to what it means to be

> and to see. . . . Such a man would be a man of great compassion, great sensitivity, and great thought. . . . And while it is true that such an open approach to life is very risky for the individual man in the short view, it is clearly more creative and productive, and therefore more viable for all men in the long run.[19]

8. Tailor your Teaching to Individualized Instruction

Madeline Hunter

Individualized instruction is one of the most popular and most misunderstood concepts in education. Some teachers view it as the act of trying to juggle twenty-five to thirty-five child-shaped balls of different activities at the same time. Others view it as an electronic arsenal with each learner plugged into his appropriate socket. Still others perceive it as turning all responsibility for learning over to the students. None of these views is accurate.

Individualized instruction is no one way of conducting education, nor any one special program. It is the process of custom-tailoring instruction so it fits a particular learner. An individualized program is not necessarily different for each learner, but must be appropriate for each. It is based on the premise that there is no one best way for all learners, but that there are best ways for each learner, which may be different from those for another learner.

How do we achieve this "perfect fit"? An educational program has three major dimensions that can be adjusted to fit any learner: *the educational task*, or what is to be learned; *the learner's behavior*, or what the learner will do to accomplish the learning; and *the teacher's behavior*, or what the teacher will do to make the student's learning more efficient and more predictably successful. Each of these factors will be discussed on the following pages.

It is important to note that the word "individualized" modifies "instruction," implying that the teacher's role is still a vital one.

Individualized instruction is not an end in itself, but rather a means to achieve learning successfully, economically, and predictably. It is an effective and efficient means for achieving learning goals as well as increasing student learning.

Adapting Learning Tasks

Individualization of learning tasks is based on two major premises, both of which have been validated by research. These premises are:

Reprinted from *Instructor* 79:53-63 (March 1970), by permission of author and publisher.

1. *Students learn at different rates.* Age and grade level are in no way guides to the appropriateness of a learning task. A task which is right for one learner will be wrong for another who has already achieved that learning, or for one who is not ready for it. We wouldn't expect children of one age or grade level all to wear all the same size clothing. Neither should we give them identical tasks.

2. *Learning is incremental.* In most instances, the child builds his learning block by block, like a wall. Some learnings act as a foundation for other learnings. It is impossible to achieve a complex learning without first having mastered the simpler component learnings, even though some children may take bigger or faster learning steps than others. For example, in order to do long division, the student must have learned to add, subtract, multiply, and divide, as well as to understand place value.

Intellectual Skills

Having accepted these two premises, we find we can no longer deal out to an entire class, on an assembly-line basis, the books and assignments of one grade level. In individualizing instruction, each objective will be custom-tailored to a particular learner, not homogenized for the whole class and in reality fitting only a few.

Individualizing instruction does not mean that we let certain students "get by" with doing less work. It means we begin where a student is able to perform and move systematically toward better and better academic performance.

Nor does individualized instruction mean that each student must work individually. What it means is that the teacher must thoughtfully and on the basis of the child's learning needs make the decision as to whether for this task he should be learning alone or in a group.

To begin the individualization of intellectual skills, we must first determine what each learner has already achieved in his learning sequence so he may move on to the next appropriate task. To identify a pupil's instructional level in reading, for example, we may listen to him read. If he misses more than two or three words on a page, the book is too hard for him. If he misses no words, the book is too easy—too easy, that is, for us to discover the level of difficulty at which he needs reading instruction. In math, we check to see if he really understands the concepts in addition and subtraction before proceeding to multiplication and division. Thus, by checking what he already knows, we don't waste his time or ours by having him work on something too simple or too advanced for him.

This determination of what each student is ready to learn has two dimensions. One dimension is that which ranges from easy learnings through learnings of increasing difficulty. An example taken from reading would be the learning progression in preprimer, primer, first-grade reader, second-grade, third-grade, and so on. For math this dimension would start with counting, addition, subtraction, multiplication, division, fractions and beyond.

The second dimension is one of increasing complexity in the student's thinking. The simplest level is where the student merely shows that he remembers what he has learned. In further steps, he demonstrates his understanding of that information; applies the information to new situations; uses that information to solve problems or generate ideas by analyzing, then synthesizing, and finally, evaluating.

To individualize instruction, a teacher can work with both of these dimensions, taking a tuck here and letting out a seam there to make the learning task fit the individual child. The task can be made easier—having the child learn addition, or use a first-grade reader. It can be made harder—teaching the child multiplication, or having him read a sixth-grade reader. An example of how a teacher may use a second dimension to adjust the learning task with a group for whom an assignment in fractions is appropriate can be charted.

Another example of this same type of individualizing takes place when a teacher reaches the subject of Daniel Boone in a class in American history. The subject remains the same, but the teacher demands different levels of thinking from each student. Billy, for example, is required only to be able to answer the question, "Who was Daniel Boone?" He is on the level of simply remembering information. Mary is expected to have some understanding—to answer a query like, "Why did Boone choose that area to explore?" Other students may be given assignments which require them to apply their knowledge *(From this group of statements, select those which could have happened to Daniel Boone)*, to analyze *(What factors made Boone's trip dangerous?)*, to synthesize *(As if you had been a member of Boone's party, write a story about your feelings and experiences)*, and evaluate *(Who do you think had the most difficult trip—Daniel Boone or the moon explorers? Support your position with evidence)*.

As you see, individualizing of instruction does not mean that each student will be on a different subject; nor does it mean that individualized instruction is instruction in isolation. Learners can be grouped. It would be a waste of time for a skilled learner to recite the "facts" about Daniel Boone; but he needs that information for analyzing, synthesizing, and/or evaluating. On the other hand, although the less able learner cannot yet perform this more complex thinking, he will benefit from hearing others deal with the information in advanced ways.

Teacher Practice

• **To individualize the difficulty of the task**—Have each child read aloud a page from his reader. Which children miss more than two or three words on a page? The book is too hard for them; use an easier book for reading instruction. Which children know all the words? For these children, the book is too easy. Find a harder book; or let each select a book of appropriate difficulty—although you must, of course, check the selections.

• **To individualize the complexity of the thinking**—Make up questions at different levels of difficulty for a story interesting to your class. If you chose *Goldilocks and the Three Bears*, for example, your questions might run like this:

1. Remembering information—What are some of the things Goldilocks did in the Bears' house?
2. Understanding—Why did Goldilocks like the Little Bear's things best?
3. Application—If Goldilocks had come into your house, what are some of the things she might have tried to use?
4. Analysis—What parts of this story could not have really happened?
5. Synthesis—How might the story be different if Goldilocks had visited the Three Fishes?
6. Evaluation—Do you think Goldilocks was "good" or "bad"? Why do you think so?

For which of your learners would each of your questions be appropriate? Try the story and questions on your class to check your judgment.

• **Reading for professional growth**—

Taxonomy of Educational Objectives, Handbook I: Cognitive Domain, Benjamin S. Bloom, Editor (Longmans, 1956).

Classroom Questions, What Kind? M. Sanders (Harper, 1966).

Attitudes and Interests

Individualization of instruction is not limited to the intellectual domain. Individualization can also be accomplished in the development of interests, attitudes, and appreciations.

You must of course first realize that these feelings *can* be taught. A myth exists that we can't teach interests and attitudes, at least not directly and systematically. But much is known about their predictable development.

The first stage of such learning is for the child to *receive* or become aware of the thing beyond himself—to recognize that there is something in which to become interested or about which to form an attitude or appreciation—whether it is an art work, a poem, or another person with rights and feelings. To teach consideration for others is a vain struggle if the student is not aware of anything beyond himself. You will be equally unsuccessful in presenting an "appreciation" lesson if a student has not experienced that which he is supposed to appreciate. Or perhaps a child has been exposed to the experience, but has paid little or no attention. He has not "received," so he cannot appreciate it.

The second step in developing an interest, attitudes, or appreciation is for the child to *respond*. He must do something. He may listen, look, think, feel, enjoy, comment, or in some other way react to that which he has *received*.

Only after he has *received* and *responded* can the student begin to value what he is learning; and, having begun, go on to make it characteristic of himself so he becomes the kind of person who "is interested in," who "feels that way about," or who "appreciates" something.

Now let's translate these ideas into the individualization of instruction. Just as with intellectual skills, children's learning interests and attitudes will differ in their stage of learning, as well as in their degree of possible development.

For example, your objective may be to develop an appreciation of poetry, and you intend to start by reading a selection aloud. To be successful, you must remember that appreciation depends first on "receiving," and select a poem that you judge your group will *listen* to. No matter how excellent a poem is or how valuable the experience would be, students will not develop an appreciation of a poem that "turns them off."

If you individualize, you will accept a wider range of student responses—from simple attending behavior to nonverbal evidence of enjoyment (such as smiles, nods, or body movements), to verbal responses indicating enjoyment or understanding. Individualization can be accomplished by requiring a particular learner only to listen; asking another which he likes better of two poems; giving a third learner a choice and hoping he will request poetry; and giving support and encouragement to a fourth when he begins to write his own poem. Future expectations for each learner will also be individualized. Your aim for the passive listener will be to get him to respond; for the learner who requests poetry, to increase his poetic literacy by teaching him to appreciate different poets and different poetic styles. In such individualized instruction, each of them will thus be given an appropriate learning task.

Similarly, we can individualize the teaching of attitudes such as "respect for the rights of others." We can expect some learners merely to become aware that there are others who are waiting to take a turn. Learners already aware of the need for taking turns can be required to do so. Some children will take turns without our intervention, even if it is only because they know we require it. Still others will take turns because the game goes better. The objective for children is for them to take turns because the other fellow has a right to one. This ideal may not be obtainable for some at this time, but we can take them a step along the way.

Teacher Practice

• **To individualize interests**—Survey your group to find out what interest each child would like to follow. After considering these interests in the light of accessibility of materials, space, and need for adult guidance, plan a program. You'll find some students will flit from one activity to another, and are unable to be independently productive; others have the maturity to pursue an interest in depth. To individualize instruction, work carefully with those who need it, and give only occasional guidance to the more independent. The dividends of such a program will be growth in productive independence, expanded fields of interest, and (most important) a growing attitude that learning is zestful and rewarding.

• **To individualize attitudes**—Together with your class, identify some school situations that cause problems. These might include having been a victim of an unfair ruling in a ball game; being teased or hit; finding the assignment too difficult; or any problem related to the attitude you are trying to build. Then ask learners to suggest as many different ways to deal with the problems as they can think of. Don't be surprised if at first students can't think of more than one way; or even if they merely parrot previously heard preaching. One reason such school problems exist is that students have not **received** and **responded** to acceptable alternative patterns of behavior. Proceed by focusing their attention on more than one possible response. When an actual problem occurs, help them identify which response they wish to use, then practice using the response.

• **Readings**—
Taxonomy of Educational Objectives: Handbook II: Affective Domain, Krathwohl and Bloom (McKay, 1964).
Developing Attitudes toward Learning, Robert F. Mager (Fearon, 1968).

Psychomotor Skills

Instruction can also be individualized for the psychomotor skills. These are movement skills through which a child expresses his feelings or demonstrates his knowledge and ability, whether by speaking, writing, jumping, dancing, playing ball, or performing on a musical instrument. Even though student aptitudes vary, each of these skills is learned by building increasingly complex and automatic movement patterns. To individualize instruction in movement skills, the teacher again must determine what the student has already accomplished, and what he is now ready to learn.

To determine the appropriate task, ask these questions:

• Has the learner perceived what he is to do—make his letters touch the line, make his voice go up or down, cup his hands to catch the ball? You can waste much time trying to teach a skill when the student has not focused on the critical elements of the task.

• Has he a "set" to perform the skill? That is, does he understand what part of his body is involved and does he know what to do with it—put the opposite foot forward, balance with his arms, place his lips correctly? Is he really trying, or simply going through the motions?

• Has the student's performance been guided physically (placing his arms for him) or verbally ("Hold your arms this way") so he will get the feel of what is expected of him?

• Has he "mechanized" his response—can he perform the sequence of movement without stopping to think what comes next?

• Has the skill become an automatic, complex response to the appropriate stimulus—does he automatically track the ball with his eyes, run to where he expects it to land, and position his hands to catch it? In language does he have the movement skills to automatically communicate?

As has been previously pointed out, a teacher who individualizes instruction will have learners working at different stages. This is as true for instruction in psychomotor skills as any other type of skill. In handwriting, for instance, some learners will be working on the correct formation of difficult letters or letter combinations. Others will be writing sentences or paragraphs, automatically using their writing skill to communicate their ideas as they proceed in their learning.

In physical education, a teacher who individualizes will be teaching some students how to use their bodies properly in throwing, catching, running, or balancing. (It is just as unrealistic to put a learner who has not accomplished these basic skills into a complex ball game as it is to expect a first-grade reader to use the encyclopedia.) Students who have mastered the basics will be given the more advanced task of practicing throwing and catching to automate their responses. Still others will be automatically using their skills in a fast ball game, in a complex type of race, or in advanced gymnastics.

Each learner in an individualized program for psychomotor instruction will be using the skills he already possesses to learn more complex patterns. No learner will be trying to work on complex skills without first having learned the simpler component skills; he will never hear, "Just get in the game and you'll learn to play."

Teacher Practice

• Make a list of students for whom you think each of the following learning tasks is appropriate: Stopping and holding a ball rolled at his feet. Catching a ball thrown to him between shoulder height and waist height. Catching a ball thrown high, low, or to one side. Tracking a ball through the air, running to place his body in the right spot, catching the "fly."

• **Readings**—

"The Classifications of Educational Objectives: Psychomotor Domain," Elizabeth Jane Simpson, in *Teacher of Home Economics*, Winter 1966-67.
Developmental Sequence of Perceptual Motor Tasks: Movement Activities for Neurologically Handicapped and Retarded Children and Youth, Bryant J. Cratty (Educational Activities, Inc.).

Providing Many Ways of Learning

Each individual finds that some learning behaviors are more productive for him than others. Some children learn more quickly if they read, some need to listen, others find it easier to learn if they talk about the material.

In planning an individualized program, a teacher should provide different types of activities so a student can participate in the ones that are best for him. History, for example, can be learned by seeing it re-enacted in a movie or a filmstrip, reading about it in a book, writing a story about it, acting it in a dramatization, painting a picture of it, discussing it with another individual or with a group, visiting one of its scenes, viewing it in another dimension through maps or on a time line, or constructing models or dioramas of it.

There are other dimensions of learning behavior which vary with individual students. Some can work productively with a friend; others are distracted. Certain children prefer to work alone and figure it out; others are more comfortable in a group. Boys tend to be active in learning styles, girls more passive.

Some students are overwhelmed by a long and complex task—they need shorter assignments which give them frequent feelings of accomplishment. Others prefer a longer learning contract so they can make their own plans and proceed at their own pace.

When instruction is individualized for a certain student, the task to be accomplished is identified first. Next, both teacher and student proceed to seek the behaviors that will help him achieve understanding and accomplish the task.

Note that this does not mean that the student will always find the same type of learning behavior productive. The choice of learning style may vary with the pupil's previous experiences, with his ability, with the task, with the current interest of the student, and even with the style of presentation. A combination of learning behaviors is reinforcing; and, when a choice of learning styles is offered, the student can and should continuously expand his repertoire of learning behaviors that work well for him.

Thus by providing for many ways of learning, the teacher is accomplishing a major objective of the individualizing of instruction, that of helping the student to learn how to learn.

Teacher Practice

• Make a list of learning behaviors which you think would be productive for your students. Be specific. You'll probably find you will have to do some careful thinking to be able to write down precise definitions of the learning behaviors. If you list "concentrate," for example, describe just what the student would have to do to convince you that he is concentrating. If you list "practice," describe what and how the student should practice. Making this list should stimulate you to increase your possibilities for individualizing learning behaviors.

• Ask students to tell you what they would do if they really wanted to learn something in a hurry. Give them specific problems such as figuring out how many bottles of soft drink would be needed for a class party, memorizing the lyrics to a new Beatle song, learning enough about Joe Namath to interview him for the school paper, perfecting a trick on the parallel bars for a gymnastic show. Try to get them to reveal some real knowledge about how they themselves work, rather than repeating platitudinous adult admonitions.

• Compare your list with the students'. You may find that you'll need to suggest some learning techniques that you know to be productive but that evidently the class does not know. A good example is making sure that pupils after learning something recall it at least once before moving on to new learning.

You may also find that your students have listed behaviors which you have not thought of. If they are productive, incorporate them in your plans.

• Start a card file on how your pupils learn. Make a card for each pupil, listing the learning methods that seem to be best for him. Just doing the cards will help you organize your thinking about how each pupil learns best. It may also point out that some use only one or two ways of learning. Plan to have these pupils experiment with other types of learning activities. If a child, for example, seems to learn only by reading and then reporting what he has read, suggest that he broaden his base by reading an article on pottery, then show what he has learned by actually making a small piece rather than by reporting verbally on what was read. As each student moves into new learning methods, add those to the cards.

• Set up a tentative plan for individualizing instruction when presenting a unit. Include activities which incorporate many ways of learning. For example, suppose your topic is the settlement of California during the 1850's. Your possibilities for learning might include: making a map showing early Spanish missions and trails; reenacting the discovery of gold at Sutter's Mill; developing a time line of California's historical events; making a report of life in a mining camp from a miner's point of view; preparing an in-depth research paper on those who came to prospect and stayed to farm and ranch.

• Include some opportunities for a long-term activity for the one or two persons in your room who learn well when they can concentrate on one topic for a long period. Often day-to-day work is frustrating to the more able student who is anxious to really attack a problem.

Adjusting Your Teaching Patterns

The third dimension in the individualizing of instruction is for the teacher to individualize his teaching behavior—to decide what he must do to make each student's learning more efficient and more successful. To accomplish this, you must gear your teaching to the needs of the individual student rather than to the demands of the large group.

Some teachers feel that teacher fairness and consistency imply identical treatment of every learner. On the contrary, it's these very qualities that require a teacher to insure that each student receives the assistance and support that are necessary to further his learning. For one student, this may mean a great deal of assistance; for another, it might mean encouraging or even insisting on independent performance.

Many teachers make these modifications in their teaching behavior unconsciously. They joke with one student, are solicitous with another; check every problem with one, spot-check another; praise one, scold another; insist that one work by himself, give continuing help to another. Although the experienced teacher automates these responses, it is important to monitor them constantly to make sure they do not become a rigid teaching pattern rather than genuinely reflecting the needs of particular students. An important factor in this aspect of individualization is the sensitivity of the teacher to varying personality patterns and needs.

This does not mean that teacher behavior can make up for errors in the individualization of the learning task or in the student's learning behavior. If the task is unattainable or the learning behavior inappropriate for a particular learner, failure is likely to occur in spite of any behavior on the part of the teacher. For example, if a student's assignment is to learn to spell words he can't read, writing them fifty times even with teacher encouragement will be a waste of time.

But when the tasks and the learning behaviors have been individualized, the next step is to ask yourself questions such as these for every student:

What can I do to increase his motivation to learn?

Should I praise him or prod him?

Should I give him many short assignments or a few long ones?

Is it better for him to experience continuing success, or does an occasional failure challenge him to greater effort?

How can I increase his speed of learning?

What kind and how much practice helps him most?

What are the reinforcers that strengthen his productive behavior?

How can I make the material meaningful and interesting to him?

How can I encourage him to take more responsibility for his own learning?

What skills and knowledge does he already possess that will help him with this new learning?

How can I make his learning experiences more vivid?

What can I do so that he will remember more surely what he's learned?

How can I add "feeling tone" that will assist his memory?

How can I help him transfer what he has learned into other situations where it is appropriate—transfer his knowledge in spelling into his written work, transfer his good behavior in the classroom to the assembly, transfer his hypothesizing in science into speculation in social studies?

How can I guide him into generalizations rather than isolated bits of knowledge?

You may be asking angrily or despairingly, "How can I possibly know all that about any *one* child, let alone all of them? Where can I find time to ponder each child's specific learning problem in such detail?" You are absolutely right; you can't possibly know all these things. But you will be amazed to find how thinking about these questions in relation to a particular child even at odd moments gives you valuable and productive insights into possible ways to individualize your teaching behavior.

Remember, however, that your purpose is to find out what behavior of yours best helps the child to learn in his own style. Don't fall into the trap of thinking that if you can just find the right technique—the right button or combination of buttons to push—all children will then move in whatever direction you have chosen, like obedient robots. Children know when a teacher is trying to manipulate them and rightfully resent it.

Another idea to watch is the notion that a child will always respond to the same teacher behavior in the same way. His needs and his responses will vary with the task, with the state of his health, with the progress of his maturity; with his mood, with your mood, and even the weather. But this flexibility is just an added dimension to your professional task of adjusting what you do to make it easier for each student to learn.

Teacher Practice

• Make a list of questions for your students which begin, "Which helps you more . . ." "When do you learn more . . ." or "When do you try harder . . ." and complete them with some of your teaching behaviors. For example,

. . . When I give you one long assignment, or several short ones?

. . . When we practice together or you practice by yourself?

. . . When I am firm or when I joke?

. . . When I tell you what to do or let you figure it out yourself?

. . . When I decide which project you should do first or let you make the choice?

Collect the answers from each child. (You may be surprised at some of the replies.) Now proceed to individualize by trying each child's suggestions, afterwards helping him see the results. "You wanted a long assignment, and you do very well when you have one," or "You said you wanted me to joke with you but now you're not settling down to business."

• If possible observe several teachers already in an individualized situation, for the specific purpose of noting the ways they adjust their teaching behaviors to the varying needs of the children. Some of these may be deliberate, some unconscious. Make a careful note of the different behaviors and how the child responds. This is even more valuable in a team-teaching situation or when a special teacher takes over your class. Then you can observe someone else with children you know, watching how specific children react to various teaching patterns.

• Try different behaviors with your group and note the children with whom they are effective. For example, tell them to be their own teacher for the next twenty minutes and see who sets to work and who takes undue advantage of the freedom. At another time let them know you will not collect their papers, and observe which children stop working or become careless. Offer a reward such as early dismissal for completed learning and see which children try harder or learn faster.

• If your school has videotape equipment, request that it be used in your room as you work with children on a particular lesson. Pick one in which you are especially confident and for which you have done some good planning. When you view the videotape later, make a list of the times when you individualized your approach to pupils, another list of times when you tried to reach the entire group. Look for these points:

Observe every person in the class. Was each being reached in some way?

What could you have done to reach the one or two who were not with you? (Perhaps only a nod, or a question worded especially for him?)

View the tape a second time. If you were teaching the same lesson again, what individualized activities would you introduce?

• Read these programmed books on learning theory and try the ideas therein with your class: *Motivation Theory for Teachers, Reinforcement Theory for Teachers, Retention Theory for Teachers,* and *Teach More—Faster,* all by Madeline Hunter, published by TIP Publications, Box 514, El Segundo, California 90245. This series of books was written to make available to teachers important psychological knowledge that will result in significantly increased student learning.

Self-contained Classroom

To individualize instruction for a self-contained class, begin by throwing out the notion that a student's age or grade determines what he should learn. You will no longer deal out the books of the grade level to everyone. You will overcome your compulsion to "cover the material." Instead, you will accept the responsibility of checking to see what each student already knows so you can plan what new material he is ready to learn. Informal tests and your own observation will show you where to start.

Begin to individualize instruction by checking each child's reading level. Have him read to you so you can see at what level he misses one to three words on a page. Then instruction can begin with groups that are able to use the same book. Slower readers will need daily instruction. More independent readers may not need to meet with you daily, but they will need instruction in certain skills and more practice in independent reading. You'll modify the complexity of the thinking task to suit each of the children reading in the same book. For some, it will be enough to know "what happened"; others in the same group should be able to use their knowledge of "what happened" to do the more complex tasks of comparing, applying, analyzing, synthesizing, evaluating.

The same procedure should be followed in math. Working usually with groups, you will teach new skills, always modifying your expectations for different students. For example, when a group is on multiplication, one learner may be doing the numerical problem, another can be solving word problems, and a third will be creating new word problems to go with the number problems.

Students will increasingly take charge of their own learning, at a rate appropriate for each. Some may work on "learning contracts," pacing themselves and designing their own ways for achieving the prescribed learning. Learning contracts may begin with a diagnostic test that will help teacher and students identify their areas of strength and weakness. Then, assuming differing degrees of responsibility, together they will design instructional procedures, making it possible for those who need to work on certain skills to work alone or in instructional groups.

At other times of day, it may be possible for students to pursue their own interests in other subject areas. However, simply scheduling "free periods" without learning expectations or without accountability is *not* individualized instruction. Other than time allowed for exploration, children should be required to make a commitment for what they intend to do and to present evidence they have done it or a reason why not.

There isn't any special way that individualized instruction should "look." But it must meet certain requirements. Each student must be working on an appropriate task, in the way most productive for him, and with the kind of teacher assistance which meets his needs.

As a Team Teacher

The staffing design of team teaching makes possible more alternatives in teaching style and competence, more dimensions in grouping, and more professional know-how in diagnosis and prescription.

In team teaching, learners are usually grouped differently for instruction in each subject. When instruction is individualized in a team-teaching setup, the grouping continues. Occasionally the total group will work together, but usually there will be many smaller, flexible groupings. Children may be grouped according to academic ability but this is only one of the many possibilities. Other bases for grouping are the style of teaching that students need, the interests or the friends they have, the skills they are ready to learn, and the amount of teacher help they require.

Most successful team teachers find that this type of organization provides a richer environment for student learning, and for teacher learning as well.

The nongraded school was created on the basic principle of individualized instruction, whether the staffing pattern is team-teaching or self-contained.

Some schools that call themselves nongraded are really levels systems; that is, all students reading on a fourth-grade level go to this room, all on a fifth-grade level go to that room, and so on. It is an attempt to *organize away* achievement differences, making it possible for one book and one assignment to be used for the entire group. True nongraded instruction is designed to *deal with differences*; in fact, this is the essence of individualized instruction.

In a nongraded school, the learner is diagnosed in terms of the style of teaching behavior that should best propel his learning. He is assigned to that kind of teacher or team. He is also diagnosed as to the kind of group in which he will learn best and assigned to that group. Only then, in an optimum environment of teaching style and peer group, is he diagnosed academically for the purpose of custom-tailoring a program to his needs.

Sometimes the teacher will work with the total class; often he will work with subgroups, and occasionally with only one or two students. If the organizational pattern in the nongraded school is self-contained, a teacher must by necessity leave some students working by themselves when he works with a group. With team teaching, another teacher is available.

When a school is nongraded and instruction is individualized, a student is always working at the academic level appropriate to his present degree of learning. He is using ways of learning and receiving teacher assistance designed to promote his success.

Questions You Might Ask

Should students always be "on their own" when instruction is individualized?

Some teachers think that individualizing instruction means turning over to students all responsibility for their own learning. This would be an abdication of professional responsibility. While it is highly desirable for a student to assume an increasing amount of responsibility for his learning, the rate of take-over must be individualized. The learning decisions a student is allowed to make should be commensurate with his ability and experience. The teacher should provide for the growth of each student toward maturity in learning decisions. He will not just hope the student will take over, nor will he expect the same degree of initiative and independence of all students.

Is individualized instruction an all-or-nothing proposition?

Completely individualized instruction and assembly-line instruction are at opposite poles, with most instruction falling somewhere between. Many learning activities are individualized in one of the dimensions of task, learning behavior, and teaching behavior, but not in the other two. Sometimes a teacher will individualize his expectations for student performance and his teaching behavior. But if he has the same performance expectations for too heterogeneous a group, he will have to adjust the difficulty of the task in order to individualize it. The behavior of the teacher who wants to individualize must at all times reflect the varying needs of each of his students. The teacher who is an instructional artist will individualize all dimensions: the task, what the learner does to achieve it, and what the teacher does to assist him.

Doesn't individualizing take more time?

If you have been arriving in school at the same time as your students and leaving when they do, you'll never be able to maintain that schedule when you individualize your instruction. In the more likely case that you have spent long hours planning and suffering with frustration when students don't learn, then individualizing instruction will save you considerable time.

All good teaching takes planning. When instruction is individualized, however, students work at a level where they can be more independent. They don't have long periods when they can't proceed because they don't understand. Nor do they have free time to get into trouble because the assignment was easy and they finished ahead of the others; so control problems take up less of your teaching time.

Many capable learners can proceed on their own with only occasional stimulation or guidance. This frees you to monitor more closely the learners who would otherwise grind to a halt. Also, as you learn to develop assignments with built-in flexibility the same assignment can be appropriate and stimulating for a greater number of students.

Yes, individualized instruction takes much planning time. But never was your time better spent.

Will my students be ready for the next grade?

Since the purpose of individualizing instruction is to increase the amount of student learning, a good program will result in students being better prepared for their next educational experience than they would have been with the typical instructional routine. Remember that good individualized instruction increases the amount of learning and decreases the time it takes to learn it. The more sturdy a child's educational foundation, the easier it is to build on it.

Doesn't it challenge a child to expose him to more advanced material?

If a student does not have the readiness and foundation for his "exposure" to any material, he will not only be unable to learn it, but precious time will be lost that could have been used to give him the learning he needs. Exposing students to fifth-grade reading when they can't read a third-grade book, or exposing them to multiplication when they don't understand addition, is actually detrimental. Imagine the rubble resulting from a bricklayer's putting in the sixth row of bricks when the first five were not securely in place. Just as real is the academic rubble which results from teaching "sixth-grade material" when previous learnings have not been thoroughly achieved.

Don't students feel that different assignments are unfair?

Do students feel it's unfair for a teacher to help a student who is having trouble with a problem and not give help to one who has solved it correctly? Of course not! Nor do they feel that assignments are unfair if each has work to do that is right for him.

Occasionally a student will ask "Why do I have to do this when he only has to do that?" or "How come he gets to do that?" Your response might be, "It's either because I'm unfair, or I like one of you better, or I have a good reason. What do you think that reason might be?" The answer is usually a perceptive one, "Because he has finished his other work," or "Because it's harder for him." If there is a need to explain further, maintain the dignity of both students.

Students usually feel individualized instruction is infinitely fairer, because everyone has a learning task he can accomplish with appropriate effort. Goldbricking no longer exists; neither are there insurmountable learning tasks.

How do I keep track of student progress?

The question of how to keep track of what students are doing is not a new one. It has always plagued conscientious teachers. Individualizing instruction merely brings into focus the fact that the question has seldom been satisfactorily answered.

The answer is not to load yourself down with bookkeeping chores, but to find ways to establish frequent learning checkpoints. Daily correction of work can be done by students who need both the responsibility and immediate feedback. For those who do not have the maturity or integrity to assume this responsibility, you may need to devise a daily monitoring system.

Your records should be simple and easily maintained. They should include this information: What has the student accomplished? Is he floundering, or is the task so easy he does not need to exert learning effort? Is he protected by a check-back system from forgetting something he once knew?

Devices can vary from checklists and anecdotal file cards to teacher-made tests and observations. It is important to have all the information you need, but on the other hand not to waste time collecting useless or obsolete data. Examine your records critically, and keep only those data that are indispensable.

Eventually, the computer will take over this chore. The machine is ready. It is waiting for humans to identify which data are most useful in making educational decisions.

Won't there be some children I just can't reach?

Regardless of your teaching procedures, there will be some children who will be very difficult to reach, especially those hardcore cases at low ability or low motivation levels. But with individualized instruction you should have less trouble. Having once accepted the idea that no materials or procedures are inappropriate for any child, you can select those which work best. And a pupil who realizes what you are trying to do is much more likely to be motivated to try harder.

Won't I need lots of materials to individualize?

A teacher who follows the ideas outlined in this feature can individualize instruction using whatever materials are available. The more good materials he has, the more alternatives he can make available to learners. No amount of materials, however, can create a good individualized program when the teacher does not have the incentive.

In short, use your materials and supplies to give direction to your individualizing, not as excuses for not doing so. This is not to say good materials are not needed. But demonstrations of good individualized education have a way of stimulating the financial support for material that will make a program even better.

How do I explain individualized instruction to parents?

Parents have been individualizing "instruction" ever since their children were born. They know that what is right for Susie can be all wrong for Marty. Although not usually at a conscious level, parents set different learning tasks for each child. Knowing Marty's clumsiness, they don't demand he make his bed as well as Susie, and so on.

Parents also know their children learn in different ways. Susie feels deserted if she does not have the support of a more knowledgeable person in new learning. Marty needs to figure out for himself; he resents assistance, and looks on it as interference.

Parents are reassured by the knowledge that at school their children are not anonymous "desk fillers"—that the individuality and learning style of each child are being taken into account so he will learn more in less time. When you explain your program to parents, don't be surprised if they respond, "Why haven't schools been doing this all along?"

9. Individualized Language Arts? Why Not!

Margery V. Northrop

The word "individualized" has been bandied about ad nauseam, but even in the near-vacuum of research evidence and of positive knowledge about the learning-teaching process, we are fairly certain that learning takes place when there is adequate feedback or knowledge of results. Ideally this feedback should contain definite information concerning the individual child's own errors received in a one-to-one relationship with the teacher. This is the advantage of the private school's small classes. Realistically, the unit count is not going to be reduced in the public school system in the near future, and the widespread use of organizational changes to facilitate small group instruction such as team teaching is still around the corner. In thousands of classrooms children are still arranged in rows or groups while a teacher instructs the group as a whole, and all work from the same book at the same time in complete defiance of our awareness of ranges of ability in any group, no matter how homogeneously they may have been sorted out. A program such as team teaching with the additional personnel and flexible scheduling will be an excellent answer to the problem of individualizing instruction, but it requires administrative authority for additional funds and changes in staff use. Yet, individualized instruction *can* be done *now*, and it can be done practically and effectively by any teacher with careful use of independent activities.

In the areas of language arts in the elementary school, it is possible and sensible to use an individualized approach to learning with children who have acquired certain basic skills in reading and writing. This can be done not only in the well-publicized area of reading, but also in the areas of writing, speaking, and listening. To bypass the sterility of most single texts in language arts, it is feasible to organize a classroom into an independently operating unit where all children are given blocks of work in spelling, composition, research, oral communication, etc., which they manipulate to their own satisfaction and at their own level of achievement. As all children are working independently on projects, the teacher is free to give individual and small group instruction. More learning can be accomplished if a child and a teacher sit down together in a conference for a few minutes to discuss that child's own work than can ever be done in a traditional program.

From *Delaware English Journal* 2:17-22 (Spring 1967). Reprinted with permission of Margery V. Northrop and publisher.

In the past the problems of individualizing class instruction with thirty or more children have appeared to be impossible to solve. With the introduction of individualized reading programs (self-selection), techniques used in this method of teaching reading have proved very successful, and can be transferred to any other curriculum area. In fact, the first prerequisite of individualizing instruction is to set up worthwhile independent activities that will vitalize the children's interest and require little attention on the part of the teacher. This leaves the teacher free to devote a large block of time to individual conferences and small group instruction in basic skills.

And *how* can this be done?

"This" can be accomplished by giving a large block of time for language arts classes—equivalent to that usually required for Reading and English subject matter classes in a departmentalized program. The class thus has a long uninterrupted time with the Language Arts teacher who is responsible for all communication skills. (This is, of course, readily accomplished in the self-contained classroom.)

Individualized Reading

The program is, first of all, based on an individualized reading program, using trade or library books but no basal readers. Each child selects his own book in special free library time slots, in addition to regular library classes, and keeps his own record of books read with short comments on each book. Reading levels are determined at the beginning of the year by spelling and informal inventories, and through individual conferences the children's skill needs are determined. This reading program has a high interest level and the children are motivated to read independently for pleasure. Small groups of children revealing need for common skills are worked with until the need of a group is satisfied, and then that group is disbanded. Children engage in book sharing—skits, puppet plays, chalk talks, TV shows, bulletin board displays, etc.—to advertise a particular book to the remainder of the class. In this way children become familiar with a wide selection of readings. The children increase their reading skills by constant, absorbing practice—in reading.

Individualized Writing

When children are established in the reading program, the writing program of individualized instruction is set up simultaneously through channels of practical and personal writing. It may take one year for the teacher to become adept at individualized reading before taking the next step. The entire group is instructed in skills of notetaking, outlining, and writing of a "research" paper. This is done in separate units based on a topic of interest to the child and selected by him. This format can also be used for social studies and science reports, and these reports can also be written in the Language Arts classes. Several short practice reports may be done before attempting a long "research" report. This could require several months, broken down into components of notetaking, outlining, rough drafts (corrected by teacher and student), and final finished report. All of this work is done independently after initial group instruction. When children encounter difficulty, the teacher assists. She is constantly helping children and checking their individual work.

The librarian is of invaluable assistance in the individualized program—a library is a must. Free library periods should be allowed for selecting and returning library books and for children to do reference work. The librarian works closely with the Language Arts teacher, and the children become familiar with the library and with a wide variety of reference materials.

In addition to practical writing of many varieties, done with correction and instruction, the children write at least one story per week for personal writing. These stories are kept by the children in a personal folder and are *not* corrected. Writing will improve by frequent highly motivated writing experiences; and, in the subjectivity of personal writing, encouragement and praise further the improvement far more than the blue pencil. The stories are read silently by the teacher and orally by the children to the class—on a voluntary basis. This is one of the highest motivating forces for writing—writing for an audience. Composition may be motivated by literary models, tall tales, classic stories, poems, etc., and, in any event, children write better about objective subjects rather than subjective ones. For example, personal writing may be initiated by any of the following suggestions after a period of introduction and discussion:

1. A story about a picture—have five or more on display
2. A story about a comic strip
3. Cartoons—to portray a story
4. Writing instructions for making a diagram so that others may draw it from these instructions
5. Discussing assigned topics in groups and then writing about them
6. Writing beginning suspenseful sentences for stories
7. Writing surprise endings
8. Tall tales
9. The school of the future
10. What would happen if we were invisible?
11. Why frogs have bulging eyes
12. The day I landed on Mars
13. If I were President
14. A girl caught in a strange, transparent bubble
15. Stories about monsters, animals, haunted houses, . . .

and so on . . .

Throughout the year, in connection with the personal writing program, the class is given instruction as a group in imagery, leading to the writing of poetry. Haiku and free verse are the most interesting vehicles for this instruction. Choral reading is also a part of this instruction in poetry. After large group choral reading, small groups of children are encouraged to practice organizing a poem of their choice for reading to the class.

Oral Communication

The oral communication skills should be emphasized in this or any program so that they will be more evenly balanced with the writing skills. Children should be given an opportunity to express themselves orally by reading their personal stories, reading exciting parts of library books, choral reading, one-to-one reading in teams of two for comprehension checks by teammates, informal speaking and formal speeches. Debating teams can be organized very simply in the elementary school with a simple ten-point system, with judges and timekeepers. Subjects such as space travel and its value, UFO's, homework, etc., can be very well debated. Group and individual instruction can be given in speaking, with attention to voice quality, interest, and organization. Tape recordings of debates, choral reading, and speeches are a very successful means of pointing out areas of difficulty.

All of these activities can be done independently by the children when properly introduced and guided. In *one* Language Arts class children can be found reading for pleasure, reading for reference work, taking notes, writing a rough draft, polishing a speech, taking a spelling list from a teammate, writing poetry or a personal story. They know what is required and when, and with few exceptions the jobs are done enthusiastically and well. Specified times are set aside for oral activities, to maintain an organized systematic program. Grades are given for most assignments, and in some areas children are given a check list with comments concerning their abilities in the subject and their need for improvement.

Individual Conferences

In the conference the teacher will attempt to determine the student's comprehension, oral expression, word attack skills, and appropriateness of reading material. From findings in the meeting, she either will assist the child in developing skills individually or will assign him to a group for work on a particular skill. Records are kept on a single sheet (ditto) containing all children's names, with blocks for comments on abilities and needs and with assignments noted. One sheet per week is used and grades can easily be assessed from these sheets. It is advisable to keep one record for reading and one for writing and speaking. Contrary to rumor, record keeping in an individualized program need not be burdensome.

The first conferences of the year should be done while the child is in his seat, to promote a ripple effect among the class. Others hearing the conference will be interested and it will reduce tensions. Children may request conferences informally or on a sign-up sheet. The conference may be two minutes or ten. However, it is hoped that the teacher will see every child as frequently as possible. Once a week or more, it is a good idea to hop rapidly around the room speaking briefly to each child.

In a conference about a child's written expression, the teacher and child correct a paragraph together, noting such things as run-on sentences, sentence fragments, poor mechanics, spelling, good thoughts, and interesting new words. If ten children show a lack of knowledge about quotations, it may be that the whole class is weak in this skill. However, the entire group may not be ready to have instruction in this. Children who cannot write a complete sentence should not be included in this group for instruction.

The chief problem of the individual conference is lack of time. It is better to point out one area of need and work on this with the child than to try to teach him everything in one conference. The mere fact that he is being treated personally does much to motivate him and encourage his improvement.

Initiating The Program

How to begin? . . . a most important question! As mentioned previously, it is best to move slowly and individuate one area at a time—reading is the appropriate choice as the children will then have something concrete to be doing while the other areas are individualized. Most important, this should not be busy work; it should be constant, absorbing reading practice, which is essential for good reading skills and comprehension.

One should not individualize until projects are well planned or outlined in advance, and the entire group has been carefully informed of requirements of the project and how to accomplish it. Projects do not have to be begun and end at the same time; staggering the work will be almost automatic because of children's varying abilities. This is an opportunity to challenge the gifted or exceptional student with assignments of graduated difficulty. Special units of work such as poetry units, debating units, sequential composition and discussion groups may be distributed during the school year, if desired.

The chief objection to a completely individualized program appears to be rooted in a fear that the teacher is not directly instructing all the children enough of the time. There is very little evidence to prove that active instruction results in learning. We are charged with instilling a love for learning in children, and we must help them learn how to learn alone. With the explosion of knowledge, we cannot possibly teach all the children all the facts, but we can teach them how to search fruitfully for knowledge above and beyond the period of formal education.

10. Improving Independent Study

Jeannette Veatch

The crux of improving independent study lies in whether or not it *IS* independent. Workbook pages and teacher-made exercises are very much *DE*pendent as they are issued by the teacher. Usually, in the elementary school we refer to independent work as that taking place during the "seatwork" time; i.e., when reading groups are meeting with the teacher.

"Seatwork" centered around such "exercises" will yield little that really educates. The appalling fact is that most teachers, as well as most people who *train* teachers, believe that such paper work is important and educative, a belief not backed up by research data. We read about "well-planned" workbooks. There are no such workbooks; nor can there be, as no author knows what a child in a given class needs at a given time. No planning is good that ignores the children to be involved, so it is nonsense to speak of "well-planned" workbooks. The only hope is that teachers may have a variety of exercises and drill pages to fit a recognized need of a child. This means a dozen different workbooks and hundreds of teacher-made exercises. Even then there is no guarantee that the best-fitting exercise will teach a child whatever that exercise is supposed to teach. We simply do not know *what* workbooks teach, if they teach anything at all. There is little except the opinion of the author of the material to justify their value, even if developed with a modicum of try-outs (but not standardization) with living, breathing children.

To develop improved independent study we need to avoid teacher-assignments of this type. Workbooks are time-killers and should be viewed as such. When and if they should be proven educative, then perhaps will be the time to use them. In the meantime let us discuss learning which can be carried out in-

---

From *Childhood Education* 43:284-288 (January 1967). Reprinted by permission of Jeannette Veatch and the Association for Childhood Education International, 3615 Wisconsin Avenue, N.W., Washington, D.C.

dependently. Children will study independently more often, with greater concentration, and certainly with greater interest when that which they study is of their own choice. Independent study means just that—*independent.* Recognizing a need, the child develops his own means of attacking a recognized problem, seeking the help he needs when he needs it.

Self-recognition of a need is a first step and certainly one of the major laws of learning. When a child *knows* he confuses "b" and "d," he can work on it. When a child realizes he is not sure of certain consonants in the beginnings of words, he can develop a project of cutting out pictures from magazines of objects that start with the needed letter. There are limitless projects in the minds of children.

One point about independent work is that it need not be hurried. When a pupil develops his own project he has the time to work on it during an independent work period without being hounded to finish. When a child is the only one doing a certain thing there is no need on the part of the teacher to rush him through. The child knows when it is time to go out and play or to go home. He can pace his work to the realistic needs of the length of the school day; if he doesn't finish one day, he can plan to stop at such a point so as to finish another. There is a matter of serenity and concentration that must not be ignored. A child works at his own project, and he works on that project at his own pace. While there is no research in the independent activities on this matter, there is plenty on self-selection in reading that supports the philosophy of this type of activity.

One interesting master's project showed children, familiar with self-selection practice in reading instruction, to be markedly more independent and resourceful in planning their independent work than were children under a traditional basal reader, workbook program.

Criteria for Improving Independent Study

Independent study requires that children make the choice as to what to do. Does the teacher make suggestions? Of course! Does the teacher check on these activities? If he wants to. But those criteria helpful in leading to the improvement of independent study are generally in the tenor of the following:

- The activities are child-chosen, self-assigned and largely self-directed, although assistance from the teacher or from friends is possible and helpful.
- The activities will require little formal checking, no red-pencil correction, but much teacher approval and knowledge.
- The activities may be long-term or short-term without regard to the length of the period devoted to their accomplishment.
- The activities must absorb children so that there is little need for the child to interrupt himself or the teacher for any purpose short of emergency.
- The activities should use materials that are easily accessible and commonplace. The creative use of ordinary materials should be a hallmark of these activities.
- The activities should be done for the pupil's personal satisfaction, producing enthusiasm rather than the feeling of doing a chore.

These activities, however, do not spring full blown out of the thin air. They require a classroom setting full of possibilities for self-determined endeavor. Most useful references describe, in some form, centers of interest that beckon to children.

Centers of Interest

With some variation, the centers of interest are set up around the following areas:

BOOK CENTER—where all the books are kept: trade, text and reference.

WRITING CENTER—where writing supplies of all kinds are kept, hopefully a typewriter or two, and including space for blackboard writing or writing on brown paper on the wall.

ART CENTER—where wet media such as clay, finger paint, water paint can be used with clean-up facilities handy; where dry media such as crayons, colored chalk, pretty paper, paste and scissors have a place of their own.

SCIENCE CENTER—where all manner of equipment such as magnets, batteries, terraria, aquaria, collections and exhibits find a spot.

DRAMATIZATION CENTER—where the unit in social studies lends itself to dramatization and exploration or where, for younger children, playing "house" is possible.

MATERIALS CENTER—where blocks and other creative toys and playthings are available for construction and similar activity.

FOLLOW-UP MATERIALS CENTER—where the teacher can assign specific exercises and other work and where children might find material to work upon for their own benefit.

With classrooms set up along these lines, independent work comes into its own. Teachers and pupils plan together so that children work through the problems that face them.

Using the Centers

Given these centers, what can a teacher expect of young children? Which activity comes when? Is there an order to activities? Briefly, order and sequence depend upon the needs of the independent work period itself. Consecutive activities are usually of two types: (1) those that occur during the reading period and (2) those that occur at some other time of the school day. The differences between these two periods lie in the noise level of the activities. In the first, because the teacher needs to be heard by the individuals and groups, a noisy activity cannot be allowed lest there be interference. But when an independent "free" time is set up when no such instruction is required, then pounding, hammering and all manner of noise can occur without causing problems. Planning for either of these two types of work periods should take place when the day is begun in the morning. Teacher-pupil planning comes into its own when there is leeway for pupil-decision.

Sequence of Activities

As far as sequence of independent activities is concerned, the independent work period during the reading time can and should begin with the silent reading of a self-chosen book. Under a program of individualization, self-selection is the motivating force behind reading. Children choose books usable by teachers to improve reading skills. Subsequent follow-up activities can be based on such book choices. A child may prepare his selection to present to his teacher during an individual conference, or he may plan a project that stems from that selection. Beyond those activities that tie directly to reading, there is really no particular need for a prescribed sequence of events. Let the child absorb himself and so be exposed to the excitement of learning independently. The prime test of such an activity is, of course, "What can the activity by itself teach the child?" Upon the answer to this question hangs learning that develops children to their potentials.

11.

Language Experience Approach in Elementary Language Arts

David C. Waterman

Criticism of the methods used to teach reading in the elementary schools has been widespread since the launching of Sputnik in 1957. Even before this event, some reading authorities recognized that we failed to teach the habit of reading—that is, the idea that reading, like breathing, is something you do throughout life. The evidence that reading has not been habitual with students after they have graduated from high school is reflected in the fact that over seventy-five per cent of high school students cease using their library cards after graduation. According to Spache, there are a number of studies which show that reading is still not a widespread leisure-time activity. Three-fourths of the flood of paperbacks is purchased by about ten per cent of the population, and only about ten per cent of adults use the library as often as once a month. Spache finds that about three-fourths of the great bulk of reading is done by less than five per cent of the adult population.[20]

From these facts, one can infer that students do not view the act of reading as a lifelong habit. Furthermore, one could ask why students do not form the habit of reading. The school accepts pupils when they are about six years of age. Perhaps the experiences of children before coming to school influence greatly their attitudes about reading but, certainly, pupils' attitudes are further influenced by what happens after they enter school. The style, vocabulary, and content of the basal readers, which are used almost exclusively, do not develop interest in reading. A major purpose of the language experience approach to teaching reading and language arts is to foster positive attitudes toward reading. As these attitudes mature, the child is encouraged to experience reading as a habit rather than a skill used primarily during the school years.

This article will describe an attempt to teach elementary language arts in first grade using the language experience approach. The term "language experience" reflects generally the concepts developed by Roach Van Allen during the time he worked with teachers in San Diego County, California. The rationale of the language experience approach, from a pupil's perspective, is as follows:

What I can think about, I can talk about.
What I can say, I can write.

Reprinted from *Contemporary Education* 40:206-211 (February 1969), by permission of author and publisher.

What I can write, I can read.

I can read what I write and what other people can write for me to read.[21] A particular strength of this approach, when compared to other approaches for teaching elementary language arts, is that pupils derive their motivation and interest from working with concepts that are already familiar to them. In contrast, a basal reading program suggests steps in nearly every lesson taught by which the teacher should provide "motivation" and "interest" to stimulate a desire on the part of pupils to read the stories.

The beginning of language experiences in first grade consists of the narrative and conversational remarks of children. Because these bits of information are to be used as "reading" materials, the teacher should have some method of preserving them. A tape recorder can be used. Children will learn to operate a tape recorder in a matter of minutes. If a child draws a picture and wants to say something about his picture, he can identify himself on tape, record his remarks, and later the teacher can transcribe these comments on paper. The comments may then be placed under the picture. The child will use the picture and his statements as "reading" material which he can repeat to others. He can also learn to recognize some of the words he has spoken in printed form. Thus, the idea that spoken language can be written is reinforced.

Using a Polaroid camera, the teacher can photograph each child. The child can build a story around the picture. For some children, this may be the first time they have ever seen a picture of themselves. The teacher can write what the child says. If a teacher does not have the camera, she can ask the children to draw a picture of themselves. These pictures, or photographs, after having been labeled and commented upon, can be displayed on a bulletin board or bound into a class book. Children will flip through the book looking for pictures of themselves as well as their friends and will also learn, through repetition and practice, to recognize many of the printed words underneath the pictures.

Concern, at this point, will be expressed by the experienced teacher because of a lack of "vocabulary control" in comparison to that exercised in a basal program. How are children going to learn so many words? The typical basal program carefully introduces about seventy-five different sight words. But, according to Heilman:

> He (the child) uses twenty to thirty times this number of words and understands many more.
>
> . . . The concern for controlling the introduction of new words puts a limit on the variety of reading material which can be accommodated within the framework of the controlled vocabularly. The teacher must motivate children to identify themselves with the characters and the situations depicted even though these may be somewhat alien to children of certain socioeconomic groups.[22]

The child learns words through the repetition that occurs naturally in his speech patterns. Furthermore, the words used in basal series are said to be based upon children's usage. An examination of the words naturally used by pupils will reveal that in a short time the child can read most of the words in the basal readers. He can read many more words that do not occur in these vocabulary-controlled readers but which do readily occur in his own speech patterns as well as in the speech patterns of his peers in the classroom.

From the first day of school, the teacher can provide a news chart. In this chart will be included items about the weather, school events, current political events, human interest items, items about "what we are going to do today," and news about the children themselves. Such charts are made upon the blackboard and copied later as displays to be read and enjoyed. The pupils are not expected to memorize the words although some will, but rather as they read and re-read these charts the words will become familiar. Children will be found looking up these news items three or four months after they were written. The discussions about what to include on these charts provides oral conversation practice. Also, children learn to edit, summarize, and review as they refer to the charts during the year.

Field trips should be planned. A visit to the furnace room, a walk to a fire station, a recess on the playground—these activities provide some common understandings and experiences about which to talk and write. During field trips, the Polaroid camera can be used to record visual images which will later refresh the pupils' memories. The pictures can be labeled and displayed along with appropriate comments. Such a display provides an illustrated textbook which whole groups can use as reading materials. Different groups can write about the same experience, which provides an opportunity to view the experience from many different angles. The children can compare versions and select the one they like best. In this process, judgments will be made which enhance the ability to analyze content and develop critical reading skills. If the classroom is fortunate enough to have teacher aides, the aides can assist by taking the dictation about the pictures and printing the necessary words. If the teacher lacks a camera, an experience chart can still be used. The children may illustrate the chart and supply the text to describe the experience.

Practice in reading occurs when the teacher has groups of children reading the charts, bulletin boards, news stories, labels, and, of course, trade books. It is suggested that at least two copies of each trade book should be available since two children can then each have a copy and can read to one another. At times, these small groups should be based upon interest; at other times, the teacher will group according to needed skills, or even permit friendship groups. As children read their own writing, then the writing of others, they gain vocabulary and comprehension skills. The teacher should label many of the objects in the room. She may also provide a Language Master which can be used as a "talking" dictionary. Thus, a child can find a word he needs to write by playing the card through the Language Master and hearing the word pronounced. The cards should be arranged alphabetically and should be recorded by the teacher using the pronunciations common to the locale. Later, these cards can be used with sentence patterns and word meanings. Pupils who need help learning alphabet letters can use cards with the letters printed and recorded. Finally, certain phonetic skills can be illustrated in both visual and oral form using the cards properly recorded.

In addition to the children's own writing and speaking, the teacher should read many stories and poems to the class. Language experiences may be broadened through the use of materials prepared outside the framework of the class. These stories and poems should be children's literature and not adult literature. In some cases, stories from a basal reader may be used. But the trade books will contain many interesting stories and an anthology of children's literature should be available as a source of stories and poems.

At some point children will begin to write their own stories. This may occur as early as October or as late as January. Their first efforts will reflect direct experiences. If the teaching processes are correctly applied, the language patterns of these stories will be natural rather than the stilted style of basal readers. Children will avoid the repetition that occurs in basal materials because they have not been exposed to this highly artificial language pattern. If they have indeed learned that writing is talking in another form, the language patterns of their first stories will resemble conversation rather than a literary style. The writing of these stories marks a significant step for each child. When these stories appear, the teacher is provided with her reading "textbooks." In some cases, the teacher may organize the stories of individual children into a "book" which contains only their stories. In other cases, she may use the stories of several children in a single "book." Books should be reproduced in sufficient quantity for each child to have his own copy. Also, the teacher may want to preserve the original spelling, punctuation, and grammar in the stories for a record of a child's progress, but the copies that are reproduced for the children to read should be edited in these areas. The content and style of the stories should be preserved in their original form.

Once books are written and reproduced by the children, their progress in reading greatly accelerates. The skills of spelling, punctuation, grammar, and proofreading are developed as children experience their handwritten stories being translated into books. The books may be bound and illustrated. The integration of language skills reaches its highest development in this approach. Spelling is taught not as an isolated skill but rather is developed as the child comes to realize that if he does not spell words correctly, others can't read them correctly. Punctuation serves a real purpose, making more precise the meaning intended. Grammar reflects the ability to express a thought clearly and to communicate that thought to others in one form or another. The teacher may add an index or a table of contents to the book. The child learns what these terms mean through working with the teacher to write books. A dictionary may be written for each book. Such a dictionary will contain the words alphabetically arranged, and, in time, simple definitions of these words as they are used in the stories.

The stories written by the children can be read, first by their original authors, then by other children. Small groups of children may form to work on a book or to discuss a story, or to read one another's stories. Individual differences emerge as the pupils progress and the use of temporary groups based upon various criteria helps the teacher deal with these variations. In addition to their own books, children will continue to read the trade books. They will also have need for other kinds of reading than the narrative reading found only in stories. A child developing an interest in fish might, for example, refer to books about fish before writing his story. If he has tropical fish at home, he may photograph his fish to illustrate his story. The children might be stimulated to organize a "unit" on fish with several children studying an aspect of the topic. A culmination of such an experience might be a presentation of a series of reports written by the pupils and presented to other groups in the school. The skills thus developed cut across subject lines. The restrictions of narrative-type reading can be avoided if the teacher encourages pupils to write units and organize materials around a theme.

The culmination of the language experiences of the child occurs when he is able to read what other people write for him to read. Early in the year, a first grade teacher might invite an intermediate grade pupil to come into her classroom and read some of the stories, charts, or news items that children wrote. This act signifies to the child that others can read what is written and establishes a goal for him.

A classroom organized around language does not resemble the traditional classroom using a basal reader. Children will be seen typically engaged in many activities. Some will be painting illustrations for their stories. Some will be lying on the floor, printing on a large sheet of white lined paper the content for their next story. Some will be grouped around a chart, reading orally and questioning each other on the chart. Some will be dictating, into a tape recorder, a story which the teacher or teacher aide will later transcribe and reproduce. There will be some children reading trade books in groups of two or more. The teacher may be circulating from one group to another giving advice as needed or perhaps meeting with a group of children to develop a particular skill in phonics, word recognition, or comprehension. There will be moments when the whole class will meet as a group; for example, during the oral reading of a story by the teacher or a pupil. Such stories will, of course, be stories that are new to the audience. Growth in the skills of language emerges as the teacher examines the original stories written by children and compares these in spelling, grammar, punctuation, story content, vocabulary, and structure to those written earlier.

Perhaps the most important by-product of this activity is the formulation of positive attitudes toward school, toward reading, and toward the expression of ideas. Given such a start, one can reasonably expect that the habit of reading will indeed occur. When children are free to express themselves, when they develop skills that clearly show the relationships of the language arts, and when they see the concrete production of books they themselves have written being read by others, they have a sense of accomplishment and pride.

Author's Note:

While such an approach is recommended for first grade, and with some modifications for second grade, the function of the school is to broaden experiences. Thus, as the child passes from second to third grade, he might logically be offered a different kind of reading program. This author thinks that the program described in Jeannette Veatch's book, *Reading in the Elementary School*, published by The Ronald Press Company in 1966, and characterized by the term "individualized reading," might suffice.

For a discussion of the weaknesses and strengths of language experience and individualized reading, the author recommends Chapters 4 and 6 of George Spache's book referenced in this article.

Notes

1. Stanley Elam, ed., *Education and the Structure of Knowledge* (Chicago: Rand McNally, 1964), pp. 4-43, and G.W. Ford and Lawrence Pugno, eds., *The Structure of Knowledge and the Curriculum* (Chicago: Rand McNally, 1964), pp. 15, 30, 71-86.
2. Benjamin S. Bloom et. al., *Taxonomy of Educational Objectives* (New York: David McKay, 1956).
3. Kate Seredy, *The Good Master* (New York: Viking Press, 1935).
4. Farley Mowat, *Westviking* (Toronto: McClelland and Stewart, 1965).
5. Walter D. Loban, *The Language of Elementary School Children* (Champaign, Ill.: National Council of Teachers of English, 1963), p. 85.
6. Ralph G. Nichols, "Factors Accounting for Differences in Comprehension of Materials Presented Orally in the Classroom," unpublished doctoral dessertation, University of Iowa, 1948.
7. E. B. White, *Charlotte's Web* (New York: Harper and Row, 1952).
8. Robert Lawson, *Rabbit Hill* (New York: Viking Press, 1944).
9. Kenneth Grahame, *Wind in the Willows* (New York: Charles Scribners Sons, 1953).
10. Noam Chomsky, *Syntatic Structures* (The Hague, The Netherlands: Mouton, 1957).
11. Graham G. Wilson, "The Structure of English," in *The Structure of Knowledge and the Curriculum*, G.W. Ford and Lawrence Pugno, eds. (Chicago: Rand McNally, 1964), p. 71.
12. *Ibid.*, pp. 73, 75.
13. C. C. Fries, "Advances in Linguistics," *College English* 23 (October 1961): 37.
14. Miriam E. Wilt, "Using the Implications of Linguistics to Improve the Teaching of the English Language Arts in the Elementary School." Published jointly by Modern Language Association of America, New York, and the National Council of Teachers of English, Champaign, Ill., p. 90.
15. Margaret Meade, "Cultural Bases for Understanding Literature," *Publication of the Modern Language Association* 68 (April 1953): 12.
16. Wilson, *op. cit.*, pp. 82, 85.
17. Joseph R. Royce, *The Encapsulated Man* (New York: D. Van Nostrand Co., 1964), p. 12.
18. Sylvia Ashton-Warner, *Spinster* (New York: Simon and Schuster, 1959), p. 52.
19. Royce, *op. cit.*, p. 199.
20. George D. Spache, *Reading in the Elementary School* (Boston: Allyn and Bacon, Inc., 1964), pp. 16-17.
21. *Ibid.*, p. 134.
22. Arthur W. Heilman, *Principles and Practices of Teaching Reading* (Columbus, Ohio: Charles E. Merrill Books, Inc., 1967), p. 115.

Selected Bibliography

Allen, Roach Van. "Grouping Through Learning Centers." *Childhood Education*, **45** (December 1968): 200-203.

Allen, Roach Van, "How a Language Experience Program Works." *A Decade of Innovations: Approaches to Beginning Reading*, **12**, Part 3 (1967) Convention Proceedings, 1-8, International Reading Association.

Ayllon, Maurie and Susan Snyder. "Behavioral Objectives in Creative Dramatics." *Journal of Educational Research*, **62** (April 1969): 355-359.

Brown, Carl F. "What Knowledge is of Most Worth in Language Arts?" *High School Journal*, **48** (February 1965): 340-345.

Cadenhead, Kenneth. "Shifting Emphasis in Language Teaching." *Elementary English*, **46**, 1 (January 1969): 36-39.

Caffyn, Lois. "Behavioral Objectives: English Style." *Elementary English*, **45** (December 1968): 1073-1074.

Crosby, Muriel. NCTE Presidential address. "Of the Times and the Language." *English Journal* (February 1967): 206-207.

Crosby, Muriel. "English: New Dimensions and New Demands." *Elementary English*, **43** (April 1966): 327-332.

Duker, Sam. "Goals of Teaching Listening Skills in the Elementary School." *Elementary English*, **38** (March 1961): 170-174.

Dyer, Prudence. "A Symposium, Language Arts in the Nongraded Schools: Symposium Introduction." *Elementary English*, **46** (February 1969): 111-118.

Evertts, Eldonna L. "The Influence of Linguistics." *Educational Leadership*, **22**, 6 (March 1965): 404-407.

Goodman, Kenneth S. "Linguistic Insights Which Teachers May Apply." *Education*, **88** (April 1968): 313-316.

Huck, Charlotte S. "Planning the Literature Program for the Elementary School." *Elementary English*, **39** (April 1962): 307-313.

Lindvall, C.M. and J.O. Bolvin. "Programmed Instruction in the Schools: An Application of Programming Principles in Individually Prescribed Instruction." In *Programed Instruction*, edited by P. Lange, pp. 217-254. Sixty-sixth Yearbook of the National Society for the Study of Education, Part II. Chicago, Ill.: University of Chicago Press, 1967.

Macintosh, Helen K. "Language Arts Curriculum: Fifty Year Highlights of the Elementary Program." *Elementary English*, **40** (January 1963): 5-14.

Moffett, James. "A Structural Curriculum in English." *Harvard Educational Review*, **36** (Winter 1966): 17-28.

Nyquist, D.L. "Grouping Other Than Ability." *English Journal*, **57** (December 1968): 1340-1344.

Purves, Alan C. "Of Behaviors, Objectives, and English." *English Journal*, **59** (September 1970): 793-797.

Reed, David W. "A Theory of Language, Speech and Writing." *Elementary English*, **42** (December 1965): 845-851.

Sanborn, Donald A. "What Can We Teach About Language." *English Journal*, **58**, 8 (November 1969): 1206-1213.

Shafer, Robert E. "Curriculum: New Perspectives." *English Journal*, **58** (May 1969): 752-756.

Shafer, Robert E. "The Changing Program in English." *Audiovisual Instruction*, **10** (April 1965): 276-280.

Smith, Rodney. "A Symposium, Language Arts in the Nongraded School: Part II, Language Arts Programs in Nongraded Schools, Problems Arising." *Elementary English*, **46** (February 1969): 126-129.

Squire, James R. "English Language Arts Education." In *Curriculum Handbook for School Administrators*, edited by Forrest E. Connor and William J. Ellena. Washington, D.C.: American Association of School Administrators, 1967.

Strickland, Ruth G. "Innovations in the Language Arts." *National Elementary Principal*, **43** (September 1963): 53-60.

Strickland, Ruth G. "Some Basic Issues in the Teaching of English." *Phi Delta Kappan*, **41** (May 1960): 332-335.

Strickland, Ruth G. "Trends and Emphases in Elementary English." In *The Range of English: NCTE 1968 Distinguished Lectures*, pp. 105-125. Champaign, Ill. : NCTE, 1968.

Thorn, E.A. "Language Experience Approach to Reading." *Reading Teacher*, **23** (October 1969): 3-8.

Townsend, Myrtle. "Integrating Language Arts in The School Program." *Grade Teacher*, **50, +88, 89, 90, 91** (April 1964).

Tyler, Priscilla. "New Concepts and Content for the English Curriculum." *The English Leaflet*, **61** (Midwinter 1962): 4-10.

Wagoner, Ralph H. "Symposium, Language Arts in the Nongraded School: Riposte, A Review." *Elementary English*, **46** (February 1969): 145-146.

PART TWO
Our Evolving Language

A. Language Heritage

As language instruction has become increasingly emancipated from the constraints of traditionalism, historical linguistics has emerged as an important part of language study. Although the English language is approximately fifteen hundred years old, it is during the present century that it has evolved as an international language. This development is a chronicle of a dynamic, changing language which reflects and unifies our culture.

Language and culture are inextricably interwoven; both are essential to an understanding of our linguistic heritage. Any attempt to segment either facet and to emphasize one over the other reduces the meaning and continuity of both. Rather than studying language as if it existed in a vacuum of "correctness" and "fixed rules," teachers and students should learn how language grew and changed within the historical context in which it was used.

The introductory article in this section traces the origin and dissemination of the English language, pointing out changes that have occurred in sound, vocabulary, grammar, and meaning. Note that these characteristics gain importance and become interesting when they are examined in relation to the motives of the persons who were responsible for the changes. The second selection also acquires a dramatic perspective as the writer briefly surveys the evolutionary development of our language and draws some conclusions regarding the contemporary uses of our speech. He observes that colloquial speech is being used increasingly in effective writing, and secondly he notes that our grammar is becoming more simplified. A revealing statistic to which he points is the rate at which new words have been added to the English language: our lexicon today contains 600,000 more words than the 140,000 recorded in Shakespeare's day.

How can we account for this explosive increase in vocabulary? Are these words primarily the product of an inventive English people, or are they largely borrowings from foreign languages? The third article explains three sources of present-day English words and describes fifteen possible methods for making a new word. The writer expresses the opinion that neologisms, "new words or old words with new meanings," are contributing significantly to our contemporary lexicon.

American slang is a major influence in the development of our language, explains the next contributor, and as such, should be an integral part of language study. Whether slang should be given the recognition of inclusion in dictionaries or whether it should be subjected to a value judgment is the subject for much debate among laymen and scholars. The concluding articles present the views of four individuals on this controversial topic.

The foregoing articles illuminate the dynamic quality of language study in historical perspective. Language begins to achieve character and meaning when we inquire into the social history and the economic, political, military, and religious lives of its speakers. It is the lore of language itself that may have the greatest appeal for students. Perhaps only after they are introduced to a flesh and blood account of those activities which have shaped speakers' words, will they appreciate the uniqueness of their own language.

12.

The English Language

Lincoln Barnett

To Americans, who use it all their lives, the English language is a commonplace thing, to be treated casually and taken entirely for granted. But few Americans realize how commonplace their language really is. Today 250 million of the world's people—nearly one in 10—use English as their primary language. And 600 million people—nearly one in four—understand it in some degree. In our own lifetime English has become the most widely spoken language on earth.

Few events in man's turbulent history compare in scope or significance with this global linguistic conquest. At the time of the Norman Conquest in 1066, English had no more than 1.5 million speakers. In the ensuing five centuries it evolved slowly into the rich, flexible medium of the Elizabethan poets who, while cherishing their language, never dreamed it might become a universal tongue. In 1582 Richard Mulcaster, the most famous English educator of his day, remarked, "The English tongue is of small reach, stretching no further than this island of ours, nay not there over all." As recently as the 18th Century, English was still outranked by French, Latin (for scholarship), German, Spanish, Russian and Italian, and European academicians deplored the fact that English writers wrote only in English.

Today English is written, spoken, broadcast and understood on every continent. There are few civilized areas where it has any competition as the international language of commerce, diplomacy, science and scholarship. Its speakers cover one quarter of the globe, ranging from the fair-skinned people of the British Isles through every gradation of color and race the world around. It is spoken by Christians, Jews, Moslems, Buddhists, Hindus and adherents of every major religious faith on earth. It is still spreading around the planet at a constantly accelerating tempo.

Among the leading disseminators of English are the Russians and Chinese, who are attempting to woo friends and influence nations with it in uncommitted regions of the earth. The Russians use English for propaganda broadcasts to the Far East. Radio listeners in Kenya, Nyasaland and Zanzibar, whose entertainment formerly came from Cairo in Arabic and Swahili, now receive loud, clear broadcasts from Peiping Radio in Red China—all in English. Freight shipments of heavy machinery and other commodities from Russia to the Near

---

Condensed by *Life* from THE TREASURE OF OUR TONGUE, published by Alfred A. Knopf, New York, 1964. Reprinted by permission of the author.

East are stamped "Made in U.S.S.R."—in English. In many cities Russian cultural offices compete with British and American centers in advertising English courses. And of the 30 million books which the Russians annually distribute to former British dominions in Africa and Asia, a large proportion are in English—among them technical books, novels and children's books, including "*Goldilocks and the Three Bears* by Leo Tolstoy" (actual author: Robert Southey).

English is also the language of international aviation, spoken by pilots and airport control tower operators on all the airways of the world. The West German Luftwaffe and even the fliers of East Germany use it. The French, though ever jealous of their proud and beautiful language, find English far more efficient for air-ground communication. It takes less time, for example, to say *jet* than *avion à réaction,* or to talk of *flaps* than *volets de flexions.* There are other areas of mankind's diverse activities within which English now reigns virtually supreme. It is the international language of sport in every country where people play *futbol* or *beisbol.* It is the international language of jazz, whose followers in all lands know the difference between *le bebop* and *buki-buki* (boogie-woogie). It is the language of international youth—of teenagers everywhere who wear *blue djins* and *pulova* sweaters, chew *gomma americana* (specifically, bubble gum), smoke *Looky Strooky* cigarets (as in Russia), and enjoy hot dogs and Coke (or, as in Japan, *Koka-Kora* and its rival *Pepusi-Kora).*

A Diplomatic Way of Saying Things

It is in the realm of statesmanship, however, that English has attained the status of a universal tongue to a degree never approached by Latin in the heyday of the Roman Empire or by French in the 18th and 19th centuries. At the Bandung Conference of 1955, attended by representatives from 29 Asian and African countries, the proceedings were conducted entirely in English—not for any love of England or America, but because it was the only means by which the multilingual delegates could communicate with one another. More recently, when Egypt and Indonesia drew up a cultural treaty, it was specified that the definitive version of the agreement between these two Moslem countries, neither one an ardent admirer of the Western world, would be the English-language copy. When a trade delegation from Ceylon journeyed to the U.S.S.R. for a conference, their Russian hosts, who met them in Kabul, greeted them in English. And when the Dalai Lama fled down from his Tibetan highlands to seek sanctuary in India, he was welcomed by Prime Minsiter Nehru on the northern frontier.

"How are you?" Nehru asked in English.

"Very nice," the Dalai Lama said.

The most spectacular advances made by English are in the so-called underdeveloped areas of the world. The polyglot populations of Asia and Africa often find it much easier to learn English than to try to comprehend the speech of their nearest neighbors. Contrary to popular supposition, languages evolve in the direction of simplicity. English, being a highly evolved, cosmopolitan, sophisticated language, has been refined and revised, planed down and polished through centuries of use so that today it is far less complex in grammar and syntax than any primitive tongue. Some of the most difficult languages in the world are spoken by some of the world's most backward people—*e.g.,* the Australian aborigines, the Eskimos, the Hottentots and the Yaghan Indians of Tierra del Fuego. In West Africa alone some 60 million tribesmen speak more than 400 different languages; hence wherever European influence has left its mark, Africans often talk to one another in English (or to a lesser extent in French) when they leave their own local language district—which in some cities may mean across the street. Ghana has proclaimed English its official language and requires English instruction from primary school on. In East Africa, whose tribes have communicated for centuries in Swahili, even rabid nationalists today favor English as the common tongue.

The swift and astonishing spread of English around the globe has not occurred without some opposition. The French in particular have endeavored to hold the linguistic lines in their former colonies in Asia and Africa. In France itself the Office du Vocabulaire Francais continually exhorts newspapers and magazines to avoid the *snobisme* of using English words where French equivalents exist. The Spanish are also reluctant to let their ancient romantic language suffer the incursions of a foreign idiom. Of all European countries Spain has been least receptive to English, partly because of its geographical isolation, partly because Spaniards historically profess little love for the homeland of Sir Francis Drake. Even in Latin America, where English is now virtually mandatory for business and professional men, purists recurrently plead for the preservation of Spanish as "the most beautiful, majestic and sonorous language in the world."

Futile Effort to 'Save Hindi'

Perhaps the most notable victory of the English language over nationalistic resistance was recently won in India. In an effort to expunge relics of the British Raj, the Central Government had proclaimed in 1950 that the official language of India would henceforth be Hindi and that the transition away from English must be complete by 1965. While this pleased the Hindu populations in the North, the reaction was quite different in the rest of the vast subcontinent, which encompasses 845 distinct languages and dialects. The Bengali-speakers in the east did not like the decree, and in the south the millions of speakers of Tamil and related Dravidian languages protested that 15 years was too brief an interval in which to adopt a tongue as alien to them as any in the Occidental world. For more than a century English has been the common tongue, and although not more than 3% of India's population of 438 million employ it with any degree of fluency, they represent the ruling 3%—administrators, judges, legislators and other educated groups. If English were expunged, they pointed out, there would be no way for all the peoples of the huge land to communicate with each other. Months of argument ensued, marred recurrently by bloody riots. At the University of Lucknow, which switched at once from English to Hindi, levels of learning went into an alarming decline. Faculty members evolved a kind of Anglo-Hindi jargon, inventing hybrid words for technical terms in an attempt to comply with the government edict. The result was Babel.

Finally the so-called "Save Hindi" campaign was called off. The announcement, significantly, was published in English. Prime Minister Nehru declared that for an indefinite period English would continue as an "associate official language." While Hindus listened in silence and non-Hindi-speaking legislators cheered, Nehru termed English "the major window for us to the outside world."

"We dare not close that window," he said. "And if we do, it will spell peril to our future."

In Nehru's words lies one explanation for the virtually unopposed diffusion of English around the globe. For not only in Asia and Africa, but in Europe, crisscrossed by linguistic frontiers and dissected by deep-rooted cultural loyalties, people of all classes now look to English as a window, a magic casement opening on every horizon of loquacious man.

West German schools require six to nine years of English. The obligation meets with no emotional resistance for the Germans, unlike the French, feel no sense of linguistic betrayal in studying English: they are eager to learn and experience little difficulty in the process. Even in East Germany (where Russian used to be, but is no longer, a compulsory subject) English holds first place among optional language courses in secondary schools, with 12 applicants for every available departmental vacancy. English classes are equally in demand in Poland and Yugoslavia. Within the U.S.S.R. itself schools offer English from the fourth or fifth grades on, and in some of the largest cities it is the one compulsory language in the curriculum. One of the best-sellers in the bookshops of Moscow is an English grammar.

The teaching of languages in schools, however, represents only one of many channels through which the torrent of English is inundating all lands. Other tributary freshets include radio and television, motion pictures, recordings of popular songs, English language publications, adult education courses, language centers, mobile libraries and exchange fellowships sponsored by government agencies and private foundations, and, perhaps most important of all, the incomputable numbers of informal encounters that occur every day among businessmen, professional men, politicians, scientists, technicians, students and just plain tourists.

Although the flood of English dates only from the end of World War II, its incipient stage actually began more than three centuries ago when British adventurers first carried their speech to the far places of the earth, erecting the initial bastions of empire. In the wake of the conquerors came traders, and after them missionaries—who still exercise a potent force in Africa and Asia. But the major catalyst in the English language explosion was war—especially the two great conflicts of this century.

"War is perhaps the most rapidly effectual excitant of language," a British etymologist has observed. The occupation troops that moved into defeated countries after World War I and on an incomparably greater scale after World War II did more to spread English (particularly American English) than any other agency of dissemination. From the hundreds of thousands of soldiers and their dependents deployed throughout both hemispheres, English words and phrases filtered down to every level of the diverse populations in every one of the nations and zones. No longer was English speech the limited possession of the educated, the wealthy and the peripatetic social elite. It became the economically valuable property of all, from shopkeepers and salesgirls, bellboys and bartenders, down to barefoot urchins in the streets of Tokyo and Teheran, Berlin and Baghdad who swiftly learned to chirp, "Hey, Joe, gimme gum."

Agencies that Spread the Words

The popular desire to learn English has increased each year as America's international interests and commercial commitments continue to radiate in widening circles across the seas. The desire has been met by a vast complex of organizations, both national and international, British and American, public and private. The U.S. Information Service maintains 389 cultural centers in 80 countries, ranging from small circulating libraries offering English books and magazines to elaborate establishments like Amerika House in Berlin which provides programs of lectures, concerts, dances and language instruction to as many as 1,800 visitors a day. During the last year 28 million persons used the facilities of USIS centers scattered around the world. Of these more than a million attended English language seminars, among them 5,000 local teachers whose combined classes represented more than two million pupils.

How can this worldwide and apparently insatiable demand for English be explained? None of the external factors—commercial motivations, the extended military and economic influence of the English-speaking people, circumglobal pathways of communications and travel—can adequately account for the phenomenon. The essential catalyst lies in the internal anatomy of the language itself.

To the advanced practitioner—the poet, novelist, essayist—English poses great difficulties by virtue of its lush vocabulary of more than half a million words and the flexibility with which they can be employed. But literature is one thing and plain talk is another. It is in the realm of plain talk that English excels. It excels by reason of its basically simple rudiments—a hard core of perhaps 1,000 energetic words which fill all the needs of ordinary communication, a few tolerant rules governing their use, and a logical underlying structure which can be taught and learned more quickly than is possible in any other language spoken today. During World War II when foreign fliers were brought to the U.S. for training, it was found that a good working knowledge of English could be imparted in about 60 hours of concentrated instruction.

Forms Reshaped by Waves of Invaders

These assets, which make English so useful as an international language, derive from its history and cosmopolitan antecedents. For in the course of centuries of development it has been periodically enriched and invigorated by elements of many other tongues. Whatever its original foundations may have been, as laid down by Germanic tribes, they were altered and revised by repeated waves of invaders that crossed the Channel in historic times—the Romans, Jutes, Saxons, Angles, Vikings and finally the Normans. Today English is classified as a member of the Teutonic linguistic family that also includes German, Dutch and the Scandinavian group. However more than half its vocabulary is of Latin origin, implanted either directly during the four centuries of the Roman occupation and the permanent Norman conquest or indirectly by borrowings from modern French, Spanish, Italian and Portuguese.

The diversified, cosmopolitan ancestry of the words in the English lexicon has been a major asset in the diffusion of the language. Of equal value is the simplicity of the grammatical conventions that govern their use. Foremost among these is the logical, down-to-earth and wholesome attitude of the English language toward sex. In the Romance languages all nouns are arbitrarily either masculine or feminine. In French, for example, *la ville* (city) and *la lune* (moon) are feminine while *le village* (village) and *le soleil* (sun) are masculine. And in German, where there are three genders to cope with, *Sonne*, (sun) is feminine, *Mond* (moon) is masculine while *Weib* (woman) is neuter. To British or American students of foreign languages such distinctions seem to impose an additional task of memorizing gender as well as meaning and make no sense in a world populated by men and woman, fathers and mothers, boys and girls.

Consider, for example, a simple French sentence: *La plume noire du vieux monsieur est perdue* (The black pen of the old gentleman is lost). The arbitrary femininity of the pen is relentlessly reiterated in the article *la*, the adjective *noire* and the participle *perdue*. There is no question, no possible shadow of doubt, that pens are female objects. But had the old gentleman lost his pencil instead of his pen, the sentence would read: *Le crayon noir du vieux monsieur est perdu*, thus establishing the maleness of pencils through every auxiliary word. And if the loss of either implement had been suffered by an old lady instead of an old gentleman, the possessive phrase would become *de la vieille dame*, involving a strikingly different form of the adjective meaning "old" and a metamorphosis of the masculine particle *du* ("of the") into the feminine *de la*.

Gender is only one of the many brier patches eliminated by common English usage through centuries of hacking and pruning in the thickets of grammar. The inflections (changes that reflect gender, tense, number, person, etc.) that complicate most other languages have almost entirely disappeared from English. Nouns change only to denote the possessive or plural forms and these variations are extremely simple ones. The possessive case is formed by the addition of *'s* (or by the apostrophe alone for some words already ending in *s*). The plural is formed by the easy addition of *s* (with a very few exceptions such as *foot, feet; child, children; mouse, mice; deer, deer; knife, knives).*

Pronouns retain some inflections, especially in the first person: *I, me, mine, we, us, ours.* But even here erosion has been at work. The second person *you* is both singular and plural, both subject and object. *Ye* has disappeared entirely, and *thou* and *thee* hold their own only among the Quakers. The relative pronoun *whom* is still mandatory in writing and in the conversation of all who cherish traditional usage, but it has given way to *who* in colloquial speech and in time will doubtless follow other inflected forms into linguistic oblivion.

English adjectives and adverbs completely ignore the words they modify. They change only to denote comparison, and there are only three degrees: *bright, brighter, brightest; brightly, more brightly, most brightly.*

Finally verbs—source of the severest headaches among language students—have lost most of their tortuous variations. In classical Greek, for example, a verb may progress through as many as 500 inflections to indicate complex interactions of tense, mood, voice, person and number. Most modern languages have reduced these complexities, but English has gone further than any other Western language in the process of evolutionary simplification. A conjugation of the English verb *to love* clearly reveals this development, when compared with conjugations of its French and Latin equivalents, *aimer* and *amare:*

I love	J'aime	Amo
You love	Tu aimes	Amas
He loves	Il aime	Amat
She loves	Elle aime	Amat
We love	Nous aimons	Amamus
You love	Vous aimez	Amatus
They love	Ils aiment	Amant
They love	Elles aiment	Amant

Thus, where Latin requires six personal endings and French five, English asks only two—the attachment of an *s* to the third person singular. And in the past tense—*I loved, you loved, he loved, she loved, we loved, you loved, they loved*—there are no inflections at all.

The absence, or decay, of inflections in English is not an unmitigated blessing to the foreign-born student. Although it vastly reduces the amount of time which he would expend in memorizing verbal mutations in another language, it may also leave him with a sense of being adrift in an uncharted sea of new words without any formal rules of navigation. It is often difficult in English to distinguish a verb from a noun. For example, one may *slice* cheese or eat a *slice* of cheese; one may *swim* or go for a *swim*; one may *call* a friend on the telephone or receive a telephone *call*, or *call* for help, or leave a *call* for 7 a.m. Such free interchange of function among the parts of speech, while one of the delights of the English language, also creates a condition which the late Edward Sapir,

Sterling Professor of Anthropology and Linguistics at Yale, described as "masked complexity." "Anyone who takes the trouble to examine these [difficulties] carefully," Sapir observed, "will soon see that behind the superficial appearance of simplicity there is concealed a perfect hornet's nest of bizarre and arbitrary usages."

The heart of the hornet's nest lies in the realm of little words. In the vast lexicon of English, thousands of precise, highly specialized and often elegant words flower side by side with small, easy-to-learn, highly flexible parts of speech. It is one of the marvelous endowments of English that these two species of words—the specialized and the general—complement, augment, define and analyze each other. Thus one may *extinguish a fire* or *put out a fire; dismount* or *get off; ascend* or *go up.*

English boiled to 850 Words

The special formula of little-verb-plus-preposition is the key to a quick grasp of English speech, if not necessarily to a gracious literary style. In 1920 two Cambridge scholars, Dr. I. A. Richards, now of Harvard, and the late C. K. Ogden, discovered while collaborating on a book about English semantics (entitled *The Meaning of Meaning*) that a few hundred key words could do all the real work in their analyses of other words and idioms. After 10 years of lexicological labor Ogden evolved what is known as Basic English—an elixer, distilled from the ancient wine of our language, of 850 volatile, versatile words that can say just about anything that needs to be said in ordinary talk.

The critical discovery made by Richards and Ogden was that their stripped-down lexicon required only 18 verbs—as against 4,000 to 10,000 that may be available in the vocabulary of a college-educated man. The 18 vital verbs are: *be, come, do, get, give, go, have, keep, let, make, may, put, say, see, seem, send, take* and *will.* The ability of these verbs to do the work of all the others stems from their gift of entering into an astonishing number of mergers with prepositions. Thus a combination like *give up* can cover the pivotal meanings of *abandon, abdicate, abjure, cease, cede, desert, desist, discontinue, forego, forsake, relinquish, renounce, resign, sacrifice, stop, succumb, surrender, vacate, withdraw* and *yield.*

It is evident that the little words of English constitute a kind of inner voice—a language within a language—capable of understudying most of the flashier ornaments of the Oxford English Dictionary and Webster's Unabridged. Because they cover so much ground they can be of enormous value to the English novitiate. Each one pinch-hits for hundreds of more complex if subtler words, and they are relatively simple to spell and pronounce.

But their simplicity is deceptive. They can be used in so many ways that their very versatility can create confusion in the mind of the learner. Contemplate, for example, the little word *up.* Most of the time it behaves like a preposition, indicating direction *(He lives up the street).* But it can also masquerade as an adverb *(It's time to get up),* a noun *(Every life has its ups and downs),* a verb *(I'll up you five dollars)* or an adjective *(The sun is up).* In addition to its multiple function in the combination *give up,* it plays a ubiquitous and sometimes superfluous role in a variety of other expressions, such as *add up, clean up, do up, drink up, hurry up, join up, line up, lock up, mix up, offer up, pay up, play up, ring up, set up, stop up, tie up, tidy up, wake up, wash up, work up, wrap up, up to now* and *up to you.* To the foreign student it seems paradoxical that the same meaning is conveyed by *his house burned up* and *his house burned down; my wife isn't up yet* and *my wife isn't down yet; the train slowed up* and *the train slowed down.* Even more bewildering are those situations where utterly unrelated concepts are evoked by one and the same phrase—*e.g., make up,* whose transient meaning depends on whether the context is cosmetics *(She takes an hour to make up her face),* indecision *(I just can't make up my mind),* domesticity *(Let's make up the bed),* forgiveness *(Kiss and make up),* fiction *(I'll make up some kind of a story)* or atonement *(Some day I'll make up for this mistake).*

Clear Meaning even without Grammar

The puzzles presented by prepositions confuse not only the foreign student but also those born to the English tongue and most particularly those teachers and writers whose obligation is to employ them correctly. The little words are sticky, fussy, elusive words even for those who have lived and worked with them all their lives. However, the pragmatic glory of English is that it is able to convey meaning even when grammar goes out the window. It matters little if a Frenchman, instead of saying, "I have been here for two hours," says "I am here since two hours." Either is intelligible to anyone who understands English. And it is because of the infinite elasticity of the English language that the many varieties of broken English have evolved, giving rise to such immortal phrases as *"Him big chief paleface"* and *"No tickee, no shirtee,"* and making possible communication without grammar the world around.

This language form recently has achieved an ultimate in richness and conciseness among its new creators in Nigeria. There, according to Professor Frederick W. Harbison, a Princeton economist who has often visited Nigeria, a boy who finishes grade school is known as a *megotbuk* (Pronounced me-got-book). A boy who graduates from college is a *bigbigbuk.* And the exceptional young man who has studied at Oxford and returns home trailing clouds of culture is a *bintojaguar-fridgful*—a handy contraction for "He has been to England and come home with a Jaguar and enough money to keep a refrigerator full of frozen foods."

The most excruciating difficulties encountered by the serious foreign student who wishes to learn to write English, as well as speak it, involve neither grammar nor syntax but rather the chaotic lack of correlation between its spelling and pronounciation. The inconsistencies are so multifarious and grotesque that foreigners are not alone in deploring them. Most Americans cannot spell correctly, and for even the most cultivated of professional men on both shores of the Atlantic the incoherent character of English orthography is a timeless problem. It is when the novice endeavors to discern some trace of conformity between the sound and spelling of English words that he gets in trouble.

The favorite scapegoat of critics of English orthography is the vestigial *ough* monstrosity, which can be pronounced in nine different ways, none of them related phonetically to the letters involved—viz., *tough, though, thought, thorough, through, bough, cough, drought, hiccough.* In another ambush the foreign student encounters homonyms—words that sound alike but are spelled differently and have different meanings—such as *pair, pear* and *pare; beat* and *beet; meat* and *meet; grate* and *great; peace* and *piece; sew* and *so; there, their* and *they're.* But in another part of the forest he is waylaid by pairs of words, twins of identical spelling, which are pronounced quite differently and serve different grammatical functions; *e.g.,* the verb *read* (present tense) and *read* (past tense); the nouns *tear* (in the eye) and *tear* (in the sheet); the verb *lead* and the noun *lead;* the noun *con' tract* and the verb *contract'.*

What does 'Ghoti' Spell?

Periodically professional and amateur apostles of consistency and simplicity have tried to get rid of these difficulties. The most notable recent crusader was the late George Bernard Shaw, who provided in his will for a bequest of £500 to be awarded to the inventor of a new alphabet that would most nearly effect a phonetic wedding of sound and symbol. As an example of the lunacy of English spelling, Shaw constructed the word *ghoti*. He pointed out that the *gh* combination is pronounced like *f* in *cough;* the vowel *o* is pronounced like a short *i* in the word *women*; and the *ti* combination is pronounced like *sh* in the word *nation*. Hence *ghoti* is pronounced *fish*.

Although Shaw's bequest was disposed of two years ago—divided equally among four contestants—the Oxford English Dictionary remains intact today. For despite all the idiosyncrasies of English spelling and the continual complaints against it, those who use the language cherish it. Defenders of the traditional spelling point out, quite correctly, that the written form of any English word reveals its etymology; it may afford no clue as to pronunciation, but its ancestry is clearly disclosed. In the diversified letter combinations of English words one may read the long, tumultuous history of the British Isles. So far as American spelling is concerned, about all that has been effected since the days of Noah Webster are a few minuscule changes: the *u* has been dropped from *honour* and *colour*, for example, and occasionally one encounters words like *tonite, thruway* and *altho*. It would seem that the English-speaking people of the U.S., like those of the U.K., are reluctant to surrender their antiquated, irrational, exasperating, obsolete, indefensible, crazy, mixed-up system of spelling. The American attitude was perhaps epitomized by Mark Twain when he remarked, "Simplified spelling is all right; but, like chastity, you can carry it too far."

For all its flaws, however, English is being adopted everywhere in the most insidious way of all, by infiltrating the other languages. Many English and American words are now completely international, not merely understood but spoken and published around the world. Among the most familiar of these, universally employed on every continent, are: *baby sitter, bar, bridge, boyfriend, bestseller, bus, beefsteak, cocktail, cover girl, cowboy, gangster, goddam, hamburger, holdup, hot dog, ice cream, jazz, juice, jeep, knockout, nightclub, party, pipeline, pin-up, racket, sandwich, shorts, sex appeal, striptease, whisky* and *weekend*. It goes without saying that for years *okay* has been a universal expression of assent. It underwent a significant variation when Premier Khrushchev added a modifier, during his tour of the U.S., by exclaiming on several occasions, "Very okay."

This diffusion would have pleased one of the great architects of the language, Dr. Samuel Johnson, who cherished his mother tongue. "Wondrous the English language," he once exclaimed, "language of live men!"

13.
Your Speech is Changing

Bergen Evans

If a contemporary Rip van Winkle had slept for 40 years and awakened today, he would have to go back to school before he could read a daily paper or a magazine. He would never have heard of atomic bombs or baby sitters, of coffee breaks, contact lenses or flying saucers—nor of eggheads, mambo or microfilm, of nylons, neptunium, parking meters or smog.

And this is the briefest sampling of the innumerable new words added to our language in a mere 40 years. Only recently, a nuclear physicist reading a year-old glossary of electronic and atomic terms, found himself saying over and over, "That's what we used to call it."

The vocabulary of physics is, plainly, exploding with a violence commensurate with the new devices it has to describe. And physics is not alone in this. Almost every major industry now finds it necessary to issue a glossary of its own special terms to its workers. Yet they are unable to keep pace with the increase of their own knowledge, and the most striking feature of these word lists is not their newness—though the ink is scarcely dry on their pages—but their obsolescence.

Since Shakespeare's time, the number of words in the English language has quintupled, increasing from about 140,000 to somewhere between 700,000 and 800,000. And most of these have come not from borrowing, but from the natural growth of the language, from the adaptation of the elements already in it.

The language has always changed, of course. But the rate of change, in some respects, has been uneven. Minor changes have slowly accumulated in every generation, but there have been periods of rapid change as well. The most important was the 2½ centuries following the conquest of England by the Normans in 1066.

At the time of the conquest, the inhabitants of England spoke Anglo-Saxon, an inflected Germanic language. The Normans were Norsemen who, after generations of raiding, had settled in North France (Normandy) in the 10th century. By 1066 they were speaking a form of French.

At the time they invaded England, Anglo-Saxon could hardly be considered one of the world's significant tongues. Certainly, there was nothing in it to suggest that it might become an important language, let alone the greatest ever known. The Normans, who were never much more than a garrison, established Norman French as the speech of the dominant group. It was the language of the

---

Reprinted from *Think*, August 1959, by permission of author and publisher.

upper classes, of law, of government and of such commerce as there was. Latin, of course, was the language of the learned.

For more than 200 years nobody who was anybody at all spoke Anglo-Saxon. It is doubtful if Richard the Lion-Hearted, for example, spoke one word of English in his entire life. Angle-ish was strictly for the churls, for the hinds and the hicks. As Wamba the Jester pointed out to Gurth the Swineherd in Scott's *Ivanhoe,* while animals were living and had to be cared for, in muck and mire, they were Saxon—as *cow, calf, sheep* and *pig.* But when they were dressed for the table—when the rewards of labor were to be enjoyed—they were Norman French: *beef, veal, mutton* and *pork.*

But the masses went right on speaking Anglo-Saxon because they didn't know anything else. There was, however, no reading or writing of it to amount to anything. There was no teaching of it. It was simply used every day for generations, by millions of common people, who just said things as effectively as they could and got on with the business of living. And never—as any schoolteacher could have foretold—did a language become more "corrupted."

But after having been submerged as a "common" language for some 300 years, Anglo-Saxon was again being spoken by the upper classes—as English. And it had become the most flexible, exact, splendid and moving instrument of expression that mankind has ever known. Norman French had become something comic, spoken by the villains in the old mystery plays just for a laugh.

There have been other periods of vigorous change. Two generations after Chaucer's death in 1400, printing was invented, and this set into motion a chain of events whose full force upon the language is only now beginning to be felt.

The 17th and 18th centuries saw the stabilization of spelling. But, even more important, they saw the establishment of colonies in America, and, from the beginning, the language in the new world and the parent language in the old world began to draw apart in many particulars (though in the past 60 years or so this tendency has been reversed). American speech developed its own rhythms and vigor, found or adapted special words for its own special needs and (more west of the Alleghenies than east) rioted with a sort of defiant exuberance. The language was for a while of the people, somewhat as Anglo-Saxon had been during the rule of the Norman overlords.

In *The Adventures of Huckleberry Finn* (1884) the full power of the American idiom was first shown. It had been heard clearly in Franklin and Thoreau. But Mark Twain first showed the passion of its cadences and the subtlety and range of which it was capable. He used the idiom of the Great Valley with no apologies and no scorn. It is true that he did it through the person of Huck, but it is equally true that in so doing he wrote not only his own greatest novel, but a novel which every American feels, somehow, speaks his language.

The liberating effect on American writing can hardly be overstated. With it we ceased to be a literary colony. The source of all modern American literature, Hemingway has said, is *Huckleberry Finn.* Of its effect on Hemingway himself there can be little doubt. One sample will suffice—a comparison of the description of Huck's diving under the paddle wheel of the riverboat, which had struck his raft, with Hemingway's description, in *A Farewell to Arms,* of Frederick Henry's plunge into the Po.

Huck says: "I dived—and I aimed to find the bottom, too, for a thirty-foot wheel had got to go over me, and I wanted it to have plenty of room. I could always stay under water a minute; this time I reckon I stayed under a minute and a half. Then I bounced for the top in a hurry, for I was nearly busting. I popped out to my armpits and blowed the water out of my nose, and puffed a bit. Of course there was a booming current; and of course that boat started her engines again ten seconds after she stopped them, for they never cared much for raftsman. . . ."

Henry says: "I ducked down, pushed between two men, and ran for the river, my head down. I tripped at the edge and went in with a splash. The water was very cold and I stayed under as long as I could. I could feel the current swirl me and I stayed under until I thought I could never come up. The minute I came up I took a breath and went down again. It was easy to stay under with so much clothing and my boots. . . ."

Colloquial vs. Formal

Anyone can hear the authentic rhythms of American speech in both passages. And anyone who thinks he can get equal action, and the same shades of menace, tension, courage and excitement in the literary idiom that such writing displaced—well, let him show us!

Though if he does, his triumph will be purely academic. For the use of the colloquial in effective writing is increasing rather than diminishing. It is one of the changes that definitely is accelerating. The purist angrily labels it "pandering to the masses" and accuses those who accept it of "debasing" the language. But the new way is better, more flexible, more expressive, communicates more directly.

Much of what is objected to in contemporary writing has been common for centuries. From all the uproar over "Winston Tastes Good *Like* a Cigarette Should," for instance, one would have assumed that the R. J. Reynolds Tobacco Company had launched a subversive attack on established English and was determined to overthrow the Constitution and set up *like* as a conjunction. But if it was a conspiracy, it had been assisted in advance by Shakespeare, Dryden, Burns, Shelley, Masefield, Maugham and millions of Americans.

Similarly, *none* has been regarded as a plural when its idea was plural (according to the King James Version of the Bible) from the very First Commandment (Deut. 5:7). And double negatives have strengthened, not denied, negation as long as men have spoken English. Purists may insist that "two negatives make a positive," but no one in his right mind has any doubt what Chaucer meant when he said that his Knight "didn't never do no villainy to no man."

Prepositions are not supposed to come at the end of sentences; but from Shakespeare ("What great ones do, the less will prattle of.") through Milton ("Thee all living things gaze on.") to G. B. Shaw ("What are the police for?") and Sir Winston Churchill's humorous rebuke ("This is pedantry, up with which I will not put."), all people who have the feel of the English sentence put them at the end to their heart's content. *That*, not *which*, has always been the common relative pronoun in English; the modern insistence that there is a clear distinction between them is pretentious nonsense.

Then there's *who* at the beginning of a question, even when in the accusative. "Who did you give it to?" would have seemed as natural and "To whom did you give it to?" as strainedly elegant 100 or 500 years ago as it does today. At least that's the way Marlowe said it ("Who have ye there, my Lordes?") and Addison ("Who should I see there but the most artful procuress?"). Noah Webster was emphatic: " 'Whom did you speak to' was never used in speaking, as I can find, and is hardly English at all."

The increased use of the colloquial in our writing is an interesting change that is bound to have far-reaching consequences. Our speech, of course, has always been colloquial. That's what the word means. The sensible man *speaks* colloquially most of the time. When he wants to be formal or unusually impressive he tries to speak as he thinks he writes. But on these occasions he often makes a pompous ass of himself and—worse—fails to convey his meaning.

Yet, whenever he stops to think, the common man feels guilty about his speech. He feels he *ought* to be more formal and that he ought not to use in writing (about which he retains a semi-literate awe) the expressions that just come naturally to his mind.

Hence, when he sees a form marked *colloq.* in the dictionary he thinks he ought not to use it at all, though actually the colloquial meaning of most words is to him the "real" meaning. For instance, *guy* in standard English means a rope, a stuffed effigy or a weirdly-dressed person. Yet no one blanched or was bewildered when Nellie Forbush sang in *South Pacific* that she was in love with a wonderful *guy*, which means, of course, *man* colloquially. A *kit*, in standard definition, can be anything from a fox to a fiddle, but its colloquial meaning of a group of separate parts ready to be assembled is the one that would first come to mind.

Some modern linguists feel that the designation *colloq.* is so often misunderstood that it might be better, a safer guide to current usage, if the term were dropped and certain words marked as *formal*, so that the ordinary speaker or writer will be warned that the word is not in everyday use.

Opposed to this increased use of the colloquial, it must be said, is a minor but increasingly vocal group that insists on "rules" and "correctness." They base their stand on a puritanical liking for absolutes, and they may be motivated in part by a sense of insecurity which the rapidly-changing social status of millions is producing. At best, the demands of this group, if acceded to, will sacrifice vigor to "propriety." And at worst it is producing a new kind of bad grammar—the uncertainty and pretentiousness which leads to the substitution of *myself* for *me* ("He gave it to John and myself."), to sticking *ly* on the end of adverbs that don't need them ("Our missile program is moving fastly." "He's doing finely.") and such vulgar elegances as "Whom shall I say is calling?"

Intimidated English

This new bad English might be called Intimidated English. No nation in the world is as afraid of its schoolteachers as we are. We have no upper or lower classes to defy them, and the new semi-literacy which has replaced the old illiteracy timidly accepts their academic pronouncements as law. This would be all right if their "laws," like other scientific "laws," were based on observation. But they are more like moral laws; they are promulgated on the assumption that there is some sanction for them beyond speech itself—logic, or decorum or social prestige.

One of the effects of this, as it relates to our speech is a belief that pronunciations which don't correspond to spelling are debased. "Slurred" is the common term for it, and those who let what their eyes have seen once overrule what their ears have heard 10,000 times have had a field day with this particular "corruption." Inspired by the humor of Orpheus C. Kerr, they have grown hilarious over such pronunciations as *mare* for *mayor*, *klōz* for *clothes*, *histri* for *history* and *ák choo uhli* for actually.

Unfortunately for the fun, however, these slurred forms happen to be accepted, standard pronunciations. Though they may not be for long. The dogmatic righteousness of the anti-slurvians is having an immense effect among the semi-literate and the insecure. Increasingly, words are being pronounced as they are spelled. The "l" in *almond*, *salmon* and *palm*, for example, is heard more and more. Only the most aristocratic and the most *un*aristocratic now dare say *Saint Looey.* One used to be able to go from *Kayroh, Illinoy* up to *Saint Looey,* but now one usually has to go from *Kyeroh, Illinoyz* to *Saint Loois.*

If this brings spelling closer to pronunciation, it will be good. But if—as seems more likely—it brings pronunciation closer to spelling, it will be bad, because spelling at the best is only an approximation of past speech and much of it is simply erroneous (like the "s" in *island,* the first "l" in *colonel,* and the "c" in *acknowledge*).

The enormous enlargement of our vocabulary, the increasing use in our writing of our spoken idiom and changes in our pronunciation are not the only changes that are taking place, however. There have also been significant grammatical changes in our language. Such changes take place only by generations or decades, at the fastest, so they pass unnoticed by all but grammarians; but even the layman can perceive them when he is told that something which seems "quite all right" to him was regarded as erroneous only a few years ago.

Take, for example, the extraordinary increase in the use of the infinitive, one of the characteristics of modern American speech and writing. Ask any educated American to point out what is "wrong" with, "The government has a duty to protect the worker," or, "We have a plan to keep the present tariff." The chances are that for the life of him he couldn't see anything wrong with either sentence. Yet in 1925 Fowler listed both of these sentences as ungrammatical. He felt they should read "of protecting " and "of keeping." Today, the old form has been completely superseded.

A further example of change in our grammar is the great increase in the use of what are called "empty" verbs. That is, where people used to say, "Let's drink," or, "Let's swim," there is now a strong tendency to say, "Let's have a drink," "Let's take a swim." Where people formerly said, "It snowed heavily," we are inclined to say, "There was a heavy snow." Our fathers *decided*; we, on the other hand, more often *reach a decision.*

Nobody knows *why* such changes are being made. Perhaps we are in the process of reducing our verbs to a few simple basic words of action—like those handy household tools where one handle serves for a blade, for a screwdriver, for a hammer, a corkscrew and a dozen other diverse implements that can be attached to it individually. That is, we may be reducing the language to an even more functional simplicity. If this is so, it may mark a change as significant as that which took place after the Norman Conquest, when the whole paraphernalia of declensions and conjugations was sloughed off.

The Big Change

One of the most remarkable grammatical changes that has been taking place is the increased use of the passive—of verb forms, that is, that indicate something is being acted upon. Some think that our increased use of the passive may indicate a decay of will. The barbarians who overran the Roman Empire, these people say, had lost most of their passive; they seemed to think only in the active voice: "I do." Those they destroyed were enfeebled in endless consideration of the way things were done *to* them. The more pessimistic of this school point out that the Russians *shot* their first satellite into space while we debated the reasons why ours *was not launched.*

Others, however, take a brighter view. They see in this same increased use of the passive an increased awareness, and increased ability to express subtleties, greater sensitivity, not decadence but greater sophistication. To them this change in our speech shows us to be increasingly a people who are interested in what was done rather than in who did it. They see it as indication that we are more detached, more scientific, more mature.

Whatever the reasons for the changes that are taking place, the vocabulary will probably continue to expand because the expansion of our knowledge and experience requires the invention of new words or the adaptation of old ones. What few inflections remain will probably disappear. Meaning will depend more and more upon word order and context. Spelling will become simpler, with fewer common variants, and pronunciation, because of the great mobility of our population and the spread of radio and TV, will tend to become more uniform.

One thing by now seems certain—that the speech of the men who lost at Hastings, the sturdy, surly, freedom-loving thegns and churls who did not attempt to ingratiate themselves with their conquerors by learning their speech—will adapt and endure.

14. Word-Making in Present-Day English

R.C. Simonini, Jr.

Words can be studied on all levels of English language teaching with reference to their *structure* (describing their morphemes) and their *etymology* (describing their origin). Students can be highly motivated to notice English vocabulary if they have a technique for classifying words etymologically. Moreover, in focusing on the study of new words in our language, one can capitalize on the teenager's penchant for innovation and inspire him to collect interesting examples of his own from everyday speech and writing about him.

How do words in English originate? What processes of word-formation operate in the language? One may begin with a corpus of new words taken from dictionary addenda or from compilations of neologisms and then proceed inductively to make classifications (see my study, "Etymological Categories of Present-Day English and Their Productivity," in *Theory and Practice in English as a Foreign Language*, University of Michigan, 1963). Or if economy of time and presentation is important, one may begin with the established categories and then deductively find examples that are plentifully about us. In any case, one must either arrive at or work with precise definitions of etymological classes that are mutually exclusive. The subtleties of defining can be readily mastered with a little practice, and before long the average student will be able to classify accurately most words without reference to a dictionary.

There are three sources of Present-Day English vocabulary: native words, loan words, and new words or neologisms. Only loan words and neologisms, of course, produce additions to our current word stock, and of the latter there are 15 possible methods of making a new word.

One principal source of Present-Day English vocabulary is *native words* or words which can be traced back to the word stock of Old English. These will be, for the most part, the short, familiar words we use most often when we speak or write informally: articles (*a, an, the*), demonstratives (*this, that,* etc.), personal pronouns (*I, me, my, mine,* etc.), interrogatives (*who, what, where,* etc.), numerals (*one, once,* etc.), prepositions (*of, to,* etc.), conjunctions (*and, since,* etc.), adverbs of time and place (*then, there,* etc.), adjectives taking inflectional suffixes (*higher, highest,* etc.), strong verbs (*sell, think, sing,* etc.), modal auxiliaries (*must, shall,* etc.), helper verbs (*prefer, avoid, do,* etc.), and

From the *English Journal* 55:752-757 (September 1966).

irregular verbs (*be, go*). About 20 percent of Modern English vocabulary can be traced to native words of Old English.

Loan words or *borrowings* are treated here separately because even though they are new words in the English language they had a previous independent existence in other languages. Borrowings from foreign languages make up about 80 percent of the total Modern English vocabulary, but loan words among new words of Present-Day English amount to less than 8 percent. This illustrates the great facility English had in the past in assimilating elements from other languages, although there is a significant tendency today—as was true of Old English—for the language to use its inner resources in word making. New loan words tend to preserve the foreign pronunciation, if not the foreign spelling, but may in the course of time undergo anglicization. Some examples of new loan words are *apartheid* (S. Afr. Dutch), *canasta* (Sp.), *montage* (Fr.), *pizza* (It.), *snorkel* (Ger.) *spelunker* (Latin), *kibitzer* (Yid). Most prevalently, however, new loan words in English are place names and proper names: *Vietnam, U Thant.*

Neologisms are new words or old words with new meanings. They can be assigned to the following classifications in order of productivity in Present-Day English:

1. **Idiomatic compounds** are highly productive in Present-Day English and account for one of the major difficulties a foreigner has in learning English. They are constructed of free base forms which, when compounded, are elliptical in meaning and must be learned in context instead of being taken literally. Some examples are *egghead, hairy dog story, atomic cocktail, top banana, brainwash.* These phrasal compounds involve distinctly new meanings and must be distinguished from self-explaining compounds which can be literally interpreted. Sometimes a phrase begins as a self-explaining compound (*iron curtain* meaning the curtain, now asbestos, that separated the stage from the orchestra in legitimate theatres), but when Winston Churchill used *iron curtain* in 1946 ("From Stettin in the Baltic to Trieste in the Adriatic, an *iron curtain* has descended across the Continent"), it immediately took on a distinctly new, figurative, and memorable meaning. Idiomatic compounds make up about 25 percent of new words in Present-Day English.

2. **Greek and Latin combining forms** are morphemes used to make modern scientific and technical vocabulary. These forms were originally bound bases in Greek and Latin, and some examples in Present-Day English are constructed of two bound bases: *astronaut, Anglophile, megapolis.* Some Greek and Latin bound bases have become free forms in Present-Day English and are combined with a bound form: *acrophobia, benthoscope, mononucleosis.* There are also examples of two free bases of Greek and Latin origin being used in combination: *psychoneurosis, homophone, audiometer.* It is also quite possible to combine a Greek or Latin form with an existing English form: *megaton, microgroove, teleprompter.* Greek and Latin combining forms are often used in what is called an "International Scientific Vocabulary," much as one would put together a chemical formula for descriptive purposes: *polyvinyl acetal, demography, pneumonoultramicroscopicsilicovolcanokoniosis* (a rare lung disease caused by inhalation of very small particles of volcanic dust). Greek and Latin combining forms are productive in Present Day English and make up about 16 percent of new words.

3. **Derivatives** come from stems to which familiar derivational affixes are added to make new words. Derivation may include the use of prefixes (*belittle, deplane, misconstrue*), suffixes (*finalize, inductee, eightish*), or both (*bizonal, unemployability, desalinization*). The vast majority of derivatives are formed

through suffixation. Derivatives make up about 13 percent of new words in Present-Day English.

4. **Semantic change words** originate from the addition of distinctly new meanings to words already existing in the language. Some people prefer to regard these as "new meanings" rather than as "new words," but this old creative process in English shows how the language can rely on its inner resources instead of borrowing from without. In Old English, for example, the meanings of the native words *speech* and *board* were extended to include the meanings of the words *treatise* and *responsibility* of French origin now used in the language to express these ideas. Important sources of semantic change words are place names and personal names. Some place names which have taken on distinctly new meanings are *bikini, cashmere, donnybrook, champagne, bologna.* Some personal names which have been generalized to describe products or processes are *Ford, mackintosh, sanforize, roentgen, Parkinson's disease.* Other examples of recent semantic change words are *bug* (microphone), *bird* (rocket), *rumble* (street fight), *gremlin* (beginning surfer), *tool* (dullard). The sources of most semantic change words are the slang of teenagers and the jargon of occupations. One should note that semantic change words are single words and that idiomatic compounds, which also show a distinct shift in meaning, are phrasal compounds. About 12 percent of new words in Present-Day English are semantic change words.

5. **Self-explaining compounds** are constructed of free base forms put together in phrasal compounds which can be interpreted literally. They differ from idiomatic compounds in that they explain themselves and from Greek and Latin combining forms in that they do not originate in classical words having special forms for combining purposes: *atomic bomb, supermarket, ballpoint pen, snow-grip tires, appointment book.* Self-explaining compounds account for about 8 percent of new words in Present-Day English.

6. **Acronyms** are formed by putting together the initial letters of a word group (*LP, TVA, VIP, GI, A-OK*) or the initial syllables of a word group (*Benelux, Texaco, Alcoa, Cominform, Comphibtralant*). The initial letters are pronounced and may be written as abbreviations (*A.M., D.D.T., Ph.D.*) or they may take the form of "cute spellings" (*emcee, teevee, veep, Esso, Seabee*). Acronyms may also form pronounceable syllables (*NATO, NASA, snafu, UNESCO, VEPCO*). Acronyms may have begun with the Roman's SPQR (Senatus Populusque Romanus) and exist today in foreign languages too: *Nazi* (Nazional-Socialist), *ONU* (Organization des Nations Unies), *FIAT* (Fabbrica Industriale Automobile di Torino). The first impetus to this kind of word-making in English came during World War I, and in World War II military bureaucracy peppered the language with shortenings of officialese. They are indeed evidence of what Henry L. Mencken called the U.S. talent for "reducing complex concepts to starkest abbreviations." In Present-Day English, acronyms make up about 5 percent of new words, but one sometimes hears nonce expressions such as "Turn on the *AC* (air conditioning) while I get the *OJ* (orange juice)."

7. **Blends** are formed by combining the first part of a word with the second part of another. One of the elements is usually a fragment of a word, but the other elements may be either fragments or full words. The process involves both shortening and compounding. Blends are sometimes called *portmanteau* words after Humpty Dumpty's term in Carroll's *Through the Looking Glass.* "Jabberwocky" has provided us with a number of curious blends remembered by readers of Alice, the Jabberwock, and the Mad Hatter: *slithy* (lithe & slimy), *chortle* (chuckle & snort), *galumphing* (galloping & triumphing). Some examples from Present-Day English are *motel, twinight, smog, cafegymtorium, slanguage.*

Some blends will by analogy inspire a series, such as the *Time* Magazine "cinema" blends (*cinemactress, cineman, cinemadoption, cinemonster, cinemasculated*) or the "sputnik" blends *muttnik, lunik, protesnik, Uncle Samnik, beatnik*). Blends comprise only about 3 percent of new words in Present-Day English, but many others are used as "nonce words," being devised for a particular occasion or effect and not heard again, at least not often enough to be recorded in a dictionary.

8. **Functional change words** are shifts from one part of speech to another without form change. In making the change to a new syntactic class, a word may not change its base form or take derivational affixes—otherwise it would be a derivative—but it may take inflectional suffixes of its new part of speech: *premiere* (n.> v.), *know how* (v.> n.), *separates* (adj. = separate items of clothing > n.). Most examples of functional change today are shifts from noun to verb and are in accord with the rhetorical technique of seeking fresh and striking verbs. Some recent examples are "Another plane was *missiled* in North Vietnam today"; Radio Hong Kong *sourced* the item in Red China"; "One wonders why those careful scholars failed to *book* it." President Eisenhower, in deploring the 1965 racial violence in Los Angeles, made a noted functional change word: "the United States is being *atmosphered* in a policy of lawlessness." Functional change words comprise 2 percent of neologisms in Present-Day English, although many more are used as nonce words for stylistic effect.

9. **Pure root creations** or **coinages** are words formed from existing possible sounds and sound sequences natural to the structure of the language. The resulting word never existed as such before in English, but it will acquire meaning through repeated use in similiar contexts. Some examples of pure root creations in recent English are *kodak, dacron, hep, zilch, shmoo.* Nonsense language, usually in the manner of Lewis Carroll, illustrates pure root creation: The *tilly zious veeps* were *dasking* the very *postest citer molently.* Reversals (pizza > *zappi)* and transpositions (kleenex > *neeklex*) also make interesting coinages; and one may note that when these processes do not produce consonant clusters, syllables, and unstressed vowels normal to the English language, changes in phonemes will occur to make the new word pronounceable *(chewing gum)* > *incha* /inca/ rather than *ingchew* /incuw/). Most slang expressions are pure root creations (*nerd, barf, dipley*), semantic change words *(fink, mouse, tool*), and idiomatic compounds *(zero cool, beard bag, huggy bear).* Coining a word which will be normal to English structure is really a highly technical process if the possibilities of phoneme combinations are analyzed. Benjamin Whorf has a formula for the phonemic combinations possible in a monosyllabic English word in John B. Carroll, editor, *Language, Thought, and Reality,* (Massachusetts Insitute of Technology Press, 1956), page 223. Pure root creations are not an important source of new words, making up only about 2 percent of neologisms in Present-Day English. Other coinages may exist, however, as nonce words.

10. **Shortenings** or **clipped words** involve the omission of one or more syllables from a word with no shift in part of speech. In that there is no change in part of speech, shortenings must be distinguished from functional change words. Shortening may be accomplished in several ways. Sometimes syllables at the beginning of a word are dropped: *phone, bus, copter, scope, plane.* The shortening may come at the end of a word: *combo, props, bra, curio, pub.* The beginning and end of a word may also be clipped, leaving what is taken to be the base form without affixes: *still, flu.* Occasionally the shortening may involve only one of several derivational affixes: *complected.* Shortenings make up about 2 percent of new words in Present-Day English.

11. **Reduplications** are compounds which have recurrent syllables, a fixed consonant framework with a variant stressed vowel, or a variant consonant framework with a recurrent stressed or unstressed vowel. Some reduplications involving whole word repetition are *hush-hush, hubba-hubba, pooh-pooh.* Examples of stressed vowel variation are *shilly-shally, wishy-washy, chit-chat.* Consonant variations are illustrated in *huff-duff, willy-nilly, razzle-dazzle.* There are several hundred reduplications in Modern English vocabulary, but this type of word-making in Present-Day English produces only about 1 percent of new words.

12. **Echoisms, onomatopoetic words,** or **imitations** attempt to imitate the sound of the real thing or activity named: *ack-ack, bebop, zipper, woofer-tweeter, zoomar. Time* Magazine recently used a combination of an echoism and eye dialect in a report on jokes about President Johnson: "Some are moderately sympathetic, such as the *yuk* that has one Texan saying to another: 'Ah think ouh President is absolutely fahn. He's the first President we've evah had who doesn't have an accent.' " Older echoisms in the language imitated animal cries (*cuckoo, meow, bobwhite, whipoorwill, hoot owl*), and at one time this method of word-making was considered important enough to be made the basis for a theory of the origin of language known as the "bow wow" theory. This theory, however, accounts for relatively few words in a language, and in Present-Day English echoisms comprise less than 1 percent of new words.

13. **Back formations** are new words formed by the shortening of an existing word taken to its derivative. It amounts to reverse derivation in that derivational suffixes are dropped as one goes "back" to the base form. Unlike shortening, the process always involves a shift in part of speech. Some recent examples are *babysit* (< babysitter), *test drive* (< test driver), *grocery shop* (< grocery shopping), *shotgun marry* (< shotgun marriage), *fact find* (< fact finder). *Time* Magazine reported that the Sinatra yacht "*opted* to drop anchor at Hyannis Port." Older back formations, now well-established in the language, are *enthuse* (< enthusiasm), *emote, sculpt, edit, orate,* and *jell* (< jelly). Although back formations seem to occur often as nonce expressions, among the recorded new words of Present-Day English they make up only about 1 percent.

14. **Sound symbolism** employs in word formation a restricted group of morphemes which in certain contexts have acquired symbolic associations. The sound / ɨ y/ has morpheme status in English as a derivational suffix when added to base forms to mean diminution or endearment: *Jimmy, tummy, hankie, sweetie, nightie.* Certain other initial and final sound clusters seem to have morpheme status in English. The initial consonant cluster /sn-/ suggests an association with the nose in *snore, sneeze, snout, sniffle, snarl,* and the final cluster /-əmp/ suggests a rounded protuberance in *bump, lump, dump, rump, hump.* Such morphemes, however, are not productive of many words, and in Present-Day English sound symbolism accounts for considerably less than 1 percent of new words.

15. **Mistaken -s singulars** are words formed through a special shortening process wherein an unusual -s singular form is mistaken for an inflectional suffix for plurality and is therefore dropped to make a base-form singular. They differ from shortenings in that mistaken -s singulars are limited to dropping the noun inflectional suffix for plurality, and they differ from back formations in that there is no change in part of speech. Some historical examples are *sherry* (< sherris), *cherry* (< cerise), *pea* (< pease). Examples from Present-Day English are rare and occur only in nonstandard speech: *Chinee, trapee, specie, aboriginee, len* (< lens), *pant* (< pants).

In Present-Day English, compounding—idiomatic, self-explaining, Greek and Latin combining forms, and blends—accounts for well over half the new words in written English. Derivatives and semantic change words are also productive categories and together with the various types of compounding account for about 80 percent of new words in the language. New loan words are of only average importance in the lexicon of Present-Day English. By using new combinations of existing words, by making old words accommodate new meanings, and by deriving new forms from existing words through a system of derivational affixes, we can readily adapt the English language to the communication needs of modern society.

This conclusion is not exactly in accord with what is said about word-making in some standard histories of the English language which emphasize the resourcefulness of Old English in using native elements in word-making and the facility of Modern English in borrowing words from other languages (see Albert C. Baugh, *A History of the English Language*, 2nd edition; Appleton-Century-Crofts, 1957, p. 75.) Rather, the processes of compounding derivation, and semantic change are highly productive of new words in both Old and Present-Day English, and if borrowing was insignificant in the ninth Century, it is of only average importance in the twentieth.

15. The Use of Slang in Teaching Linguistics

Ernest Heiman

Much of the language instruction given to students is accomplished incidentally, when it is apropos, or as it arises out of a related activity. The bombastic boasts of beleaguered Beowulf will teach the student one aspect of the nature of using language; the rosy-fingered lines of wine-dark Homer will teach him yet another. But occasionally, it is helpful to set aside a block of time to present a small unit of linguistic material as a unit, or as an introduction to a continuing study of the nature of our language. Such an activity is a discussion of the characteristics of slang.

So often we hold a stigmatic view of slang. We red-pencil it in compositions; we correct it in class recitations; and we are amused by it, or ignore it in the corridors, where the classroom dialect we foster within our own rooms seems somehow to have lost its franchise.

Over the years of teaching standard English, teachers have developed the idea that slang is a use of the language which needs to be squelched or at least resisted. Yet slang is undeniably a part of the language. It may even be considered a distinct dialect, and sometimes it is almost a second language within the school. It is impossible to squelch and difficult to resist. Perhaps by recognizing it, analyzing it as English, and putting it to use, we might teach its users some things they may not know about the language, the way they use it, and, the way we would like them to use it. We may even discover that some of the excitement students exhibit in using a slang dialect can be transferred to their learning the standard dialect.

The advantages then to using slang as a basis for language study are twofold: a high interest level on the part of the students and a presentation of a great variety of language principles which are applicable to standard English.

Teachers may feel somewhat chagrined at dealing with language on a student level, but I have found that the rewards are well worth the extension of one's vocabulary. Those who may not be acquainted with the wide range of student vernacular will find that a little practice in tuning one's ear to it while walking the halls will usually give a wealth of material from which to work.

From *English Journal* 56:249-252 (February 1967).

In beginning a discussion of slang in the classroom, writing on the blackboard statements dictated by students is one way of inductively introducing the following points:

- a definition of slang
- where slang originates
- what happens to slang words after they are put into use

Out of these introductory discussions and the work that follows, students should deduce that within slang are elements of jargon, shop talk, and cant, and that it can originate from a great variety of sources. They should also see that, unlike standard English, slang normally originates through a conscious spontaneity. However, though the creation of slang words is often deliberate, the linguistic principles of word formation used are usually traditional. Finally, students should determine that the life history of a slang term depends to a great extent upon the need it serves within the language, and will follow generally one of three courses: (a) that most frequently a slang term is born, becomes popular, is used in excess, recedes, and dies [*skidoo*]; (b) that sometimes it is born, becomes popular, and remains as a slang term [*booze, beat it*]; (c) and that occasionally the word is born, is popularized, and leaves the area of slang to become accepted as standard English [*walkie-talkie*].

A study of language which compares slang to standard English can relate to four linguistic areas:

(1) CLASSIFICATION OF VARIOUS FIGURES OF SPEECH

(2) PRINCIPLES OF LANGUAGE FORMATION

(3) PRINCIPLES OF LANGUAGE CHANGE

(4) SEMANTICS.

Figures of speech are condensed analogies which by their very nature lend themselves easily to the world of slang. They are intentional departures from the normal use of words, created to add strength and freshness to otherwise matter-of-fact descriptions.

1. **Similes**—Within slang, the best example in use currently is the practice of prefacing introductory and exclamatory statements with the term *like:* "Like where ya goin' man?", "Like now, man!" Standard English examples of simile can be supplied from the teacher's own knowledge of literary analysis.

2. **Metaphors**—Though examples of metaphoric slang are seemingly limitless in number and variety, a great many terms have originated from (1) analogies to the human body and its parts: *half-pint, gorilla, pony tail, meat hooks,* and especially the human head: *rocker, bean, nut, gourd;* (2) comparisons to food: a *prune*, a *greaser*, a *pickle*, a *honey, lettuce*, to be *kosher;* and (3) references to the five senses: *rough* (situation), *smooth*, to *touch* (for money), to *smell.* Here too, standard English examples of metaphor can be supplied from the teacher's own knowledge of literary technique.

3. **Metonymy**—This figure of speech describes by substituting a term thought to be closely associated with an object for the object itself. Some examples found in slang are: a *breadline*, a *company man*, a *brain*, *Ivy League*, a *long hair.* Some examples from standard English are: the *crown* (for king), the *White House* (for President), "In the *sweat* of thy face shalt thou eat *bread.*" (Genesis, 3:19)

4. **Synecdoche**—A form of metaphor, this technique is used to describe by having a part signify the whole, or the whole signify a part, (the latter sometimes being confused with hyperbole or exaggeration). Slang examples are: *wheels* (for car), a *skirt* (for girl), a *pad* (for home), a *library* (when referring to several books). Standard examples would be: to *motor* (drive a car), a *foot soldier*, a *roof* (over one's head).

Though the use and durability of words vary greatly between standard English and slang, rarely do slang terms come into being without conforming to traditional principles of word origin. Thus, the student who creates or uses such expressions to color his speech is often unknowingly exhibiting one of many standard principles of language formation.

1. **Onomatopoeia (or echoism)**—This is the use of words in which their pronunciation suggests their meaning. In slang: *whammo, yuk-yuk, slurp*, a *tick-tock* (for watch). In standard: *buzz, bang, whirr, hiss.*

2. **Iteration (or reduplication)**—Also phonetic, this principle uses the suggested repetition of sounds; as in slang: the *heeby-jeebies*, the *bees knees, long-gone, a booboo, hankie-pankie.* In standard: *Piggly Wiggly, zig-zag, pitter-patter, walkie-talkie.*

3. **Compounding**—This principle simply places two words in juxtaposition, at times combining them into one word. In slang: *plow jockey, egghead, brain trust, hillbilly.* In standard: *blackberry, cupboard, stone wall, soap opera.*

4. **Shortening**—Though other methods exist, the most common form of shortening is simple abbreviation. In slang: a *hood*, a *collēge* (a person), *specks, biochem;* and, of course, "Hey, *teach.*" In standard: *gym, taxi, math, bus.*

5. **Conversion (or functional shift)**—This principle takes advantage of the lack of morphological inflection in modern English to create new words by changing the function of form words or parts of speech. The process usually results in a refinement or specialization of meaning. In slang: to *stomach* (from the noun form), to *bug* (from the noun form), a *find* (from the verb form), the *ins and outs* (from the adverb forms). In standard: to *stone*, to *ink*, to *paper*, to *bridge* (all from the noun forms).

6. **Derivation**—This very common principle of language growth forms new words through the affixing of prefixes and suffixes, ("Having forgotten several items, I found I had to go *re*Kroger*ing*".) A great variety of word forms can be illustrated by the students, and, if desired by the teacher, a thorough study of affix etymology can be undertaken. In light of this, rather than have the students suggest examples of the technique involved, as recommended in illustrating the previous principles of word origin, the teacher may wish to place affixes of various origins on the blackboard and have the students suggest examples of their use in both slang and standard English. The following is given as a partial list:

Anglo-Saxon: *be-, mis-, -ness, -less, -ful, -y*, and *ish*
Latin: *pro-, post-, pre-, ante-, super-, -ation, -ative*
French: *dis-, en-, -al, -ment, -able, -ous, -ary*
Greek: *a-, hyper-, -ist, -ize, -ic, -itis, -ism*

7. **Acronyms**—With the impatience of modern generations has come a seige of words using this principle of formation. Acronyms are formed by using the initial letters or syllables of a phrase to form a new word. This abbreviated form then is either pronounced as a phonetic morpheme or by reciting the alphabetic letters it is composed of. In the use of slang are found: *TV, SNAFU, OK, UNCLE.*

In standard English are found: *CARE, NATO, UN, SNCC.*

Of the types of historical change in meaning which words can undergo, only two principles are readily applicable to slang. Since linguistic change evolves so slowly, it generally takes too long to affect slang words with their ephemeral nature.

1. **Hyperbole**—It is difficult to imagine words being "used up," but with the influence of modern technology and the appetite of the advertising world, many of the descriptive and superlative adjectives of the language have lost much of their force. In addition, the very human habit of using a strong word on a light occasion causes the intense word to lose some of its impact or strength. As a result, even stronger substitutes are used, or adverbs are "tacked on" to bolster the weakened word, and so the self-degenerating process continues. Both the slang and standard English examples below should clearly illustrate this principle of change.

Slang: *jillion, miraculous* (when used outside of its biblical connotation), *super, the most.*

Standard: *stupendous, absolutely unique, perfect, custom* (of special manufacture).

It is interesting to note that in today's feminine world, a permanent isn't, nor in the masculine world is a two-by-four any longer two-by-four.

2. **Euphemism**—Since the accepted use of slang is restricted, and the principle of euphemism involves the replacing of one term with a more acceptable one, slang does not frequently qualify as a substitute term.

Slang: *kicked the bucket*, a *"nice guy"* (meaning the opposite), *strip, cracked* (for insane).

Standard: *passed away, disrobe, funeral home, mental institution.*

With an understanding of the nature of slang, along with the knowledge gained in previous introductions of semantic principles, the students should be capable of determining inductively the advantages and disadvantages of using slang in their writing. Slang, when used with discretion, will add color and force, of a type, to compositions. However, the great disadvantage to the indiscriminate use of slang is its lack of precise denotation.

Compare the following two lists of slang terms which are often used as either adjectives or counterwords (single word responses of acceptance or rejection). The list of older terms is still in use. However, even these expressions in their ambiguity (have the students try to define them) are being hyperbolically replaced by the second list of newer slang descriptions.

Older terms: *nice, swell, fair, neat, awful, keen, sharp.*

New terms: *way-out, gone, kooky, square, cool, sick, groovy.*

In discussing the meaning of slang terms, most teachers can readily tell their students the disadvantages of using slang in their writing. But I believe it is important that in such a discussion we do not deride the use of slang in general, or worse yet, ignore its existence. The simple fact that slang crops up so often where it is neither rhetorically desired nor needed in student communication should not negate for us a recognition of slang as a useful area of language study. Our task necessitates our communicating with the Pepsi generation. And in so doing, if we can give them a better understanding of all areas of language, it just might help them make the scene in English. It might even help them Ace the course, man!

16.

'dik-shə-ner-ēs 'ōld &'n(y)ü

Bergen Evans

The first English dictionary was Robert Cawdrey's *A Table Alphabeticall . . . of hard usual English Wordes*, gathered, so the title page tells us, "for the benefit and helpe of Ladies, Gentlewomen" and "other unskilfull persons."

It was published in 1604 and, although ludicrously meager in comparison to any modern dictionary, is still of value to the discerning. The very date of publication, for example, reminds us that Chaucer, Langland, Wycliffe, Skelton, Tyndale, More, Marlowe, and probably Shakespeare, Bacon, Ben Jonson, Lancelot Andrewes, and John Donne (not to mention several million others) never consulted a dictionary in their lives and yet managed to write and speak effectively. That is, the date of publication of our first dictionary emphasizes the fact that language takes precedence of lexicons and that dictionaries do not dictate but record dictation.

Cawdrey was an intelligent man. His definition of *degenerate* as "unlike his auncestours" is a brilliant piece of insight. And "pleasing" for *plausible*, "heathen" for *ethnick* and "nigardness" for *tenacity* are still something to think about. Finding "orphan" spelled *orphant* in Cawdrey, the modern reader may be charmed to realize that some Elizabethan pronunciations lingered on in rural Indiana as late as 1885 when James Whitcomb Riley wrote *Little Orphant Annie*. Or, finding that Cawdrey listed *imply* and *inferre* as synonyms, meaning "to signifie," and then having this synonymity excoriated in one of the zippiest, most-up-to-the-minute newsmagazines as "an atrocity which has crept into current usage," he may be surprised to discover that the newsmagazine is at least 365 years behind the times. Or, finding their interchangeable use condemned as a corruption by 92 percent of a panel of savants consulted by our most recent dictionary, he may question the value of consulting such savants or of consulting a dictionary that consults them.

There is no better beginning for the study of lexicography than a mistrust of lexicons.

Nineteen years after Cawdrey, there appeared Henry Cockeram's *New Interpreter of Hard English Words*, which offered to assist its readers to "a speedy attaining of an Elegant Perfection" in their speech, just as *The American Heritage Dictionary*, in 1969, was to offer its readers "guidance toward grace and precision." Cockeram, however, was enough of a linguist (or humorist)

From *Today's Education* 59:24-7 (February 1970). Reprinted by permission of National Education Association and Bergen Evans.

to add that "Elegant Perfection" was for those "who study rather to hear themselves speak than to understand themselves."

Other dictionaries followed, and all of these were drawn upon and enlarged by Nathaniel Bailey's *Universal Etymological English Dictionary* which, between 1721 and 1802, ran through 30 editions. It was from Bailey that the ill-starred poet Chatterton obtained many of the phony antique terms that were to prove his undoing. More important, Bailey's dictionary was the first one that sought to include all the words in the language. And most important of all, it was the foundation of Samuel Johnson's *A Dictionary of the English Language.*

The success of Bailey's dictionary had convinced a group of London booksellers (publishers, we call them) that there was a market for a definitive lexicon, one that would list all the words in the language, define each one, and give its pronunciation. An additional function, perhaps its greatest, would be to "fix" the language, to halt its "corruption" and "decay." Then, as now, a process of degeneration was thought to have progressed so far under the pressure of the "vulgar" that unless something drastic was done immediately, the language would be rendered useless and all communication would necessarily cease—among the elegant, that is, since the vulgar, presumably, would go on making their vulgar sounds.

To avert this calamity, they selected Samuel Johnson as editor. His qualifications were immense learning, a style marked by ponderous Latinity (the antithesis of "vulgar"), and unsurpassed dogmatism, and a deep piety.

Johnson, who was desperately poor and needed employment, announced (in 1747) his willingness to be the linguistic dictator that the emergency demanded. He was prepared to "fix" the pronunciation of English, "preserve the purity of its idiom," and hold back the flood of "low terms" that was overwhelming it.

In 1755, the *Dictionary* appeared in two folio volumes, magnificently printed and prefaced by an essay on language and lexicography that must be classed with Wordsworth's *Preface to the Lyrical Ballads* and Shelley's *Defence of Poetry* as one of the intellectual landmarks of the English-speaking people.

In this document, Johnson confessed that eight years of "sluggishly treading the track of the alphabet" had taught him that talk of "fixing" a language or of "preserving its purity" was ignorant, silly, and pretentious: "the dream of a poet doomed at last to wake a lexicographer." He had perceived that irregularities were inherent in "the boundless chaos of living speech," were, indeed, indications of its profusion and vitality. As for academies, panels of experts, and others who sought or were besought to place official seals of approval or disapproval on this or that form, he hoped that "the spirit of English liberty" would destroy them as fast as vanity could set them up.

Finding that there were no guides but experience and analogy, Johnson illustrated the meanings of words by quotations from the writings of well-known authors. And in so doing he established the lexicographic principle that language is what usage makes it and that custom, in the long run, is the ultimate and only court of appeal in linguistic matters.

In selecting his illustrative quotations, by the way, Johnson took his passages, whenever he could, from writers whose works had a moral and religious tone he approved of. One would smile at the quaintness of this were it not for the uproar made over the fact that *Webster's Third New International* illustrated one meaning of *shake* by a quotation from Polly Adler's *A House is not a Home.*

Johnson's dictionary was an immediate and great success and for almost a century its two stately folios upheld the dignity of every manorial collection of English books that professed to be a library. Soon after its first appearance, he published an abridgment, and this not only graced humbler households but was the standard prize in school exercises. It was undoubtedly a later edition of this work that Miss Becky Sharp hurled back over the wall of Miss Pinkerton's Academy as a supreme gesture of disrespect for the established order.

Although other dictionaries appeared as time went on, Johnson was not displaced as the ultimate authority until the publication of *The Oxford English Dictionary*, now commonly called the OED. And in many ways this was not so much a displacement as an extension. Many of Johnson's definitions are retained simply because better ones have not been invented. And the OED was based on the idea that meaning and form are determined by usage and can best be displayed in authenticated, dated contexts.

The statistics of this great work are staggering. Its 13 huge volumes, representing 75 years of labor by some 800 (*unpaid*) readers, appeared in sections between 1884 and 1928. It is built on historical principles, tracing every word in the language from Anglo-Saxon times down to the date of its volume's publication and illustrating the development of every meaning of every word, as well as its spelling and pronunciation, by illustrative quotations.

In America, Johnson was gradually replaced by *The American Dictionary of the English Language*, the work of an energetic, learned, cranky Yankee, Noah Webster, a man more contentious than even the Great Cham himself. His prospectus provided a storm of derision. The Boston *Palladium* insisted that the whole thing was unnecessary, since English had reached perfection and no new words were needed. The Boston *Aurora* dismissed as "preposterous" the suggestion that new words and meanings had been introduced by semiliterate Colonials. The *Gazette of the United States*, convulsed with merriment, demanded to know if Webster proposed to include such "low" words as *hominy*, *possum*, and *banjo*.

But Webster was unabashed. He went right ahead and included such "corruptions" as *applicant*, *lengthy*, *congressional*, and *presidential* for no better reason than that Americans used them. And he indicated that while he was reforming the dictionary, he was willing to reform our spelling as well. It may be one of our national misfortunes that the ridicule of the ignorant frightened his publishers and prevented them from letting him do the thorough job he wanted to do.

To his lifelong work, we owe three things: (a) the slight simplification of our spelling that allows us to write *color*, *labor*, and the like instead of *colour* and *labour*, and *theater* and *center* instead of *theatre* and *centre*; (b) the sense, derived to some extent from these spellings, that our language could accept its own usages as standard and need not assume that every deviation from British usage was a corruption; and (c) the establishment and growth of the chain of Merriam-Webster dictionaries.

Webster lived to revise his 1828 dictionary, the revised version coming from the press in 1840 when he was 82 years old. He had to finance and publish this revision himself and died indebted to his printers, George and Charles Merriam, of Springfield, Massachusetts. These brothers secured the rights to his book and copyrighted *Merriam-Webster*. But they failed to copyright the single word *Webster*, which is now in the public domain and may be used by anyone who publishes a dictionary that he feels incorporates some or all of Noah Webster's lexicographical methods.

In 1847, the first *Merriam-Webster Unabridged Dictionary* appeared. Revisions of this came out in 1864, 1890, and 1909, and these were followed, in 1934, by *Merriam-Webster's New International Dictionary, Second Edition* (MW2). This was replaced, in 1961, by *Webster's Third New International Dictionary of the English Language, Unabridged* (MW3), the book that brought Johnson's lexicographical findings to the attention of newspaper editors and moved them to antediluvian indignation.

No account of English dictionaries, however superficial, could neglect to mention *The Century Dictionary and Cyclopedia*, an American dictionary that was published in 1889 and was revised and enlarged (into 10 volumes) in 17 subsequent printings. It has been out of print for almost fifty years and is, therefore, out of date. But within its limitations it is a very great dictionary, especially in the fullness of its definitions and the richness of its illustrative quotations.

Of general dictionaries, there is now God's plenty from which to choose. First, in its solitary grandeur, is the OED, access to which is indispensable to any student of language or literature. Equally unrivalled in its profusion of entries, its accuracy, the excellence of its definitions, the richness of its illustrative quotations, and its conformance to the standards of modern lexicography is *Webster's Third New International.* It is a very great book. No scholar, no teacher of literature, no library, no lawyer, no editor, no business office can afford to be without it.

Just below this in its number of entries—lighter, easier to handle, and at about half the price—is the *Random House Dictionary of the English Language.* Every household, especially if it includes children of school or college age, should have this as one of its dictionaries. For one cannot overemphasize the fact that dictionaries differ, that the idea of *the* dictionary (as in "Is that word in the dictionary?") is dangerously misleading. Similar to the *Random House Dictionary* is *Funk and Wagnalls Standard Dictionary, International Edition,* edited by Allen Walker Read.

There is also a host of desk dictionaries, such as G. & C. Merriam's *Seventh New Collegiate*, Random House's *American College Dictionary* and the college edition of their *Dictionary of the English Language*, the Thorndike-Barnhart *Comprehensive Desk Dictionary*, and *Webster's New World Dictionary, Second Edition.* All are excellent buys and one or two should always be within easy reach.

The most recent of the desk dictionaries—*The American Heritage Dictionary*—merits special comment because it repudiates what has come to be the basic principle of dictionary making: It is designed to protect the English language rather than to report on it.

In most respects it is a good desk dictionary. It has about the same number of entries as the other desk dictionaries. Its range of meanings is adequate for its level.

But its chief distinction—the one most touted—is that it offers "that sensible guidance toward grace and precision which intelligent people seek in a dictionary." This was accomplished by submitting "dubious or controversial locutions" to a panel of outstanding speakers and writers, whose names are listed in the book's prefatory material. There are 104 of them—as against MW3's 14,000, with the added difference that AHD's authorities stated what *should* be done, whereas MW3's citations show what *is* done—a significant difference.

The value of the panel's pronouncements may be illustrated by their treatment of *gift*, used as a transitive verb (as seen in "The Lord gifted him above his brethren."). *The American Heritage Dictionary* informs us that this, a "recent" use of the word, was voted "unacceptable" by 94 percent of the panel, and a publicity release supplies us with a few names and specific opinions.

Sidney Harris characterized *gift* as a transitive verb with the one word "Ghastly!" Walter W. (Red) Smith apparently fell back on the assumption that verbs are verbs and nouns are nouns and never the twain should meet—despite some 50,000 or more instances to the contrary in our speech. William Zinsser dismissed it with lofty scorn in a sentence ("I never saw it and I never want to."), which reveals that he has never consulted the OED and has never read the English ballads, Fielding's *Tom Jones*, or the works of Mrs. Browning. And, what's more, seems proud of it. That, of course, is his privilege, but it is a puzzling qualification for being selected as an expert in English usage. *Gift* as a verb has been in common use for at least 400 years and is listed as standard in every major dictionary.

The 104 members of the panel are certainly men and women of distinction. But less than a score of them could be regarded as creative writers—who are likely to be familiar with current idiom—and less than half that many are trained linguists. Most of them are editors, commentators, critics, librarians, and government officials—men and women, that is, who by profession tend to have strong opinions. Their average age is 64.

But even so, even with this very small and relatively homogenous group, we are told (p. xxiv) that out of the 600 questions submitted to them the panel members were in complete agreement on only one! Their decisions are presented in percentages. But the reader is not told who's who in these percentages. He has no way of identifying the informed statements of the linguists—who, one assumes, must have been acutely embarrassed by the rodomontade of some of their colleagues. Not that it matters. Here, as everywhere, usage is determined by the practice of the majority. But the reader has a right to ask that the group consulted be as large and as representative as possible.

B. Linguistics

The recent impact of linguistic science on the teaching of language is known as the "new English." Linguistic scholarship is advancing new theories that are displacing outmoded schools of thought. What the individual considers the content of language to be varies in accordance with his interests and educational pursuits. An examination of current language arts publications reveals that the impact of the "new English" has been erratic.

The variety of adaptations and the lack of an authoritative voice in linguistics has grown out of the recent history following the "Sputnik crisis" in education. In an effort to achieve academic respectability during this era, English educators initiated a debate over what should comprise the "new English." Within a short time the deliberation, which was narrowly defined, focused on which grammar to teach: traditional, structural, or transformational. Each of these approaches had its vigorous advocates. The controversy centered on this rather singular aspect of linguistics, even though research and opinion have long questioned whether the study of grammar has ever improved children's uses of their native language at all.

The discursive nature of what grammar to use merely compounded the problems of conscientious elementary teachers who were attempting to introduce new math, science and social studies into their curriculum. How were they to provide language programs that assured some measure of sequence and continuity with those in the high schools?

Although at present there is little agreement concerning the appropriate emphasis in content at each level, a trend is emerging. The writer of the overview to language study which follows cites a number of linguistic concepts. He cites, for example, the impact that research in language development and history has had on etymology, the traditional science of word derivations and on phonology, the study of speech sounds. He notes the growing awareness of social and regional dialects. And finally he elaborates on the structure of language, discussing several important language concepts that are fundamental to the teaching of English grammar.

Although the controversy concerning the merits of the various grammars persists, educators are beginning to synthesize the best of the "old" and "new" grammatical principles into an eclectic program of pedagogically useful concepts. The two selections following the overview discuss the study of grammar. One summarizes information and definitions for the most commonly used linguistic terminology, while the other uses three lesson plans to demonstrate how to apply grammatical concepts to language in a spirit of rational inquiry.

Even though the foregoing articles seem to lend credence to the viewpoint that the "new grammar" is alive and well, there are those who state that the once heralded grammatical revolution has failed. The last contributor in this section cites three mistakes made since 1954 which have contributed to the revolutionaries' demise: (1) their theory was too scientific, (2) it lacked practical applications, and most important (3) their theory failed to recognize the humanizing qualities of language.

Hopefully, these objections will be met by language scholars in this decade. Now that the fadishness of doing something "linguistic" is passing, those concepts which meet the test of reasoned evaluation will begin to emerge on a persisting basis.

17.

Language Study Today—An Overview

Kent Gill

Even though I begin this presentation with a parable, I urge you not to view me as a minister preaching a narrow gospel or as a missionary proselyting for a strange new faith. I hope rather that you will think of me as a teacher talking with you about some concepts basic to the English language and to classroom instruction in English. But to my parable:

> Once there was a botanist, Linny von Taxonomy, who was interested in naming the members of the plant kingdom. He applied a series of Latin terms to phylum, class, order, and family, resulting in specific genus and species designations. As a result, around the world the dogwood is known as *cornus alba* and the yew pine as *Podocarpus macrophylla.* Thereafter, he busied himself giving names to the tallest trees of the forest and the tiniest flowers of the desert.
>
> In the meantime fellow scientists developed a strange instrument called a microscope and they began to examine cells; but Dr. von Taxonomy heeded the cytologist not. Other men of science, called chemists, began to explore the intricacies of plant systems, discovering protoplasm and chlorophyll. Ecologists examined the plant in its relationships with its neighbors—plants and animals, atmosphere and minerals. Geneticists moved toward cracking the code which would explain the heredity of the specific plant.
>
> But Dr. von Taxonomy went vigorously on, giving names right and left till he had named every plant in sight, pausing only to throw rocks at the other scientists and to dodge the missiles thrown in return. But, alas, he was no longer a botanist. Without his really noticing, the fund of botanical knowledge had expanded, leaving him only a small fraction of the field as his specialty; the many significant changes had left him with an incomplete and imperfect understanding. Without the new insights available, he found it impossible even to extend with any precision his own predilection for giving names. So he now occupies the furthermost cell in the

From *New Directions in Language, Composition, and Literature,* pp. 33-44, (Area III English Project, California, A Third Report, December 1967), edited by Wayne Harsh and Helen Strickland. Reprinted with permission of Helen Strickland, Area III English Project Director, and Kent Gill.

most remote of the ivory towers, muttering to himself *lewisii, linnaeus,* and *pseudotsoga taxifolia.*

As in biological and psychological studies, as in chemistry and physics and geology, much systematic and objective study has been made recently in language—one of the most basic human activities. This study of language has resulted in promising discoveries, insights, and theories. A brief historical view of language scholarship may help us take our bearings as teachers of English.

Let's begin with the language study which all of us suppose we learned and which most of us think we teach. Known as traditional or schoolroom grammar, this grammar has an eminently respectable history, based on logic and rooted in classical studies. It was written down for us by eighteenth-century scholars, who applied Latin and Greek names and concepts to English with the goal of bringing regularity and respectability to a vernacular which was fast gaining precedence over Latin. These scholars—a London bishop, an Oxford professor of geometry—set standards and prescribed rules, basing their rules on how language *should be* used rather than on how it actually *was* used, giving, for instance, specific rules for *can* and *may, will* and *shall.* Over the years, traditional grammar has increasingly focused on usage rules, prescribing which verb tense, what pronoun case. The traditional approach has not expanded with continuing language study, has not grown, but has actually shrunk as some of its tenets have become so obviously at odds with the facts.

Language scholarship has advanced dramatically during the last century, even though, until recently, it has affected schoolroom grammar very little. Historical grammarians in the nineteenth century documented the language actually used by English writers. Earlier in that century, comparative studies of languages as remote in time and space as Sanskrit, Greek, and German began to reveal similarities so striking that a hypothetical Indo-European language could be reconstructed, and regular laws could be stated to explain its sound changes.

In the United States and in England, dialect began to assume some importance in literature, exemplified by Mark Twain and by Kipling. This use of dialect suggested an increased awareness of speech differences within a single language. As early as 1910, a linguistic atlas was published in France, mapping geographic variations in speech. European nations, both because of missionary zeal and imperialistic desires, faced the problem of learning other languages and teaching others to speak their languages. They developed that branch of linguistics which focused on the sound systems of language and revealed the fact that spoken and written language do not uniformly correspond.

Similarly, American missionaries, anthropologists, and language scholars, who were originally interested in American Indian languages, turned their attention to English, producing phonemic transcriptions which demonstrate that English utilizes 26 alphabetic notations but some 40 or more meaningful or *phonemic* sound variations. The last century has seen much pulling together of various branches of language scholarship, much pooling of linguistic knowledge, much new scholarship. But until recently, linguistic studies have had little influence on the teaching of English.

As a result of language scholarship we now define language as systematized but arbitrary combinations of sounds which have meaning for people in a given culture. And we are better able to say what knowledge about language is pertinent to the teaching of English. The chart below suggests several areas of language study which need to be incorporated in the English curriculum.

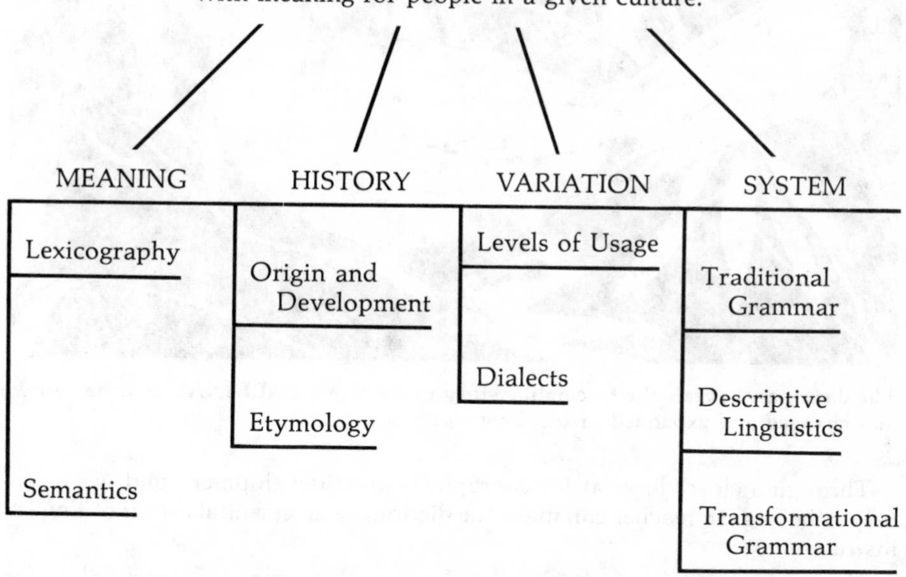

Language study begins and ends with a consideration of meaning, and meaning we can immediately associate with vocabulary. Yet, as teachers, we know the futility of direct teaching of vocabulary. Learning about words—in context, in situation, in life—is much more fruitful that the rote learning of word lists. Learning words to express meaning, and through words learning new meanings, is quite obviously a matter for students in an English class.

Let's examine first the matter of lexicography. Teachers have long taught dictionary skills, and some students have become competent, if perhaps not too willing, at "looking it up." Even when the student is able to use the dictionary, however, there is much he might not know about it. He is probably not certain whether the dictionary is telling him what to do or whether it is offering him alternatives by describing what has been done. The student may be unaware of the shades of meaning differentiated in synonymy or the diversity of meaning suggested for some of the common words: the word *head*, for example, has 39 definitions, 51 compounds, and 6 derived or inflected forms. Often the student doesn't understand changes in meaning which most words have undergone over a long period of linguistic history.

CARDINAL

- **a hinge**
- **that on which something turns or depends**
- **fundamental or principal**
- **one of the principal Roman Catholic churches**
- **the heads of these churches**
- **the cloak worn by these churchmen**
- **bright red, the color of these cloaks**
- **a bird of bright red hue**

The dictionary reveals the fascinating story of the word CARDINAL as it has grown and changed and expanded in our language.

Through a closer look at lexicography—word development and word history—the English teacher can make the dictionary an essential aspect of English instruction.

The subject matter of semantics offers another important possibility for enriching the English curriculum. Semantics illustrates the arbitrary nature of language, that is, the ways in which we associate words and meanings, so that even onomatopoetic words are different in each language. Semantics is concerned with the emotional element in language and recognizes the connotations which are basic to our understanding and selection of words. What, for instance, do we call a traveler?

It is important that students realize the tremendous, significant potential in the manipulation of language and that they learn to use language so that they express adequately their own meanings and feelings. Students need to recognize how language is used, ranging from the mass hysteria in the *Sieg Heil* of Nazi Germany to the soothing murmurings of the television commercial or the "subtlety" of cigarette names. We can help the student to recognize the existence of occupational or special-interest language—referred to as cant, argot, or jargon—language which, when carried to the extreme, becomes incomprehensible to the outsider. Examples are *hot rods, slicks,* and *4-barrels,* or our own professional jargon— *percentiles, stanines, culturally-deprived children.* We can assist students to cut through the language of propaganda, through the undefined abstractions and loaded words, the glittering generalities and false analogies, to get to meaning.

Language history is another area of English study that we need to include in a meaningful curriculum. The generalization that English comes from Latin is inaccurate. English is a Germanic language, which has borrowed much of its vocabulary from Latin and Greek (as well as some fifty other languages), and has patterned some of its grammatical structures after the classical languages. Students need to develop some comprehension of what language is and how it developed; they need to know that around the world there are probably as many as 3000 languages. Students also need to see how languages are related, which languages have influenced the development of English, and to understand how historical events have affected the language.

We should not overlook etymology—a study which traces the historical development of individual words, revealing clues to meaning, sound changes, historical influences, and the diversities of English.

By tracing processes involved in word-formation and in word-change, etymology reveals much about linguistic methods and about psychological relationships. The single modern word *telecast* shows something of the polyglot history of the English language.

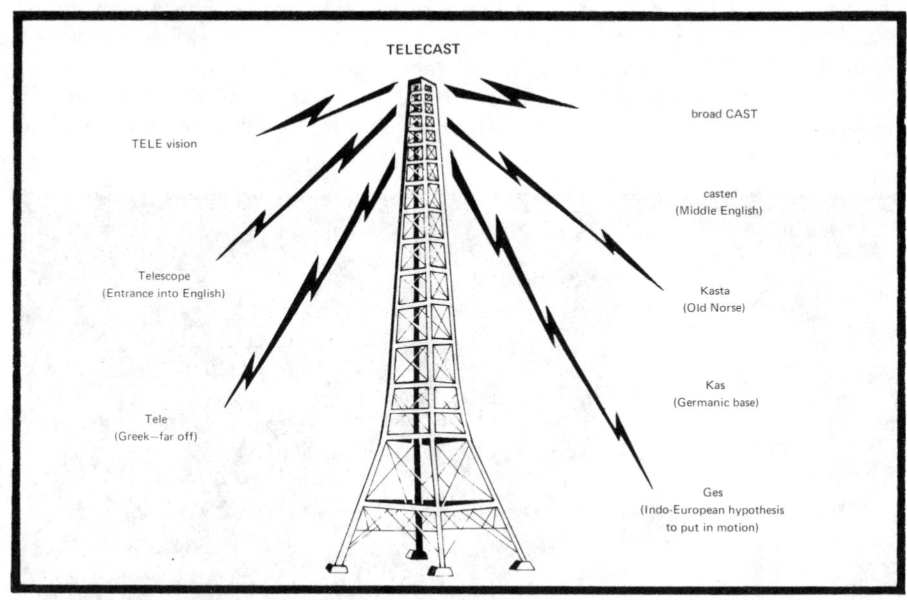

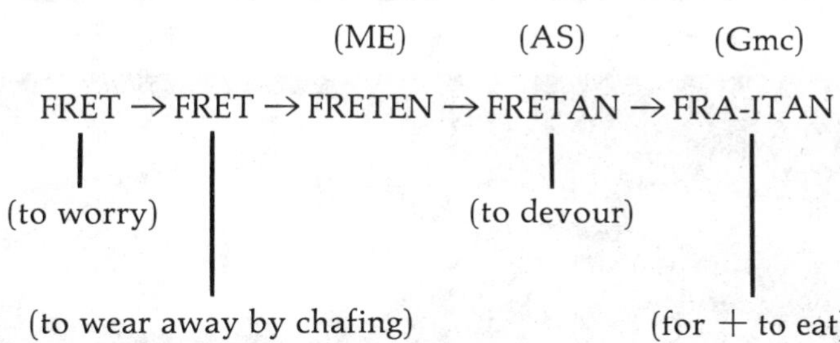

A Germanic base (kas) coming from a hypothetical Indo-European root (ges), and changed in its linguistic development to cast, is combined with a borrowing from Greek (tele-) to form a new word for a new activity. In fret, etymology shows the metaphorical application which resulted in a new meaning: the word for eating, in its development from Germanic to present-day English, became the word for worrying.

Dialects and levels of language usage, significant areas in linguistic study, deal with language variation. Much previous teaching of English has been based on the assumption that there is one single standard, or one "correct," form of English. In reality, our language exists in many variant forms and is constantly changing. *Correctness* and *standard* must be defined by considering usage and by considering regional variations or dialects.

One of the first concerns is with levels of usage. Each individual person adjusts his language to fit each of his language needs and situations. No hard and fast rules govern usage, though we are able to recognize a *norm* or *norms* in the speech and writing of educated people. We pay attention to vocabulary choices, as well as verb tense and pronoun case, in formal situations; we can let them fall as they may in less formal language situations. Few of us move with linguistic ease in all language situations without making a conscious effort, such as we make, for example, in formal writing or teaching. The student who, because of cultural or social deprivation, is unable to deal with a variety of language patterns presents one of our most serious pedagogical problems. The school must teach these students a second dialect—at times, a second language—which approximates the language spoken by educated members of the community.

The diagrams above illustrate levels of usage, the variations made both by linguistic maturity and by linguistic situation, and the regional dialect forms for one object. No one would be surprised to hear the same paternal figure referred to in all of these variants at different times and in different circumstances. The spider of the New England speaker becomes the skillet for the Southern speaker.

The knowledge of regional dialects can be of value both in language study and in literature. Dialects are distinguished by variations in pronunciation, vocabulary and grammatical constructions. Linguists have identified a number of regional dialects in American English. A study of dialect variations—both social and regional—should lead to a student's recognizing that he himself speaks in a dialect and that he can accept dialects different from his own.

Although we have demonstrated that language study need not be grammar alone, we must not overlook the fact that language does have structure, and that grammar is an explanation of this structure. Grammar has been a primary focus of interest and controversy since World War II. During this short period, linguists have contributed two new approaches to the study of grammar: *structural* (or *descriptive*) *linguistics* and *transformational-generative grammar.* The concepts and methods made available by these approaches have enabled classroom teachers to modify and enlarge the somewhat narrow description of the English language given by traditional schoolroom grammar. Linguists define grammar as the systematic description of how language elements work together to produce meaning, or, as generative grammarians say, the way in which a language produces an infinite number of grammatical sentences from a finite number of words and basic sentence forms.

Descriptive linguists stress several significant language concepts as fundamental to the teaching of English grammar:

First, word order is basic to meaning:
Willie hit the ball means something quite different from *The ball hit Willie.*
Second, changes in word form (inflections), although few are left in English, are important to meaning.
We recognize nonsense sentences because of these inflections:
The bleenest blugs bliffled very bleebly.
-est, -s, -ed, -ly.
Third, signal or structure words are very significant in the grammar of English: words such as *a, an, the,* which point to nouns; or verb auxiliaries, *may, shall, will,* which point to verbs.
Fourth, elements of intonation (stress, pitch, juncture) affect meaning in important ways.
Fifth, parts of speech can be more precisely defined by reference to form and position than by reference to lexical meaning.

The most dramatic product of linguistic research during the last decade is the system known as transformational-generative grammar. Noam Chomsky, a linguist at Massachusetts Institute of Technology, pointed out that every speaker of a language—even a child of four or five years—has an intuitive and relatively complete command of the grammar necessary for his communication. Chomsky further proposes that most of the speaker's multitudinous grammatical choices, after his initial years of experimenting, produce grammatical sentences. Because language is based on sets of rules, speakers can form and understand an infinite number of sentences. Chomsky contends that formulating such sets of rules is possible and that these rules will demonstrate how language "makes infinite use of finite means." These rules will show how each of us—each day—uses or understands hundreds, even thousands, of different sentences.

The underlying theory of transformational grammar is that language utilizes a small number of *kernel,* or *basic,* sentence patterns. These simple, declarative sentences can be derived by *generative (phrase structure) rules* and can be added to, rearranged, and combined by *transformational rules.*

The premise is that every sentence has two basic parts, each of which is formed by making choices from a limited number of options. These options are formulated in the phrase structure rules which utilize a system of symbolic notations.

The premise is that every sentence has two basic parts, each of which is formed by making choices from a limited number of options. These options are formulated in the phrase structure rules which utilize a system of symbolic notations.

THE BOY THREW THE BALL

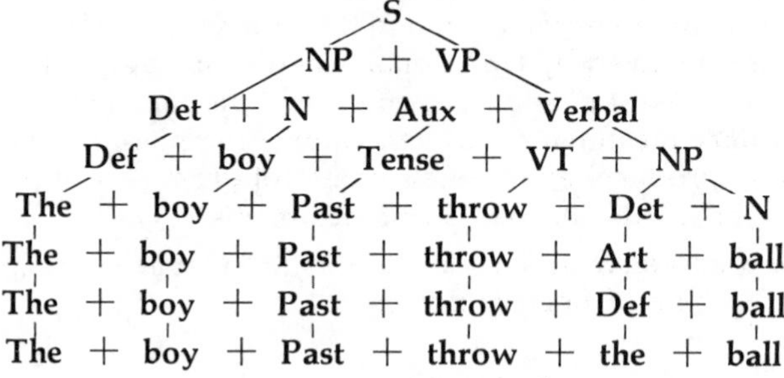

The boy did throw the ball.
Did the boy throw the ball?
Who threw the ball?
What did the boy throw?
The ball was thrown by the boy.
The boy did not throw the ball.
The skinny boy threw the ball.
Which boy threw the ball?
The boy threw the ball yesterday.
When did the boy throw the ball?

The basic phrase structure rule or formula is S → NP + VP, which is read as S (Sentence) is rewritten as NP (Noun Phrase) plus VP (Verb Phrase). (A single arrow means "rewrite as"; a double arrow, used in stating transformational rules, means "change to.") Phrase structure rules tell us that NP may be written as a Det (Determiner) plus N (Noun), that we may select *the* or *a* as the Det if we select such a noun as *boy*, that a verb or a verb phrase (symbolized by *Aux* plus MV) must indicate tense, and that the verb phrase may consist of (1) a transitive verb with an NP direct object, (2) a *be*-verb plus predicate, (3) an intransitive verb, (4) a copulative verb plus complement. Phrase structure rules include several other choices, such as sentence-final adverbs. Once all phrase structure symbols required for a kernel sentence have been selected, the *terminal string* of symbols can be replaced with words.

Transformational grammarians use a pictorial representation of sentences known as a *branching tree diagram*. This diagram, shown in the upper half of the illustration above, has the advantage of maintaining word order so essential for indicating meaning in English. The diagram also illustrates the pattern of every sentence which has an identical *syntactic* structure.

Once the kernel sentences have been "generated" by applying the appropriate phrase structure rules, the sentences can be added to, rearranged, or combined to form *derived* sentences—sentences which are longer, more complex, and more usual in mature speech and writing than are the kernel sentences. Examples of some of the possible transformational rules through which kernel sentences may be combined (or by which they can be rearranged) include those listed below. (The resulting derived sentences are given in the lower half of the diagram above.)

(1) the emphatic transformation,
(2) the *yes* - *no* question transformation,
(3) the *wh* - question transformation,
(4) a second example of the *wh* - question transformation,
(5) the passive transformation,
(6) the negative transformation,
(7) the transformation for embedding the adjective *skinny*,
(8) a third example of the *wh* - question transformation,
(9) a kernel sentence with the adverb included,
(10) a fourth example of the *wh* - question transformation.

As this abbreviated and partial description indicates, transformational grammar works with a set of precise, almost mathematical, rules by which sentences are generated and transformed to produce the infinite variety of English sentences. Transformationalists utilize some of the concepts of descriptive linguistics to describe the sounds of English, the methods of word formation, and the types of words. (In other words, though they may use somewhat different terms and definitions, transformational grammarians use the concepts of *phonemes, graphemes, class words* and *structure (function) words.)* Transformationalists also use certain descriptions and terminology from traditional schoolroom grammar. We need to remember, however, that though terms may be the same, the definitions frequently are not the same.

If such a system with its formulas and notations at first seem formidable, remember that a five-year-old child—by experimentation and intuition—controls it even if he cannot describe it. If the child learns at school to make formal application of what he already knows intuitively, he will be able to use his language better than he does now.

In summary, let me repeat that I am not proselyting for any particular new contract or any particular new methods for public-school language study. Rather, I suggest that teachers supplement the best of the traditional with the most valuable concepts and methods given by recent linguistic study. Perhaps we still will not have a "new English." We will have a more complete, a more honest, and a more accurate one.

18.

The Role of Linguistics in the Elementary School Curriculum

Samuel Jay Keyser

The study of grammar is a traditional part of the elementary and secondary school curriculum. The question which is raised in this discussion is 'should it be?' The answer depends on what one conceives the study of grammar to be. If one conceives of the study of grammar in the same terms as the theoretical linguist, then surely grammar has no more place in the elementary school curriculum than does the study of mechanics or high temperature physics. Linguistics is concerned with developing a theory to formally characterize the knowledge which a speaker of a natural language possesses. The questions which he asks are questions about formal properties of grammars based upon the facts of a natural language.[1] A study of such facts and correspondences can tell him a great deal about the abstract principles according to which natural languages appear to be constructed. One thing which this inquiry will not tell the linguist, however, is how to read better, or write better, or speak better, or listen better. There is little reason to suppose, then, that what linguistics does not do for its practitioners it will do for elementary school children.

This is not to say that the subject matter of linguistics is irrelevant to elementary school teaching. It does say, however, that the linguist's concern with language is quite different from the educator's concern with language and while the linguist can tell the educator a great deal about language, even his own, what the educator is to do with that knowledge is quite a different matter. It is the purpose of this discussion to attempt to demonstrate a (hopefully) fruitful way in which the educator might make use of linguistic insights in the elementary and secondary school curriculum.

In the pursuit of their discipline, linguists discover a great many things about natural language. Sometimes these discoveries are quite unexpected and sometimes they are merely extensions of previous insights. In any case these discoveries have two important properties which recommend them for use by educators in the classroom. First, these discoveries deal with knowledge which every speaker of a language is master of, including, of course, the student and the teacher. Second, this knowledge is immediately available to the student

From *Elementary English* 47:39-45 (January 1970).

and the teacher through introspection. Each student and each teacher constitutes, as it were, a ready-made laboratory in which it is possible to conduct instantaneous experiments in language.

These properties suggest a possible reformulation of grammar as a subject. Instead of viewing the intellectual goal of grammar as the categorizing of parts of speech and the instilling of certain (to a large extent) ad hoc principles of diagramming, it is possible to look at grammar as attempting to teach children how to make, critically examine, and reformulate hypotheses about language—using as evidence their own knowledge of English.

In other words, grammar can be viewed as an opportunity for students to learn how to engage in rational inquiry—at least with respect to the facts of their language. An inevitable partner of this kind of inquiry, however, will be the expansion of the linguistic experience of both the student and the teacher. Thus a great many kinds of sentences which one would not normally encounter will arise in the course of discussion. (Examples will follow.) Indeed, it is hoped that the creation of strange and unusual sentences will be encouraged.

To demonstrate how this might be done, three lesson plans are presented later. Each plan includes a brief grammatical analysis of a part of English which seems suitable to the kind of inquiry suggested above. The analysis is followed by an approach section which suggests how a class might be led to achieve the grammatical insight described in the analysis section on their own. Then follows an analysis section in which the grammatical insight is used in analyzing larger linguistic structures including poetry, maxims, aphorisms and arguments. The lesson plans were designed for the elementary school level. There is no reason why the same strategy cannot be used at higher levels of secondary education. Indeed, it is conceivable that this kind of inquiry might culminate at the highest level in a theoretical course in linguistics in which the facts of language which have been brought out in earlier grades are then viewed as evidence for one linguistic theory over another.

Lesson Plan No. 1[2]

Purpose: The goal of this lesson is to teach children how to make hypotheses about their language. We focus attention on a particular restriction between verbs and the nouns which these verbs select.

Grammatical analysis: There are many verbs in English which impose special restrictions on their subjects and objects. Speakers of English observe these restrictions, often unconsiously. In this lesson we look at one such restriction. Consider the verb *to frighten.* It may take either an animate or inanimate subject, but may only take an animate object. Thus one may say *the girl (or the table) frightened the boy.* But it is not grammatical to say *The girl (or the boy) frightened the table.* One may capture these facts about English by noting that the verb *to frighten* requires an animate object, but is unrestricted (with respect to animacy) as to subject. Like *frighten* are *amaze, astonish, amuse,* and *surprise.*

Again focusing strictly on animacy, we note that certain verbs require only inanimate objects. Thus one can build *a house,* but not *a boy, a cat, a mouse,* etc. Like *build* are *solve, polish, write* and so on, all of which require inanimate objects.

If we shift attention to the requirements of verbs and their subjects, we find similar kinds of restrictions. Thus verbs like *eat, drink, sleep, cook, sew,* etc. all require animate subjects while verbs like *elapse, evaporate, trickle,* etc. require inanimate subjects.

Approach: Rather than simply reveal the distinctions among verbs and their subjects and objects, it might be useful to engage the students in an exercise which leads them to make these distinctions for themselves. Suppose, for example, one were to ask them to list the kinds of things one can *frighten* and the kinds of things one cannot *frighten.* As the list becomes representative, one might ask the pupils to attempt to make a generalization about the items on each list so that one can, in fact, replace the list by the generalization. An important part of the lesson, of course, will be in testing each hypothesis, as it is suggested, to see if it works; and if it doesn't, to modify it.

For example, in a combined 4th and 5th grade class using this lesson plan, pupils were asked to supply the names of things which could be frightened. As each name was given, the pupils were instructed to write it down and think about it to see if, in fact, it could be frightened. A typical agreed upon list included things like *a deer, a mouse, a person, a horse, a dog,* and *a cat.* A list of things which could not be frightened included *a rock, a tree, an idea, a car.* Items like *a brave man* were excluded on the grounds that only those things were included which could not possibly, under any circumstances, be frightened. (The teacher will often have to use great ingenuity in excluding such things as 'my dog,' 'Scott Carpenter,' 'Mickey Mantle,' etc.)

After the lists were made, the pupils were asked to say what each list had in common. An immediate response to the first list was that all the things were living. But this was soon seen to be false since a tree was alive, but not frightenable. Then it was suggested that things which moved could be frightened. This was false because of entries like *a car.* Finally, it was suggested that *living things which move on their own accord* can be frightened. In other words, left to their own devices and with minimum guidance, the students essentially defined the term *animate* for themselves. The items in the second list, then, were either non-living things (as opposed to things which were once alive) or living things which could not move on their own accord.

Once the distinction is made for *frighten,* it can then be expanded to a whole class of verbs like *surprise, astonish, amaze.* In this regard, the students can be asked to determine whether a given verb is like *frighten,* and if not, how it differs.

Other verbs (perhaps those mentioned earlier) can be studied to see if the students can classify them according to the animacy of their subjects and objects. Moreover, similarities between verbs can be studied.

For example, the students can be led to observe that the same things that can be frightened can also eat, while the same class of things which can be built cannot be frightened, and so on.

Analysis: A useful exercise to do, once the distinction is made perfectly clear, is to analyze a poem with respect to the verbs and subjects and objects it contains. One poem which is suitable is:

Little Miss Muffet sat on a tuffet
Eating her curds and whey.
Along came a spider and sat down beside her
And frightened Miss Muffet away.

In this poem, the humor comes from supposing that spiders, like people, can sit. Note, also, the use of frighten.

Conclusion: In effect the above lesson plan represents a kind of instantaneous experiment. The pupils are asked to make hypotheses about their language and then to examine the implications of those hypotheses with respect to a wider sample of language and to modify the hypotheses to account for the largest number of examples. As always, the goal is to make the children look closely at what their language actually does and especially what it implies, rather than at the ways in which its sentences might be parsed.

Lesson Plan No. 2

Purpose: The goal of this lesson is to try to point out differences between syntactic and semantic aspects of plurality of nouns in English and to try to bring the children to formulate generalizations about the nouns under discussion.

Grammatical analysis: There are certain nouns in English which occur only in the plural form. Among these are *scissors, trousers, pants, pliers, forceps, glasses, spectacles,* and *binoculars.* These nouns always take a plural verb. Thus one can say *The scissors are on the table* but not *The scissors is on the table.* However, these nouns, although they always require a syntactic plural are semantically ambiguous. Thus the sentence *The scissors are on the table* can mean any number of *scissors* from a single pair on. There are, however, certain adjectives in English which may only occur with semantically plural subjects. Among these are *numerous, plentiful, abundant.* If such adjectives occur in a sentence with one of the nouns cited above, then that noun is immediately understood in the plural sense. Thus *The scissors are numerous* can only mean that several pairs are available.

On the other hand, there are certain nouns in American usage of English which occur with singular forms of verbs but which, nevertheless, require a semantically plural meaning. For example, one may say *The membership is disgruntled* but not *The membership are disgruntled.* There are, however, certain verbs in English which require plural subjects. Among these are *surround, disband, disperse, scatter.* Thus one may say *The girls surrounded the house* but not *The girl surrounded the house.* Notice, however, that the sentence *The membership has surrounded the platform* is a perfectly good sentence and, although the verb form is singular, i.e. *has surrounded,* the meaning is plural. Thus *scissors,* a syntactic plural, can have a semantic meaning of singular while *membership,* a syntactic singular, has a semantic meaning of plural.

Approach: The purpose of this lesson will be to show the students that syntactic and semantic number do not always go together. A useful way to start out, then, would be to consider examples in which they do. This can be done by simply considering pairs of sentences in which nouns which can be counted occur. Thus *one chair is by the window,* but *two chairs are by the window.* The alternation between a singular noun and the singular *is* and a plural noun and the plural *are* must be firmly grasped. Once this is done, the instructor might then place a pair of scissors in view of the class and ask the class to talk about them. Hopefully a response such as *The scissors are on the table* will be forthcoming. Then the instructor can proceed to ask why a plural *are* since there is only one scissors. This will lead to a discussion of the two parts of the scissors, but the teacher can point out that neither part makes up the scissors but only both together. Then the class might be asked to consider what other objects are made up of two parts, but which function as a unit and which, even though they take a plural verb, can be either singular or plural.

Next, the instructor can examine with the class the relationship between syntactic and semantic number in such words as *class, membership, team,* etc. using as evidence the behavior of the words with verbs such as *scatter, disband, disperse, surround* which also require a plural meaning for the subject even though the syntactic number can be singular.[3] The point in these nouns is that the syntactic number is based upon the notion of a unit while the semantic number is based upon the individuals which make up the unit.

Analysis: The distinction between semantic and syntactic plurality can be made the basis of a discussion of the kinds of effects it is possible to achieve in language by subtle manipulations of categories. Consider, for example, the following non-sentence (due to Noam Chomsky and used to illustrate a quite different point):

1. *The boy who had been changed by magic into a swarm of bees dispersed.

What is operative in this non-sentence is (1) the conflict between the fact that *boy* is syntactically and semantically singular and therefore cannot occur with a verb like *disperse* so that one cannot say **The boy dispersed* and (2) the fact that the relative clause *who had been changed by magic into a swarm of bees* provides the boy with precisely the necessary semantic property required in order to disperse. The point of this example is that, while it is ungrammatical, it exhibits the kind of linguistic adroitness characteristic of a certain kind of writing, most conspicuously poetry. A useful exercise, then, would be to have the children construct similiar non-sentences, for example:

1. *The boy who had been changed by magic into a glass of water trickled into the room.

Conclusion: This lesson plan has attempted to make children aware of a distinction in the language which they know but are not aware that they know and, once having made it, to use it creatively in new constructions, including ungrammatical ones. It is hoped that this kind of experience with language will not only develop their ability to analyze what they read but also to enliven what they write.

Lesson Plan No. 3

Purpose: The goal of this lesson is to focus the pupil's attention on a certain distinction in the English language. Once the distinction is grasped it is then used to analyze certain statements in the English language. Thus the overall goal is to have them look closely at their language and then to use the results of their scrutiny to analyze and criticize statements which use this distinction implicitly.

Grammatical analysis: There are two types of adjectives in English: those which describe activities and those which merely describe states or conditions. The active adjectives can occur in imperative sentences: *be good, be nice, be quiet.* The state adjectives cannot occur in imperatives **be fat,* **be brilliant,* **be hungry.* The semantic difference between the two is that active adjectives describe things which people can do, whereas stative adjectives describe states that people can be in, but not things that they can do. This difference is reflected in the fact that active adjectives are about things which are under our control; stative adjectives are about things which are not under our control. Thus we can *be good* because there are things under our control which we can do. We cannot *be old* because there is nothing under our control which we can actively do to *be old.*

Approach: There are certain verbs in English which, when they occur with adjectives, must occur only with active adjectives. *Tell* and *persuade* are examples of such verbs: *I told John to be quiet, I persuaded John to be reasonable* but not **I told John to be fat,* **I persuaded John to be rich.* Using this fact (which the children ought to know—hopefully!—intuitively), one might begin by asking the students to list all kinds of things people can be; guiding them to use adjectives only. A list of their responses should include active as well as non-active (stative) adjectives. If particularly clear cases do not arise, the teacher can supply his own. (Adjectives like *hungry, thirsty, hot, cold, rich, fat, thin, young, old* are good non-active examples. Adjectives like *happy, polite, nice, sensible, thoughtful, helpful* imply that there is some course of action which the person is able to pursue which leads to *happiness, politeness,* etc.)

Next the teacher might ask the student to list what kinds of things they can *tell* someone to be. This list will contain only active adjectives. (There will be some adjectives which certain students will treat as actives, for example, *smart*, while others will not treat them as active. The difference between individuals in their usage of these adjectives is useful in making the point that not every question has a black and white answer, a fact which is much in evidence in language. However, universal agreement over adjectives like *quiet, good, nice* as active and *hungry, thirsty, tired* as non-active will very likely occur.)

Finally, the teacher might return to the first list and weed out those adjectives which cannot co-occur with *tell*, namely the non-active adjectives. Thus we end up with two lists as a basis for discussion; the teacher might then induce the essential difference between the two, namely that in the one list, activity under the person's control is implied while in the second list, no such activity is implied.

Analysis: Having secured as well as possible the distinction of active versus non-active adjectives, it is possible to turn to certain examples in English and discuss them from the point of view of this distinction. First, one might consider the Boy Scout Law and ask if the adjectives in it are active or non-active:

1. A scout is trustworthy, loyal, helpful, friendly, courteous, kind, obedient, cheerful, thrifty, brave, clean and reverent.

Then one might analyze the poem, *Jack, Be Nimble* from this point of view:

2. Jack, be nimble, Jack be quick.
   Jack, jump over the candlestick.

Thirdly, one might consider the following maxim:

3. Early to bed and early to rise makes a man healthy, wealthy and wise.

Here the adjectives *healthy, wealthy* and *wise* are non-active adjectives. (Thus, you cannot say: **Be healthy, *Be wealthy, *Be wise.)* You can, however, tell someone to go to bed early and get up early. The point of the maxim is that by doing something which is under your control (going to bed early), you may become something which is not under your control (being healthy).

Finally, one might consider the following argument and see if the children are in a position to determine whether it could possibly be true. The argument is:

> John is very persuasive. He can persuade you to be anything he wants you to be.

The argument must be false. The reason is that it is possible for John to want someone to be both *good* and *tall,* but he could only persuade someone to be *good.*

Conclusion: The lesson outlined above tries to make students look closely at their language in an attempt to show that there are certain things which they know but which they may not realize they know. Thus every student will be able to make this distinction. Furthermore, given this basis, they are in a position to refer to it in looking critically at examples such as the Scout Law.

It is perhaps worth emphasizing that these lesson plans exploit facts which provide evidence for selecting one linguistic theory over another. They can perform quite a different function in an elementary school classroom. They can provide the raw material from which an educator can develop a lesson in rational inquiry in which children examine their own language and, in effect, construct their own theories to account for what they observe. Notational questions such as *what is a noun phrase* and *what is an adjective* play a subordinate role in this kind of inquiry. Indeed, they should be introduced only to help the inquiry along rather than be considered the central goal of a grammar lesson.

A second fact worth mentioning is that the distinctions which these lesson plans exploit are distinctions which are available both to the student and the teacher. From this it follows that while in the beginning it may be necessary for the teacher to expose himself to linguistic research in order to learn what sorts of processes and distinctions are actually operative in English, because they are available to his own intuitions as well as to the linguist, he should at some point be able to move independently in making his own discoveries about his language and in constructing appropriate lesson plans around them. What is especially valuable about this is that it provides the teacher with an opportunity to become actively and creatively involved in developing the grammatical portion of the curriculum.

If this sounds as if the traditional role of the teacher is being shifted from one who depends on textbook lesson plans to one who, in essence, writes his own each year, then that is precisely what is intended. There are no sources of such lesson plans currently available and the teacher who chooses the method described above will have no other alternative. This, however, is a good thing. It is difficult to see how a teacher can be effective unless he is actively involved in his work; and rational inquiry into the facts of English provides a golden opportunity for both the teacher and the student to exercise their creativity and imagination together.

19.

Linguistics in Modern Grammar

Harry W. Sartain

The word *grammar* is commonly used with more than one meaning. In this discussion it refers to *the arrangements and forms of words in sentences.* It includes the standard patterns of various kinds of sentence constructions, the standard patterns of word forms indicating changes in function or meaning, and to some degree, the standard intonation patterns that contribute to the expression of meaning in speech.

The summarizing of information on modern grammar is made somewhat difficult by disagreement among linguists on terms and on certain details of language analysis. In this discussion the most common and readily understandable terms are used; in addition, frequently used alternative terms are given as an aid to teachers who read from other sources.

1. **Parts of Speech.** The words which are classified by the linguists as the four major parts of speech—nouns, verbs, adjectives, and adverbs—are the words which carry most of the meaning in English sentences. (A few linguists give the four major parts of speech form-class names: nouns are called form-class I words; verbs, form-class II words; adjectives, form-class III words; and adverbs, form-class IV words.) Some linguists add a fifth part of speech, personal pronouns. Others regard personal pronouns as structure words.

2. **Structure Words.** Those words in a sentence that are not classified by the linguists as major parts of speech are called *structure words* because they are used to show the structural relationships of the major parts of speech. Below is a common classification of the structure words with a few examples.

a. NOUN MARKERS (sometimes called *noun determiners*). Typically, they begin a noun group (a noun and the modifiers related to it), thus signaling that some following word is a noun or has noun function. The articles (*the, a, an*) are always noun markers. Other kinds of words often used as noun markers are:
Possessives: *my, our, your, their,* and others in certain situations
Demonstratives (sometimes): *this, that, these, those*

From *Language Monograph*, D.C. Heath and Company (Reprinted from Guides for Teaching, *English Is Our Language*, Third Edition, Books 3-6, © 1966, D.C. Heath and Company). Reprinted with permission of the publisher and the author.

Quantitative terms (sometimes): *one, two, all, every, each, many, several, some,* etc.

b. VERB MARKERS, or auxiliaries. They indicate that a verb form will soon follow.
   Examples: *have, had, has, will, may, did, ought,* etc.

c. QUALIFIERS(sometimes called *intensifiers*). They precede and modify adjectives and adverbs, showing the strength of the adjective or adverb.
   Examples: a *very* slow train, a *rather* slow train; running *quite* rapidly, running *extremely* rapidly
   Others: *more, most, less, least, so, somewhat, too, mighty,* etc.

d. NEGATIVES. They show that a structural unit is negative instead of positive.
   Examples: *no, not, never,* etc.

e. QUESTION MARKERS. Their placement at the beginning of a sentence shows that the sentence should be interpreted as a question.
   Examples: *why, how, what, where, when, who, whom,* etc.

f. COORDINATORS, or coordinating conjunctions. They join words and constructions having the same grammatical functions, as in compound subjects, compound predicates, compound objects, and compound sentences.
   Examples: John *and* Mary played *and* sang. We saw *neither* rain *nor* snow. I would like to come, *but* I have a previous engagement.

g. PREPOSITIONS (sometimes called *phrase markers*). They precede nouns or other nominal elements, combining with them to make phrases that typically act as modifiers.
   Examples: *after, against, around, at, below, in, off, over, toward, under, up,* etc.

h. SUBORDINATORS (sometimes called *clause markers*). They begin dependent clauses. Kinds of words often used as subordinators are:
   Relative pronouns: *who, whom, whoever, which, whichever, what, that,* etc.
   Subordinating conjunctions: *after, although, because, before, if, until, since, though, as soon as, when, while, unless,* etc.

3. **Classification of Words as Parts of Speech.** Traditional grammar sometimes classifies words as parts of speech according to definitions based on the meanings of the words—"nouns are words that name," "verbs are words that show action," etc. Linguists feel that a classification according to definitions based on meaning lacks exactness because often a word has different meanings depending upon its grammatical class—for example, the word *heat* in "too much heat" and in "heat the water."

Linguists prefer to classify words as parts of speech according to clues other than meaning. The main clues derive from (1) syntax, the positions of words in constructions, and (2) morphology, the forms of words, including affixes and inflectional endings.

a. WORD-ORDER (SYNTAX) CLUES TO CLASSIFICATION. Most linguists define a noun as a word that patterns in the same way as the italicized words in these sentences:

   The happy *child* ran quickly out the *door*.
   That *man* is a *teacher*.

Because of his experience in using and studying language, any intelligent adult can utilize this definition in picking out the nouns in the following nonsense sentences:

The donnel pludder silled rinly in a glig.
That silfa gars the flod.

In the first sentence the reader can decide that *pludder* and *glig* are the nouns, not because of their meanings, which are unknown, but because of their positions in the sentence. The essential clues are the articles, which always indicate that some following word is a noun (or has noun function). Because of his language experience since infancy, he automatically expects a noun to follow an article or other noun marker. Since the reader also knows that an adjective may come between the marker and the noun, he may have momentary difficulty determining whether *donnel* or *pludder* is the noun. This is solved, however, upon reading the words *silled* and *rinly*. He guesses that *silled* is a verb because it has a standard ending showing past tense (a word-form clue). The word *rinly* has an ending which suggests it is an adverb (also a word-form clue), and its position after *silled* is further evidence that *silled* is a verb. Because a verb often follows a noun group, it seems logical to designate *The donnel pludder* as a noun group; and since the noun usually is the last word in a noun group, he can be quite certain that *pludder* is the noun. The intelligent adult does all this reasoning in a flash instead of in the longer time required to read the explanation.

The word *glig* in the same sentence is easily classified as a noun because it alone follows the noun marker *a*, where no other part of speech could be used in an English sentence.

The nonsense words in the second sentence can be identified just as readily as those in the first.

b. WORD-FORM (MORPHOLOGY) CLUES TO CLASSIFICATION. Nouns can sometimes be identified by the endings *s* and *es*, used to change them from singular to plural forms, as well as by possessive endings. Verbs are often recognized by the variant endings *s*, *es*, *ed* and *ing*. Words ending with *ness (kindness, baldness)*, *ity (proximity, fluidity)*, *er (dancer, speaker)*, and *ment (statement, judgement)* frequently are nouns. Words ending with *ous (joyous, humorous)*, *y (noisy, risky)*, and *ish (blackish, fiendish)* often are adjectives. Words ending with *ly (bravely, quietly)* often are adverbs. There are a number of additional clues that could be included in a more detailed discussion.

Although a single clue based on word order or on word form will not always provide enough information to classify a word as a certain part of speech, a combination of such clues makes possible a rather objective categorization of most words.

Linguistic facts of this type will be of help to young students in grammatical word classification. However, it seems likely that some of the traditional definitions also may be of value. It may be helpful, for example, for a student to learn that a word which names a person, place, or thing is a noun; learning this does not prevent him from also learning, at a later time, that some other words are nouns, too. However, the teacher is advised to conscientiously avoid teaching those traditional definitions that are very ambiguous and confusing. An example is "A preposition shows the relationship between its object and another word." Obviously this vague definition would include some verbs, too.

4. **Sentence Patterns.** The meaning of English sentences is highly dependent upon word order. The three words *chase dogs boys* mean nothing in that order, but they make sense when stated as *Dogs chase boys.* A different meaning is expressed when they are placed in a third order: *Boys chase dogs.*

Although children have learned appropriate word order for sentence constructions through observation and analogy long before coming to school, they have never consciously analyzed their sentences to see what the regular structural patterns are. Such an analysis will serve to help them understand the nature of the English language and perhaps to make their speech and writing patterns more varied and interesting.

Sentence patterns are based upon the order of the words that carry the major portion of the meaning in sentences—the nouns (or pronouns), verbs, and adjectives that serve as simple subjects, simple predicates, complements, and objects in sentences. Structure words and modifiers are not of significance in determining basic sentence patterns. Pronouns may function as nouns in the patterns.

Five common sentence patterns are described below.

a. PATTERN N-V (Noun-intransitive verb, or subject-verb)

Fish swim.
N V

Many old ladies knit beautifully.
N V

He sings happily hour after hour.
N V

b. PATTERN N-V-N (Noun-transitive verb-noun, or subject-verb-direct object)

Billy threw the ball.
N V N

The hungry rabbit chewed the carrot rapidly.
N V N

I found three beautiful shells on the beach.
N V N

c. PATTERN N-V-N-N (Noun-transitive verb-noun-noun, or subject-verb-indirect object-direct object)

Billy threw Jack the ball.
N V N N

The new teacher gave the little girl a pencil.
N V N N

Mother bought me a pretty new dress.
N V N N

At the elementary level each of the following types of sentences may also be classed under the N-V-N-N pattern.

John gave the book to Mary. (Subject-verb-direct object-object of preposition)

The class voted Jim chairman. (Subject-verb-direct object-objective complement)

d. PATTERN N-V^{be}-N (Noun-linking verb-noun, or subject-verb-predicate noun)

Miss Smith is a teacher.
N V^{be} N

The animal was a little dog.
N V^{be} N

They are my cousins from California.
N V^{be} N

e. PATTERN N-V^{be}-ADJ. (Noun-linking verb-adjective, or subject-verb-predicate adjective)

Her father is tall.
N V^{be} Adj.

The first step is extremely slippery today.
N V^{be} Adj.

I was late for lunch yesterday.
N V^{be} Adj.

5. **Sentence Transformations.** The five common patterns explained above occur in declarative sentences stated in the active voice. The study of processes for changing basic sentences to other forms is called *transformational grammar.* Among the other forms that can be made from simple declarative sentences are (*a*) sentences in the passive voice, (*b*) questions, (*c*) negative sentences, (*d*) imperative sentences with the subject omitted, and (*e*) sentences beginning with the expletives *it* and *there.* These transformations are made according to certain regular processes and may require changes in word order, word form, or both. Even when there is no plan for teaching the transformational patterns at the elementary level, some able pupils could be led to discover them inductively.

6. **Sentence Expansions and Combinations.** The emphasis in traditional grammar study is on analysis and dissection of sentences. The emphasis in modern grammar study is on building, or generating, new sentences that are needed for accuracy and economy in expression. Sometimes this means merely the addition of modifiers to provide more detail. At other times it means the use of structures that combine monotonous sentences into more interesting or more succinct sentences.

Several types of expansion are appropriate:

a. COMPOUNDING—the combining of words, phrases, and independent clauses to form compound subjects, compound predicates, compound objects, and compound sentences.

Basic sentences: Della waited. She watched.
N V N V

Betsy waited. She watched, too.
N V N V

Expansion: Della and Betsy waited and watched.
Comp. subj. Comp. pred.

b. MODIFICATION—the addition of adjectives, adverbs, qualifiers, adjective and adverbial phrases, and adjective and adverbial clauses.

Basic sentence: The boy sold his sheep.
N V N

Expansion: The ragged little boy who came first sold his five woolly sheep
Adj. Adj. N Adj. clause V Adj. Adj. N

before ten o'clock.
Adv. phrase

c. APPOSITION—the addition of words, phrases, or clauses that are in apposition with nouns in the sentence.

Basic sentence: Fido chased the strange dog.
N V N

Expansion: Fido, the small puppy's mother, chased the strange dog.
N Appositive V N

d. SUBORDINATION—the addition of words, phrases, and clauses that convey ideas closely associated with, but secondary in importance to, the main idea of the sentence.

Modification and apposition are considered to be specific types of subordination. The additional examples of subordination given below are limited to clauses that begin with subordinators.

Basic sentence: Dick soon went home.
N V

Expansions: Dick, who arrived late, soon went home.
N Subord. adj. clause V

Although he arrived late, Dick soon went home.
Subord. adv. clause N V

e. PARALLEL STRUCTURES—the addition of a series of ideas in the form of equally important phrases or clauses.

Each of the examples below obviously could have been constructed by expanding a basic sentence to include ideas from several short sentences.

When planning a story, a pupil should be advised to outline a lively plot, to make his characters true to life, and to select words that are succinct and colorful.

Wanting to attend the party but also wanting to finish preparing for an examination, Dick decided to make only a brief appearance.

It is apparent that elementary school pupils will not often expand sentences in this manner unless they are assisted by the teacher.

7. **Intonation.** This is the term for such vocal effects as pitch variation and "phrasing" which contribute to the meanings of sentences in speech. The function of intonation is similar to that of punctuation in writing, but the two systems are not in exact correspondence. Usually linguists divide patterns of intonation into stress, pitch, and juncture.

a. STRESS. Most linguists identify four degrees of stress in English, but the discrimination of all four generally requires some training. Three degrees can be noticed, however, in such a word as *elevator*. The first of the four syllables has primary stress; the second and last have the lowest degree, called "zero"; and the third has some degree less than primary but more than zero.

Every English construction has a pattern of stresses as well as a pattern of words. If one says the following sentence without giving special emphasis to any word in it, primary stress ordinarily falls on the last word.

Mary boiled some éggs.

Now notice the changes produced by shifting the primary stress to other words. This is called emphatic stress.

Máry (not Jane) boiled some eggs.
Mary bóiled (not fried) some eggs.
Mary boiled sóme (not all the) eggs.

The use of stress is not, however, confined to showing emphasis. A few nouns and verbs are distinguished by a difference in the syllable which carries the greater stress.

NOUN	VERB
próject	projéct
cóntract	contráct
súbject	subjéct
próduce	prodúce

A difference in stress pattern also distinguishes compound nouns from sequences of modifier and noun.

COMPOUND NOUN	MODIFIER PLUS NOUN
gréenhouse	green hóuse
Whíte House	white hóuse
báby-sitter	baby rábbit

Also a stress difference distinguishes a preposition from the second element of a "two-word verb." Compare:

He rán in the field. He ran ín the thief.
He túrned up the street. He turned úp some evidence.

b. PITCH. When one speaks an English sentence, he varies the pitch of his voice to produce a kind of tune. Most linguists recognize four levels of pitch as significant, numbering them 1, 2, 3, and 4, from lowest to highest. The basic pitch of a person's voice, regardless of whether the person is a man or a woman, is designated as pitch 2, and the others are relative to this. There is a high correlation between pitch level and degree of stress, but the fact that they are distinct can be seen from such sentences as the following, in which the italicized words are given lower pitch than the others, even when stress is not reduced:

He knows you are here, *doesn't he*?
These books, *however*, will not be needed.

c. JUNCTURE. This term is used for the vocal effects that cut the stream of speech into segments so that words and constructions can be recognized.

Open juncture is the vocal signal that usually divides words from each other. Notice that in the word *strong* the second and third consonants are pronounced so as to produce a kind of blend. In *most wrong* the same consonant sounds appear in the same order, but are not blended as they are in *strong* because open juncture separates them. Its existence makes possible such jokes as pronouncing "syntax" as "sin tax."

Terminal junctures are the vocal signals that usually divide sequences of words into constructions. There are three types. All impress the ear as pauses, but the significant element is not the length of the pause. Instead, it is the direction of change in pitch, if any, as the voice fades into the pause.

Falling terminal juncture (or fall-fade juncture) is the type of terminal juncture that ordinarily ends a statement.

Mr. Jones is a baker.

If one reads this sentence aloud with no special emphasis on any of its words, his voice remains on nearly the same pitch (pitch 2) until the last word. For the first syllable of this word (last stressed syllable before juncture), his voice goes up to pitch 3 and then rapidly down through the second syllable to pitch 1. The pitch falls before or as the voice fades. This is the usual end-of-sentence voice signal.

Rising terminal juncture (or rise-fade juncture) can be illustrated by the same sequence of words if the sequence is spoken as a question.

Mr. Jones is a baker?

The pitch is the same as for a statement until the last syllable is reached. To make the sequence of words a question, one continues at pitch 3 through the last syllable. The pitch rises as the voice fades. If one wishes to show surprise that Mr. Jones is a baker, he uses a still higher pitch—pitch 4 rather than pitch 3.

Sustained terminal juncture conveys the effect of an interruption without any significant change in pitch. This type of juncture is not used at the end of a complete sentence but serves to mark divisions between certain constructions within a sentence.

In the last quarter of the game the home team made two touchdowns.

Spoken with ordinary tempo, the preceding sentence will require a sustained terminal juncture after the word *game*, at least. Some people will use more sustained terminal junctures in the sentence. Also, if a person speaks a sentence in a deliberate manner, he will use more sustained terminal junctures than if he speaks it with rapid tempo.

d. TERMINAL JUNCTURE PATTERNS IN SENTENCES. Although terminal juncture patterns may differ somewhat in various parts of the country, those described below are frequently found. Arrows pointing in appropriate directions will be used to show terminal junctures:

↘ Falling terminal juncture (contour of high to low pitch followed by pause)
↗ Rising terminal juncture (rising pitch followed by pause)
→ Sustained terminal juncture (pause with no significant change in pitch)

(1) Most statements end with a falling terminal juncture.

Johnny ran home.↘
Jean baked a pie.↘

(2) Many questions end with a falling terminal juncture.

When did you expect Dorothy?↘
What did you do over the weekend?↘

It is not uncommon for a person, if he is anxious, to raise the whole pitch level of the last word of a question. In calm tones the first four words in the first example above would be spoken at level 2; the pitch would rise to level 3 at the beginning of *Dorothy* and fall to level 1 at the end. An anxious person seems to begin *Dorothy* on the higher level 4 and drop only to level 2 at the end. The general contour still is a quick rise followed by a fall-fade.

(3) A question which usually ends with a falling terminal juncture may end with a rising terminal juncture if it is intended to express surprise, doubt, regret, or other emotion.

Did you see that good TV program last night? ↘ (no emotion)
Did you read the whole book in one evening? ↗ (surprise)

(4) A question that is worded like a statement ends with a rising terminal juncture.

You went to the movie?↗

(5) Short questions that can be answered with one word usually end with a rising terminal juncture.

Who?↗ Did you win?↗

(6) Sustained terminal junctures sometimes separate phrases in sentences.

The funny little man → stomped out the door.↘

(7) Rising terminal junctures at the ends of words or word groups within a sentence signal the listener that the sentence is still not completed.

We ate cookies, ↗ candy, ↗ and nuts.↘
They looked for him in the attic, ↗ in the yard, ↗ and in the basement.↘

(8) A nonrestrictive modifier is distinguished from a restrictive modifier by the type of juncture that is used before it. To indicate that a nonrestrictive element is to follow, a more prominent juncture is used than the syntax would otherwise require. Usually there is also a drop in pitch for the nonrestrictive element.

A sustained terminal juncture is more prominent than an open juncture.

Restrictive: A stream which flowed nearby, → supplied water.↘
Nonrestrictive: A stream,→which flowed nearby,→supplied water.↘

A rising terminal juncture is more prominent than a sustained terminal juncture.

Restrictive: A clear and sparkling stream → which flowed nearby → supplied water.↘
Nonrestrictive: A clear and sparkling stream, ↗ which flowed nearby, → supplied water.↘

When a rising terminal juncture marks the beginning of a nonrestrictive element, the juncture marking the end may be a rising terminal juncture rather than a sustained terminal juncture.

(9) A descriptive appositive is set off by the use of more prominent junctures than the syntax would otherwise require.

Person addressed: Mr. Brown, → the school principal called the police.↘

Apposition: Mr. Brown,→ the school principal, → called the police. ↘

In either instance, the juncture after *Mr. Brown* may be a rising terminal juncture rather than a sustained terminal juncture.

Of course the addition of varied stress patterns will further affect the intonation of the sentence examples given on the preceding page.

8. **Inductive Approach.** It is always preferable that youngsters be led to discover the various language patterns themselves. The sequence of steps in inductive thinking may be initiated by the teacher either by asking questions that focus attention on common patterns or by taking advantage of a minor misunderstanding to do so.

As an example of the latter situation, one pupil might say, "You're all finished," with indefinite intonation. Another might respond, "Are you asking me or telling me?" At this point the teacher could comment, "That's a reasonable and interesting response. How do we generally tell whether a group of words such as 'You're all finished' is a question or a statement?" This comment should lead to the development of a tentative hypothesis by the pupils. Then a series of similar utterances should be elicited, listed on the chalkboard, studied for patterns, and grouped into categories based on characteristics observed. Finally, the pupils should state the principle or principles of intonation or syntax that have been discovered and verified through the experience. The satisfaction attained thereby should make children interested in offering and checking other hypotheses about language structure.

20.

The Grammatical Revolution that Failed

A. M. Tibbetts

In 1954, W. N. Francis published in *The Quarterly Journal of Speech* an article that was to become the most reprinted essay on its subject in modern times. The article, called "Revolution in Grammar," appeared at the right moment, when it seemed that the scholars fighting for the New Grammar[4] were winning the battle. The article also had the right tone, which may partly account for its immediate popularity and subsequent appearance in many anthologies dealing with the problems of language. Francis presented, calmly and in detail, the case for the "long overdue revolution" that was in 1954 "taking place in the study of English grammar—a revolution as sweeping in its consequences as the Darwinian revolution in biology. . . . To anyone at all interested in language, it is challenging; to those concerned with the teaching of English (including parents), it presents the necessity of radically revising both the substance and the methods of their teaching."[5]

But over a decade after Francis published his article, it is evident to observers that the revolution failed. There have been no "sweeping consequences," at least not in favor of the New Grammar. Its "challenge" has in the main disappeared. In most parts of the United States, parents, teachers, and the general public have rejected it (sometimes violently). Even many of the most ardent revolutionaries have modified their views.

Why did the revolution fail? In 1954, it seemed to have everything on its side. The answer to such a question is bound to be complex. (For one thing, the revolution was not a total failure. There are, for example, certain small pieces of the New Grammar that are being taken up and used in some high school classrooms.) The most satisfactory answer lies, I believe, in the fact that the revolutionaries made three important mistakes, which can be listed briefly as follows:

1. They made mistakes in *theory*.
2. They failed to derive many useful *practical applications* from their theory.
3. They forgot the importance of language as a *civilizing force*.

A brief study of these three mistakes should be of considerable value to persons interested in grammar and linguistic study.

I

A major mistake in theory made by the New Grammarians was that they tried to attach grammar to the coat-tails of science. In his "Revolution in Grammar," Francis stated that the phenomena of language "can be observed, recorded, classified, and compared; and general laws of their behavior can be made by the same inductive process that is used to produce the 'laws' of physics, chemistry, and the other sciences."[6] It is a curious (and sometimes horrifying) fact that the New Grammarians knew almost nothing about the nature of modern science, which is by no means merely an "inductive process." Not even an experimental laboratory science can be safely called "inductive," for there are large amounts of deduction, intuition, and just plain luck in laboratory work.

"Science" is not a discipline but many disciplines. To be accurate, perhaps one should use the plural—the "sciences"—for scientific disciplines can be as different from each other as grammar is from descriptive geometry. T. H. Huxley wrote: "Science is, I believe, nothing but *trained and organized common-sense*. . . . "[7] Huxley was right, but he failed to note the paradox that flows from this idea. Common sense, for instance, in the study of biology is not the same thing as common sense in the study of grammar, although—and here is the paradox—a certain amount of the same kind of common sense is needed in both disciplines. That is to say, if the biologist and the grammarian are not *curious, careful,* and *skeptical*—commonsensical, in other words—they will make bad mistakes. The great researchers in most fields, scientific or not, have been to some degree curious, careful, and skeptical. This does not imply a method but a particular attitude and a rigorous training. When the linguist John Hughes wrote that "the first step in the scientific study of anything is to gather and classify all available data . . . ,"[8] he made the typical error of the New Grammarian. He implied that there is a fixed scientific method and that one can study "anything" with it. It is worth adding that usually the first step in the study of "anything" is to sit down and think.

Their rigid, almost medieval, belief in science with a capital S was perhaps the most important force behind the New Grammarians' desire to create closed theoretical systems of grammatical philosophy. It is only a short step from believing that there is a perfect scientific method to believing that one can create a perfect system of grammar by using that method. (The modern sciences, generally speaking, are remarkably "open" and not very systematic, but the New Grammarians did not know this.) To those who are familiar with the histories of closed systems, the next event is predictable. Grammatical splinter groups arose, each insisting that its own system was the true one. Many of the New Grammarians stopped fighting in their own revolution against the traditionalist enemy and started fighting each other. Linguist Raven McDavid described this unfortunate situation in 1965:

> In this field [syntax] we seem to be in the unhappy lot of Christianity in the third century, Protestantism in the sixteenth and seventeenth, or Communism in its salad days of the 1920's. Each sect and subsect has its theoretical major prophets and many have their hatchet-men, less concerned with arriving objectively at the truth than with discouraging other approaches than their own.

This practice is particularly distressing in the transformational Reich, where not content with the contributions they can make to the study of syntax, Chomsky and his satellites seem to disparage all research accomplished by other schools. Nor is the situation any better in lexicography, where we have managed to produce better dictionaries than our fathers did, but have not managed to explain their excellence to the public who must use them—even though we are proceeding in a well-formed tradition of some three hundred years.[9]

Splinter groups typically produce public proclamations justifying themselves. For the last few years the air has been full of grammatical "scientoid manifestoes"[10] that make no bones about where they stand and customarily avoid making qualifications. Such a theoretical manifesto was printed in 1964 in the journal of the Modern Language Association. *PMLA* seldom prints anything that is not qualified and documented to an alarming degree. Therefore, it was surprising to find in a *PMLA* article based on "a conference on linguistics and language learning held at the MLA" a twelve-point manifesto, from which I quote three unqualified statements:

No. 4: "Changes in language depend on time, place, social level, stylistic level. These changes are *not* corruptions but normal features of *all* languages."

No. 6: "Language has *nothing* to do with race."

No. 11: "*No* language is inherently difficult; if it were, the people who speak it *would soon simplify it.*"[11]

The striking characteristic of such statements is their perfect dogmatism. Without a hint of qualification, they make flat statements about language, which is one of the most complex and mysterious products of human nature. As one might expect, such dogmatism has led to more than one error when a New Grammarian tried to construct a grammar for the schools. For example, on p. 3 of his high school text, Paul Roberts gives us this sentence: *Horses that think for themselves smoke filter cigarettes.* Roberts says of the sentence: "Of course it is grammatical." Three lines down, he adds that this sentence conforms "perfectly to the rules of English sentence structure. We see then that by *grammatical* we don't necessarily mean 'meaningful' or 'true.'" On p. 208 of the same text, Roberts employs another nonsense statement: *The intention took it into account.* Of this sentence Roberts says: "This is ungrammatical. An intention cannot take something into account and consequently can't fail to do so. Only a person can take something into account."[12]

A sharper contradiction it would be hard to find. One should feel sympathy for Professor Roberts because contradictions in statements about grammar are very easy to fall into. But, in one sense, he brought that contradiction upon himself because, like so many New Grammarians, he was excessively positive in his attempt to create a closed theoretical system.

II

The difficulty that Paul Roberts had with the term *grammatical* is a small example of the multitude of difficulties that the New Grammarians faced when they tried to make practical applications using the theory they had created. Since they tried to create closed systems, their idea of grammar was often too narrow and technical. Take, for example, their belief, as stated by Francis, that "the spoken language is primary, at least for the original study of language."[13]

Unquestionably, this can be a useful working hypothesis, but employed—as it often was—as a premise in the classroom study of language, it led to confusion.

Almost all of the models used for grammatical study in the classroom are of necessity prose models, with the hesitancies, stresses, and ellipses of speech weeded out. If such speech "flaws" are not omitted, the student finds that studying grammatical models becomes unnecessarily complicated. In the classroom grammars written by New Grammarians, such complications of speech were introduced and as a result the student had to learn and use a mixed technical diction; *e.g.*: *noun, adjective, headword, juncture, stress, pitch, intonation.* He even found trigonometric symbols like / ↗ /, / ↙ /, and /→/. The standard complaint of students was not only that the New Grammar was harder to learn, but also that it was less relevant to their everyday problems in using English.

The belief in the primacy of speech may be harmless if one is studying the physiology or structure of a language. But in modern America, grammar is used mainly in pedagogy, and the pedagogy of grammar is concerned with more than speech. If language is primarily speech, then a student already knows his "grammar" without studying it. In his review of Ralph Long's textbook, *The Sentence and Its Parts,* linguist Karl Dykema stated: "The student whose native language is English has already mastered the language; his primary objective is appreciative, to understand consciously what he controls subconsciously."[14] The fact is that relatively few students of English who study grammar have "mastered the language"—if by *mastery* we mean that they can think and write well. They can order a cup of coffee, talk to girl friends, spell out road signs, or read a James Bond novel, but these activities are not signs of mastery. Some students never master English, as anyone who teaches college seniors can testify.

When one starts to teach grammar in the classroom, he soon discovers that mastery comprises many elements, one of the most important being that of meaning. But the New Grammarians typically fought against the use of meaning in the study of grammar. Wrote Francis: "Most shaky of all bases for grammatical analysis is meaning."[15] The limitations of this premise are shown by the examples Francis employed to support it. One example is a telegraphic sentence borrowed from C.C. Fries: *ship sails today.* Another is the phrase *a dog's life,* about which, Francis says, "there can be endless futile argument about whether *'dog's'* is a noun or an adjective."[16] Both examples are of minor importance and somewhat eccentric. A student does not ordinarily speak or write in telegraphic sentences, and the argument about *a dog's life* is in the practical student's world worth barely a moment's thought.

In the practical world, a teacher soon learns that meaning is very important indeed and sometimes must be the first thing considered. As Boris Pasternak once remarked, "In writing as in speaking, the music of the word is never just a matter of sound. It does not result from the harmony of vowels and consonants. It results from the relation between the speech and its meaning. And meaning—content—must always lead."[17] The teacher often finds himself drawn to explicating grammatical problems in terms of meaning. If he does not do so, he will generally lose the interest and respect of his students who care little for the fancy intellectual footwork of grammatical theology. It may matter less, for example, that a word is called a "preposition" than that it can express precise meaning in a special context. For illustration, there is the vivid story of Hugh Blair's:

> The proper distinction in the use of these particles [*with* and *by*], is elegantly marked in a passage of Dr. Robertson's History of Scot-

> land. When one of the old Scottish kings was making an enquiry into the tenure *by* which his nobles held their lands, they started up, and drew their swords: "*By* these," said they, "we acquired our lands, and *with* these, we will defend them."[18]

So far as the teacher is concerned, perhaps the weakest element in the New Grammar is that practical textbooks have not been forthcoming. It is hard to keep a grammar simple and useful. The first test of a new book is that it be at least as simple and useful as the older ones available. The texts published by New Grammarians are generally more complex than the older grammars. A closed grammatical system requires a great deal of modifying, restricting, and hedging to keep it closed; consequently the newer texts are often loaded with excessive detail and elaborate quasi-philosophical commentary. As an example, we can take the definition of the term *sentence.*

The older texts defined the term concisely. A sentence, wrote Barrett Wendell, in 1908, is "a series of words so composed as to make complete sense. In its simplest form it consists of a subject—the thing concerning which a completely sensible assertion is made—and a predicate, the assertion made."[19] A grammar of the same period defined *sentence* as "a group of words which expresses a complete thought."[20] As practical definitions made for the school room, these work quite well. By contrast, the definitions constructed by the New Grammarians are based on a more philosophical reasoning like that of C. C. Fries who was following the logic and terminology of Leonard Bloomfield: "Each sentence is an independent linguistic form, not included by virtue of any grammatical construction in any larger linguistic form."[21] There are several unexplained abstractions lurking here, and if a grammarian tries to use this or similar philosophical formulations in his textbook he is likely to confuse the student (and probably the teacher) with wordy circumlocutions. It takes well over one hundred words and symbols for James Sledd to define *sentence* in his text.[22] In a recent text by Sumner Ives, *sentence* is defined as follows:

> *Sentence:* When we speak or write something more than a simple response to a question, our discourse almost surely consists of one or more sentences. Like words, sentences are generally recognized as such by native speakers of a language, unless they are confused by misleading definitions. The important thing to remember is that a sentence is primarily a unit in grammar, and only secondarily a unit in meaning. Sentences are made by putting words together according to certain established patterns. The essential characteristic of the sentence is its independence. Its words are related to each other, but the sentence as a whole is not grammatically a part of any larger unit; its boundaries are the boundaries of grammatical ties between its words. For example, the words in "He sees a monkey" are related, and the total unit is independent of other units, although *he* might be a grammatical echo of some previously used word. This independence is taken away if *when* is added, thus: "When he sees a monkey." The initial word alerts the reader or listener to expect something which will tell what happens when the monkey is seen.[23]

Like many New Grammarians, Ives tends less to define a term than to philosophize about it. It is small wonder that students find such discussion dull and irrelevant, for a definition in the schoolroom is generally made to be *used.* Unfortunately, the latest development in defining *sentence* is, apparently, not to define it at all. W. N. Francis' new textbook on language has only one listing in the index for *sentence*. In his discussion of the term, he quotes Bloomfield (as did Fries) and then adds: "A completely accurate definition would have to be a detailed description, considerably longer than this chapter or even this book, of all the kinds of grammatical constructions that native speakers of English accept as sentences."[24] In Roberts' high school text, *English Sentences*, the definition of *sentence* is not listed in the index, nor is a definition given in any of the sections called "Summary of Terms" in the book, although *sentence* is talked about at considerable length.

The New Grammarians also failed to give practical applications for their theories when they worked in the areas of usage and lexicography. One of their ruling theoretical principles was a belief, which amounted to a fighting faith, in linguistic change. Patrick Kilburn, for instance, reminded his readers that "Heraclitus long ago observed that one cannot step in the same river twice. No more can one use the same words twice, for they are changed by the preceding use of them."[25] Louis Muinzer spoke of linguistic change with similar enthusiasm: "Change, the very *life* of a language, moves relentlessly towards the future."[26]

When men believe so passionately in change, they are likely to demand that the old should be replaced whether it needs replacement or not. Thus the first edition of Fowler's *Modern English Usage* has long been condemned as archaic and Webster's *Second* was called outmoded. Wrote Bergen Evans, the foremost apologist for Webster's *Third:* "New dictionaries are needed because English has changed more in the past two generations than at any other time in its history.. . . Every publication in America today includes pages that would appear, to the purist of forty years ago, unbuttoned gibberish." These remarks to the contrary, a reasonably bright eighteen year old can still read the prose of Dryden, Swift, and Johnson with ease. And most of that prose was written over two hundred years ago.

The arguments over Fowler and the *Third* are too well known for me to recapitulate them here. Suffice it to say that the New Grammarians' belief in linguistic mutability led them to ask for changes in dictionaries that turned out to be impractical. No publisher has been willing to publish a truly relativistic dictionary of usage. Bergen Evans' *A Dictionary of Contemporary American Usage* (1957), written with Cornelia Evans, makes a number of theoretical bows to change, but from a practical standpoint the book is only a little less prescriptive than Fowler—and Fowler, when examined carefully, turns out to be far less prescriptive than the public has been led to believe. When Sir Ernest Gowers revised Fowler, he made no sweeping changes in the book.

Only in Webster's *Third* did the New Grammarians have their way to any extent. They loaded the big new dictionary with changes, many of which turned out to be remarkably impractical. The omission of status labels, the foggy rewriting of definitions, the inaccuracy of certain definitions, the mispunctuation and stylistic deficiencies—all of these made the dictionary hard to use. Most impractical of all was the elaborate pronunciation key that required users to learn a new system before they could discover the pronunciation of unfamiliar words. In sum, the *Third* is an unsuccessful dictionary simply on a practical level: it is inaccurate, carelessly written, and difficult to use.

III

Perhaps the most important mistake made by the revolutionaries of the New Grammar was that they forgot that language is, or should be, a civilizing force.

One looks in vain through their theoretical works for a recognition of language as a *human* thing. "A word," Edith Hamilton has written, "is no light matter. Words have with truth been called fossil poetry, each, that is, a symbol of a creative thought. The whole philosophy of human nature is implicit in human speech."[27] Human nature is a paradoxical mixture of qualities and characteristics—good and evil, right and wrong, intelligent and stupid, known and unknown. The nature of language reflects the nature of man; for, paradoxically, language too is a mixture of conflicting qualities and characteristics. To civilize language is to civilize man; to allow language its head, as the New Grammarians wished to do, is to give man his head, which is a thoroughly dangerous and uncivilized thing to do.

Language is for thinking and feeling. Insofar as we are able to describe our feelings and think with precision we can civilize ourselves and others. This is the ultimate pragmatism—the *use* of language to make men better than they are; or, at least, to keep them from being no worse than they are. The study of language, therefore, is both a means and an end. And that end is partly a moral one. When Professor Francis stated in his famous article that "moral judgments . . . are repulsive to the linguistic scholar,"[28] he cut the very heart out of linguistic studies. To treat words as things is to treat men as things, things to be manipulated rather than human beings to be civilized.

It was this last mistake—dismissing language as a civilizing force—that more than anything else weakened the grammatical revolution. In the long run, a revolution must have a viable ideology to survive. With no moral weight behind them, the revolutionists could not construct an ideology that would permanently stand the test of philosophy and experience. Civilized man needs—and apparently will fight for—a civilized language. For, as Jacques Barzun has written, "the state of the mother tongue is in fact the index of our control over destiny."[29] The revolutionists took away the linguistic controls that we had, but offered nothing better in their place. So the grammatical revolution, like so many other revolutions in history, failed at last.

Notes

1. For example, it is a fact of English that reflexive pronouns never occur in a subject position. Thus, one may not say **Himself shaved Bill* or **Himself was shaved by Bill,* though one can say *Bill shaved himself.* It is also a fact of English that reflexive pronouns may never appear as the agent in a passive sentence. Thus under normal intonation **Bill was shaved by himself* is also ungrammatical. These facts interest the linguist because reflexive pronouns in other languages exhibit correspondingly similar constraints. This similarity intrigues the linguist and suggests to him that the restriction which prevents the above cited English sentences from being grammatical might not be a specific fact about English, but rather the English data might reflect a general principle about language.
2. This and the following lesson plans were used in the classrooms of the Needham school system and the Gloucester school system. Thanks are due to Mr. Lee Allen of Needham and Mr. Herbert Wostrel of Gloucester for making the presentations possible. Also to Miss Ardena Manahan and Mrs. Mildred Finn thanks are due for making their classrooms, their time and their pupils available to me.
3. Two possible difficulties that might arise are worth noting. First, while words like *membership, class* and *team* may not occur with syntactic plurals in my own dialect, there are dialects in which sentences like *The membership are assembled* are acceptable. I believe this to be true of certain British dialects. Note also that while these words can be made plural, i.e., *the memberships, classes, teams,* they need not be in order to satisfy the subject requirement of verbs like *scatter, disperse,* etc.

   A second difficulty has to do with verbs like *scatter.* The appropriate generalization is that *scatter,* etc., require plural subjects. An apparent counterexample is a sentence like *the boy scattered the seed.* Note, however, that in this sentence the relationship of *seed* to *scatter* is identical to the relationship of the subject and the verb in a sentence like *the seed scattered.* Indeed, there is a real intuition that the latter sentence is somehow contained in the former. The way linguists go about capturing generalizations of this kind goes beyond the intent of this lesson plan. However, for purposes of classroom discussion it would be extremely interesting, I think, to observe that the relationship between a verb and a related noun (in this instance, *scatter* and *seed*) can remain the same even though the noun might be subject of the verb in one sentence and object in another.
4. The term *New Grammar* is not entirely satisfactory, but it does keep one from repeating long expressions like *structural linguistics* and *transformationalism.* I use the term *New Grammarians* to refer to those scholars who are against traditional grammar and who are in favor of one of the newer scientific grammars.
5. W. Nelson Francis, "Revolution in Grammar," *The Quarterly Journal of Speech* 40 (October 1954): 299.
6. *Ibid.*, p. 300.
7. "On the Educational Value of the Natural History Sciences," in *Thomas Huxley [on] Science and Education,* introduction by Charles Winick (New York: 1964), p. 46.
8. *The Science of Language* (New York, 1962), p. 73.
9. "The Cultural Matrix of American English," *Elementary English* 42 (January 1965): 18.
10. The term was invented by an unidentified editorial writer of *The American Behavioral Scientist* 4 (May 1961): 36. Wrote the editorialist: "By 'scientoid'

we mean, wearing the robes of scientific language and logico-empiricism, rationalistic. It [the scientoid manifesto] will carry statistics, trend, data, and a hundred 'oughts' recorded as 'is'."

11. Donald Walsh, "The FL Program in 1963," *PMLA* 79 (May 1964): 26. Italics added.
12. *English Sentences* (New York, 1962).
13. Francis, *op. cit.*, p. 302.
14. "Review of Ralph Long's *The Sentence and Its Parts*," *American Speech* 37 (October 1962): 213.
15. Francis, *op. cit.*, p. 304.
16. *Ibid.*, pp. 304-305.
17. *Writers at Work: The Paris Review Interviews*, Sec. Ser. (New York, 1963), p. 118.
18. H.F. Harding, ed., *Lectures on Rhetoric and Belles Lettres*, I (Carbondale: Southern Illinois University Press, 1965), p. 201.
19. *English Composition* (New York, 1908), p. 76.
20. G.L. Kittredge and F.E. Farley, *An Advanced English Grammar* (Boston, 1913), p. 1.
21. *The Structure of English* (New York, 1952), p. 21.
22. *A Short Introduction to English Grammar* (Chicago, 1959), pp. 246-247.
23. *A New Handbook for Writers* (New York, 1962), pp. 31-32.
24. *The English Language: An Introduction* (New York: 1965), p. 61.
25. "Ruckus in the Reference Room," in *Dictionaries and THAT Dictionary*, James Sledd and Wilma Ebbitt, eds. (Chicago, 1962), p. 218.
26. "History: The Life in Language," *Illinois English Bulletin* 48 (November 1960): 8.
27. *The Greek Way* (New York, 1952), p. 230.
28. Francis, *op. cit.*, p. 302.
29. *The House of Intellect* (New York, 1959), p. 27.

Selected Bibliography

Alego, John. "Linguistic Marys, Linguistic Marthas: The Scope of Language Study." *College English*, **31** (December 1969): 273-279.

Alego, John. "Linguistics: Where Do We Go From Here?" *English Journal*, **58** (January 1969): 102-112.

Ashley, Rosalind. "Linguistic Games and Fun Exercise." *Elementary English*, **44** (November 1967): 765-767.

Brazil, D. "Kinds of English: Spoken, Written, Literary." *Educational Review*, **22** (November 1969): 78-92.

Burgess, Anthony. "The Future of Anglo-American." *Harper's Magazine*, **236** (February 1968): 53-56.

Burns, Paul C. "Linguistics: A Brief Guide for Principals." *The National Elementary Principal*, **45** (September 1965): 37-42.

Chomsky, Noam. "The Current Scene in Linguistics." *College English*, **27** (May 1966): 587-595.

Chomsky, Noam. "Should Traditional Grammar Be Ended or Mended?—I." *Educational Review*, **22** (November 1969): 5-17.

Crews, Ruthellen. "Linguistics in the Elementary School Classroom." *NEA Journal*, **57**, 2 (February 1968): 26-28.

Crowell, Michael G. "American Traditions of Language Use: Their Relevance Today." *English Journal*, **59** (January 1970): 109-115.

Dawkins, John. "Linguistics in the Elementary Grades." *Elementary English*, **42** (November 1965): 762-768, +786.

Evertts, Eldonna L. "The Influence of Linguistics." *Educational Leadership*, **22**, 6 (March 1965): 404-407.

Foley, L. "Ain't Them Grammar Rules No Good?" *Educational Forum*, **34** (May 1970): 527-531.

Fries, Charles C. "Advances in Linguistics." *College English*, **25** (October 1961): 30-37.

Geach, Peter. "Should Traditional Grammar Be Ended or Mended?—II." *Educational Review*, **22** (November 1969): 5-17.

Gilbert, Donald. "I'm Sold on the New Grammar." *Grade Teacher*, **86** (March 1969): 160-64.

Gleason, H.A., Jr. "The Relevance of Linguistics?" Paper presented at the Ontario Council of Teachers of English Convention, March 17, 1969, in Toronto. *English Quarterly*, **2** (June 1969): 7-13.

Goba, R.J. "Grammar, Usage, Teachers of English, and Paul Roberts." *English Journal*, **58** (September 1969): 886-891.

Goodman, Kenneth S. "Let's Dump the Uptight Model in English." *Elementary School Journal*, **70** (October 1969): 1-13.

Goodman, Kenneth S. "Linguistic Insights Which Teachers May Apply." *Education*, **88** (April 1968): 313-316.

Grimm, Gary D. "Our Language." *Grade Teacher*, **87** (April 1970): 76-80.

Groff, Patrick J. "Is Knowledge of Parts of Speech Necessary?" *English Journal*, **50** (September 1961): 413-415.

Hedley, C.N. "Language in the Classroom: Or Every Teacher a Teacher of Semantics." *Elementary English*, **47** (March 1970): 361-362.

Hodges, Richard E. "Linguistics, Psychology, and the Teaching of English." *The Elementary School Journal*, **66** (January 1966): 208-213.

Hoey, Edwin A. "History Might Help." *English Journal*, **57** (October 1968): 1041-1044.

Johnson, Falk S. "Grammars: A Working Classification." *Elementary English*, **44** (April 1967): 349-353.

Keyser, Samuel J. "The Role of Linguistics in the Elementary School Curriculum." *Elementary English*, **47** (January 1970): 13-16.

Kreidler, Charles W. "The Influence of Linguistics in School Grammar." *The Linguistic Reporter*, **8** (December 1966): 1-4.

Lefevre, Carl A. "The Contribution of Linguistics." *The Instructor*, **74** (March 1965): 77+.

Lenneberg, Eric. "On Explaining Language." *Science*, **164** (May 1969): 635-643.

Lund, Thomas A. "Grammar Should Be Groovier." *Today's Education*, **57** (December 1968): 61-62.

Marckwardt, Albert H. "The Structure and Operation of Language." *Language Linguistics and School Programs*, pp. 17-27. Champaign, Ill.: NCTE, 1963.

May, Frank B. "Composition and the New Grammar." *Elementary English*, **44** (November 1967): 762-764.

Miller, James E. "The Linguistic Imagination." *Elementary English*, **47** (April 1970): 467-475.

Morris, W. "Dictionary as a Tool in Vocabulary Development Programs." *English Journal*, **59** (May 1970): 669-671.

Nelson, Francis W. "The Present State of Grammar." *The English Journal*, **52** (May 1963): 317-321.

Owen, George H. "Linguistics: An Overview." *Elementary English*, **39** (May 1962): 421-425.

Pei, Mario. "How Did Language Begin." *Saturday Review*, **50** (September 7, 1967): 54-55.

Reynolds, William. "Ten Commandments for Teachers of English." *English Journal*, **59** (May 1970): 672.

Sklar, R. "Chomsky's Revolution in Linguistics." *Nation*, **207** (September 9, 1968): 213-217.

Sledd, James. "On Not Teaching English Usage." *English Journal*, **54** (November 1965): 698-703.

Stanford, B.D. "Is Teaching Grammar Immoral?" *Changing Education*, **4** (Spring 1970): 24.

Strickland, Ruth G. "The Contribution of Linguistics in Reading, Spelling, Grammar." *The Instructor*, **75** (March 1966): 73, 78-79.

Ulin, Richard O. "Linguistics: Mission Impossible?" *Educational Forum*, **33** (March 1969): 329-335.

White, Evelyn Mae. "Teaching Discovery Linguistics." *Elementary English*, **45** (March 1968): 342-345.

PART THREE
Language in the Classroom

A.
Language Development

By the time children enter school they have acquired most of the basic grammatical constructions used by adults. Interestingly, this process of language acquisition has taken place without the benefit of formal instruction. For all practical purposes each child, regardless of his native tongue, appears to possess intuitive linguistic abilities which permit him to learn language within the perimeter of his society. Empirical evidence suggests that a child's personal language serves him quite well in his cultural milieu, but in the classroom he may be considered linguistically deficient. Thus, the problem becomes one of determining how to help him attain a literate level of English without destroying his language heritage.

How language learning experiences are structured and how children perceive these experiences are of considerable concern to educators, for each child's self concept is deeply rooted in language and thought. The recent unprecedented interest in cognition during early childhood has carried over into language programs. There is a virtual plethora of linguistically based programs now in existence. Private and public schools, Project Head Start, and educational television series such as Sesame Street have all sought to capitalize upon language enrichment as the major vehicle in overcoming children's learning deficiencies.

As yet we know very little about the possible psychological effects various language teaching approaches have on children. It may be that the unstructured, "natural" instructional methods used with linguistically adept speakers are not effective for language deficient children. It may be necessary to use a more structured, drill-type approach to train these children. The educational process is infused with a diversity of opinions regarding the appropriateness and effectiveness of various language improvement programs. These opinions are among the topics given consideration in Part III. Research data are presented to balance these opinions.

This theoretical discussion of varying opinions in the developmental nature of language is directed toward one major thesis—that teachers must expand upon children's language resources instead of attempting to replace their "undesirable" grammatical forms with new language patterns. They caution teachers to be particularly sensitive to such considerations. Too much prescriptive teaching of grammatical constructs having little reality for the child may actually retard language growth.

21. Suggestions from Studies of Early Language Acquisition

Courtney B. Cazden

When we say that a child has learned his native language by the time he enters first grade, what do we mean he has learned? A set of sentences from which he chooses the right one when he wants to say something? The *meaning* of a set of sentences from which he chooses the right interpretation for the sentences he hears? Even if the sets of sentences and interpretations were enormous, the result would still be inadequate. Outside of a small and unimportant list of greetings like *Good morning* and cliches like *My, it's hot today,* few sentences are spoken or heard more than once. Any speaker, child or adult, is continuously saying and comprehending sentences he has never heard before and will never hear or comprehend again in the same way. Creativity in expressing and understanding particular meanings in particular settings to and from particular listeners is the heart of human language ability.

The only adequate explanation for what we call "knowing a language" is that the child learns a limited set of rules. On the basis of these rules he can produce and comprehend an infinite set of sentences. Such a set of rules is called a grammar, and the study of how a child learns the structure of his native language is called the study of the child's acquisition of grammar.

When we say that a child knows a set of rules, of course we don't mean that he knows them in any conscious way. The rules are known nonconsciously, out of awareness, as a kind of tacit knowledge. This way of knowing is true for adults too. Few of us can state the rules for adding /s/ or /z/ or /iz/ sounds to form plural nouns. Yet if asked to supply the plurals for nonsense syllables such as *bik* or *wug* or *gutch*, all who are native speakers of English could do so with ease.[1] Most six-year-old children can too. We infer knowledge of the rules from what adults or children can say and understand.

From *Childhood Education* 46:127-131 (December 1969). Reprinted by permission of Courtney B. Cazden and the Association for Childhood Education International, 3615 Wisconsin Avenue, N.W., Washington, D.C.

Children learn the grammar of their native language gradually. Might one assume, therefore, that the stages they pass through on their way to mature knowledge could be characterized as partial versions of adult knowledge? Not so! One of the most dramatic findings of studies of child language acquisition is that these stages show striking similarities across children but equally striking deviations from the adult grammar.

For example, while children are learning to form noun and verb endings, at a certain period in their development they will say *foots* instead of *feet, goed* instead of *went, mines* instead of *mine.*[2] Children do not hear *foots* or *goed* or *mines.* These words are overgeneralizations of rules that each child is somehow extracting from the language he does hear. He hears *his, hers, ours, yours* and *theirs;* and he hypothesizes that the first person singular should be *mines.* Human beings are pattern- or rule-discovering animals, and these overgeneralizations of tacitly discovered rules are actively constructed in each child's mind as economical representations of the structure of the language he hears.

Rules for formation of sentences show the same kinds of deviations. In learning how to ask a question, children will say, *Why I can't go?*, neglecting temporarily to reverse the auxiliary and pronoun.[3] And their answer to the often-asked question *What are you doing?*, will temporarily be, *I am doing dancing.*[4] If the answer to *What are you eating?* takes the form, *I am eating X,* the child hypothesizes that the answer to *What are you doing?* is, *I am doing X-ing.* Only later does he learn that answers with *doing* require the exceptional form *I am X-ing.*

The commonsense view of how children learn to speak is that they imitate the language they hear around them. In a general way, this must be true. A child in an English-speaking home grows up to speak English, not French or Hindi or some language of his own. But in the fine details of the language-learning process, imitation cannot be the whole answer, as the above examples show.

Sometimes we get even more dramatic evidence of how impervious to external alteration the child's rule system can be. Jean Berko Gleason's conversation with a four-year-old is an example:

She said, *My teacher holded the baby rabbits and we patted them.*
I asked. *Did you say your teacher held the baby rabbits?*
She answered. *Yes.*
I then asked, *What did you say she did?*
She answered, again, *She holded the baby rabbits and we patted them.*
Did you say she held them tightly? I asked.
No, she answered, *she holded them loosely.*[5]

Impressed by the confidence with which the child continued to use her own constructions despite hearing and comprehending the adult form, Gleason conducted a variation of her older test with first-, second- and third-grade children.[6] She asked the children to give irregular plural nouns or past tense verbs after she had supplied the correct form as she asked the question. "In the case of the verbs, they were shown a bell that could ring and told that yesterday it rang; then they were asked what the bell did yesterday."[7] Even under these conditions, only 50 percent of the first-graders (7 out of 14) said *rang;* 6 said *ringed* and one said *rung.* Gleason concludes:

> In listening to us, the children attended to the sense of what we said, and not the form. And the plurals and past tenses they offered

were products of their own linguistic systems, and not imitations of us.[8]

When sophisticated parents try deliberately to teach a child a form that does not fit his present rule system, the same filtering process occurs. The following conversation took place when a psychologist tried to correct an immaturity in her daughter's speech:

C. *Nobody don't like me.*
M. *No, say "Nobody likes me."*
C. *Nobody don't like me.*
(eight repetitions of this dialogue)
M. *No. Now listen carefully; say "Nobody likes me."*
C. *Oh! Nobody don't likes me!*[9]

It happens that irregular verbs such as *went* and *came* are among the most common verbs in English. Children usually learn the irregular forms first, evidently as isolated vocabulary words, and later start constructing their own overgeneralizations *goed* and *comed* when they reach the stage of tacitly discovering that particular rule. Finally, they achieve the mature pattern of rule plus exceptions. Stages on the way to the child's acquisition of mature behavior may look for the moment like regressions, like new errors in terms of adult standards, and yet be significant evidence of intellectual work and linguistic progress.

With a very few pathological exceptions, all children learn to speak the language of their parents and home community. They do so with such speed and ease, at an age when other seemingly simpler learnings such as identification of colors are absent, that one wonders how the environment helps the process along. Just as the commonsense view holds that the child's process is basically imitation, so it implies that the adult's contribution is to shape the child's speech by correcting him when he is "wrong" and reinforcing him when he is "correct." Here too the commonsense view seems invalid. So far no evidence exists to show that either correction or reinforcement of the learning of grammar occurs with sufficient frequency to be a potent force. Analysis of conversations between only a few parents and children are available, but that generalization holds for them without exception.

Brown and his colleagues have found corrections of mis-statements of fact but not correction of immature grammatical forms in hundreds of hours of recordings of three children—Adam, Eve and Sarah—and their parents.[10] Horner found only correction of "bad language" (*pee-pee*) in her study of conversation between parents and two three-year-old lower-class children.[11] Finally, students recording the acquisition of language in such farflung areas of the world as India, California and Samoa report the same lack of correction.[12]

Reinforcement of immature constructions could be expressed in many ways. Brown et al have looked for two kinds of reinforcement: verbal signs of approval and disapproval and differential communication effectiveness. In either case, the critical requirement for the operation of reinforcement is that the parent's utterance must be supplied contingently—supplied when the child speaks maturely and denied when he speaks in an immature fashion. Without that contingent relationship, the adult behavior cannot reinforce the child's mature utterance and make it more likely to occur again. Brown et al examined parental response to specific constructions—such as questions—at times when the children were oscillating between mature and immature forms (as with *went* and *goed* above). They found no evidence of differential approval or of differential communication effectiveness.[13] Analyzing these same parent-child conversations, Bellugi-Klima concludes:

> The mother and child are concerned with daily activities, not grammatical instruction. Adam breaks something, looks for a nail to repair it with, finally throws pencils and nails around the room. He pulls his favorite animals in a toy wagon; fiddles with the television set; and tries to put together a puzzle. His mother is concerned primarily with modifying his behavior. She gives him information about the world around him and corrects facts. Neither of the two seems overtly concerned with the problems that we shall pursue so avidly: the acquisition of syntax.[14]

In modifying behavior, supplying information about the world and correcting facts, mothers of young children do seem to use simpler language than they address to other adults. At least, this is indicated in the only study in which the mother's utterances to her child and to another adult have been compared. The utterances to her child were both shorter and simpler.[15] Presumably, as the child's utterances become longer and more complex, so do the mother's. Other than this simplification, there is no sequencing of what the child has to learn. He is offered a cafeteria, not a carefully prescribed diet. And, seemingly impelled from within, he participates in the give-and-take of conversation as best he can from the very beginning, in the process takes what he needs to build his own language system and practices new forms to himself, often at bedtime.[16] As far as we can tell now, all that the child needs is exposure to well-formed sentences in the context of conversation that is meaningful and sufficiently personally important to command attention. Whether the child could learn as well from an exclusive diet of monologues or dialogues in which he did not participate—as he could get from television—we don't know and, for ethical reasons, may never be able to find out.

The foregoing picture of how children learn their native language *before* school is fairly certain, though still incomplete. Implications for how to help childern continue their learning *in* school are far less certain—indeed, are controversial in the extreme—and evidence on which the controversy might be resolved is insufficient. The most obvious implication is that teachers should act the way parents have acted: talk with children about topics of mutual interest in the context of the child's ongoing work and play. This recommendation is made by many people in early childhood education in this country and in infant schools in England.[17] And see Hawkins' sensitive account of "the language of action and its logic" in six four-year-old children who are deaf.[18] Controversy arises because so far experimental comparison of various preschool programs that focus on language development have failed to demonstrate the effectiveness of those programs based on the above philosophy.[19]

Two different explanations of this apparent anomaly can be very tentatively suggested. First, our diagnosis of children's communication problems may be inadequate. Children who need help with language may need very specific kinds of help: help in specific language knowledge such as word meanings, in specific communication skills such as communicating information accurately through words alone, in specific school language games such as answering questions posed by an adult who obviously knows the answers; or help in very general cognitive strategies like focusing attention in school and on tests. In short, maybe the kind of linguistic knowledge that has developed so well in the conversational setting of the home is not a problem in school at all, even for children from disadvantaged environments, and the problems that do exist respond better to more structured educational programs. Second, the test results in the more structured programs may look deceptively good. What the child has learned well enough to express on a test may not have been assimilated into his total linguistic and cognitive system.[20]

Hopefully, this controversy will be resolved in the near future. It is an issue of both practical and theoretical importance.

22.

Language and the School Child

Martin Joos

> The trouble was arithmetic and grammar. My thick skull for mathematics was a source of humiliation. For a year or two I slaved over the subject. As a spur I announced my intention of becoming a civil engineer. The results of these efforts were peculiar. Occasionally I would come up with the solution of a complicated problem—and then miss a string of simple ones. This created suspicions that I had been helped with the hard problem. So, in the end, I just gave up mathematics.
>
> Grammar I wasn't obliged to give up, not having paid it any mind to begin with. I had no intention of doing so now. My position on grammar was that it served no useful purpose. This business of learning which words were verbs and which words nouns; what was the subject of a sentence and what the predicate; and that mumbo-jumbo about moods and tenses—there seemed no more sense to it than learning the alphabet backward (which one teacher required her kids to do). My teachers and my parents said grammar was necessary, to know how to read and write properly. *Bushwa.* As often as any other kid I was asked to read my compositions before the class.[21]

Now if I had good sense, I suppose I'd stop right here; for I surely can't hope to do any better than Marquis James did, and my message is exactly the same as his. However, I have been told that a contribution is wanted from me, no matter how little I could possibly say that is new. I must not try too hard to discover the reason, for fear that it should turn out to be invidious. For instance, I hope that very few of the readers of this journal need to be told how utterly mistaken my class of forty English teachers in the 1958 Summer Session was when they concluded, by a majority of thirty-four to six, that the quoted text was the work of a backward teenager, messily constructed and everywhere incoherent, foolish in its message, and saturated with slang and grammatical errors. I was partly at fault, I admit, for I had asked them to 'criticize' the text; and, much as I regret to, I must also admit that it is possible to get a first impression of incongruity from the way the writer's point of view

From Harvard Educational Review 34:203-210 (Spring 1964). Reprinted by permission of Martin Joos and *Harvard Educational Review.*

wavers between reliving and retrospection. The fifty-year-old winner of two Pulitzer prizes was not entirely successful in getting back into the twelve-year-old's frame of reference, and there is certainly some clashing between the mature wording and a few juvenile words. But it remains clear that nobody ought to be allowed to criticize English composition who is unable to perceive that this text is wise, mature, skillfully and nearly everywhere gracefully composed, grammatical, and unblemished by its single slang item, though it suffers from journalism.[22]

Were they too scared to understand it? Can it be that the plain sense of the message so appalled them that they suppressed it, repressed it into the subconscious, so as to escape consciously acknowledging a truth which would have convicted them of having committed emotional and intellectual mayhem upon their own pupils? There was evidence of that.

This child, they said—in each of the things I report next, I am quoting at least six of those thirty-four teachers—was incompetent in both arithmetic and grammar: when he grew up he would be unable to use arithmetic for practical purposes, and he would never learn to write 'acceptably'—their favorite term, and one which still makes me shudder. If he had paid attention to his arithmetic teacher instead of copying the work of brighter students, he could have learned arithmetic too; and if he had buckled down to the study of grammar he would have learned to write, instead of continuing to write so badly that he was exposed to the mockery of his classmates by being forced to read his compositions allowed (this spelling was used only once). Not one of those thirty-four teachers was able to see what was meant by a pupil using a declaration of specific ambition as a spur to his own efforts in school, so little did they understand how a boy's mind works; most of them thought he meant thereby to gain the teacher's indulgence for his remaining mistakes in arithmetic. Not one of them could concede that his listening ear could tell him anything about what he wrote; after all, it was their job to teach him the language, and to the extent that he failed to learn from his teachers he would have no language at all. And not one saw that the two paragraphs have a single message presented twice over.

It is only fair to report that after I had spent a two-hour period discussing the rhetoric of the text and explicating its message, a good many of those thirty-four teachers came to me in office-hours to say that they felt self-convicted of incompetence and were ready to learn. I say this in justice to them, not to claim the equivalent from my present audience with its far higher level of sophistication. If I now go further, it is only because I have been given to understand that some interest attaches to seeing what one linguist's formulation of all this may look like.

The twelve-year-old Marquis James rejected discipline and felt free to write by ear; writing and listening, he congratulated himself that he was free of the trammels that his elders wanted to impose from outside. But he was not aware that by the time he was eight years old he had trammeled and disciplined his own language (in accordance with what he had read or heard men or older boys say—the girls don't count) to the point where he had entirely lost the freedom of his babyhood. The native language is learned in stages, each stage completed while the next is in progress. The first stage is the learning of the complete pronunciation-system, and normally the books are closed on that before schooling begins. The second stage is learning the grammatical system; this begins about one year later than the first stage began, and it is complete—and the books are closed on it!—at about eight years of age. It is not normal to learn any more grammar beyond that age. Presumably there is some connection between the fact and the traditional postponing of grammar study in school to somewhat beyond that age. In my part of the world, the last two grammar items learned seem to be: (1) The possibility of beginning a sentence with an infinitive, as in 'To err is human' and 'To sing that song is hard'; (2) The forms and the standard-language meaning of the past perfect. On the latter, I can report the statistics from foreign-language teaching: more than sixty percent of our college students have no past perfect in the English that they can control, so that they are utterly baffled by the pluperfect of French or German. It appears that any who had not learned it by age eight were destined never to learn it, for after that it was too late.

The third stage begins at about the time when the first stage is ending. At that time, probably at about age four or a little later—the exact time is rather hard to determine—the meanings of the words currently known begin to get organized into semantic systems of similarity, contrast, and hierarchy. This process continues uninterruptedly for a good many years, long past the end of grammar learning; but it slows down somewhat in the teenage years and in the majority of the population it comes to a halt before they are over. The number of words known increases fairly constantly too: a normal vocabulary is about one thousands words per year of age, from about age three to about age twenty. But in the majority of the population that number hardly increases significantly beyond that age: from then on, new words are either proper names or else are learned as if they were proper names—that is to say, without analysis and without getting firmly located in any semantic hierarchy: new words are learned by normal mature people only the way the term *transistor* is learned by people who are not specialists in electronics, learning it only in its social functions and not at all in its technical significance and hierarchic placement. That minority of the population which continues adding new words to the personal vocabulary, and continues refining the understanding of them, after the age of about twenty, can be called 'academic' persons. Both normal and academic persons have been President of the United States; for example, Eisenhower is a normal person and Truman is an academic with a vocabulary considerably more than twice as large. Similarly, both types are common in fairly low-ranking employments: your mail-carrier may even be an academic, and most competent registered nurses are too.

With these few remarks I can dismiss the vocabulary and return to grammar picking it up again at the point where I said that Marquis James had learned the grammar of English completely, thus replacing his baby freedom with strict social discipline, several years before the epoch that the text speaks of. At that time he did not know that he was obeying any rules of grammar, because he could not perceive them any more than a fish can perceive the water he swims in. Nothing can be perceived except by being an obstacle. I feel the table that I am touching because it is an obstacle to my pressing finger; I see that table only because it was an obstacle to the light that struck it, and bounced some of that light towards my waiting eyes. And there can be no obstacle in a habit that is identical with a community custom. He never knew it, but he was speaking grammatically, for grammar is nothing but custom and habit.

When a child is said to speak 'ungrammatically' the fact is always that he is obeying a vast number of grammatical rules, a very small fraction of which happen to be different grammar rules from the ones that the critic subscribes to. The critic does not notice, for the reason already given, that the child is obeying any rules at all. For that vast majority in which there is identity between the child's grammar and the critic's grammar, the critic notices no rules because there is no conflict; in that small minority of all the rules for which there is conflict instead of identity, the critic notices only the conflict and does not recognize that the child's pattern has its own logic and is part of a different grammar just as rigid as the critic's own. Hence the critic says that the child has no grammar at all, when in fact he has just as much grammar as anybody, very little of it non-standard.

Normal fluent speech obeys about five or six grammar rules per second; a critic can seldom detect, in a child's speech, more than one conflict with standard grammar per ten seconds on the average. And the one time that he was 'incorrect' feels no different, to the child speaker, than the fifty times when he was 'correct.' This means that the child must feel every critical intervention to be an unjustified interruption of his fluent speech, and must regard the form of every correction as completely arbitrary, not conceivably motivated otherwise than by some mysterious urge to interfere with normal human behavior and to distort it into a kind of marionette-dance. There are several possible outcomes of this predicament that the child now feels that he has gotten involved in through no fault of his own. Let me consider them.

The principal lesson that the child learns from this predicament, the lesson that is the most important of all because its application is not confined to linguistic usage, is a lesson that no sane teacher intends to teach, of course, but which he is bound to teach anyhow unless he is almost superhumanly cautious. It is the lesson that unreality is the norm in school, that the laws of the universe have been banished from the schoolroom, so that within its walls the normal laws of cause and effect are not necessarily valid and a whole new way of thinking has to be put on like a smock to replace the outdoors clothing taken off on entering. One result is that the same child who is brilliant in school arithmetic will still rearrange furniture by shoving the pieces into new places to see if they will fit: it does not occur to him to use a yardstick or to add and subtract inches to see whether they will fit, because that's school stuff and school ain't for real anyhow. Or it never occurs to him that there is such a thing as a geography of his home town, or a rhetoric of persuasion within his circle of friends. And when he is required to learn, and to attempt to apply, the definition of 'work' used in his physics textbook, he doesn't have the foggiest notion of what is being done to him; instead he assumes that this is more of the same crazy distortion that has been imposed on him ever since his grammar was first corrected, and that the textbook definition of work is a flat lie to which he must give lip-service. It is a wonder that he ever learns anything useful.

In a peculiar sense, the situation is not as bad as it might be, because there is the settled custom of continually reminding the pupil of where he is by employing special schoolroom voice-qualities, melodies, and of course words and grammar-patterns; the intelligent pupil adopts these himself, of course, for use exclusively within the schoolroom, so that he can swiftly and completely switch between reality outside it and unreality within it. This means that he can earn high grades if he tries; the fact that it blocks him from making practical applications of his 'knowledge' is of course irrelevant.

I turn now to the effects of his predicament upon the child's language. But these can't be disentangled from the effects upon those matters which in real life are most closely correlated with usage differences, namely the judging of personalities and social status. When the artificial school treatment of usage impinges on what the child already knows about personalities and society, there is necessarily a powerful reflex action upon the child's image of himself and his associates. Long before any teacher began to correct his English, the child has learned all he needs to know, at his age, about people and their places;

he has developed considerable skill in judging adults by their speech; he has built up a sufficient repertory of shibboleths and touchstones for judging them —partly what we call usages and partly consisting of voice qualities, gestures, favorite messages, and other such details.

He has not only learned to judge people by this method; he has also learned that people differ from each other in many ways, that people can be similar in several details and yet differ in many others—technically speaking, he has learned that human differences have many dimensions. It is part of the pervasive unreality of the schoolroom that he is now required to junk his elaborate map of society and replace all his speech-tests with a single yardstick that has no scale: its two ends are labeled 'correct' and 'incorrect' and that's all. By tone of voice and by precept he is indoctrinated into the theory that correct language is the same as morality, that only the Bad Guys talk with native freedom.

The effects of this intellectual and emotional assault and battery are too numerous for me to list in full. Today few teachers go as far as what was formerly customary, when what the teacher said could be condensed quite fairly into: "Johnny! Do not let me hear you say 'ain't' again! Yes, I know that your father says 'ain't,' but your father is only an ignorant farmer, and I am here to teach you to be a better man than your father!" Our teachers are more urbane today, but the difference is only that the same assault is spread out thin into a decade of unremitting nagging whose natural effect is linguistic and social schizophrenia and hypocrisy, a precarious balance that must be protected by either sullen withdrawal or violent reaction when it is threatened by such things as a new edition of a dictionary or a new treatment of grammar in the schools. This is the middle-class syndrome; in the slum schools the children react earlier and more fatefully. Their social self-defense has been precarious enough already, and nearly every child has been continuously on the edge of disaster as long as he can remember; now he is superciliously informed that the rhetoric he has been protecting himself with is essentially rotten and that the school language will take him many years to learn—years during which he will be unable to fight his battles with either the one or the other! There is no need for me to remind you what that is costing us in the normal sequence of events: terrified, the school child barricades himself behind what he already knows how to do and refuses to be trapped into learning anything economically significant, occupies himself with what we call juvenile delinquency, and ultimately becomes a school drop-out with all the rest that follows.

That is too grim for me to pursue any farther. Have I exaggerated? Yes, but only to the extent that a good many children are tough enough to beat the odds. I insist that I have not exaggerated in stating the nature of the conflict and the naturalness of the disastrous outcome.

Is there a way out? I know of only one, and I'm afraid it's almost a counsel of perfection. Teachers must simply abandon the theory that usages differ in quality, as between good and bad, correct and incorrect, and instead build their methods and reconstruct their emotional reactions on the plain facts that are already known in part to their pupils. Teacher and pupil must come to terms with each other—and of course all the burden of coming to terms must rest upon the one who is supposed to be wiser and better informed—on the basis that usages can be learned without condemning those which they replace, that the learner has an indefeasible right to speak as he likes without school penalties, while the teacher has no rights in this respect but only the duty to demonstrate what usages are profitable in the adult world.

It follows that the teacher must know the facts, and use only facts; he must abandon any schoolbook pretence that conflicts with the facts. It is a monstrous demand, but nothing less will suffice in theory; in actual practice, the teacher can afford to be ignorant of quite a few details provided that he cheerfully confesses it and promptly shows how the facts can be uncovered. What he must not do is to be sure when he is wrong, for the children will see through the deception and apply the maxim 'false in one thing, false in all.' For example, most children, long before the point ever comes up in school, have learned that any number of well-educated and trustworthy adults say 'It's me.' That teacher who prides himself on his tolerance and is presumptuous enough to forgive those people, to be indulgent with them because they are too busy being useful to have any time for correctness, is choosing the wrong path. With that attitude, he can accomplish only one of two things: either he succeeds in distorting the child's whole frame of reference and weakening the child's ability to find his way around in the world, or else he is detected in the falsity of his position and forfeits the child's respect. The teacher would be far wiser to say frankly that 'It is I' and especially that 'This is she' is a school invention which has become fashionable for certain purposes; that the girl pupil who aspires to be a receptionist will do well to adopt this mode of speech, since it goes well with the brilliant pink fingernails and the upswept hairdo, but that if she wants to be a pediatrician she had better learn to switch styles between one usage and another to suit her interlocutors: 'That's me all over' when consulting with another physician, but 'This is she' when she recognizes certain voices on the phone.

At this point I switch to my final topic, the teaching of composition in writing, perhaps the teaching of effective speaking for formal addresses. I am not an insider in the professional teaching of composition, but I have had as much opportunity to observe the methods and results as a linguist needs for my present purposes.

Fortunately, grammatical errors are no problem: either the pupil already knows the 'correct' form and has inhibited it by trying to guess what the teacher will pass as correct, or else he is at the wrong stage for learning it. Correct what you absolutely must, of course, to salve your conscience, but don't call attention to what you are doing; instead, try to give the impression that you have heedlessly written your own forms without noticing what the pupil wrote; for instance, you must not circle or cross out what he wrote—you owe at least this much to common decency.

Your aim should be to make the child's own resources available to him. He comes to you able, apparently, only to write simple sentences eight to twelve words long. Why? He is afraid to write the long compound sentences which he can and does use lavishly in conversation, because he has been regularly condemned for 'comma-faults'; he is afraid of complex sentences because his teachers have foolishly insisted that he was making the wrong clause subordinate; he has not been encouraged to experiment with devices like saying 'without noticing' and 'heedlessly' instead of adding two more clauses to the sentence, but has instead been slapped down for beginning a sentence with 'The trouble being. . . . ' He confines himself to the eight-to-twelve-word simple sentence for one reason only: self-defense. In other words, he is inhibited.

Your ostensible goal for him should be nothing but completeness: finding room in his composition for everything that needs saying, including the linkages between the items. You find awkwardness in his drafts; each one is to be treated simply as an obstacle completeness: it has interfered with something that he surely wants to put in.

Can you tell him how to clear away the obstacles? No, you can't; he has to invent his own devices. All you can do is to encourage experimenting with grammatical and derivational transformations—the only proper employment of grammar-theory in composition—by demonstrating them and never condemning any that he performs. Condemnation is nothing but inhibition again; just encourage him to make still more transformations until he accidentally hits upon one that satisfies him. If his ear is still too young, it isn't you that can age it.

23. The Nature of Nonstandard Dialect Divergence

Walter A. Wolfram

Within the last decade, we have witnessed an expanding interest in the study of nonstandard dialects from a number of different vantage points. Various aspects of nonstandard dialects and their relation to standard dialects have now been investigated. With the increasing number of perspectives on a theme, it has become correspondingly more difficult to keep abreast of all the developments in the field. The various approaches to the problem may keep one rightly perplexed, for the conclusions drawn from similar data may differ dramatically. With the proliferation of papers on a general theme, it also has become increasingly difficult to select a subtopic from a larger area which may be of concern to the potential reader. Finally, the limited and delayed availability of papers through the normal channels of publication may keep one in a constant state of frustration. (Because of this problem, the reader should keep in mind that this description only includes ERIC documents which were processed prior to the fall of 1969.)

The development of ERIC has certainly helped alleviate the problem of limited and delayed availability, but the relevance of various papers to a specific issue and the relative merit of these papers is outside the scope of ERIC. Yet, it is apparent that such evaluative judgments might be of great service to the reader who has neither the time nor interest to survey the many divergent aspects of nonstandard dialects for himself.

The primary purpose of this paper is therefore evaluative. It is designed to investigate a specific issue in the area of nonstandard dialects and to evaluate

---

ERIC documents dealing with this issue. Obviously, not all of the articles will be of equal relevance to the specific issue being investigated here. The relative importance will be implicit in the comments concerning each article. In addition, special notation will be made of crucial articles in the notes.

The issue reviewed here is the manner in which nonstandard dialects differ from standard English. In other words, possible answers are explored concerning the question of *how* nonstandard dialects differ from standard dialects.

Deficiency versus Difference

Although it may seem somewhat over-simplified, the current viewpoints on how nonstandard dialects differ from standard dialects can be subsumed under two theoretical positions: either nonstandard dialects are viewed as a *deficient* form of standard English or they are viewed as a *different* but equal language system. In a *deficit* model, speech differences are viewed and described with reference to a norm and deviation from that norm. The control group for describing deviation is middle-class speech behavior. From this perspective, nonconformity to the norm is seen as an indication of retarded language acquisition or under-developed language capacity. Nonstandard pronunciation and grammatical patterns are sometimes viewed as inaccurate and unworthy approximations of standard English. Nonstandard dialects are considered as "the pathology of non-organic speech deficiencies," and the patterns of these dialects are labeled with such terms as "misarticulations," "deviations," "replacements," "faulty pronunciations," and the like.

On the other hand, the *difference* model considers each language variety to be a self-contained system which is inherently neither superior nor deficient. Nonstandard dialects are systems in their own right, with their own pronunciation and grammatical rules. Although these rules may differ from standard English, they are no less consistent or logical than the rules of the socially prestigious dialect. That one language variety is associated with a socially subordinate group and, therefore, socially stigmatized has nothing to do with the actual linguistic capacity of the system. From this viewpoint, one must be very careful not to confuse the social connotations of a language system and its linguistic capacity as a communicative code.

Although the deficit perspective has enjoyed considerable popularity in a number of disciplines, it conflicts with some basic assumptions about the nature of language.[23] In the first place, empirical evidence suggests that all languages are capable of conceptualization and expressing logical operations. It is therefore assumed that different surface forms for expression have nothing to do with the underlying logic of a sentence, since there is nothing inherent in a given language variety which will interfere with the development of conceptualization. This is not to say that differences between the handling of logical operations may never correlate with social class. However, social class categories cannot be explained by language differences alone, since all language varieties provide for the expression of syllogistic reasoning.

A second linguistic premise is that all languages and dialects are adequate as communicative systems. It has been established that language is a human phenomenon which characterizes every social group, and that all language systems are perfectly adequate for communication by the members of the social group. The social acceptability of a particular language or dialect, considered nonstandard because of its association with a subordinate social group, is totally unrelated to its adequacy for communication. The question for the linguist is not the *what* but the *how* of communication.

Another linguistic premise relating to the adequacy of all language systems is that languages are systematic and ordered. Technically speaking, there is no such thing as a "primitive" language or dialect. All languages and dialects are highly developed and complex systems in their internal organization. Furthermore, affinities between the pronunciation and grammatical patterns of related dialects are consistent and regular, not haphazard and random.

Finally, language is learned in the context of the community. All linguistic evidence points to the conclusion that children have acquired a fairly complete language system by the age of five or six, with minor adjustments in language competence sometimes occurring until eight or nine. This system is acquired from contact with individuals in the immediate environment. Whether the source for this acquisition is parental, sibling, or peer group interaction is only incidental from a linguistic viewpoint. What is more important is the fact that the rate of language development is approximately parallel across cultures and sub-cultures. That is, lower-class children learn nonstandard dialects at approximately the same rate as middle-class children learn standard English.

Nonstandard Dialects as Deficient

Although the linguistic premises concerning the nature of language have been basic to the discipline of linguistics for decades now, when the speech patterns of the so-called disadvantaged became an area of high priority for educators in the early sixties, it was the *deficit* model which provided a framework for this discussion. On this basis, programs were devised to describe and change the speech patterns of these children. One of the earlier programs designed to deal with the speech of these children was the Institute for Developmental Studies, founded and directed by Martin Deutsch.

Deutsch and his staff describe a "language intervention" program, an attempt to intervene with the development of speech patterns at a preschool period in order to prepare and equip the child with the linguistic capacity for success in school. In other words, the program is set up to remedy the presumed deficits of these children before entering school.[24] Three major premises are enumerated as the theoretical basis for this program: (1) the intellectual deficit caused by early cultural deprivation cannot be made up for by putting children in a middle-class school; they need more direct emphasis on cognition; (2) to overcome deficiences, there must be a carefully planned match between specific deficits and remedial measures; and (3) to alleviate the language handicap of disadvantaged children, they must be motivated to learn a standard pattern.

The Deutsch model for intervention is based on the theory that environment plays a major role in the development of cognitive skills, and that language skills and cognitive skills go hand in hand. Because of a "noisy environment" and the inaccessibility of adults in the home, the language and cognitive skills of these children are deficient.

The theoretical basis of Deutsch's position suggests that behavioral characteristics different from middle-class norms are inherently lacking in culture. Such ethnocentric norms for comparison are, of course, at variance with basic understandings of the nature of culture. That ghetto culture is different is not disputed here, but a *de facto* interpretation that this difference is equivalent to deficiency is difficult to justify. When the implicit criteria for viewing differences as deficiencies are looked at closely, the main criterion which emerges is conformity to middle-class patterns, as if there were some inherent "correctness" in this way of doing things. Attributing speech deficiencies to the unavailability of adults for interaction, for example, takes into account only one model for language acquisition—parent-child interaction. Sibling or peer group interaction, which may be quite extensive at a relatively young age for ghetto children, is not considered.

Furthermore, the relationship of language development and cognitive development has often been misunderstood. That language is integral to the cognitive development of an individual is not at issue here, but empirical linguistic evidence demonstrates that all languages and dialects provide for syllogistic reasoning. Every bit of linguistic data points to the fact that any logical operation possible in a standard dialect is also possible in a nonstandard dialect. The linguistic expression of logical operations may be different from dialect to dialect, but the underlying logic is quite intact. For example, both standard English and nonstandard English provide for making "identity statements" such as *The box is blue*, but in the dialect spoken by many lower-class Negro children, this construction is *The box blue*. That the copula form *be* is not found in this instance has no effect on the ability to form an identity statement. Rather, this dialect, like languages such as Russian, Thai, and Hungarian, may not have any copula in certain types of constructions. This is not a matter of deficiency but a difference in linguistic expression.

In "The Disadvantaged Child and the Learning Process," Deutsch is somewhat more detailed in his discussion of the environmental and psychological factors which contribute to the presumed verbal deficiency.[25] Factors such as the lack of toys and books, an unstable family life, and substandard housing may leave a child deficient in perceptual discrimination, attentional mechanisms, expectation of rewards, and the ability to use adults as sources of information. All of these tasks are skills required for learning in schools, at least those of the sixties. Due to the "non-verbal" slum home, the child may fail to acquire a language-concept system which fits the school's instructional patterns.

As we had suggested above, correlations between learning ability and the language of these children are misleading. What is considered to be a lack of syntactic organization and inadequate perceptual ability may emerge only because of the external norms of acquisition, the white middle-class behavior which serves as a measure of "normalcy." Dialect-fair and culture-fair measurements of perceptual ability and syntactic organization have only recently come under consideration. Furthermore, claims about the non-verbalness of slum homes are not based on formal research evidence. As mentioned above, the ghetto homes may well be the predominant source for verbal interaction in this cultural setting.

Cynthia Deutsch measured the auditory discrimination abilities of lower-class black children on the premise that "a particular minimum level of auditory discrimination skill is necessary for the acquisition of reading and general verbal skills."[26] A basic assumption was that lowerclass children are deficient in the development of auditory attentiveness and discrimination because of an excessively noisy, overcrowded environment.

The basis for measuring perception was the Wepman Auditory Discrimination Test, one of the standard tests for discrimination development. Several important limitations of the Wepman Test must be identified. In the first place, the Wepman Test is constructed without reference to legitimate dialect differences. Thus, the failure to discriminate between *wreath* and *reef* or *lave* and *lathe* by young black children is interpreted as indicative of underdeveloped auditory discrimination. Actually, such pairs are the result of a systematic pattern in which *th* in *wreath* and *f* at the end of a word and *th* in *lathe* and *v* in *lave* are both pronounced as *v* in the dialect spoken by many black children in the ghetto. This, however, is not the result of retarded speech development, but the result of a legitimate dialect difference which may be maintained by adults as well as children. In essence, this homophony (i.e., the pronunciation of two different words alike) is no different from that of the New England middle-class child who does not discriminate between *caught*, the past tense of *catch*, and *cot*, the object for resting, or *taught*, the past tense of *teach*, and *torte*, the pastry. The learning of standard English measured by the Wepman Test is not differentiated from the language development of a different dialect. Without taking such dialect differences into account, one can only arrive at erroneous conclusions.

Even if a dialect-fair test indicated that some of these children did reveal developmental retardation, asserting that this might be attributed to the noisy home environment of the child seems to be a simplistic explanation. The social dynamics of the ghetto home, although much mentioned, are just beginning to be researched from an anthropologically valid perspective.

In "The Role of Social Class in Language Development and Cognition," Martin Deutsch attempts to identify background patterns at two developmental stages and relate them to specific cognitive and linguistic patterns.[27] His conclusions are based on a four year "verbal survey" of 292 Negro and white children in the lower and middle socioeconomic groups. The data indicate that being lower-class and/or Negro contributes to lower language scores. On the basis of these data Deutsch suggests that there is a "cumulative language deficit." That is, language deficits become more marked as the child progresses through school, showing the increasing disparity between the school expectations and performance of these children with respect to the prescribed mold. The finding that the language deficits become more marked as the child progresses through school is significant; the assumptions and interpretations as to the cause of these differences, however, bear closer examination.

Labov and Robins for example, in their study of Harlem teenagers, have shown that there is a direct relation between peer group involvement and reading achievement.[28] On this basis, it might more reasonably be suggested that as the child becomes older, the values of the peer group, in direct conflict with the school-imposed value system, are basically responsible for the increasing alienation of ghetto children in middle-class oriented classrooms.

John has set forth the early stages of language acquisition as they relate to social environment in "The Social Context of Language Acquisition."[29] She suggests that a child, surrounded by a sea of words, selectively and sequentially acquires the names of objects and actions. The learning of new responses is facilitated by "the relative invariance of the environment where the social context of learning as well as the stability of the bond between word and referent is being acquired." Differences in the rate and breadth of acquisition can be influenced by the nature of verbal interaction with those caring for the child. Using the Peabody Picture Vocabularly Test as a basis for measurement, it is found that three clusters of words are difficult for low-income children: words relating to rural living, words whose referents are rare in low-income homes, and action words, particularly those dealing with gerundives (e.g., *lying, running*). That these children have difficulty with the first two types is not surprising to John, because of sub-cultural differences; however, she suggests that the relatively little opportunity these children have to engage in active dialogue must be considered as a reasonable explanation for their difficulties with action words. The children did not have difficulty in experience with the referent, but had trouble fitting the label to the varying forms of the action.

The assumptions and methods of John follow those of Deutsch; therefore, the limitations ascribed earlier to Deutsch pertain also to John: (1) the assumptions concerning the social environment of these children are not research based; and (2) the investigators fail to recognize legitimate form differences between dialects in discussing linguistic capacity. Nowhere, for example, is the possibility explored that difficulties with standard English gerundives might be attributed to form differences in the linguistic structure of the dialects investigated.

In all fairness to John and other members of the Institute for Developmental Studies, we must mention that all the above articles were written before the issue of difference versus deficiency was clearly articulated. Characteristically, these articles did not even recognize the existence of the difference alternative. However, with the more recent explication of this issue, current literature dealing with this topic must bear the full responsibility for considering and examining alternatives to the deficit view of language differences in the lower class child in its assumptions, interpretations, and applications.

A slightly different approach to the speech of the economically impoverished is offered in Osser's "The Syntactic Structures of 5-Year-Old Culturally Deprived Children."[30] Osser has compared the syntactic structures of middle-class children and black ghetto children in an attempt to discover how much environmental stimulation is necessary for language development. Using the total number of sentences the children used in the experimental session, the total number of different syntactic structures, and the average "complexity score," a difference favoring the middle-class group is found. Osser also observes that the lower-class group does not show homogeneous speech behavior, a fact he interprets to support the position that environmental differences may not only account for large differences *between* divergent groups, but large differences *within* groups.

Although Osser is treated here along with other studies of nonstandard dialects from a deficit model, he shows considerably more respect for the legitimacy of nonstandard speech as a linguistic system than other approaches from this perspective. It is for this reason that he recognizes the concept of *functional equivalence* in syntactic structures. This refers to "the fact that sequences of words in one dialect may be something different in the other dialect, yet the two sequences are syntactically functionally equivalent, e.g., *his sister hat* in the nonstandard dialect is functionally equivalent to *his sister's hat* in the standard dialect."

Despite the caution found in Osser's conclusions, several exceptions to his interpretations must be taken. We have already seen the need to justify statements about the influence of verbal environment on speech by correlational studies, so we need not elaborate this criticism again. The conclusions about the syntax of these children must also be viewed suspiciously, as Osser himself has cautioned. The total number of sentences used in an experimental situation may not have any direct relationship to the communicative adequacy of speech in a natural speech situation. Furthermore, the number of sentences used is significantly intercorrelated with the diversity and complexity of structures. Is, for example, the absence of relatives among the lower-class children representative of the actual linguistic capacity or a function of the failure to elicit a sufficient speech sample? Unfortunately, the legitimacy of cultural differences affecting the experimental situation has not been recognized.

Nonstandard Dialects as Different

One of the first important attempts to explicate the different approaches to the study of nonstandard speech was Cazden's "Subcultural Differences in Child Language: An Interdisciplinary Review.[31] Although this article refects the fact that it was written at the inception of much of the current research on nonstandard speech, it is still quite useful. Disciplines included in Cazden's review are linguistics, experimental psychology, anthropology, and sociology. Three main areas of inter-disciplinary convergence are reviewed: (1) nonstandard versus standard English; (2) stages in the developmental continuum; and (3) different modes of communication.

In her discussion of the relation of standard to nonstandard dialects, Cazden delimits several methods of describing differences, including frequency of errors, contrastive analysis, and transformational grammar. The first method, describing errors, is associated with the deficit view of language described above. Cazden is rightly skeptical of studies which assess the status of nonstandard dialects as a cognitive liability, although not as polemical as most linguists dealing with this issue might be. The other two methods, contrastive analysis and transformational grammar, assume a difference view of nonstandard languages. Cazden's distinction of contrastive analysis from transformational grammar, however, is nebulous. For one, these two approaches are not mutually exclusive. Contrastive analyses can, and often do, employ the methods of transformational analysis. Furthermore, transformational grammar is only one linguistic model which might be used in the description of a language or dialect. What is more important than the particular linguistic model is the general linguistic perspective which recognizes the structure of different languages and dialects as systems in their own right, with both similarities and differences to related varieties.

With reference to the stages of the developmental continuum, Cazden summarizes work in this area by noting that children of upper socioeconomic status are generally evaluated as more advanced than those of lower socioeconomic status. But she correctly points out that studies are only valid if evaluated in terms of the norms of a child's own speech community. In this regard, she anticipates the significance of constructing dialect-fair tests.

The final area, the different modes of communication, reviews research on both the intra-and inter-individual aspects of communication. Essentially, this concerns the importance of what, to whom, how, and in what situation we are speaking. She concludes that we know very little about differences in language function.

As a review of the literature up to 1965 on the subcultural differences in the language of children, this can be recommended as a thorough reference. It is less evaluative than might be hoped for with respect to the crucial issue of difference versus deficit, but the period in which it was written may have called for a more cautionary evaluation.

The most explicit sources on the difference/deficit issue are several papers by Joan C. Baratz. In "A Bi-Dialectal Task for Determining Language Proficiency in Economically Disadvantaged Negro Children,"[32] the major dispute about this issue in the literature is outlined, and experimental evidence for her own conclusion is offered.

Baratz suggests that there are three main viewpoints concerning the linguistic system of low income Negro children. First is the view that such children are verbally destitute, not having yet developed a functionally adequate or structurally systematic language code. This viewpoint is rejected by Baratz because of the biased testing procedures, e.g., the use of middle-class testing situations such as the classroom.

The second viewpoint considers these children to have systematic but underdeveloped language behavior, their underdeveloped system leading to cognitive deficits. Again the viewpoint is considered invalid because of the use of middle-class oriented tasks and norms which serve as a standard of normalcy.

The third viewpoint is that these children have a fully developed but different system from standard English. In support of this viewpoint, Baratz has conducted a bidialectal test in which she assesses the proficiency of black ghetto children and middle-class white children in repeating standard English and nonstandard Negro English. The black children were significantly more proficient in repeating the nonstandard Negro dialect sentences than the white children, but when they repeated the standard English sentences there were predictable differences in their repetitions based on interference from the nonstandard dialect. When the same test was given to the white children, the standard English sentences were repeated quite adequately, but predictable differences in their repetitions of the nonstandard sentences, based on interference from the standard English system, were observed. The results of this study show that: (1) there are two dialects involved in the educational complex of black children; (2) neither white nor black children are bidialectal; and (3) there is interference from their dialect when black children attempt to use standard English. This type of evidence, Baratz points out, indicates the bias of testing which uses standard English as a yardstick of language development.

The conclusions that Baratz reaches on the basis of her study are important support for the viewpoint which maintains that we are dealing with different but equal systems. Furthermore, the concise discussion of the deficit/difference controversy makes this one of the most essential articles for anyone interested in the issue.

A slightly different emphasis on this issue is given in Baratz's article "Language and Cognitive Assessment of Negro Children: Assumptions and Research Needs."[33] In this article Baratz examines the speech of lower-class children in relation to cognitive ability. Several of the problems confronting a primarily psychological approach to the language assessment of black children are pointed out: (1) the assumption that language development is synonymous with the acquisition of standard English; (2) the tendency to equate cognition with rationality, i.e., the tacit acceptance of external norms resulting in the description of cognitive abilities of black children in terms of a developmental lag; and (3) the conclusion that some environments are inherently more adequate than others for stimulating general language and cognitive growth. The foregoing problems seem to have evolved from misconceptions of what language is and how it functions.

Like the previous article by Baratz, the explication of the different viewpoints in approaching the speech of low-income children makes this an invaluable contribution to the field. Without taking issue with the essential contribution of this article, it is necessary to point out one example in which the position of Englemann and Bereiter is misrepresented.

One of the prime illustrations in her refutation of the Bereiter-Englemann position of language deficits is the treatment of the *if-then* construction; they claim that children are unable to handle this construction in deductive reasoning, e.g., *If this block is big, then the other is small.* Baratz understands this use of it to be the same as the "question" *if* in a sentence such as *He asked John if he could come.* Because black children may not use *if* in the second type of construction (*He asked John could he come* being appropriate in the dialect of these children), she assumes that Bereiter and Englemann have interpreted a legitimate dialect difference as a cognitive liability. But one cannot argue the case of *if-then* deductions on the basis of question *if* since the two uses of *if* have quite different syntactical functions. Although Baratz's general criticism of the reasoning of Bereiter and Englemann is quite defensible, the particular example chosen to refute their position is, in this case, unfortunate.

In "Grammatical Constructions in the Language of the Negro Preschool Child," Baratz and Povich compare the language development of a group of Head Start children with the results obtained for middle-class preschoolers, using Lee's Developmental Sentence Type model.[34] This article chronologically preceded the papers discussed above, but probably has been pre-empted by them in terms of relevance to the deficiency/difference issue. It is, nevertheless, important because the analytical method used by Baratz and Povich is different from that described in the articles of Baratz which were discussed in the above paragraphs.

The majority of utterances by the lower-class children are on the kernel and transformational levels of Lee's developmental model, according to the investigators. Although the language of economically impoverished Negro children indicates that their language contains a number of structures which would be considered as "restricted forms" when they are compared with standard English, they conclude that these forms are not only acceptable in lower-class dialect, but also indicate a level of syntactic development where transformations are being used appropriately. Inasmuch as the lower-class Negro child is using the same forms as the lower-class Negro adult, Baratz and Povich conclude that he has adequately acquired the forms of his linguistic environment.

Although the vast majority of the controversy over the difference/deficit model in describing speech differences concerns the speech of ghetto Negro children, Vincent P. Skinner looks at the speech of low-income families in Appalachia from this perspective in "Mountaineers Aren't Really Illiterate."[35] Because of the paucity of material on Appalachian speech, the article is mentioned here, despite the fact that it is lacking in detail. Skinner does, however, note that this dialect is sophisticated language which is quite effective for the communicative purposes of the community. The dialect spoken by these mountaineers tends to preserve a more archiac form of English, due to the geographical and social isolation of this group from mainstream American culture. Unfortunately, this article is much too brief and sketchy to be useful as more than an illustration of the status of white nonstandard Appalachian speech as a different but equal system.

Summary

We have seen that there is considerable difference in how nonstandard dialects are viewed as represented in ERIC documents. It should be apparent that one's view of this divergence is crucial for our educational system. For one, the view of a child's dialect will have a direct bearing on teachers' attitudes toward the dialect with which the child comes to school. The attitudinal biases toward linguistically adequate but socially stigmatized language varieties is no doubt the biggest problem we face.

There are also practical reasons for understanding how nonstandard dialects differ from standard English. With respect to testing language proficiency, it means that we must strive to design dialect-fair measures of language proficiency. Only such tests can authentically indicate where a child is in terms of language development. Our viewpoint of nonstandard dialects is also crucial if we propose teaching standard English to nonstandard dialect speakers. A thorough understanding of the systematic and regular differences between standard and nonstandard English must serve as a basis for the most effective teaching of standard English in our schools.

B.
Language Diversities

The facility with which a child learns language skills is influenced, to a significant degree, by the cultural background of the child. Environmental circumstances influence the child's ability to conceptualize clearly and to verbalize adequately. Unfortunately, the preschool cultural environment of many children has not provided the variety and quality of experiences that are necessary for normal language development. These children have been isolated by poverty, by illiteracy in the home, or by indifference within the community. And opportunities for language building experiences outside this socially impoverished environment have been limited.

Children enter school from varied cultural backgrounds. If teachers have an understanding and appreciation of the cultural heritage of the children they will be able to plan effective learning experiences for them. This knowledge helps the teachers to relate to the total class and to establish a better climate for the language growth of each child.

The articles in this section discuss the effect of cultural background on language development. In the articles on black culture, for example, the writers regard the Negro dialect as a consistent, formally developed linguistic system that is only superficially similar to standard English. Because of this, they assert, it may be as difficult for black ghetto children to learn standard English as a second dialect as it is for Indian or Mexican-American children to become bilingual. There has been, to date, little basic research to deny or support their thesis; it stands, therefore, as an academic hypothesis. As the articles herein suggest, our history of attempting to teach English to children who live in environments where a language other than English is the major form of communication has not shown the most gratifying results.

Bi-dialectalism and bilingualism are growing issues. Increasing concern is being paid by educators to the philosophical and pedagogical questions of how to preserve respect for language differences while helping children develop the linguistic abilities needed to function effectively in a society in which standard English is the dominant language. This section is concerned with the psychological impact of the interrelationship of language, culture, and social attitudes upon young language learners; methods of instruction are given but cursory consideration.

24. On Valuing Diversity in Language

Kenneth S. Goodman

Language, in its many, many forms, is man's most useful and most marvelous possession. It is uniquely his. He alone among the animals has achieved the ability to represent in a symbolic encoding the experiences he has and his reflections upon these experiences. He alone has achieved a medium of communication with others of his species so flexible and so effective that he may not only make them aware of his needs, feelings and insights but may actually transmit knowledge to them and influence their behavior and attitudes.

Man alone has a fully functioning medium of thought that makes it possible to multiply the effectiveness of his intellectual capacity as thought is captured and manipulated through language.

What is perhaps even more remarkable is that every human society has developed language. Stone-age man is no less a user of language than atomic-age man. Each group has a language that is suitable for dealing with the experiences and communicative needs of its members. Furthermore, each language is open-ended—dynamic, changing constantly as indeed it must to perform its changing functions.

Each child creates language for himself, moving toward the language forms of his community, as he strives for effective communication. His success is so obvious that it is taken for granted by most adults. By the time a child is five or six, regardless of the culture into which he is born, he is fully competent to use his mother tongue to meet his own needs in communication, thought and learning. And he has the ability to continue developing language as he grows and learns and as his needs become more complex.

The language he comes to control is that of his family and, as such, is closely interrelated with the culture of the community. It has developed categories and structures that represent well the community's mores, beliefs, values—not only for the child to communicate with those around him but for him to discuss and react to his experiences on their terms. As the life-view of a group or a subgroup or individual within it changes, language in turn changes. Hippies offer the most recent example, but adolescents in general find it necessary to change, alter or invert language as they reject adult values. Scientists are another group that must create language as it gains new insights and develops new

---

From *Childhood Education* 46:123-126 (December 1969). Reprinted by permission of Kenneth S. Goodman and the Association for Childhood Education International, 3615 Wisconsin Avenue, N.W. Washington, D. C.

theories to explain our experiences with each other and the universe in which we live.

Language is not the private property of any one culture, society, nation, race, ethnic group or socioeconomic class. Nor is the language of any group superior to that of any other group. Each group's language is best for its needs. Most people will agree that French, German, English, Chinese and Russian are equally useful to their users and that Navajo, Ashanti and Hawaiian are admirably suited to the communicative needs of their respective users.

But when it comes to comparing dialects of a single widely used language such as English, many of us, including some educators, are reluctant to extend the concept. We find that our views of correct English, proper English or standard English conflict—leaving us with the inconsistent conclusion that black speakers of Ashanti in West Africa have adequate language but black speakers of English in Chicago's ghetto do not.

Superimposed on our perceptions of differences in the way English is spoken is our perception of the status of speakers. In England that perception would make the King's English better than anyone else's since the class system makes royalty better than anyone else. An inferior speaker speaks poorly, then, because he's inferior; and he's inferior because he speaks poorly. This circular logic has led us away from seeing the social basis for attitudes toward language difference. It has led us to consider low-status dialects as corruptions of high-status ones, though in fact the historical facts do not support such conclusions.

Educators for generations have assumed that getting a pupil to speak more "properly" automatically made him more effective. The language of low-status groups has been characterized as sloppy, incomplete, ineffective and inadequate. The confusion between language difference and language deficiency permeates texts, tests and curricula in wide use today.

Educators have fallen prey to the elitist notion that they speak a superior form of the language and in fact the only form suitable for learning. Armed with righteousness, they have sought to make their pupils over in their own linguistic image. They have exhorted their pupils to learn the language of the teacher while disdaining to listen carefully themselves to the language of the learners.

The effect of this confusion has been to create learning disadvantages where none need exist. The impact has been hardest on the poor, on ethnic minorities, on the culturally divergent. Even those who have succeeded in school have frequently done so by rejecting themselves, their cultures, their people, as well as their language.

The disadvantages need not exist because the alternatives are basic and simple once we have purged ourselves as educators of our elitism. What has been treated as weakness emerges then as strength. The children we are teaching are found to have language. They have learned the language of their communities in the same manner as any other children. They have a language medium that, regardless of its social status, is the flexible tool of communication, thought and learning.

As we listen we discover that their language is systematic, that they can communicate with each other effectively, that once confident we will listen and accept their language they can discuss their experiences with us and can deal with new concepts using the language they bring to school.

If we can accept without prejudice—not just tolerate—dialects divergent from our own, then we can truly "start where the child is." We can help the learner to build on a base of pride and confidence instead of negating his language competence in a cloud of shame and confusion.

We must accept his experience as legitimate too because only then can we build a curriculum that is relevant. No child is devoid of experiences. From the time of his birth his world is bombarding him with sensory input. A ghetto child or a migrant worker's child clearly has experiences useful to him in building concepts and offering a base for further learning, however different from the experiences of more economically privileged children.

Building on the language and experience of all learners, we will find that we are working with them in the natural direction of growth because new experience creates the need for language growth and expanded language makes it possible for learners to cope with new experiences. The irony is that we may even achieve the goal of making it possible for learners to control a second dialect of English as they expand outward (not upward) on the base of their own dialect and encounter situations in which they are likely to be more effective in an increasingly familiar alternate form. They will acquire this ability to shift if and when it is useful for them to do so.

The legitimate goal of education is to assist each learner to become all that he is capable of being. The goal is not to force him to become something he is not. For too long we have defined equal education as the equal opportunity to become carbon copies of ourselves. It is time that we understood that we can help children to grow without forcing them into a mold of conformity. Indeed, if we learn this lesson we will experience success where previously we have had repeated failure.

25.

Negro Ghetto Children and Urban Education: A Cultural Solution

Stephen S. Baratz and Joan C. Baratz

The failure of urban education to educate Negro ghetto children has reached crisis proportions. At a recent conference on "Race and Education" sponsored by the Civil Rights Commission in Washington on November 16-18, 1968, a crystallization of the two polar solutions on urban education became apparent.

One solution offered by the Civil Rights Commission in its report on Equal Educational Opportunities suggests massive metropolitan area-wide bussing to achieve integrated classes. The second solution, exemplified by New York's More Effective Schools project, suggests that quality education for ghetto children can only be achieved by massive updating of ghetto school facilities, reduction of pupil-teacher ratios, and community control of curriculum.

To each of the possible solutions to urban education—the virtues of integrated education as espoused by the Civil Rights Commission report on the one hand and quality ghetto education as advanced by More Effective Schools on the other—one could say "You're right, you're right." For each is right as far as it goes. However, the difficulties with educating inner-city Negro children will not be solved simply by seating them next to white middle-class children. This solution is unrealistic in that it does not take into account the extent of suburban white resistance to the suggestion of massive bussing to achieve an interchange of the urban Negro school child with children from the surrounding suburbs. Nor does it recognize the resistance of the Negro community to the underlying assumption of this solution: that something about sitting next to a white child "rubs off" and allows the Negro child, by virtue of a bus ride, to become more educable. For that matter, even if both Negro and white communities were clamoring for such a solution to educational problems, the traffic congestion posed by such a solution to the already suffocating city would make the bussing untenable.

Nor will heavy concentrations of traditional compensatory education alone succeed. Larger doses of the same medicine in a new bottle do not appear capable of curing the ills of urban education. The recent evaluations contained in the Coleman report on compensatory education and the reports of the Center for Urban Education on the More Effective Schools confirm these assertions. Change is surely needed. But social change alone is not equivalent to educational change. We must not let our search for social solutions divert us from the fact that the basic problem posed by the ghetto school is an educational one—ghetto children are not learning as much as the children outside the ghetto.

Negro Non-Standard Dialect—Cause and Effect

Reading ability is the important measure of success in our educational establishment. Both our schools and the children in them are evaluated on the basis of reading scores, or achievement tests that rely heavily upon reading ability. Progress in school depends on the constant development of reading skills. Yet, the one major fault of our urban educational system is its failure to understand why teaching an urban Negro child to read is so difficult. But the explanation is really quite simple. A cultural variable is at work which is basic to the difficulty that the Negro child experiences in attempting to learn to read. Evidence has been accumulating that the Negro ghetto child has a different language system, (call it Negro nonstandard dialect) which is a part of his culture and which interferes with his learning to read. Unless and until this variable is considered, and specific educational innovation based upon it, the majority of the inner-city Negro children will continue to fail despite the introduction of all sorts of social improvements to the educational setting.

The recent subcommittee hearings on bilingual education recognized the need for teaching children in their native tongue (here Negro nonstandard English) and then in standard English. The low income Negro child who is speaking Negro nonstandard dialect is hindered by a linguistic problem more elusive in character than that confronting the Spanish speaking Mexican American. The Spanish speaker possesses a recognized, certified and "legitimate" language system. Everyone knows he speaks a different language. Negro nonstandard dialect, on the other hand, has not been accepted by the educational establishment as an orderly, formally structured linguistic sustem. Yet studies of the language of the ghetto Negro child have shown that his language, while equally expressive, is sufficiently different from standard English as spoken by middle-class Americans, that it poses serious communication problems. Like the Spanish speaking Mexican American the Negro American cannot always understand what he is taught in school because he does not always understand or use the standard language. But, unlike the Spanish speaker, the Negro American is said to be using poor, underdeveloped English, rather than a highly developed, highly sophisticated language system.

Need to Recognize Significance of Negro Dialect

When linguists use the word dialect, they do not limit themselves to the way that people in different regions of a country pronounce words. They refer to a total linguistic structure—the organized way that the language grammatically relates certain words to other words: a dialect is a fully developed linguistic system. But dialect is a dirty word in American public schools. The schools tend to regard standard English as "right" and dialects as "wrong." Therefore, instead of recognizing that the ghetto child is speaking a well-developed language, and then using that language to teach him standard English (something that he must acquire if he wishes to compete in the middle-class world), the teacher defines her goal in regard to the Negro ghetto child as that of stamping out his "bad" language (which relates to his culture and his basic Negro identity) and replacing the child's language with standard middle-class English.

The Spanish speaking Mexican American does not speak English because no one in his home or his peer group speaks English. The child is not presumed to have a language problem that is pathological in nature. The school system recognizes that it must teach him standard English in addition to his knowledge of Spanish. He is not necessarily expected to lose or get rid of his Spanish. The Negro child, on the other hand, is viewed as a "sick speaker" of English. His dialect is viewed as aberrant and underdeveloped, and therefore the school system does not consider teaching him another language in addition to his own, but rather thinks only of "remediating" his language—i.e., erasing it and replacing it with standard English.

The lower income Negro child has learned to speak; he has acquired a formally structured linguistic system. However, the child's linguistic system interferes with his learning when he is placed in a middle-class school system which fails to give validity to his language. Our schools punish the child when he says or reads "he sit" for "he sits." But, in his dialect, there is no obligatory "-s" in the third person singular. Again we presume that he is ignorant and unable to understand concepts when, if we teach the rhyming concept in reading, he replies that han' ("hand") rhymes with "man." When we tell him that he is wrong, we confuse him, for he was right: han' and man do in fact rhyme in his speech.

We must separate the concepts to be learned (rhyming, etc.) from the teaching of details of standard English. Until we do this, Negro children will be confused, and will have great difficulty learning to read standard English.

Why Dialect Has Not Received Recognition

But why have we not given recognition to Negro nonstandard dialect? Perhaps the most obvious explanation is the dialect's superficial similarity to standard English. Boy means "boy" and two means "two." Yet when combined into "two boy," the result, while not standard English, is nevertheless proper Negro nonstandard dialect. William A. Stewart, a linguist, has shown that grammatical patterns are such that when pluralization is clearly indicated by some other device, e.g., a number word, then there is no further need to indicate pluralization again. Consequently the standard English "-s" in "boys" is not obligatory from the point of view of the dialect speaker when following the marker "two." Again, using the same English words, our confusion grows when we describe an action attributed to our two boy(s). As Stewart has indicated, "two boy be workin' " is not standard English, but is correct Negro nonstandard dialect. That sentence indicates that two boys are habitually working; as opposed to "two boy workin' " which indicates only that two boys are working at the moment. The syntax of the Negro nonstandard English is complex.

A highly revealing incident which recently took place in Washington, D.C. will illustrate the necessity of recognizing the operation of dialect differences in the teaching of reading. For the text on a Christmas card associated with a project to study the nonstandard dialect of the nation's capital, William A. Stewart had been translating the familiar "Night Before Christmas" into nonstandard dialect. For various reasons, he preserved the standard English spellings of the words, but arranged them according to the dialect's syntax (word order). Thus, the first part of the poem ran as follows:

It's the night before Christmas, and all through the house
Ain't nobody moving, not even a mouse.

There go them stocking, hanging up on the wall.
So Santa Claus can full them up, if he pay our house a call.

While he was still engaging in translating the poem, one of the project's young informants, Lenora, happened to observe the nonstandard dialect text. This 10-year-old Washingtonian was not only a speaker of nonstandard dialect, but was also a school reading problem. Yet, without assistance, she read the dialect text with a degree of speed and accuracy which surprised even herself. Struck by the implications of her success, Stewart then had her attempt to read the original standard English version. All of the behavioral symptoms of a poor reader came back. It was clear that Lenora's problem was not that of being unable to read, but rather that she was unable to read standard English. The fact that words in the nonstandard version were spelled in the standard way, yet caused no reading problem, suggests quite clearly that syntax (rather than spelling, pronunciation, or word-recognition) constitutes the central reading difficulty.

Another reason that the ghetto dialect does not attain legitimacy is its threat to the middle-class Negro. Most successful Negroes who have escaped the ghetto have done so by denying their basic Negro-ness. In so doing, they must also deny the existence of Negro dialect in most rigid fashion. Most, middle-class Negroes speak impeccable (though measured and sometimes strained) standard English. Nevertheless, at times of great emotional stress (listen to some of our Black Civil Rights leaders during their hellfire and brimstone speeches), the nonstandard dialect creeps in. The dialect is inaccurately viewed by both Negro and white as a defect to be hidden. This fact becomes critical when we realize that most black children in this country who come to school speaking Negro nonstandard dialect are taught by the middle-class Negroes who regard that dialect as a defect. Yet when it is necessary for communication, most middle-class Negroes can speak, or at least interpret, ghetto dialect. But in teaching, they seek to destroy the dialect first and then build standard English. On the other hand, the white teacher of Negro children has never learned the dialect and hence does not understand it. Her communication with her nonstandard dialect speaking children may result in meaningless rote recitation, silence, or frustration and anger. In fact, one may speculate that the first systematized indication of discrimination that a Negro child experiences occurs when the elementary school teacher communicates her disapproval and lack of understanding of the child's language. This experience may be so traumatic to the child that he may stop talking altogether while in school. By dealing with the child's language system as one would deal with a defect, the teacher closes off, perhaps altogether, the most significant mode of communication available to the child.

This leads to a final, frequently used explanation for the refusal to accept the legitimacy of the dialect. Language is a part of the culture. The current white liberal doctrine insists that the American Negro is "just like" the American white person. The few anthropological studies of the black ghetto seem to indicate otherwise. Rather than supporting an egalitarian doctrine erroneously defined as sameness, the literature seems to indicate striking and significant differences, as well as interrelationships, between the two cultures. In their efforts to save the Negro from the myth of genetic racial inferiority, liberals may well be consigning him to an equally bad fate—that of considering himself an abnormal white man. A cultural explanation, as in our example of the dialects, describes cultural differences without making value judgments.

One need only to ask "Is Hindustani a better language than Urdu?" to see the nonsense of a value-laden cultural comparison.

Confusion of Equality with Sameness

Solutions to urban problems have to be related to cultural variables despite the fact that they are controversial. We are only dimly aware of the emptiness of our myth-laden "egalitarian" dogma. To say that the Negro is different is not to say that he is inferior. One should not confuse a political and moral position with a cultural fact. Most proposed solutions to our social ills vis-a-vis the Negro have been couched in the whiteness of their creators. They do not give acceptance or legitimacy to the Negro or his culture. Black Nationalism implores the Negro to see himself for what he is and accept what he sees. The white world could learn from the increasing emphasis placed on differences by the "militants" instead of remaining fixed on misleading racist or egalitarian dogma. Instead of being confined by an egalitarian doctrine that confuses equality with sameness, we would do well to recognize that American society is a pluralistic one, and that in a pluralistic society, political and social equality are not incompatible with cultural differences.

The relevance of the issue of dialect and cultural differences to the school is clear if we understand that the controversy in educating the black child has completely ignored the legitimacy of the ghetto culture. Of course, those few Negroes in integrated schools may well be better achievers. Not because they are sitting beside a white student but because standard English is the lingua franca of their environment. Massive bussing does not provide a practical educational solution to the failure of lower-class Negro children to learn to read. Black children may learn in all black schools if their teachers help them translate (not read) standard English. The problem with the More Effective Schools approach is that it too is not necessarily innovative educationally. The MES Solution stresses more of the same, i.e., smaller classes doing the same thing that larger classes had been doing previously. However Negro children do not need as their first priority smaller classes, intensive social programs, etc. What they need most is an educational system that first recognizes their abilities and their culture, that draws upon these strengths, and that incorporates them into the teaching process.

The white man should not be afraid of feeling that a Negro is different from his white brother. To be different is not to be inferior, or superior. Racial harmony can occur if the black man "tells it as it is" and the white man understands him as he is. One should not become annoyed with the Negro for failing to mold himself to our distorted vision. We can not blame him for being unable to learn when we have not yet learned how to teach him. Our social system says to the Negro, "If you want to make it in the white world you have to deny your self and your culture." It can be done. He can move into the white world, but with bitterness and impotence as the end products. The white world has kept the black man segregated in ghettos and hence insured the development in isolation of a visible and often beautiful language and culture. Let us not in our haste demand the destruction of the culture and the man as the price of integration. Rather, let us allow each culture to adapt to the other (a privilege we have allowed every other minority group). Social assimilation comes from shared knowledge. The past few summers have demonstrated that the white world has much to learn about the black world in a short time. We have to meet the Negro in his world; explore his ghetto for its strengths; and understand the processes whereby this seemingly wicked environment sustains a viable culture. We must not confuse the ghetto environment with the culture flourishing in it. We should be open to the world as seen by the black man and not demand his changes as the price of acculturation. We have perpetuated the dependence of a "child people" by our lack of understanding. It is time to relinquish this arrogant parental role and see the emergence of a beautiful culture too long held in the cocoon of our ignorance.

26.

Bi-Dialectalism: The Linguistics of White Supremacy

James Sledd

Because people who rarely talk together will talk differently, differences in speech tell what groups a man belongs to. He uses them to claim and proclaim his identity, and society uses them to keep him under control. The person who talks right, as we do, is one of us. The person who talks wrong is an outsider, strange and suspicious, and we must make him feel inferior if we can. That is one purpose of education. In a school system run like ours by white businessmen, instruction in the mother tongue includes formal initiation into the linguistic prejudices of the middle class.

Making children who talk wrong get right with the world has traditionally been the work of English teachers, and more recently of teachers of that strange conglomerate subject which we call speech. The English teacher in the role of linguistic censor was once a kind of folk heroine (or anti-heroine), the Miss Fidditch of the linguists' diatribes. Miss Fidditch believed in taking a strong stand. It never occurred to her that her main job was making the lower classes feel so low that they would try to climb higher. Instead, Miss Fidditch taught generations of schoolchildren, including future linguists, to avoid *ain't* and double negatives and *used to could* and *hadn't ought*, not because *ain't* would keep them from getting ahead in the world, but because *ain't* was wrong, no matter who used it, and deserved no encouragement from decent people who valued the English language. She did her job all the better for thinking that she was doing something else.

Miss Fidditch is not popular any longer among educators. Though the world at large is still inclined to agree with her, the vulgarizers of linguistics drove her out of the academic fashion years ago, when they replaced her misguided idealism with open-eyed hypocrisy. To the popular linguists, one kind of Eng-

---

From the *English Journal* 58:1307-1315 (December 1969).

lish is as good as another, and judgments to the contrary are only folklore; but since the object of life in the U.S.A. is for everybody to get ahead of everybody else, and since linguistic prejudice can keep a man from moving up to Schlitz, the linguists still teach that people who want to be decision-makers had better talk and write like the people who make decisions. The schools must therefore continue to cultivate the linguistic insecurity which is already a national characteristic but must teach the youngsters to manipulate that as they manipulate everything else; for neither Miss Fidditch's dream of a language intrinsically good, nor a humbler ideal of realizing the various potentialities of the existing language in its responsible use, can get in the way of the citizenry in its upward anguish through the pecking order. The linguists think that people who do knowingly what Miss Fidditch did in her innocence, will do it more efficiently, as if eating the apple made a skilled worker out of Eve.

As long as most people agreed that up is toward Schlitz and another TV set, and as long as they could pretend that every American eaglet can soar to those great heights, Fidditch McFidditch the dialectologist could enforce the speech-taboos of the great white middle class without complaint: either the child learned the taboos and observed them, or he was systematically penalized. But the damage done to the Wasps' nest by World War II made difficulties. People who talked all wrong, and especially black people, began to ask for their share of the loot in a world that had given them an argument by calling itself free, while a minority of the people who talked right began to bad-mouth respectability and joined the blacks in arguing that it was time for a real change. Some black people burned up the black parts of town, and some students made study impossible at the universities, and in general there was a Crisis. Optimists even talked of a revolution.

The predictable response of the frightened white businessman's society was to go right on doing what it had done before—which had caused the crisis—but to do it harder and to spend more money at it. Education was no exception. Government and the foundations began to spray money over the academic landscape like liquid fertilizer, and the professional societies began to bray and paw at the rich new grass. In that proud hour, any teacher who could dream up an expensive scheme for keeping things as they were while pretending to make a change was sure of becoming the director of a project or a center and of flying first-class to Washington twice a month. The white businessman strengthened his control of the educational system while giving the impression of vast humanitarian activity.

Black English provided the most lucrative new industry for white linguists, who found the mother lode when they discovered the interesting locutions which the less protected employ to the detriment of their chances for upward mobility. In the annals of free enterprise, the early sixties will be memorable for the invention of functional bi-dialectalism, a scheme best described by an elderly and unregenerate Southern dame as "turning black trash into white trash." Despite some signs of wear, this cloak for white supremacy has kept its shape for almost a decade now, and it is best described in the inimitable words of those who made it. Otherwise the description might be dismissed as a malicious caricature.

The basic assumption of bi-dialectalism is that the prejudices of middle-class whites cannot be changed but must be accepted and indeed enforced on lesser breeds. Upward mobility, it is assumed, is the end of education, but white power will deny upward mobility to speakers of black English, who must therefore be made to talk white English in their contacts with the white world.

An adequate florilegium may be assembled from a volume entitled *Social Dialects and Language Learning* (NCTE, 1964), the proceedings of a conference of bi-dialectalists which was held in 1964. William A. Stewart of the Center for Applied Linguistics begins the chorus (p. 13) by observing among our educators "a commendable desire to emphasize the potential of the Negro to be identical to white Americans"—a desire which is apparently not overwhelming, however, among the Black Muslims or among the young men who have enjoyed pot-shooting policemen for the past few summers. Editor Roger W. Shuy next speaks up (p. 53) for social climbing by our American Indians, who have been notably reluctant, throughout their unfortunate association with their conquerors, to adopt our conquering ways. Our linguistic studies, Shuy remarks in the purest accents of fidditchery, "should reveal those elements, both in speech and writing, which prevent Indians from attaining the social status which, with socially acceptable language, they might otherwise attain." A similiar desire to be at peace with status-holders is suggested (p. 66) by Ruth I. Golden, who opines that "a human being wants most of all to be recognized as an individual, to be accepted, and to be approved." Since Southern speech brings "negative reactions when heard by employers in Detroit," where Dr. Golden labors in the schools, she devotes herself to stamping out /i/ for /e/ in *penny* and to restoring /l/ in *help* (pp. 63 f.).

An admirable scholar from New York, William Labov, then agrees (p. 88) that "recognition of an external standard of correctness is an inevitable accompaniment of upward social aspirations and upward social mobility," and advises that people who (like Jesus) prefer not to take excessive thought for the morrow can probably be made to. In Labov's own words, "since the homes of many lower class and working people do not provide the pressures toward upward social mobility that middle-class homes provide," and since adults in those lower reaches are sometimes resistant to middle-class values, we must "build into the community a tolerance for style shifting which is helpful in educational and occupational advancement," and we must build into the children, "starting from a level not much above the nursery school and going on through high school, a tolerance for practice in second role playing" (pp. 94-97, 104).

Presumably Labov sees nothing wrong in thus initiating children into the world of hypercorrection, insecurity, and "linguistic self-hatred" which marks, as he has said elsewhere, "the average New Yorker" *(The Social Stratification of English in New York City*, Center for Applied Linguistics, 1966, Chapter XIII); and Charles Ferguson, the eminent ex-director of the Center for Applied Linguistics, is equally confident of *his* right and duty to remake his fellow men in his directorial image. Talking about the Negroes in our Northern cities, Ferguson says that "we have to face a rather difficult decision as to whether we want to make these people bi-dialectal. . . [please to remark Ferguson's choice of verbs] or whether we want. . . to impose some kind of standard English on these people and to eradicate the kind of substandard English they speak" (p. 116). To cite another NCTE volume *(Language Programs for the Disadvantaged* [NCTE, 1965], p. 222), if the black children of the ghetto "do not learn a second kind of dialect, they will be forever prevented from access to economic opportunity and social acceptance." Middle-class white prejudice will rule eternally.

The bi-dialectalists, of course, would not be so popular with government and the foundations if they spoke openly of the supremacy of white prejudice; but they make it perfectly clear that what they are dealing with deserves no better name. No dialect, they keep repeating, is better than any other—yet poor and ignorant children must change theirs unless they want to stay poor and ignorant. When an NCTE "Task Force" set out to devise *Language Programs for the Disadvantaged* (NCTE, 1965), it laid down a perfect smoke screen of such hypocrisy, as one would expect from persons who felt called upon to inform the world that "without the experience of literature, the individual is denied the very dignity that makes him human" (p. v) but that not "all disadvantaged children are apathetic or dull" (pp. 24 f.).

"In this report" (p. 117), "teachers are asked to begin by accepting the dialect of their students for what it is, one form of oral communication. . . " Teachers are warned particularly that they "need to accept the language which Negro children bring to school, to recognize that it is a perfectly appropriate vehicle for communicating ideas in the Negro home and subculture" (p. 215), that it is "essentially respectable and good" (p. 227). But though teachers must not attack "the dialect which children associate with their homes and their identity as Negroes" (p. 215), they must still use all the adult authority of the school to "teach standard informal English as a second dialect" (p. 137), because the youngster who cannot speak standard informal English "will not be able to get certain kinds of jobs" (p. 228).

The most common result of such teaching will be that white middle-class Midwestern speech will be imposed as mandatory for all those situations which middle-class white businessmen think it worth their while to regulate. In the words of Chicago's Professors Austin and McDavid (p. 245), "future educational programs should be developed in terms of substituting for the grammatical system of lower-class Southern speech [read: black Chicago speech] that of middle-class Chicago white speech—at least for those economic and social situations where grammatical norms are important." Labov goes so far as to ask *(Social Dialects and Language Learning,* p. 102*)* whether Northern schools should tolerate Southern speech at all—whether they should not also correct the "cultivated Southern speech" of privileged children who move North.

The description of compulsory bi-dialectalism may be completed by examining the methods which its proponents advocate for perpetuating the supremacy of white prejudice. Essentially, those methods are derived by analogy from structuralist methods of teaching foreign languages—methods whose superiority has been claimed but never demonstrated and whose intellectual foundations vanished with the demise of structuralist ideas. As an eminent grammarian privately observed after a recent conference, "The achievements of the operators will continue to lie in the field of getting and spending government money. . . . They seem to have an unerring instinct for finding ways of spending it unprofitably—on conferences at which they listen to each other, for example. Now they're out to teach standard English as a second dialect through techniques that have served very poorly in teaching second languages."

High on the list of those techniques is incessant drill on inessentials. In theory, the drills are the end-product of a long process of systematic comparison of the children's nonstandard dialects with the standard dialect which they are to be taught; but since the systematic comparisons have never been made, the bi-dialectalists fall back on a simple enumeration of a few dozen "features of pronunciation, grammar, and vocabulary which can be considered indices of social stratification" (Roger Shuy, "Detroit Speech," in A. L. Davis, ed., *On the Dialects of Children,* p. 13). Professor Rudolph Troike of the University of Texas was thus simply platitudinizing piously when he told the TESOL convention in 1968 that "any instructional program . . . must begin with as full an *objective* knowledge as possible" of both or all the dialects involved. The escape hatch in Troike's statement is the phrase *as full as possible.* What is usually possible is an unsystematic list of shibboleths— the simplification of consonant clusters, the Southern pronunciations *of walk* and *right, ax* for *ask*, the dropping of postvocalic /r/, *ain't* and *fixin' to, bofe* and *mouf* for *both* and *mouth*, and the like. These innocent usages, which are as familiar as the sun in the late Confederacy, are apparently the terror of Northern employers, who the bi-dialectalists assume are almost suicidally unconcerned with such details as character, intelligence, and training for the job. The fact is, of course, that Northern employers and labor leaders dislike black faces but use black English as an excuse.

Having established, however, that a child of darkness under her tutelage says *mouf*, the pretty white lady sets out to rescue his soul. First she plays tapes of Southern speech to convince her victims, who understand Southern speech far better than they understand hers, that Southern speech often makes "complete understanding of content . . . difficult," "not readily comprehensible"—as is demonstrated by the fact that the pretty white lady would never have detected her victim's four-letter word just by listening and without watching his lips (New York Board of Education, *Nonstandard Dialect*, pp. 1, 14, 17). The difficulty of detecting him is all the more reason for fearing the iniquitous *mouf* sayer: it proves he is a cunning devil who probably says *dentissoffice* too and who perpetrates such subversive "malapropisms" as "The food in the lunch room is not fitting to eat" (*On the Dialects of Children*, p. 23). How else *would* he spell *fitten?* But for such a hardened rogue, a good many "motivational activities" are likely to be necessary before the pretty white lady can really start twisting the thumbscrew with her drills.

Yet the drills are available, and the pretty white lady will use them when she sees her time. She has drills of all kinds—repetition drills, substitution drills, replacement drills, conversion drills, cued answer drills, the reading in unison of long list of words like *teeth / reef, toothbrush / waffle, bathtub / alphabet, weather / weaver*. To get rid of *dentissoffice*, she may have students debate such propositions as "Ghosts do exist" or "Formal school tests should be eliminated;" and before a really "culminating activity" like playing "Pack the Trunk" she may "divide the class into consonant-cluster committees to seek out words containing" clusters like *sks, sps*, or *kt (Nonstandard Dialect, passim)*. At this point the class might be invited to suggest a context for a replacement drill—maybe something like "Teacher! teacher! Billy Joe say that Tommy———— Bessy!" This last suggestion, it must be confessed, has not yet been made in the literature, but it seems considerably more stimulating than choral recitation of Poe's "Bells" *(ibid.*, p. 35*)*.

Perhaps it need not be added that existing tests and evaluations of such "instructional materials" are something of a farce. If bi-dialectalism is really harder to acquire than bilingualism (Einar Haugen in *Social Dialects and Language Learning*, p. 125), teachers and texts ought surely to be superb, and judgments on them ought to be severe; but New York City's curriculum developers can give "highest priority" to making the children change *a* to *an* before nouns beginning with a vowel (*Nonstandard Dialect*, p. 14), and Texas' Professor Troike can argue the success of his methods by showing that after six months of drills a little black girl could repeat *his hat* after her teacher, instead of translating automatically to *he hat*. Unfortunately tapes do not record psychological damage, or compare the effectiveness of other ways of teaching, or show what might better have been learned in the same time instead of learning to repeat *his hat*.

So much for a description of mandatory bi-dialectalism, a bit enlivened (since the subject is dreary) by irreverent comment, but not distorted in any essential way. In the U. S. A., we are being told, everybody wants approval—

not approval for doing anything worth approving, but approval for doing whatever happens to be approved. Because approval goes to upward mobility, everybody should be upwardly mobile; and because upward mobility is impossible for underdogs who have not learned middle-dog barking, we must teach it to them for use in their excursions into the middle-dog world. There is no possibility either that the present middle class can be brought to tolerate lower-class English or that upward mobility, as a national aspiration, will be questioned. Those are the pillars on which the state is built, and the compassionate teacher, knowing the ways of his society, will change the color of his students' vowels although he cannot change the color of their skins.

It is not at all certain that the bi-dialectalists, for all their absurdities, can be dislodged from their well-carpeted offices. They are supported by the National Council of Teachers of English, the Modern Language Association of America, the Center for Applied Linguistics, the federal government, the foundations, the governments of a number of major cities, and by black people who have made it into the middle class and so despise their origins and their less efficient fellows. In the best of times our top dogs are pleased by docility, if not mobility, among the beasts below; and in 1969 a new ice age is beginning. Newspaper headlines tell us that the Department of Health, Education, and Welfare has been urged to relax its requirements for desegregation of schools immediately but quietly, and President Nixon loses his Miami tan at the thought that militant students will "politicize" our universities—as if government grants to upwardly mobile faculty had not politicized them long ago. In Lyndon Johnson's Texas the citizens of Austin vote down an open housing law, their board of education then justifies segregated schooling by the established pattern of segregated housing, and the governor of the state praises the state university as the source of brain-power to assist the businessman in the lucrative exploitation of what the governor proudly calls the "insatiable appetite" of Texans. The only revolution we are likely to see is the continued subversion, by the dominant white businessman, of the political and religious principles on which the nation was founded.

Yet though the times are bad, they are not hopeless, at least not in the small, undramatic world of English education; and the bi-dialectalists are so gorgeously absurd that the breath of laughter may collapse their card-house if only enough people can be brought to see it as it is. It is not simply quixotic, then, to add to a laughing description of imposed bi-dialectalism a more serious statement of reasons why it cannot succeed and should not be tolerated even if it could—a statement which can lead, in conclusion, to the proposing of an alternative policy.

The argument that bi-dialectalism cannot be forced is easy to make out, even, in part, from the reluctant admissions of some of its proponents. Two principal reasons have already been suggested, the ignorance and unproved methods of the bi-dialectalists. The term *ignorance* is used literally, and in all fairness. Whatever one thinks of teaching standard English by methods like those for teaching foreign languages, contrastive analyses of our different dialects are a prerequisite—but a prerequisite which has not yet been supplied. Until very recently, the principal sources of information were the collections for the *Linguistic Atlas;* but they are unsystematic, partially out-of-date, and in some respects inaccurate and superficial. Where, for example, should one go for descriptions of intonation and its dialectal variants, for accurate accounts of the system or systems of verbal auxiliaries, for analyses of the speech of ghetto children instead of rustic ancients? Such minimal essentials are simply lacking. In fact, it might be said that for all the talk about revolutionary advances in linguistics, neither the structural nor the generative grammarians have yet produced a satisfactory basic description of even standard English.

The best descriptions of all our kinds of English would still not be enough to make coercive bi-dialectalism a success. The English teacher's forty-five minutes a day for five days in the week will never counteract the influence, and sometimes the hostility, of playmates and friends and family during much the larger part of the student's time. Formal education could produce real bi-dialectals only in a vast system of state nurseries and boarding schools to which the children of the poor and ignorant would be consigned at an early age; but such establishments would be prohibitively expensive, intolerable to the people, and still not absolutely certain of success, because the most essential of all conditions might not be met—namely, the desire of the children to talk like the white middle class.

When one thinks about it in these realistic terms, the whole argument about bi-dialectalism begins to look schizophrenic, as out-of-this-world as an argument whether Lee should surrender at Appomattox or fight back. There is no evidence that the bi-dialectalists, if they actually had good textbooks, better teachers, and as much money as the country is spending to devastate Vietnam, would really know what to do with those fictional resources. Instead of clear ideas, they offer cliches, like the familiar attacks on "traditional methods and approaches" or the protected pedagogue's arrogant assurance that illiterates can have no human dignity. They fly off quickly into high-sounding vaguenesses, talking (for example) about "differences in social dialect and associated versions of reality" (*Social Dialects and Language Learning*, p. 68), as if metaphysics rested on a preconsonantal /r/. At their most precise, they suggest the prudential avoidance of Southern pronunciations of *walk* and *cough* in Washington because Negroes there look down on new arrivals from Georgia and the Carolinas. They happily assume what they should prove—that intensive training in "standard informal English as a second dialect" has produced or can produce large numbers of psychologically undamaged bi-dialectals, whose new accomplishment has won them or will win them jobs that otherwise would have been impossible for them to get. When their guard is down, the bi-dialectists actually confess that they *have* no concrete program, since "no one program at any level yet seems applicable to a significant number of other classes at the respective level" (*Language Programs for the Disadvantaged*, pp. 30 ff.).

Some awareness of their difficulties, and some uncertainty about priorities, seem indeed to be spreading among the bi-dialectalists (though it would be too much to hope that if their present bandwagon falls apart they will consider themselves discredited and resign their membership in the Society of Mandarin.) For one thing, they have become aware of the significance of reading, which William A. Stewart, as late as 1964, could reduce to the level of "socially desirable embellishments" (*Social Dialects and Language Learning*, p. 10). In his latest book, however, *Teaching Black Children To Read*, Editor Shuy announces "the simple truth that speaking standard English, however desirable it may be, is not as important as learning to read" (p. 118). His colleagues Walter A. Wolfram and Ralph W. Fasold are even closer to enlightenment. In the same new volume (p. 143), they hesitantly admit that "there is some question about the degree to which Standard English can be taught to the ghetto child in the classroom at all"; and Fasold meant what he said, for he had said it before at the Milwaukee convention of the NCTE. Though that august body was still congratulating itself on its concern with "a language component for the so-called culturally divergent," it had to bear with Fasold's embarrassing confession: "Because of the operation of social forces in the use of language," he said, "forces which are only poorly understood, it may not be possible to teach Standard English as a second language to Black English speaking children unless they are interacting with Standard English speakers in a meaningful way outside the classroom" (*Convention Concerns—1968*, p. 10). The Center's linguistician came as close as standard English would allow to saying that it is segregation which makes black people talk different and that there would be no slum children if there were no slums.

No doubt the most important of Fasold's poorly understood social forces is one which everybody but white linguists has understood for a long time: black people may just not want to talk white English. Several years ago, Labov observed that some of his more rebellious New York subjects were deliberately turning away from social-climbing New York speech toward a black Southern model (*Social Dialects and Language Learning*, pp. 96 f.), and today comment on "the new feeling of racial pride among black Americans" (*Teaching Black Children to Read*, p. 142) is a platitude. Wolfram and Fasold go on to the quite unsurprising speculation that that pride may even extend to the Negro's speech. "If a realization develops that this dialect, an important part of black culture, is as distinctively Afro-American as anything in the culture, the result may well be a new respect for Black English within the community" (p. 143). More plainly, condescending middle-class white charity is not wanted any more, if it ever was, in language-teaching or anywhere else. We should learn from the example of the British: the social cataclysm of the Second World War, and the achievement of political power by labor, did more to give the "disadvantaged" English youngster an equal chance than charitable bi-dialectalism ever did. We are past the stage when white teachers, whether Africans or Caucasians, can think well of themselves for trying to turn black people into uneasy imitations of the whites.

The immorality of that effort is the chief reason why enforced bi-dialectalism should not be tolerated even if it were possible. Predators can and do use dialect differences to exploit and oppress, because ordinary people can be made to doubt their own value and to accept subservience if they can be made to despise the speech of their fathers. Obligatory bi-dialectalism for minorities is only another mode of exploitation, another way of making blacks behave as whites would like them to. It is unnecessary for communication, since the ability to understand other dialects is easily attained, as the black child shows when she translates her teacher's prissy white model *"his hat"* into *"he hat."* Its psychological consequences are likely to be nervous affectation, self-distrust, dislike for everyone not equally afflicted with the itch to get ahead, and eventual frustration by the discovery that the reward for so much suffering is intolerably small. At best the altered student will get a somewhat better job and will move up a few places in the rat-race of the underlings. At worst he will be cut off from other blacks, still not accepted among whites, and economically no better off than he was before.

White teachers should hope, then, that their black students will be recalcitrant, so that bi-dialectalism as a unilateral condition for employment can be forgotten. It would make better sense, if pedagogues insist on living in a fantasy world, to require whites to speak black English in their dealings with blacks, since the whites have more advantages than the blacks and consider themselves more intelligent; or perhaps we should be hard-headedly consistent in our brutalities and try to eradicate the vices which really do enrage employers—like intellectual questioning, or the suspicion that ours is not the best of possible worlds.

Indeed, the educationists' faith in education would be touching if it were not their way of keeping up their wages. Nothing the schools can do about black English or white English either will do much for racial peace and social justice as long as the black and white worlds are separate and hostile. The measure of our educational absurdity is the necessity of saying once again that regimented bi-dialectalism is no substitute for sweeping social change—*necessity* being defined by the alternative of dropping out and waiting quietly for destruction if the white businessman continues to have his way.

The reply that the educational system should not be politicized is impossible for bi-dialectalists, since bi-dialectalism is itself a political instrument. They may purge themselves of inconsistency, and do what little good is possible for English teachers as political reformers, if instead of teaching standard English as a second dialect they teach getting out of Vietnam, getting out of the missile race, and stopping the deadly pollution of the one world we have, as horribly exemplified by the current vandalism in Alaska.

One use for a small fraction of the resources that would thus be saved would be to improve the teaching of the English language. Bi-dialectalism would never have been invented if our society were not divided into the dominant white majority and the exploited minorities. Children should be taught that. They should be taught the relations between group differences and speech differences, and the good and bad uses of speech differences by groups and by individuals. The teaching would require a more serious study of grammar, lexicography, dialectology, and linguistic history than our educational system now provides—require it at least of prospective English teachers.

In the immediate present, the time and money now wasted on bi-dialectalism should be spent on teaching the children of the minorities to read. Already some of the universal experts among the linguists have boarded this new bandwagon, and the next round of government grants may very well be for programs in reading and writing in black English. That might be a good thing, particularly if we could somehow get rid of the tired little clique of operators who have run the professional societies of English teachers for so long. Anyway, the direct attack on minority language, the attempt to compel bi-dialectalism, should be abandoned for an attempt to open the minds and enhance the lives of the poor and ignorant. At the same time, every attempt should be made to teach the majority to understand the life and language of the oppressed. Linguistic change is the effect and not the cause of social change. If the majority can rid itself of its prejudices, and if the minorities can get or be given an education, differences between dialects are unlikely to hurt anybody much.

(The phoniest objections to this proposal will be those that talk about social realism, about the necessity for doing something even—or should one say particularly?—if it's wrong. That kind of talk makes real change impossible, but makes money for bi-dialectalists.)

27. Mexican-Americans and Language Learning

Richard D. Arnold and Thomasine H. Taylor

One and nine-tenths of the population of the United States is made up of persons with Spanish surnames. They live in various geographic areas but are concentrated primarily in the Southwest. In south Texas they represent the majority ethnic group.

School failure of Spanish-speaking children provides cause for concern to their parents and to educators alike. As of 1962, 82 percent of these children "failed" in their first year of school; their high school dropout rate was twice that of Anglo-Americans, and they dropped out earlier.[36] Today these data are being viewed from new perspectives by educators concerned with valuing cultural diversity. They are asking, "Does the alleged retardation of the Spanish-speaking child really represent, at least in part, inadequacies within the school systems that fail to reach him?"

As one way of attacking the problem, many programs are concentrating on first and second language development activities for Spanish-speaking children, in the belief that language deficiency is a major barrier to their academic growth in school. Low socioeconomic status and general social deprivation are also considered important contributing factors that compound the language problem of many Mexican-American children.

The literature is filled with descriptions of "experimental" studies and opinions as to good methodological approaches to teaching Mexican-American children, but there is disagreement among the leaders in this field. For example, a considerable difference of opinion was expressed between representatives of California and Texas in a recent seminar at the University of Texas at Austin. Further, numerous meetings held at the national level bog down in semantics, often resulting in hampered progress because of decision-making based on opinion and poor dissemination of few empirical findings. While it is recognized that experimentation must start somewhere, hopefully efforts will go beyond the reporting of what school systems "think" is good.

From *Childhood Education* 46:149-154 (December 1969). Reprinted by permission of Richard D. Arnold and Thomasine H. Taylor and the Association for Childhood Education International, 3615 Wisconsin Avenue, N.W., Washington, D.C.

Native Language Acquisition

Unless physically handicapped in some way, all learners of language have the same physiological equipment with which to speak.[37] Development from unintelligible infant noises to meaningful speech in the native tongue follows a sequential pattern,[38] with a significant landmark in terms of meaning and understanding occurring when the child understands utterances from intonation.[39] How a child learns to put sentences together and learns language rules is unknown. Chomsky feels this is a human "species-specific" ability that defies any known explanation at present.[40] Generally, linguists feel that when children enter school they have internalized their native language and use it automatically and creatively without thinking about it—thereby being able to communicate in their native speech environment even though it may be different from the speech used in the school.

Second Language Acquisition

The sequence outlined above has yet to be observed in the acquisition of a second language. Learners must have something to say; they can invent the message but not the language with which to communicate it.[41]

Lado claims that each language has its own habits, conscious and subconscious.[42] To change any part of the language habit—be it an emotional, muscular or intellectual process—is a major undertaking; to set up a parallel system for learning a new language is a formidable task. Fortunately, some native language patterns or habits often can be used to help teach another language. Where the components of the languages are complementary, little difficulty for the learner should be expected. Where the languages differ greatly, learning a second language becomes more difficult and contrastive analyses assist in determining how to help children learn in special problem areas.

With younger children untaught analogy functions liberally in acquiring the mother tongue as well as the second language.[43] Frequent pattern practice that is related to analogy is an effective learning tool because it depends upon the reaction to hidden samenesses as contrasted with minimal differences.[44] Slot substitution, where all words but one in a particular structure are held constant, is a recommended technique in teaching by analogy. An example is a simple statement with the noun being the slot to teach other nouns: "The (*lamp*) is on the table," "The (*book*) is on the table."[45]

Fluency in a second language depends to a large degree on previously learned, modelled utterances that may be recalled in a specific situation. Sentences or utterances that have been learned in connection with specific situations are likely to suggest themselves again as models in similar situations; thus, content used is vital in language learning. Sentences and utterances learned which have not been associated with meaningful experiences are not likely to occur to the learner again.

The San Antonio Language Project: An Example

A program dealing with language learning of Mexican-Americans was conducted in San Antonio, Texas.[46] The primary purpose of the five-year longitudinal study was to compare three treatment groups: intensive oral-aural English, intensive oral-aural Spanish, and various control groups.

Five main line research studies followed Sample I children for five years and Sample II children, a replication of the study beginning in 1965, for four years.

Results of Horn's study for Year I identified no significant differences among treatment groups.[47] Problems of instrumentation for the target population were then stressed. Year II results revealed that the experimental treatments at second-grade level were essentially ineffective, while the first-grade replication suggested the English treatment to be somewhat superior.[48] Year III results showed inconsistencies at the third-grade level slightly favoring the control treatment.[49] The second-grade replication generally revealed findings favoring the English treatment. Preliminary findings from Year IV indicate that the English treatment excelled at the fourth-grade level, while at the third-grade level generally the control treatment appeared best.[50] Even though control was exercised through analysis of covariance, wide differences in intelligence favored the control treatment and tended to mitigate the findings. The criteria for the first four years of the research were usually intelligence, reading, and reading related tests.

In Year V the criterion measure was oral language proficiency.[51] In fifth grade the Spanish treatment generally excelled, and in the fourth grade the tendency to favor the Spanish treatment was also somewhat apparent. Ancillary studies by Ott and Arnold were supportive of the experimental treatments in terms of language growth in English at the first-grade level and retention in reading over the summer months between second and third grades.[52] Space does not permit discussion of other relevant studies and articles.[53]

Suggestions for Teaching Techniques

Many of the teaching techniques used in the San Antonio Research Project were adapted and modified to fit the Mexican-American children. Such classic books as Lado, Brooks, Finocchiaro and various other sources such as FLES, MLA, and TESOL publications were used in the development of materials and teaching techniques.[54]

Some of the objectives of the five-year longitudinal study were: to teach language through academic content and experiences the school could provide; to use extensive pattern practice to teach habituation of basic language structures; to provide for informal, incidental language practice in other less structured content areas; and to improve self-concept. Several others are outlined in Horn's original U.S. office report and elaborated by Stemmler.[55]

The basic teaching techniques were teacher modeling, teacher cueing, and student response. The modeling-response procedure followed the sequence from the total group, to various smaller subgroups, to individual students. As the children matured in their language learning, new structures, transformations, and more difficult language processes were added. A few examples follow.

		Student Response
1) Teacher model:	This is a circle. (holds up her circle)	This is a circle. (holds up own circle)
Teacher cues:	Triangle	This is a triangle. (holds up triangle)
	Book	This is a book. (holds up a book)
2) Teacher questions:	Is this a house? (shows picture of house)	Yes, it is.
	Is this a moon? (shows picture of house)	No, it's not.

3) Pupils' dialogue with questions and answers using concrete objects and pictures

4) Pronoun Substitution		*Student Response*
Teacher model:	We made a picture.	We made a picture.
Teacher cues:	You	You made a picture.
	I	I made a picture.
	He	He made a picture.
	etc.	

5) Verb Tense Substitution		*Student Response*
Teacher model: (Pres. Prog.)	We are making a number line.	We are making a number line.
Teacher cues:		
(Past Prog.)	were making	We were making a number line.
(Past)	made	We made a number line.
(Future)	will make	We will make a number line.
	etc.	

Similar models and cues were used with other linguistic elements. Progressive substitution is one of the more difficult procedures used in later grades.

		Student Response
Teacher model:	We made a time line.	We made a time line.
Teacher cues:	They	They made a time line.
	will make	They will make a time line
	some	They will make some time lines.
	We	We will make some time lines.
	blue	We will make some blue time lines.
	arrows	We will make some blue arrows.

The original project reported herein is being continued and modified by the Southwest Educational Development Laboratory (further information can be obtained from Edwin Hindsman or Elizabeth Ott). The Regional Laboratory is also developing and pilot testing a bilingual reading program to complement the language program described.[56]

Summary

While it is acknowledged that the traditional methods of teaching language and reading have been unsuccessful in the past, no precise teaching methodology to use with Mexican-American children has yet been agreed upon. Pattern practice, coupled with meaningful learning situations, appears most promising, along with the use of analogy and incidental learning situations in content areas controlled by the school. General and specific examples of techniques for teaching Mexican-American children have been cited. But beyond any methodology, the school and the teacher must come to know the children, to understand their language strengths and weaknesses, as well as the total social and cultural milieu in which they live both in and out of school. The challenge then for effective growth in learning lies with the informed, accepting, creative, and hard-working teacher.

Editor's note: For a very different approach to furthering language growth and valuing the cultural diversity of children of Mexican descent, readers are urged to see Luis F. Hernandez' pamphlet, *A Forgotten American: A Resource Unit for Teachers of the Mexican American* (Anti-Defamation League of B'nai B'rith, 1969—315 Lexington Avenue, New York, New York 10016. 75¢. Mr. Hernandez, assistant professor of Education at San Fernando Valley State College and a Los Angeles public school teacher for over ten years is consultant to the Mexican American Studies Program of the Los Angeles city schools.

His study, developed pursuant to a grant from the U.S. Office of Education Department of Health, Education and Welfare, affords teachers many insights into the background, acculturation, value-systems, and family life of Mexican American students. Included are some practical suggestions for positive approaches in the classroom, recommended readings and sources of information, and a good short chronological outline of Mexican history.

28.
Language Learning at Rough Rock

Virginia Hoffman

"Lamb it for fence I can make . . . Mud it can make house like that one." The nine-year-old Navajo girl was talking eagerly as she walked around the teacher work center looking at photographs, toy animals and other objects. "My mother—he can brought back the furnitures from the Gallup," she said, talking of a trip her mother had made recently to the Navajo Reservation bordertown in New Mexico, where many reservation-dwellers go regularly to shop.

Darlene obviously loved to talk, and she continued to do so for more than an hour in her highly expressive—but mixed-up—brand of English.

It was August 1966, and the little girl was to enter the third grade at the new Rough Rock Demonstration School in September. Her typical Navajo version of English was as old as the Anglo-American school systems which have guided Navajo education for nearly 100 years.

Since the 1870's children like Darlene have left the warm family circle of their hogan camps to enter a foreign world—school. It has been a world where age-old Navajo beliefs and social rules have been considered valueless, if indeed they were even considered at all. Their Navajo language, too, has been virtually useless at school. It is still a rare teacher who encourages beginning school children to communicate in Navajo, the only language most children can speak when they enter reservation schools. This has been with good reason, too, for most teachers on the reservation are not Navajo and cannot speak the language. The school curriculum has been the same that Anglo-American children in the distant cities have had—immersion into the life and language of urban America.

Since the beginning of Navajo education, the children have faced rejection, either explicit or implicit, of their culture, language—and therefore of them, some psychologists observe—upon entering school. Darlene came to Rough Rock after several years in this typical educational situation, and she was a typical result of it as far as her academic progress showed. About to enter third grade at age nine, her achievement test scores indicated that she was already more than a year behind her Anglo-American counterparts at the same grade level. Typically this gap widens as the Navajo child continues through the elementary grades, and a high dropout rate before high school may well indicate

---

From *Childhood Education* 46:155-157 (December 1969). Reprinted by permission of Virginia Hoffman and the Association for Childhood Education International, 3615 Wisconsin Avenue, N.W., Washington, D.C.

the students' feelings toward school. Darlene had not learned fluent American English in spite of her love to talk and in spite of the total immersion policy.

Her probable future had already been experienced by thousands of Navajo children who went before her. Navajo sixteen-year-olds, overage and underachieving, commonly drop out of elementary school to become babysitters, school janitors, cooks, and similiar members of the Navajo working society. Many are needed at home to assist in the traditional farming and livestock enterprises of the Navajo people. They then face the myriad problems of people who would like some of the benefits of the general American society—a steady and livable income, electricity, running water and modern transportation—but who do not have the means to acquire them. They also often face the dubious courtesy of bordertown shopkeepers, some of whom equate nonfluent English with mental "retardation."

Either out to the general American society or back to the hogan and a per capita income of about $600 annually—such has been the implicit force behind the education of Darlene and 40,000 of her peers annually. Personal choice of the Navajo people has had little to do with it.

These youngsters have missed the education their parents would have provided them to help them become good Navajos, a highly valued but unachieved goal according to Navajo elders. Had they not been away at boarding school, many would have become knowledgeable medicine men, successful ranchers or skilled weavers. But they have not gained these skills, nor have they gained skills they need to operate successfully in the non-Indian world. Worse, they are poorly equipped to build a modern Navajo world of their own design. Only a rare few have become comfortable with skills they need so as to choose when, and where, and how they wish to function.

Rough Rock Demonstration School was about to change Darlene's school experience abruptly.

Indian education pioneer Robert A. Roessel, Jr., initiated the new school in 1966 with the idea that Navajo people have the right to a more hopeful future, that Navajo parents have both a right and an obligation to be involved in educational decision-making, that children need to have knowledge of and pride in their native heritage—rather than to have to face rejection of it. He worked closely with Navajo governmental leaders, who formed the first Navajo Board of Directors to oversee a Navajo Reservation school. Backed by funds from the Bureau of Indian Affairs and the Office of Economic Opportunity, they took the first step in the sparse and scattered community of Rough Rock, located at the Base of Black Mountain approximately fifty miles south of Monument Valley, Arizona. A local Board of Education was elected by the Navajo community, and Rough Rock opened its doors.

The innovations flowed in a steady stream, centered on parental involvement, community participation, and a curriculum that offers Navajo and Anglo-American curriculum content on equal footing. Parents, invited to come into the school whenever they wished, were encouraged to take part in the school's adult education program, which offers training in Navajo silverwork, rug-weaving, and other traditional arts and crafts, as well as standard American school subjects. Their own Navajo Board of Education asked them to come to school-community meetings so that ideas and decisions could come from the people being served. Because vast distances, poor roads, and limited means of transportation (many still use horsedrawn wagons) necessitated a boarding school situation, parents were hired to live in the dormitories with the children, and another "first" came out. Children returning from classrooms could walk into the dormitories and feel at home with familiar faces, language and custom. As

Dr. Roessel pointed out, being able to provide love for young children does not require a formal education and these parents filled a need long felt in dormitories. In the mornings parents walk with the children to breakfast and the classrooms. In the evenings they counsel, tell stories and mend clothes, just as they would in their own homes.

Qualified Navajos were sought as teachers and administrators to work side by side with non-Indian educators. After his second year as school director, Dr. Roessel handed his position to Dillon Platero, a recognized leader in Navajo education, chosen by the Board of Education.

But parental participation and Navajo decision-making were only part of the objective. The classroom came under close scrutiny as an environment that needed changing, if the children were to gain a good feeling about themselves through pride in their Navajo background. A Navajo Curriculum Center was initiated at the school, staffed by educators, Navajo artists and interpreters. Soon courses of study were evolving in Navajo culture, history and language. From the first day of school at Rough Rock, children have been able to walk into a classroom and find their ways and language not only accepted, but encouraged. At the same time, they began to learn English in a new way, through a systematic approach that encourages creative usage rather than parroted drill, a program contributed by Robert D. Wilson, linguistic consultant.

The curriculum center invited Navajo people to come in and tell the old stories Navajo children have loved for generations—coyote stories being special favorites. These stories become books printed in English to be used as supplementary reading material, as well as the basis for Navajo courses of study. *Coyote Stories* was followed by *Black Mountain Boy*, the true story of the boyhood of a Navajo medicine man known by many of the Rough Rock children. *Grandfather Stories* was next, and then came *Denetsosie*, the autobiography of a medicine man. *Lucy Learns To Weave* was published as the first of a primary reading series based on Navajo life. Two books for educators, *Navajo Education at Rough Rock* and *Oral English at Rough Rock* were other curriculum center projects. *Navajo Biographies*, the most comprehensive book about Navajo people from the center, was published this fall, designed to bring the lives of fifteen Navajo leaders from the eighteenth century through the present to upper elementary students. *Navajo History* is one of the center's current projects.

During the schools third year, an experimental Navajo reading program was developed, with Oswald Werner and Caleb Gattegno giving workshops and acting as consultants to the curriculum builders at Rough Rock. This program begins with first-year children who may be ready to read but who are not familiar enough with English to enter the English reading program and continues through the elementary levels. To Navajo parents, the important fact is that their children are learning to read and write their native language as well as their second language. In both Navajo and English language programs, a systematic approach to familiarization and usage is the key. Up-to-date programs in math, science and social studies are also part of the curriculum. But through all classrooms, the Navajo view of the universe is just as important a part of the curriculum as the standard American school courses in science and social studies. Primary children have all subjects, except English language study, in the Navajo language. When they reach upper primary levels, they continue the courses using English as the language of communication.

For Darlene, Rough Rock Demonstration School meant that she could communicate fluently and freely in her own language with her teacher, a Navajo. She gained standard American English fluency through daily lessons and also began to explore in her native language the wealth of cultural knowledge the Navajos possess. Darlene's bilingual, bicultural school experience resulted in a 3.8 grade level achievement on a standardized test at the end of her first year at Rough Rock, a marked improvement in nine months' time.

She and her classmates are no longer passive recipients in an Anglo-American-oriented school program. They take field trips to off-reservation cities where they delight in shopping in modern shopping centers and where they speak fluent English with the sales people. They keep up with the latest developments in hair and clothing fashion in their home economics class. The boys gain practical skills in shop class and in 4-H livestock projects and are especially enthusiastic basketball players. But they also listen with keen interest to their Navajo teachers and respected older community members, who speak to them in class about their own Navajo history and their highly refined traditional view of the universe. They wear traditional Navajo clothing with pride when school occasions call for it, and they use their best Navajo manners in showing parents through the school on community days. The student newspaper publishes stories written in both languages, some in English and others in Navajo. The important point is that the children now have an opportunity to choose which language they wish to use and when they wish to use it. They are at ease in both.

Another happy result may also be forthcoming from using the youngsters' native culture as the foundation for their education. During a trial run with *Navajo Biographies* in one upper-level Navajo history class, the students were discussing the early nineteenth century period, when Spain dominated the Southwest. One boy observed, "Yes, but this is all about us Navajos. What was going on in the rest of the country?"

Many teachers on the Navajo Reservation would find a question like that a delight equal to a month's extra pay. At Rough Rock such academic curiousity is less of a surprise with each passing week.

Other indicators of Rough Rock's success appear, too. Parents feel welcome to give ideas and often make excellent suggestions. A parent-teacher-child "learn-in" has been initiated, with parents recommending to teachers what they would like to teach their children at home for a week. Navajo botany was one such suggestion, a traditional study as refined and as complex as any standard text on the subject. All involved in the trial run of this program vowed it such a success that it has been instituted as a regular part of the curriculum. Each semester for one week, children, parents and teachers confer and particpate in teaching the children in their homes. Several specific objectives are decided for each "learn-in," and thorough evaluation of the home study takes place with the participants after the week is over.

Navajo parents are employed at every level of the school's operation, whether or not they are fluent in English, an economic opportunity hitherto unavailable at most reservation schools. Thus encouraged, the parents respond by encouraging their own children to continue in education. Rough Rock's dropout rate today is nonexistent. Another indicator of success may be in the way the spark is catching. Hundreds of Navajo parents from all over the 25,000-square-mile reservation attended a two-day school board conference sponsored by Rough Rock Demonstration School last spring. Their keenest interest was in finding out how they might make the schools in their own communities Navajo schools like Rough Rock.

Typical of Rough Rock's appeal to the community it serves was the 1969 summer program. Based on success of the 1968 summer program, school administrators opened two additional "schools" away from the main school—using as classrooms brush shelters at hogan camps miles from the main school. Teachers who expected twenty children at each field school faced more than fifty each on the first morning of class, and things continued this way. Success of the summer school and regular program is in no small way due to the dedication of Rough Rock teachers, who are called on to design the curriculum, guide many extra-curricular activities of children, visit homes of children, and teach as well.

It is still early to judge Rough Rock's approach fairly, but two major points stand in its favor: (1) the Navajo people themselves are closely involved in the education of their own children and (2) at last a Navajo school has totally dedicated itself to experimentation and to documentation of the experimentation for the benefit of the total Navajo community. Present indications are that Rough Rock Demonstration School may be the most hopeful step forward in a century of Navajo education.

C.
Language Teaching

Each year there is a growing body of students in our schools for whom English is not the mother tongue. An increasing number of children are speaking the language of American Indians, Mexican-Americans, Cuban exiles, or Puerto Rican-Americans. Most of these children are faced with the task of learning English as a second language. Those students speaking a nonstandard dialect of a particular social class constitute an even larger element among the student population. They are found in most of our classrooms. What techniques can be used by the schools to help these students cope with the learning problems inherent in their multi-linguistic environment?

There are, as was forcefully asserted in the preceding section, scholars who believe that there is little merit in commencing with standard English in attempting to teach language skills to children who speak a different social class dialect. Rather, these scholars advocate accepting the validity of a child's native speech and culture and using them to develop beginning reading materials. Research shows that the foreign-speaking child learns English best if he first learns the concepts in his native language and then learns the English words for these concepts. Although the simultaneous acquisition of both languages is deemed ideal for producing literate, well-adjusted bilingual children, its cost has, however, negated its wide adoption.

While recognizing the limitations on a child's language development that are imposed by a culturally restricted environment, we must nevertheless, attempt without reluctance to improve his language habits. Assuming these specific goals, considerable disagreement may arise concerning the methodologies by which they may be most effectively achieved. Patterned drill, "modeling," and more eclectic approaches to teaching language are being discussed in the literature. The philosophy and method that an individual teacher adopts vary with the social attitudes and prior experiences of that teacher. These factors determine whether he prescribes the language of educated persons or orients his instruction toward the descriptive potential of the learners. Which of these theoretical positions is adopted depends on whether the teacher believes that the dialect offers a complete system of communication. As the following articles suggest, each of these polar positions has its scholarly advocates.

29.

An Approach to Language Learning

Celia Stendler Lavatelli

A noted authority on the study of language has said, "The ability to learn language is so deeply rooted in man that children learn it even in the face of dramatic handicaps." The grammar that they acquire may not be the King's English, but even children from impoverished, disorganized homes know and use all parts of speech by the time they enter kindergarten. Their very mistakes reveal that they have acquired the rules. When a child says "footses" for "feet," he is revealing a knowledge of one of our rules of forming plurals; he is simply not aware of all the exceptions.

But despite the child's natural capacity for language and his remarkable progress in this area in a few years time, the school must assume considerable responsibility for language development. Children need help in making words do what they want them to do—namely, to express ideas clearly. And in the search for the right words to express ideas, children may also find that ideas lose some of their fuzziness and become clearer and more logical. Thought and language are interrelated; language is "the handmaiden of thought," as Vygotsky put it, but thought also serves language.

Piaget's recent work on the development of causality is interesting in this connection.[57] He describes three stages in the young child's thinking about causality. In the first stage, explanations tend to be "finalistic;" that is, the child finds purpose in natural events. Asked why water flows downhill, he says, "because it has to go into the lake." In the second stage, explanations are characterized by "dynamism;" the child attributes a kind of animate power to water, and the water flows downhill "because it has movement."

Later, in the third stage, the child gives mechanistic explanations; water flows downhill "because it is heavy" or "because of gravity." Note that the word "because" appears in all three explanations. The use of the word does not denote that the child in this case has an accurate notion of causality; he uses "because" in a very loose way to denote a relationship between ideas which may or may not be causal.

Early childhood curricula typically list, and rightly so, the development of language competence as a goal; language is the vehicle of school instruction and the child who does not have adequate possession of language is handicapped in school learning. The lower-class child in particular is handicapped

---

Reprinted from *Young Children* 24:368-376 (September 1969), by permission of author and publisher.

in school learning; standardized tests of school achievement show that scores on such tests are correlated with socioeconomic status and the lower the class, the greater the number of students who score below grade. Particularly in reading is the disability marked; disadvantaged seventh and eighth graders who test at the third-grade level are not uncommon. Such low scores have been attributed to many factors: little desire to succeed in school, lack of readiness for school learning, poor teaching and most frequently to a language disability.

What aspect of the lower-class child's language deficit affects school achievement is still a matter of study. It is generally agreed that the disadvantaged child has a smaller vocabulary than his middle-class peer, and that he uses substandard English. But whether vocabulary size or syntax *per se* affects school learning is debatable. Not knowing five synonyms for beautiful and saying "He done it" are unlikely to impede school learning. What is more likely to interfere, and there is a growing conviction on this point, is the disadvantaged child's inability to use language to meet the demands of the school. When he is asked to follow directions, participate in discussion, compare two objects or events, and make discriminations between them, classify or draw inferences, he is often at a loss to do so. In a word, he does not know how to use language to meet cognitive demands.

A number of writers have theorized about the antecedents of this specific disability. From an early study by Milner came the thesis that patterns of family life, including opportunity for two-way conversations in the family, might account for differences.[58] She investigated two groups of Negro children, high and low scorers on the language criteria of the California Test of Mental Maturity. She studied the patterns of parent-child interaction, and found striking differences between the two groups. Families of high scorers had meals together and engaged in two-way conversation at the meals. Such two-way conversations were lacking in the families of low scorers. Differences described by Milner are usually associated with socioeconomic differences. Lower-class, disorganized families are more likely to contain the patterns of family living Milner found in low scorers.

Bernstein in several provocative papers noted that lower-class parents tend to use a "restricted" code in talking to their children, in contrast to the "elaborated" one used by middle-class parents.[59] In the restricted code, only short, grammatically simple sentences are used, with little use of subordinate clauses, limited use of adjectives and adverbs, frequent instances of illogical statements and few specific referents, with the speaker often taking it for granted that the listener knows what he's talking about.

Parents Assist in Teaching

Hess and Shipman studied parent-teaching styles, in an effort to describe more precisely how mothers influence language development.[60] Mothers and children, both low and middle class, all black, were brought to the laboratory at the University of Chicago Early Education Research Center, where each mother was to teach the same content to her child. The investigators analyzed what went on in the lessons in terms of how well the mothers transmitted information, as well as in terms of other variables. The tasks involved sorting objects into groups and explaining the sorting principles. To be effective, the mothers had to be able to communicate specific meanings clearly and precisely. The teaching of many mothers, however, was poorly organized or incomplete. Some mothers simply said, "That's not right," when the child made a mistake, leaving him in the dark as to what to do next. In contrast, some mothers would point to the erroneously placed block and the other block and say, "No, see, this block has an *O* on it and these have *X*. You don't want to mix up the *Os* and the *Xs*, so you have to put this block where there are some other blocks that have *O* on them, too." Children of such mothers were more successful in completing the task than were mothers who could not transmit information specifically enough to teach the child what to do.

In addition, successful mothers used praise and encouragement rather than criticism and coercive control to motivate their children. The contrast between the two is shown in the following example:

1a "I've got another game to teach you."	1b "There's another thing you have to learn here, so sit down and pay attention."
2a "Now listen to Mommy carefully and watch what I do because I'm going to show you how we play the game."	2b "Pay attention now and get it right, 'cause you're gonna have to show the lady how to do it later."
3a "No, Johnny. That's a big one. Remember were going to keep the big ones separate from the little ones."	3b "No, that's not what I showed you! Put that with the big ones where it belongs."
4a "Wait a minute, Johnny. You have to look at the block first before you try to find where it goes. Now pick it up again and look at it—is it big or small? . . . Now put it where it goes."	4b "That doesn't go there — you're just guessing. I'm trying to show you how to do this and you're just putting them any old place. Now pick it up and do it again and this time don't mess up."
5a "No, we can't stop now, Johnny, Mrs. Smith wants me to show you how to do this so you can do it for her. Now if you pay close attention and let Mommy teach you, you can learn how to do it and show her, and then you'll have some time to play."	5b "Now you're playing around and you don't even know how to do this. You want me to call the lady? You better listen to what I'm saying and quit playing around or I'm gonna call the lady in on you and see how you like that."

Note that the successful mothers made the task seem desirable, rather than a chore, with the mother in the role of supportive sponsor or helper rather than an impersonal or punitive authority figure. Affective behavior of the mother contributes to her effectiveness as a teacher.

Hess and Shipman found social class differences in the teaching behaviors of the mothers. All mothers in the study were black but were from four different social groups: a college-educated professional, executive and managerial level, a skilled blue-collar level, a semi-skilled level with a predominantly elementary school education, and a lower-level class group on Aid to Families of Dependent Children. Lower-class mothers, poorly educated, and with the lowest IQs, were the least effective in teaching; upper-middle-class mothers were most effective. One can safely predict which children are going to be successful school learners.

One additional analysis of the needs of the lower-class child might be mentioned here. Moore has reviewed the literature on subcultural differences in children's language abilities and finds two major problems that contribute to the learning difficulties of the lower-class child.[61] One is the inability to use a "language of reference," to describe precisely by use of appropriate modifiers what he is talking about, and the other, the inability to use language in the "abstract" where the objects or events under discussion are not present and so the bulk of the communication burden falls upon language.

Schools obviously have a remedial job to do in the case of the many lower-class children whose training in the use of language has been inadequate. But middle-class children also need help. They may speak the King's English but still have difficulty putting thoughts into words, in expressing ideas sequentially, in keeping to the subject in a speech sequence and in stating reasons for actions. They may need help in giving precise descriptions of objects and events and in giving logical explanations of actions or phenomena.

The problem is obviously more than one of increasing the child's vocabulary or eliminating "ain't" from his grammatical repertoire. It is one of teaching him the language essential for receiving and communicating ideas. And, as we have pointed out, this kind of language is closely tied to thought; we want the child to grow more logical in his thinking and to be able to express his logical thought adequately.

One of the widely publicized approaches to improve language development is that in which English is taught as if children were learning a second language. In parts of large metropolitan areas populated by Puerto Ricans and in the Southwest with large populations of Spanish-American or Indian children, English may indeed be a second language. Even where it is not, however, some investigators maintain that the children's handicap is sufficiently great to warrant a drastic new approach to language teaching, an approach which is patterned after contemporary methods of teaching foreign languages.

Patterned Drill is Basic

Basic to the teaching method is the patterned drill. Two educational psychologists, Bereiter and Engelmann developed a preschool program for disadvantaged four-year-old children which relies solely upon patterned drill.[62] The program has been so widely publicized that it will not be described in detail here. To review briefly, 15 subjects received three periods of 20-minute instruction a day in subject-matter areas—language, arithmetic and reading. All three subjects were taught by the same method, that of having children repeat statement patterns; all instruction was verbal and no toys or other concrete objects were used. For example, language instruction began by teaching children basic identity patterns by verbatim repetition:

1. *Verbatim repetition:*
   Teacher: This block is red. Say it . . .
   Children: This block is red.
2. *Yes-no questions:*
   Teacher: Is this block red?
   Children: No, this block is not red.
3. *Location tasks:*
   Teacher: Show me a block that is red.
   Children: This block is red.
4. *Statement production:*
   Teacher: Tell me about this piece of chalk.
   Children: This piece of chalk is red.
   Teacher: Tell me about what this piece of chalk is *not.*

Children: (ad lib) This piece of chalk is not green . . . not blue, etc.

5. *Deduction problems:*

Teacher: (With piece of chalk hidden in hand) This piece of chalk is not red. Do you know what color it is?

Children: No. Maybe it is blue . . . maybe it is yellow . . . (p. 134)

Bereiter reports that it takes four-year-old children considerable time to learn these statement patterns with their plural variations and sub-class nouns (e.g., "This animal is a tiger"). The length of time varies considerably—from six or seven months for those who came in with practically no spoken language to two or three months for those of near normal language competence, at the end of which time the children can recite such statements as, "If it's a hammer, then it's a tool" which purportedly illustrates proficiency in class inclusion (knowing that "hammer" is a subclass in the more general class, "tool") and in inferencing (knowing that *if* something is true, *then* we can infer that something else is true).

Critics of such an approach to language training argue that the grammatical sentences children give are evidence of response learning; they doubt that patterned drill affects language and thought processes any more effectively than memorizing nursery rhymes and learning to respond, "Dickory comes after Hickory," and, "The mouse ran down the clock; the mouse did not run up the clock."

Critics of patterned drill also contend that it is too limited a program. In language lessons, for example, the children in patterned drill classes are exposed to a very limited variety of syntactical forms including a limited number of verbs, mostly in the present tense. Yet we know that human beings have a natural capacity for language and acquire it often in the face of great difficulties. With sufficient exposure to a rich vocabulary and a complex syntax in interactions with adults, children can process data and put together utterances which they have never heard themselves. If a mother says to her three-year-old, "Find Daddy and tell him supper is ready," the child does not find his father and say, "Find Daddy and tell him supper is ready," as a child might parrot in patterned drill. Instead he says to his father, "Daddy, Mommy says supper's ready." Young children acquire the structure of the language by listening to what is said to them, processing the information, figuring out the rules, and *using what they have figured out in reply*.

Results Favor "Modeling"

Some support for the "natural" method of language training is to be found in Cazden's research.[63] Cazden exposed a small group of preschool children to a treatment she called "modeling;" that is, a tutor would reply to a child's utterances in a conversational manner, modeling as she did so a rich variety of syntactical forms. While differences between modeling and a second treatment were not significant, results favored modeling.

But the natural method of acquiring language is only effective if the child has sufficient chance to interact with adults who use language effectively. Jensen who has been a major investigator in the area of language learning, states, "The degree of subtletly, diversity, and complexity, of the verbal environment will determine the nature of the syntactical processes incorporated by the developing child.[64] The extent to which these structures become incorporated is a function of the frequency with which they are experienced in the environment, the degree to which the social environment reinforces their overt manifestation, and the individual's basic capacity for learning."

In Cazden's research, the tutor worked with *three* children at a time, and there was no attempt to structure the language training. Comparison of her research with one carried out by Blank raises interesting questions.[65]

Blank provided training on a one-to-one basis and makes a strong case for such a tutorial language program. She points out that the usual classroom situation does not require overt responses by the child; the teacher gives directions to which the child does not have to perform verbally and which he can carry out by imitating other students. In a one-to-one tutorial session with the teacher, the teacher not only ensures that the child uses language, but she can also plan the tutorial sessions to meet the special needs of the child. Blank sees these needs as related to the child's deficit in abstract thinking, and has developed a program in which such abilities are developed as attending selectively to phenomena, dealing with exclusions, categorizing, dealing with cause and effect, separating words from their referents, etc. Blank reported gains of 14 IQ points for children tutored for 15-20 minutes daily over a four-month period.

How many children can a teacher work with at one time and still have the sessions be tutorial in nature? Should the training be on a one-to-one basis, as provided by Blank? Can one work with more than one child at a time, and, if so, what is the maximum number? The question is obviously a practical one for which we need an answer. We also need to know how the sessions should be structured. Tutors in the Cazden program let the children play and paint and they read stories to them. Blank provided language training that in Blank's judgment might influence thought processes.

The question of number of children to receive training at a time and the question of structure are interrelated. That is, where structure is provided in the training sessions, more children can be active at a time. When children are moving freely about the room, it is difficult for the teacher to carry on a conversation with more than one at a time. The situation is easier when children are seated around a table, engaged in a common enterprise that is language-provoking. It is possible under such circumstances for the teacher to carry on interactions with groups of four, five or six children (depending upon age and need) during the same session.

What Role does Language Play?

Before considering the question of content or structure of training sessions, the relationship between language and thought processes must be considered. Can we use language training sessions to sharpen thought processes? There has been considerable debate in the literature over the role language plays in facilitating logical development. Much of the controversy stems over Piaget's thesis that language is an expression of underlying thinking processes, and is the handmaiden of cognition, rather than the other way around. Yet, there are those who maintain that logical operations are only possible because of language; that as the child becomes able to express relationships of comparison and causality, thought becomes logical.

The position taken in this paper is that language plays a strong supportive role in the development of logical intelligence. It is true that thinking can take place subverbally, and that ideas may emerge from logical operations that we perform without words. But verbalizing these ideas is a way of refining them so that the ideas are clearer and more precise. It is this role of language that writers have in mind when they say that to learn something well one must teach it.

Granted that language training should take place in small groups so that there is considerable adult-child interaction. Granted that in the training the child should be exposed to a rich variety of syntactical forms and particularly those that might conceivably aid logical development. How can such training be systematized so as to make sure that what is known about language and logical development is fully utilized? Many present preschool programs leave everything up to the teacher who may not be aware of the tremendous amount of knowledge about development accumulated in the last few years. Present research programs decide on the content of the training program on the basis of whatever items the investigator thinks to be important. Thus, thousands of children in the country are being trained on a few limited syntactical forms and a few limited logical operations, the choice of which is personal to the investigator and indeed whimsical.

A systematic approach should have a firm foundation in theory. It should be based upon a grand plan of how intellectual development takes place, a plan that is adequately supported by research. Fortunately, in the area of logical development such a grand plan is available in the developmental theory of Piaget. We can take what he has discovered about the emergence of schemes of classification, conservation and seriation and build a training program from it.

And in the area of syntactical structures we can turn to the field of developmental psycholinguistics for an analysis of syntax and how syntactical forms emerge. Bellugi-Klima, for example, has studied the emergence of negation in the speech of the young child.[66] First it appears that the child negates by commencing sentences with "No" as in, "No can do it;" "No get jelly;" next the child positions *no, not, don't* or *can't* in a sentence, but not always grammatically as in, "He not waking up." A new development is the appearance of multiple negation, with the child sprinkling several negatives in one sentence: "No one didn't took it." Tag questions appear still later. In the sentence, "You understand, don't you?," "don't you" is a tag. Tag questions are quite involved, for the child must make a decision about affirmative and negative forms. If the sentence is negative, the tag is affirmative: "He isn't here, is he?" If the sentence is affirmative, the tag is negative: "He's here, isn't he?"

The National Laboratory on Early Childhood Education is presently engaged in collaborative research to shed some light on training for language competence. Research Centers at Cornell and Syracuse Universities, University of Chicago and University of Arizona under the direction of Marion Potts, Vernon Hall, Wilbur Hass and Arline Hobson have structured a research project part of which is to be carried out at each of the Centers simultaneously. Child populations include poor rural whites, poor urban blacks and Mexican-American children.

The main questions to be answered in the research are as follows:

- Is patterned drill or extension method more effective in influencing acquisition of syntax?
- Is modeling of syntactic structures alone in a tightly controlled sequence enough to elicit the target syntax in the context of new materials and situations (generalizations)?
- Does the use of material objects in teaching syntax aid its acquisition?
- Does acquisition of syntax by any method contribute to logical development?
- Which aspects of syntax appear to contribute most to logical development?

30. Language Learning and the Teaching Process

Janet Ann Emig

The British linguists Halliday, McIntosh, and Strevens divide the teaching of the native language into three major modes. These they called (1) the prescriptive, (2) the descriptive, and (3) the productive teaching of language.[67] This discussion will emanate from their distinction. I believe that most teachers engage in all modes when they teach the native language, although their exemplifying of each and their apportioning of time among the three modes vary stunningly. I also believe that this apportioning exemplifies in part the philosophy of language of a teacher, a department chairman, or indeed, of anyone who shapes the curriculum in a school or school system.

Prescriptive teaching of language is the mode many linguists would regard as the least interesting and significant. Prescriptive teaching involves teaching children to replace language patterns which are regarded as unacceptable with other patterns that are regarded as acceptable. As with the other two approaches, prescriptive teaching of language can deal with either or both oral and written modes of discourse. Dialect I will use throughout my discussion as one example of oral discourse to which any three of the approaches can be applied.

If a teacher proceeds prescriptively, he treats the student's original dialect as inadequate, inaccurate, illiterate, or just plain cussed and wrong-headed. He often makes statements of the following sort: "John, you must sound the *g* in *ing* at the end of words. Educated people always do. Don't say *singin'*; say sing*ing* if you want to sound and be educated. Dropping your *g's* is just sheer laziness and indifference." Or: "Educated people never say 'You is,' or 'They is, Millicent'; Say 'You are'; 'They are.'" It is, incidentally, this kind of teaching that leads to one of two reactions almost all of us have experienced at any cocktail party or for many square miles around any NCTE convention. Query; "You one of those English teachers?" Reaction 1: "I'd better watch what I say." Reaction 2: "Oh!" Then the lapse into total silence.

A certain kind of evaluation of student themes qualifies as an example of prescriptive teaching directed toward the child's written language. It involves positively profligate use of margins, backs of pages, and even whole extra sheets

From *Elementary English* 44:602-608, 709 (October 1967).

of paper where the prescriptive teacher makes such mute imprecations as *awk! wc!* and *dang part!*

Both of these examples—indeed, all examples of prescriptive teaching—proceed from at least two hidden assumptions that are, to say it as gently as possible, suspect. The first is that there are absolute standards, which are known and unanimously shared by educated adults, to which a student's oral and written language should attain. The standards in the case of child's oral language might be—if the student is lucky—the style of Huntley-Brinkley or Walter Cronkite, depending on the teacher's network loyalty; or if he is unlucky—that of Gladstone or William Pitt, or evenDemosthenes—in translation, of course.

The standards in the case of the child's written language might be the immortal prose of the Harbrace Handbook or, if the teacher is sufficiently anachronistic, the essays of Gibbon or Sir Thomas Browne. My reason for reaching into the past for models of excellence is that prescriptive teachers do, when they are not proceeding from negative instances a la Lindley Murray and other sterling school grammarians. Often there is not even a specific model or era in mind so that the teachers, when pressed, just lyricize over some Golden Age of perfect language—with time and place carefully unspecified.

A second assumption in prescriptive teaching is that prescriptive teacher intervention can effect significant changes in oral and written language patterns of late adolescents, of early adolescents, or even of elementary children. One wonders if teachers who proceed wholly prescriptively have read any recent research on the child's initial acquistion of language. Take these three quotations:

The first is from a summary of research on language development by the psycholinguists Susan Ervin and Wick Miller:

> What material is available suggests that by the age of four most children have learned the fundamental structural features of their language and many of the details.[68]

The second is by the psychologist John B. Carroll:

> By the age of about six, the average child has mastered nearly all its common grammatical forms and constructions—at least those used by adults and older children in his environment. After the age of six there is relatively little in the grammar or syntax of the language that the average child needs to learn, except to achieve a school-imposed standard of speech or writing to which he may not be accustomed in his home environment. Vocabulary learning, however, continues until late in adult life.[69]

And here is the linguist Martin Joos in his essay "Language and the School Child":

> It [learning the grammatical system of the native language] is complete—and the books are closed on it!—at about eight years of age. It is not normal to learn any more grammar beyond that age.[70]

Let's combine these statements by linguists for a moment with the thesis developed with convincing data by the psychologist Benjamin Bloom in his study *Stability and Change in Human Characteristics*.[71] Bloom's thesis is that certain human characteristics are increasingly impervious to change with increasing chronological age. Language is strongly implied as a cluster of characteristics especially impervious to change. Bloom means through any form of intervention, of which I believe prescriptive teaching to be a powerful instance.

There are assumptions not only about the nature of language but about the nature of learning and teaching in prescriptive teaching of language [indeed, in all three modes]. For a moment let me make these explicit for prescriptive teaching.

The psychologist Jacob Getzels has devised a very useful set of distinctions about teaching and learning which might be called "Knowledge, Knowledge, Who's Got the Knowledge?" There are four possible situations: The first—and this order is arbitrary—is that the teacher knows something which the student does not. A second is that both teacher and student know something. A third is that the student knows something the teacher does not. A fourth, of course, is that neither knows.

Each of these situations I'd like to suggest requires a different role or set of roles for both teacher and learner. Prescriptive teaching is, I think, clearly and wholly an example of a situation where the teacher knows something the student doesn't (since there is often no match in his own experience). One way to put the relation between teacher and student is the classic metaphor of student as pitcher, to be filled with new oral or written dialect. What would be the role of teacher here? Teacher as water carrier or—if the teaching were for some reason reported on the society page, the article would begin, "Miss Fidditch poured."

If one preferred a more active metaphor for prescriptive teaching, the teacher of course could become sculptor with the student here a raw lump of clay to be pummeled finally into a member of the English-Speaking Union. Perhaps the most accurate metaphor from what I've said thus far about prescriptive teaching might be teacher as Sisyphus with the student as stone, rolling relentlessly down the hill again.

The wholly prescriptive teacher might at this moment be rue-ing "Othello's occupation's gone." He might also be asking, "Are there no components of my student's language still pervious to change at the high school level?" The answer seems to be *perhaps* usage or other specific components in student dialect, if he wants to try.

Several important considerations to note here. First, only tough, systematic, long-term effort will make any change at all. And with constant, carefully programmed drilling. Since what is required here is really teaching a foreign dialect, the teacher who wants to take on the task—and let's leave aside the ethics involved in such a decision—probably should learn the latest techniques in the teaching of a second language, especially the outstanding work in motivation accomplished by the second language teacher.—May I just pause to note the metaphor inherent in this form of prescriptive teaching: which is of course teacher as top sergeant, student as buck private.

The second consideration in deciding what to teach prescriptively is efficiency, or the time-and-motion factor. *If*—and again please note the conditional state of my utterance—the teacher plans to try to change the near-impervious, it is important not to proceed in a scattershot method and deal with all matters of usage or phonology discretely or randomly. There are now excellent studies available of the dialects indigenous to many, if not most, parts of the fifty states. As just three examples, Lee Pederson's work on the dialects of Chicago, William Labov's on New York and Richard Larson's on Hawaii.[72] If I may be prescriptive, read the appropriate studies for your section of the country; select a brace of phonological and syntactic deviances; and focus on these, excluding all others. In the Chicago dialect, for example, drill on agreement with second person singular and plural, and third person plural with verbs *to be*, because therein lies one of the most persistent deviances from standard English.

Since the amount of time I spend on a mode may be regarded as a value judgment on how important I think it is, let me move quickly to the second—the descriptive teaching of English.

This is the mode in which descriptions are delineated of how language actually works; its general nature; and, if this can be separated, its specifically human characteristics. Because I think the subject matters and the approaches to them in descriptive teaching are more broad and varied, teachers and students assume a far greater range of roles. I will try to suggest many of these forms of variety in descriptive teaching.

Let's start here with the uniquely human nature of language, as contrasted with animal communication. A description of both can form a fascinating subject matter from grade one through graduate school, with the focus and the sophistication of treatment determining the grade level for presentation. One can imagine a likely discussion in the very early grades of "Can Flipper Talk?" or a consideration in late secondary school or college of certain physiologic correlates with and psychological propensities to language as noted, say, by the physiologist-psychologist Eric Lenneberg.[73] Lenneberg points out, for example, that no animal masters the concepts and principles of language well enough to apply or engage in phonemic analysis, to produce an infinitely large and original set of utterances from his basic stock of sounds, or to impart what Lenneberg calls the "total semantic domain" of word.

A second subject-matter in emphasizing the uniquely human nature of language is a description of how a child initially acquires language. Here, as with specific regional or group dialects, the teacher needs to add reading of current research to observations, and remembrance of how his own children, or babies he knew, acquired language. Some authors here, if you are interested, are Bellugi and Brown; Carroll; Ervin and Miller; and Weir.[74]

Students can learn the basic data about how children learn language by the same route adults follow—that is, by observation systematized by reading, with both supplemented by teacher aid in establishing categories and generalizations. Here teacher and student become field linguists together using as subjects siblings and neighbor children as they answer such questions as "What sounds does a baby make first? When? Why?" "What kinds of responses do babies and small children make when you say a word to them? Why?" "How can you decide when a baby says his first word?" "When do children talk in sentences? What do you mean by sentences?" "What parts of speech do small children learn first? Last? Why?" "Which sex speaks earlier? Why? Later? Why?"

The next subject matter to approach descriptively is grammar. And of course the question becomes "What Grammar?" To answer this question, one needs to establish the criteria for what constitutes a satisfactory description. For me these criteria are the following: A satisfactory descriptive theory of grammar is (1) accurate, (2) comprehensive, (3) elegant, and (4) self-correcting. This means the mode of grammar I teach is the latest version of Noam Chomsky's evolving transformational-generative grammar as presented in his study, "Aspects of the Theory of Syntax." My choice I do not regard, I must say, as an edict from the dais: it is simply my personal preference for the reason I have cited.

One of the crucial concepts—I might say deep structures—in what I will call *t-g* grammar is that every native speaker, from the time he acquires syntax, possesses a profound intuitive knowledge of his own language. A major question in teaching the native language today is how, when, and why should this knowledge be made explicit and conscious? I cannot within the scope of this paper do more than suggest a few dimensions of this decision.

If Joos is right in saying that a child completes learning the grammar of his language by the time he is age eight—and I think it is clear from the context he means the unconscious mastery—is the child then immediately ready to have this knowledge made conscious and explicit? Should there be a hiatus of a year or two to allow this knowledge to deepen? Should we wait until the age Piaget and Whitehead agree is the age of the first coping with formal propositions—that is, between twelve and fourteen? Is a conscious knowledge of grammar necessary or useful at any age? If so, how? Should the teaching be regarded non-pragmatically? That is, grammar is one of the most profound whorls of identifying our humanity, and as a humanistic endeavor, it is self-justifying?

Why teach a student two types of subject matter? To instigate awe in what he has already achieved as a learner. One differentiation between prescriptive-proscriptive, and descriptive and productive teaching of language is the stress. Prescriptive teaching focuses on the miniscule failures—often matters of maturation or socio-economic status—in a student's mastery of language; descriptive and productive, on his fantastic actual and potential attainments. Especially to children who regard themselves as academic failures, there should be enormous assurance and support in the fact that by the time they enter school they have already learned enough to assure their human membership for their lifetime.

What roles do teachers and students assume in this particular segment of the descriptive mode? To return to the Getzels distinction both teachers and students at once know and do not know. The teacher has conscious, explicit, and systematic knowledge of both animal communication and the initial acquisition of language; the child unconscious and implicit. Yet they are in other ways fellow discoverers together. The teacher has another role here—one I mentioned earlier. He is instigator of awe. What is the concomitant role for the learner? He is apprentice in appreciation, of his own accomplishments.

With this descriptive mode of teaching grammar, as with teaching the initial acquisition of language, the teacher may have the role of explicator and organizer. The student then is provider of data: a more classic metaphor here, if you prefer, for teacher in this inductive role is teacher as Socrates; students as his students.

Other phases of language teaching that can be approached descriptively are the teaching of lexicography, semantics, the history of language, and dialectology. Our own teaching imaginations can supply ways of approaching these so as to intrigue the interest and to insure the participation of the students.

All of these segments deal with *oral* phases of language teaching. What opportunities are there for teaching the written language descriptively? The teacher can deal with actual calligraphy, using perhaps such beautiful new sources as *The Art of Writing*, the UNESCO publication available at the last NCTE Convention. The class can also examine the process of composing. How can this be done given the fragmentary nature of our formal knowledge about how we compose? There are two rich resources: introspection in our own experience; and analysis of other writers' accounts, both student and professional. The two sources can be joined if students are asked to keep a writer's diary in which they describe how they feel about writing they are doing. Did they like the theme assigned or not? Why? If there was no topic assigned, what kind of search did they make for one? How long were they engaged in pre-writing? In what context or environment? If they revised, how long after a draft? What did their revisions consist of?

Professional authors can be approached through the number of analyses by the authors themselves and others of styles of working, of attitudes positive and negative to the act of writing. Anthologies of interviews such as *Writers at Work,* Volumes I and II,[75] and *Counterpoint,* edited by Roy Newquist,[76] present the statements about composing by nearly a hundred professional writers. An article which examines a number of such writers' statements is one I wrote in February, 1964, in the *CCC Journal,* "The Uses of the Unconscious in Composing."

There are also for student examination writers' drafts and revisions—in far greater number than we might suppose. For juniors and seniors, there is a new anthology *Word for Word: A Study of Authors' Alterations, with Exercises,* by Wallace Hildick with segments of revisions from *Middlemarch, Mrs. Dalloway,* and six other selections, along with excellent questions about why certain changes were made.[77]

There are many other sources as well. Two examples are M. R. Ridley's study of the manuscripts connected with the major odes by Keats and Thomas Parkinson's recent study of Yeats, *W. B. Yeats: Later Poetry.*[78]

Some of you might say with this or other parts of what I've described thus far: "I'd call that productive, not descriptive, teaching." Perhaps it is. The categories are not tidy, nor have I suggested—I hope—that there is some kind of mystic matching between certain subject-matters and certain teaching modes.

The productive mode of teaching Halliday, McIntosh, and Strevens describe as helping the student extend the use of his native language in the most effective way. Teachers of course will interpret and implement "in the most effective way" very individualistically. I would like to suggest one or two ways for both oral and written features of discourse. Many British linguists employ a term *register* which some of you might find as useful as I do. It refers to specific realms of language usage, such as the realm of professional jargon or a style directed to a given sort of audience. The emphasis then, in a broad sense, is rhetorical.

The major emphasis in productive teaching of English then might be said to be the extension of student registers, both in oral and written discourse. How might this work with each? Despite protestations and sillinesses I have heard to the contrary, children from a very early age govern features of their oral discourse according to audience. This adjustment, which is sometimes called social rather than linguistic awareness, is analogous, I think, to grammatical skill in that it is unconscious and unsystematized, but *there*. Again, as with grammar, the role of the teacher is as explicator; the role of the student is as purveyor or supplier of raw data. Students at all levels can be trained to listen to themselves and others speaking to many kinds of audience, to observe and systematize differences, and eventually to practice specific roles.

They probably need to experience a range of styles. In school too often we teach but few varieties of jargon. One constant example is lexis of whatever critical theory of literature we happen to espouse. We are elaborate in our treatment of the jargons of academe which only some students will ever have to handle, while slighting or forgetting entirely the jargons of the marketplace in which all students will be dealing for significant parts of their future life. One thinks here of the language of advertising, of propaganda—indeed of all forms of slanted writing and talking. A useful study here would be the rhetorics of political movements, such as Civil Rights—the style of a Martin Luther King against the style of a Stokely Carmichael, and both against a Malcolm X. Or the prose of actual campaigners, such as the recent pottage of rhetoric.

Both written and oral targets of productive teaching—indeed of any of the three modes—can I think be approached playfully rather than grimly, with the students engaging in all kinds of autoletics of discourse, trying on different styles and roles, without fear of mature responsibilities or reprisals.

With written discourse this approach can take many guises. Students can imitate a range of stylistic models of their own choosing. They can choose to be for a given assignment Virginia Woolf or Ian Fleming. Some might ask, "How can imitation of models be a form of productive teaching?" Fortunately, we are all such inevitable individualists that perfect and literal imitation is impossible—some cadence or flavor of our own gets into whatever we write, as all of us who have taught modeled writing are well aware.

Or we can watch the transmogrification of a story or other content through the employment of many styles or voices. A new almost-classic source is Raymond Queneau's *Exercises de Style*;[79] another just published is a book by Walker Gibson wonderfully entitled *Tough, Sweet and Stuffy*.[80]

In all these forms of productive teaching we have a double role. We are at once fellow performer and director—Gielguds and Oliviers of our classrooms. Fellow performers because we produce too. We write not only because of the models we hope to set but because of inner compulsions for order and beauty that we at times talk about with our students; directors, because we try to create a context that is safe and free enough that students will find courage to extend their public and private expressions of heart and mind, thinking and feeling.

What kind of teacher does the most powerful and successful teaching of language require?

1) He has formidable substantive command of his discipline of language. If he teaches prescriptively, he has to know what standards he holds and why, as well as the formidable barriers that threaten even a most modest success. If he proceeds descriptively, he must have accurate descriptions of many phenomena involving the general nature of language and of human acquisition of it. This means, ideally, for the purposes of given classroom segments—or to use the chic word, modules—he is a historical linguist; for others, a dialectician; for others, a grammarian. If he proceeds productively, he needs a strong knowledge of processes. If he does not keep this knowledge in his head, he needs to keep it on his book shelves or in a nearby library to which he has ready access.

2) He has knowledge as well about the nature of the learner, of the teacher, as well as a repertoire of ways in which they interact. He is aware of implications about learning theory of a given role he may assume and/or ask a student to assume. As important, he has the cluster of strategies to assure he and his students will be playing the role appropriate to the nature of the subject he is teaching, as well as those which enable him to stay in these roles or shift to another as their needs and the requests demand from the subject matter required.

3) Both of these imply a third, a human category. The teacher must possess certain personal attributes that make possible his movement along modes. Clearly, the key attribute here is flexibility. Another—a closing way—to put the matter, he needs an incredibly wide range of registers which he can play like the virtuoso performer the good teacher ideally is.

31. Teaching Children Who Speak Social Class Dialects

Walter Loban

American *regional accent* rarely causes serious educational or social problems. In every region of this nation, Americans speak with rhythms and intonations that vary from New England to the South to the Far West. Here in Hawaii, where we are convening, educated and cultured people have—as in all other regions—a delightful and special way of speaking standard English. In Georgia, teachers and community leaders speak *their* standard English—like Georgian Southerners. A man can speak with one of the New England accents and become President of the United States. President Kennedy never voiced the *R* in "Hahvahd" but he had no difficulty putting it in "idear." Similarly one can speak with the regional accents of Texas and be elected to the highest office in the land. In any sizable nation, regional variation is inevitable, with syntax or grammar remarkably standard but with pronunciations, rhythms, and subtle idiosyncracies of usage providing a desirable range of variety.

What does cause problems is *dialect, social class dialect:* Pidgin, Cajun, Appalachian, Ozark, various Negro dialects, the many variations of English usually spoken by poorly educated or culturally different Americans. These dialects differ enough from standard structure and usage to cause problems in communication as well as in social and personal relationships. To deal with such problems in schools requires sound knowledge, humane values, and great delicacy, for nothing less than human dignity and the pupil's self image are at stake.

In the old closed societies of the past, each class spoke differently, and language was one of the most effective means of maintaining the stability, the unchanging nature of those class societies. In Denmark a tart saying illuminates this relation of language to class distinction: "In the old days our Danish nobility spoke French to one another, German to their merchants, and Danish to their dogs." The implications of this saying are not limited to Denmark; we know from history that aristocrats in all nations separated themselves from the masses by means of language. Tolstoi, in *War and Peace*, depicts this same linguistic separation. At the time of Napoleon's invasion, as the Russian people began to unite against the French, the aristocrats at their soirees began to play "*Forfeit*, a delightful patriotic game." They reinstated standard Russian as their means of communication, and anyone who lapsed into French forfeited some small possession or was punished in some amusing way. Such language separation of the classes was not so much a deliberate plan as it was the natural result of differences in the quality of daily living.

As long as class societies remain stable, the variations in language cause few problems. In fact the language differences support and stabilize class societies. In any kind of society language represents tremendous social power, and the Establishment speaks one kind of dialect, the established standard dialect. For example, until recently the Tyneshire man rising to political position in England has had a language problem. The purely historical accident that Tuscan became standard Italian, rather than Venetian or Sicilian, is an illustration of how standard speech begins as merely another dialect. However, we need to remind ourselves often of the sociological relationship between poverty, with its waste of human potential, and language itself. Closed societies have always used language and education as one means of maintaining the *status quo* and of perpetuating a large class of peons or peasants. In a fluid society like that of the United States, we act to diminish this ancient element of social control, this extraneous determination of individual destiny.

Even in an open society such as ours, however, where individual worth and aspiration are intended to count for more than fortunate or unfortunate birth, language still operates to preserve social class distinctions and remains one of the major barriers to crossing social lines. In a free and open society schools should assist all other institutions in making equality of opportunity a reality. To do this teachers need to understand how language and social caste are linked and why many middle-class people naively condemn the language of the least favored economic groups. On attitudes concerning language, teachers can learn much from sociology. "We fear lower class speech and are inclined to give it no quarter. The more precarious our social status in the higher classes—that is, the closer we are to the line that divides the middle from the lower classes or the more recent our ascent from the lower strata—the more insistent we are on the purity of our linguistic credentials."[81]

Realizing that human worth cannot be measured by the language or dialect a man uses, teachers will be more likely to help children acquire standard English without making them ashamed of their own way of speaking. Such an addition—not "improvement"—of language is much more possible through instruction where drill and directed effort are oral and where they are not separated or long separated from language used to express ideas, attitudes, and values of genuine concern to the learners. Not only different usage but also awareness of situation, of how listeners are helped or hindered by one's language, proves to be the need of most learners. To achieve language flexibility a pupil must apply whatever is studied to situations in which he has something to say, a deep desire to say it, and someone to whom he genuinely wants to say it.

Children need to perfect or acquire the prestige dialect—not because standare English is correct or superior in itself but because society exacts severe penalties from those who do not speak it. Unless they can learn to use standard English, many pupils will be denied access to economic opportunities or entrance to social groups. The leaders of most communities are sensitive to departures from the informal English, the standard, accepted language of their communities. Whether we like it or not, children who speak a social class dialect need the opportunity to learn standard usage if they are ever to be free to choose whether or not they will use it.

One nation so far in history has approached quite closely the elimination of poverty and class differences. This nation, Sweden, is also large enough in population and space to have a history both of regional accents and social class dialects. Today regional accents—such as Skane (in Southern Sweden), Dalarna (in Central Sweden), and Norrland (in Northern Sweden)—still persist, similarly to our regional accents. But under the leveling influences of education and the highest average standard of living in the world, social class dialects in modern Sweden have rapidly withered. One must talk quite some time to a man to discover his economic condition. His interests and vocabulary will constitute the difference—not his usage or syntax. Thus in Sweden we can see a striking illustration of how language relates to education.

The popular idea of language differences mistakenly sees them in terms of black and white, right or wrong, correct or incorrect. This past summer I read with interest an account of an excellent address given by Hawaii's Lieutenant Governor Thomas P. Gill at the Konawaena High School's commencement exercises. In his address, one newspaper quoted him as follows:

"Language is an expression of culture and often social attitudes. If Pidgin is important to the people of an area, it should not be destroyed, but accepted and supplemented. Of course, we also learn good English so that we are not trapped in one corner of a fluid and changing society."

The lieutenant governor also told the graduates that Kona will not long remain a quiet, remote section of Hawaii. "The flood of tourism which flows across Hawaii today, and in substantial part touches your coast, has still not hit you with the surge you are likely to see tomorrow," he said. "You are still a small and quiet place. Competition is still not keen; you have not yet lost the ability to be personal in your relationships; an individual can still be gauged for what you know him to be. This is good, but it will change. You will be part of the change. We all hope you can be ready. Our attitudes in Hawaii, and here in Kona, will be important to us in the years ahead if we are not to disappear as a people with a character of our own."

Yet almost as soon as the Lieutenant Governor's sensible and restrained remarks appeared in print, opposing voices rose to charge him with condoning sloppy English. Letters to the editor flayed Pidgin as "bad" and "incorrect." Many lay people are indeed sensitive about language and not everyone feels secure enough to view language with true perspective and objectivity.

In a nation where space is shrinking and everyone is becoming more interdependent, certainly the value of a widely used standard language is scarcely arguable. Without adopting condescending attitudes toward class dialects, we ought to be able to help as many children as possible to speak the prestige dialect—standard English. As citizens of Hawaii know, it is entirely possible to speak both standard and Pidgin. Many who use standard English at work lapse back into the intimacy and warmth of Pidgin during coffee breaks and at home. As one young lady on Kaui says, "Using the Island dialect, for me, is like taking off my high-heeled shoes and getting into comfortable slippers. It's the real me; it's my deepest feeling." Eventually, as social and educational forces continue, her children or grandchildren will more and more speak standard; Pidgin will gradually diminish. Even now Pidgin is changing; the need for it is not urgent as it once was in the nineteenth century when at least eight different nationality groups speaking widely dissimilar languages had to communicate with one another.

Today in an open and heterogeneous society such as ours, what actions are the schools and teachers to take concerning social class dialects? The major course of action seems quite clear. Teachers must proceed on the principle of adding standard English to the dialect of pupils whose speech reflects economic disadvantage. The other alternative, substituting standard English and eliminating the dialect, is neither feasible on sociological grounds nor sensible on psychological grounds. Least of all is it humane. A speaker who is made to feel ashamed of his own language habits suffers a basic injury as a human being. Only an infinitesimally small number of pupils can deny their family and community to the point of *eliminating* their dialect. Although not easy, either, an addition of a second dialect is far more possible in American society, and in education we are developing the means of accomplishing it.

In pre-school, headstart programs, the kindergarten and the earliest years of school, the emphasis should be upon the child's using *whatever dialect of the language he already speaks* as the means of thinking, exploring, and imagining. But language is also more than a tool of thought: it is a way of expressing emotions and feelings, it is a way of adjusting to other people, of expressing solidarity with the human race. Language has many important functions, but one of the most important we can agree is its use as a means of developing the powers of reason without denying and neglecting the other functions.

If the kindergarten child who speaks a dialect says, "Them magnets pickin' up them nails," the teacher need not at this point worry about "Them magnets" or the omission of *are*. That usage will not interfere with the crucial cognitive or communicative processes. If we do not first encourage the child to use his own indigenous language in its full range, we will diminish his desire to use language in school. Therefore, first of all, orally he must develop and amplify sentences until he is using the full range of his mental, emotional, and linguistic potential. It is much easier for him to achieve such powers in the dialect he already uses. Nor should anyone worry that he is to be left to do this forever in school. The strategy is merely that the pre-school stage and kindergarten are much too early to press him to be concerned about using standard dialect continuously. Such teaching only confuses small children, causing them to speak much less frequently in school. Usually from grade three and after, the children's daily recitation should adhere to standard English, but in the early years the teacher would accept "Him a good dog." At this stage the teacher would be more interested in eliciting from the child, "Him a good dog *but with three fleas*"; indeed, the teacher would be very much interested in such qualification and amplification.

However non-standard oral language cannot be left entirely untouched, even this early. If children do not soon begin to practice all the phonemes in the English language, eventually they will find it difficult or almost impossible to sound some of the phonemes (as, for instance, English speakers have difficulty with the Spanish "r"). Children who speak a dialect must practice early the phonemes not in their dialect. Therefore, in the primary grades, in primary school, teachers should introduce a great many listening experiences for pupils to imitate and dramatize. These would be taped—short little skits, riddles, or dialogues, repeated twice on the tape, once in the dialect with which the child is familiar and once in standard English. The purpose: to focus the pupil's attention upon *differences* (but not "correct" or "incorrect"!); otherwise he will not hear them. To him the phonemes, morphemes, and usage sound at first just as he always says them; he must be helped to hear that they are not exactly the same. One of the major tasks of the linguistically trained elementary school teacher is to focus the child's attention upon the contrasting distinctions presented in these skits which use both the standard and nonstandard dialects.

Reading is another educational avenue for helping dialect speaking pupils. Initial reading instruction for these children should utilize the language experience approach in which the child dictates his own brief "stories." Teachers using this method often worry about their procedure when the child uses dialect. If he says, "Da cah wen heet da dog," the teacher hesitates to write such Pidgin usage. I recommend that she do so the *first few times* in order to help the child comprehend a basic concept: that what he can think and say can also be turned into written symbols. After one or two such dictations, however, the teacher can say, "Joseph, there is another way to say the same thing: 'The car hit the dog.' Can you say it *both* ways?" If the child resists, the teacher quickly says "Well, all right, let's write it *your* way." But gradually she presses —as rapidly as her sensitive understanding of the child's readiness and her artistry as a teacher permits—toward what will probably be termed "school language." Always she is exerting a mild pressure toward standard usage, but she is ever ready to relax the pressure if she deems it alienating or upsetting to the child. When the child *is* willing to try saying something two ways, she compliments him, writes the dictation both ways and requests the child to read it *both* ways, and very soon she has at least accustomed him to the *idea* of "school language." Never, never, does she speak slightingly or reproachingly of "home language" nor in her inmost thoughts does she ever call it substandard, wrong, incorrect, or bad. It is merely nonstandard, a valuable human way of communicating in its own proper surroundings.[82] On the other hand she does not dawdle; as rapidly as possible she establishes the concept that there are several useful ways of talking. One of those useful ways is school language, and as soon as possible and as much as possible the child will try to use school language in class. Actually, children accept this concept very quickly and shift almost as easily as American children sojourning in Chile, who use Spanish with their playmates and English with their parents.

Equally important, at this stage, is a method of classroom oral-aural dialogues, built upon linguistic analysis of the major contrasts between the dialect and standard speech. These oral dialogues, exemplified by instruction now being carried on in Hilo and Detroit, deserve our careful attention. These dialogues have built into them the pattern practice of the oral-aural methodology of modern foreign language instruction.

At Keaukaha Elementary School in Hilo, where I am familiar with the procedures, the lessons are composed of riddles, short dialogues, narratives, or poems for memorization. Various drills, guided conversations or games follow each dialogue in order to give the pupils practice with the new material in *varied situations.* Visual aids, puppets, and role playing are devices used to hold interest and facilitate practice.

In Hilo, goals chosen for inclusion in each lesson are embedded in content interesting to children. Some lessons are based on children's interests or compelling aspects of another part of the curriculum. The lessons also use children's literature, children's poetry, and books of riddles. In sequence, the dialogues usually proceed as follows:

> Children listen to the teacher's model, that is, she reads the dialogue in lively fashion.
>
> Children imitate and practice the teacher's model, first in unison, then individually.

The teacher listens and makes judgments about the accuracy of the child's production.

The teacher may alter the child's imitation at the time; not with a negative reprimand, but always with two or three more repetitions as models to imitate. The teacher maintains a smiling, pleasant manner throughout.

The teacher may choose to overlook the child's nonstandard imitation at the time, and focus on it again in the next exercise, the next day, or later.

For instance, one dialogue that interested the third-grade children at Keaukaha—one they recited with genuine zest—dealt with summer safety. Mrs. Anna Chow's class was in session just a few weeks before the close of school. The lesson focused on gerund phrases, a structure of language not used in Pidgin.

Vacation Safety

Mrs. Chow: Summer vacation is a happy time for us all. We have more time to do the things we enjoy doing: swimming, camping, boating, or whatever. It can also be an unhappy time if we aren't careful. Now, here are two boys talking about vacation.

Dialogue

George: School's almost over this year.

Robert: Yes, and I like the summer vacation. I can go swimming every day with my friends.

George: Does your Mother let you swim all by yourself?

Robert: No. I can't go swimming unless my older brother's there.

George: I'm going to ride my bicycle every day this summer.

Robert: Me, too. It's fun!

George: Right! But we should be careful about riding in traffic.

Robert: That's right. And vacation is no fun if we get hurt.

The children then imitated the dialogue, first in groups, then as individuals. Mrs. Chow sometimes repeated a line or word, reinforcing the model when necessary.

Riding in traffic

Group I	*Group II*
We should be careful about riding in traffic.	That's right. *Riding in traffic* is dangerous.
swimming alone.	*etc.*
climbing trees.	*etc.*
hiking alone.	*etc.*
petting strange dogs.	*etc.*
playing with fire.	*etc.*

At the close of the dialogue and the exercises, Mrs. Chow moved to a very important step, *transfer* of the learning. She said, "Very good! Very good! Now *what else* can we think of that we must be careful not to do if we want a happy vacation?" Eager hands moved to add new, original ideas:

We must be careful about swimming near vanna.*
We must be careful about eating too many macadamia nuts.
We must be careful about walking under mango trees with ripe fruit.

The exercise had been transferred to a functional creative phase. The new language seeds had been planted and were germinating.

In Detroit, although I have not observed their work, Ruth Golden and Robert L. Donald have moved in a similar oral-aural direction. To reach (as is desperately needed) large numbers of teachers and children, they have placed lessons-for-imitation on tapes.

The problems of dialect, we should realize, require sustained, cumulative instruction, and cannot be completed in the primary grades. Therefore, during grades four, five, and six, teachers should introduce a range of English in different dialects so pupils become accustomed to the fact of many dialects. Children imitate skillfully; this is why they pick up foreign languages so quickly. These pupils in the middle grades should listen to Scotch, Australian, and Appalachian dialects, to Pidgin, to Cajun, to the Beatles' Liverpoolese. They should sing songs, recite rhymes, and engage in choral speaking in their own dialect and in the standard dialect, trying also to become somewhat flexible, imitating all the dialects presented, producing a range of sounds.

In grades four, five, and six, then, there would be an emphasis upon imitation and upon playing out short skits, reading plays aloud and improvising in creative dramatics. Drama is thus particularly important in the theory of this articulated, sequential program. Often the drama would require puppets because many children readily identify with puppets. Simple hand puppets presented on a stage made from grocery cardboard boxes provide an incentive for children to write their own brief skits. Then they practice them, standing securely concealed behind the stage. Throughout all this they would be imitating different dialects, but *always with an increasing emphasis on the established standard English*—one more tongue to imitate in the same way that Scotch, Pidgin or other dialects are imitated.

Never at any time throughout this elementary school period would the teacher indicate to the child that there is the slightest thing wrong with his dialect, because the teacher would not, in his own heart, believe this. We need teachers who know that such dialects are essentially respectable and good, although the teachers would realize these children must also learn the dialect accepted by convention. Thus there should never be any invidious comparisons, any criticism, at the pre-school and primary school stage of the child's education.

However, before language habits become inflexible, teachers should begin to work on some of the more crucial items of usage by means of oral training as in Hilo and Detroit. This would involve emphasis on usage *through the ear*. If "Him a good dog" exemplifies a crucial usage for a class of Negro pupils, the teacher begins to identify "He is a good dog," and drills orally on case of pronouns—but does *not* employ grammatical analysis. Sometimes the teacher reads ten sentences aloud, explaining first which is standard dialect and which is not. The children listen to these sentences to hear whether or not the teacher expresses the point at issue in established dialect or in non-standard. Often the pupils would number from one to ten on a sheet and write an S (for standard if the teacher uses an expression appropriately) and NS (if the expression is non-standard). The teacher would begin, "Listen for the sentences I read in standard

*Standard (Hawaiian) English for sea urchins armed with dangerous spikes.

and the ones in nonstandard": (1) He is a good dog. (2) She is my friend. (3) Him a happy fellow," and so forth up to 10, the pupils listening and repeating. Such oral-aural drill can be placed on tapes also and used in language laboratories or, more humbly, in one corner of the room while other pupils work with the teacher.

Eventually the time comes when the teacher must talk over with these pupils the facts of social language discrimination, and that time, to my way of thinking, usually is grade five, six, or seven. Teachers differ on the ideal age for introducing the concept, but I see no point in telling children this earlier. Before they can really see the value of learning standard English, pupils need to understand the social consequences the world will exact of them if they cannot handle the established dialect. Grade five, six, or seven, therefore, would be the point at which the concept would be discussed although parts of the total concept might be sketched in earlier as answers to questions children ask. At this upper grade level I would select most carefully teachers who had no snobbish attitudes about language, the scholar-linguist-humanists whom the school could most safely entrust with the important task of explaining sociological truth to these children, aged 11 and 12. "Although the language your parents use is a perfectly good language and we have used it in this class, it is not the only way of speaking English. Have you ever noticed that the textbooks are printed in only one of the English dialects we have heard? The day we went down to visit the juvenile court, the judges and lawyers all talked that standard language. When we had that speaker in assembly the other day and she told us about her work as a judge in the courts, even though she belongs to our same ethnic group, she was using the standard English dialect you hear television announcers use. Now, here is something you need to know. Many business and professional people and many people who hire teachers, architects, clerks, and stenographers just will not hire or encourage people who do not speak the standard dialect. And so, we must begin to speak this special standard way even better than we have so far. We'll have to work on it much more, and I'll help you." Then from grades six through twelve the teacher and pupils would avoid as far as possible the use of social class dialect *in school.* The aim in school during these secondary years would be to help young people acquire this very important kind of dialect, this second language they need. Much of this would require oral-aural pattern practice with taped exercises.

In acquiring the standard dialect, pupils should continue to amplify, embroider, and extend sentences. Thus, they should begin in grades four, five, and six a special kinesthetic method of sentence study. The teacher gives some of the children individual words printed on cards. These pupils come up to the front of the room where they arrange and rearrange themselves, determining how many possible ways they can make sentences with the words they are carrying. Then those not in front of the room practice saying the sentences aloud, using intonation patterns: Where do we drop the voice? Where do we pause? What words should we stress? Can we rearrange the words? Teachers may have other children waiting with extra cards, ready to come up in front to extend the sentences, to see how long they can make them without awkwardness, and then again how short they can make a sentence and still make sense: "What's wrong when we just have, The great white horse. . . ? What's wrong with that? What do we have to do? More words, more words! What words? All right—add them!"

After the pupils have worked with words in front of the room, the next step would be to provide smaller cards for seatwork; everybody rearranges his stack of word cards and works out different solutions and problems as a game.

Next the pupils write compositions and with the opaque projector or some other projector, the teacher throws on the wall some of the papers for reading aloud and for discussion of powerful sentence syntax. At other times a group of children may suggest better sentences as they read aloud each other's papers. Always, the teacher relates the study to the spoken language, to oral intonation, to pause, pitch, emphasis, and all verbal signalling necessary to the melody of standard English usage.

In addition to these strategies there should be much oral reading—especially of literature—by the teacher, through tapes, records, and television, by older pupils invited into the class, and by the pupils themselves. We need very much to restore the oral tradition to English instruction, beginning at pre-school levels. In grades eleven through twelve, the teacher would use drill tapes and language laboratories in order to accomplish ear training, alternating such drill with dramatics, literature, discussion, and writing. The tapes would sometimes focus on usage, pronounciation, vocabulary, and idiom. At other times the tapes would present literature and the pupils would follow the printed page as they listened.

Through the ear all of us learned to speak before we came to school. Only through the ear will any of us ever add a second language, dialect, usage, or pronunciation. The addition of a second dialect will require sustained, cumulative instruction over many school years, but it is a realistic educational goal in a free society seeking to free itself from arbitrary class distinctions.

32. Methods for the Bilingual Child

Doris C. Ching

The problems of the bilingual child continue to be of interest and concern to educators. Bilingualism is still prevalent in our large metropolitan areas, in the rural areas of the Middle West, in the five southwestern states, and in Hawaii.

When the term *bilingualism* is used, there is frequently a vagueness of meaning attached to it. Some people think of a bilingual as an equilingual, a person who can perform proficiently in all aspects of both languages. However, when the term *bilingualism* is used in its broadest sense, it is considered without qualification as to the degree of difference between the two languages or systems known; it is immaterial whether the two systems are "languages," "dialects of the same language," or "varieties of the same dialect."[83]

Thus, a bilingual's achievement may be limited to one aspect of a language, dialect, or variety of a dialect, such as understanding, speaking, reading, writing; or he may have varying degrees of ability in all these aspects. Actually, bilingualism and monolingualism can be thought of as opposite extremes of a continuum, with a continuum for each aspect of language, dialect, or variety of a dialect.[84]

Teachers who work with bilingual children are often confronted with pupils who have handicaps in relation to the language background necessary for successful reading. Investigation has revealed that bilingual children enrolled in the first four grades of the elementary school have difficulties with meanings of words in readers. Before the child with a language handicap can begin to read successfully, he must command a meaningful English vocabulary based on the interests of his age group and including the concepts needed in beginning reading. The task confronting the teacher of a child such as this is much greater than that of a teacher of English-speaking children. The bilingual child with a language handicap needs to receive special attention and instruction.[85]

Various methods of teaching the bilinguals in different parts of the United States have been used, and there have been numerous articles with many suggestions for helping the bilingual child overcome his language deficiencies. Unfortunately there has been a paucity of carefully designed experimental studies concerned with this aspect of the problem of bilingualism; that is, trying to find the best methods that teachers can use to help bilingual children. The

---

studies bearing on this topic which could be located and which have implications for the classroom teacher of bilingual children are summarized below.

Pioneer Experimental Studies

Fuller conducted a four-year study in which successive groups of children in the kindergarten of the Grant School in San Jose, California, were given special language training.[86] Units of work, games, visual aids, and dramatizations were utilized for vocabulary building. The understanding and speaking of the English language was emphasized in all activities. The effectiveness of the special language training given to pupils in the kindergarten was measured by comparing twenty-nine pupils with no speech training and thirty pupils with a year of speech training in the kindergarten as to amount of failure and reading ability during the early elementary school years. The results showed that pupils with special language training in kindergarden made fewer failures in the first grade than those without special training and made better scores on reading tests (names of tests used were not given) when they were tested after three years of schooling. However, because the children were not equated on intelligence, it is difficult to interpret the findings of this study. Fuller concluded that "the problem of providing adequate educational opportunities for those children who are handicapped in language by reason of foreign parentage is of such importance as to warrant further intensive study and experimentation under conditions where more factors can be controlled with larger groups of pupils than was possible in this study. Such research should yield rich returns in the solution of the problem of providing those school experiences which are necessary to meet the needs of pupils with language handicaps."

Unfortunately, though many educators have recognized this need for special methods, there has not been much carefully controlled experimentation in this area.

The San Jose Experimental School study, however, seems to have been a carefully planned experimental study. It was carried on over a period of eight years in New Mexico.[87] The subjects of the experiment were 2,312 pupils in the first through the eighth grades. All the children came from Spanish-speaking homes. The battery of tests administered to San Jose and also to two control schools (with 1,331 and 1,320 pupils respectively) included individual and group intelligence tests and various achievement tests. The children in the control schools were Spanish-speaking and of the same general background as the San Jose youngsters, the number of pupils per teacher was about the same, and the length of the school term was approximately the same, so the author declared that the type of educational program was the large differential factor.

In the school program adopted at San Jose, special emphasis was given to reading and oral English. Extensive room libraries were provided, the work in social sciences was considered as one part of the reading program, and a minimum vocabulary list was taught the first-grade child before the regular work was undertaken.

A comparison of the relative achievements of the three schools in the achievement tests administered; that is, the Gates Reading Test and the New Stanford Achievement Test, showed that when the schools were compared grade by grade according to the averages of the medians for five years, San Jose was in the lead on the Gates by differences which were large enough to prove that they were real and not chance differences. On the Stanford, San Jose was again superior although the differences were not statistically reliable until the fifth grade. However, this report is difficult to interpret because data concerning intelligence were not presented. Furthermore, there was no measure of the extent of bilingualism present in the children studied.

In another study, Herr, like Fuller, was interested in the effect of pre-first-grade training on the bilingual child's achievement when he entered elementary school.[88] This study was somewhat of an improvement on Fuller's because the investigator attempted to equate the children on vocabulary ability, home environment, chronological age, and intelligence. The first two factors were equated by "subjective analysis," and the Pintner-Cunningham Primary Intelligence Test was used to equate the children on intelligence. Two groups of five-year-olds were selected from nine towns in New Mexico. The control group did not attend school and was subjected to no special training, while the experimental group attended school and received special training directed toward the development of their vocabulary, auditory perception, and visual perception.

Another form of the Pintner-Cunningham Intelligence Test was given to both the control and experimental groups when they entered the first grade, and the results showed that the IQ's of the children in the experimental group had increased by 29.91 points (from 66.01 to 95.92), while those of the control group had increased by only 9.56 points (from 68.9 to 78.46). However, since the intelligence tests were verbal and the children had only a limited English vocabulary, the results serve merely as a basis for comparison and diagnosis and not as a true measure of intelligence.

Both groups were introduced to reading in the first grade through the use of experience charts and the preprimer was used when the pupil showed a definite desire to read. At the end of the school year the Metropolitan Achievement Test was given to both groups, and the results showed that all the children in the control group attained a grade placement of 1.5 or below in reading achievement, while in the experimental group 20% achieved a grade placement of 2.1 or over, 67% had 1.9 or over, and not one received a grade placement below 1.5. The investigator concluded that Spanish-American children with pre-first-grade training have a decided advantage over the children who do not have the experience of pre-first-grade training, and that such training is an important factor in success in learning to read and could eliminate a large percentage of failures in the lower grades.

It is unfortunate that Herr did not also give the children a non-verbal intelligence test and that she did not use some of the various measures available for measuring extent of bilingualism instead of just doing it by "subjective analysis." However, the investigator must be commended for her efforts toward a carefully controlled experimental study.

Recent Experimental Studies

The experimental phase of J. Cayce Morrison's *The Puerto Rican Study* is one of the more recent research studies concerning methods of teaching bilingual children.[89] The study was conducted in the first, fourth, and seventh grades of seven schools. In each experimental class one half hour was given to teaching English to Puerto Rican pupils selected as language learners. Language learners were those Puerto Rican children who were not able to communicate effectively in English in the school situation. During the half hour period the teacher emphasized one of three variants of methods. These were: vocabulary, structure or language pattern, and experience. Each teacher used three types of materials: (1) resource units with suggestions for helping the child who needed help in learning English; (2) variant brochures which were manuals of procedure that described the variant to be emphasized and suggested devices, illustrative English-language-learning situations, procedures, and practices; and (3) variant supplements which provided the specific words, the structural patterns or the experiential situations to be developed from day to day.

The testing program was carried on at the beginning and near the close of the school year to obtain measures of pupils' learning in understanding spoken English and in speaking, reading, and writing English. The Gates Reading Test was used to measure English reading ability and all other tests used were constructed by those involved in the study. Data were reported separately for the fourth and seventh grades, but none were given for the first grade. The total numbers of language learners assigned to the experimental classes were 146 in the fourth grade and 462 in the seventh grade. Comparisons were made of the differential gains between variant groups and of the gains from pre-testing to post-testing. The results of the study led the author to conclude that "the three variants had differential strengths, and that all variants were weak in promoting development of English reading skills. The strength of an experiential emphasis seems to be in the area of improving the pupil's ability to understand spoken English. The strength of the vocabulary emphasis is in improving the pupil's ability both to speak and to write English. The strength of a structural emphasis is in improving the pupil's ability to write English. For any one goal, a particular variant may be more effective. For an integrated attack on all four areas of English—understanding, reading, writing, and speaking—a combination of the three emphases together with a more direct attack on reading would seem to be most desirable."

Unfortunately no control group was used in this study and the mental ability of the pupils in the variant groups was not measured. The Puerto Rican pupils may have made gains in the four areas of English without the special instruction and emphasis on teaching English, and the intelligence variable may have had an influence on the results of the study. These factors must, therefore, be considered when interpreting the results of this study.

In another recent study by Ching, a remedial English program was carried on with third-grade bilingual children over a period of six months.[90] The subjects of this investigation were 246 children, 123 each in the experimental and control groups. The experimental and control groups were comparable to each other in regard to chronological age, intelligence, reading and English language ability, and various factors of their personal and environmental backgrounds. The testing instruments used to secure data during the pre-testing and post-testing were the California Short-Form Test of Mental Maturity, the California Reading Test, and two original tests devised by the investigator, the Written English Test and the Oral English Test.

The experimental language program was carried on in the experimental classrooms twenty minutes daily for a six-month period. Approximately two weeks were spent on each of the ten lessons in this program. The lessons were primarily oral in nature. Each lesson was devoted to the correction of a specific type of error in usage and consisted of six main parts: oral drill with sentences; dramatizations; stories; and games which gave the children practice in the correct use of the words being emphasized; and regular checks and regular reviews of what had been taught.

Comparisons of the final scores of the experimental and the control groups in reading and in written and oral English tests showed that the experimental group was significantly superior to the control group in reading and English language ability. Over the six-month period the experimental group made gains in reading and written English which were significantly greater than those of the control group and only the experimental group made a significant gain in oral English.

Other Methods Used with Bilinguals

The preceding are all that can be presented in the way of research reviews in methods for bilingual children. However, the professional literature reveals other methods of teaching bilingual children that have been tried in different parts of the United States. These methods are summarized in an article by Burbeck.[91]

Patterson and Johnson of Santa Barbara, California, worked with a Mexican group using both the informal methods of experience-activity charts and the textbook method of teaching reading.[92] Their conclusions were that these children learned more words from their own charts than from the textbooks and ready-made materials.

Stone made a survey of a school system in California consisting of thirteen schools where there was a considerable number of Mexicans and Italians.[93] Stone felt that the reasons for failure among these children were that the course of study was inflexible, that the material used was too difficult, and that too much time was being devoted to formal vocabulary drills. His experiences with bilingual children led him to conclude that the experience-activity method of teaching reading gave the children a poor start in reading.

Here we have conflicting findings and ideas as to the best methods to use with bilinguals. The reasons for this apparent disagreement may be the manner in which the experience-activity method was used and the different purposes for which it was used. In Patterson and Johnson's study the children may have learned more words from the charts because they had developed the charts themselves from the background of their own experiences and, therefore, the words in the reading material were meaningful and real to them. However, the experience-activity method has its shortcomings as well as its advantages. Although it may be valuable in building interest in reading, in laying the foundation for certain reading mechanics, and in developing comprehension, it cannot be used to teach all children to read because experiences are varied and, therefore, vocabulary to express such experiences must be varied. Consequently, vocabulary is introduced at such a rapid rate that only the exceptional child can keep pace. The teacher can control the vocabulary to some extent, but the control necessary for adequate repetition demands skill and time that the average teacher cannot afford. In addition, expression is stilted by too much control. Stone probably concluded that the method was not a good one for bilinguals because of these reasons. Actually the use of experience charts is a sound method, providing it is not the only method used for developing reading skills with bilingual children.

In the La Jolla School in southern California a method called "incidental" was tried for seven years with "very satisfactory progress." The children were Mexican and Japanese and entered school with scarcely any knowledge of the English language. The curriculum in this school consisted of the study of nature and industrial activities, the enjoyment of songs and stories (through retelling, dramatization, and other activities), and handiwork. Formal subjects, such as arithmetic and grammar, were not taught. Very little writing was done in the primary grades. In this way the teaching of English was incidental, for the main objective was the "improvement of pupils' activities in normal life." It was reported that when this group was tested on formal subjects, the norms compared favorably with average American schools.

One can easily see how the incidental method can be used to advantage in the elementary grades, especially at the primary levels, because it can help to enrich the child's background of experiences and give him many opportunities for oral speaking; but if the method were used for an indefinite period of time, the child would be penalized in other aspects of his school work. There is no reference as to where Burbeck learned about the above situation, and a search of the literature in this area has not uncovered it. It would be of interest to know which test was given to the group in which the norms of the group compared favorably with average American schools, the grade level of the group that was tested, the length of time during which the children were taught by the incidental method, and whether or not the children attended classes in regular schools after they had gained a sufficient knowledge of English.

In Seattle, Washington, Japanese-American bilinguals were segregated and placed in special groups. In their school program, emphasis was placed on pitch and intonation of speech, drill on exercises for the speech organs to obtain correct articulation of English, and drills on the sounds of the letters. Each child progressed at his own rate, and at the end of one and a half to two years, he was able to enter the grade in his own district in which he belonged. At the time the report was written, none of the children had had to return to the special classes for additional work.

There was no description as to the extent of bilingualism present in the children; but the above method, it seems, would be insufficient for children with little knowledge of English. Such children would also need many opportunities for oral speaking and various experiences to broaden their concepts.

Thus, we see that several different methods have been tried with bilinguals in the United States. There is a need now for carefully controlled experimental studies using each of the different methods or combinations of methods to appraise the effectiveness of each with bilingual children. In these studies there should be valid pre-test and post-test measurements of ability and achievement, followed by rigorous and searching statistical analyses of the data. There should also be adequate measurements and descriptions of bilingualism present in the children studied and specific definitions and descriptions of the methods of teaching used to improve the bilingual children's language and reading, as well as the progress, if any, shown by the bilinguals as a result of such methods being used.

Notes

1. Jean Berko, "The Child's Learning of English Morphology," *Word* 14 (1958): 150-177. Also in *Psycholinguistics*, Sol Saporta, ed. (New York: Holt, Rinehart and Winston, 1961), pp. 359-375.
2. Courtney B. Cazden, "The Acquisition of Noun and Verb Inflections," *Child Development 39 (1968)*: 433-448.
3. U. Bellugi and G. Klima, *The Acquisition of the System of Negation in Children's Speech* (Cambridge, Mass.: MIT Press, in press). Quoted material reprinted by permission of MIT Press.
4. Cazden, *op. cit.*
5. Jean Berko Gleason, "Do Children Imitate?" *Proceedings of the International Conference on Oral Education of the Deaf, June 17-24 1967*, Vol. II, 1441-1448, copyright 1967 by the Alexander Graham Bell Association for the Deaf, Washington, D.C. Quoted material reprinted by permission of Alexander Graham Bell Association for the Deaf.
6. Berko, *op. cit.*
7. Gleason, *op. cit.*, p. 3.
8. *Ibid.*, p. 8.
9. D. McNeill, "Developmental Psycholinguistics," in *The Genesis of Language: A Psycholinguistic Approach*, F. Smith and G. A. Miller, eds. (Cambridge, Mass.: MIT Press, 1966), pp. 15-84. Quoted material reprinted by permission of MIT Press.
10. R. Brown and C. Hanlon, "Derivational Complexity and Order of Acquisition in Child Speech," in *Carnegie-Mellon Symposium on Cognitive Psychology*, J. Hayes, ed., in press. R. Brown, C. B. Cazden and U. Bellugi, "The Child's Grammar from I to III," in *1967 Minnesota Symposium on Child Psychology*, J. P. Hill, ed. (Minneapolis: University of Minnesota Press, 1969), pp. 28-73.
11. V. M. Horner, "The Verbal World of the Lower-class Three-year-old: A Pilot Study in Linguistic Ecology," unpublished doctoral dissertation, University of Rochester, 1968.
12. D. I. Slobin, "Questions of Language Development in Cross-cultural Perspective," paper prepared for symposium on "Language Learning in Cross-cultural Perspective" (East Lansing: Michigan State University, September 1968). University, September 1968).
13. Brown, Cazden and Bellugi, *op. cit.*, and Brown and Hanlon, *op. cit.*
14. Bellugi-Klima, *op. cit.*
15. Slobin, *op. cit.*
16. R. H. Weir, *Language in the Crib* (The Hague, The Netherlands: Monton, 1962).
17. Courtney B. Cazden, "Evaluating Language Learning in Early Childhood Education," in *Formative and Summative Evaluation of Student Learning*, B. S. Bloom, T. Hastings and G. Madaus, eds. (New York: McGraw Hill, in press). See also "Language Programs for Young Children: Notes from England," in *Preschool Language Training*, C. B. Lavatelli, ed. (Urbana: University of Illinois Press, in press).
18. F. P. Hawkins, *The Logic of Action: From a Teacher's Notebook* (Boulder: University of Colorado Elementary Science Advisory Center, 1969).
19. See M. Blank and F. Solomon, "How Shall the Disadvantaged Be Taught," *Child Development* 40 (1969): 47-61, for one such comparison.
20. For words of caution see J. Glick, "Some Problems in the Evaluation of Preschool Intervention Programs," in *Early Education*, R. D. Hess and R. M. Bear, eds. (Chicago: Aldine Press, 1968), pp. 215-221, and L. Kohlberg, "Early Education: A Cognitive-Developmental View," *Child Development* 39 (1968): 1013-1062.
21. Marquis James, *The Cherokee Strip* (New York: Viking Press, 1945), p. 120f.
22. There is one spot in the text that can technically be called a flaw in the grammar: the skillful anacoluthon at the dash in the second paragraph. Not one of the thirty-four noticed it; instead they gave

the name of 'grammatical error' to these details: (1) 'was' is wrong with two nouns in the predicate, they said, and corrected it to 'troubles were'; (2) in the second sentence the subject of 'was' should not be 'skull' but 'thickness'; (3) 'As a spur I. . . ' makes the boy himself a spur; (4) should be 'intention to become'; (5) inversion at the beginning of the second paragraph is ungrammatical; (6) 'not having' is slang (!) for 'since I had not'; (7) 'to begin with' puts the preposition at the end of the sentence, a common error; (8) the same sentence has a double negative; (9) 'had no intention' is in the wrong tense, since 'now' refers to present time; (10) 'it' in 'it served' has no antecedent, 'grammar' being ineligible because it is the object of a preposition; (11) 'business of learning'; (12) 'were verbs' should be 'are verbs'; (13) 'which words nouns' should be 'which are nouns'; (14) 'seemed' should be 'seemed to be'; (15) 'than learning' should be 'than to learning'; (16) 'my parents' has a redundant 'my'; (17) 'necessary, to' should be 'necessary in order to' without the comma; (18) 'bushwa': all slang is ungrammatical.

This is grammar? My sample of teachers may not be statistically representative, but it remains clear that grammatical nit-picking inevitably leads to such excesses if it is ever allowed to get started. The only cure is never to start it at all; see later.

23. Walter A. Wolfram, "Sociolinguistic Perspectives on the Speech of the Disadvantaged," ED 029 280, 1969.
24. Martin Deutsch, et. al., "The Deutsch Model—Institute for Developmental Studies," ED 020 009, 1964.
25. Martin Deutsch, "The Disadvantaged Child and the Learning Process," ED 021 721, 1963.
26. Cynthia Deutsch, "Auditory Discrimination and Learning: Social Factors," ED 001 116, 1964.
27. Martin Deutsch, "The Role of Social Class in Language Development and Cognition," ED 011 329, 1966.
28. William Labov and Clarence Robins, "A Note on the Relation of Reading Failure to Peer-Group Status in Urban Ghettos," in *Linguistic-Cultural Differences and American Education*, Alfred C. Aarons, Barbara Y. Gordon, and William A. Stewart, eds., Special Anthology Issue, *The Florida FL Reporter* 7, 1 (Spring/Summer 1969).
29. Vera P. John, "The Social Context of Language Acquisition," ED 001 494.
30. Harry Osser, "The Syntactic Structures of 5-Year-Old Culturally Deprived Children," ED 020 788, 1966.
31. Courtney B. Cazden, "Subcultural Differences in Child Language: an Interdisciplinary Review," ED 011 325, 1966. *Merrill-Palmer Quarterly of Behavior and Development* 12 (1966): 185-219.
32. Joan C. Baratz, "A Bi-Dialectal Test for Determining Language Proficiency," ED 020 519, 1968.
33. Joan C. Baratz, "Language and Cognitive Assessment of Negro Children: Assumptions and Research Needs," ED 020 518, 1968.
34. Joan C. Baratz and Edna Povich, "Grammatical Constructions in the Language of the Negro Preschool Child," ED 022 157, 1968. See also Laura L. Lee. "Developmental Sentence Types: A Method for Comparing Normal and Deviant Syntactic Development," *Journal of Speech and Hearing Disorders* 31 (1966).
35. Vincent P. Skinner, "Mountaineers Aren't Really Illiterate," ED 020 236, 1967. *Southern Education Report* 3 (1967): 18-19.
36. Texas Education Agency, *Report on the Preschool Instructional Program for Non-English Speaking Children* (Austin: Author, 1962).
37. Nelson Brooks, *Language and Language Learning*, 2nd ed. (New York: Harcourt, Brace and World, Inc., 1964), and Werner F. Leopold, "Patterning in Children's Language Learning," in *Psycholinguistics*, Sol Saporta, ed. (New York: Holt, Rinehart and Winston, 1961).
38. John B. Carroll, "Language Development in Children," *Encyclopedia of Educational Research* (New York: Macmillan Company, 1960).
39. Roger Brown, *Words and Things* (New York: Free Press, 1966).
40. Noam Chomsky, *Language and Mind* (New York: Harcourt, Brace and World, 1968).
41. Brooks. *op. cit.*
42. Robert Lado, *Language Teaching* (New York: McGraw-Hill, Inc., 1964).
43. Brooks, *op. cit.*, and Wilga M. Rivers, *The Psychologist and the Foreign-Language Teacher* (Chicago: University of Chicago Press, 1964).
44. Carl Bereiter and Siegfried Engelmann, *Teaching Disadvantaged Children in the Preschool* (Englewood Cliffs, N. J.: Prentice-Hall, 1966). See also Joe L. Frost, *Early Childhood Education Rediscovered* (New York: Holt, Rinehart and Winston, 1968).
45. Brooks, *op. cit.*; Lado, *op. cit.*, and Harold B. Dunkel, *Second Language Learning* (Boston: Ginn and Company, 1948).
46. Thomas D. Horn, "Three Methods of Developing Reading Readiness in Spanish-Speaking Children in First Grade," *The Reading Teacher* 20 (October 1966): 38-42.

47. Thomas D. Horn, *A Study of the Effects of Intensive Oral-Aural English Language Instruction, Oral-Aural Spanish Language Instruction, and Non-Oral-Aural Instruction of Reading Readiness in Grade One* (Austin: University of Texas, 1966).
48. Richard D. Arnold, *1965-66 (Year Two) Findings, San Antonio Language Research Project*, Thomas D. Horn, Director (Austin: University of Texas, 1968).
49. Lester N. Knight, *A Comparison of the Effectivness of Intensive Oral-Aural English Instruction, Intensive Oral-Aural Spanish Instruction, and Non-Oral-Aural Instruction on the Oral Language and Reading Achievement of Spanish-Speaking Second- and Third-Graders* (Austin: University of Texas, 1969).
50. Mary E. Swanson, *A Comparative Study on the Effects of Oral-Aural Teaching Techniques on Pupils' Gains in Reading, Language and Work Study Skills in Grades Three and Four* (Austin: University of Texas, in Press).
51. Thomasine H. Taylor, *A Comparative Study on the Effects of Oral-Aural Language Training on Gains in English for Fourth and Fifth-Grade Disadvantaged Mexican-American Children* (Austin: University of Texas, 1969).
52. Elizabeth H. Ott, *A Study of Levels of Fluency and Proficiency in Oral English of Spanish-Speaking School Beginners* (Austin: University of Texas, 1967).
53. Richard D. Arnold, "Reliability of Test Scores for the Young 'Bilingual' Disadvantaged," *The Reading Teacher* 22 (January 1969): 341-345, and "Social Studies for the Culturally and Linguistically Different Learners," *Social Education* 33 (January 1969): 73-76; Elaine D. Fowler, *An Evaluation of Brengleman-Manning Linguistic Capacity Index as a Predictor of Reading Achievement of Spanish-Speaking First-Grade Students* (Austin: University of Texas, 1969); Gloria R. Jameson, *The Development of a Phonemic Analysis for an Oral English Proficiency Test for Spanish-Speaking School Beginners* (Austin: University of Texas, 1967); Neil A. McDowell, *A Study of the Academic Capabilities and Achievements of Three Ethnic Groups: Anglo, Negro and Spanish Surname;* Fredrich G. Pauck, *An Evaluation of the Self-Test as a Predictor of Reading Achievement of Spanish-Speaking First-Grade Children* (Austin: University of Texas, 1968); Albar A. Pena, *A Comparative Study of Selected Syntactical Structures of the Oral Language Status in Spanish and English of Disadvantaged First-Grade Spanish-Speaking Children* (Austin: University of Texas, 1967).
54. Lado, *op. cit.*; Brooks, *op. cit.;* and Mary Finocchiaro, *Teaching English as a Second Language* (New York: Harper and Row, 1958).
55. Anne O. Stemmler, "An Experimental Approach to the Teaching of Oral Language and Readings," *Harvard Educational Review* 36 (Winter 1966): 42-59; Horn, *op. cit.*
56. Richard D. Arnold, "English as a Second Language," *The Reading Teacher* 21 April 1968): 634-639.
57. Jean Piaget, "Notions of Causality," in *Newsletter* 9 (Winter 1967). Science Curriculum Improvement Study, University of California at Berkeley.
58. E. Milner, "A Study of the Relationship between Reading Readiness in Grade One School Children and Patterns of Parent-Child Interaction," *Child Development* 22 (1951): 95-112.
59. B. Bernstein, "Social Structure, Language and Learning," *Educational Research;* 3, 3 (1961): 163-167.
60. R. Hess and V. Shipman, *Parents as Teachers,* ERIC (Urbana, Ill.: National Laboratory for Early Childhood Education, 1968).
61. D. Moore, "A Comparison of Two Methods of Teaching Specific Language Skills to Lower Class Preschool Children, a Research Proposal," mimeographed (Cambridge, Mass.: Harvard Graduate School of Education, 1968).
62. Bereiter and Engelmann, *op. cit.*
63. Courtney B. Cazden, "Environmental Assistance to the Child's Acquisition of Grammar," unpublished doctoral thesis, Harvard University, 1965.
64. A. Jensen, "Social Class and Verbal Learning," in *Social Class, Race, and Psychological Development*, Martin Deutsch, I. Katz, and A. Jensen, eds. (New York: Holt, Rinehart and Winston, 1968), pp. 115-174.
65. M. Blank and F. A. Solomon, "A Tutorial Language Program to Develop Abstract Thinking in Socially Disadvantaged Preschool Children," *Child Development* 39, 2 (1968): 379-390.
66. Bellugi-Klima, *op. cit.*
67. Michael A. K. Halliday, Angus McIntosh, and Peter Strevens, *The Linguistic Sciences and Language Teaching* (Bloomington: Indiana University Press, 1965), Chap. 7.
68. Susan M. Ervin and Wick R. Miller, "Language Development," *Child Psychology*, Sixty-Second Yearbook of the National Society for the Study of Education, Part I (Chicago: The University of Chicago Press, 1963), p. 125.
69. John B. Carroll, *op. cit.*, p. 748.
70. Martin Joos, "Language and the School Child," in *Language and Learning* (New

York: Harcourt, Brace and World, 1966), p. 205.
71. Benjamin S. Bloom, *Stability and Change in Human Characteristics* (New York: John Wiley, 1964).
72. Lee A. Pederson, "The Pronunciation of English in Metropolitan Chicago: Vowels and Consonants," unpublished doctoral dissertation, the University of Chicago, 1964; William Labov, *The Social Stratification of English in New York City* (Washington, D. C.: Center for Applied Linguistics, 1966); Richard L. Larson, "An Inquiry into Possible Relationships Between the Place of Students' Upbringing and the Characteristics of Their Written and Spoken English," 1966 (in progress).
73. Eric H. Lenneberg, "A Biological Perspective of Language," *New Directions in the Study of Language* (Cambridge, Mass.: MIT Press, 1964), pp. 67-68.
74. Ursula Bellugi and Roger Brown, *The Acquisition of Language* (Lafayette, Ind.: Child Development Monograph of the Society for Research in Child Development, 1964); John B. Carroll, *op. cit.*; Susan M. Ervin and Wick R. Miller, *op. cit.*; Ruth H. Weir, *op. cit.*
75. *Writers at Work: The Paris Review Interviews*, Vol. I, Malcolm Cowley, ed., (New York: Viking Press, Inc., 1958); Vol. II, introduction by Van Wyck Brooks (New York: Viking Press, Inc., 1963).
76. *Counterpoint*, Roy Newquist, ed. (Chicago: Rand McNally Company, 1964).
77. Wallace Hildick, *Word for Word: A Study of Authors' Alterations, with Exercises* (New York: W. W. Norton and Company, Inc., 1966.).
78. Thomas Parkinson, *W. B. Yeats: Later Poetry* (Calif.: University of California Press, 1966).
79. Raymond Queneau, *Exercises de Style* (New York: French and European Publications, Inc., 1966).
80. Walker Gibson, *Tough, Sweet and Stuffy* (Bloomington: Indiana University Press, 1966).
81. Werner Cohn, "On the Language of Lower Class Children," *School Review* (Winter 1959): 35-40.
82. At one time, as Richard Foster Jones shows in *The Triumph of the English Language*, Stanford University Press, 1966, all English was regarded as a vulgar, inferior tongue incapable of sufficient development for use in the arts, law, or civilized society.
83. Uriel Weinrich, *Languages in Contact: Findings and Problems* (New York: Publication of the Linguistic Circle of New York, 1953), p. 1-2.
84. Harry Singer, "Bilingualism and Elementary Education," *Modern Language Journal* 40 (December 1956): 445-446.
85. Sister M. Timothy, "The Reading Problem of a Bilingual Child," *Elementary English* 41 (March 1964): 235-237.
86. Lorraine Fuller, "The Effect of Kindergarten Speech Training on Primary Grade Progress and Achievement of Children with Foreign Language Handicaps," *California Journal of Elementary Education* 4 (February 1936): 165-173.
87. San Jose Experimental School, *We Learn English: A Preliminary Report of the Achievement of Spanish-Speaking Pupils in New Mexico* (Albuquerque: University of New Mexico, 1936).
88. Selma E. Herr, "The Effect of Pre-First Grade Training upon Reading Readiness and Reading Achievement among Spanish-American Children," *Journal of Educational Psychology* 37 (February 1946): 87-102.
89. J. Cayce Morrison, *The Puerto Rican Study, 1953-1957* (New York: Board of Education, 1958).
90. Doris C. Ching, "Effects of a Six Month Remedial English Program on Oral, Writing, and Reading Skills of Third-Grade Hawaiian Bilingual Children," *Journal of Experimental Education* 32 (Winter 1963): 133-145.
91. Edith Burbeck, "Problems Presented to Teachers of Bilingual Pupils," *California Journal of Elementary Education* 8 (August 1939): 49-54.
92. Inez Patterson and Hazel M. Johnson, "Methods for Mexicans," *Sierra Educational News* 33 (September 1937): 12.
93. Clarence R. Stone, "How to Adapt Reading Instruction to the Varying Needs of Children," *California Journal of Elementary Education* 5 (Feburary 1936): 91-99.

Selected Bibliography

Adams, L.S. "If FLES is to Succeed: Foreign Languages in the Elementary School." *N.E.A. Journal,* **56** (December 1967): 72.

Arnold, Richard D. "Mexican Americans and Language Learning." *Childhood Education,* **46** (December 1969): 149-154.

Bailey, Beryl Loftman. "Some Aspects of the Impact of Linguistics on Language Teaching in Disadvantaged Communities." *Elementary English,* **45** (May 1968): 570-578.

Bosmajian, Haig A. "The Language of White Racism." *College English,* **31** (December 1969): 263-72.

Burrows, Alvina T. "Children's Language: Insights for the Language Arts." *National Elementary Principal,* **40** (September 1965): 16-21.

Cassidy, Frederic G. "American Regionalisms in the Classroom." *English Journal,* **57** (March 1968): 375-379.

Clapp, Ouida. "Language Arts, Why Color it White?" *Instructor,* **80** (October 1965): 74-75.

Cohen, Dorothy H. "Language and Experience: The Setting." *Childhood Education,* **42** (November 1965): 139-142.

Conville, Mozella P. "Language Improvement for Disadvantaged Elementary School Youngsters." *Speech Teacher,* **18** (March 1969): 120-123.

Dale, Edgar. "Vocabulary Development of the Underprivileged Child." *Elementary English,* **42** (November 1965): 778-786.

Day, D. E., and J. R. Nurss. "Effects of Instruction on Language Development." *Elementary School Journal,* **70** (January 1970): 225-231.

DeBoer, John. "Some Sociological Factors in Language Development." In *Child Development and the Language Arts,* National Conference on Research in English, pp. 6-16. Champaign, Ill.: NCTE, 1963.

Deutsch, Martin. "The Role of Social Class in Language Development and Cognition." *American Journal of Orthopsychiatry,* **35** (January 1965): 78-88.

Goodman, Kenneth S. "Let's Dump the Uptight Model in English." *Elementary School Journal,* **70** (October 1969): 1-3.

Gunderson, D.V. "Language Development in its Social Context." Conference on Reading, Report 23, University of Pittsburgh, 1967, pp. 39-46.

Heffron, Pearl M. "Our American Slang." *Elementary English,* **39** (May 1962): 429-434, 465.

Hornburger, Jane M. "Bringing Their Own: Language Development in the Middle Grades." *Childhood Education,* **46** (December 1969): 155-157.

Kaplan, Robert B. "On a Note of Protest (In a Minor Key): Bidialectalism vs. Bidialectism." *College English,* **30** (February 1969): 386-389.

Krear, S. E. "Role of the Mother Tongue at Home and at School in the Development of Bilingualism." *English Language Teacher,* **24** (October 1969): 2-4.

Lenneberg, Eric H. "On Explaining Language." *Science,* **164** (May 9, 1969): 635-643.

Loban, Walter. "What Language Reveals." In *Language and Meaning,* Association for Supervision and Curriculum Development, N.E.A., pp. 63-73, 1966.

MacGinitie, Walter M. "Language Development." In *Encyclopedia of Educational Research,* 4th edition, edited by L. L. Ebel, V. H. Noll and R. M. Bauer, pp. 686-699. Toronto, Can.: The Macmillan Company, 1969.

McCarthy, Dorthea A. "Language Development in Children." In *Manual of Child Psychology,* 2nd edition, edited by Leonard Carmichael. New York: John Wiley and Sons, Inc., 1954.

McDavid, Raven F. "Variations in Standard American English." *Elementary English,* **45** (May 1968): 561-564, 608.

Nielsen, Wilhelime R. "Experiences and Language Development." *Childhood Education,* **46** (December 1969): 135-138.

Ralph, Jane B. "Language Development in Socially Disadvantaged Children." *Review of Educational Research,* **35** (December 1965): 389-400.

Ratte, E. H. "Foreign Language and the Elementary School Language Arts Program." *French Review,* **42** (October 1968): 80-85.

Shuy, Roger W. "Detroit Speech: Careless, Awkward, and Inconsistent, or Systematic, Graceful, and Regular?" *Elementary English,* **45** (May 1968): 565-569.

Smith, Dora V. "Developmental Language Patterns of Children." In *Reading and the Related Arts,* A Report of the Twenty-first Annual Conference on Reading, University of Pittsburgh, 1965, pp. 19-28.

Strickland, Ruth. "Language Learning: Modes, Models and Mystique." In *Claremont Reading Conference,* 29th Yearbook, edited by Malcolm P. Douglass, pp. 81-89. 1965.

PART FOUR
Oral Language Experiences

A.
Listening

More attention should be given by the elementary school teacher to instructing the learners how to listen. Normal children learn first to listen, then to speak, next to read, and last to write. Listening skills establish the basis for achievement in speaking, reading, and writing. The ability to think and to solve problems is directly related to skill in listening. Despite its importance to communication, listening is probably the most neglected skill in classroom instruction. Evidence indicates that listening instruction in the elmentary school is almost exclusively restricted to admonitions of "pay attention" and "listen carefully."

It is now apparent that the ability to listen well is not innate. The ability to listen effectively must be taught. Research data indicate that listening skills can be taught and that listening ability does improve substantially when specific instruction is provided. Therefore, it is essential that elementary teachers make children aware of the importance of listening and provide specific guidance in the development of needed listening skills. By encouraging children to talk, share, plan, discuss, report, evaluate, and express their creative thinking, many meaningful opportunities for listening will arise throughout the school day. Listening instruction should not be based on incidental experiences because such isolated opportunities to listen do not teach a child to listen effectively. The development of listening skill is the result of carefully planned programs that are carried out in daily classroom activities.

The following articles discuss the serious neglect of listening instruction in our elementary schools today. The authors point out the urgent need for greater emphasis on teaching the skill of effective listening and offer valuable suggestions for developing good listening habits in the classroom.

33.
The Concept of Oracy

Andrew Wilkinson

It would be inappropriate for a visitor such as myself to make prescriptions as to what should be going on in English teaching in North America. The most I can do is to describe what seems to me to be liberal, suitable, good British practice, and where it has relevance to the American situation you will obviously be able to make your own comparisons; where it hasn't relevance you will be able to make your own rejections. First of all then I would like to talk about the fundamental processes going on in English teaching because it is impossible for me to talk about the aspect indicated in my title without going a little deeper. If I were asked to write a book on the teaching of English in a time of great shortage, and the publisher allowed me three words only, this would present me with something of a problem. Eventually I would produce three words which would seem to me to describe the essential process that we are concerned with in the teaching of English. These words would be the *verbalization of experience*. In other words, it's encouraging people to put what they have experienced into words—when I'm writing I'm putting something that happened to me into words, when I'm speaking I'm putting something that this—literature for instance. So obviously my definition is incomplete. My publisher, however, is adamant; I can only have three words. This is an even greater problem, but at last I have an inspiration. I switch them around. The other part of the process encouraging English teaching is the *experience of verbalization*. "Verbalization" is what other people write and what other people say. And we as readers read what they write and we as listeners listen to what they are speaking. The definition seems to include something essential, expressed fairly simply. It seems to me that one cannot subtract any more words from it. But if I had to, at this publisher's command, I'd have to leave out anything but the word "experience." I'd have to say that this is where we start from, this is the first thing in the teaching of English.

We would have to consider what one meant by experience, what sort of experiences must one build into the English class teaching. We might think first of the students. What sort of experiences would be meaningful to them. For instance, what has happened to them; what has happened to their brothers and sisters; what when they were lost; what when their father or mother went

From the *English Journal* 59:70-77 (January 1970).

away; what happened to a girl when she fell down? And what happens to the child in the classroom when we bring in a pipe of soap bubbles and we begin to blow it and we say—now look at that bubble; describe it in words; now can you describe that infinitesimally tiny noise it makes when it bursts? And we bring other experiences into the classroom; the sound of a bell, just a single stroke of a bell and what it evokes in their minds; or we circulate a bottle with a strange scent in—what does this evoke? These are experiences. Or we circulate a piece of rusty iron, or driftwood. How evocative this can be, like Henry Moore's statues. And there are the experiences when the students go out and visit places, or when they read things; when they read *Huck Finn;* or when they read *The Old Man and the Sea,* and they suddenly become old, and they suddenly become courageous and noble. And when they see a film of, for instance, a bullfight and the beauty and the cruelty cause them to really assess what's been happening to them during this film. Or when they see pictures of children or old people or young people or happiness. And when they see a sparrow peck about in the gravel as Keats saw a sparrow peck about in the gravel. The point about mentioning Keats here or any other writer, is that we are realizing the same process of creation goes on within a child as in a great creative artist—an excited response to and an organization of experience. I think it is summed up by what Coleridge said: "I cannot write without body of thought." And by thought he means more than thought in the limited sense. He means the interreactions of the whole sensibility—of thought, of feeling.

Now, if one makes this basic assumption, one can proceed to look at the implications this kind of statement has for our varied approaches to the teaching of English.

In the past, we in England certainly, have tended to start with a group of skills, we've made goals or objectives of a variety of skills. And these skills tend to be those we can define pretty clearly; skills of grammar, for instance, and spelling and paragraphing and topic sentences. We tend to spend so much time with these things that it's easy to forget the central activity. Now the switch in emphasis in English teaching is a switch to the centrality of experience so that the skills emerge in the *process* of verbalizing the experience, and they don't have the status of immediate goals. The experience is the thing one starts with. This I think is a shift of emphasis. Now, again, we tend conventionally, and I think this is useful, to think of English as having three facets. We tend to think of it as having the facets of language, literature, and composition. Now this may be an example of the way that words determine our thought processes rather than our thought processes choose words in which to express themselves. Language, literature, and composition, we tend to think of as either reading skills or writing skills. This certainly has been the tendency in the past, and this had made our thinking about English teaching very *literary, i.e.,* based on reading and writing. Supposing however we don't start with those three headings, but with the verbalization of experience; and the experience of verbalization. One starts with the verbalization of experience, that is one starts with producing language, and of course we call this *production.* Now the way we produce language is twofold—by speaking it and by writing it. And then we come to consider the other aspect—the *reception* of language. We receive it by reading and we receive it by listening. Reading and writing are the skills of literacy. When you look at speaking and listening, however, we find that we heve hitherto had no word in which to make a description of those two skills. And to come back to a point I made earlier in a slightly different connection, our thinking is often determined by the words we have, and not to have a word for a concept may be not to think at all about that concept.

	production	reception
	speaking	listening
LITERACY	writing	reading

When we came to carry out research into the spoken language in the University of Birmingham, England, we found that there were no words for a large number of features of the spoken language. For instance, what sort of word, what grammatical term, can you apply to a word which is the most common in the English language, the word *er*? It is a language feature, not just a mistake. The more we look at language we realize that to *er* is human, may even be divine. For words like *er*, and pauses and hesitations, and groups like *you know, you mean, know what I mean,* which have been called faults in the past, have really definite virtues (we have called them stabilizers). And they are just one more indication of the way we tended to look at the spoken language in the way that we look at the written language and yet these two are not the same at all. The examples here are fairly lighthearted, but the serious point is that for the central concept of speaking and listening there was no term and so we offered in all deference the term "oracy," to describe these skills as a parallel to literacy (Wilkinson and others, University of Birmingham School of Education, 1965). Thus our model is completed.

	production	reception
ORACY	speaking	listening
LITERACY	writing	reading

Now in England this seems to fulfill a need. One can't foist off a word onto an unwilling public: either a word fulfills a need and it's used and it lives, or it doesn't and it dies. It seems in this case, at the moment, it is fulfilling a certain need, the point being that it is a word which enables one to think about the importance of these skills of speaking and listening; and these skills are, of course, not only important but fundamental. Our communication is most of the time through speaking and listening, and very little of the time through reading and writing, and the less able our children are, the more this is true and will ever be true. Psychologists have led us to see how fundamental the spoken language is to the development, not only of the human ability to speak, not only of the human ability to communicate, but the human ability to develop fully a personality, and to develop cognitively. An English document, called the Newson Report (1963), I would just like to read you a little bit of because it seems to me that this does sum up some of the importance that we now attach to the spoken language. "There is no gift like the gift of speech, and the level at which people have learned to use it determines the level of their companionship and the level at which their life is lived." Speech determines the level of our companionship, the level at which our lives are lived. This is very different from the old attitude towards speech and listening which was a kind of frill subject, perhaps taught by someone coming in from outside. The report goes on:

> This matter of communication affects all aspects of social and intellectual growth. There is a gulf between those who have, and the many who have not, sufficient command of words to be able to listen and discuss rationally; to express ideas and feelings clearly; and even to have any ideas at all. We simply do not know how many people are frustrated in their lives by inability ever to express themselves adequately; or how many never develop intellectually because they lack the words with which to think and reason. This is a matter as important to economic life as it is to personal living; industrial relations as well as marriages come to grief on failures in communication.

There we have it. Speech (including listening) is a central factor in the development of the personality and closely related to human happiness and well being. And so, with those fairly preliminary but important remarks, I want to turn in a little more detail to these two aspects of oracy—speaking and listening.

I am now concerned with speaking or talking. We should teach speech in the way that we learn speech, and this is not by having speech lessons separated from English lessons, it's not by having drama lessons separated from English lessons, it's not by having elocution lessons separated from English lessons. What we mean by speech is not interpretative language, it's not reciting a poem, or even giving a public speech (very few people ever have to give public speeches). What we are concerned with is a certain quality of language which consists, not in interpreting other people's words, but in putting one word of our own, next to another word of our own, next to another word of our own, and so on in the creative utterance which we are all using all the time while we are speaking. So it follows that we must start with situation. The task of any teacher of English, and this applies to literacy as well as oracy, is the creation of situations in which language is the natural outcome. When I speak to you, you must answer; when you speak to me I must answer, unless I contract out (by for instance being rude or embarrassed). Ninety-nine times out of a hundred the speech situation is compulsory; we must communicate when we are in the situation. If I am in an elevator and there is only one other person in it, perhaps a person of the opposite sex, the elements in the compulsory speech situation are all there but something is lacking. Englishmen certainly would probably avoid eye contact with English women in this lift because that is almost the equivalent of assault (I have yet to find out what the American custom is on this!). But the lift stops between floors and the elements in the compulsory speech situation are all present and in addition that little bit of tension which compels speech. There's a speaker, there's a listener, there's a context, and there's a subject, a desperate need to talk. The illustration is silly but the point is serious. We do find words, we do talk, in conversations when we have to answer, in discussions when we are confronted with points, in lifts when there are some things that must be said. There's that little bit of compulsion about it.

Now this, it seems to me, is the basic device for speech training, a *compulsory situation*. I am not meaning compulsory in any authoritarian sense. I think I have defined sufficiently the kind of thing I mean. Now the normal classroom school situation does not provide these compulsory situations in profusion. In fact, it scarcely provides them at all in many cases, because in the conventional classroom we often get to have a gigantic prestige figure, to use the language of the social-psychologists, and you have a series of low prestige figures, and they're seated in rows, so that the communication tends to go one way only. There may be a question-and-answer session, but the whole purpose of much fast questioning is to preclude anything but a single response. The teacher knows the answer, and there's only one possible answer he will accept. The others can only say one thing. We can't develop speech under those circumstances. Now the whole richness of conversation is that you can say absolutely anything to anybody in answer to anything. Remember King Henry IV, Part I, when Prince Hal is teasing Falstaff and he keeps reminding him of the gallows. Falstaff replies, "By the Lord, thou sayest true, Lad. . . And is not my hostess of the tavern a most sweet wench?" (I.ii.34). This is certainly a creative response, a creative strategy for moving away. It comes out from that situation.

The basic conversational situation, the basic discussion situation, is one in which two or three or half-a-dozen are sitting around, and ideas get discussed and pushed around. So the basic situation for development of oracy, for oral production, is the group situation; and the practice in the English classrooms that I am thinking of is to have a large amount of splitting children up into groups and working in that way. There's a point in the California State film on English teaching—that children should have an opportunity sometimes to take the equal or even the superior role. I think that's a very wise statement. But it is not of course appropriate all the time. The teacher's function is crucial. It's the teacher who directs the students' language. Adults stretch children's language. The basic device is to split the grade into small groups, sometimes only of two. Very withdrawn children may be helped by only having one other to talk to, and by not being overwhelmed by very loquacious students. It is a big undertaking to discuss the sort of work that one would think is appropriate in groups, and obviously I can't go into it in detail, I would just like to take one or two examples. One I'm going to take from my limited experience of America. I saw recently some very interesting work in inter-age teaching whereby older children, after a training session, are given the responsibility for teaching younger children certain things. In their training session they discuss tapes and interviews of these younger children, and they discuss these in a certain type of language. They discuss this in the sort of language which you do discuss things objectively in. Then they go and teach these young children and they adopt a slightly different language, an expository language that we would adopt in simplifying your language for younger children. We don't talk to everybody like it. And these are genuine situations. The fourteen-year-old students have to communicate with one another, with their group leaders; they have to communicate with young children, they have to explain. And the situations are compulsory.

We may mention briefly other examples, more conventional for the English classroom. For instance children come in to a new grade, perhaps a new school as they do in England at eleven. The teacher splits them up into groups and announces the topic is "schools." One group discusses schools their parents went to, another the difficulties of getting to school, the third schools they went to before, the fourth their impressions of the new school. They discuss these things and then one of their number in each group reports back to the whole class and then, perhaps as a further exercise, they write something about their ideal school. Their responses then are both oral and written because oracy and literacy move in and out of one another. Again, younger students may be split into groups to discuss a picnic. Perhaps they are given certain guidance. In the United Kingdom in both the elementary schools in the higher grades and in our secondary schools, some teachers give little sheets with discussion hints on. Discussion hints are very simple; about the picnic for instance—where shall we go; who shall we invite; what food shall we take with us; what shall we do when we get there. Such headings give that little bit of necessary guidance. Meanwhile the teacher is going around to these groups, and giving that little bit of lift; saying, "Yes, but haven't you forgotten so and so?" and, to a higher group of students, "What exactly do you mean by that?" or "Shouldn't you consider this?"

This group situation can be extended in the field of literacy. Some of our children write group novels for instance. They discuss the plot and characters first and then write, section by section. Some of our children discuss poems in groups and then read them back to the rest of the form or discuss them. In each case different kinds of language will be used because we all have, as I have tried to imply, varieties of language for different situations. We do not speak to everybody in the same way, and sometimes we are unaware that we make all kinds of subtle changes. A man doesn't speak to his employer in the terms he uses for his wife or somebody else's wife.

I have been hinting that there is guidance implicit in the learning situation. Of course, it's terribly important to get children to talk, especially younger children. They need to build confidence, but when all is said and done, it is not just one gigantic village pub gossip we are aiming at. Children are being gradually moved in the directions of *relevance*, of *objectivity*, of *depth*, and of *reciprocity*. I needn't perhaps go into this, but if you have suffered like I have, attending numerous meetings in which every single further point raised seems to be off the issue, and the chairman follows it up off the issue, it does seem to me that the sense of relevance is one of the most serious drawbacks in our speech skills. Depth of course is obvious; objectivity is obvious. This is what educated human beings ought to be able to attain to. Reciprocity is of course the sense of the other person, that delicate sense of somebody else with rights, the way that you get the emanations coming from them, and the way you get on their wavelength, and *listen* to them. These are very important things. The kind of discussion I am thinking of should gradually encourage these things.

May I now turn to listening, because if speaking is neglected, listening is unheard of in common educational practice. The new linguistics, I think, has contributed a great deal to our knowledge of the spoken language, and has modified our attitudes towards it. It has much to contribute to our teaching but not the sort of contribution that some people are suggesting it should make in English schools. I would be very suspicious of formal grammatical training derived from the new linguistics, or anything resembling it, but the spoken language I think is a field in which we can interest children in language. There's a magnificent passage in the preface to that great 1765 dictionary of Samuel Johnson. He's talking about the words he has put in and the words he has left out and, quite clearly, he's not very enthusiastic about certain words. These are the words which he dubs in his dictionary *low* or *mean* or *barbarous* or *bad*. It is very interesting that many of them are spoken and not written words. Here is the passage.

> That many terms of art and manufacture are omitted, must be frankly acknowledged; but for this defect I may boldly allege that it was unavoidable; I could not visit caverns to learn the miner's language, nor take a voyage to perfect my skill in the dialect of navigation, nor visit the warehouses of merchants, and shops of

> artificers to gain the name of wares, tools, and operations, of which no mention is found in books; what favorable accident or easy enquiry brought within my reach, has not been neglected, but it had been a hopeless labor to glean up words by courting living information, and contesting with the sullenness of one, and the roughness of another.

What does Johnson mean by courting living information? He means that he is not going to listen to words as they are on the tongues of men, nor to have words which are not found in books, nor to listen to living speech. Johnson was deaf, and he hadn't time. What he did do was a monument, and he was anyway within the assumptions of his age. But we are not any longer bound by those assumptions. What I am saying is that listening in schools could be made fascinating by providing what Johnson called "living information," by providing tapes and records and perhaps videotapes of the spoken language. In England there are radio plays, in both countries there are records available; but more there are tape recorders. We have the ability to get conversations down on tape or to make conversations, to put specially on tape, to record different dialects, different idiolects, to ask questions about the difference between the spoken and the written language, to ask questions about the sorts of relationships which are going on as expressed through language. The conventional training in listening, both in England and America, and particularly in America, has been skill training, and the conventional listening tests have been skills. The American teachers have started off, not with the linguistic material, not with this rich, living information, but with psychological skills, the ability to separate the main from the subordinate point, the ability to recognize signposts in information. There is nothing wrong with this, of course, but it's all the time a question of emphasis, what the priorities are. The material has been testing material, not teaching material. Listening tests so far have taken a piece of written English which has then been read aloud. Scholars have then been surprised that the correlations with reading skills are pretty high. It was Lindquist in 1959 in the *Yearbook of Mental Measurements* (Gryphon Press, 1959) who made this point, though he probably didn't realize that what was wrong was that they were testing the same material. What we want in the listening field is "living information," and I think the time is right, both in the United Kingdom and in America, for the construction of a new spoken literature (the word *literature* is question begging), a new body of "living information" which will motivate our children, including the less able children who are not terribly interested in books but who are listening and speaking all the time.

To summarize, I have been arguing that we cannot separate oracy from literacy; in describing the concept of oracy I am not advocating something off track. It is part and parcel of the verbalization of experience. I would like also to add that not only can we not separate it from literacy, but also that we cannot separate English from other subjects in the timetable, because the verbalization of experience is going on the whole time in these areas, using different sorts of language. My suggestions as far as the spoken language is concerned have been that we could profitably (certainly in the United Kingdom) pay much more attention to the kinds of situations which are not so prestige ridden, more group situations which produce natural speaking, that we could pay more attention to the living language, and that we could, in Johnson's words, "court living information."

34.

Teaching Listening in the Elementary School

Paul M. Hollingsworth

Listening improvement begins in the elementary school classroom. Canfield had this to say about listening: "Day in and day out our ears are bombarded by volleys of spoken words. To interpret verbal messages and to tune out verbal noise are essential skills in out time. How to teach these listening skills is a vital question for the classroom teacher."[1]

In teaching these listening skills, several characteristics should be involved in a listening improvement program in the elementary school.

Characteristics of Listening Improvement Programs

If you as a teacher wish an effective listening improvement program in the classroom, it should contain some of these basic characteristics.

1. **Direct instruction in listening skills.** There have been many research studies which indicated that listening comprehension can be improved through direct instruction. If maximum improvement of the listening skills is expected, a program must be planned to aid the pupil in the listening skills that are necessary to good listening.

A teacher must develop within each child the proper attitudes toward listening. These attitudes affecting listening comprehension are the listener's attitude toward the speaker, the attitude of the listener to the subject matter, and the attitude of the listener toward the listening situation.

Listening should be taught to the pupils so that they will comprehend that listening is an active process. It requires active participation, although the skill is an assimilative one. A combination of visual and auditory presentation of materials leads to more efficient comprehension.[2] It would seem quite evident that the speaker's visible actions would contribute to the ability of the listener to understand and remember the ideas expressed.

Before each listening situation, purpose for listening should be established for each child. Three general principles could improve listening comprehension. First, the teacher must establish for the pupil a desirable goal in listening. A

Reprinted from *Education* 89:103-104 (November-December 1968), by permission of author and publisher, The Bobbs-Merrill Company, Inc.

child's tendency is to listen to what he perceives as important.[3] Second, an opportunity for practice must be offered, with attention directed toward the desired goal. Last, some evaluation or appraisal of the degree of accomplishment of the goal must be made.

A major task in helping pupils to improve listening is that of teaching them to use their spare thinking time efficiently as they listen. First, the listener should think ahead of the speaker to draw conclusions from the words spoken at the moment. Second, the listener should weigh the verbal evidence used by the speaker to support the points that he makes. Third, periodically the listener should review the portion of the talk completed thus far. Last, the listener should search for meaning that is not necessarily put into spoken words.[4]

2. **Reinforcement of good listening habits throughout the school day.** For listening comprehension to be improved, a planned program in which the teacher reinforces and gives his pupils many hours of practice in these listening skills is necessary. Skills necessary in listening must be strengthened throughout the school day by an alert teacher if the pupil is to benefit from listening programs.[5]

3. **Careful listening on the part of teachers.** Example is the great teaching factor in many aspects of learning, and so it is with listening. The teacher must take the first step in teaching listening by the teacher analyzing his own listening habits.[6] The teacher who cannot stop his activities and listen to the pupil will not be doing that which is necessary in teaching listening habits for good comprehension.

4. **Awareness of the world of sound.** Teachers must help the children to become aware of the large world of sound. The teaching of listening is not an extending but enriching process to be carried on throughout the school day. An alert teacher has an opportunity to improve the listening of children as he makes their worthwhile out-of-school listening and viewing contribute to the school program. Never lose an opportunity to show the importance of listening well.[7]

Summary

A major task before us is that of developing in the elementary school curriculum a program for listening improvement. Listening comprehension can be improved if the teacher will take time to make a worthwhile contribution to listening in the pupil's school day. The characteristics of a good listening-improvement program include involvement by both teachers and pupils.

35.

The Neglect of Listening

Donald L. Landry

Although research has consistently shown that pupils spend more time listening than in any other language arts activity, a serious lack of programs which develop listening skills is evident in most elementary schools. What has caused this seeming unawareness? There are, of course, numerous factors which are involved in this neglect of listening. These factors are interrelated. However, three major factors seem to cause this neglect of listening—traditions, time, and training.

There are numerous traditions which play a vital role in causing neglect in the teaching of listening in our elementary schools. Is it because we have not been able to separate listening from hearing? Is it because we have considered listening, like walking, to be an area which develops naturally? Is it because the intangibleness of listening has frightened us? Or is it because other, more fully organized areas such as reading have crowded out listening in our elementary schools?

Time for listening must also be recognized as a vital factor which causes our neglect in teaching listening skills. With the already over-crowded curriculum, is there really time to teach listening?

Training, the third major factor, must also be included in the possible causes of our neglect in teaching listening. Do we know how to teach listening? What training has been available to us in order to at least explore this area? Moreover, what materials are available to us to at least try to use in our own classrooms?

Listening, like walking, is naturally developed. Traditionally, many teachers have believed that listening, like walking, is developed naturally by the child on his own. It is, perhaps, the primary nature of listening which has caused many to consider listening as a natural skill, one that is known by everyone and one which does not require teaching. We seem to be believing that because a child has two legs, he can walk; therefore, a child who has two ears can listen. However, we fully realize in our schools, that although a child does have two eyes, it is still very necessary to teach him how to read. Could we then assume that although a child has two ears, it is still very necessary to teach him how to listen?

The mistaken belief that a child grows in listening by merely growing up is

---

one which is gradually changing. Within the last twenty years, researchers have investigated the nature of listening and the success with which we are able to listen. Consistently, studies have proven that instruction in listening does improve listening abilities. We are just beginning to fully realize that children do have a potentiality for listening as they do for reading. We are just beginning to fully realize, too, that training is necessary to develop that potential. This type of research should make a difference in the teaching which we do in the classroom. However, as Anderson has indicated: "Except in isolated instances, virtually the only instruction in listening that children and young persons receive in the schools is the quite useless admonition of 'pay attention' and to 'listen carefully.' Listening, at all educational levels, has been the forgotten language arts for generations."[8]

Studies also indicate that without instruction there is little improvement in listening from junior high school level through college level. Indeed, when mental age is taken into consideration, children in the primary grades are the best listeners. The level of listening decreases as the age of an individual increases. According to Logan, adults are the worst listeners.[9]

Moreover, investigations have shown that most of us listen badly. Some studies show that most people absorb only 30% of what they hear; other studies show that most of us remember less than a quarter of what we hear. This would, indeed, imply that instruction in listening could add much to our learning and living.

Still another area which must be realized is that there are strong indications that we have learned even not to listen by building up strong resistances to listening as a result of circumstances in our own environment. Traditionally, we have always developed a natural defense against the bombardment of partially useless information and sounds which assault the ear in our environment. Because we are now engulfed by sounds, we have had to learn to shut some of them out, to ignore some of them, and to insulate ourselves against some of them. We need these defenses in order to function in our present society. However, we have not learned to use these various devices as effectively as is needed today. We still need to develop skill in using these devices even more effectively in order to be able to receive those sounds we want to receive and/or need to receive. Hook indicated that "in our society-filled world we need a strainer over our ears, a strainer that will automatically exclude the sounds of no significance to us but allow the others to filter through to a responsive brain."[10]

There is still other proof to us that listening cannot be considered as an area which is naturally developed. With the bombardment of radio, television, and tapes and records, interests and emphasis has shifted from reading back to listening to a considerable extent. We are suddenly realizing, however, that more and more of our children are not able to appreciate and evaluate what they listen to as we had assumed. Research and personal experiences have clearly indicated this fact to us.

Without question then, the purposes, values, and procedures necessary for competent listening need to be developed by teaching as well as merely by living.

Listening is difficult to measure. Traditionally, we have a strong tendency to want to be able to measure and evaluate the areas which are part of our school programs. Since listening is an area which tends to be difficult to measure and evaluate concretely, some schools frown upon it as an acceptable part in today's curriculum. One of the difficulties has been the lack of instruments to measure and evaluate listening.

The audiometer can test the pupil's auditory acuity. However, there is no mechanical instrument which can measure how well a pupil has listened. In the past, we have equated the medical report which shows no physical impairment of hearing with listening. Unless there is some response and although the pupil may have the physiological equipment to hear, he may not have listened.

Although much of the success of the learning process depends upon the development of reading and listening skill, little effort has been made to evaluate listening. Some measures of listening have been attempted. Betts suggests an informal way of using graded reading materials in order to determine the hearing comprehension of a pupil. Durrell's test of hearing comprehension is a pioneer attempt at determining the hearing comprehension of an elementary pupil.[11]

Although reading tests have been used for more than twenty-five years, it was not until the spring of 1959 that a standardized measure of listening was introduced. This test was the Listening Comprehension Test, part of the Sequential Tests of Educational Progress series. It can be used with pupils in the fourth through sixth grades, as well as upper grades. This test still remains the only one available for the elementary grades.[12]

At present, informal check lists and tests created by the classroom teachers and applied to daily activities are the most useful measures available to us. However, even these must be highly questioned in light of the knowledge gained concerning teacher awareness in the field of listening.

Perhaps, we must consider more fully the implication of Miriam Wilt's statement:

> Tests can't measure listening; living can. We would be indeed fortunate if we could measure listening ability with standardized tests and say a listening level of 6.5. This, however, cannot tell the story. Even if we develop listening tests with their grade or age equivalents, we are measuring only the minutest aspect of the total listening act. A good listener evidences a constellation of behaviorism: he is intellectually curious, selective, courteous, accurate, tolerant, and understanding. But you will say these are not listening skills; this is life—and you will be right.[13]

These indeed are the skills involved in effective living. The real evaluation of listening skills cannot totally be devoid of skills considered necessary for more effective living.

Listening is hearing. Traditionally, teachers have equated listening with hearing. We have assumed that what we have said has been heard, and consequently, must have been understood. We have assumed that if the pupil had the ability to hear, he also had the ability to listen.

Listening can be differentiated from hearing in numerous ways. Hearing depends primarily upon the proper functioning of the ears, the brain and the coordinating nervous pathways. Hearing is a relatively simple registration of sound stimuli which uses the ears as the receptors and the brain as the area of registration. Listening, on the other hand, is much more complex. Listening implies more than just hearing. It involves giving active and conscious attention to the sounds for the purposes of gaining meaning. Listening involves comprehension of meanings heard as well as the relating of these sounds to our experiences.

According to Hampleman, as in the field of reading, authorities in the field of listening have finally discovered that a child must bring a combination of experience and intelligence to the listening situation. "It is at this point, where intelligence must be applied to symbols, that listening is distinguished from mere hearing. It is here that we discover the focal point to attack in helping children to listen better. Children need to be assisted to use the proper techniques for applying intelligence to that which is heard."[14]

Listening crowded out by reading. The final tradition in listening deals with the importance of the other language arts, especially reading, in crowding out listening as an individual area. Our school curricula has been traditionally reading and writing. Teachers have always felt a deep responsibility for teaching a child to read well. The education conviction, "Every teacher is a teacher of reading," has permeated our total outlook.

Listening has been neglected, not only as an area of instruction in our schools, but also as an area of research. It was not until 1917 that the first research in listening appeared, while 1881 marked the beginning of reading research. By 1948 only three research reports in the field of listening had been published, while over 3,000 studies had been published in the field of reading. Even by 1961, according to Duker's extensive bibliography on professional articles and studies in listening, only 725 items appeared.[15]

Moreover, it was not until April 1955 that the *Review of Educational Research* even contained a summary of the studies of the listening field.[16] Still further, it was not until 1960 that the *Encyclopedia of Educational Research* included "Listening: Teaching of" and "Tests of."

There has, to be sure, been a greater upsurge of emphasis upon listening in research. Horrworth, referring to Duker's 1964 *Listening Bibliography* writes "A recently published listening bibliography annotating 880 articles, many of a research nature, confirms the observation that the information-getting phase in this area of language is well under way, and there is no evidence of abatement."[17] However, when compared with the quantity of research in the other areas of the language arts, especially reading, this emphasis is still minor.

Time for Listening

With the already over-crowded school curriculum, many teachers feel that there is no time to add another subject. In fact, in spite of the importance of listening, apparently no authority advocates the addition of listening as another course to the elementary curriculum. Generally, authorities on listening recommend that there not be separated periods for providing lessons in listening. Hildreth states: "In view of the relatedness that exists among these different phases of language expression, more integration should be achieved in language instruction in school experiences. All can be taught more meaningfully and economically through capitalizing on the interrelationships that exist among these skills." Another widely known source, Lewis and Nichols also recommend this integrated approach to the teaching of listening. They wrote that the "best approach to classroom training in listening appears to be through a coordination of listening and speech instruction. In schools where no immediate opportunity exists to institute a course labeled 'listening,' the next best alternative has frequently seemed to be the dovetailing of listening assignments into routines already established in speech classes."[18] The feeling that listening skills should be developed in the general language arts context and indeed in the total setting of the elementary school is realistic and workable *only to a degree.*

The language arts areas are not academic subjects. They are constantly used media which can be enlarged and refined on the pupil's level through experiences in using them. The development of language areas occupies the entire school day. Language is utilized in nearly everything that is done throughout the day. Language is taught by the teacher directly and indirectly. Listening, as do the other language arts areas, needs a content in which to operate effectively. Although there are understandings to be developed and knowledge of operation procedures to be learned in listening, it is not a subject per se. As a pupil does not read reading nor write writing, he does not listen listening. When a pupil reads, writes, or listens, he must read, write or listen about *something*. Because listening is inherent in many of the classroom activities, the teaching of listening merely capitalizes upon those experiences which are already a part of the school day and uses them to make living and learning even more effective. Effective methods of actually teaching in the context of the various content areas need to be developed. The teacher needs to assume responsibility for providing those methods which will, indeed, provide for development in listening skills. As a result, listening becomes one of the media through which other areas can be studied and learned. As a result, too, pupils learn by listening as well as by learning to listen.

If we consider two other areas involved in the language arts programs we can further clarify the above descriptions. Handwriting is another area which integrates itself effectively in all areas and contents of school life. Although handwriting is so vital throughout the total school day, many still find it necessary to develop programs which actually teach the pupils the skills, techniques and understandings of handwriting. With these skills, handwriting does serve its purpose as a tool. Let us now consider a second language arts area which easily integrates itself in the curriculum, spelling. There are, of course, numerous programs which teach pupils how to spell more effectively. With competency in spelling, the pupil uses it as a useful tool in many aspects of the total school day. It is the opinion of this writer that listening must be likewise considered: listening must be *taught* in order to function as effectively as a tool of communication in our schools.

Training in Listening

The third major factor which has caused teachers to neglect listening has been their own training. Many teachers do not know how to provide meaningful instruction in listening because they themselves have never received training in this vital area. Little, if any, emphasis upon the teaching of listening skills is given in most language arts courses in teaching training institutions. Kellogg adds more insight into this area for us. He was recently engaged in one of the twenty-seven research projects funded by the U.S. Office of Education in studying first grade reading and language arts methodologies. "Fifty teachers in San Diego County, California, selected because of their teaching competency utilizing the traditional method language arts program and the experience approach language arts program, included little direct instruction in listening skill development. These teachers are judged to be typical of the best elementary teachers across the nation."[19]

Still another factor in the training programs would be the actual language arts textbooks utilized in the language arts courses. It is not uncommon to find language arts textbooks which do not include any more than a few pages concerning the area of listening. Some even exclude listening entirely from its contents. Many which do include listening blend the area strongly with speaking, or oral language. It is interesting to note in a recent publication, a chapter dealing with innovations in the language arts contained no mention of listening at all. Moreover, in another recent publication dealing with reading in the language arts, only one article dealing with listening was included. This article was one which was seven years old by the time it was reprinted in this publication. By the way, this article was only eight pages long. In still another recent publication, only five pages from 450 dealt with listening. Even in 1969 this seems to reflect the status of listening, the neglected language arts area!

In addition to the obvious lack of training afforded our teachers by way of courses and textbooks, still another major factor influences the neglect of listening programs within the classrooms. In examining the language arts books which are utilized in the elementary schools, a similar pattern can easily be observed. It is not uncommon to find any more than a few pages concerning listening. Even when it is included, it is not emphasized as a distinct language arts area. Some texts merely mention listening in passing with such admonitions as "Listen courteously," "Listen carefully," or "Sit up straight." In a recent report by Kenneth Brown, this lack of concern was made even more pronounced. After analyzing fourteen language arts series that were published from 1959 through 1964, he found that even though authorities claim that listening is the language arts medium children used more frequently, it was rarely stressed in these texts.[20]

Conclusion

Because of the constantly growing awareness of the neglect of listening programs in the elementary schools and the realization of the need for developing listening skills, some progress is being made. Some researchers have developed a series of lessons which can be utilized for a portion of a year at a grade level. Some programs which utilize tapes and records and earphones are being developed in order to encourage effective listening. However, much remains to be done.

Even in spite of all of this neglect of listening, there still remains encouragement. In spite of this lack of training in colleges, in spite of the lack of educational insight in the writing of language arts textbooks, in spite of the crying need for language arts series which recognize listening as a major learning force, and in spite of the lack of available programs in listening, the development of listening skill can become an effective part of the competent teacher's language arts program in the elementary school. Very gradually, but also very surely, the factors which have caused the neglect of listening—traditions, time, and training—will be the very forces which will make listening fulfill its potential and promise.

36.

Listening: A Facet of Oral Language

Gloria Horrworth

As recently as 1958, textbooks used in graduate courses on research in the teaching of the language arts described such arts as consisting of reading, writing, speaking, and spelling. Although probes into the mysteries surrounding listening had begun, the gap between practice and research was great, due to difficulties of data retrieval, lack of a conceptual framework, and the scarcity of tools and techniques for making teaching of listening operational for the classroom teacher.

More recently the gap between research and practice has narrowed, and tools and techniques have appeared. However, a considerable disparity still exists and a conceptual framework for choosing tools and techniques and using them is only in the process of development. This report furthers this development by suggesting a conceptual model based on research findings and indicates methods and techniques for making the teaching of listening practicable for teachers.

An Overview

In the quadratic context of the language arts, the receptive language functions of listening and reading and the expressive functions of speaking and writing, listening occupies a baseline position and may be diagrammed as follows:

Table I

Listening Occupying a Baseline Position

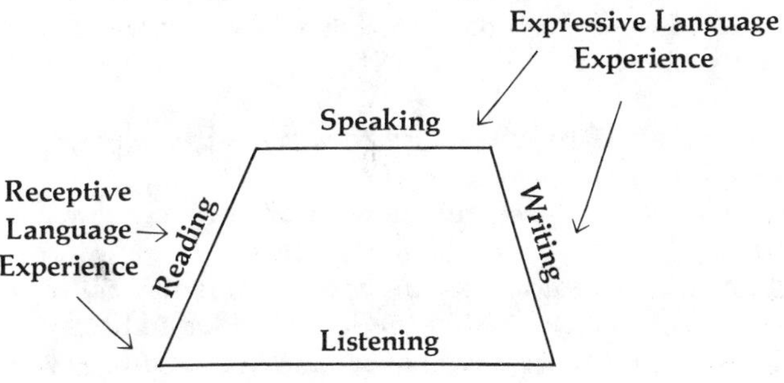

From *Elementary English* 43:856-864,868 (December 1966).

In addition to increasing concern being shown for the teaching of listening, the importance of its role in the entire language function has recently received significant attention. Historically, constructive discontent led first to research regarding the graphic phases of communication; this was followed by investigations into the nature of oral language and its development, investigations which have resulted in a revision of the simplistic view of listening long held by many educators. Thus, that everyone who can hear knows how to listen has been experimentally discredited. A recently published listening bibliography annotating 880 articles, many of a research nature, confirms the observation that the information-getting phase in this area of language is well under way, and there is no evidence of abatement.[21] The titles of the articles in this bibliography, and the annotations of these, indicate many differences in the uses of terminology. Thus the appearance of semantic swamps suggests the need for a definition of terms.

Definitions and Guidelines

Auding: In this review auding is defined as the gross process of listening to, recognizing, and interpreting spoken symbols. This definition is holistic in nature and embraces the hearing act, the listening act, and the comprehending act. Thus auding herein is not defined as a distinguishable stage of listening; that is, hearing, listening, and auding are not recognized as separate stages.[22]

This reviewer's interpretation of the research findings of Brown, Caffrey, Furness, and others is expressed in the following paradigm: Auding = Hearing + Listening + Cognizing.
This paradigm is operational from at least three points of view.[23]

1. It is consistent with findings in learning theory which recognize that cognition is the central process or intermediary within the organism involved in all communications.[24]
2. By considering aspects of auding relational and configurational rather than as discrete, hierarchial stages, we will come closer to its actual nature.
3. Researchers and teachers using this lexicon will not be flying in the face of the general public's definition of listening, to give attention with the ear for the purpose of hearing.

Hearing: Hearing is the process by which sound waves are received, modified, and relayed along the nervous system by the ear. Factors affecting the hearing act are those of:

1. Acuity or the ability to respond to various frequencies (tones) at various intensities (loudness levels).
2. Binaurality or the fused functioning of both ears in coordination with each other.
3. Masking or the simultaneous input of extraneous sound which can cover, drown out, or otherwise alter the sound under audition.
4. Auditory fatigue or the effects of sustained exposure to sounds of the same frequency or intensity which can induce lowered levels of efficiency; this is especially true for sounds in the speech range which are most likely to produce fatigue.[25]

Listening: Listening is the process of directing attention to and thereby becoming aware of sound sequences. Archaic meanings of the Old English derivative word *list* include "to like" and "to choose." In modern usage, "to heed" or "to yield to advice" are common dictionary meanings. Affective behavior or attitudinal responses are clearly implied. In a bulletin to teachers entitled "What Can Be Done About Listening," Ralph Nichols describes ten poor habits as a listener's roadblocks to effective oral-aural communication. They are as follows:

*1. Calling a subject dull
*2. Criticizing a speaker
*3. Getting overstimulated
*4. Listening only for facts
5. Trying to outline everything
*6. Faking attention
*7. Tolerating distractions
*8. Choosing only what is easy
*9. Allowing emotion-laden words to interfere with listening
10. Wasting differential time between speech and thought speed.[26]

All of the starred items of poor listening behavior seem to be affective behaviors; that is, they reflect interests, attitudes, and values.

Cognizing: Cognition is a generic term used often to denote all of the various aspects of knowing, including perception, judgment, reasoning, remembering; and thinking and imagining. A more specific meaning exists for cognitive theorists who have suggested that an organism's response is largely determined by a central process (rather than peripheral intermediaries) within the organism. This central process influences an individual's reactions to stimuli and provides him with a representation of it. Field theorists refer to this representational process as cognition.[27] That such a process is part of the auding experience is helpful in explaining its complexity and in gaining the understanding that auding consists of more than hearing (sensation) and listening (affect factors). Relative to the auding phenomenon subfactors (abilities or skills) in cognizing would at least consist of these aspects of conceptualizing experiences:

1. Making comparisons
2. Noting sequences of details
3. Indexing
4. Categorizing
5. Drawing inferences
6. Drawing conclusions
7. Recognizing relationships, noting associations
8. Mentally reorganizing in terms of past experience (reordering)
9. Abstracting main ideas
10. Forming sensory images.

The Role of Auding in Oral Language

Auding is the first language art that the child develops. He learns his language by ear, and whatever skills he brings to school were first learned by his listening and attending to the speech of those around him. This can seem to complicate the problem of the teaching of listening because it suggests a variety of individual differences in learning styles that are quite firmly developed when the child enters school. Many classroom teachers who prefer teaching in the lower elementary grades when queried respond that by choosing a primary grade level they do not have to undo, reteach, or help the child unlearn aspects of reading and writing. There is a high motivation on the part of the learners, and a clear road ahead. Attention directed to improving auding skills might not hold this same kind of appeal. It has been observed and verified objectively that school children spend 54 percent of the instructional day learning by listening, yet only 16 percent of teachers questioned ranked listening as the most important language skill.[28]

Auding is a people process as well as a language process; it is reciprocal, and in order to listen, an individual needs to have experienced an attentive listener interested in him and in what he is saying. Kindergarten teachers report that their good listeners, most often, have a mother or some other adult who is an attentive listener to the child.

The auditor, not the speaker, is the prime director of the learning process.[29] He controls the input of oral communication. Among the four facets of language, only in auding is there no overt control over the flow of words. The speaker can stop speaking, the reader can lay aside his book, the writer can put down his pen. In each case there is no longer visible involvement in the activity, if such is the desire. The listener, however, remains visibly involved. But because of this people-process nature of aural communication, the listener learns ways of covertly tuning out, when he becomes aurally fatigued or disinterested. The listener may stop the flow of words by directing thought processes elsewhere, or through sporadic flights of fantasy. More significant to the learning process is the fact that he is often unaware of the tactics he employs.

The Relationship of Speech Competency to Listening Comprehension

Research does not yet reveal a clear picture of the nature of the relationship between speaking and listening effectiveness. Whether or not a valid measurable relationship exists has been questioned.[30] Working with a large number of adults, 180 panels, each having twelve members, Black reports correlations between listening and speaking scores ranging from .02 to .87, with a median of .21.

Stark, using 175 college speech students as subjects, found vocal speech capacity and listening to have a .36 correlation. Howe's study, also with college students, shows a correlation of .43 between speech effectiveness as judged by a panel of college speech instructors and listening as measured by the Brown-Carlsen Listening Comprehension Test.[31]

Everts reported a definite and positive relationship between children's oral language structure and their listening ability as measured by the Marten Test. Other studies undertaken with children of early elementary school age report much higher correlations than do those studies previously described in which the subjects have been adults. Thus it would appear that while factors of interdependency and interaction between speech and auding in the young child exist, the nature and extent of this interdependency and interaction are assumed rather than supported by research.[32]

Other Related Findings

The coefficients of correlation found suggest also that there are different components of listening ability and that these vary in their relationships to other factors. Listening is not a discrete skill, neither is it a generalized ability; it is a cluster of specific abilities closely related to those needed in the reading task.[33]

Due to the tendency of some writers to view the process of auding as a generalized ability, a question has been raised as to whether or not knowledge about listening contributes to the ability to listen.[34] However, the overwhelming majority of researchers state that listening skills can be taught; and as early as 1949, articles appearing in *School Review, Education Research Bulletin, Journal of Education,* and many other journals stressed that the school has a responsibility for the teaching of listening. Many courses of study and curriculum guides now approach listening as a separate language arts ability, making it incumbent upon the classroom teacher to improve the quality of the teaching-learning act in this area.

Measures to Improve Auding Capabilities

Lasting improvement in any performance usually occurs as a result of a strengthening of many factors requisite to that performance. Any attempt to improve the quality of aural communication must be based on the knowledge that all aspects of the auding process—hearing, listening, cognizing—are of significance. Learning tasks should be so structured that skills in all three areas are at some point being stressed. No one lesson or brief series of lessons, drills, or activities will make the desired improvement in listening ability. A plan of action must also include measures (exercises, games, *etc.*) for strengthening specific skills as well as ways of integrating these skills and learnings with all subject matter. Specific suggestions for activities are now included in texts on the teaching of reading. The development of listening centers in classrooms is an example of attempts to optimize more than one aspect of auding. Such centers include an auto-instructional device consisting of a record player or tape recorder, earphones (varying numbers of), and response sheets which are completed by the listeners through the course of the listening experience.[35]

Observations on Listening Centers

This writer for the past several years has worked in various school jurisdictions with children and teachers setting up such centers, helping in the acquisition and organization of equipment, helping to develop teacher skills in producing taped lessons. Descriptions of such listening centers are increasingly appearing in periodicals on local, state, and national coverage levels and should prove helpful for schools wishing to pursue this development.[36] The following observations regarding listening centers are pertinent here:

> An individual child listening through earphones is at work improving auding abilities optimally on two levels: at the hearing level because problems of masking, binaurality, and often acuity are minimized, and at the cognitive level because he is guided into thinking, making judgments, and following directions. Carefully structured taped lessons tighten teacher-prepared lessons, extraneous and confusing verbalisms are reduced, and the listener receives immediate feedback as to the appropriateness of his written response.

Tapes are most often developed with a particular subject matter as the organizing factor (reading skills, literature, spelling). Cognitive functioning could be more effectively strengthened if the previously mentioned factors in aural cognizing served as guidelines for lesson construction.

It has been the experience of this writer that the use of listening center equipment did little to improve what has been herein described as the level of listening or the affective aspect of the act. Empathic listening, reactive listening, projective listening, and interpretive listening are some of the kinds of listening that develop in face-to-face relationships where one speaks and one listens. The utilization of a listening center can do much to improve many auding skills but no machined device can provide the most essential components for producing good listeners. These the classroom teacher must provide.

The Role of the Teacher and Implications of Effects on Listening Behavior

Classroom climate which emanates from the leadership style that is set and generated by the teacher has far greater impact on the auding experience than does any other factor. Reasons for this have been explored in terms of effect cues in communication through the work of J.R. Gibb.[37] In an article, "Defensive Communication," Gibb discusses the necessity of reducing group defensiveness. Defensive behavior occurs when an individual perceives threat or anticipates threat in the group. Defensive behavior engenders defensive listening and this, in turn, produces postural, facial, and verbal cues which raise the defense level of the original communicator. This defense-arousal prevents the listener from concentrating on the message.

Teachers who generate a supportive climate through their own behavior and reactions in verbal and silent language produce learners with improved listening skills and are effective teachers of listening whether they are conscious of it or not. Perhaps such a teacher has never had access to the Russells' excellent *Listening Aids Through the Grades,* nor has had the opportunity to benefit from Miriam Wilt's suggestions of activities in the teaching of listening.[38] These writers, aware of the central significance of a teacher's speaking and listening behavior, stress that the first step in teaching listening is taken by the teacher in analyzing his own listening habits.

Gibb asks teachers, parents, and managers to examine the total communication climate since, if the climate is defense reductive or supportive, the listener will not distort from his own projections.[39] Gibb suggests that the listener will be better able to concentrate on the structure, the content, and the cognitive meaning of the message in such a climate.

A Look at Listening Climates

In recent developments in the psychology of learning, there is an appreciation of the fact that learning takes place within a total context that is more than just the sum of the components of learning. There are specific content and skills to be learned which adds to the store of competence; there are also the pervasive qualitative aspects of the learning situation which affect the self-feeling, the images of authority, the delineation of psychological planes of safety and adventure. These inevitably affect each other.[40]

How does a listening-learning climate which is alive with the spirit of adventure differ from one which is not? If the affect cues sent out by the speaker (teacher) are defense reductive, positive attitudes for learning which include curiosity, manipulation (of ideas), spontaneity, and awareness will be sustained and nurtured.

Gibb says "Defense reductive climates result when the speech behavior which a listener perceives possesses characteristics of:

1. Description—rather than evaluation
2. Problem orientation—as opposed to control
3. Spontaneity—rather than strategy
4. Empathy—not neutrality

5. Equality—as opposed to superiority
6. Provisionalism—rather than certainty.[41]

Children perceived by other children as good leaders and good sports, those who are listened to by peers, often seem to automatically employ defense reductive techniques. Listen in on a playground argument—one which was repetitive many times in the writer's experience and is familiar to classroom teachers. The participants are fifth-grade children playing a game of baseball. Two are fighting. The combatants are separated. Their respective friends are yelling as to who started it, and the yard duty teacher is asked to arbitrate. One boy speaks up; the others begin listening. He says something of this nature:

> We didn't see what happened, but they're fighting over who has next ups. (pause) Bill's nose is bleeding; maybe he should go to the nurse. (pause) What about the game, you guys; we have only five minutes left.

The children listen; they take their positions; the game continues.

An adult hearing this might comment that the children listened because what the one said was reasonable. Specifically what he said was descriptive (he made no attempt to place blame) and problem-oriented (how to get the nose bleed taken care of and how to get the game going again). A "natural" leader? Perhaps. A defense reductive communicator? Yes.

A New View of Empathy

Empathy and neutrality as aspects of the listener's environment merit special attention by the classroom teacher because it has somehow seemed in the past (perhaps as a misapplication of non-directive counseling techniques) to be sound pedagogical practice to be emotionally neutral, to withhold how one feels, and in certain specific instances, such reaction is warranted. However, when neutrality in speech appears to the listener to indicate a lack of concern for his welfare, he becomes defensive. Group members usually desire to be perceived as valued persons, as individuals of special worth, and as objects of concern and affection.[42]

Bruno Bettleheim, working in a consultative role with teachers concerned with problems of the disadvantaged, relates a dialogue between himself and a particular teacher who was having problems with a little girl.[43] The child alternated between extremely aggressive and extremely dependent behavior, making comments to the teacher such as "you ugly old white woman." When asked how she reacts, the teacher said, "Well, I think I try to get her to sit down or something like that and actually ignore the problem. I never take her comments personally."

"Now, that is hard for me to believe," Dr. Bettleheim replies, "if someone says to you, 'I hate your ugly white face,' you are certainly going to be bothered unless you don't take the child seriously. This is what I'm driving at. If we don't take a person's nasty remarks seriously, that means that we don't take him seriously. It implies you're irresponsible, no good, of no account. Because if a person is of any account, then it seems to me that we must take seriously what he says . . . In a situation like that, I'm shocked each time they do it; and the more shocked I am, the sooner they stop . . . If you pay no attention to a remark like this, the child will be driven to keep it up all year long. . . . If, on the other hand, she can hurt you, she might think 'Do I really want to hurt my teacher?' And that is what we're striving for."

"Speech with low-affect that communicates little warmth or caring is in such contrast with the affect-laden speech in social situations that it sometimes communicates rejection."[44]

In the teacher's attempt to de-emotionalize much of the living-learning process with children, he often doesn't listen or does not take seriously or personally their remarks, and by so doing can be communicating rejection and feeding a defense arousal that prevents a listener from concentrating on any message under audition.

An anthropologist working in a volunteer community action group with high school drop-outs reports a conversation with one young man who implored him to "teach me to listen to the teachers—I want to—I hear what they're saying, and I can understand but I just can't listen to some of them."

A Look at the Future

The teaching of listening has gone through many of the same phases as has the teaching of reading: periods of componential analysis—defining and refining requisite sequential skills and attitudes. The pace has been more rapid in listening for many reasons now taken for granted by mid-twentieth century educators. When some of the pieces of the puzzle of learning to read were placed in frameworks called the language experience approach to reading or individualized reading, the new emphasis was upon the "who" in the process; and what we now do depends on the individual involved. It is reasonable to assume that the teaching of listening will reach this point also. For example, we now have available lists of sequences of skills as well as skill building techniques described in new texts (usually chapters in books of the teaching of reading or language arts).

When teachers become more familiar with the totality of the auding process, along with a deeper knowledge of the learner, more individualization of instruction in listening will be possible. An incident which occurred in this writer's experience might help to strengthen this assumption for the reader.

While working with a group of fourth graders in an attempt to improve their skill in forming sensory images, a record album, *Creative Thinking Through Aural Imagery*, was used. A band of the record (consisting of a sequence of sounds—footsteps, a chain being pulled, crickets, frogs, a sudden splashing of water, the rhythmic splashing of water) was played. The students were instructed to listen first and then to draw what they thought those sounds could mean. All of them did this. Most of the children drew and later discussed someone taking a boat ride on a pond. However, one boy produced an entirely different and quite unusual picture using the footsteps and chain sound cues only. When questioned by the other children about why he didn't include a body of water, he said he didn't hear any water, nor did he hear the crickets, frogs, *etc.* Later in talking with his classroom teacher, she asserted that this was the boy's chief problem—that although his intelligence quotient was the highest in the class, much higher than the next closest, he seldom listened long enough to anything to get it right. We then together explored the possibility that perhaps this boy's brightness was a contributing factor in his poor critical listening habits. Perhaps his store of stimuli of meaningful association was so rich that he became totally involved cognitively and couldn't continue listening. It was suggested also that it might be well for him to understand this about himself or about his listening habits. Many adults while listening to talks or lectures find it helpful to "doodle." Reasons for the doodling on paper are certainly varied, but one bright adult student when queried about it said to this writer that he did it to get extra ideas out of his head so that he could go on listening. Such self-help techniques point to the possibility that more attention in the future should be given to the individualized nature of the auding experience.

B.
Speaking

Oral language is the foundation of the language arts program. Growth in oral communication should be an important goal at all levels of the elementary school. We can hardly overemphasize the importance of speaking as a means of communication. We speak far more frequently than we read or write. The evidence of available research suggests a high degree of interrelatedness among the communication skills. A child's ability to comprehend written material and to express himself through writing appears to be directly related to his ability to communicate orally.

Recent research emphasizes the effect a child's language has upon his self-concept. Linguistic studies indicate a relationship between a child's ability to use the language orally and his success in beginning reading instruction. As a result of these findings, many educators now stress the importance of oral language instruction. The results of this research have had surprisingly little effect on the language arts program in the elementary school. Such a great emphasis has been put on reading instruction in the primary grades that little time has been set aside for meaningful oral language experiences. This neglect has caused serious problems for the educational and personal growth of many children.

Classroom teachers should become more sensitive to each child's needs for extensive oral language development. Systematic instruction in oral language cannot begin too soon. This instruction must be provided if the basic attitudes, skills, and abilities needed for speaking are to be developed and reinforced and if their use in meaningful communication situations is to be implemented. Sporadic drill and incidental instruction is not enough. Every opportunity should be taken to present the principles of speaking; this instruction should not be confined to the language arts period alone, but should be developed through rich and varied experiences and constant practice.

Specific guidelines for developing oral language skills are presented in the articles in this section. The direct relationship between oral language facility and the other language art skills is discussed. The negative effects of teachers verbally dominating the classroom are pointed out and a plea is made for greater oral participation on the part of the pupils.

37. Developing Oral Expression

Ruth Strang

At the turn of the century, oral expression flourished. It was called elocution, defined by one youngster as "the method used to put criminals to death." A child's competence in reading was judged by his gestures, his inflections, and his "expression," as well as by the clearness and correctness of his pronunciation of each word. Exercises suggested rising and falling inflection:

Did he act pru- dent- ly?

Has he come?

Has he gone to town to- day, or will he go to-morrow?

In the 1920's and 1930's, the popularity of oral expression, and particularly of oral reading, declined. Since research had shown that the rate of oral reading is slower than that of mature silent reading, overemphasis on oral reading would tend to slow down the rate of silent reading. It was also pointed out that oral reading had little social utility. The proportion of oral reading to silent reading in life situations was very low.

Since 1940, however, oral communication has been recognized as a vital part of the child's life both at school and at home. The child's first experience with words is with spoken words. He uses them to get people to meet his needs and do what he wants them to do. Words help him to organize his experience and communicate it to others. One of the most important values of nursery school and kindergarten is the opportunity they provide for oral expression and the language growth that it stimulates.

During the last decade, the linguists have given a new emphasis to oral expression. They recognize the primacy of the spoken word. According to many linguists, reading is the process by which printed words are translated into spoken words, and then endowed with the meanings that are already associated with the spoken words. They also emphasize that the stress, rhythm, and intonation of oral expression are important clues to the meanings of printed words. Several competent scientists have even advocated indicating, in printed materials, the words that should be stressed. "It has been discovered that readers who stress words, which the author indicates should be stressed, obtain significantly superior scores when given a written comprehension test on the same reading material."[45]

In a 1964 series of textbooks designed to give a mastery of the English language,[46] we find indications, like those given in textbooks of the previous century, for the inflection of each sentence:

I / doubt / that I'll do / any / thing tomorrow.

Thus through the years we have observed a decline and a resurgence of emphasis on oral expression. Before 1900, elocution was an end in itself. Today, oral expression is recognized both as an important part of living and as a means to more effective reading through the interpretation of printed material as it would be spoken.

In general, we talk more than we listen and much more than we read. Studies have shown that people spend 75 per cent of their communicative effort in speaking and listening, as compared with 25 per cent in writing and reading.[47]

The quality of oral expression leaves much to be desired. Some people are like the woman whose husband wanted to get a divorce. "What's the trouble?" the judge asked.

"Oh, my wife just talks, and talks, and talks," the husband said.

"What does she talk about?" the judge asked.

"She doesn't say," the man replied.

Others are afflicted with total recall like the nurse in *Romeo and Juliet.* Many of us have never learned in speaking or writing what a French literary critic called "the art of not saying everything."

Importance and Values of Oral Expression

Language, particularly speech, is an important indicator, a linguistic barometer, of the state of an individual's mental health.[48] Disturbed people use language quite differently from the way those who are well adjusted do. The oral expression of brain-damaged children is characteristically confused and incoherent.

Speech is a most important form of behavior. It is an expression of personality; it also contributes to personality development. In the broadest sense, the study of human behavior depends heavily upon the study of language behavior. A child's language development reflects the quality of his relationship with his mother and of the experiences afforded by his home and neighborhood.

Oral expression is particularly important in efforts to aid the disadvantaged and the culturally different. These children tend to speak little in the classroom, and what they say is often poorly expressed. This is due to several factors. If they come from homes where they hear only a foreign language, a dialect of English, or substandard English, they are unfamiliar with our speech sounds, our idioms, our standard sentence patterns. They are unable to hear the sounds of standard English speech clearly and accurately. Consequently, their efforts to reproduce the spoken language are inaccurate. Their vocabularies are small and unique to a given environment. Their sentence structure differs from that used in books and by the teacher. It is not the language expected in school.

Though easily explained, these differences are less easily remedied. Some of these children have never been outside their immediate neighborhoods. Others, such as the children of migrant workers, have traveled, but have not talked about what they have seen and done. They may hesitate to speak up in class because they fear that their remarks will not be acceptable. In many homes where the parents are poorly educated, the children have had little stimulation and practice in verbal thinking. They have not developed verbal fluency. Thus their reported low IQ's may not represent their true intellectual capacity.

These pupils may talk freely among themselves, but say little in class.[49] They do not have the same kind of experiences to relate that other children have. They do not have the words to express their ideas. They are afraid of saying the wrong thing. And often the teacher's questions can be answered merely by "yes" or "no."

Pre-school programs will help these children to develop language learning during the years when this can be most readily done. "Project Headstart" was a dramatic and widespread effort to make up for this kind of language deficiency.

Facility in oral expression is a prerequisite to success in beginning reading. Reading should be geared into the oral language that a child has already mastered. The first words to be learned at sight should be words that have personal significance for the child. Beginning instruction in phonics should deal with meaningful words. The child should become aware at once that stress, pitch, and pauses at significant points are all important clues to the meaning of sentences.

An individual's social status is reflected in his speech. In *My Fair Lady*, based on George Bernard Shaw's play *Pygmalion*, Eliza Doolittle's speech identified her immediately as an uneducated Cockney flower girl. After she had been taught correct English, she spoke like a duchess and was treated like a person of quality. Whether we like it or not, people make judgements about a person's character from his speech. Slovenly speech and poor grammar handicap a young person. They set him apart from his better educated classmates and make him feel "different." Oral expression both creates and reflects his concept of himself. In the *Fables of Phaedrus* (25 B.C.) we find this statement: "Nothing is more useful to man than to speak correctly."

Oral expression helps to clarify thought as well as to communicate it. The Greeks had one word for both language and thought. The little child, in the effort to tell mother something, finds out what he himself is thinking. An adolescent girl said to her boy friend, "I talk so I'll know what I think, don't you?" Some authorities say that the idea must be in the mind before one can express it in speech. This is true for the more mature speaker. For the less mature, the effort to express an idea is an effective way of clarifying it.

In the classroom, oral expression motivates more effective composition. To impress and instruct an audience, a talk must be well organized, have a main point, supply a variety of information to explain or prove the point, and use words accurately and vividly.[50] Even knowing that he will be expected to take part in class discussion of a topic assigned as homework will cause the pupil to read with a more definite purpose than he otherwise would. He not only will look for points that he can raise, but also will have a mind set to remember them.

The importance of oral expression in the appreciation of poetry is generally recognized. In teaching a given poem, the teacher often begins by reading it aloud or playing a recording of it by a well-known actor or actress. Voice quality, articulation, phrasing, stress, intonation, and rhythm convey meaning that is not revealed by the printed words.

To help pupils appraise their own interpretation of a selection, tape recordings of their oral expression are very helpful. As they listen, they can recognize their strengths and weaknesses. They are often delighted with the improvement shown in a selection recording of the same selection.

A pupil who cannot express himself easily through speech is seriously handicapped both academically and socially. With help he can analyze his speech problem and learn how to cope with the multiple factors that produce it.

What Is Oral Expression?

First of all, oral expression represents thought; it is a vehicle of thought. To neglect this element reduces oral expression to "sound and fury, signifying nothing." In colloquial language, it is merely "talking through one's hat," or, a little more scientifically, "talking with one's larynx."

A second component is sentence structure or syntax—the way words or word groups make up sentences. One must sense the syntax in order to convey the thought to an audience. One must also pay attention to the organization of the talk as a whole—central point, sequence of events, place, cause and effect, main ideas and supporting details. All of these factors need to be taught.

Meaning is also conveyed by stress, pitch, and the rise and fall of the voice at the juncture of thought units. This is a third element in oral expression. Stressed syllables are spoken in a louder voice and held longer. Stress, pitch, and juncture all stem from thought; they depend on the meaning the speaker wants to communicate.

Body mechanics is the fourth component. Some speakers have an initial advantage in voice quality. This is one of Richard Burton's assets as a great actor; his voice has a depth and richness of tone that communicates emotion in a remarkable way.

The fifth element involves the depth of the speaker's knowledge and the extent of his vocabulary. Technique will avail him little if he does not know what he is talking about.

Finally, the speaker must have a need to communicate. A speaker may have a thought and may express it in appropriate words, arranged in the correct order, with proper stress and intonation; but he will be ineffective if he does not make connection with his audience. Some pupils fail in their oral expression because "they couldn't care less" about conveying their ideas to the audience. Others fail because they doubt the value of what they have to say. Still others provoke their listeners' antagonism by adopting an air of superiority.

In brief, the essentials of effective oral expression are a thought to begin with, expressed in grammatically approved sentence structure, in precise and vivid words, spoken with appropriate stress, pitch, and intonation, and pleasing quality of voice—plus a command of the subject and a desire to communicate it to the audience.

Relation to Other Language Arts

An element that underlies all of the language arts is the need for something worthwhile to listen to, to tell someone else, to write about, or to read. The thought element is central, and basic ways of teaching the language arts also have much in common. The same principles of learning apply to all; all can be taught.

From several standpoints, listening precedes speaking and reading. Children acquire their native language through listening to and imitating the speech of their parents. The ability to learn language in this way seems to reach a peak at about three years of age. Children who have not learned to speak English before they come to school learn it most easily from their Anglo playmates. Until the age of fourteen or fifteen, most non-English speaking pupils pick up the second language quite easily if most of their classmates speak standard English—unless they have strong outside interests that involve their native language.

Most children learn to become independent readers by associating the sounds in familiar words with the corresponding printed symbols. This is the phonic approach, which forms a part of almost all reading programs.

One simple and useful way of determining whether a given child has the ability to read better than he does is to note his ability to comprehend when listening to a selection read aloud. A pupil who shows superior listening comprehension would seem to have developed potential for reading.

Oral communication presupposes one or more listeners.

There are also reciprocal relations between writing and speaking. Writing is "speech written down." It is a somewhat imperfect representation of speech because it does not indicate stress, intonation, or other spoken clues to meaning. Speaking transmits meaning to the ear and mind of the listener; writing transmits meaning to the eye and mind of the reader. The wider and more diversified their speaking experience, and the fewer their errors in speech, the better and more grammatically will children learn to write.

Speaking is basic to both reading and writing. Speech involves voice quality, enunciation, pronunciation, gesture, and other mechanics. Writing involves such elements as spelling, capitalization, punctuation, and penmanship. Both require organization of ideas, selection of precise and convincing words, and use of correct and appropriate sentence structure. Reading is writing in reverse: the writer creates a pattern of thought, the reader discovers the thought. Unexpected poetry crops out in children's spontaneous speech; it will be recognized by the alert teacher who listens for it as Hughes Mearns did.

Oral expression is clearly related to oral reading ability. Speech supplies the basis for beginning reading in most classrooms. Oral reading depends on many of the same processes that are involved in effective speech. Children who make many speech errors such as "Wet me thee it" for "Let me see it," or "jist," for "just," or "whu cha doin?" for "What are you doing?" tend to develop wrong sound-letter associations that are difficult to correct. Many of the "boners" reported by teachers seem to arise from faulty perception and pronunciation of words:

"Acumen is the white of an egg."
"Robinson Caruso was a great singer who lived on an island."
"In mathematics Persia gave us the dismal system."
"The clown in *As You Like It* was named Touchdown."
"Tennyson betrayed women very successfully."
"In this country a man can have only one wife. This is called monotony."[51]

A child who has imitated the incorrect speech of his parents or of other people in his environment may be puzzled when the teacher pronounces a word differently. When confronted by the same word in print, he does not know which way to pronounce it. Even though he does not have a speech defect at the present time, these incorrect letter-sound associations may persist.

The relation of faulty oral expression and speech defects to silent reading ability is less clear. If a child whose speech habits are poor has been able to develop word analysis skills, he may be an excellent silent reader.

Though speech improvement programs have fostered mastery of the mechanics of reading, they have done little for reading comprehension. Studies of children with severe speech difficulties caused by physical defects showed that speech therapy did not improve their reading.

Favorable effects on silent reading achievement were obtained by a program that included the following features:[52] The subjects were average third grade pupils who were given a series of thirty-six half-hour speech improvement lessons during one semester. The program included instruction in attentive listening, methods of observation, techniques of self-expression, practice in speech sound discrimination, and practice in speech production. The pupils' self-confidence increased as they were given opportunities to lead the group in discussion and in choral speaking. The teacher tried to create an appreciation of good speech, to present a model of correct speech herself, and to encourage the children to comment favorably on the improved speech of their classmates. Five or ten minutes of each lesson were devoted to an activity requiring attentive listening. The rest of the time was spent in choral speaking, discussion, speech games, and the dramatization of stories and poems. The pupils were encouraged not only to improve their speech, but also to think about the ideas they gained and apply them to their own experiences. During the last eleven lessons, they listened to a story or poem for the first part of the period and then dramatized it during the remainder.

This combined language arts program had a positive effect on the silent reading achievement of the experimental group of third grade pupils, compared with their matched counterparts who did not receive this special instruction.

Difficulties in oral reading and other aspects of oral expression appear to be associated with at least two personality types—the timid, shy, immature, anxious child; and the aggressive, hostile child. In both cases, underlying personality factors seem to affect both speech and reading.

Oral reading has a legitimate place in the classroom in varying amounts with varying grade levels. Oral reading is essential in the primary grades to prevent the children from persisting in errors that may go undetected when they read silently. However, continuous "round-the-room" oral reading is definitely without justification. This practice dies hard, despite all the legitimate criticism of it. Oral reading is a legitimate means of giving information or directions, presenting problems or riddles to the group, proving a point by reading from an original source, and sharing good literature or otherwise imparting entertainment. Oral reading should be preceded by silent reading. It should involve a natural audience situation. These same conditions apply to other kinds of oral expression.

Methods of Developing Oral Skills

As "stimulator of ideas" and "creator of opportunities" for teachers to improve their present practice, the principal needs a reservoir of valid theory and concrete suggestions on which to draw.

He will encourage teachers to give their pupils many opportunities for oral expression. Among these are choral speaking, informal conversation, planning, sharing experiences, discussing books they have read and other topics, reporting on individual or group projects, and evaluating their own performance and that of others. Dramatization of many kinds appeals to pupils of all ages. First graders like to repeat Dick's and Jane's remarks the way they would say them. Shy children will feel free to speak through puppets. The chance to give a dramatization in reading a story or play appeals to children of all ages. Creative dramatics covers a wide range of enjoyable experiences—role playing, presenting a radio script, presenting class plays and plays for PTA meetings and assembly programs.

The principal will help teachers to recognize the importance of developing children's faith in their ability to speak clearly and fluently. This confidence is built by teachers who listen with understanding and appreciation, rather than by teachers who pounce upon errors. Children need to have comfortable and successful experiences in listening and in speaking. The memory of these successes builds the confidence that is so essential to effective oral expression. When a child has learned to speak freely and naturally and to use language with pleasure and satisfaction, he is usually eager to read and write it correctly. The emphasis should be on the ideas to be communicated. From this focus arises the desire to think straight and to use language appropriately and effectively.

At the same time, the mechanics of oral expression should not be neglected. The teacher should repeatedly guide the class through the process of preparing, giving, and evaluating various kinds of oral reports. Together, teacher and pupils set up criteria for effective oral expression:

Can I be heard and understood?
Is my talk clear and well organized?
Will it be enjoyed by the audience?

It is also the principal's responsibility to provide time and equipment for the various kinds of oral expression. A flexible time schedule enables the creative teacher to include oral expression in connection with any subject, or to devote occasional afternoons to the presentation of plays prepared by groups of children Classes may exchange programs that have grown out of their class work. Pupils and teachers should have access to recordings by outstanding readers and speakers, a tape recorder for class use, and other instructional materials cooperatively chosen after judicious appraisal of the wealth of devices now on the market.

By visiting classrooms, the principal increases his own knowledge of the teaching of the language arts. He takes special note of the good features that he finds. In every classroom he is likely to observe at least one effective procedure. Comment upon it helps the teacher to feel that his efforts are appreciated.

The forward-looking principal encourages teachers to survey children's needs for oral expression, to build up files of materials, to plan classroom activities more carefully, to improve teaching procedures, and to coordinate their efforts with those of other members of the staff.

38.

Oral Language and the Development of Other Language Skills

Robert B. Ruddell

Understanding the contribution of oral language to the development of other basic communication skills is vital to the classroom teacher. Such an understanding should enable the teacher to utilize better the transfer potential present in the interrelatedness of all communication skills.

A major purpose of the language arts program in the elementary school is the development of each child's ability to utilize his skill in oral and written expression for effective communication. This communication can be considered to be of two major types: first, interpersonal communication (verbal interaction with others); and second, intrapersonal communication (verbal interaction with self). Research studies focusing on the interrelationships of language skills in achieving the communicative objective have been described; this report is an extension of the past writing with emphasis upon oral language skills as related to the development of other language skills.[53]

Vocabulary and Syntactical Language Development

The five to seven years of pre-school experience has afforded most children opportunity for vigorous oral language interaction with environment and self. During these years the average child's vocabulary increases dramatically from a minute number of words used by the one year old to many hundreds of basic and derivative words recognized by the average first grader. The grammatical development of children's language likewise increases at a rapid rate from one word utterances at the end of the first year to lexical class substitution by the second year. The mastery of most basic grammatical fundamentals has occurred by the fourth year. By the time the child enters the first grade, he has achieved a high degree of sophistication in his oral language development.[54]

It must be recognized of course that these findings represent the language development of "average" children. The very nature of inferential research requires that the researcher test major hypotheses by relying on significant differences derived from large sample averages, which may result in conclusions of a general nature. Thus the practitioner must be alert to the developmental ranges

From *Elementary English* 43:489-498 (May 1966).

in language growth as related to factors in each child's language environment. For example, Bernstein's research with British youth points to middle and lower working class language differences. The speech patterns of the middle-class children reflected greater individual variation and greater meaning clarity through the utilization of the available possibilities of sentence organization. This presented a marked contrast with patterns of lower working class children who were found to have a comparatively rigid and limited use of the organizational possibilities of sentence construction. Templin's findings also suggest that socioeconomic level is related to the grammatical complexity of responses and vocabulary development of children.[55]

The frequency of the child's opportunity to participate verbally with adults in the family and the language model available would appear to have a direct bearing on the rate of language development.[56] In families with a single child, the child's language facility was found to develop more rapidly than that of children with siblings; the latter children were found to develop language facility faster than twins only.

Thus oral language development of the individual child must be carefully assessed for present achievement and for future potential in light of related environmental factors. The following discussion will focus on research dealing with the relationship between the development of oral language skills (speech, listening) and written language skills (reading, writing), the interrelatedness of language skill development, and the implications from this research for the teaching of language skills.

Oral Language Development and Reading Achievement

The relationship between oral language development and reading achievement is evidenced either directly or tangentially from a number of significant investigations.

Strickland's study of children's oral language development and reading achievement at the sixth-grade level revealed a significant relationship between the use of movables and elements of subordination in oral language and oral reading interpretation.[57] Children who ranked high on measures of comprehension in silent reading and listening were found to make greater use of movables and elements of subordination in their oral language than did children who ranked low on measures of these variables. This finding suggests that a child's ability to utilize subordination and movables in oral expression is closely related to his ability to comprehend written language.

The longitudinal study of children's language development by Loban revealed that children who were advanced in general language ability, as determined by vocabulary scores at the kindergarten level and language ratings by teachers, were also advanced in reading ability.[58] The inverse was found for those low in general language ability. Language achievement differences between the high and low groups were found to increase from year to year with the low group using many more partial expressions or incomplete sentence patterns. Loban concluded that competence in spoken language appears to be a necessary base for competence in reading.

Further evidence of this relationship was supplied by Milner's investigation of the use of language in the home and reading achievement at the first-grade level.[59] She found that the high achieving readers came from an enriched verbal environment which, as contrasted with that of the low achieving readers, included having more books available and being read to more often by high-esteemed adults. The high-scoring children also engaged in conversations with their parents more often than the low-scoring children.

Gibbons used a "disarranged phase test" to study the relationship between third-grade children's ability to understand the structure of sentences and their reading achievement. She found a correlation of .89 between the ability to see the relationship between parts of a sentence and the ability to understand the sentence, when intelligence was partialled out. A correlation of .72 was found between the ability to see the relationship between parts of sentences and total reading achievement.[60]

The significant finding highlighted in both Strickland's and Loban's studies, emphasizing the relationship between children's demonstrated use of movables and subordination in oral language and their reading and listening achievement, has an interesting parallel in Thorndike's early descriptive study of mistakes in paragraph reading.[61] Thorndike concluded from his study of sixth-grade children that in "correct reading" each element of meaning must be given appropriate weight in comparison to other elements and that ideas presented must be examined and validated to make sure that they satisfy the mental set or purpose of reading. He further concluded that understanding a paragraph is dependent upon the reader's selection of the right elements and synthesizing them in the right relationships. These conclusions point to the importance of seeing relationships among contextual elements—the movables and various forms of subordination—to reading comprehension. Again it would seem to follow logically that the child who demonstrates control over movables and subordination in his oral language will better comprehend written or spoken language emphasizing these features than will the child who has little facility in using movables or in subordinating.

A reading program encompassing oral patterns of language structure, identified by the Strickland study, was developed at the first grade-level by Ruddell.[62] In the early stages of the program, meaning change in oral and written language as conveyed by intonation patterns (pitch, stress, juncture) and punctuation was stressed. In a later phase of the program, emphasis was placed on the relationships which exist among words in sentences by developing meaning change through manipulation of specific elements in the sentence. The sentences used were developed in the context of a paragraph or story. Findings at mid-year in this first-grade study showed significant differences in reading comprehension skills favoring the basal reading programs using the special supplement emphasizing language structure as related to meaning when contrasted with identical basal reading programs not using the special supplement. This study reported correlations of .68 and .44 between children's syntactical language development measured early in grade one and the respective factors of vocabulary achievement and comprehension achievement measured at mid-year.

At the fourth-grade level the same researcher examined the effect on reading comprehension of patterns of language structure which occur with high and low frequency in children's oral language.[63] When the readability level of reading passages was controlled, comprehension scores on material written with high frequency patterns of language structure were found to be significantly superior to comprehension scores on passages written with low frequency patterns of language structure.

The research reviewed here strongly suggests that facility in oral expression, particularly vocabulary knowledge and an understanding of sentence structure, is basic to the development of reading comprehension skill.

Listening Development and Reading Achievement

Kelty investigated the effect of training in listening for certain purposes upon the ability of fourth-grade pupils to read for the same purposes.[64] She found that practice in listening to note the details of a selection produced a significant gain in reading for the same purpose. However training in listening to decide upon the main idea and to draw a conclusion produced a positive but not significant change in reading for these purposes.

The research by Hampleman indicated that the listening comprehension of fourth- and sixth-grade children was superior to their reading comprehension of easy material when compared to the comprehension of more difficult verbal context.[65] Listening comprehension was found to be significantly superior to reading comprehension for both fourth- and sixth-grade pupils, but an increase in mental age resulted in a decrease in the difference between listening and reading comprehension.

Young[66] found that children retained more from an oral presentation by the teacher than from silent reading by themselves. The oral presentation plus simultaneous silent reading by the pupils was equally as effective as the oral presentation of the teacher alone. Children who did poorly in comprehension through listening were also found to perform poorly in comprehension through reading. Young concluded that throughout the intermediate grades children improve their ability to comprehend through reading at the same rate that they improve their ability to comprehend through listening.

A number of correlational studies have examined the relationship between listening and reading comprehension. At the fifth-grade level Lundsteen reported a correlation of .52 between critical listening and reading achievement. Plessas reported correlation coefficients between a listening test and various aspects of reading achievement ranging from .27 to .80. Trivette found a correlation between listening and reading comprehension of .61 and Hollow found a correlation of .55, at the fifth-grade level. From a study at the sixth-grade level Pratt reported a correlation of .64 while Devine at the high school level found a correlation of .65. High relationships between listening and reading comprehension were also reported in early studies by Larsen and Feder and by Young.[67]

The correlations from the majority of these studies suggest that factors in listening comprehension account for approximately twenty-five to sixty percent of the variance in the reading comprehension scores, depending on the types of listening and reading skills measured. It must be emphasized, however, that correlational studies are limited as to the clarity of relationships between variables. This is to say that a cause-and-effect relationship is not established through correlational analysis. The common, but imperfectly defined, variable of intelligence, for instance, may account for a significant portion of the relationship observed between listening comprehension and reading comprehension.

The research of Caffrey and the study by Spearritt suggest that ability in listening, or "auding," may be constituted of verbal comprehension factors differing from those involved in reading. Russell has emphasized the need for a theory of listening which would enable researchers to generate fruitful hypotheses for examination and allow practitioners to apply findings in developing this phase of the language arts curriculum.[68]

In summary, the relationship between listening and reading is shown to be of significant magnitude, with common factors accounting for a degree of the positive correlations; however, the evidence indicates that each receptive skill may contain verbal factors individually unique.

Oral Language Development and Writing

The research evidence concerning the relationship between oral language and writing is comparatively limited. Loban reported from evidence obtained in his longitudinal study that children who were rated superior and above average in oral language usage were also rated above average in writing, and those below average in oral language were also below average in written language.[69]

Although specific data were not reported, Winter's findings of "low stable relationships" between oral language vocabularies and writing abilities of first- and second-grade children, substantiate Loban's research.[70]

Hughes also concluded from his investigation of 332 fifth-grade children that high achievement in any one of the language abilities examined (e.g., language usage) tended to be associated with above average achievement in the other areas, studied (*e.g.*, sentence sense, paragraph organization).[71] The inverse was true with low achievement in any one of the abilities. Correlations between language usage and the two factors of sentence sense and paragraph organization were found to be .46 and .39 respectively. The correlations reflected a positive relationship between each of the selected language variables independent of intelligence.

A detailed study by Harrell compared selected language variables in the speech and writing of 320 children of ages nine, eleven, thirteen, and fifteen. A short movie was used as the stimulus for securing the speech and writing samples.[72] The investigator found that the length of the compositions and clauses used in oral and written expression increased with age, with a larger percentage of subordinate clauses being used by the older children in both written and spoken composition. The children were found to use a larger percentage of subordinate clauses in writing than in speaking. More adverb and adjective clauses were used in written compositions while a larger number of noun clauses were used in speaking. A larger percentage of adverbial clauses, excepting those of time and cause, were used in the children's speech. The developmental increase of each language variable in relation to age was found to be greater for written compositions than for oral.

Working with tenth-grade students Bushnell compared each student's oral and written compositions of the same topic.[73] He found that higher scores on measures of thought content and sentence structure were obtained on the written themes than on the oral compositions. Correlations between the scores on oral and written thought content and oral and written sentence structure were found to be .42 and .35 respectively. Bushnell concluded that the most important difference between the two forms of expression was the more precise and logical organization of written language in contrast to the less precise and loosely organized oral language.

By examining research which contrasts the language development of children possessing defective hearing with that of children having normal hearing, the relationship between oral language development and writing achievement is brought into sharper focus. Heider and Heider used a motion picture as a stimulus for securing written compositions from 301 deaf and 817 hearing children ranging in age from eleven to seventeen years and eight to fourteen years respectively.[74] Although the deaf children were three years older their compositions were found to resemble the less mature hearing children. The deaf children were found to use fewer numbers of words and clauses than the hearing children. The hearing children used more compound and complex sentences with a larger number of verbs in coordinate and subordinate clauses, indicating a more advanced development in written language.

The written language of normal and defective hearing children was also examined by Templin.[75] Children having defective hearing were found to use more words in their explanations of natural phenomena than hearing children. This was interpreted as reflecting less adequate control over vocabulary, rather than representing a more complex type of expression. The children with defective hearing apparently needed more words to express a concept because of their inability to use precise vocabulary. Templin concluded that the written language of the defective hearing child is more immature than that of the hearing child of the same age, grade, and intelligence.

These investigations point to similarities in the growth patterns of oral and written language development. Achievement in oral language appears to be directly associated with written language achievement although some variance in the organizational quality of oral and written expression of older children is evidenced.

Summary: Interrelationships of Language Skills

Research evidence available strongly suggest a high degree of interrelatedness among the various communication skills. The functional understanding of vocabulary and the ability to comprehend relationships between elements of vocabulary in structural patterns appear to encompass common communication components in the language arts.

The research reviewed indicates that oral language development serves as the underlying base for the development of reading and writing achievement. The child's ability to comprehend written material through reading and to express himself through written communication appears directly related to his maturity in the speaking and listening phases of language development.

The findings reported suggest that the receptive skills of listening and reading are closely related and utilize similar verbal factors but may encompass factors unique to each skill.

The relationship between the receptive skill of listening and the expressive skill of writing was explored in the research on normal and hearing handicapped children. Hearing children were found to use more complex types of language structure and more concise composition, reflecting a higher degree of maturity in written expression than that of deaf or partially hearing children.

The expressive skills of speaking and writing appear to parallel closely each other in developmental growth. With older children, however, some variance is noted in the types of subordination and the degree of organization utilized in oral and written compositions.

Interrelationships among the language arts skills are very much apparent in the research examined. These interrelationships deserve careful consideration by the classroom teacher if full utilization is to be made of the learning transfer potential in language skills.

Implications for Teaching the Language Skills

The research evidence presented in this discussion suggests a number of implications for teaching language skills. These include the following:

1. The teacher of basic language skills must be aware of the wide range in language development which can be anticipated in the elementary classroom. His understanding of individual children will be more complete, enabling the planning of a more adequate language program, if the possible factors which may have precipitated the range of individual language differences can be accounted for. These factors may include the language models presented in the home, the degree of language interaction between the parents and the child, the

value placed by the home on the importance of language development, the dialect differences between home and school, and individual pupil characteristics such as hearing acuity loss and intellectual development.

2. Children's language is greatly influenced by the models presented in their environmental settings. Although the early home environment plays a major role in a child's language development, it would seem that the teacher's model and that of other children could also exert a positive influence on children's language development in the classroom setting. Such devices as the tape recorder should be considered for individual or group listening activities in presenting appropriate and contrasting language models to the children. Oral language enrichment activities such as role playing, storytelling, and group discussions of direct experiences, deserve strong emphasis, particularly with children from culturally disadvantaged backgrounds. In this manner a language base can be established for the development of reading and writing skills.

3. Consideration should be given to language difficulties impairing children's reading and listening comprehension and clarity of oral and written expression. Vocabulary enrichment and the development of functional utilization of movables and subordinating elements in improving sentence meaning may require special emphasis. Consideration should be given to the following types of structural meaning changes: word substitution (*e.g.*, Bill hit the *ball.* Bill hit the *girl.*); expansion of patterns (*e.g.*, Tim had a wagon. Tim had a wagon *yesterday.* Tim *my brother* had a wagon yesterday.); inversion of sentence elements (*e.g.*, Sam hit the ball. *The ball* hit Sam.); transformations of basic structural patterns (*e.g.*, Ann is in the house. *Is* Ann in the house?). By a careful appraisal of language skill development, the language arts program can be based on the children's specific needs.

4. Oral language development can provide a basis for written language skill development in the integrated language skills curriculum. Oral language activities such as reading literature to children, dramatic play and dialogue, combined with extensive use of experience charts, can serve to help children understand how intonation and punctuation may be used to convey meaning in oral and written expression. Such activities also provide an excellent way to show children how descriptive language can be used in developing story characters and story settings, and how certain parts of sentences can be expanded to provide the listener or reader more precise information in an interesting way.

5. An increased awareness of the interrelatedness of listening comprehension and reading comprehension skills should be fostered in the classroom. Listening and reading activities should encompass a variety of purposes, ranging from direct recall to critical evaluation of material. In practice the development of these skills may evolve through the careful development of purposes for listening and reading. For example, news articles and advertisements found in the daily newspaper or on television may be used in fostering critical comprehension skills. Listening comprehension skills can be taught and would seem to enhance reading comprehension skills. This consideration in the instructional program is essential if children are to obtain maximum benefit from the language environment which surrounds them.

6. Careful consideration should be given to children's concept development in relation to their own experiences. The child must have a firm grasp of the concept he is attempting to express in oral or written form if his communication attempt is to be successful. The teacher should attempt to develop and expand concepts through concrete experiences in the classroom and field trips, and by showing children how words convey different meanings in a variety

of oral and written sentence contexts.

7. Language educators must consider the implementation of two types of research in the further exploration of the nature of interrelationships among the language arts and in testing the hypotheses embodied in the procedures and materials of language programs. The first type of research is the action research study carried out in individual classroom settings. In practice, this means using procedures and materials with children and noting in a descriptive manner the success and difficulty experienced in improving language skills within the limitations of the classroom. The second type of research is the carefully controlled research study carried out in an experimental setting. This type of evaluation must be effected with groups of children taught by distinct and contrastingly different programs with provision for control of important variables such as intelligence and socioeconomic background.

Although past research on children's language development has explored only a small segment of the vast cognitive realm, the high degree of interrelatedness between oral and written language skill development is evident. Through cooperative efforts psychologists, linguists, and language educators have recently forged new tools providing for more precise descriptive analysis of children's language. The value of such analysis techniques has been demonstrated in the studies of Strickland and Loban and should facilitate the exploration of the future language researcher. These techniques, new hypotheses, and development of new curriculum materials all require added understanding of factors leading to the improvement of children's language achievement. These must be carefully studied in classroom settings if knowledge is to be furthered and methodology of language arts instruction is to be improved.

39.

Too Much Shushing—Let Children Talk

Betty L. Broman

A dead quiet room is a danger sign. A danger sign that learning is not taking place. Not a question asked, not a question answered. Not a comment made. Not a moment shared. No scraping chairs, no grating pencil sharpener, no swish of the paper cutter, no rattling crayon box, no rustling brown wrapping paper, no talk in the science corner, no talk as a social studies panel is planned. In this room the only talk is teacher talk.

The buzzing room of children's talk and movement is a learning sign. A sign that ideas are taking form, questions being asked, thoughts being shared, objects being created, discussions being planned, children learning from children, and children learning from the teacher.

Why do teachers shush? Some teachers shush all activity while others shush activity that is "noisy." The emphasis of keeping children under control often deadens rich teaching opportunities. The fear of being accused of having a noisy room prompts a teacher to shush the children. A classroom is supposed to be a learning room. A learning room for learning how to talk, to listen, to write, to spell, to read, to be mathematical wizards, to be beginning scientists, to be potential baseball stars, to be good citizens, and to be creative in all of the arts.

What is noise? Noise is knocked over chairs; dropped books; loud voices; children wandering aimlessly around the room, humming, whistling; chatter; unrelated activities; children calling across the room to other children or to the teacher. Any one of these "noises" happens occasionally in any classroom but the difference between a good learning room and a noisy room is that, in the latter, all of them are happening concurrently. This kind of noise is aimless and purposeless.

Children learn to talk and to listen by talking and listening under the guidance of the teacher. The guiding teacher in turn listens for areas of weakness in content knowledge while the children are planning and sharing ideas and materials. She listens for weakness in pronunciation, enunciation, vocabulary and sentence patterns as they are reporting, participating on panels and leading discussions. Teachers know what they need to teach, reteach or stress only if they listen to children's talk. Research has shown children listen 50 to 75 percent of a school day—more confirmation that teachers talk too much and children talk too little.

From *Childhood Education* 46:132-134 (December 1969). Reprinted by permission of Betty L. Broman and the Association for Childhood Education International, 3615 Wisconsin Avenue, N.W. Washington, D.C.

The *other* child, the child who comes from the disadvantaged home, comes to school with a language pattern that has been adequate and meaningful in his own environment. Suddenly he is thrust into a totally new situation, one demanding correct pronunciation, enunciation, grammar, and word meaning that is very sophisticated. All of the old habits are wrong and he must become a "new child" if he is to succeed in school.

Many of our curriculum rigidities are holdovers from a generation when only those who could succeed stayed in school. Today we require all children to stay in school, regardless of how well they succeed in any of the subject areas or of whether we have a curriculum designed for an individual's ability and needs or not.

The experts have been telling us for years to teach children on the level where we find them. In many school systems this excellent advice has been followed, but the disadvantaged child has been disadvantaged in many ways other than having limited home and enrichment opportunities. This child attends the poorer schools and hasn't been accepted and taught at his own level. The lack of emphasis on teaching individuals in our ghetto schools has made these children second-class citizens.

Teachers who provide a classroom atmosphere that allows discussion, sharing, group work; who develop the elements of the arts in all subject areas; and who stimulate as well as permit their students to talk will improve the language of children.

In setting up a learning room the teacher should:

- establish rules of conduct with the children
- provide guidance to the children for helping them to learn how to control themselves
- be consistent in the ways he handles discipline problems
- be aware of the natural growth tendencies of the age of children he teaches
- plan lessons that are conducive for group discussions, panels, reporting, small group planning and buddy teaching
- allow time for children to enrich and develop the general plans of the teacher for answering their questions and interests
- always provide an excellent example of language himself.

Teaching language requires teachers to provide conditions that are conducive for children to talk. The following suggestions will aid the teacher in providing these conditions for language growth. A teacher should:

- provide proper physical conditions for individual and small group work
- speak in an animated and pleasing voice
- always use correct language
- avoid speaking when children should be doing the talking
- help children eliminate bad language habits
- praise the children for correct language usage
- avoid needless criticism
- provide language opportunities that are purposeful, accurate, and fulfill a language need
- check the children's use of language through listening as they talk to each other, as they talk to other adults, and as they talk to the teacher
- plan for an integrated language development program in all subject areas, as well as for daily language skill classes.

Teachers must design a language curriculum that provides sequential experiences that are integrated within the entire instructional program (social studies, mathematics, science, art, music, physical education, health and language arts).

The following ideas can be varied to meet the needs of many ages in the elementary school:

Social studies language activities: Have children (1) tape their social studies reports; (2) give oral directions for driving to the nearest city.

Mathematics language activities: Have children (1) create oral mathematical puzzles; (2) work in groups of four, each taking turns asking mathematical questions.

Science language activities: Have children (1) give oral description of the natural phenomena in the school yard; (2) present monthly, weekly and daily weather reports.

Art language activities: Have children (1) explain how they formed a papier-mache animal; (2) give directions for an art activity.

Music language activities: Have children (1) present oral reports on composers; (2) discuss the language of a variety of music, such as folk ballads, classical music, jazz and popular songs.

Physical education language activities: Have children (1) give directions for a new game; (2) direct physical exercises.

Health language activities: Have children (1) prepare and present a panel discussion on the care of the body; (2) tape short discussions on daily diet needs, mental health, and hygiene.

Language arts language activities: Have children (1) listen to oral reports in instructional areas other than language arts; (2) write a book report to be read orally; (3) look up words they mispronounce and learn to spell them correctly; (4) read aloud a poem; (5) compose an original story and read it to the class; (6) analyze the speech of others.

Children from all cultures need to use as much oral language as possible. Through using ideas and questions they begin to define, amplify and enrich. The purpose of these activities is to develop the length and complexities of the sentences they use.

Language growth is not developed by a separate language class alone. Language growth should be stressed throughout the day, including those language skills that need to be corrected, improved and extended. As the teacher listens, he hears the language problems of the children and from these problems develops his lesson plans.

Along with setting an example of standard English, a teacher must always accept the language of the child without criticizing, degrading or ignoring him; and he must build upon this language to provide success in later instructional learning. To do this the teacher must listen more than he talks and the children must talk more than they listen.

40.

What the Classroom Teacher Can Do for the Child with Speech Defects

Evelyn Young Allen

Even though people assume that speaking must be a simple function because almost everyone speaks, no process performed by human beings is more complex. It is not surprising, therefore, that youngsters with speech problems make up our largest group of exceptional children.

The need for speech therapy is great, and the number of speech therapists is small. Many schools have no speech programs of any kind, and in those that do, the speech-handicapped child probably receives only one or two brief speech therapy sessions per week. As a result, much of the responsibility for helping children to overcome speech handicaps or to succeed in school and in life in spite of persistent ones rests with the classroom teacher.

Most classes include at least one child with a speech problem. How can the classroom teacher meet his responsibility to this child?

The speech-handicapped child thrives in the same warm, supportive classroom climate that agrees with other children. By adding some special emphases to this climate, the teacher can help him improve his speech and, in the case of a child who is receiving speech therapy, can expedite the therapy.

The classroom teacher must receive the speech-handicapped child as a welcome member of the group. The child's speech attempts must never be criticized. Such a remark as, "Say it again; I can't understand a word you say," is catastrophic. On the other hand, encouraging comments like, "Let's listen carefully so we can understand what Bob has to tell us," and "Tom has been working hard to say the *s* sound correctly; do you hear his new way of saying *saw, bus,* and *missing*?" are valuable.

Accepting the child as he is and being pleased with any growth he makes are basic keys to helping him improve his speech. It is as if the teacher is saying, "It will be fine if we can help you to talk more distinctly, but I like you and approve of you just as you are." Not only is this attitude healthful but it is also contagious and will spread to the children in the classroom.

The ideal classroom climate holds no threat or penalty to the child who cannot measure up orally. Children with speech problems are expected to do the classroom assignments and take the tests required of all children, though it may be necessary in some cases to modify assignments from oral to written.

Reprinted from *N.E.A. Journal* 56:35-36, (November 1967), by permission of author and publisher.

As Roberta Gibson, a speech correctionist formerly on the staff of the public schools in Kansas City, Missouri, points out, the speech-handicapped child "should be helped to understand that speech is a tool and that his lack of proficiency with this one instrument does not minimize his value as a member of the group. Abilities in other fields, such as art, athletics, mathematics, and music, should be emphasized. He should be helped to discuss his problem calmly, without the feeling that it is something to be ashamed of."

Articulation defects (the substitution of one sound for another, the complete omission of a sound, or the distortion of a sound) account for the majority of speech problems among children. Often these articulation errors result from a child's inability to listen to different sounds and distinguish between them.

It is definitely helpful to the child with an articulation problem for the teacher to use every opportunity to build awareness of sounds so that the child learns to identify specific phonemes or sound units.

The classroom teacher is not expected to become a speech clinician, correctionist, or therapist, but he can find many ways in which the daily classroom program can focus on specific articulation defects. Learning to listen and learning about listening can benefit the children with speech problems and at the same time improve the auditory discrimination skills of all children.

The teacher can develop many creative listening games based on words starting with sounds that are difficult for children to differentiate—*pan, fan; day, gay; cold, gold; let, wet; round, wound; sick, thick; they, day.*

Speech-oriented activities, such as reciting rhymes and poetry, taking part in dramatics, telling stories, and singing songs that contain sounds the class has worked on, can provide valuable experiences for both handicapped and normal speakers. Similarly, all will benefit from learning how to introduce and identify themselves, introduce others, express social amenities, answer the telephone, and give messages orally.

Many teachers worry about how best to help the stutterer, the child whose speech is interrupted by pauses, blockings, repetitions, hesitations, and bodily contortions. Although speech correctionists, pathologists, and psychologists disagree as to the causes of stuttering, they are in agreement that the child's environment and the attitude others show toward his manner of speech affect his stuttering. Following are some ways in which a classroom teacher can help a child who stutters.

- Establish a favorable atmosphere for speaking in the classroom.
- Try to help the stuttering child maintain a calm and happy attitude toward school and himself.
- Try to speak in an unhurried manner with a pleasant, low-pitched voice.
- Learn to accept the way the stutterer speaks. Show patience and kindness but not pity. Look directly at the stutterer's eyes and don't turn away when he encounters speaking difficulties.
- Help the stutterer feel that he is a worthy member of his group.
- Give him opportunities to develop and express abilities in areas other than speech, so that he can experience success.
- Encourage him to participate in group activities like games, singing, dancing, and discussions.
- Encourage the stutterer to speak in the classroom; expect him to take part in class recitations and fulfill all assignments, oral and written; help him to know that even though he may stutter, he can speak in the classroom with no fear of ridicule.
- Do not compare the stutterer's speech or other skills with those of siblings or classmates.

• Do not tell him not to stutter—the harder he tries not to stutter, the greater will be the tensions and the worse the stuttering.

• Do not tell him to take a deep breath before speaking, to think before he starts, or to stop and start over.

• Do not praise the stutterer when he doesn't stutter. Praise his speech on the basis of adequate preparation, clearness, good expression, and calm manner.

• Do not tell the stutterer the word he is trying to say or cut his speech off unfinished.

• Encourage the stutterer to realize that it is not important for him to have fluent speech, but that it is very important for him to speak in all situations, regardless of stuttering.

In schools which have therapists, the teacher should discuss with the therapist and the parents the step-by-step program for the child who has speech problems. The classroom teacher's greatest contribution in these cases, however, is a positive attitude. If classroom teachers believe in and express enthusiasm for the speech therapy program, the children and their parents are likely to share the enthusiasm.

Some children referred for speech therapy are apprehensive about going to the speech room for the first lesson. They may fear that something unpleasant or painful will occur or that they will miss important classroom work. They may feel ashamed because they do not speak as well as other children. These fears can be minimized or even banished by understanding teachers.

By following any or all of the suggestions below, the classroom teacher can help to create a positive, wholesome attitude about the speech program.

• Have a short class discussion on speech therapy in which children exchange ideas and ask questions.

• Invite the speech therapist to visit the room, tell about the program, and answer questions.

• If the speech therapy room is in the building, arrange for the children to visit it briefly, possibly to observe a lesson.

• Speak of a child's appointment for speech therapy as a fine opportunity and privilege, rather than as something unpleasant which he must do.

• Let children who are having therapy report to the class on the lessons.

• Encourage parents to cooperate by assisting with assignments to be carried out at home.

Another way in which the teacher can help the therapy program is by following up the speech lessons in the classroom. When the therapist feels that a child has mastered a sound, he will notify the teacher, who can then encourage the child to make correct use of the sound in reading and speaking. In this way the child comes to integrate his newly learned sounds with his total speech pattern. Even more important, this makes him realize that his classroom teacher appreciates him and his efforts to improve his speech.

C.
Creative Expression

Developing creativity has long been considered one of the primary goals of the elementary school. Recently, fostering creativity within each child has emerged as one of our greatest educational concerns. In the past, creativity was restricted to some aspect of the "arts" and only a few children were regarded as being creative. This narrow view of creativity is no longer widely held and it is generally felt that all children possess creativity to some degree.

Children show great variation in the manner in which their creative expression emerges. Some are born storytellers, many excel in dramatics, while others create original plays or verse. Creativity can be displayed through many different avenues and teachers must provide a rich variety of opportunities for each child to express himself according to his special aptitudes and interests. Children must be given the chance to express their ideas and feelings in their own way.

Numerous conditions affect any attempt to develop each child's creative potential. Evidence seems to indicate that the teacher is the single most influential factor in any program attempting to release or guide creativity within the classroom. A positive attitude by the teacher toward creativity is imperative. The example the teacher sets in showing creativity in his own expression and appreciation of creativity in others is of utmost importance. It is necessary for the teacher to establish conditions within the classroom which foster creativity. Willingness to encourage and recognize children's creative efforts would be a vital part of these necessary conditions.

The following articles represent diverse approaches to creative expression in the elementary school. Motivational techniques and instructional suggestions are presented for a variety of creative activities. The authors discuss the role of the teacher as he attempts to create an atmosphere conducive to releasing the creative potential within each student.

41.

'Let Not Young Souls Be Smothered Out...'

R. Van Allen

Let not young souls be smothered out before
They do quaint deeds and fully flaunt their pride.
It is the world's one crime its babes grow dull . . .*

Bill was in a third-year class with a teacher who valued his uniqueness of expression above everything else in language development. She helped him to realize that no one else could *really* say anything for him. He had to rely on himself. This did not mean that she neglected to help Bill and the others in assimilating our language heritage and societal expectancies. These demands could be achieved at the same time that Bill's individuality, his uniqueness, was being preserved. One result follows:

THE VOLCANO

Tumbling boulders
Fiery river
Very, very hot!
It boils and it bubbles
And sizzles and crashes.
It comes out in rock and in lava it flows
Through the streets of the town
And nothing can stop it.
It hits the sea!
It smokes and it bubbles.
It steams, it fizzes,
It hisses and billows.

Bill B. (Age 9)

From *Childhood Education* 44:354-357 (February 1968). Reprinted with permission of R. Van Allen and the Association for Childhood Education International, 3615 Wisconsin Avenue, N.W., Washington, D.C.

*Reprinted with permission of The Macmillan Company from *Collected Poems* by Vachel Lindsay. Copyright 1914 by The Macmillan Company, renewed 1942 by Elizabeth C. Lindsay.

Constant pressure is still being exerted, in the interest of convergent thinking and response, to extinguish young children's spark of uniqueness, despite the fact that many teachers and parents value individuality of oral and written expression. Perhaps all of us need to pause and consider our contribution to this "crime of dullness" in children and youth. At the same time we need to consider anew some of the values of keeping children happily adjusted to language opportunities and to personal ways of expressing ideas and feelings.

• **Creative language experiences provide for individual differences.** Children think and reason differently. They have varying abilities, interests, drives and talents. Teachers who live and work with children soon realize that each must be dealt with differently. They realize that children work best when their tasks and responsibilities are appropriate to their age and abilities and flexible enough to permit individual ways of thinking and working.

A well-developed program of oral and written communication provides richly for individual differences. The child develops a style of expression typically his own. As the adults in his life let him know that they appreciate his style and value his ideas, the child gains confidence and extends his efforts to produce something that is truly his.

The teacher should guard against preconceived ideas about what children's language should be—how it should be spoken, written, dramatized or painted. It is his task to create the learning environment in which spontaneous language expression can flourish. The attitude of the teacher will result in language experiences which either express individuality or show that unfortunate similarity which reflects teacher dominance.

• **Creative language experiences develop imagination.** All children are endowed with the power of imagination—the power to form mental images of ideas, things and people not actually present. This resource is available in every classroom at no extra cost, but in the process of what we call "education" somehow the power of imagination diminishes as other facets of the personality are developed.

Teachers working with children should be careful not to destroy or discourage the gift of imagination in children. As they work to increase their ability in oral and written communication, children should have great freedom to draw upon their imagination for content, settings, situations and characters. Through imaginary characters and plots, a child can express his innermost concerns and feelings with a sensitivity and a frankness seldom reflected in real character and setting assignments. Dramatizations and all forms of creative writing invite children to maintain and continue to develop their powers of imagination.

• **Creative language experiences build self-confidence.** A child must rely on himself when he is engaged in creative language production. He should search in his own storehouse of experiences for skills and knowledge which he possesses when using his own language to solve speech and writing problems.

Evidence of pleasing results gives the child a feeling of satisfaction. A measure of success from something of his own thinking inspires him to further achievements. It helps him to set his own standards rather than being judged always by uniform standards, rivalry or competition. Some measure of praise may be used wisely. However, strong, exaggerated praise can be damaging, for the child may recognize its falseness or become discouraged by the fact that he cannot live up to the high expectation implied in the praise. Self-confidence is strengthened more through gratification a person derives from completing a task in a way that meets his own standards.

• **Creative language experiences provide for emotional expression.** Children need socially acceptable outlets for their emotions. They need some dramatic ways to do this so they can observe the response of other people. Dramatization and creative writing activities depend upon expression of emotions for an important part of their power to communicate. When the emotions of the child are deeply involved with his subject—whether oral or written—his output will contain an element to which others can respond. Masterpieces in writing are usually expressions of basic emotions to which people have long responded.

In creative language activities, children combine their ideas and experiences with their emotional attitudes and, as they do this, select words and phrases put into appropriate arrangements so that they will communicate feelings. All these processes help children express their emotions in orderly and acceptable ways.

• **Creative language experiences develop the esthetic sense.** Although emotional and social improvements are valid goals of rich language programs at school, they should be accompanied by goals which build appreciation for quality and beauty in speech and literature. As the level of awareness to the beauty around them is raised, children increase their delight in the treasures of the world near them. Through their work in writing, children gain the power to distinguish quality in thought and expression of others who have described the world as they see it.

Children need exposure to the great works of literature of the past and of their own time. Oral reading by the teacher or by a child who is a good reader is a way to give an exposure to which most children can listen, absorb, enjoy and respond. Few young children can do the reading themselves and get the sheer enjoyment from artistic language. They need oral exposure.

Children who have engaged in abundant writing of their own ideas and have experimented with many forms of writing are the ones who are best prepared to appreciate good writing of others when they encounter it. Whether a child becomes an author is not the major consideration. Every person needs to be able to make quality judgments and selections of reading material in everyday life.

• **Creative language experiences deepen appreciation of other people.** A language program focused on the thinking of individuals and uniqueness of expression provides opportunity for appreciation of the work of other children in the classroom. A child who has struggled to communicate his ideas, orally or in writing, is appreciative of other children who have solved their problems in a variety of ways that not only communicate ideas clearly but bring pleasure as well. He expects and looks forward to diversity in self-expression. He is released from the shackles of believing that "correctness" and "conformity" are synonymous.

• **Creative language experiences bring balance to educational activities.** Children need the educational balance of a program which takes into account their creative powers at the same time they are learning fundamental skills of handwriting, spelling, mechanics of English, and reading. They need time to consider their own ideas, feelings and aspirations.

Freeing children to independently create something different is a necessary balance to requiring them to arrive at the same solution. Both play a part in helping a child improve his oral and written communication.

42.

Techniques for the Creative Reading or Telling of Stories to Children

Sue Ann Martin

"There was a child went forth every day, and the first object he look'd upon, that object he became, and that object became part of him for the day or a certain part of the day: Or for many years." These words, found in Walt Whitman's *Leaves of Grass*, illustrate two things: first, that Mr. Whitman had a good understanding of the heart of the child; and second, that the imagination runs joyfully rampant through childhood.

Unfortunately, this fresh imaginative romp gradually slows down to a crawl as the years pass. Perhaps too much rote learning, too much reliance on routine, too much organization, and too much interference by society are the germs in this crippling disease. "Those ears born cocked to celestial tunes, are forced to grow dull listening to what uncles, aunts and neighbors say, what teachers and other classmates say."[76] Intense exposure to stories and storytelling, however, is an effective antidote. The sooner the treatment is begun, the better the prognosis.

"Truly thrice blessed is the child who has experienced such art through the listening years. For these are the years a child can be so easily played on, when to be filled to the brimming means that the years ahead will never run dry."[77] Thus, it is imperative to give storytelling prime time in the social and pyschological diet of children.

Storytelling stirs and develops the imagination. As educators we should be concerned with this stirring and developing because it is directly related to mental growth. Gesell says that "in the play of phantasy, the child projects his private mental images in a practical spirit. He manipulates them in order to organize his concepts of reality and not to deepen his self-illusion."[78]

But how do you tell a story? The answer to this question is usually never a satisfactory one. There are numerous publications dealing with how to select stories for children, when to tell stories to children, and why storytelling is important. And while knowledge in these areas is necessary for every teacher, there can be no practical application of it unless the teacher also has a knowledge of how to tell a story.

"The storyteller," says Leland Jacobs, "uses distinctive talents and abilities; his background of experience in the comedy and tragedy of life; his joy in language; his sensitivity to what is of spiritual and moral import; and his delight in aesthetic responses to nature and to what man has created that is beautiful."[79] With these tools that Jacobs speaks of, the storyteller can develop techniques for creative storytelling. The most important of these are the techniques of characterization, imagery, the vocal pause, comic techniques, and animation.

Characterization

Characterizations have a great deal to do with the success and life of a story. The storyteller must first keep in mind that most characters in children's literature are exaggerated figures. The younger the child audience, the more exaggerated these figures must be to communicate. Therefore, the storyteller must be concerned with those one or two outstanding characteristics that identify each figure rather than with analyzing the characters in depth and searching for their motivations.

Little Red Riding Hood, for instance, is an exaggerated figure. Consequently, the storyteller must look for her most dominant characteristics. In this case, little girl sweetness and naivete would be the predominant ones to exaggerate in the portrayal. This exaggeration should not only be auditory, but also visual.

In *Many Moons*, James Thurber describes the Royal Mathematician as being a "bald-headed, nearsighted man, with a skullcap on his head and a pencil behind each ear." Here the storyteller may commence to draw an exaggeration by portraying him as an old man who squints, talks with a frail voice, and whose speech is made hesitant by a pre-occupation with figures and numbers. In contrast to this character, the author gives the storyteller a lively image of the Court Jester. "The Jester came bounding into the throne room in his motley and his cap and bells and sat at the foot of the throne." Consequently, for the Court Jester, the storyteller needs to draw a brighter, happier, and more youthful character. The voice needs to be melodic, quick and full of enthusiasm. The eyes need to be open wide and eyebrows lifted with bright expectation.

The "big bad wolf" in "Little Red Riding Hood" is also an exaggerated figure. This wolf is not just an ordinary wolf; rather, he is a cross between a human and a wolf. He uses human language and dresses in human clothes, but, at the same time, he still growls and flashes his big teeth. The storyteller must keep this in mind when creating the wolf.

Once the storyteller decides upon the most outstanding characteristics to be emphasized, he must go ahead and emphasize. Have a sinister laugh. Growl! "One of the most important artifices in storytelling to young children is the use of mimicry—the imitation of animal's voices and sounds in general is of never ending joy to the listener."[80] Exaggerate! Really *be* the big, bad wolf. Forget about yourself and have fun! This philosophy of becoming the character is very important. Give full range to your imagination and put aside your inhibitions. If the storyteller really believes that he is the big bad wolf for that moment, the children will also believe it for that moment.

Dialogue Is Important

Children like to hear characters talk directly to each other through dialogue. Dialogue, or direct discourse, is closer to real life than a third person account. Whenever a story is written indirectly, the storyteller should change it grammatically to direct discourse. "Direct discourse should be used almost entirely when telling the story. Even when conversation is indirect in the written form, the teller will do well to make it direct."[81] For instance, if Jack in the story of

"Jack and the Beanstalk" simply says that when the giant came in he shouted "fee, fie, fo, fum" in a very loud voice, change it to read: The giant came in. "Fee, Fie, Fo, Fum!" And say it in a loud voice. *Be* the giant. This direct approach is much more dramatic and life-like than mere narration.

Character Delineation

The storyteller should avoid, when there is more than one character in an episode or scene, looking in one direction when one character speaks and in another direction when another character speaks. In other words, there is absolutely no need to turn the head toward the left when Mama Bear speaks and to the right when Papa Bear speaks. This artificial technique borders on the ridiculous situation of putting a white hat on when the hero talks and a black hat on when the villain talks. Such a technique is not only ineffectual, but is an insult to the imaginative powers of a child. It marks the storyteller as being too disinterested to study the literature for a real basis of character delineation. The characterizations will only be real and the delineation will only be clear, if the storyteller understands each character and is actively involved in being that character.

Imagery

> The special training for the storyteller should consist . . . above all in power of the delicate suggestion which cannot always be used on the stage because that is hampered by the presence of actual things to the more delicate organism of the "inward eye."[82]

This "inward eye" theory is a wonderful way of describing the imaginary canvas on which the storyteller and each listener paints, image by image, the whole story. All images stake their lives on the ability of the storyteller to stir the senses. Among these are the visual sense, auditory sense, the olfactory sense, the tactile sense, the gustatory sense, and the kinesthetic sense. The storyteller must be capable of concentrating on an image to such a degree that he sees, feels, hears, tastes, and smells the image before he verbalized it. "Impression precedes expression—this is the ever secret of art." The only way these images, the building blocks of all stories, come to life is through complete and total concentration. This takes a lot of discipline. However, it is absolutely necessary in order to keep out all interference and allow the image to be met and experienced as if it were the first meeting. "To be able to create a story, to make it live during the moment of telling, to arouse emotions—wonder, laughter, joy, amazement—this is the only goal a storyteller may have." If the storyteller brings these images to life by experiencing them firsthand, they will be as vivid and real as life itself. Consequently, the listener can experience the story in deeper, fuller and more meaningful ways.[83]

Tactile Imagery

How do images actually enter into a story? Let's start with the tactile image, or image of touch. In Joseph Jacobs' version of "Jack and the Beanstalk," Jack's mother slaps him three times when she hears about the trade he has made. "Have you been such a fool, such a dolt, such an idiot, as to give away my Milkywhite, the best milker in the parish, and prime beef to boot, for a set of paltry beans? Take that! Take that! Take that!"[84] These slaps are predominantly tactile images, although they also contain some kinesthetic imagery. (Seldom is a particular type of imagery completely isolated from at least one of the other types.) The storyteller must really feel the slaps on the back of the neck. If he does not take time to recall the way slaps on the back of the neck feel, there will be no image. Consequently, he will be reading or saying words rather than creating vivid word pictures.

Olfactory Imagery

A good olfactory image, an image of a smell, takes place when the giant says, "Fee. Fie. Fo. Fum. I smell the blood of an Englishman."[85] Of course, the storyteller has no idea how the blood of an Englishman smells to a giant! But, the storyteller does know what it is to smell something unusual. This, then, is probably as close to the image as the storyteller can get in this case. Here, too, the storyteller must recognize that the giant's attitude toward Englishmen will also color this olfactory image. In fact, any character's attitude to any image, whether it be an olfactory, visual, or any other type, will, indeed, impose a shade of meaning on that image. Consequently, it is the storyteller's responsibility to actually relive the smelling of some unusual odor. If he does this, the image will be so vivid that the listener will experience a similar image.

Auditory Imagery

After the giant eats his dinner he calls for his harp. The Jacobs' version of the tale describes how beautifully the harp sings. "And it went on singing till the ogre fell asleep and commenced to snore like thunder."[86] This in an auditory image, something that one hears. If the storyteller concentrates so that he hears not only the music of the harp, but also the loud thunder of the giant's snoring, he is provided with a vivid contrast.

Kinesthetic Imagery

The kinesthetic sense is a very important one in reading or telling a story. It has to do with the description of the physical movement of an object. For instance, kinesthetic imagery is used to get the feeling of a chase and scramble down the beanstalk in this following passage. "Jack ran as fast as he could and the ogre came rushing after. . . when he got to the beanstalk the ogre was not more than twenty yards away. . . the ogre swung himself down on the beanstalk, which shook with his weight. Down climbs Jack, and after him climbed the ogre. By this time Jack had climbed down, and climbed down, and climbed down till he was very nearly home."[87] The storyteller must really participate in this chase by mentally running along with Jack and the ogre. The physical motion in this image will be communicated through the storyteller's muscle tension and body rigidity. Consequently, if the storyteller does not concentrate so that he mentally participates in the chase, his muscles and body will be totally detached from the image and there will be nothing from which the audience can get the communication.

Visual Imagery

Visual, or sight, imagery is the most commonly used imagery for describing people and places. When Jack's mother heard her son yelling for an axe she ran out of the house, "but when she came to the beanstalk she stood stock still with fright for there she saw the ogre with his legs just through the clouds."[88] This visual image of the ogre is communicated very vividly if the storyteller takes the time to actually see in his mind's eye the ogre's legs poking through the clouds.

The Vocal Pause

This article has been referring to the taking of time to see, feel, hear, smell, taste, or experience movement of each image. But, where does the storyteller get the time necessary to do all this when telling or reading a story? The answer to this is found in the vocal pause. A vocal pause is a space of silence during which the storyteller mentally paints the next image in his own mind's eye before verbalizing the experience for the audience. It also gives the audience time to digest one image before the next one is piled on top of it. This is one of the basic functions of the vocal pause.

Suspense

The suspense of the story is also controlled by the vocal pause. Marie Shedlock speaks of the "judicious art of pausing" by saying, "With children it means an unconscious curiosity which expresses itself in a sudden muscular tension. There is just enough time during that instant's pause to feel, though not to formulate, the question." This will create a suspense, and an excitement. Beware of making it merely a technical device. "It must be fraught with meaning and arouse the most intense interest in what is to follow." In the Chinese folktale, "The Tale of Turtle Mountain," these words are found: "Suddenly, about midnight, the rich man and the crew where terrified by a noise coming from the turtle's head, but the geomancer quickly ordered them to lift up the coffin and cast it into the turbulent river, where, seized in the maelstrom, it vanished in a flash." Now reread this passage and place a vocal pause between the following words: about, midnight, terrified, noise, head, seized and vanished. By doing this the suspense has time to grow and intensify. "A long pause before a significant idea creates suspense. It might almost be said that the longer the pause, the greater the suspense and hence the more dramatic the effect."[89]

Emphasis can be obtained by the placement of a vocal pause after the word, phrase, or sentence. This will draw attention to what has been spoken. "An abrupt pause after an idea strengthens the effect of the words."[90]

Comic Techniques

Humor is an important element in many children's stories. Humor is usually created from a situation containing an element of incongruity. "Laughter is the result of the sudden recognition of the wide difference between what is and what ought to be." Humor has been more colorfully described by Max Eastman as " . . . a kind of disappointment. If you expect to drive a tack in the carpet and drive your thumb instead, that is funny."[91] In children's literature these situations are plentiful.

Exaggeration

Incongruity can be emphasized by exaggerating the images through the manipulation of the words and sounds. Extreme vocal inflection is a sure way to emphasize humorous words. In Laura Richards' *Tirra Lirra*, for example, there are many humorous words in the poem "Eletelephony." "Once there was an elephant who tried to use the telephant. No! No! I mean an elephone, who tried to use the telephone.. . . "[92] Here the words *telephant* and *elephone* contain the incongruity because the beginning of the words do not go with the ending of the words. Consequently, these words must be exaggerated if the humor is to be emphasized. Inflective slides up and down the vocal scale will aid exaggeration. Taking the word *elephant*, for example, the storyteller might let his voice start high on *el*, a little lower on *e*, still lower on *pha*, and slide the *nt* all the way back up the scale.

Prolonging words is yet another technique for exaggerating the humor contained in the sounds. This can be accomplished by sustaining the vowel sounds, *m, n, ng, w, l, r,* and *y*. Over-articulation of sounds and increased volume add to the exaggeration. Since children delight in funny sounds, the storyteller should never fail to exaggerate them. For instance, Dr. Seuss' words such as *grickily gratus, schnamikkd schnopp,* and *beezlenut trees* may be prolonged, over-articulated, and given increased volume.

Comic Timing

The vocal pause is found also in the delivery of humorous material. "A pause just before the word or phrase which carries humor points up the meaning. This technique of pausing just before the word, phrase, or line is sometimes called 'planting' the line." For instance, in *Many Moons,* the Royal Mathematician lists the things that he has figured out for the King. "I have computed how far is Up, how long it takes to get Away, and what becomes of Gone. I have discovered the length of the sea-serpent, the price of priceless, and square of the hippopotamus." The words in this passage containing the humor are *away, gone, priceless,* and *hippopotamus.* A vocal pause just prior to each of these words will "set up" or plant the humor. The storyteller may also employ vocal pauses after humorous material so that he will not interrupt audience reaction by going ahead with the next detail of the story. "The amateur is inclined to keep the humor away from the audience by going on with new ideas before the audience has had time to fully grasp preceding ideas. The creative reader holds pauses sufficiently long for the audience to catch the humor and respond with a chuckle, or more enthusiastic evidence of enjoyment." This is the heart of timing.[93]

Humor Is Serious

Humor is a "funny" thing, for if it is not executed in a serious manner it will rarely be funny. Dr. Eugene Bahn of the Wayne State University Interpretative Reading Department has stated, "Usually, in reading humor, the situation will seem serious to characters who find themselves in a distressing plight." Remembering that humor may stem from incongruity, the storyteller must beware of destroying the degree of incongruity by laughing at the situation himself. He must be serious in relating the situation no matter how ridiculous it may be. If he is not, if he laughs at the situation, the incongruity will usually be lessened, and, so will the humor. For instance, when portraying the wolf in "The Three Pigs," the storyteller must be serious in his attempt to blow down the house of bricks. If, however, the storyteller, as the wolf, starts to laugh at his huffing and puffing, he might be suggesting that the wolf is not really taking the situation seriously. The incongruity of trying to blow down a house of bricks by mere breath, then, is gone. And, therefore, the humor is lessened.

This also applies to the situation where the wolf tries to enter the pig's house by preparing to jump down the chimney. The incongruity is found in the difference between what the wolf expects to find at the end of the jump and the pot of boiling water that is really waiting for him at the end of the plunge. "The unexpected indication of the absence of perfection (what ought to be) constitutes the comic situation."[94]

Forecasting

Inherent in this scene, too, is another factor that appeals to children, forecasting. Children delight in being in on what is going to happen long before the character in the story realizes what the future holds. In other words, the fact that a pot of boiling water awaits Mr. Wolf is forecast to the children. Now they know something the wolf does not. This technique always adds to the humor.

Animation

"For the sake of the child we must recover, if we have lost it, the speaking face, animated body, and eloquent hand of our childhood."[95] The old adage that one picture is worth one hundred words is especially true in the art of storytelling. The visual code, what a child sees, appeals to him because it is action-packed and communicates all at once, in a presentational manner. On the other hand, the verbal code, word by word, is a much slower communication. One visual sign can say immediately what it takes a whole sentence to say.

Gestures

Gestures should not be prepared, planned, and practiced ahead of time. On this subject the writer is in conflict with the "practice gestures before the mirror" supporters. Gestures should not be rehearshed! By their very nature they must be spontaneous action arising from an involvement on the storyteller's part with the literature. If rehearsed, the gesture's timing will be off because that gesture will usually *follow* the spoken word rather than precede it by a split second, as it does in normal speech. This delayed action, then, is incongruous and, consequently, a visual technique of humor. Hours of practice in front of the mirror will not help.

Two things to remember when executing your gestures for children are boldness and follow through. First, most gestures should be literal rather than suggestive. Since, as discussed earlier in this article, most characters residing in children's literature are exaggerated figures, generally, literal gestures will aid in the creation of these characters. Children like a lot of movement. Subtle gestures are not exciting for them. The younger the child-audience, the bigger the gestures should be. Second, "follow-through" should be employed. In other words, when the storyteller starts a gesture, the motion should be completed rather than drawn back in the middle of the movement. Half-executed gestures are also half-sincere. The storyteller must speak with his hands, eyes, body, and spirit. He must be mobile. He must flex his arms! He must raise his eyebrows! And think animated!

Storytelling is a most challenging and satisfying activity. It should not be taken casually. As Ruth Sawyer states, ". . . there is a kind of death to every story when it leaves the speaker and becomes impaled for all time on clay tablets or the written or printed page. To take it from the page, to create it again into living substance, this is the challenge—not only for the storyteller from 4,000 B.C. through the Middle Ages, but for the storyteller of today."

43.

Where are We Going with Poetry for Children?

Patrick J. Groff

Those concerned with poetry for children are faced today with several perplexities about this form of literature. Among these are the basic problems of defining the term, poetry for children, and finding the best way to attract children to poetry. If we are to develop children's esteem for poetry, we are inescapably influenced by these two considerations.

A survey of the writing on poetry for children over the past ten years convinces one that the first question has no dearth of answers. There appears to be no reluctance on the part of different writers to rush in with various opinions; and often each new response appears more grand and splendiferous than the last.

We are continually pressed to accept definitions of poetry that are based on emotional reactions. For example, Myra Cohn Livingston, a children's poet, believes that

> Poetry is after all a personal thing; its meaning to each human being is private. It invades the innermost thoughts; it clings to and bolsters the inner life. It is not something to be rationalized or explained. . . .

(Happily, the last view is not accepted everywhere. If it were, the result would be the reduced employment of thousands of English teachers.) Often the emotional approach is carried forward in a train of excessive language. Lindley Stiles, the long-time dean of education at the University of Wisconsin, recently gave one of these effusive paeans to poetry. According to this sometime poet, "Without poetry, learning becomes pedantic and life becomes existence merely, devoid of ideals and inspiration." And he further declares that "the poet has the greatest sensitivity, analytical ability, wisdom of interpretation, and skill with ideas, imagery, and language." His overly dramatic defense of poetry cannot but be seen as an intentional downgrading of prose literature and therefore must be both unfair and unwarranted. Worst of all, the very idea that poetry has such high-class distinctions acts to frighten away the middle-brow adult on whom the child depends for his literature.

From *The Horn Book Magazine* 42:454-463 (August 1966). Reprinted with the permission of the author and publisher.

Others have claimed that poetry has many psychological values for children. It is not unusual to hear it said that poetry for children allows them to experience life in a deeper sense, acts as an antidote for violence, recreates the emotions, passes on wisdom, stimulates the imagination, enhances the appreciation of nature, stirs the emotions, develops a feeling for beauty, develops an awareness of the spiritual elements of life, is a source of courage, provides for relaxation.

Poetry may very well do some of these things on the occasions when a poem and a child hit it off. Nevertheless, few, if any, of these definitions of the uses of poetry give us any significant clues as to the characteristics that make it distinct from prose literature. Every objective implicit in each of the definitions could be accomplished just as well, or perhaps better, with prose. Little, if any, evidence shows that poetry accomplishes for the child the host of things commonly attributed to it. Available is more than a little thinking to support the belief that if children's literature were able to do these things, they would be done much more effectively with the sustained effect a child gets from a novel than with the transitory images he gains from a poem.

Others profess what I consider a false bewilderment, as did the late Eleanor Farjeon:

> What is Poetry? Who knows?
> Not a rose, but the scent of the rose;
> . . . .
> Not myself, but what makes me
> See, hear, and feel something that prose
> Cannot: And what it is, who knows?*

The need for such artificial humility about poetry on Miss Farjeon's part seems uncalled for. She must have known very well what was good poetry for children, or she could not have written so much of it. Those who are seeking after some way to find the standards of poetry are nonplused by such elusiveness.

On the other hand, Flora Arnstein argues that poetry is quite simple. In her words, it is an uncomplicated record of experiences and, therefore, should be readily and completely understandable. "Boiled down to its essence, it is merely a reconstruction of an experience. And, here is the point, all poetry is just that: the presentation, in words, of experience . . ." The example she uses to demonstrate the thesis is "The Pasture" by Robert Frost, the meaning of which is very apparent:

> I'm going out to clean the pasture spring;
> I'll only stop to rake the leaves away
> . . . .
> I sha'n't be gone long.—You come too.†

Mrs. Arnstein's unsophisticated definition of any kind of poetry, including that written for children, should not be accepted, however, since the objections to it are many. Our senses often deceive and distort experience. May Swenson,

---

*From "Poetry" from *Poems for Children,* J.B. Lippincott Company. Reprinted by permission of the publisher.

†From "The Pasture" from *You Come Too* by Robert Frost. Copyright 1930, 1939 by Holt, Rinehart and Winston, Inc. Copyright ©1958 by Robert Frost. Reprinted by permission of Holt, Rinehart and Winston, Inc.

for instance, has remarked on the crudeness of our experience:

Hold a dandelion and look at the sun.
Two spheres are side by side.
Each has a yellow ruff.

Eye, you tell a lie,
That Near is Large, that Far is Small.
There must be other deceits.*

A simplistic definition of poetry is wrong. Poetry must surely go beyond the flat surface of experience and physical phenomena.

There seems to be a more precise definition of poetry that not only can remove it from the never-never land of mysticism set up by Eleanor Farjeon and others, but also will allow a working definition of it so that one will not be afraid to form judgments about what is and what is not poetry. Especially we need this to rid ourselves of such illogical statements as: "What is poetry for one person is not poetry for another." There is an explanation of poetry that will disentangle the confusion.

The definition is apprehensible and to the point: poetry for children is writing that (in addition to using, in most cases, the mechanics of poetry) transcends the literal meaning of expository writing. It is not the kind of writing that appears in newspapers and popular media or the kind of writing that is found in classroom textbooks. It is writing that goes beyond the immediately obvious. Poetry, then, consists of those aspects of writing that cannot be readily explained, unless one has some knowledge of what is going on. In contrast to that which is readily and completely understandable to all, poetry is often ambiguous.

"The Pasture," tested against this definition is revealed as a poem only in the mechanical sense. True, it has some poetic features: a certain cadence, rhyme, and some slight inversion of sentence pattern—"And wait to watch the water clear, I may." (The word order seems used largely to satisfy a rhyme scheme, "away-may.") The poem does have a refrain, and even a colloquial word, "sha'n't" (if colloquialisms are poetic). But these are all a part of the mechanics of poetry. To identify a poem on the basis of such elements is too easy. For example, a child recently said when asked what a poem was, "It's lines that are all capitalized and even on the left side, and all squiggily on the right." Another said, "Poetry is what rhymes." Obviously, to define poetry merely in terms of its mechanical features does not take much perception or maturity.

In another sense, "The Pasture" is not exceptional poetry because with startlingly few changes the poem could be made into a paragraph of prose. To show this, drop the first refrain in the poem and put the third line into a regular pattern.

Compare the result with "Afternoon on a Hill," by Edna St. Vincent Millay:

I will be the gladdest thing
   Under the sun!
I will touch a hundred flowers
   And not pick one.

. . . . .

*"Hold a dandelion" was included in "The Poet as Anti-Specialist," *Saturday Review*, January 30, 1965. It appears in Miss Swenson's essay "The Experience of Poetry in a Scientific Age" in *Poets on Poetry*, edited by Howard Nemerov, published by Basic Books, Copyright © 1966, and is reprinted with the permission of May Swenson, *Saturday Review*, and Basic Books.

And when lights begin to show
  Up from the town,
I will mark which must be mine
  And then start down.*

Try as one might, one cannot reduce the poem to prose as can so easily be done with "The Pasture." One mark of poetry, then, is that it is not translatable into prose.

Here I want to stress that the use of original combinations of words is probably the easiest, the best, and the most obvious way to write poetry that transcends the literal and goes beyond a complete or obvious meaning. Consequently, in poetry a word has much more meaning than a word in prose. In the former the emphasis is connotative rather than denotative. Words possess suggested significances apart from their explicit and recognized meanings. It is the guessing element that requires the reader to go below the surface of words, to plumb their literal meanings. Figurative language most often provides the guessing element. A poem without metaphor, simile, hyperbole, personification, metonymy must compensate for the loss of these poetic devices in some other way. Sometimes it is in the use of words of a certain tone, for in poetry the language, not the subject, is of utmost importance. Ultimately, as Archibald MacLeish says, "A poem should not mean, but be." Its subject is not presented by means of language. Rather the reverse is true: language is presented with the aid of its subject matter. In "The Pasture" the emphasis on subject denies the poem much status as poetry.

It may seem paradoxical after the foregoing to say that the best way to attract children to poetry (our second major problem) is to pay the closest attention to the subject matter of poems chosen for them. This does not contradict the premise of the importance of language, however. Unless a poem says something to a child, tells him a story, titillates his ego, strikes up a happy recollection, bumps his funny bone—in other words, delights him—he will not be attracted to poetry, regardless of the language it uses. Many have known the agony of going through highly-thought-of anthologies of children's verse-poetry to find them full of "my dears" and lyrical odes to fairies and nature. Most of this whimsey and sentimentality is due to false notions about children held by misguided adults. The child of today is not attracted to archness, coyness, or mere prettiness. While it may be true that some very conventional modern girls might still like poetry such as that by Rose Fyleman, the reaction from the modern boy will be without doubt something like "Stop! You're putting me on!" Therefore, let us give a decent but definite burial to such bathos as:

I wish I were a bumble bee
  So merry, blithe and gay,
To buzz and hum from flower to flower
  All on a summer's day.

I wish I were a butterfly
  Upon a buttercup.
I'd flutter down the woodland paths
  And then I'd flutter up.

---

*From "Afternoon on a Hill." From *Collected Poems,* Harper & Row, Publishers. Copyright 1917, 1945 by Edna St. Vincent Millay.

I wish I were—but then, oh dear!
  A sudden thought strikes me:
For if I were a butterfly,
  I could not be a bee.

I'd love to be a bumble bee
  All summer time, and so
I'm glad I'm not a butterfly
  To flutter to and fro.*

If we find such poems in present anthologies, let us ignore them in the hope they will wither away. Or better yet, replace them with poems of real life in an honest world like the one portrayed by Gwendolyn Brooks:

These buildings are too close to me.
I'd like to PUSH away.
I'd like to live in the country.
And spread my arms all day.†

Despite an agreement to spare the modern child "sissy" or "flighty" poetry, there nevertheless remain two schools of thought as to how to select poetry for him. One of these decries the use of poetry especially written for children. Its most pertinent argument is that one cannot present well a poem that he cannot read with some enjoyment. There is little doubt that much of the poetry written especially for children offends an adult's intelligence. The other side strongly supports the work of children's poets who write little or not at all for adults, and contends that children need special consideration. The battle seems to be worth fighting, regardless of the side one is on, for if we have only children's poetry, we run the risk of beginning with something less than the best. Surely, we should not believe that the young child can be gradually led to excellence through acquaintance with poems of lesser quality. The achievement of excellence is seldom accomplished in this way. Start with the best must be the maxim. On the other hand, one commits a capital offense by believing that it makes little difference where the poetry that children read and hear is chosen from. This opinion leads to the choice of the overly abstruse, the ancient, or the "cute." A selection from the first two categories may surely be poetry, but children are often overwhelmed by the strange vocabulary, antiquated subject matter, and rusty language. The last inevitably misses the mark of poetry that we have set up here.

When working with the youngest it is important, therefore, to keep in mind two criteria for the selection of poetry. The first is that the subject matter delight children. The second is that the language actually be poetic. The younger the children are, the more important is the former. As they grow older, language assumes primary importance. Moreover, the process of selection seems one of only two variables, the second being accepting children as they are. Consequently, the variables appear to be, first, the poems to be used and, second, the means used to attract children to them.

In schools, still another controversy has centered around how to attract chil-

*"A Thought" by James Reeves, not intended for serious publication. From *Teaching Poetry*, Heinemann Educational Books Ltd., 1958.

†Four lines from "Rudolph Is Tired of the City" from *Bronzeville Boys and Girls* by Gwendolyn Brooks. Reprinted with permission of Harper & Row, Publishers.

dren to poetry. First is the "hands-off" approach to poetry. Its advocates make no place for memorization, study, or activity connected with the use of poetry. Poetry is introduced in an entirely incidental way. "Forget any obligation to appreciate poetry or to indulge in any critical appraisal of it" expresses the feeling of this group. Teachers who have this opinion really would not touch poetry with a ten-foot pole, even though they continually say that poetry must be "caught not taught." The stand apparently stems from a negative reaction to the unfortunate days of forced memorization, analytic scanning of meter, and the testing of the content of poems. If the feeling of "hands-off" has done any good, it has been through the removal of some of the unfortunate practices in the use of poetry.

What the "hands-off" policy has not done, unfortunately (if a cliche is permitted), is to fish out the poetry baby before the dirty water of forced memorization and other disagreeable practices is flung away. Too, as courses of poetry are successively dropped as a result of this overreaction, it has been felt increasingly that poetry is too precious and fragile a literary commodity to be handled in the way other writings are. What seems left in the schools are sporadic readings by teachers or an occasional reading of a poem by children out of the basal reader. Poetry, a high literary form, apparently holds at present the lowest priority of utility in the language program.

While the actual teaching of poetry in elementary schools has largely disappeared (but not in other English-speaking countries, one would gladly hasten to add), a most curious practice has taken its place—teaching children to write poetry before they have had opportunities to truly learn about it. (See, for example, the suggestions in Nina Walter's book, *Let Them Write Poetry*, or those in Flora Arnstein's *Poetry in the Elementary Classroom.*) Staggering the imagination are suggestions of how children can be taught to write poetry, the most demanding of all literary forms, before they have learned to understand what is is, to react to it, and to distinguish it from prose, before they have learned to appreciate either prose or poetry. The growth of this practice is explained by the unfortunate belief, which schools perpetuate, that any writing put together in a certain distinguishable form can thereby be called poetry. Hence the flood of execrable doggerel that goes under the name "creative writing."

While all is not lost, to arrest the seeming downward plunge of the status of poetry and to forestall the misunderstanding, suspicion, and, finally, dislike for poetry so common in children by the time they reach the ages of ten or eleven, a drastic reversal of directions in the use of poetry for children is called for. First, we should emphasize the few "new" (if not young) poets for children who have pushed the art forward from the days of Walter de la Mare and Rachel Field. The new poetry is found in the social realism of Gwendolyn Brooks, the unpretentious warmth of Eve Merriam, the exhaustive imagery of Mary O'Neill, the gentle persuasion of Harry Behn, and in the urbane versatility of James Reeves (the single Briton of this group). Second, we should renew the teaching of poetry as such so that an understanding of it can be used as the basis upon which to build trust and appreciation of poetry as children grow older. Finally, we need to encourage publishers to look for children's poetry where it naturally emerges. We have seen that the commissioned book of poems for children by the established adult poet has been much less the success than was hoped for. For as Christopher Morley said, "poetry . . . does not often visit groups of citizens sitting down to be literary together."

44. Creative Drama

Ronald Side

Creativity has been receiving increased attention from educators at all levels in recent years. Creative language activities that deal with written language forms have become established parts of most language arts programmes. Creative language activities that are principally oral, are also now beginning to become accepted parts of many language arts programmes. Creative drama is one important phase of such oral work. Like other creative activities, children benefit from creative drama, not when they are told *about* it, but when they participate *in* it. Therefore, our principal concern must be to give students an opportunity to express their creativity, by 'setting the stage' for the work, and leading students through a series of activities that will encourage them, and promote creative growth.

Creative drama is a particularly apt method of encouraging such growth of creativity, through self-expression. Drama is a form of play; in fact this is an activity in which it is often difficult to distinguish between work or play. Small children playing among themselves commonly dramatize events and situations in order to entertain themselves. As drama is play, and play activities are ones in which most people expend considerable amounts of energy, dramatic play is a way of utilizing and channeling some of this energy.

Creative drama contains many of the elements so frequently associated with creativity, and considered a part of creativity. Pupils are given encouragement to become both more aware, and more capable of using effectively: concentration, imagination, the senses, the voice, emotion, and intellect. Pupils are encouraged to recognize, in both themselves and in others, their capabilities in all of these areas. Improvised situations encourage the development of fluency and clarity of language. Originality is encouraged, for creative drama could well be called 'imaginative drama.' The creation of characters and of situations demands a degree of persistence; this is usually more likely to occur in a play situation than in a work situation. Increased knowledge and understanding of oneself, and one's capabilities is also frequently derived from participation in creative drama. All of these items are commonly considered parts of creativity, and all are expanded through the use of creative drama.

Creative drama is sometimes presented, not so much as a subject in itself, but

From *Elementary English* 46:431-435 (April 1969).

as a method, or way of teaching, a number of subjects. Although this is true—*when* a class is proficient in creative drama, unfortunately it has proven a pitfall for many teachers. Pupils are not taught to write, rather than print, during a Science lesson, or a History lesson. They are given specific instruction in handwriting, *before* they are required to put the newly acquired skill to use. Spelling is taught in a similar fashion, and by the same token, creative drama should be handled in this manner. Once the children have mastered the elements of creative drama suitable for their age level, then it is time to apply this skill, and use it in a variety of other subject areas. Many teachers have unfortunately attempted to begin work in creative drama by applying it, as a method, to a subject such as Social Studies. An attempt to dramatize an incident from history, without prior preparation, has done much to discourage both teachers and students. With sufficient preparatory work, such disappointments are not likely to occur.

Like other areas of endeavour, creative drama consists of a number of skills that contribute importantly to it. These skills may be practised and improved upon separately, prior to actual creative-playmaking. Concentration (often coupled with imagination), movement (often coupled with rhythmic activities) and dialogue (often coupled with speech activities) are the preparatory skills given consideration in this paper. They are actually simple types of creative drama, all of which are necessary for improvisations, or playmaking. Therefore it is suggested here that creative drama be treated separately, as a subject rather than a method of teaching several subjects, and that this separate programme should give pupils an opportunity to facilitate their abilities in each of these elements: concentration, movement, and dialogue—prior to improvisations, and playmaking. Once the children have proven to the teacher, and more importantly to themselves, that they are capable of playmaking itself, then creative drama might as well be put to practical use, treated as a teaching method, and put to use in a variety of subject fields as a means to an end, rather than an end in itself.

If it seems as if such a programme as described above would be a great deal of work, and that considerable time might pass before children could successfully apply their skills, it should be noted that each of the basic elements suggested as pre-requisites to playmaking has practical applications. After pupils have become capable of any one of the areas: concentration, movement, and dialogue, this experience could be put to practical use. Tableaux can be used after work in concentration has been completed, and it should prove useful as a method in numerous other subject areas. Pantomime, likewise, is a practical application of work in movement, and puppet plays and radio plays can prove useful applications of work in dialogue.

The actual teaching of these elements need not take place within the language arts programme itself. In fact, both concentration and movement are frequently better suited for teaching in other times and subjects. The work in concentration might well be done in Art, as an aspect of art appreciation. The composition of a good picture contains the same points as tableaux. Work in movement might well be done in physical education, as part of the creative movement, or creative dance, programme. Creative dance deals with many points identical to those of pantomime. If speech or speech activities form a part of the language arts programme, work in dialogue might be done in conjunction with speech activities. Although it has been suggested that creative drama not be used as a means to an end (a teaching device) until the pupils are proficient in it, there are other subjects that sometimes lend themselves to being a means of teaching creative drama.

Creative drama, or aspects of it, is not confined to specific grade or age levels.

As pupils mature they are capable of more involved work. Treating each of the aspects of creative drama separately at each new level is not the waste of time it appears to be initially. With each of these aspects, pupils are capable of expressing themselves, perhaps more effectively, and certainly differently. Topics and subjects of interest will vary at different levels as well, depending upon the maturity of the students involved. The preparatory work may be quite intensive, because the pupils indicate a need for further work of this type. But, it is also possible that such work may be quite intensive, not because the pupils actually need any further work of this sort, but simply because it suits the needs of both the teacher and the pupils at that time. On the other hand, if actual playmaking is the immediate goal, then the preparatory work may be only as intensive as the teacher believes necessary, at each level.

Although reference has been made to the three elements of: concentration, movement, and dialogue, in that order, this was not done to suggest in any way that this particular order should be followed. Each of these three sections is basically independent of the other two sections, as each deals with a different aspect of creative drama. Dialogue could be the first topic to be given consideration, or movement, or concentration. The actual choice should be made by the teacher, and should be determined by the classroom situation. Whichever of these three items lends itself most readily as a natural beginning may be used to begin a creative drama program. If the three aspects are being dealt with in different subject areas, as was suggested earlier, then all three could well be done concurrently. If one activity must be suggested, as a beginning, then it would be the activity that the teacher believes would be the easiest, for both teacher and pupils, as success is often a strong motivation for continuation of a program.

As pupils may be somewhat self-conscious if put on display in front of their peers, when this work is beginning, it is usually wise to avoid an audience—performer relationship. This can be done in several ways. The entire classroom should be used for creative drama activities, and not the front of the room. Within most classrooms the front of the room is "the stage." Desks may be pushed back, and the entire room used, so as to eliminate this feeling toward the front of the classroom. An audience can be eliminated very quickly, by having all pupils participate at the same time. None will have any time to watch others. By having each pupil work individually at first, the students do not feel that the others, even within a small group, are watching them. As the pupils grow more confident, more likely than not some students will ask for an opportunity to see what the others are doing. Some students may be permitted to observe various others engaged in the activity. When this observation ceases to have an obvious adverse effect upon the participants, the teacher may generally be assured that the pupils are ready for more involved activities. The next step might well be to have the pupils work in small groups. Groups of two or three keep the audience-participant relationship quite close, and therefore tend to be less inhibiting than larger groups. At first the pupils might be permitted to choose their own groups, as social groups are usually somewhat easier for the pupils to work in. Again, when the pupils indicate they are capable of working in such a situation, the groups may be changed. Larger groups may result. These groups should be chosen by the teacher to insure there is an adequate distribution of leadership qualities, pupils of both sexes, and a reasonable distribution of talent. Again, when the pupils seem sufficiently self-confident to be eager to see what the other groups are doing, an opportunity might be given to one or two groups at a time. Perhaps one group will profess a willingness to perform for the others. If this is the case, it is usually wise to use the center of the classroom, seating students around the 'playing' area, as with arena-type staging. This avoids a large segment of the audience being in front of the pupils, and lessens the likelihood of pupils being inhibited by their audience. As has been mentioned earlier, once the pupils have mastered a specific aspect of the work, they can then apply it to another subject area. It is usually wisest to retain groupings formerly used when beginning to apply any creative drama situations to content areas, so as to ensure success to as great a degree as possible. When material from another subject area is being used in creative drama, the pupils are responsible for both the content of the subject area, and the skills of creative drama. It is therefore necessary for the teacher to prepare the class well before the class is expected to use creative drama as a teaching method applicable to a variety of subjects. However, the result is well-worth the effort, for after having been thoroughly introduced in the manner described above, creative drama will become an effective and an enjoyable method of learning.

Summary

A Suggested Programme for Creative Drama at Various Levels

Aim: To provide pupils with **opportunities**
for the growth of **creativity,**
through **oral language** activities,
utilizing **play-type situations.**

Principal Topic	Secondary Topic	Activities	Pupil Participation	
a. Concentration (Interchangeable with b. or c.)	Imaginative Activities	Exercises	Individual work Small groups	Art: —composition —appreciation
		Tableaux	Small groups Large groups	
		Materials from other subject fields	Large groups	History Literature Guidance
b. Movement (Interchangeable with a. or c.)	Rhythmic Activities	Exercises	Individual work Small groups	Physical Education: —creative movement
		Pantomime and Shadow Plays	Small groups Large groups	—creative dance
		Materials from other subject fields	Large groups	History Literature Guidance
c. Dialogue (Interchangeable with a. or b.)	Speech Activities	Exercises	Individual work Small groups	English: —creative writing —composition (oral)
		Radio and puppet plays	Small groups Large groups	
		Materials from other subject fields	Large groups	History Literature Guidance
d. Improvised Scenes (To follow above three items.)	Interaction	Exercises	Small groups	English: —creative writing —composition (written)

Principal Topic	Secondary Topic	Activities	Pupil Participation	
		Scenes and playlets	Small groups	
		Materials from other subject fields	Large groups	History Literature Guidance
e. Play-making (To follow above item, d.)	Incorporates: —imaginative activities —rhythmic activities —speech activities —interaction	Exercises	Small groups Large groups	English: —creative writing —composition (written)
		Plays	Large groups	
		Materials from other subject fields	Large groups	History Literature Guidance etc.

45.

Choral Reading in the Elementary School

Milton M. Sankar

Choral reading or choral speaking is the revival of an ancient art. The United States was one of the last countries to become interested in the revival of choral reading and it is only since 1933 that the interest has become general. Extension and summer courses that emphasize this art are now being offered in many universities throughout the United States. Some universities have well-developed programs while others ignore it entirely.

The Greeks engaged in choral speaking as early as 500 B.C. when they held their harvest festivals honoring Dionysus, the wine god. In the ancient classics of Sophocles, Aeschylus and Euripides the chorus was frequently accompanied by stylized movements conducted to explain to the audience what had happened, was happening, or was going to happen. A chorus was used to heighten the effect and sometimes to supplement the unfolding of a story in these dramas. Some of the passages in the Old Testament, particularly the Psalms, are good for choral speech. The minstrels and troubadours of medieval Britain used this form of rhythmic expression. At his festivals, the American Indian engaged in certain physical rhythmic responses such as swaying to the beat of the tom-tom or to the rain chant of the tribal group.

Cecile DeBanke lists as the five most prominent uses of the Choral Chant in ancient times: "to praise, propitiate and supplicate the deity, to incite warriors to unrelenting slaughter, to celebrate victory in battle, to taunt the vanquished and to lament the dead."[96]

Modern choral reading had its birth in a musical festival—the Glasgow Festival in Scotland in 1922. According to Agnes Hamm of Marquette University it grew out of the suggestion of John Masefield, later Poet Laureate of England and adjudicator at the festival. At this event Marjorie Gullan and her students presented a program interpreting poetry. "He was so impressed," writes Miss Hamm, "by the beauty of their voices and the interpretation that he suggested that they try interpreting poetry in unison. Miss Gullan experimented, and being delighted with the results, she moved to London where she had greater scope for her work; it was there that interest grew very rapidly and began spreading throughout the British Isles, the continent and to the United States."[97]

Reprinted from *Contemporary Education* 50:233-239 (February 1969), by permission of author and publisher.

The first modern choral reading involved adults and performances. The adults were judged on voice control, diction and interpretation. Valuable prizes were awarded to both men and women who best met these requirements. Many verse choirs were established. As its values were noted, educators became interested. During the 1930's choral reading was introduced into many language arts programs. Today choral reading is considered by many to be an important technique in teaching the language arts. In many ways it may be considered to be a synchronization of three important elements of language —*listening, reading,* and *speaking.* It combines these activities in a manner designed to encourage a broader appreciation of literature.

What is Choral Reading?

Choral reading has been defined by a number of people and in numerous ways. One of the most concise yet all-inclusive definitions, probably, is expressed by Abney and Rowe, who have defined it as "the interpretation of poetry or poetic prose, by several or many voices speaking as one in unison, in groups and by parts."[98]

Technically speaking, choral speaking (reading) is the interpretation of poetry by two or more voices speaking as one. For over twenty-five hundred years choral speaking has been one of the most effective ways of interpreting literature orally. While it is true that the materials for choral speaking are most often poetry, selections of rhythmic prose from the Bible and certain "participation" stories in prose are considered to be choric in nature also.

Miss Marjorie Gullan believes that choral reading is group interpretation of prose and poetry.[99] Miss Gullan lectured widely in the British Isles, in Canada, on the Continent and in the United States and is considered the pioneer authority on choral speaking.

Good choral speech is a technique which is highly specialized and requires unity in the following:

1. **Articulation:** Good diction and articulation must be accomplished first. Individuals who speak at various rates of speed must say each word at the exact time in group work. The blending of many voices and the clear *enunciation* of every word can give to certain poems the same richness that an orchestra gives to music.
2. **Pitch:** This requires a blending of voices. As the children develop better understanding of poetry and as they become accustomed to the voices of those around them, the pitch will become more uniform.
3. **Inflection:** Unity in modulation of the voice is difficult to accomplish because of the tendency to end sentences on an upward inflection. It is first of all necessary that each speaker hear himself so he can correct this habit.
4. **Thought:** All the participants must have the same understanding of the poem. The meaning is obvious in most, but not all, poems.
5. **Feeling:** To interpret poetry it is necessary to have a sensitivity to words and to have great depth of feeling. This is most difficult to develop in a group. [100]

The Values of Choral Reading

According to DeBanke there are four objectives in the teaching of choral speaking (reading), namely: "the revival of pride in correct and expressive speech, the restoration of the art of spoken poetry, the encouragement of individual creative work, and the recognition of the value of group achievement."

One of the best reasons for having choral reading in the elementary school is that it improves the everyday speech of children who tend to have diction difficulties because it requires the correct forming of vowels and sharp, clear articulation of consonants. This is not a speech fault limited to children, however, because speech training is needed at all levels in America. As a nation, our speech is slovenly. Our most glaring weaknesses appear to be *lip, tongue* and *jaw* laziness; dropping of consonants, especially *t, d, ng;* changing the medial *t* to *d,* and *dudy,* for *duty;* using contractions such as *woncha* and *lemme.*[101]

Because people do not hear their mistakes, ear training is the first requisite in acquiring good diction. Choral reading gives children a chance to hear themselves.

In choral reading, the timid child gains self-reliance, because he does not speak alone, and the exhibitionist learns the value of group participation.

The imagination of the child is developed, because to interpret a piece of literature one must feel and see the things the writer expresses. Reading gives joy to the participants, and it can be correlated with every subject in the curriculum.

There are also many other benefits in the practice of choral reading. The speech becomes more accurate and enunciation is more clear. The appreciation of poetry is heightened. The speaking group becomes a more cohesive social unit from having worked together. The children in this situation are engaged in an active endeavor rather than a passive one. An element of entertainment is introduced into the class proceedings. The shy child learns to contribute to a shared undertaking, and the bold child learns to submerge himself for the good of the group.

Like music, poetry must be read aloud or listened to, to be really enjoyed and appreciated, for rhythm and rhyme can be taken in through the ear better than through the eye. In choral reading, literary skills are developed, including the ability to sense mood and color, understand rhythm, and appreciate the significance of voice tone, quality and volume. It also develops good listening habits as the group strives for a common effect. It provides an opportunity to read more poems orally. It increases and enriches the child's vocabulary and his ability to phrase. Choral reading helps to develop poise for standing before an audience.

Types of Choral Speaking (Readings)

Choral speaking is known by many names—choral reading-group speaking (in the primary grades), choric speech (combined with music)—and is distinguished by six major methods of arrangement.

Just as children in a group tend to sing too loudly, so in a choral reading this same tendency is likely to appear. If any one voice is clearly dominant, the total effect is spoiled. Enunciation must be clear and precise, the voice flexible and well controlled. Whenever voices grow loud, it is best to stop at once, recall the meanings and feelings to be expressed, and encourage light but rich tones on the part of the speakers. One child with poor enunciation can destroy the clarity of the unison voice, so each child must be able to sense the need for speaking with clarity, with expression and with precision.

For choral speaking purposes, poetry may be divided into the following types or arrangements:

a) **Refrain** (chorus). If either the teacher or the children has not had previous experience in choral speaking this is an easy type with which to begin, especially in the primary grades. A soloist reads the body of the poem while the rest of the group or one of the voice groups joins in the chorus or refrain.

In the primary grades the soloist is invariably the "best" reader. Refrain poems, such as "Shop Windows," "Hickory, Dickory, Dock," and "The Mysterious Cat," are excellent for instructing the group in basic rhythm and the various moods that poems may have. The nursery rhymes and the Mother Goose rhymes provide an endless array of refrain materials for the primary grade teacher.

Arrangements other than the basic one may be tried after experience has been gained. In the refrain type of reading the teacher, or perhaps a more accomplished or confident child, reads the major part of the poem while the group chimes in on the refrain, such as saying "Dinkums, dunkums, littly gray Billy Goat."

b) **Line-a-child.** A single child (or a group of two or three children) speaks a line or couplet. Then another individual or group picks up and continues, one after another. I have found this arrangement very useful with different groups of children saying the "Beatitudes" and the "Ten Commandments" of the Bible.

Poems that have relatively short lines or couplets ending with punctuation are best. Examples include "The Barnyard" and "Gump or Giggle." The director must see to it that children come in on cue; otherwise, continuity may fail and the poem may become dismembered and meaningless. Early efforts with line-a-child should find the children standing in the order in which they present their lines. A very good example for introducing this type of speaking is the rhyme "One, Two, Buckle My Shoe."

c) **Antiphonal or Two-Part Arrangement.** This type is the simplest type of dialogue as far as participation and direction are concerned. The antiphonal arrangement is one of the most enjoyable ways of encouraging children in choral reading. This type of orchestration balances one group of voices with another. The balanced-voice groups may be *light voices* against *heavy voices,* boys versus girls, or the poems used may be of the question and answer variety.

Because of the precision demanded, antiphonal choral work is primarily for middle- and upper-grade children. Poems selected should be of high quality so that interest in them will not wane as practice proceeds. "Puppy and I," "Wishes," and "Laughter" are examples of antiphonal poetry that serve well. Dialogue poems and poems of contrast make very good antiphonal pieces.

d) **Unison.** In this type of reading the whole group speaks as one. This is the most difficult because the voices must blend and the articulation and timing must be perfect. A short poem such as Victor Hugo's "Good Night" is a good one to use in introducing this type of reading. Small children should not be given a heavy dose of unison experience because of the problems of coordinating timing and inflection.

Unison poems may be acted out and pantomimed. Nursery rhymes lend themselves to such interpretation, for example, "Ride a Cock Horse" and "Little Miss Muffet." Blending the volume, rhythms and tones, and the various voices is the key to successful unison work. Particularly apt poems include "A Kitten," "The Bells," and many of the Mother Goose rhymes which are filled with action, and which contain scanty dialogue and little change in mood.

e) **Cumulative Arrangement.** This is used when the poem calls for a "building to a climax" effect. It is the crescendo arrangement in choral reading. The group may be divided into such groups whose voices gradually build, one topping the other, until a climax has been reached. Young children will frequently decide upon a certain sound which complements both rhythm and meaning of the poem such as "Trains" by James Tippett. The volume of tone is regulated by adding or subtracting groups of voices so that the selection seems to increase or decrease in intensity. Psalm 150 can be very effectively done in this arrangement by the upper-grade children.

f) **Deletion.** This is the arrangement where the voices gradually move away from the climax to the conclusion. It is similar to the diminuendo effect in a musical rendition. The poem "Trains" is suitable for this type of arrangement. The arrangement of the voices gradually moving away may give the effect of the noise of the train gradually dying away in the distance. Such an orchestration demands a real understanding and appreciation of the content of the poem.

Some Teaching Techniques in Choral Reading

The teacher should direct the choral reading choir in much the same manner as she would direct a singing choir. The pupils need signals to begin and end together, to know when to speak loudly and when to speak softly. As the pupils gain in experience, fewer signals will be needed, resulting in fewer distractions for the audience.

A choir should have between fifteen and twenty-four voices for the best results. If it has more than thirty voices it becomes difficult to handle while fewer than twelve voices makes it difficult to establish unity. After the children have acquired experience, a small choir of eight to eleven voices can be very effective with a delicate type of poetry.

Elementary pupils can be divided into groups of high, medium and low voices. Most authorities seem to favor a wedge shape formation of the group, with the apex in the front, rather than a widespread line, especially for unison work. However, the speakers who form the apex should not be regarded as leaders; each member of the group must assume equal responsibility.

Introduce choral reading techniques to children through jingles which are very easy. Kindergarten, first- and even many second-graders love Mother Goose rhymes because of the rhythmical swing and the sound of the words. They help children to realize that they can run, skip, hop, march or sway to the rhythm of a poem as well as to the music. Most of these children have given little or no thought to the meaning of the rhymes so they sing-song the words. Let them say such a rhyme as "Pussy Cat, Pussy Cat, Where Have You Been?" Then ask them, "Who do you think was talking to the cat? What did the cat say?" Then have one group of children recite the jingle by asking the questions and the other group be pussy cats and answer the questions. As the children learn to interpret the rhymes, much of the sing-song will disappear.[102]

The pupils in the intermediate grades should also begin choral reading with jingles. They will not enjoy them as do the primary children, but they can be made to realize that through jingles they can concentrate on learning to repeat lines in unity, recognize great varieties in rhythm and change in tempo, become conscious of faulty diction while having fun speaking together. All of this would be ruinous to real poetry. When the children have learned to interpret simple rhymes, other kinds of poetry may be attempted. Each child should have a copy of the poem which should be read at least once and discussed. The thought of the poem is the prime consideration. Rhythm and action are secondary considerations. With experience and practice the group will develop the ability to keep the same rate of speed and pause in the same places for the same length of time. Be sure there are no dominating voices. Insist on soft tones. Stress good articulation and enunciation.

The teacher who is to make the most effective use of choral reading must understand its basic philosophy and phrases before she attempts to use this method. There are many pitfalls and both teacher and pupils may easily become discouraged. To prevent this, a teacher needs to learn how to work with the tools of choral reading and place the whole experience in proper perspective. Before she attempts to lead a group of children, she must learn for herself the progressive phases through which a choral reading moves, and place the whole experience in proper perspective.[103]

The first phase is the understanding of rhythm and tempo. Little children who delight in nursery rhymes are not interested in the words or the meaning. It is the rhythm, the flow of the words and the pattern of the flow that delights them. Skipping out the rhythm of "Jack and Jill," clapping out the "Hickory, Dickory, Dock," and swaying to the rhythm of "Little Boy Blue" offers the children a chance to feel and become part of the rhythm. Encouraging the children to suggest different ways to express the rhythm of nursery rhymes is a broadening of their experience. The purpose of this phase is to encourage the child to sense the rhythm and tempo through the whole body. Exploring the rhythm and tempo underlying A.A. Milne's "The King's Breakfast" may prove to be lots of fun.

The second phase which the teacher must understand is the color and quality of the voices. She needs to understand the meaning of choral reading terms. It is not necessary that the children know them as definitions but the teacher needs to be aware of them. She must know that *inflection* is the rise and fall within a phrase and *pitch levels* refer to the change between one phrase and another. *Emphasis* is the pointing up of the most important word and *intensity* is the term used to indicate the loudness and softness of the voices. These terms will have meaning to the teacher as she reads about the art of choral reading. Children learning to be sensitive to pitch, inflection and intensity are more likely to comprehend and enjoy the experience if they are learning through a poem such as "I Have Known Rivers."

The third phase that the teacher must understand is the arrangement. This is the orchestration of choral reading. It is the creative aspect of the project. Here the children and the teacher work together to find the best arrangement for emphasizing and clarifying what the poet meant to convey in the poem. The teacher needs to understand the different ways in which this meaning may be expressed. The readings that have been arranged by the children and the teacher working together have much more value.

The preparation of the poem before the phases of choral speaking are begun, builds a basis for success or failure. Careful analysis through discussion is vitally important. Questions such as the following may help to assure successful choral reading: a) What is the poem about? b) What kind of poem is it? c) What is the author trying to say? d) Did you feel happy and gay or did it make you feel gloomy? e) What type of music does it bring to your mind? f) What do you think we can do to best express the ideas and feelings? g) Does it build to a climax? h) Is it stately and slow? Such questions as these have been found to be good and workable. This does not mean that new techniques should not be investigated.[104]

Here are some procedures to be employed in the presentation of a choral selection of a group of children, and the group before an audience, that may be of use to the reader. The suggestions that follow are not the only ones possible.

1. Choose a poem that will be of interest to the children.
2. Read the poem aloud to the class. Be *sure you are the only one* with a copy or read the poem from the chalk board. Know the poem well enough to be able to develop enthusiasm in the group at the first reading.
3. Talk over the poem with the children, clarifying the images in the poem,

defining the words, and answering questions about pronunciation. However, *do not over analyze* the poem.

4. Read the poem aloud a second time, asking the group to reflect on the rhythm. Active interpretation may be brought about by having one or two children "skip" or "walk" to the poem.

5. Read the poem aloud a third time, having the children follow along with fingertip tapping, or light handclapping.

6. Distribute copies of the poem to the children. Invite the class to participate in the next reading. Direct as you do in music, *one hand controlling the rate, the other hand minding the volume.* Do not over do the directing.

7. Clear up any tendencies toward awkward phrasing and intonation, heavy voices and sing-song patterns.

8. Assign solo parts. After a number of choral-speaking experiences, boys and girls will be able to nominate classmates for solo parts. Pupils may now begin to memorize their parts if this is required.

9. Total group recital of the poem begins, the teacher-leader fading more and more into the background with each rendition until she discontinues speaking with the group.[105]

Conclusion

Programs of choral speaking by children should be easy, natural outgrowths of what they have been doing in class. Special costumes are neither necessary nor desirable, and colored lights and dramatic gestures are both anathema. Light, pleasant voices, intelligent interpretation of the poems, and a quiet enjoyment of what they are speaking—these are the essentials of a good performance, whether it is for the class next door or the P.T.A. or visiting celebrities. Anything that smacks of the theatrical is out of place. Poetry is precious because of its melodies, its meaning, its beauty, or its laughter, and these rather than choir vestments or elaborate staging are valuable both to the children and to their hearers.

Obviously, successful choral speaking requires considerable preparation on the part of a teacher and practice on the part of the children. Interestingly enough, the first testimonial of anyone who has worked with choral speaking groups, whether young children, pre-adolescents, youths or adults, is that the work is tremendously exhilarating. "It's fun!" the children say. Poetry is therapeutic just as music is. Occasionally a prose selection may be effectively spoken by experienced choirs. Story poems like "The Pied Piper of Hamlin" have been superbly spoken by solo voices, choirs, and choruses, and in a great variety of ways. "The Pirate Don Durk of Dowdee" is also amusing in choir form. The class can be divided for this colorful jingle on the basis of sex and make a very funny performance of it. The boys can speak of his wickedness while the girls can reply simperingly, "But, oh, he was perfectly gorgeous to see! The Pirate Don Durk of Dowdee."[106]

Children who have been roughly treated at home, who have heard coarse, harsh speech and use it themselves, speak quietly and gently in a verse choir, in pleasant voices they hardly know they possess. To see and hear rough boys speak richly and longingly "I must go down to the seas again, to the lonely sea and the sky," is to feel the power of words and ideas penetrating the hard crust of youthful bravado to the spirit of youth that somehow or other holds fast its dreams.

In speaking together, some remarkable personal changes in children are noticeable. The over-aggressive child who monopolizes class discussions or activities is suddenly dropped into the background. If he is an intelligent child, he listens and becomes sensitive to the beauty of group voices speaking together quietly in pleasant harmony. This is corrective for his exhibitionism. He adds his good voice to the others, and the result is pleasing. The over-timid, self-conscious child really comes into his own. As one of the group, he speaks confidently, perhaps aggressively, and is not even surprised at himself. One of these days, the teacher gives him a solo line and he speaks it without thinking twice. A milestone for him! Try it and enrich your language arts program by choral reading.

46.

Puppetry, A Means of Creativity in the Language Arts

Mary S. Etter

"Tell the class how you get started with puppets each year in your classroom," said the instructor of the college class in Language Arts after a group of my fourth graders had presented *Many Moons* by James Thurber and had demonstrated ways of making various kinds of puppets. We had been invited to the college by student observers in our school, who had heard our discussion of the story and seen the puppet show. Thus, I explained to the college class.

It has always been easy to motivate puppetry in the schools where I have taught because a professional company has usually given a show for the students. The next day during the sharing period, in discussion and evaluating the presentation, boys and girls usually displayed puppets they had bought or made. Immediately other pupils want to make puppets and begin looking for stories to write into puppet shows.

This year an incident added to our study of puppetry, as mothers bought detergents and soap with puppets attached to the packages. Soon pupils had all the characters for *The Wizard of Oz* and a group began working on the play.

The school has a puppet stage that we move into the classroom each year. From a file of scenery that pupils have made to fit the stage, they choose appropriate backdrops or make changes in the scenery, creating new ones as needed.

Pupils use any materials at hand to make furniture and articles required. Small boxes, spools, and miniature objects are useful in creating the proper settings. A box with colorful cloth curtains was made by a boy for the princess' bed in *Many Moons*.

With coupons from the detergents, we ordered the castle, script, and Wizard puppet. The pupils, however, had already written their own script and did not use the one received. They worked diligently on their show for our class. The librarian, having seen the group rehearsing, requested that it be repeated in the library for the primary grades during National Library Week. This was gladly done.

All the pupils worked in small groups, writing scripts, making puppets, arranging scenery, and then rehearsing for presentation of their puppet shows. Pupils wanted the shows to go well and prompted one another behind the scenes. Many times the teacher would be called in to give suggestions.

Reprinted from *Virginia Journal of Education* 61:13,33 (November 1967), by permission of author and publisher.

Among the shows, the pupils gave *Johnny Cake, Rumplestiltskin, The Cobbler*, and many original plays on good manners, health, science, and history.

Always the teacher needed to guide and assist each group to be certain that each pupil was carrying his share of the work and doing his job well. Pupils in my classes have always shared their puppets with others and have been considerate in caring for puppets. Discarded card racks from a gift center store hold the puppets when they are not in use.

In making puppets, paper mache heads or elaborate ones are not always necessary. Pupils have originated many puppets. Various colored socks with yarn hair and magic markings for faces have made announcers and been used by some groups for their presentation. The socks can be stuffed with cloth, cotton, or paper or used over the hands without stuffing. One pupil made puppets from paper bags, sewed on yarn for hair, and painted the faces.

These puppets were used to evaluate our work and citizenship at various times. Puppets, too, could get across to the pupils in a humorous way many suggestions for improvements in work methods and conduct.

Paper puppets, made to fit over the fingers in the form of rolls of paper with appendages pasted on and the paper designs and painted faces were quite effective.

One pupil, who was very retiring, made puppets from large wooden spoons and milk cartons with painted faces and cloth clothing. She wrote her own script which she called *The Lost Red Slippers*. Her presentation was most effective, delighted the other pupils, and helped to overcome some of her timidity.

A most creative boy made marionettes with strings attached to wood that danced, walked, and sat down easily.

Puppetry not only helps in teaching language arts (English, reading, writing, spelling), but art was used in making the scenery and puppets; music was related when some used songs and background music played on recordings. At times pupils used their flutophones in the shows.

Other classes were invited one at a time to our classroom to see our puppet shows. In this way all could see from the small stage and everyone could hear, since pupils were behind the stage and only the puppets showing. It was difficult in the auditorium for the audience to see and hear. While some teachers think it a waste of time to work with puppets and such foolishness, I have found the following values in using puppets in my classes:

1. Pupils who have been shy and retiring have overcome some of their timidity in presenting puppet shows.

2. Pupils who have felt insecure in the group have gained security when their shows were accepted by the class.

3. A well-presented puppet show helps pupils to feel successful where they may not have been successful in some of their other school subjects.

4. Pupils must know a story before it can be written into a script for presentation. Poor readers get others to help them with a story so they can do a good job in the puppet show. Some with reading difficulties improve in reading skills after working with puppet shows.

5. By working in groups to give a puppet show, pupils gain a feeling of belonging to some group and being wanted and needed in the group.

6. Puppetry gives a change of pace from routine studies, and pupils welcome this change. They are still learning many subjects as they present various types of shows, but they work harder because of the novel presentation and fun they get from such work.

7. Pupils gain aesthetic satisfaction from creating attractive scenery and puppets, and from discovering good literature in the stories used.

8. Pupils learn by doing, not just watching, and gain enjoyment and understanding.

9. Pupils get lasting experiences in creative interpretation as they work to present puppet shows.

10. Pupils do not easily forget a story they have presented in a puppet show. Seventh grade teachers have said pupils still remembered stories they had presented in puppet shows in the lower grades.

Those boys and girls of the fourth grade who travelled to the college for the puppet demonstration that beautiful May morning will not forget *Many Moons* and the lovely mountain scene as we assembled on the campus, facing Massanutten Peak, shrouded in pale mist, and talked a few moments about the mountains we had discussed in social studies.

Members of the college class visited wrote us appreciative letters after our presentation. One letter said in part: "Did you realize you were teaching future teachers? You did a very good job. Now we know more about making different kinds of puppets. Some day the boys and girls in our classrooms may be having fun and learning through puppet shows because you taught us more about them."

47.

Pantomime: Another Language

Paul S. Graubard

The language arts have received a great deal of recognition and emphasis in the curriculum of most schools. Countless studies have been made on the most frequently mispelled words, self-selective reading programs, TV viewing, and other facets of this discipline. But non-verbal communication, a creative and essential aspect of the language arts, has been glossed over in the classroom.

The author believes that the study of non-verbal communication has been omitted for essentially two reasons—(1) that this area of communication is taken for granted and is not considered important enough to merit inclusion in an already crowded curriculum, and (2) that room teachers are not equipped with the specific skills to teach this aspect of the language arts.

Upon close examination of language one may realize that words are at best only close approximations of feelings. Long before words were spoken, man could read on the face of his fellow man feelings such as love, pain, and hate. A person's physical expressions are a form of universal communication, whereas words by themselves often fail to tell a complete story, and must leave a great deal to the imagination. There are usually many meanings for individual words, and it is sometimes necessary to watch the expression of the one who delivers the words to get any real meaning from them. Telephone communication is often unsatisfactory for this reason.

Skills of both interpreting and delivering these facial and physical movements are developed by people in the same way that one learns to speak the English language without a grammar book. But it is obvious that people speak more intelligibly for having studied their language. So, too, children will benefit by not leaving non-verbal communication to chance.

Mime, the formal use of non-verbal communication, develops the art of giving a shrug or using a facial or hand gesture to convey a very special meaning. Because mime by definition is without words it heightens an appreciation of the significance of words along with understanding of how their delivery may be reinforced. The directness of mime makes one aware of how much non-essential verbiage clouds meaning. Through the study of mime, children's ability to communicate verbally and be direct, precise, and economical is sharpened.

The purposes for which mime can be used are varied, and it can reach individual

---

From *Elementary English* 37:302-306 (May 1960).

children and groups in many ways. Mime is a great equalizer in group situations and can enable most children, not only those who are verbally talented, to release and communicate their feelings. Some mime games also help to develop a group cohesiveness which comes about quite spontaneously. Groups with a common purpose must work together, and it is sometimes surprising to find out which children will exhibit leadership qualities in activities of this sort.

Mime reaches the individual children on many different levels. Especially appreciated by the bright child is the fact that it stimulates creativity, and makes him think of how to explore new concepts and express ideas independently of cliches or props. Because mime is a medium through which people can express themselves with their bodies, it can especially reach the withdrawn child, the non-verbal child, and even the overly verbal child who has not learned how to coordinate his body, though he may be brilliant in oral language.

The author recently worked with a fifth grade class of bright children. One youngster in the class, who was extremely adept at mathematics and science, had great difficulty in communicating with people, and refused to participate in such activities as music, dancing, and art. At first J . . . also refused to participate in the mime games which the class was playing. At last he consented to be one of the guessers in a mime game where he did not have to act anything out and enjoyed the game immensely. Because it was so spontaneous, the game carried him along without his even realizing it, to the point where he was willing to join the group and participate in activities. This situation helped him along the road to sharing group experiences and communicating his own feelings toward other people and himself. Another youngster in the same group was also extremely bright, but had problems with physical coordination. He came from a home with a European background where scholarship was placed above everything else. He liked sports, but only as a spectator. The mime games in which this child participated helped him to coordinate his body, and enabled him to loosen up to the point where he could effectively use his body as he wanted to.

Mime skills can best be taught in the classroom within the framework of games. These games can also be useful during indoor recess and while projectors are being assembled and in other short breaks during the school day. They can be a boon in teaching reading and writing as well. Some mime games (for example, Crambo, which will be described in detail later in the article) are made to order for teaching word families. Even the most resistant child will enjoy these activities and still learn the content of the word family. Creative writing skills might profitably follow the experiences of some mime games. After having pantomimed various occupations and feelings, the teacher can ask the children to write as directly as possible to describe what the carpenter feels and hears and sees; what sounds he will make and the way he moves.

Mime does not have the wide range or discrimination of the spoken word, but it can lead to the development of an interest in acting and giving plays and a sharpening of insight into words themselves and their connotative value. Mime is a form of non-verbal communication which everyone can learn. One does not have to be a trained or skilled actor to participate in mime activities. Actually, the real value of these games lies in their spontaneity. The activities which are described should serve only as a framework, and each teacher should bring his own interpretation and skills to them. The framework of these games is elastic enough so that each game can be adapted to the developmental level of a particular group. In many instances these games also blend well with the academic curriculum.

Dumb Crambo

This game is well-suited for teaching word families. A person is picked to be "It." "It" then thinks of a word and tells the audience a word that rhymes with the one he selected. For example, if the word he chooses is "fall," he might say his word rhymes with "ball." "It" then picks an individual from the audience to act in pantomime the word that he is thinking of. If the word that is acted out is the one that "It" is thinking of he says, "Yes, the word is 'fall," and the actor becomes "It." Or if the word that is being acted out is "call," "It" says, "No, the word is not 'call'," and a new person is selected from the audience to guess and act out "Its" word. The third alternative that "It" has is to say, "I don't understand what word you're acting out," in which case the actor must try a different approach to get his word across.

A more complicated version of the game will actively involve more people. If "It" cannot guess the word which is being portrayed, and someone in the audience thinks that he has guessed the word being acted out, he whispers his guess to the actor. If the word he guessed is incorrect he sits down, but if the word has been guessed correctly then he and the actor together do a skit in pantomime to portray the word, until either "It" guesses correctly or another person from the audience who thinks he has guessed the right word joins in. In the event that "It" still cannot guess the word, the person who first acted out the word becomes "It" and selects a new word. This game can also be played as a team game, with the class divided into small groups which act out the words together.

Charades

There are hundreds of variations of this ever popular game, but this writer has found this one to be most fruitful in terms of developing mime into a part of the language arts program: Divide the class into three or four groups. Each group selects a word of more than one syllable; each syllable is depicted in a pantomime skit, and one skit is used for the entire word. Initially, it is best to select two-syllable words, leaving longer words for later. The group which guesses correctly then acts out its own word, and so the game progresses. In this way each group acts out a word for another group and has a chance to guess its opponent's word. Some good words to act out are: Ideal, Quarrelsome, Penmanship, Restaurant, Surprise, Tidewater, Uproar, Youngster, Youthful, etc.

History Dramatizations

In this activity the role of the teacher is crucial. Every member of every group should be encouraged to participate, and the teacher must discourage the dramatization of important events which do not lend themselves to dramatic depiction, such as the signing of the Declaration of Independence. An event like Ethan Allen's capture of Fort Ticonderoga would be much more effective. The secret of making this game a success is to give no more than five minutes for rehearsing, gathering props, and assigning parts. Each act should take no longer than sixty seconds. A good technique used to stimulate the groups and to exact discipline is to tell the groups to rehearse as quietly and as secretly as possible, so that no group will have an advantage when it comes to guessing the dramatization. By this time your groups should be quite impatient to begin, and the teacher will have successfully blended the language arts program with the social studies curriculum.

Notes

1. G. Robert Canfield, "How Useful Are Lessons on Listening?" *Elementary School Journal* 62 (December 1961): 147.
2. Sam Duker, "Listening and Reading," *Elementary School Journal* 65 (March 1965): 321-329.
3. Ramon Ross, "Teaching the Listener: Old Mistakes and a Fresh Beginning," *Elementary School Journal* 66 (February 1966): 239-244.
4. Ralph G. Nichols and Leonard A. Stevens, *Are You Listening?* (New York: McGraw-Hill Book Company, Inc., 1957).
5. Paul M. Hollingsworth, "So They Listened: The Effect of a Listening Program," *The Journal of Communication* 15 (March 1965): 14-16.
6. Gloria L. Horrworth, "Listening: A Facet of Oral Language," *Elementary English* 43 (December 1966): 856-864.
7. Joseph Mersand, "How to Train Pupils to Listen," *Senior Scholastic* 85 (November 4, 1964): 9.
8. Harold A. Anderson, "Needed Research in Listening," *Elementary English* 29 (April 1954): 215-224.
9. Lillian M. Logan, *Teaching the Young Child* (Boston: Houghton Mifflin Co., 1960).
10. J. N. Hook, *The Teaching of High School English* (New York: The Ronald Press, 1965).
11. Emmett A. Betts, *Foundations of Reading Instruction* (New York: American Book Co., 1946), and Donald D. Durrell, *Improvement of Basic Reading Abilities* (Yonkers-on-Hudson: World Book Co., 1940).
12. *Sequential Tests of Educational Progress,* Cooperative Test Division, Educational Testing Service, Princeton, New Jersey.
13. Miriam E. Wilt, "Children's Experiences in Listening," in *Children and the Language Arts,* Virgil E. Herrick and Leland B. Jacobs, eds. (Englewood Cliffs, N.J.: Prentice-Hall, Inc., 1955), Chap. 7.
14. Richard S. Hampleman, "Comparison of Listening and Reading Comprehension Ability of Fourth and Sixth Grade Pupils," *Elementary English* 35 (January 1958): 49-53.
15. Sam Duker, *Listening Bibliography* (New York: The Scarecrow Press, Inc., 1964).
16. Caffrey John, "Auding," *Review of Educational Research* 25 (April 1955): 121-132.
17. Horrworth, *op. cit.,* pp. 856-864, 868.
18. Thomas Lewis and Ralph G. Nichols, *Speaking and Listening* (Dubuque, Iowa: William C. Brown Company, 1965).
19. Ralph E. Kellogg, "Listening," in *Guiding Children's Language Learning,* Pose Lamb, planning editor (Dubuque, Iowa: William C. Brown Company, 1967), Chap. 5.
20. Kenneth L. Brown, "Speech and Listening in Language Arts Textbooks: Part I," *Elementary English* 44 (April 1967): 336-341.
21. Duker, *op. cit.*
22. Donald Pardie Brown, "And Having Ears They Hear Not," *NEA Journal* 39 (November 1950): 586-587; John Gardner Caffrey, "Auding as a Research Problem," *California Journal of Educational Research* 4 (September 1953): 155-161.
23. Stanford E. Taylor, "Listening," *NEA What Research Says Series Bulletin* 29 (April 1964).
24. Emerald V. Dechant, *Improving the Teaching of Reading* (Englewood Cliffs, N. J.: Prentice-Hall, Inc., 1964), p. 488.
25. Ira J. Hirsh, *The Measurement of Hearing* (New York: McGraw-Hill Book Company, 1952); G. A. Miller, "The Masking of Speech," *Psychological Bulletin* 44 (March 1947): 105-129; Stanford E. Taylor, *What Research Says to the Teacher: Listening* (Washington, D. C.: National Education Association, April 1964), p. 8.
26. Ralph Nichols, "What Can Be Done About Listening?" *Supervisor's Notebook,* Scott Foresman Service Bulletin 22 (Spring 1960): 1-4.
27. Edward Joseph Shoban, "Viewpoint from Related Disciplines," *Teachers College Record* 60 (February 1960): 272-282.

28. Miriam E. Wilt, "A Study of Teacher Awareness of Listening As a Factor in Elementary Education," *Journal of Educational Research* 43 (April 1950): 626-636.
29. Dechant, *op. cit.*, p. 95.
30. John W. Black, "A Relationship Between Speaking and Listening," *Joint Project Report No. NM 001 104 500, 54,* Ohio State University and Acoustic Laboratory, 1955.
31. Joel Stark, "An Investigation of the Relationship of the Vocal and Communicative Aspects of Speech Competency with Listening Comprehension," *Speech Monographs* 24 (June 1957): 98-99; Doris L. Howe, *"An Exploratory Study Concerning Listening Comprehension and Speaking Effectiveness,"* unpublished master's thesis, University of Arizona, 1960.
32. Eldonna L. Evertts, "An Investigation of the Structure of Children's Oral Language Compared with Silent Reading, Oral Reading, and Listening Comprehension," *Dissertation Abstracts* 22 (1962): 3038; Annetta Vester Evans, "Listening Related to Speaking in the First Grade," unpublished master's thesis, Atlanta University, 1960.
33. David H. Russell, "A Conspectus of Recent Research on Listening Abilities," *Elementary English* 41 (March 1964): 262-267; Hampleman, *op. cit.*
34. Herbert Hackett, "A Null Hypothesis, There Is Not Enough Evidence," *Education* 75 (January 1955): 149-151.
35. Arthur Heilman, *Principles and Practices of Teaching Reading* (Columbus, Ohio: Charles E. Merrill Books, Inc., 1961), pp. 45-50; Dechant, *op. cit.*, pp. 97-100.
36. Gloria L. Horrworth, "The Listening Center," *Maryland Teachers Journal* (January 1964); Miriam Hoffman, "Our Listening Center Livens Language Arts," *Elementary School Journal* 63 (April 1963): 381-385.
37. Jack R. Gibb, "Defensive Communication," *Reading in Managerial Psychology* (1964): 191-192.
38. David H. Russell and Elizabeth F. Russell, *Listening Aids Through the Grades* (New York: Bureau of Publications, Teachers College, Columbia University, 1959); Miriam E. Wilt, "Let's Teach Listening," in *Creative Ways of Teaching the Language Arts* (Champaign, Ill.: National Council of Teachers of English, 1957).
39. J. R. Gibb, "Defense Level and Influence in Small Groups," *Leadership and Interpersonal Behavior* (1961): 66-81.
40. Barbara Biber, Elizabeth Gilkeson and Charlotte Winsor, "Teacher Education at Bank Street College," *Personnel and Guidance Journal* 37 (April 1959); 550-568.
41. J. R. Gibb, "Sociopsychological Processes of Group Instruction," *The Dynamics of Instructional Groups,* Fifty-Ninth Yearbook of the National Society for the Study of Education, Part II (Chicago: University of Chicago Press, 1960), pp. 115-135.
42. Gibb, "Defensive Communication," *op. cit.*
43. Bruno Bettleheim, "Teaching the Disadvantaged," *NEA Journal* 54, 6 (September 1965): 11-12.
44. Gibb, "Defensive Communication," *op. cit.*
45. W. F. Dearborn, P. W. Johnson and L. Carmichael, "Oral Stress and Meaning in Printed Material," *Science* 110 (October 14, 1949): 404.
46. English Language Services, Inc., *English 900* (New York: The Macmillan Company, 1964).
47. John J. Carney, Jr., "Anyone Who Writes Well Can Speak Well," *Improving College and University Teaching* 12 (Autumn 1964): 207-211.
48. Dorothy McCarthy, "Language Disorders and Parent Child Relationships," *Journal of Speech and Hearing Disorders* 19 (December 1954): 514.
49. James Olsen, "The Verbal Ability of the Culturally Different," *The Reading Teacher* 18 (April 1965): 552-556.
50. Wilbert Pronorost and Louise Kingman, *Speaking and Listening in the Elementary School* (New York: Longmans, Green and Company, 1959).
51. *Bigger and Better Boners* (New York: The Viking Press, 1952).
52. N. V. Jones, "The Effect of Speech Training on Silent Reading Achievement," *Journal of Speech and Hearing Disorders* 16 (September 1951): 258-263.
53. A. Sterl Artley, "Research Concerning Interrelationships among the Language Arts," *Elementary English* 27 (December 1950): 527-537; Mildred A. Dawson, "Interrelationships Between Speech and Other Language Arts Areas," *Elementary English* 31 (April 1954): 223-233; John J. DeBoer, "Composition, Handwriting, and Spelling," *Review of Educational Research* 31 (April 1961): 161-172; Gertrude Hildreth, "Interrelationships among the Language Arts," *Elementary School Journal* 48 (June 1948): 538-549.
54. Mary K. Smith, "Measurement of the Size of General English Vocabulary Through the Elementary Grades and High School," *Genetic Psychological Monographs* 24 (1941): 311-345; Ruth Weir, *Language in the Crib* (The Hague, The Netherlands: Mouton and Company,

1962); Susan M. Ervin and Wick R. Miller, *Language Development*, Sixty-second Yearbook of the National Society for the Study of Education, Part I (Chicago: University of Chicago Press, 1963), pp. 108-143; Ruth G. Strickland, "The Language of Elementary School Children: Its Relationship to the Language of Reading Textbooks and the Quality of Reading of Selected Children," *Bulletin of the School of Education* 38, Indiana University, Bloomington (July 1962).

55. *Ibid.;* Smith, *loc. cit.;* Basil Bernstein, "Language and Social Class," *British Journal of Sociology* 11 (1960): 271-276; Mildred C. Templin, *Certain Language Skills in Children: Their Development and Interrelationships* (Minneapolis: University of Minnesota Press, 1957).
56. Edith A. Davis, *The Development of Linguistic Skill in Twins, Singletons with Siblings, and Only Children from Ages Five to Ten Years* (Minneapolis: University of Minnesota Press, 1937).
57. Strickland, *loc. cit.*
58. Walter D. Loban, *The Language of Elementary School Children* (Champaign, Ill.: National Council of Teachers of English, 1963).
59. Esther Milner, "A Sudy of the Relationship Between Reading Readiness in Grade One School Children and Patterns of Parent-Child Interaction," *Child Development* 22 (June 1951): 95-112.
60. Helen D. Gibbons, "Reading and Sentence Elements," *Elementary English Review* 18 (February 1941): 42-46.
61. E. L. Thorndike, "Reading and Reasoning, A Study of Mistakes in Paragraph Reading," *Journal of Educational Psychology* 8 (June 1917): 323-332.
62. Robert B. Ruddell, "The Effect of Four Programs of Reading Instruction with Varying Emphasis on the Regularity of Grapheme-Phoneme Correspondences and the Relationship of Language Structure to Meaning of Achievement in First Grade Reading: A First Progress Report," in *Psycholinguistic Nature of the Reading Process*, Kenneth Goodman, ed. (Detroit: Wayne State University Press, in press).
63. Robert B. Ruddell, "The Effect of the Similarity of Oral and Written Patterns of Language Structure on Reading Comprehension," *Elementary English* 42 (April 1965): 403-410.
64. Annette P. Kelty, "An Experimental Study to Determine the Effect of Listening for Certain Purposes upon Achievement in Reading for These Purposes," *Abstracts of Field Studies for the Degree of Doctor of Education* 15, Greeley, Colo.: Colorado State College of Education (1954): 82-95.
65. Richard S. Hampleman, "Comparison of Listening and Reading Comprehension Ability of Fourth and Sixth Grade Pupils," unpublished doctoral dissertation, Indiana University, 1955.
66. William E. Young, "The Relation of Reading Comprehension and Retention to Hearing Comprehension and Retention," *Journal of Experimental Education* 5 (September 1936): 30-39.
67. Sara Lundsteen, "Teaching Abilities in Critical Listening in the Fifth and Sixth Grades," unpublished doctoral dissertation, University of California, 1963; G. P. Plessas, "Reading Abilities and Intelligence Factors of Children Having High and Low Auding Ability," unpublished doctoral dissertation, University of California, 1957; Sue E. Trivette, "The Effect of Training in Listening for Specific Purposes," *Journal of Educational Research* 54 (March 1961): 276-277; Sister M. K. Hollow, "Listening Comprehension at the Intermediate Grade Level," *Elementary School Journal* (December 1955): 158-161; Edward Pratt, "Experimental Evaluation of a Program for the Improvement of Listening," *Elementary School Journal* (March 1956): 315-320; Thomas G. Devine, "The Development and Evaluation of a Series of Recordings for Teaching Certain Critical Listening Abilities," unpublished doctoral dissertation, Boston University, 1961; Robert P. Larsen and Daniel D. Feder, "Common and Differential Factors in Reading and Hearing Comprehension," *Journal of Educational Psychology* 31 (April 1940): 241-252; Young, *loc, cit.*
68. J. G. Caffrey, "Auding Ability as a Function of Certain Psychometric Variables," unpublished doctoral dissertation, University of California, 1953; Donald Spearritt, *Listening Comprehension—A Factoral Analysis*, Australian Council for Educational Research, Research Series No. 76 (Melbourne: G. W. Green and Sons, Ltd., 1962); David H. Russell, "A Conspectus of Recent Research on Listening Abilities," *Elementary English* 41 (March 1964): 262-267.
69. Loban, *loc. cit.*
70. Clotilda Winter, "Interrelationships among Language Variables in Children for the First and Second Grades," *Elementary English* 34 (February 1957): 108-113.
71. Virgil Hughes, "Study of the Relationships among Selected Language Abilities," *Journal of Educational Research* 47 (October 1953): 97-106.
72. Lester E. Harrell, Jr., "An Inter-Comparison of the Quality and Rate of the Development of Oral and Written Language in Children," *Monographs of the*

Society for Research in Child Development 22, 3 (1957).

73. Paul Bushnell, "An Analytical Contrast of Oral with Written English," *Contributions to Education*, 451 (New York: Teachers College, Columbia University, 1930).
74. F. K. Heider and Grace M. Heider, "A Comparison of Sentence Structure of Deaf and Hearing Children," *Psychological Monographs* 52 (1940): 42-103.
75. Mildred C. Templin, *The Development of Reasoning in Children with Normal and Defective Hearing* (Minneapolis: University of Minnesota Press, 1950).
76. Ruth Sawyer, *The Way of the Storyteller* (New York: The Viking Press, 1942), p. 118.
77. *Ibid.*, p. 18.
78. Arnold Gesell and Frances Ilg, *The Child From Five to Ten* (New York: Harper Brothers, 1946), p. 365.
79. Leland Jacobs, "Telling Stories to Young Children," in *Using Literature with Children* (New York: Columbia University Teacher's College Press, 1965), p. 16.
80. Marie Shedlock, *The Art of the Storyteller* (New York: Dover Publications, Inc., 1952), p. 136.
81. Winifred Ward, *Playmaking with Children* (New York: Appleton-Century-Crofts, Inc., 1951), p. 122.
82. Shedlock, *op. cit.*, p. 31.
83. Laura Emerson, *Storytelling* (Grand Rapids, Mich: Zondervan Publishing House, 1959), p. 65.
84. Joseph Jacobs, "Jack and the Beanstalk," in *English Fairy Tales* (New York: G. P Putnam's Sons, 1902), p. 61.
85. *Ibid.*, p. 63.
86. *Ibid.*, p. 66.
87. *Ibid.*, p. 67.
88. *Ibid.*
89. Shedlock, *op. cit.*, p. 34; Ward, *op. cit.*, p. 123; Wolfram Eberhard, "The Tale of Turtle Mountain," *Folktales of China* (Chicago: University of Chicago Press, 1965), p. 76; Sara Lowrey and Gertrude Johnson, *Interpretative Reading* (New York: Appleton-Century-Crofts, Inc., 1942), p. 83.
90. *Ibid.*
91. James Feibleman, *In Praise of Comedy* (London: George Allen and Unwin, Ltd., 1939), p. 191; Max Eastman, *Enjoyment of Laughter* (New York: Simon and Schuster, 1936), p. 7.
92. Laura Richards, "Eletelephony," *Tirra Lirra* (Boston: Little, Brown and Company, 1932), p. 31.
93. Lowry and Johnson, *op. cit.*, p. 84-85.
94. Feibleman, *op. cit.*, p. 180.
95. Angela Keyes, *Stories and Storytelling* (New York: D. Appleton and Company, 1916), p. 51.
96. Cecile DeBanke, *The Art of Choral Speaking* (Boston: Baker's Plays, 1937), p. 18.
97. Agnes C. Hamm, *Choral Speaking Technique* (Milwaukee: Tower Press, 1941), p. 1.
98. Louise Abney and Grace Rowe, *Choral Speaking Arrangements for the Lower Grades* (Boston: Expression Company).
99. Marjorie Gullan, *Choral Speaking* (London: Methuen and Company, 1934), p. 2
100. Josephine Tronsberg, "Choral Reading At All Grade Levels," *Pittsburgh University Conference on Reading*, June 17-June 28, 1957, pp. 136-137.
101. Carrie Rasmussen, "Choral Reading In The Elementary School," *NEA Journal* 19 (November 1960): 26.
102. Robert Whitehead, *Children's Literature: Strategies of Teaching* (Englewood Cliffs, N. J.: Prentice-Hall, Inc., 1968), p. 121.
103. Tronsberg, *op. cit.*, pp. 135-140.
104. Barbara McIntyre, "The Art of Teaching Choral Reading," *Conference on Reading—Pittsburgh University*, July 6-16, 1965, pp. 74-75.
105. Whitehead, *op. cit.*, pp. 122-125.
106. May Hill Arbuthnot and Shelton L. Root, Jr., *Time for Poetry* (New York: Scott, Foresman and Company, 1968), pp. 244-245.

Selected Bibliography

Ackerlund, Sylvia. "Poetry in the Elementary School." *Elementary English*, **46** (May 1969): 431-435.

Anderson, William. "Poetry in the Elementary Classroom." *California English Journal*, **5** (January 1969): 39-48.

Bloom, Robert M. "A Program for Oral English." *Elementary English*, **41** (February 1964): 158-164.

Bolz, George C. "Promoting Oral Expression." *The National Elementary Principal*, **42** (April 1963): 41-43.

Botel, Morton, and John Dawkins. "Tune In on Oral Communication." *The Instructor*, **79** (April 1970): 56.

Burns, Paul C. "Teaching Listening in Elementary Schools." *Elementary English*, **38** (January 1961): 11-14.

Denby, Robert V. "NCTE/ERIC Report on Research in Listening and Listening Skills." *Elementary English*, **46** (April 1969): 511-517.

Duker, Sam. "Listening." In *Encyclopedia of Educational Research*, 4th edition, edited by Robert L. Ebel, pp. 747-753. New York, London: Collier-Macmillan, 1969.

Evertts, Eldonna L. "Dinosaurs, Witches, and Anti-Aircraft: Primary Composition." *Elementary English*, **43** (January 1966): 109-114.

Hall, Edward T. "Listening Behavior: Some Cultural Differences." *Phi Delta Kappan*, **50** (March 1969): 379-380.

Hayes, Eloise. "Creative Drama at Kaliki-Uka." *Today's Education*, **57** (September 1968): 30-32.

Hayes, Eloise. "Drama, Big News in English." *Elementary English*, **47** (January 1970): 13-16.

Hollingsworth, Paul M. "The Classroom Teacher as a Speech Teacher." *Education*, **85** (January 1965): 270-273.

Lake, Mary Louise. "First Aid for Vocabularies." *Elementary English*, **44** (November 1967): 783-784.

Lewis, G. M. "Releasing Creativity." *Childhood Education*, **41** (February 1965): 295-300.

Lindberg, Lucile. "Oral Language or Else." *Elementary English*, **42** (November 1965): 760-761, 804.

Lundsteen, Sara W. "Critical Listening and Thinking: A Recommended Goal for Future Research." *Journal of Research and Development in Education*, **31** (1969): 119-133.

May, Frank B. "Effects of Environment on Oral Language Development." *Elementary English*, **43** (November 1966): 720-729.

Meyerson, Marion. "The Bilingual Child." *Childhood Education*, **45** (May 1969): 525-527.

Moffett, James. *Drama: What is Happening? The Use of Dramatic Activities in the Teaching of English.* Champaign, Ill.: NCTE, 1967.

Nichols, Ralph G. "What Can Be Done About Listening?" *The Supervisor's Notebook* **22**, No. 1, Spring 1960. Glenview, Ill.: Scott, Foresman and Company, 1960.

Petty, Walter T. and Roberta Starkey. "Oral Language and Personal and Social Development." *Elementary English*, **43** (April 1966): 386-394.

Prescott, Elaine, et al. "Are You Teaching Auding? A Review of the Literature." *Peabody Journal of Education*, **46** (November 1968): 150-154.

Putt, Robert C. "Improving Speech Habits." *Instructor*, **78** (February 1969): 108-109.

Siks, Geraldine B. "Creative Dramatics for Children." *Contributions in Reading*, No. 26, Ginn and Co.

Spencer, Robert J. "Mastering the Art of Storytelling." *Grade Teacher*, **85** (January 1968): 80-82.

Stahl, Dona K. "A Look at Listening." *Instructor*, **79** (April 1970): 65-66.

Thornley, Gwendella. "Storytelling is Fairy Gold." *Elementary English*, **45** (January 1968): 67-79, 88.

Wagner, Guy. "What Schools are Doing: Teaching Listening." *Education*, **88** (November 1967): 183-188.

Wallen, Norman E. "Creativity-Fantasy and Fact." *The Elementary School Journal*, **64** (May 1964): 438-443.

Wilt, Miriam. "Talk—Talk—Talk." *The Reading Teacher*, **21** (April 1968): 611-617.

Woods, Margaret S. "Learning Through Creative Dramatics." *Educational Leadership*, **18** (October 1960): 19-23.

PART FIVE
Written Language Experiences

A.
Literature

Developing reading habits is an integral part of the language arts program. Too many teachers feel that their responsibility is limited to teaching children how to read, and they do not extend their efforts beyond this singular goal. Far too few teachers are concerned that children read extensively or question what they read. The real value of the printed page is not derived from knowing *how* to read, but is derived *from* reading. Few children develop a love for reading as a result of their lessons in reading skills. Therefore, it is necessary that a literature, not just a reading, program be an integral part of the elementary curriculum.

A child's reading habits are developed during the years he spends in the elementary school. His classroom teachers have a tremendous influence upon the quality and quantity of his reading. The teacher should enjoy reading and in some way allow the children to share in his enthusiasm for books. It is also necessary for the teacher to become as familiar as possible with a wide selection of children's literature and be able to recommend books and authors to meet the needs and interests of the individual child. A planned literature program takes time. Periods must be set aside for introducing, reading, and sharing a variety of books.

The influence of good literature on the speech and writing of children is undeniably important. Literature must be made an essential part of the elementary school curriculum, not just an "extra."

What is literature? What should be included in an elementary school literature program? How should the literature program be planned? What is the role of the classroom teacher? These and many other questions pertaining to the literature program for children are discussed by the authors of the following articles.

48.

Planning an Elementary School Literature Program

Iris M. Tiedt

In considering the development of an elementary school literature program, there are a number of basic questions or issues that should be explored. The answers to these questions will serve to guide the planning of a scope and sequence, the selection of appropriate materials for use in the program, and the determination of methodology to be utilized.

It should be noted, first of all, that the questions posed here are not ones to which there are simple answers or even questions to which there are clearcut "right" answers. They are questions, however, that require careful consideration as we conceive of an ideal, yet feasible, literature program.

Why should Literature be included in the Elementary School Program?

Very few persons would deny the wisdom, the desirability, of including literature in the elementary school curriculum, but the reasons given for including literature are often vague and varied. In general, they might be listed as the following:

—to transmit the cultural heritage
—to help children understand other people
—to increase the child's understanding of himself
—to expose children to excellent writing
—to stimulate the child's enjoyment of reading
—to teach children concepts about literature

When considering the types of concepts we might include in a literature program, we often think of the following group: (1) plot or story line, (2) theme, (3) characterization, (4) setting, and (5) imagery. These concepts are important as the student discovers how the author manipulates the English language, how he organizes his ideas, how he achieves a desired effect. The student becomes aware of the author's many skills as he himself writes original stories.

Also to be considered, however, is another type of concept that we might

---

better term "understandings." Literature presents values; it teaches sensitivity, for E.B. White not only tells the child Charlotte and Wilbur's adventures but he also conveys mature concepts of friendship, loneliness and death. We could begin a list of these understandings to be gained from literature, thus:

a. Everybody has problems.
b. Problems are to be solved.
c. Appearances may be deceiving.
d. People are not all "good" or all "bad."
e. People are much the same all over the world.

As is readily seen, this list will prove to be inexhaustible and will need constant revision.

Is There a Need for a Planned Scope and Sequence in Literature?

In all other subjects taught in the elementary school curriculum there has been developed a carefully delineated scope and sequence that is followed at least to some extent. There are those, however, who hesitate to submit literature to this type of structure. "We must feel free to present the 'right' book at the exact moment it is appropriate," they say. One would question whether many teachers take full advantage of this idealized approach which even at best remains incidental and may be just as often *ex*cluded as *in*cluded.

The advantages of the planned scope and sequence lie not in the elimination of incidental, enriching experiences with literature but rather in the addition of a planned presentation of quality works that are selected for specific purposes. The planned literature program is directed at providing instruction about literature, the teaching of concepts that young children can absorb at their individual levels of understanding.

The carefully developed program, furthermore, avoids the unfortunate repetition that occurs as every teacher "discovers" haiku with her students or "shares" *Charlotte's Web*. Even the best of literature becomes distasteful when repeated in this unorganized manner. One could anticipate the result that children would dislike writing haiku or resent hearing the adventures of Charlotte and Wilbur for the third time.

The planned program not only eliminates this repetition but it also ensures continuity. Developed both vertically and horizontally, it includes selections designed to instruct as well as to please. A number of contemporary reading texts now include "good" literature by known authors. English, and even spelling, texts are also including literature as part of the learning experiences presented. What they lack, however, in most cases, is the planned scope and sequence of literature concepts and the close interrelationship with other language learnings, the reading of poetry, for example, which results in the composition of poetry. Little effort is made to teach literature concepts in these texts, and of course, the child is never provided with the rich experience of studying a whole book, a novel such as Madeline L'Engle's *A Wrinkle in Time*, for instance, with its introduction to symbolism.

Where does Literature fit into the Present Elementary School Curriculum?

The elementary school daily schedule is already bursting at the seams so that it is no idle question to consider just where this new content is to be placed. There are several possibilities: (1) it could be given a small portion of time labeled "literature;" (2) it could be part of the English program; or (3) it could be part of the reading program.

Ideally the "language arts" in the elementary school would consist of a well-integrated program focused directly on the English language. English would, thus, be studied through reading, writing, speaking, and listening. Certainly the interrelationship between encoding and decoding should be observed as the child visualizes himself as both a reader and a writer. He not only appreciates the writing of others, but as a young author, he, too, can produce "literature." The literature he reads may serve as a model for his own creative efforts.

Again, pleading for a well-organized, integrated language program, the author would suggest the approach illustrated in this diagram.

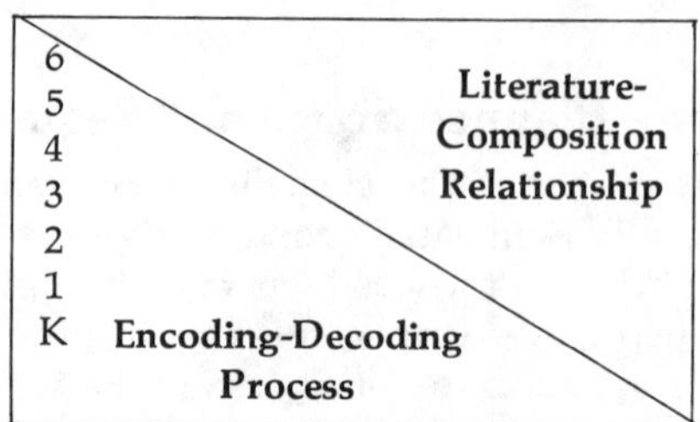

The encoding-decoding process is a unified approach to the teaching of linguistic skills basic to reading and spelling, both of which are essential to developing skills of composition and to studying literature. While linguistic abilities are developing, a large amount of language time is devoted to teaching children the phoneme-grapheme relationship in English. Less time is necessarily allotted to the *study* of literature and composition during this period although oral approaches are used to begin instruction as soon as possible.

As less time is required for the encoding-decoding skills, more time is available for the study of literature in close relationship to its companion, composition. This time allotment, it should be stressed, is for formal instruction. It does not include the exciting incidental experiences with literature that may occur as the teacher reads Evelyn Lampman's *A City Under the Back Steps* to the group that has been very active and needs time to rest or the sharing of "Velvet Shoes" by Elinor Wylie as the first flakes of winter suddenly appear. These experiences are enriching and stimulating, but their very spontaneity means that they are irregular and unplanned so they cannot be counted as part of the continuity necessary for a literature program. And will remain "frosting on the cake."

How will Literature be Selected for This Program?

It is common for teachers and librarians to share the responsibility for ordering trade books for school libraries, and this tradition will probably be followed to some extent in selecting books to be included in a literature program. Another group, however, that should have something to contribute to this selection process consists of the children themselves. We don't always take full advantage of utilizing the opinions of children which in many cases would assist us in avoiding poor choices.

As we decide who will make the selection, we must also enumerate the criteria which will guide the selection of individual items. Our objectives in including a literature program and the concepts we wish to teach will, of course, directly influence selection. Certainly quality of writing, recommendation by experts, and enjoyment by children will require evaluation.

Published aids for book selection will prove helpful, especially those which are kept up-to-date. The following will be useful:

The Booklist and Subscription Books Bulletin, A Guide to Current Books, American Library Association. 60 E. Huron St., Chicago, Ill.

Children's Books Too Good to Miss, May Hill Arbuthnot, comp., Cleveland, Ohio: Western Reserve University Press, 1963.

Children's Catalog, New York: H.W. Wilson Company. With regular supplements.

Fare for the Reluctant Reader, 3rd ed., Anita E. Dunn, comp., Capital Area School Development Assn., State University of New York, Albany, New York.

Gateways to Readable Books, 3rd ed., Ruth Strang, *et al.*, eds., New York: Wilson.

The Horn Book Magazine, The Horn Book, Ind., 585 Boylston St., Boston, Mass. 02116.

Reading Ladders for Human Relations, Muriel Crosby, ed., American Council of Education, 1963. Primary to adult books.

A Teacher's Guide to Children's Books, Nancy Larrick, Columbus, Ohio: Merrill, 1960.

When we think of literature for the elementary school, we usually mean books. Within the broad category of books, however, there are subclassifications to be examined, for example, the various genres. We should aim at including contemporary novels (*And Now, Miguel*), nonfiction (*From Drumbeat to Tickertape*), poetry (*Cricket Songs*), short stories (*Homer Price*), and drama (*Peter Pan*).

Contemporary emphasis on media should lead us to remember that literature also includes more than books. Excellent films and filmstrips have much to offer a literature program. *The Red Balloon, Hailstones and Halibut Bones,* and *Rainshower* are but three excellent films that offer the same fine qualities found in books plus the visual imagery contributed by outstanding photography and imagination. *The Red Balloon* contains the same elements that a printed story would offer in a literature program, for example, characterization, foreshadowing, and plot structure.

Records, too, serve to present literature through another sense. *Ruth Sawyer, Story Teller* and *The Just So Stories* are examples of recordings by skilled storytellers who share quality literature with young children. Recordings, as well as films, can aid a child in stretching to learn as he is exposed to new vocabulary and interesting ideas.

How will Teaching Literature differ from Teaching Reading?

The teaching of reading will focus on skills, the teaching of the phoneme-grapheme relationship. It will move into the study of morphology or word forms as children learn to read these forms which are also presented in grammar instruction. *The teaching of literature, on the other hand, remains focused on ideas and the appreciation of the writer's performance with words.* The child will thus be led to express his own ideas and to manipulate words as he, too, develops a style of writing.

Any literature program must be sufficiently flexible to permit growth at the upper levels as well as to encourage development by students who are slower learners. Provision must be made, too, for additional enrichment for disadvantaged children who may need more time for building a background of literature experiences. Building around a core of materials that all children will experience, the ideal program will then suggest further lessons to extend the learning of able students. It will also suggest enrichment activities at the same level for those who need to develop a rich background before moving on.

In order for the teacher to present well-organized literature lessons, it will be necessary to have carefully prepared materials that will bring out concepts and take advantage of the offerings of each selection, for example, the contrast of British and American English in *The Children of Green Knowe.* Not every teacher can be expected to have the background information needed to present topics of this sort as they occur. The classroom teacher has neither the time nor the training required to prepare the needed materials for a top quality program.

Not only are new materials needed but also new instructional strategies. *The most useful organization for studying literature will probably be a combination of individual study and the seminar approach, for work in large groups does not make for student involvement. Certainly we must discard the antiquated book report which is still being used in many classrooms serving only to stifle interest in reading. More creative approaches to reacting to a book or sharing it with classmates include the following:*

> *The *diorama* is an excellent medium for depicting a scene from a story. Homer Price (cardboard or papier mache figure) could be shown with Aroma, his pet skunk, as they creep up on the robbers who are camping in the woods. The diorama also can be used to portray a scene from historical fiction or from the life of a figure in American history.
>
> A *mobile* can present a book by displaying the characters as well as objects or ideas essential to the story. *The 500 Hats of Bartholomew Cubbins* might, for instance, be interpreted through a mobile which features many unusual hats created in three dimensions.
>
> *Music* can be related to book sharing as a student or a small group of students composes a ballad about *Mary Poppins.* Older students might write a calypso or a folk song about the adventures of Huckleberry Finn or a real person about whom they have read.
>
> A *collage* is an intriguing method of combining art with literature. *Chitty-Chitty-Bang-Bang,* for example, might be depicted on a large poster which includes a cut-out drawing of this distinctive green car, the faces of Man-Mountain Fink, Joe, the Monster, and the twins. Portions of a map of England, the English Channel and northern France might be worked into the background as would be other illustrative ideas from the story. Words can also be incorporated in the collage—*Paris, transmogrifications, Paragon Panther, Ian Fleming,* and so on.

Summary

As we plan an elementary school literature program, there are many questions and issues to be considered. We have discussed the ramifications of five such questions:

1. Why should literature be included in the elementary school program?
2. Is there a need for a planned scope and sequence in literature?
3. Where does literature fit into the present elementary school curriculum?
4. How will literature be selected for this program?
5. How will teaching *literature* differ from teaching *reading*?

*From *Contemporary English in the Elementary School* by Iris M. Tiedt and Sidney W. Tiedt, Englewood Cliffs, New Jersey: Prentice-Hall, 1967. pp. 298-99.

In developing an elementary school literature program we should strive to achieve an exciting, stimulating curriculum that will truly involve children in their literature. The teaching of literature learnings at this level should be aimed at opening the door to an extended and expanded literature program at the secondary school level.

49.

Building on Experiences in Literature

Marjorie L. Paige

There are poems for blue moods and giggly moods. There are tales about death and baby's birth. Literature is very much attuned to the marrow and grist of life . . . of children's lives. Let's bring children and books together.

Experiences with literature tie together and echo for us many of our life experiences. What greater gift can we give to the children with whom we come in contact than the opportunity to relate the impact of stories and poems to their own lives? It is a privilege to introduce the friends we know in books to the children who are our friends and the excitement we feel, contagious. It has been well said that the love of literature must be caught rather than taught.

Books, stories and poems are too often used to fill incidental moments in the school lives of young children. "Library time" is one way of keeping children quietly occupied. Stories are frequently used as "fillers" in the program or told during the final moments of the day. As parents arrive to collect their offspring, the interruptions are many and only the children of dilatory parents are able to enjoy the ending. Even when a more appropriate time is set aside for stories and poems, this is not enough. If the teacher knows both children and their literature, she will be able to bring them together through the events of the day for many unifying and enriching moments.

Poetry, especially, knows no set time or place. The teacher who has some degree of familiarity with poetry and is able to recite it without searching out the place in the book, is often able to use a poem at the precise moment that it is wanted. On any puddly or slushy morning, the chore of too many too-small boots can be lightened by . . .

John had
Great Big
Waterproof
Boots on;

Reprinted from *Young Children* 25:85-88 (December 1969), by permission of author and publisher.

Susie's galoshes
Makes splishes and sploshes

A glimpse of a squirrel scampering up a tree in the playground can be made more meaningful by the sound of

Whisky, frisky,
Hippity hop;
Up he goes
To the tree top.

as the rhythm of the lines simulates the movements of the animal.

The verbal accompaniment of

Christopher Robin goes
Hoppity, hoppity,
Hoppity, hoppity, hop.

reinforces and gives added pleasure to spontaneous activity.

And

When I was One
I had just begun.

makes the importance of being six years old very plain.

This is not to say that a poem should commemorate each event, but having these things at our fingertips permits us to enjoy them when the time is right. One cannot, of course, commit to memory all of the poetry that one might want to share with a group of children. The teacher may keep a card file on her desk or table with the poems classified in whichever way is best suited to her needs, readily available to offer as the occasion arises. The value of the file may be enhanced by clues appropriately marked on the cards as to ways that the poems may be used to encourage children to express themselves—their reactions—in order to help them relate the content of the story to their own experience.

Poetry is meant to be spoken as well as heard. Children will join in when favorites are repeated. The rhythm and sound of the words, the feel of them in the mouth, are fun.

The pictures that the words conjure up for a child create, in his mind's eye, something that is different for each one. He relates it to his own experiences—his own feelings. Poems can be funny or sad; about things that are familiar or things that are mysterious. Even poetry that is not wholly understood can often be appreciated because of the lilt or the delicious way the words are put together. If the child has enjoyed it and has acquired impressions and images, there is no need to have everything explained. For the teacher to give a literal interpretation, or suggest that each person should get the identical meaning from a poem, is to rob the listener of his right to make the poem his own.

There are many ways, too, that we can help children to make stories and poems more their own. Through the use of puppets, by "playing the story," helping them do song stories, using a flannel board, by drawing or painting about the story children can, each in his own way, recreate that which has particular meaning and importance for him. Some experiences in literature may have such general impact that the entire group will want to use them in many ways—others may appeal on a more individual basis.

Hand puppets made of felt, and provided with a simple interchangeable wardrobe, can be readily available for spur of the moment use. Materials for creating puppets—paper bags, cardboard, toilet tissue rolls, sticks, bits of fur, feathers and buttons—are easy to acquire for those children who choose to make their own.

Song stories seem to emanate naturally from the repetition or rhythm of some stories and poems—they cry to be sung! "Caps for sale! Caps for sale! Fifty cents a ca-ap!" the chant of the street peddler, is a refrain in the taunting rhythm of childhood, familiar to all and so suggestive of music and action that it almost creates itself. The way in which the peddler carries his wares on his head—first his own checked cap, then the gray caps, then the brown caps, then the blue caps, then the red caps on the very top forms a rising tonal sequence. And, surely, the teasing "Tsz, tsz, tsz," of the monkeys and the increasing anger of the peddler move toward a crescendo which is quickly diminished as the caps fall to the ground.

Any story or poem that has a strongly accented beat, a frequently repeated phrase or a cumulative pattern lends itself to adaptation as a song story, by children who are sufficiently familiar with the content and tempo to blend them in their own way.

Marchette Chute's *Sea Song* is great fun to use with the flannel board. The doodle bug and the creatures of the sea are easily made of felt, sequins, shells, or whatever other materials imagination suggests. Children, singly or in small groups, enjoy manipulating them to accompany the quick action of the verse. So many stories and poems lend themselves to flannel board use that the group may enjoy building a shoebox library of their favorites to add pleasure to retelling of tales.

Children begin to strengthen and deepen their awareness of the outside world and to explore the world of feelings within by assuming the attitudes and motivations of literary characters well known to them. Stories will seldom be used in their entirety. No attempt is made when "playing the story" to memorize the lines. In fact, only snatches of it may be chosen to be played and replayed. The most simple props, if any, are needed and the children are ready to try on new feelings and ideas. Nursery rhymes lend themselves readily to simple creative dramatization.

It is, in part, through the experiences one has with literature that life is "tried on," new insights and understandings gained, thinking stimulated, language appreciated and knowledge achieved. The important thing is for the teacher to love his story so well that he is eager to share it. If his enthusiasm is genuine and his material well suited to the interest and age level of the group, it will be a satisfying experience to which children can respond.

There is, in children, great response to the language and magic of Rose Fyleman's *Very Lovely* in which she turns an ordinary rainy day into a provocative situation. The easy rhythmic meter and imaginative content combine to create a picture in verse, so vivid that the child will enjoy recreating his impressions through the use of art media.

Many sensory feelings are shared by children and poets. They know that

Mud is very nice to feel
All Squishy-squash between the toes

and appreciate the sensation produced by going

Round about
And round about
And round about and round about

An appreciation of literature develops gradually in children, as it is a part of their daily living. They become selective. Many stories are enjoyed, but some, as they meet the needs of a particular child, are held and treasured by him for a time or forever.

With so much excellent material available it is no problem to find well done books to suit a variety of tastes. Children's feelings as well as their interests must be considered—their desire for facts as well as fantasy; for humor and suspense; for the plebian as well as the glamourous. Books can be a comfort and a friend to children in some of their concerns, and it is the challenging function of the teacher to bring them together—not only in acceptance but in genuine excitement.

Are You my Mother? (Eastman) is a book that has direct appeal for a child concerned about his own identy. *The Dead Bird* (Brown) helps to make death somewhat comprehensible and quite normal in the cycle of life. *The Quarreling Book* (Zolotow) gives an understanding of the power of gray days and displacement of anger.

The child who needs to be bigger and more controlling than he is will identify strongly with Tommy (de Regniers) who is busy all day being a Giant and becomes smaller as bedtime approaches. For the one who is coping with the problem of being too big in relation to the new baby, *Peter's Chair* (Keats), *The New Pet* (Flack), or *Little* (Aldis) might have great meaning.

If it is through humor or the use of words that the added ingredient is supplied, *Which Witch?* (Lasson) may be just the right story. Or perhaps *Horton*, his plight and his refrain will provide whatever is needed to make a book special for a child. *The Terrrrible Tigerrr* (Brown) and his quest for four-year-old meat may well strike a spark—but if not, there are many more from which to choose.

In order to achieve a measure of success, however, it is necessary for the teacher to be familiar with the variety and scope of children's literature. It is surely not enough to order by title from book lists suggested by librarians or publishers. One must feel and taste of books before selecting those which have greatest appeal and whose total effect incorporates literary and aesthetic values.

Keep a poem in your pocket
and a picture in your head

is excellent advice to all who are aware that literature can be a friend to children—a source of pleasure in itself and a source of stimulation for creative expression.

50.

Toward a Rationale for Teaching Literature to Children

Arthur T. Allen and Dorothy I. Seaberg

At a time when the teaching of literature in the American elementary school is as unsettling and challenging as it is in high school, it is imperative that the researcher, curriculum specialist, and classroom-teacher become vigorously involved with curriculum development. College students display an extraordinary ignorance in the literary tradition and in the face of this ignorance usually have to be taught what literature is and why great literature is great. The teaching we have done in the past has not produced very good results, and the time is right for creating and experimenting with more promising rationales for programs in literature for the young.

The opening phase of English projects sponsored by the U. S. Office of Education came to their conclusion in September, 1967. Several study-demonstration centers and individual research projects were developed. Their programs have been tried out in various classrooms and school systems throughout the country. These exciting, and even imaginative approaches, need further testing in elementary classrooms to determine their effectiveness for teaching literature meaningfully outside a basal and/or some other type reading program. The trend in these projects appear to be one in which the teaching of literature is organized uniquely as a separate but close ancillary to the reading program. Possibly we are going back to the "old days" when the "literature period" was just as important as the reading period now is. If this trend becomes reality, we dare not retreat to the old methods of reading and discussing great literature for the purpose of instilling the techniques of literary criticism. Most of us can recall reading a selection of prose or poetry to find its "true" meaning! This was accomplished by first being text-readers and then proceeding immediately to dissecting, analyzing and finally giving succinct summaries of what the authors were attempting to communicate to us, the readers. This approach turned most of us off and away from literature and we came to view it not as an encounter with life as it is or as it might be, but rather as a formal, dull learning experience in which the teacher engaged in literary criticism with an uninvolved and unappreciative audience.

From *Elementary English* 45:1043-1047 (December 1968). Reprinted by permission of the National Council of Teachers of English and Arthur T. Allen and Dorothy I. Seaberg.

A literature program should have, instead, teaching strategies in its overarching structure that will allow the child's own experience to open the poem or story to him, and conversly, have the poem or story open the child to his own experience. As one of the authors said in a different context:

> Simply let him live it. Let him grow through literature for a long time before we attempt to teach him how to analyze it. Let him open the treasures found in literature at will, not by coercion. Out of his own inner thoughts and feelings, the "reader-child" is capable of making a new ordering, the product of creative endeavor carried on by the reader under the guidance of the text and teacher.[1]

With this viewpoint in mind an NDEA Institute in Children's Literature was organized at Brooklyn College for experienced teachers and supervisors who for the most part would be revisiting literature for children after a long separation. The staff provided opportunities for renewed contacts with sufficient samples of the enduring great books for children as well as with the outstanding contemporary works. The participants, therefore, had a first-hand engagement with children's books; they did not study *about* literature. The study of criticism was dealt with only incidentally as a result of questions. Interspersed with independent reading of children's books, the participants were shown how to present various literary genre to children. They in turn attempted to execute these suggestions as they taught children in special summer school classrooms. In analyzing their teaching, they saw that children first become story-listeners or if not story-listeners, text-readers. Then they become active participants through pantomime, creative dramatics, or choral speaking, overtly expressing their own personal ordering of the text or tale; and finally they become dreamer-creators by making judgments of value based on the rich and multiple associations they encounter in literature compared with their own lives. After responding *feelingly* to what they had read or heard, the children could more easily express their thoughts and emotions. The literature resource teachers realized that only at this point can we, as teachers, intervene to teach about theme, plot, and characterization.

In contrast to this procedure, an informal survey of the newer curriculum guides reveals that suggestions to teachers are continuing to urge high level abstraction, offering few ideas for developing appreciation through active re-creation of the text. Rather they are providing helps to the teacher on how to study a particular literary genre with children from grades one through six. One wonders whether teachers, given these suggestions will simply, in desperation, assign the standard written book report or have pupils construct dioramas to depict the theme as follow-up activities.

In one of the new innovations, *A Curriculum for English* (grades 1-6), prepared by the Nebraska Curriculum Development Center, children are introduced to all the major types of literary genre through units progressing from folk and fanciful literature at one end of the continuum to historical fiction and biography at the other. The Nebraska guides have been developed using basic assumptions set forth by Northrop Frye in *The Educated Imagination.* However, Frye's assumptions have been followed only in part, for it is noticeable that even at first grade level children are introduced to factual prose. Frye believes that "if literature is to be properly taught, we must start at its center which is poetry, then work outward to literary prose, and from there work outward to the applied languages of business and professions and ordinary life."[2]

It is noteworthy to compare the hypotheses developed by Frye with the ideas expressed by the Soviet children's writer, Kornei Chukovsky, in his book, *From Two to Five.* Chukovsky, too, believes the young child should be allowed to dabble in poetry and thence immerse himself in the fairy tale, but not necessarily for the reasons Frye suggests. He advocates that children as young as age two should be immersed in nonsense verse because his own spirit demands it just as his spirit later demands the wish-fulfilling fairy tale. Chukovsky reasons that "topsy-turvy" poems filled with incongruities such as

> He rode on a dapple wagon
> Tied to a wooden horse.[3]

are a means of clarifying the world of reality to the child because the imaginary sharpens the norms of the real world when placed in juxtaposition. Both writers point out that fanciful literature helps to develop the powers of the imagination. Frye, pursuing this theme, explains the difference between art and science as they relate to the use of language. He says:

> Perhaps on this basis, (i.e. the literary language of poems and novels vs. the language of practical sense) we can distinguish the arts from the sciences. Science begins with the world we live in, accepting its data and trying to explain its laws. From there, it moves toward the imagination: it becomes a mental construct, a model of a possible way of interpreting experience . . . Art, on the other hand, begins with the world we construct, not with the world we see. It starts with the imagination, and then works toward ordinary experience . . . You can see why we tend to think of the sciences as intellectual and the arts as emotional: one starts with the world as it is, the other with the world we want to have.[4]

The assumptions of Chukovsky and Frye make sense. Through observation one can see that the young child, like the intuitive artist, first structures his world, through his imagination, as he would like it to be. Later he arrives at a stage of realism (as characterized by the scientist) helping him to live and cope with the world as it actually is.

We find in Frye, the literary critic, and Chukovsky, the children's writer, three arguments for first starting with poetry at the elementary level and then moving on to imaginary prose before tackling other types of literature: (1) Structurally, poetry is the simplest of literary genre. A poem does not explain; it simply *is.* (2) Developmentally, the child needs to deal with the wish-fulfilling, imaginary world to clarify the world as it really is. Only then is he ready to discard the fanciful and move on to the real; and (3) Humanistically, imaginative literature develops creative power which permits the individual to construct, in Frye's words, "possible models of human experience."[5] This highly developed ability may later lead to breakthroughs in solving either human or scientific problems.

In analyzing final evaluations of teaching written by the Institute participants, the writers found that experientially many of them had verified the assumptions made by Frye and Chukovsky. A content analysis revealed these views as well as other significant observations which are summarized as follows:

1. Most children respond enthusiastically to poetry and rhythmical prose. Perhaps there is evidence to support Frye's contention found in *The Educated Imagination* that poetry should be the foundation of all literature teaching.

2. Folk literature and fantastical fiction seem to have the greatest appeal of all types of literary genre for the urban child.
3. If realistic fiction is employed with the urban young, it must possess realism related to the real life experiences of the child. It is only then that identification can take place.
4. Story selection is a critical factor in developing appreciation and enjoyment of literature. When using the newer works, the teacher should select those books that possess the same qualities as the timeless and ageless books (that is authenticity of theme, plot, and characterization).
5. When a teacher is sharing literature in a group experience with children, opportunities should follow for the youngsters to participate actively and expressively in response to the literary work. This is an intermediate step or the free and uncritical literary response that children make before they are able to verbalize in the abstract.
6. Children must encounter good literature in a meaningful and organized way.

Bringing together the theoretical assumptions of Frye and Chukovsky, the experimental data provided by the Institute participants and the writers' own knowledge, experience and insights, we offer the following as a rationale for developing elementary-school programs of literature:

Rather than beginning with informational prose and proceeding to the poetic forms of literature found in poetry, folklore, and fantastical fiction, we believe the curriculum should proceed from rich exposure to simple rhythmical poetry including nursery rhymes, the fairy and folk tale, and modern fiction fantasy. Given this foundation, children are ready to move to realistic prose. We are saying that at the primary school level children should be immersed first in poetry, folklore, and fantasy by providing sufficient samples rather than by a systematic treatment of samplings from a range of literary genre. Here is where the writers might differ with the Nebraska Curriculum Center in their emphasis on providing structured study in each of the literary genre from grade one onward. This is done to help the child develop a sense of structure for each literary type.

We are not saying that simple realistic prose (e. g. the informational picture book) should be excluded from the primary curriculum. Children do want to discover more about the world in which they live. Possibly our orientation, like that of Chukovsky, would focus on the child and his personal use of poetical language which he readily employs in his eagerness to describe feelingly the experiences he encounters in daily living. The child's language is poetic, therefore, the poetry of the poet is something he not only hears but reacts to with his senses because the imagery of poetry quickens the senses that are so very much alive in the growing child. Modern fantasy is a form of poetry and the poetry of folklore is a means of uncovering the nature of the child's physical and biological worlds. Poetry explores in depth for the child the great natural phenomena of wind, water, and wilderness. It provides satisfying answers to children's global questions such as "Who can see the wind?" After this, the child needs to be guided into prose that has natural rhythm comparable to the poetry he speaks. The informational type prose that is stilted, bookish, and not at all like the way he talks is an enigma to the child.

When teaching for appreciation it is necessary to allow children time to express overtly their responses through appropriate dramatic activities. When the child acts it out through many strategies, he is better able to find words for his thoughts and feelings and grasps intuitively the importance of theme, plot and characterization.

The authors are postulating that if youngsters are saturated in a particular literary genre, they will not only emerge with appreciation but also with an intuitive feel for the structure of a particular literary form. We are not advocating that they come up with structure perse but that they are able to detect some of the features that characterize a particular genre. We do not believe they are ready to extrapolate structural elements that are basic to a literary type. In other words, the major focus should be on appreciation and the by-product would be the child's own intuitive feel for the structure. The writers are of the opinion that some of the new curricula are pushing the child too quickly into a structured study of literature rather than releasing his aesthetic appreciation for literary works. The writers infer that Chukovsky is also saying children need imaginative literature for the feeding of their own souls.

With poetry and fanciful literature as the fundamental base at the primary school level, we should be able in the middle grades to build upon the genre of the folk tale and then move onward to realistic adventure, stories of other lands and people, and simple historical fiction and biography. They are now able to enjoy and understand the myth and fable as well. Although the emphasis will be proportionately greater in realistic prose, this does not infer that the imaginative poetic literature should be reduced at the expense of introducing children to the realistic prose forms. We need to strive for balance in literary materials in executing a literature program for the young.

In other words, we are taking the developmental point of view as emphasized by Chukovsky rather than the structural point of view as inferred by Frye. However these views are not mutually exclusive but, as pointed out earlier in this article, support each other. We are saying that the child should first of all enjoy literature of the kind he likes in a given point in his life cycle for what it can mean to him. Developmentally this coincides with the unfolding of literary structure so that structure also emerges as a by-product in the mind of the child but not as the primary focus.

In the period of curriculum reform, it is important that we direct our efforts to literature along with mathematics, science, and the social studies, if we are to formulate a vital humanities program for the elementary school. If we overlook this important aspect, the soul and spirit will be missing from the substance of the curriculum. The authors submit this proposal for the reader's critical examination as one possibility for engaging the child with life through the medium of literature.

51.
A-V Media Support Children's Literature

Susan Camp

Books are *in* and so is the use of other materials to develop a love for them. New dimensions in instruction have appeared with the development of audiovisual materials and equipment. The term *media center* or *learning center* is replacing the word *library* in many schools as more and more filmstrips, records, tapes, and films become part of the circulating collection of all media available to teachers and students.

Although it is hard for some librarians and teachers to realize, the medium doesn't determine whether a story, verse, or play is literature. It once needed to be a book, but the so-called "print culture" of the first half of the twentieth century is gradually being replaced by an "all-media culture." As proof, just as films and filmstrips are created from books, so are books being written from films and filmstrips.

The special advantage of the book is that it allows the child to create his own image of setting and action—of all media, books intrude least on the user. But because of this, as every librarian knows, they are also the most easily rejected. Many children need some outside incentive.

Media Guidelines

What sort of guidelines might be set up for the cooperative use of all media in supporting children's literature?

1. Do a variety of different things, and not always in the same order. Sometimes start with audiovisual media, but at other times start with the book.
2. Vary the size of your group. Often it will be the whole class, but at other times give children the option of attending, and use noontimes and after school for crossage experiences.
3. Always have the book at hand, with as many copies as possible available immediately afterward.
4. In addition to commercially produced audiovisual materials, develop your own or encourage children to make or collect them. Transparencies, puppets, and realia are all good motivators for reading.
5. Include related activities but don't force them. Role playing, singing, rhyth-

mics, and impromptu skits provide logical accompaniment, but they should be a natural part of the experience.

6. Make all media equally attractive. If children who see a film about a book go scot-free, while those who read the book have to write a report on what they read, they will equate the film with pleasure and the book with toil.

7. Use many forms of differentiated instruction. Seminars are excellent, so are small groups, and nothing beats a totally individual experience in hearing the spoken word.

8. Encourage spontaneous comments and actions from the children. Avoid being the dominant figure—let the audiovisual media and the book be paramount in the minds of the children.

Filmstrips

Filmstrips offer variety in the presentation of books for the primary grades, whether to introduce a new story or to present a new type of literature such as a fable. Weston Woods Studios produce many excellent filmstrips of well-known picture books using the illustrations from the books themselves. Sound filmstrips, or filmstrips with a companion record, are available; however, it is also effective to read the story from the booklet which accompanies the strip, or to tell it as the illustrations appear. One advantage to reading yourself is that timing is more flexible and can be varied to accommodate a particular group. If comments or discussion is forthcoming, there is no need to hurry on to the next frame.

Once children are familiar with a picture book, it is fun to show a filmstrip of the book and have them tell the story in their own words. Stories with much action and few words, or repetitive tales, lend themselves to this type of presentation. Books such as Maurice Sendak's *Where the Wild Things Are* (Harper, 1963) present the opportunity for the class to become actively involved. For example, during the "wild rumpus" scene in the filmstrip (Weston Woods), several children may act out their own "wild rumpus."

When showing a filmstrip with captions, such as one of the *Fables of Aesop* produced by Warren Schloat Productions, children may take turns in reading the captions. This kind of strip also lends itself readily to individual or small-group viewing.

Tapes and Records

Recordings of poetry readily spark an interest and appreciation for this art form. Spoken Arts has a record of John Ciardi's book *You Read to Me, I'll Read to You* (Lippincott, 1962), and I find that both boys and girls enjoy hearing Mr. Ciardi and his own children read poetry to each other. When using this record I often suggest that a few children read along with Mr. Ciardi or read aloud to the class after listening to a poem recited on the record. Transparencies made of a poem and flashed on the screen allow the entire class to read together.

Other recordings of poets reading their own works include *Robert Frost Reads His Poetry* and *Carl Sandburg's Poems for Children*, both available on Caedmon Records (Houghton Mifflin). A volume of poetry entitled *Miracles—Poems Written by Children of the English-Speaking World* (Simon and Schuster) has a companion record of the same title (also Caedmon).

Recordings are often effectively used as an extension of a previously stimulated situation. For example, *Jack Tales* (Folk Legacy Records, Inc.) is so authentic that the vernacular of the South Carolinian hillbilly may immediately cause the children to tune out unless they have previously heard or read the

Jack Tales and are aware of the setting. Hearing the recording after they have become familiar with the tales serves to enhance their appreciation and total understanding of this folk literature.

Many tapes of favorite children's stories and fairy tales are produced by Imperial International Learning. A set entitled *Palace in the Sky* contains twenty tapes of high quality, usable in many ways.

Taped interviews with well-known authors such as Eleanor Estes, Marguerite de Angeli and Marguerite Henry are available through the University of Michigan A-V Service. These can be used to introduce a group to an author and his works or as a follow-up after the author's books have been circulated and read by several in the class. They also provide information for author study reports.

Sometimes a musical recording related to a story or a book can enhance a literature experience. One of my favorite lessons consists of reading the picture book *John Henry* by Ezra Jack Keats (Pantheon), and following it with a musical interpretation. To hear this dramatic tale set to music is a thrilling experience and provides much active involvement of the children. They are quick to pick up some type of rhythmical activity such as clapping their hands or swaying to the music. It's fun, too, to appoint one child to be John Henry, swinging his mighty hammer to the rhythm of the music. On more than one occasion "John Henry" has become so involved that when the final climax of John Henry's dying is reached, he dramatically falls to the floor to imitate the death of that great steel-driving man. The best recording that I have found is from a new music series, *Exploring Music* (Holt, Rinehart and Winston).

In addition to listening to tapes, the making of a tape can be a very worthwhile experience for a class. A third grade worked together to produce a tape of Edward Lear's *The Scroobious Pip.* Some read solo parts while others joined in choral reading. As they made the tape the story became a part of the children. Indeed, in the last library period of the year, the class delighted everyone present by spontaneously bursting into a recitation of the story, which they had learned by heart.

Films

Films are an excellent medium for introducing children to literature. The Weston Woods productions of picture books such as *A Snowy Day* and *Mike Mulligan and His Steam Shovel* are extremely good. One unusual movie distributed by Weston Woods, *Alexander and the Car With the Missing Headlight,* won a first prize at the Venice Film Festival in 1966. In this original film, created by Peter Fleischmann, the illustrations were drawn by four- and five-year-old Parisians, the sound effects were produced by German children, and the story was narrated by children from the United States. In 1967, this film appeared in book form under the same title (Viking), using the illustrations from the film.

Other outstanding movies which I have used include "The Doughnuts" (Weston Woods), a humorous incident from Robert McCloskey's *Homer Price* (Viking), and National Film Board of Canada's production of *Paddle-to-the-Sea,* adapted from the book by Holling C. Holling (Houghton Mifflin). Each film authentically interprets the book and produces an incentive for reading.

The appreciation of poetry may also be augmented through the use of films. I know of no better way to introduce the poetry of Robert Frost than by showing Norwood Film's production *Robert Frost,* which provides the viewer an experience that is tantamount to roaming through the Vermont countryside. Filmed in the environment which inspired much of Frost's poetry, it shows Frost as poet and philosopher and reveals the depth of his poetry which he recites throughout.

Mary O'Neill's *Hailstones and Halibut Bones* (Doubleday), a small book of poems relating color to ways of feeling, has been produced on film by Sterling Educational Films. The recitation of the poems combined with animated drawings interpreting the poems results in a film worth showing to all age groups.

Films which acquaint children with the authors and illustrators and deal with the process of book production serve to inspire creativity. *The Story of a Book* (Churchill Films) shows each step that was used in writing, illustrating, and publishing Holling C. Holling's *Pagoo* (Houghton Mifflin). A Weston Woods film, *The Lively Art of the Picture Book*, introduces several artists of picture books which have won the Caldecott Award. A third-grade teacher showed this film to her class after having discussed and read many of the Caldecott books; then many of her children wrote and illustrated their own books. In a sixth grade a similar assignment proved most successful. Creative activities inspired by films are numerous.

Though this discussion of the uses of media relating to literature has been limited to group use, it should be emphasized that individual children benefit from and enjoy viewing and listening during their leisure time. Last year a fifth grader came many afternoons to listen to the Audio Book Company's recording of *Call of the Wild* and *Alice in Wonderland* while she read the books to herself. Very often children ask to listen to a record or a tape or to view a filmstrip just for their own enjoyment.

Problems to Consider

What difficulties might you expect? One question is how far to go. If you are showing a film based on a book, should you stop before the climax lest the child feel he doesn't need to read the book because he already knows what happened?

It has been my experience and that of teachers and librarians with whom I have worked that withholding the end is not wise except in unusual cases. If you are motivational in your presentation and the film or filmstrip is good, you don't need to worry that children will not read the book. For further proof, think how a popular movie stimulates book sales. The *Dr. Doolittle* film resulted in several new printings of the book.

A second consideration lies in differences between the book and the film or filmstrip—a different emphasis, an overstressed character, a setting not true to the author's intent. If the difference is too great, and you feel it is in poor taste, then of course you must make the decision not to show it. But I also utter a caution—the difference may be only that the visuals contradict *your* visual images. Also, children seem more able to handle these discrepancies than adults.

A third problem, more anticipated than real, is that the film or filmstrip can have a glamour that a book can't compete with. If this is true, then the only long-range answer would be to phase out books, but I have found that books are both compatible and competitive with all other media. Airports that show free movies report that far more people read while waiting for planes. So are children entranced with good books.

Yes, books are in and so is the use of machinery in developing a love for books. The impact of the multisensory presentation of worthwhile literature is indeed immeasurable.

B.

Composition

Writing is one of the most difficult of the language skills for the elementary school child. Many children who read well and have an excellent mastery of oral communication are not good writers. Other children who write reasonably well do not enjoy expressing themselves in writing and do so only when they feel a dire obligation.

Unfortunately, classroom methodology has contributed to the negative attitude that many children have toward written communication. In many instances the technical and mechanical skills of handwriting, spelling, punctuation, and capitalization have been overemphasized. The pressure of learning the skills of writing has frequently jeopardized its function as a medium of expression. These skills should not be allowed to get in the way of the idea, story, or tale which the child is attempting to express. Primary stress should be on content. Too much emphasis has been placed on "correctness" with little regard for the development of positive attitudes toward writing. Children have often been so burdened by the *how* of writing that the *why* has been lost and communication of experiences has been mired in anxiety for correctness.

Three basic guidelines should underlie the composition program of the elementary school. First, when children write there should be a real purpose for this written expression. It is imperative that the children recognize this purpose or need so that they have a genuine desire to participate in that particular activity. A second guideline should be that children must have something to write. Experience must precede expression. A child cannot be expected to create in a vacuum. Children who have had a background of rich experiences which were based on their individual interests and needs will seldom be at a loss for ideas to express. A third requisite for a successful writing program is that the children's products should be used. Something must be done with each written compositon when it is finished. Children should write for a larger audience than the teacher; their contributions should be shared with fellow classmates, posted on attractive bulletin boards, published in a school newspaper, or bound in a permanent classroom notebook.

The children need to see that their products serve some real purpose and that their ideas are being communicated to others, which is the basic reason for writing in the first place.

Various techniques and activities for developing a sincere interest in written composition are discussed in the articles of this section. Suggestions are given for reaching children with varying degrees of ability. Recommendations are made for establishing an atmosphere conducive to writing in the classroom. Many valuable tips are offered for giving guidance in creative writing.

52. Composition Through Literature

Eldonna L. Evertts

The elementary-school teacher who frequently reads quality literature to primary or intermediate pupils not only provides enjoyable listening experiences but contributes to their own satisfaction in composing stories. These listening opportunities build a reservoir or background of literary experience which the pupil uses not only in his own compositions but also for understanding how language functions.

Models in Literature

The rationale and early teaching units for grades K-12 from the Nebraska Curriculum Development Center reasoned that a curriculum should be approached through a study of literature. Literature, then, became the focal point for the study of language and composition. Composition was not isolated but was viewed as closely related to literature and language.

A similar view is held by Northrop Frye in his book *Design for Learning* (University of Toronto Press). He states that those who read widely are the best writers, with a complimentary relationship between literature and writing. Direct experience with literature and the study of models, together with the imitation of their structure and form in larger and smaller composition units—the whole composition and the sentence—should accompany the writing process.

Pupils become aware of the larger elements of structure in literary selections or stories through listening and discussing stories read aloud. Stories not necessarily within the child's own reading vocabulary can be enjoyed and appreciated if the teacher reads well orally and understands principles of literary analysis and criticism.

Old favorites as "The Story of Sleeping Beauty," "The Three Bears," "Cinderella," "The Lion and the Mouse," or "The Ant and the Grasshopper" illustrate the basic structural plot motifs of folktales. Paul Olson, co-director of the Nebraska Curriculum Development Center, identifies these motifs as follows:

1. The journey from home to isolation.
2. The journey from home to confrontation with a monster.
3. The rescue from a harsh home and the miraculous creation of a secure home.

Reprinted from *Instructor* 75:105-108 (March 1966), by permission of author and publisher.

4. The conflict between the wise beast and the foolish beast.

These motifs may seem an oversimplification of plot structure, but, they help young pupils recognize what "constitutes" a story, and they note the variations of these plots with interest and delight. Pupils who have gained a *gentle*, inductive approach to these concepts of plot motifs through many, many contacts with good literature are able to use the simple folktales as models for their own writing. Most elementary pupils attending the pilot schools in Lincoln, Omaha, and West Side Omaha, Nebraska, have produced excellent compositions at all elementary grade levels using this approach. Accompanying the writing of stories based on literature has been an oral sharing of these stories.

An understanding of the structure of literature is further explored by students in the junior high school with units on *The Making of Stories*, *The Meaning of Stories*, and *The Making of Heroes*. Units on *Satire*, *Comedy*, and *Tragedy* are a few of the many packets designed for high-school use. This Nebraska English program has been planned as a sequential, spiral curriculum with elements presented in simple fashion in the early grades and than reintroduced with increasingly sophisticated writings at later grade levels.

Sentences of recognized authors become models to help pupils understand how words can be strung together to form familiar patterns of English sentences. Primary pupils learn how words in simple sentences can be rearranged to form sentences of similar contrasting meaning and how to expand basic sentences. These activities are begun in the earliest units of literature with such stories as *Little Tim and the Brave Sea Captain* by Ardizzone and *Charlotte's Web* by E. B. White. By the time sixth-graders are studying *The Wind in the Willows* by Kenneth Grahame, they are able to understand the expansion of sentences by the compounding of the verb slot, the compounding of the object of the preposition, or the compounding of the preposition itself. After having been introduced to these sentence expansions in the elementary program, junior- and senior-high school students learn to develop the concept of the multilevel sentence in their composition and rhetoric units. Sentences which occur frequently in the literature that the teacher reads orally are discussed and analyzed.

Oral Composition

Oral composition and its interpretation has always been important to man. The tribal storyteller was esteemed because of his ability to describe customs and mores of his time entertainingly for the education of the young and the delight of the elderly. Even today the storyteller is popular with young and old alike.

The sincere, honest response of children to a tale well told is ample reward for the time and effort spent on its preparation. The small child in the kindergarden or the more mature elementary pupil both sense the feeling of his audience when he becomes a storyteller. If the selection is well organized and clearly stated, he gets approval. A rich and extensive vocabulary enables him to vary his sentences and to add interest to his tale. Oral storytelling should parallel written composition throughout the grades. No one ever outgrows the need for communicating orally and for achieving better communication between himself and his audience.

The Nebraska English Curriculum at the elementary level stresses the importance of many opportunities for oral interpretation. Pupils retell familiar tales and create original stories. They also dramatize these stories, create simplified puppet or marionette shows, and experiment with choric verse. Such activities extended over a school year provide firsthand experiences requiring a wide range of oral language experimentation.

Oral composition is the pathway from the passive enjoyment of stories created by others to the active enjoyment of one's own efforts. Written composition further involves the thought processes of oral composition and logically grows out of it.

Mechanical Skills

Technical and mechanical skills related to handwriting, spelling, punctuation, or capitalization should never get in the way of the idea, story, or tale which is being developed and written. Primary stress should be on content. Gradually a child learns how punctuation and spelling help transmit the content accurately to the reading audience.

In the Nebraska English Curriculum, no formal set of prearranged exercises or lesson plans in usage, spelling, punctuation, or capitalization are advocated. Rather, the teacher is advised to select skills which need to be taught to individuals, small groups, and the entire class, and to arrange her instructional program accordingly.

After reading written compositions, the teacher comments on the good ideas and notes mechanical skills that helped convey these ideas to the reader. Only then are pupils taught refinements of these skills to be used in further writing.

The teacher is advised to take time to build skills of handwriting and spelling as they are needed. She plans a program involving instruction and practice which contributes to growth in these skills by pupils.

The Writing Assignment

Creativity and imagination can be expressed in compositions based on literature that a class is reading. For example, while hearing *The Door in the Wall* by Marguerite de Angeli, a pupil may write a letter such as Robin might have written to his father who is fighting for the king. He can describe what has happened at the castle where he is serving as a page, experimenting as he writes, with the language characteristic of that period in history.

From the story of *Cartier Sails the St. Lawrence* by Esther Averill, can come letters or articles to the people back home in France describing some of the new foods, impressions of land forms, or unusual animals, written by make-believe members of the exploration party. Pupils enjoy assignments which provide opportunities to develop visual and auditory perceptions, the senses of touch and smell.

Competency in composition skills is not acquired through a single assignment, or a few units, nor can it be done within a specified period of time. Growth, rather, is sometimes slow and difficult to evaluate, but continued writing under the supervision of a sensitive, competent teacher encourages increased skills in written composition. Says an old Chinese proverb: "All the flowers of all the tomorrows are in the seeds of today."

53. Teaching Composition in the Elementary School

Mary J. Tingle

When the kindergarten child announces to the teacher, "I have a new baby brother," he has engaged in the whole complex process of composing: he has abstracted from his whole repertory of experiences something that is significant to him, he has identified the audience with whom he wishes to communicate; he has been motivated by a purpose—to inform, to establish rapport; he has chosen the language and syntax to convey his communication; he has received some kind of response to his communication and has, through it, made a judgment about its effectiveness in relation to his purpose and audience. If he is encouraged by questions or comments, he will expand his composition to include related details which, in his mind, belong to this experience. He has somehow categorized the elements of the experience and brought them together to serve his purpose.

The tendency to categorize, to bring order to his personal world, seems to be intuitive to a child. The process of categorizing begins as soon as the individual becomes aware of any two elements of his environment that seem to belong together—a soft voice and presence of another person, gentle handling and food, loud voices and discomfort. How the individual does this is a matter of theory, but at a very early age—how early we do not know—he can sort out aspects of his total environment, bring certain ones together as a focus for a response, and eliminate others. The infant, through nervous responses and sensory perceptions, begins the process of grouping his experiences and responding to sets of circumstances by behaving one way in one set of conditions and another way in another.

As he grows, he learns that adults organize things differently from the way he would do it. He learns that you put a cap on the head, but not a bowl of Pablum; you wash hands in water but not in milk; you eat a cracker, but not soap; you kiss your mother but not the puppy. All around him are models of behavior, situations in which certain kinds of behaviors go together. Most of the models are called to his attention on his initial contact with them, but gradually he begins to observe and imitate. He comes to realize that certain

---

From *Elementary English* 47:70-73 (January 1970).

things go together and make a unit of experience. He learns to make associations and differentiations; he learns that his experiences center about events—mealtime, bathtime, bedtime, storytime, the groupings of the routine day, and those of special occasions such as a visit to the grocery store or to grandmother's. He learns that events have beginnings, a main part, and a conclusion. A three-year-old girl watched her mother begin to clean up after her birthday party and said, "The happy birthday is all gone." For her this statement covered the beginning, the middle, and the end of an incident. The excitement of anticipation was gone, the surprise of opening packages was gone, the ice cream was gone. The significance of her simple statement is that she had identified a unit of experience. She could not retell the whole incident, but she was sensitive to the wholeness of it. A more mature person might have given an accurate report of it or drawn upon it for material for a personal essay, a satire, a bitterly realistic drama, or a poem. She could not do this, but someday in retrospect she may, for she had recognized the unitary nature of the experience.

By the age of two the child has learned the names of many items in his environment. He can see similarities among items to which a common term applies. He experiments, explores, talks, and questions, and as his range of experiences broadens, he develops confidence in making comparisons and in proposing cause and effect relationships through relating the unknown to the known. A young friend of mine explained that he put lightning bugs in the refrigerator because their tails were too hot. Chukovsky in his book, *From Two to Five*, cites many illustrations of children's attempts to express their perceptions:

> The ostrich is a giraffe bird.
> A turkey is a duck with a bow around its neck.
> Make a fire, Daddy, so that it can fly up to the sky and make the sun and stars.

These childish mistakes, delightful as they are to adults, are the child's serious and determined effort to bring order into his limited and fragmentary knowledge of the world. That the child attempts to classify objects of the material world and to compare them with other objects is evidence of his potential for flexible but orderly thought.

All that a speaker or writer has to draw upon for content of his composition is his own experiences, and all that he can do is present them as he sees them. They may be direct, vicarious, or imaginative, but in some way they become a part of him and he interprets their meaning to him whenever he chooses what he will tell about them. The teacher's responsibility in helping the learner broaden his base of choice lies in two directions: (1) to lead him to see in his experiences meanings that he has not previously seen and consequently to reevaluate their significance and (2) to open the way to new experiences.

The child may have to learn that he does have something to think, talk, or write about. He is a member of the human race and has participated in the affairs of a particular culture; he has only to recognize the significance of everyday experiences to have a limitless source of ideas to think and talk about. In addition to sharing the common experiences of mankind, he has had experiences that are peculiarly his own; he has perceptions that give particular meaning to his experiences; he is unique: he is a very special person with very special things to say.

However exhausting to adults may be the endless why, how, and what-does-it-do questions of three and four year olds, it is probable that the nature of the adult responses at this time determines the extent to which the child believes that the world is worth exploring, thinking about, and talking about. Without these beliefs he is not likely to learn either to talk or to write very well—certainly not as early as he might and perhaps never.

As the child grows through the experiences of infancy, he also develops a command of language. At first he is in a world of undifferentiated sounds, but from this mass of sound, some emerge as significant: footsteps, closing of a door, speech sounds associated with activities related directly to him. He makes sounds and finds that some of them are more important than others because they evoke responses that are consistent and meaningful. As conceptualization of experiences progresses, he develops a vocabulary and a grammar through which he can express his understandings. By the age of thirty-six months some children can produce most of the major varieties of English simple sentences up to a length of ten or twelve words. They have control of the common kernel sentences of the English language and are rapidly learning the transformations that can be derived from them.

The language the child uses is the language that he can use—whatever it is, it is all he has. It is a part of him. He learns it from the people who make his childhood world; through it he is able to establish himself as a member of the group that affords him all of the security that he knows, and if it enables him to live comfortably within his group, he has every reason to believe that it is the language valued by everyone.

When the child comes to school where everyone is not like him and where his language is not the only language spoken, he may become sensitive to the difference or he may be subjected to criticism by his peers and possibly by his teacher. Since he has no alternative language and therefore no way to meet the demands of his critics, he is reduced to silence, to active resentment, or to recurring frustrations, none of which is likely to lead to fluency in the use of language. If, however, he can be respected as a person who has something to say, just as everyone does, and as a person who uses the dialect of the community, just as everyone does, his interest and pleasure in communicating his ideas will make it reasonable to him to learn standard dialect so that his range of communication can encompass people other than those with whom he lives; he will be willing to risk experimenting with composition.

So when the child comes to school he brings with him the foundations for growth in the composing process: a background of experiences, the ability to make association and discriminations, a vocabulary through which either literally or metaphorically he can express a wide range of meanings, a knowledge of the syntax of the language, and the ability to use all of these in simple oral compositions. We as teachers must take him from there.

Basic to the child's growth in composing is the development of sensitivity to a unit of experience—the beginning, the development, and the conclusion. There are several procedures that seem useful in developing this process.

(1) Retelling well-structured stories.

The child that has had contact with good literature all of his life has had a model of how man shapes his thoughts. He becomes sensitive to order, to sequence, to climax and to ending.

When he reads stories like "The Three Little Bears" he is able to retell the story by recognizing the parts of the story, the sequence of actions, and the repetition that ties one incident to another. The structure is obvious enough to become a pattern in the child's thinking, and he can relate the story. He is composing and producing an oral composition but under conditions of minimal demand because the entire story is already a part of his consciousness, the structure is ready-made, much of the language is already available to him, and he knows when he has completed the story.

As students grow older and the literature that they read becomes more complex, the teacher can help improve the skills of composition—oral and written—by teaching students the conventional structures of literature and helping them to recognize the ways in which an author composes a story, shows relationships, and chooses language to express his ideas.

(2) Developing compositions in structured situations.

Giving some cues to the structure of a story and yet permitting freedom in response to the cues enables a child to use his own judgment in shaping a sequence and selecting details but he does not have to determine the structure. A teacher can provide such situations through using pictures about which stories can be told, stopping at a crucial point in a story that the teacher is reading and asking children to tell what they think will happen, asking children to watch a pet and tell what he did, asking children to tell the story about a picture they have painted.

(3) Developing compositions in unstructured situations.

The child has the freedom to choose his subject, develop his own plan for telling the story, and tell it in his own way. The sharing periods are such situations. The teacher has the opportunity to ask questions and make comments that can help the child recognize relevant information that may be added, supply kinds of details that will help the audience see, feel, hear more than he has provided or help him devise a suitable conclusion.

Thus far I have talked about the child at the pre-writing stage; however, much of our concern in schools is about teaching written composition.

By the time a child is ready to learn to write, he can talk very well. If he has had many contacts with good literature and has had many opportunities to talk, both under the carefully planned direction of a teacher, he has begun to understand what a person does when he makes a composition.

Between his skill in telling a story and in writing the story equally well is the necessity for learning to make letters, to put them together in special arrangements, and to design those arrangements in special ways. Learning to manipulate a pencil is a laborious and tension-producing experience. Learning to move the pencil fast enough to catch a thought is impossible. Thoughts have to be slowed down to accommodate the pencil. Perhaps success in accomplishment of writing is sometimes adequate compensation to the child for the loss of the fluency which is his in oral composition; however, the time spent in learning to write (and also learning to read) should not substitute, in the child's experiences, for time spent in talking and in hearing and responding to literature. His ability to think, to organize his thoughts, and to verbalize them should be at the highest level possible when the time comes that he has sufficiently mastered the skills of writing and of reading to use them without having them interfere with his intellectual growth. This means that probably through the first, second, and third grades, and for some children longer, the program in composition must include extensive, well-planned experiences in oral composition through which the child can experiement with organization and vocabulary in ways that let him stretch his intellectual capacities to his limits without the restrictions of handwriting, punctuation, and spelling. Paralleling this are experiences in writing that are leading to the time when the written composition is as satisfying to the child as are his oral compositions.

54. Writing Poetry in the Elementary School

Moira Dunn

Poetry has been defined as "the best words in the best order." It can be thought of also as a story succinctly told; or as a truth, a little philosophy or observation of life; or that it combines some of the finest ingredients of language.

So it would be only the most churlish of us who would fail to recognize the necessity of poetry in education. Let us consider its value to children.

a) It can tell a story, read silently or listened to as stories are (E. Farjeon's "Absolutely Nothing").

b) It has the humor of verse and doggerel (Lewis Carroll's "Jabberwocky").

c) Its imagery encourages imagination (Walt Whitman's "The Stallion").

d) There is pleasure in its rhyme and rhythm (de la Mare's "Off the Ground").

e) There is excitement in dramatic poetry (W. Scott's "Lochinvar").

f) It sets a standard in writing succinctly and beautifully.

In her poetry lesson the teacher may include listening, speaking, discussion, and drawing or dramatic activity.

But the subtle values of poetry can also be exploited when they are presented spontaneously. Children love the unexpected. Some poems naturally blend in with a prevalent theme. In nature, for instance, one could cite "Sea Shell," "Rabbits," "Little Brown Seed," "White Fields." An example for history might be Auden's "What is that sound which so thrills the ear?" "Pine Trees" and "Once you have slept on an Island" in geography. Or, apart from particular lessons, during a general classroom discussion, there may come to mind a poem which would throw new light on the subject. Poetry can be a contrast with previous activity; it may even be listened to more avidly because of this. Towards the end of the afternoon, a painting lesson over perhaps, the children would enjoy the humor of Eleanor Farjeon's "Wheelbarrow." It is essential that the teacher have a personal collection of poems always available so that suitable ones can be found quickly.

Through familiarity children come to sense what is poetry. They have a knowledge of its variety of theme and form. And they grow to realize, perhaps unconsciously, how it can vividly and sensitively express their thoughts and

---

emotions. Poetry can bring to the surface and air for us feelings and ideas which we only dimly realized we had. This seems to suggest that some of our thoughts can be best expressed in poetry—in fact may *only* be expressed so.

How then can poetic expression in children be engendered and achieved? And how can this be a natural expression for, "if poetry comes not as naturally as the leaves to a tree, it had better not come at all."

We assume first that children recognize what is poetry, and that this recognition could be geared to their own writing. We can use five points as a basis of approach:

1. theme
2. mood
3. discussion
4. teacher-involvement
5. setting down.

1. Theme

Any *theme* which the teacher feels will lend itself to poetic expression can be used. Aspects of life important to children like holidays, fire, people, water, the fair, shopping, animals, the sea and traffic may be suitable. Weather (wind, sun, rain, snow, storms) and the seasons can be exciting to children and provide ideal themes. Conditions and incidents arising spontaneously from school life may also provoke and inspire.

Barbara writes of "The Horse."

With his velvet muzzle
And his well-groomed coat,
And his graceful head
And his soft coat,
The horse loved by all men
Lies peacefully in the field.
See him canter, see him trot,
See him gallop round the field
With his graceful head held high
Like a king he proudly gallops by
I wish he was mine, the horse.

The teacher must be alive to the possibilities inherent in situations and judge for herself whether or not certain themes are apt for poetry-writing. She must recognize that in some instances a poetic interpretation would be unsuitable; yet in others it may be the only possible medium. [Indeed, sometimes the child could himself choose between writing prose or poetry.]

2. Mood

Our second point in this basis of approach is *mood*. This must go hand in hand with theme. Poetry has been said to "take its origin from emotion recollected in tranquillity." And so one can find with children that some situations (like storms) are best "recollected in tranquillity." Sometimes in life we need to "sleep on it" to get our ideas and attitudes into perspective.

Teachers become sensitive to the mood of children and know the importance of catching the right moment. Sometimes an opportunity has to be seized quickly as theme and mood simultaneously present themselves; or a theme may need to be contained until the right mood exists. Some poetry to be quoted was written immediately following a movement lesson. Aspects of movement had been explored and this led on naturally to discussion of the theme in the classroom. The previous physical activity engendered ideas which threw open the door to a deeper appreciation of movement as a whole. And in writing on this theme each child interpreted it in his own way.

Anthony wrote:

As the flowers gently sway
As the clouds fly away
As the sea breaks away
The sun rises in the sky,
Night has gone
And,
Day has come.
As you get out of bed
You stretch and twist and turn your head,
You go down the stairs very slowly.

On one occasion "Color" fell easily into a prevalent mood and situation. On a bright spring day, when the classroom looked particularly colorful and after an art lesson had taken place, the significance of color in our lives was discussed. The right conditions and mood prevailed and were exploited, to write on this theme. Sometimes the teacher may choose a theme and then foster a mood. There may be a discussion about old people in which she points out that though years may bring wisdom they also bring incapacity. She can call upon the children's sympathy, respect, pity, consideration, helpfulness; for these initiate awareness, which is the stuff of poetry.

3. Discussion

Two points have been noted so far: our concern with theme and with mood. Our third concern is with *discussion*.

Discussion engenders thought and thought engenders emotion and emotion creates more thought. This is invaluable to children because they are challenged to examine their own ideas and have respect for others. There is a pooling of experiences and opinions. So there can emerge from children discussing, a kaleidoscopic view of a subject. There may be words jotted down in books, there will be words on the board, and there will be ideas simply voiced. After absorption in a theme by everyone, each child then creates his own conception of it. This is how Jaqueline interpreted "Color."

The color of birds
Their yellow beaks
And beautiful wings,
The cockatoos white crests
On their proud heads,
The color of green leaves
And the fresh grass,
The clouds are sometimes silver
And sometimes smoky grey,
The rainbow and its wonderful mauve,
Milk as white as snow,
The giraffe's yellow and black neck,

Horses dappled and brown,
Dogs and cats black and white,
The orange and yellow of the sunset,
Artists pictures are full of color.

4. Teacher-Involvement

Our fourth consideration is *the involvement of the teacher* at the stage of discussion. She has a delicate role to play. A balance has to be struck between the immediate spontaneous response of children and the teacher's unobtrusive generation of deeper and wider complexities. She can remind of texture, touch, smell, strength, fragility, excitement, power, humor. She can "stimulate the inward eye." Heightening of awareness we also seek and the teacher can nurture this. We want children to observe with thought; not to see just a building but also its height, color, construction, age, usefulness. Teacher involvement then implies attempting to stimulate ideas, develop the "inward eye" and heighten awareness. These, together with the children's own naturalness and spontaneity can be infused into their writing. The expressing of emotions must seem as natural as to feel them.

So, through theme, mood and discussion the teacher is contriving opportunities for poetic expression.

5. Setting Down

With point five we reach the actual *writing down* of poetry. Here there is but one simple guide; *each new thought begins with a new line.*

Nothing more need be stressed. From their familiarity with poetry as a whole the children sense the general truth of this. There is freedom in writing down ideas in simple lines. Indeed, expression and motion can drown in the sheer pedestrianism of prose; but live and glow in the vivid flashes and spontaneity of poetry. The elusive idea can be captured in a few words. Less able children respond surprisingly well to poetry-writing perhaps because of this freedom. Without rambling they write down simply what they think and feel. And they are not restricted by grammatical rules.

The Importance of Truth

There are two aspects of truth in poetry. The first is the obvious one that a statement should be factually correct. It has been said that "poetry is certainly something more than good sense, but it must be good sense at all events." Truthfulness needs stressing to children because they, like adults, can sometimes luxuriate in the sounds of words without understanding their meaning. And of course untrue statements can be made in all innocence. The second aspect of truth in poetry is rightness of expression or beauty of expression. One would not ask children to write something "beautiful," but one can point out particularly attractive passages in poems. They are said to be examples of truth—just the right words chosen to say something—an idea written rather beautifully. In this way we hope to inject self-criticism in children while still retaining their spontaneity. And we are setting standards towards which they may strive.

Barbara wrote on "The Stream":

The smooth tranquil water
In all its beauty

Flows before me
Agile fairies
Gently stepping lightly over the turquoise ripples.
Now it is night, and all that is left
Of the beautiful stream
Is an inky pool of black water
Stretching as far as I can see.
Gone are the delicate ripples,
Gone like a ghost
Like something in a dream.
Now the moon will shine
Down on the black dull water,
The stream is a silvery color
Like a miracle.

Hearing this poem the children acknowledged its rightness of words, its truth. Barbara has naturally and sensitively used metaphor. She has intuitively sensed its aptness. It seems that children do, of their own volition, find out these poetic "mannerisms" or "devices."

Most of the poetry the children come across in their general reading is in regularly rhythmic and rhyming verses. This is pleasurable to the ear and children will imitate its style. But adherence to formality, particularly in rhyming, can restrict spontaneity and flow. It is not superficial juggling with words that we seek but a maturing and enriching of individual style. The child must feel encouraged to write freely and not be hide-bound by rules. If, in spite of this freedom, he still writes in rhythmic and rhyming verses, it is usually done successfully. His discipline has been self-imposed.

Repetition can be effective in poetry though it can be used simply because of lack of ideas. If the teacher finds instances of this latter she may wonder whether or not to point out the failing. She could praise the poem as a whole but indicate that a certain part doesn't seem to fit in well, and perhaps needs a little more thought. Children know themselves where they have or have not succeeded.

Alan was happy with the simple rhyme and repetition of his "Flight":

A bird is great for its flight,
A bird can fly up to a great height,
A bird can soar and hover up high,
I should think it would be lovely to be able to fly.
A bird can look on all that's below,
A bird is free, free to go,
A bird can fly high in the sky,
I should think it would be lovely to be able to fly.

In our appreciation of poetry we can feel close to the poet and enriched by his wisdom, his highlighting of a truth, his philosophy of life. Picasso said that arts create "weapons of war against brutality and darkness." We can override inhumanity and ignorance with sensitivity and truth. Poetry at its finest does this and is, in a simple way, recognized and respected as such by children. If they reveal a little wisdom in their own writing, the teacher has a gift.

Margaret (2) observes that "Color is in the nature of every day." Howard pinpointed a truth when he wrote:

Birds have the secret of flight.

And Maxine writing of trees says:

The heavy bulk taken only by the trunk
So the tall twisted branches are free.

Jaqueline (1) tells us that:

Animals and humans move to be useful
Or just to please themselves.

Kevin writes:

You feel free, when you move.

Elaine writing of the tide says,

Every day this action is the same
No one will stop it,
Ever.

In the poems quoted we have seen use of metaphor, simile, rhyme, rhythm, imagery, alliteration, repetition, contrast and comment on life; and the children have done this with no prompting. They have, admittedly, been influenced by poems read to them, but in their own writing have instinctively chosen satisfying phrases to convey ideas. It would seem that the teacher must simply bring about right situations; the children will do the rest. She can provide the instruments but the children will make the music.

The poem written, the subject is dismissed; but temporarily because children value individual discussion with the teacher on their work. They want to have correctly-spelled words and their intention to be clear. And, essentially, they need and delight in appreciation. Final copies of poems, perhaps illustrated, should be accessible for reading at leisure.

The teacher will find in children's writing instances of poetry verging on prose and prose verging on poetry. It does not matter; that the child expresses himself as best he can is our only concern. Certainly it is impossible to gauge any influence that poetry-making may exert on other writings. But with its call for succinctness, spontaneity, imagery, and beauty of expression, these qualities may also be injected into prose.

In concluding, perhaps it may be said that if poetry writing in school has some success, then its values are synonymous with those for poetry as a whole. "Setting of a standard in writing succinctly and beautifully" may be its greatest merit, for this is what we seek in all writing. Indeed, if children writing poetry are attempting to create its values and if this has influence on other writings, then standards are being set and striven for in the whole realm of language.

55.

Encouraging Talented Children to Write

Alvina Treut Burrows

Tell me, where is fancy bred,
Or in the heart, or in the head?
How begot, how nourished?
—William Shakespeare,
The Merchant of Venice

Three hundred years after the Bard posed these questions, we are still searching for their answers. Many of us believe that fancy—or imagination, or creativity—is bred in *both* heart and head. Affect and intellect appear to sustain each other in bringing fancy into form, whether to be seen or heard or felt.

Though we may know comparatively little about how fancy is *begot*, we do know a respectable number of things about how it is *nourished*. Creativity in children is nourished by contact with supportive people and by a richly invigorating environment. Gifted and less well endowed children as well respond productively to encouraging human companions and to materials that both suggest ideas and respond to their ideas.

To cite some of the ways in which people and things spark creative enterprise in the elementary classroom and to give some special attention to the needs and potentials of verbally gifted youth will be the two purposes of this article.

Stimulating All Children to Write

Almost every report on teaching procedures that have produced many original responses has highlighted the necessity of the teacher's respecting individuals. Differences are to be valued, not regretted. It is important to show warm approval for the honest efforts of children who are exploring many ways of expressing their ideas. Trying a new technique of characterization or planning a surprise ending for a story is far better for a child's growth than writing a smooth imitation of an already written tale. Courage to invent must be supported.

Reprinted from *Education* 88:31-34 (September-October 1967), by permission of author and publisher, The Bobbs-Merrill Company, Inc.

As important as the cultivation of individuality is the task of establishing communication among individuals. Children paint pictures to be seen; they produce plays to be viewed; they write to be heard, or read, or both. They want —and need—the face-to-face responses of their associates.

Developing one's ego is a pervasive task throughout the elementary school years, and the responses of one's peers are as essential to a positive feeling about oneself as is the approval of power-wielding adults. Hence, the creative teacher conditions the class audience to look for opportunities to give honest approval.

It is far more productive to note the techniques that hold audience attention, that pique curiosity, that present sensory detail than to look for what is poor. Imitative phasing, pointless exaggeration, flatly repetitive statements when ignored in the brief time available for comments after hearing children's stories are likewise ignored in further writing. Focusing upon honest and colorful expression, upon movement and suspense, upon varied and pleasing sentence forms used in a story immediately upon hearing these elements of style reinforces them when the learners are most vulnerable. It is the principle of almost instant reinforcement that the supportive teacher applies in orienting classwork toward creativity. Comments upon parts that were alive, that made us "hear the roar of the waves," or "scared us with the buzz of a thousand angry hornets" help to increase sensitivity to vivid communication for both writer and audience.

We have long wondered why reading aloud seemed a more potent use of a story for teaching purposes than posting it, even in glamorous trappings. Now that we know more about immediate reinforcement and more about the power of oral, face-to-face language than even a decade ago, we can be quite certain that this experience is valid teaching, not mere entertainment.

In addition to these teaching-learning situations, children also need to savor literature read aloud by their teacher, read aloud by individual children, read silently, often and by everyone, read and recited chorally by groups and by the whole class. Stories and poems should be enjoyed and talked about; they should at times be examined briefly for what makes them strong and clear and memorable. Children who are trying to hold their listeners are acutely sensitive to the techinques and the style used by fine authors. They are open to learning from the great and near great whose works they hear because they are not on the defensive about their own writing. Children who feel their own success can learn from the success of others.

Once writing has become established as one of the ways to enjoy one's own efforts, little direct stimulus is needed. However, when the urge to write has been supplanted by other pressures for a considerable time, it can often be reawakened by one of a number of activities. Reading aloud some of their old stories, playing "out loud" with new adventures for Paul Bunyan or Ulysses or for our modern Space Heros, scribbling new tricks for a mischievous pet, and best of all adopting a set of animal characters to write about—these and other story starters often get lagging authorship moving again into enthusiastic production.

The foregoing conditions and procedures for fostering invention and fluency nurture the talents of all children. The work of the writer is his—to be shared and enjoyed but not to be taken apart or negated. Individuals are not queer because they like to write or paint or compose music. Audiences are receptive, but they need not assume synthetic delight with everything they hear. Approval is given, not in general, but to a powerful phrase, to a surprising but appropriate episode, to the poem's refrain that holds several verses together. Both intellectual and social-emotional factors operate in the communication between author and listener.

Special Needs of the Gifted Pupil

Risks of conforming to the ideas of others are greatest for those whose ideas are the most unique and daring. Whether the strongly gifted child needs authoritative approval less than does the more nearly average is not clearly established. Even if he is more self sufficient, it is essential that he be strengthened rather than punished for his autonomy. Hence, the teacher needs to be aware of the risks of non-conformity to ensure the optimum productivity of gifted pupils.

Further, the highly original child may himself be concerned at times about his "crazy ideas," whether he or his associates apply the derogatory term. It is important to defend the fantasy life of children; it is also important for them to check many of their ideas. It is this testing against some grid of reality that helps to distinguish between aberration and healthy imagination.[6] Fortunately elementary school children can and should try out their inventions in many media. The test of a new way of setting wings on a glider is readily observable. The success or failure of a new way of mixing colors can be seen. Finding out for sure what does work and what does not work is a healthful discipline.

In writing, however, highly subjective elements of personal judgment enter the testing. Here, as in other realms of esthetics, the work of art belongs to the artist. No one is required to like or dislike a total product. Looking for what is clear, convincing, and colorful helps both writer and hearer to focus upon those elements that communicate most effectively. It is highly unusual for even a gifted child to withdraw from the satisfaction of holding an audience of his peers. But a few children do so withdraw, and their wish not to read a poem or story aloud must be respected.

At times, a very able writer is so far beyond the capacity of his peers that little of what he writes engages them. Here the teacher must offer extra response to the more mature style and substance than the class can appreciate. Occasionally, it is wise to arrange for the gifted pupil to read to an older class or to a group of interested and able children from various classes. And the reward of collecting his stories in a book of his own making adds further satisfaction to the prolific writer whose work is beyond the horizons of many of his classmates.

In addition to protecting a gifted child from conformity of various sorts, it is likewise necessary to protect him from school expectations that he has an obligation always to do better than others. Few strictures freeze output more than a sense of duty. Moreover, we have some research evidence that the superior adult writer varies more in quality from time to time than does the less able.[7] We have no research evidence on this variation among children, but we have case studies of children that bear out this truth about adults.[8] Here is yet another area in which careful research is needed.

Still another characteristic of many, though certainly not all, highly creative youngsters is their tendency to be all-concerned with what they write, not with neatness and other externals. The cluttered desk, the smudgy paper are likely to accompany zeal for "the greatest story yet." How much correct form should these children apply? Certainly the minimums, but not at the expense of fluency of imagination. When a report or other piece of factual writing is to be displayed, then it must be edited, corrected, and copied. Letters must be in good form before they are sent. For the young pupil, the teacher can write or type the last fatiguing lines if need be.

Stories are to be read aloud and should be enjoyed, then filed in private folder or portfolio. They remain private and need not be corrected. More is to be gained for the pupil's originality by his using this time for more writing, more painting, more dramatics. From many experiences in editing and rewriting communications to be *seen* by others the pupil learns the realistic standard that public writing must be corrected but that private writing need not be.

Human Relations Can Foster Creativity

To further the creativity of all children can be one of the joys of teaching. To sense the energy released and the satisfaction engendered by invention is to sense the joy of communication in a common endeavor. When such common endeavor includes the unique responses of many individuals, then a true community of feeling and of intellect has come into being. In such a community the gifted as well as their associates can reach toward the stars.

56. Fostering Creative Expression

Elizabeth Hunter

While there is some argument about whether or not creativity can be "taught," there seems to be no question that this aspect of human capability can be encouraged and nurtured. This article will not delve into the differences and similarities of meaning between the words "encourage" and "teach" but will suggest specific methods and ideas which teachers can use with children to foster creative written and oral expression. It is undoubtedly true that a rigid and stultifying classroom, where only the teacher's way of doing things is "right," will discourage creative expression on the part of children. In addition to providing an accepting classroom environment in which participation in planning is encouraged, alternatives are recognized, and children's ideas and feelings have worth, teachers need to give children quite specific help with speaking and writing ideas.

Some teachers attempt to create a mood for writing by playing music, reading poetry or displaying "lovely" paintings; and while this may encourage some children, others find themselves with the same dearth of ideas after the mood experience as before. Other commonly used means to further children's writing consist of giving such assignments as: write a story of what you did over the weekend or, simply, write a story. Since many children do not know how to make commonplace happenings interesting and are at a loss for story ideas, they do not find these instructions helpful. Directions such as: "Think of an appropriate title, start in a way which will capture the reader's interest, make sure the central portions are sequential and logical and finish up with an interesting paragraph," will also leave many children where they started—without ideas which they can get hold of and with little knowledge of how to proceed.

How, then, can teachers help children express themselves with originality and imagination? How can a teacher foster creative expression? Three categories need to be considered.

(1). Children need help with ideas for plot and content.

(2). Children need language help: increasing the effectiveness and range of words and learning new and interesting ways of sending messages.

(3). While utilizing the first two categories, children need help with process—

From *Childhood Education* 44:369-373 (February 1968). Reprinted by permission of Elizabeth Hunter and the Association for Childhood Education International, 3615 Wisconsin Avenue, N.W., Washington, D.C.

methods of getting started, of gathering and examining ideas and words and exchanging them with others.

The last category will be discussed first.

Process Help

Many children have little idea of how to get started with stories or poems and not much past experience to draw upon, even though they may be in the intermediate grades. One useful way to help children begin is to do some whole-class writing; that is, the teacher takes over the mechanics of writing while the class talks out the ideas and plot. The teacher may participate as a group member and act as secretary as well. Rather than use the chalkboard, in this kind of exercise, the teacher may jot down ideas on a pad of paper as they come forth and later transfer the finished product to chart paper, the chalkboard, or hexographed sheets. In this stage, much can be talked and re-talked—plot ideas and language to be used—without making final decisions. No final product need be written out; it can be talked and left at that. After all, stories were handed down orally for generations, both before the development of writing and before large numbers of people could read.

The teacher will want to be accepting of all ideas at this stage, neither criticizing nor praising, but utilizing such verbal behavior as, "That's one idea." "Would someone like to add to Jack's idea?" "All right." "You're suggesting then, that the old man should be a kind person." "That's another thought." The use of praise or rejection discourages the variety and number of contributions, for children will try to outguess the teacher about what is *good* and, therefore, *right*. Negative criticism should probably be non-existent at this stage and even later in the year as criteria are developed. It is wiser to encourage progress through positive means: "Might you have asked a question at that stage?" "Is there any possible ending which might permit the boy to give up the puppy in another way?" "A bit of conversation might be useful at this point." To be avoided are negative comments: "Your language is not very colorful." "Your ending is poor."

The class may continue to work as a total group from time to time throughout the year, at the same time that they begin to work as individuals and in small groups. Working in small groups is fruitful for exchanging ideas. The group may compose stories or poems together or merely meet to talk and then separate to write individually. Again, there need not be writing at all; talk can be the means and the final product, especially where writing skills are far below verbal skills. In nursery school and kindergarten children, of course, cannot write, but throughout the grades the mechanics of writing may inhibit creative expression.

When teachers are somewhat hesitant about putting children into groups because they have not had this kind of classroom experience and do not know how to work in small group situations, it may be wise, after some initial whole-class experiences, for the teacher to work with one group of perhaps five to eight children, while the rest of the class observes. This might be done several times, with different pupils participating. Next, one group might work by itself while the rest of the class is involved in something else, then a second group can be added, and so on. When the total class is working in small groups, the teacher will want to be available for help, moving from group to group as the need arises. Groups may be made up of only two pupils, if this seems most feasible, and again, the partners may exchange ideas and then work on their own; they may work together in the actual writing, or they may just talk their ideas and not write at all.

Plot and Content Ideas

Children may have few resources for actually tapping their thoughts and need, at least in the beginning, "pump primers." The sources for ideas are many. Thought-provoking pictures (as differentiated from "lovely" pictures) are valuable. Pictures which show people, particularly children, in varying moods and situations—pictures which provoke speculation—can be helpful in stimulating pupils' writing and speaking. Teachers may want to collect folders of such *story idea* pictures.

Many specific assignments may be used as starters. The following list is indicative of the variety of plot suggestions and "pump primers":

- Tell or read a story to the class and stop at a logical point, letting the children supply a variety of endings. Then examine the author's ending.
- Read or tell a story in its entirety and then invent other possible endings.
- Make up sad or happy endings for the same story.
- Extend the adventures of the characters in a story which the children know.
- Write a novel, or serial, using the same key characters, perhaps persons known to the class.
- Tell the beginning and end of a story and let the children speculate on a variety of middles. Then examine the central portion of the original story.
- Make up stories from the viewpoint of another character in the story; for example, from the point of view of the wolf in *Red Riding Hood*, the stepsisters in *Cinderella*, the giant in *Jack and the Beanstalk*, the rat in *Charlotte's Web*. The task ordinarily would be to make these characters more sympathetic without changing the essential storyline.
- Speculate about some "ifs": "What would it be like if I were an only child?" or, ". . . if I had ten brothers and sisters?" "What if our teachers could only say 'yes'?" "What if there were no schools?" "If I could be any animal I chose, what would I want to be?"
- Make up myths: why Santa wears a red suit; why the witch flies on a broomstick; why we cry when we're sad instead of laughing.
- Provide beginning sentences or portions of beginning sentences: "Suddenly I knew the reason why no one would look at me." " 'Stop, Stop,' I yelled." "The little boy cried so hard he thought he would never stop." "Everything looked marvelous, but then I realized that something was dreadfully wrong." "Jane's mother would never let her . . ." "When the colt tried to run away he . . ." "I was really mad because . . ." "My perfect friend would be someone who . . ."
- Provide ending sentences: "And that's why the two girls never spoke to each other again." "Well, after that I never loaned my bicycle to anyone again." "And so the catastrophe had a happy ending after all—I think!"
- Make up stories incorporating certain words: a teacher, a bug and a motorcycle; a bear, a bowl of fruit and a book; a spaceman, a candy bar and an overcoat.
- Put objects into paper bags and ask the children to invent stories about them. The bags might include: a pencil, a nail and a glove; a piece of paper, a picture and a pair of eyeglasses.
- Pretend that inanimate objects can speak and make up stories utilizing their conversation: "What does my math book say about me after I've gone home?" "What does our chalkboard think about us?" "What does my bed say about me after I get up in the morning?"

Children can begin to work on their own ideas and suggest ideas to others, more or less gradually depending upon individuals and classroom make-up.

The teacher will want to be ready to provide plot and content help when necessary throughout the year.

Plot and content ideas should probably be worked on first, with much emphasis on the outpouring and exchange of ideas. The language to be used can be worked out after the content ideas are somewhat arranged. While some children and some classes need more process help than others, all children need varying degrees of continuing assistance in gathering, examining and exchanging ideas.

Language Help

Once children are helped with ideas or are able to draw upon their own store of experiences, they often become quite skillful in the area of plot and content sequence. However, they usually require help with language, to add interest to their work and make ideas more vivid and expressive. Children often do not realize that one reason why certain stories and poems are more interesting than others is because the author has used words well. Children tend to utilize the same rather limited store of words over and over, despite the fact that they own a more varied language supply. Creative expression assignments help increase word supplies.

Children will not necessarily know (to indicate one area of possible language help) that conversation can add interest to stories. Rather than use the actual spoken words of characters, they will tend to relate incidents without employing conversation. ("He told his mother he didn't want to go," rather than " 'Ma,' he said, 'I won't go to school, and I won't, I won't, I won't!' ") When using conversation they often rely heavily upon the verb *said*, usually placing it at the beginning of sentences. They can be helped to see that varying the position of the speaker's identification and the verbs used will increase the story's interest. (" 'Why won't you do it?' she asked. 'Because, if I do, then I'll miss the picnic,' he replied," rather than, "She said, 'Why won't you do it?' and he said, 'Because if I do, then I'll miss the picnic.' ") Teachers can point up the many variations for *said, asked* and *replied* by helping children toward: " 'Well,' he smiled." " 'No,' she frowned." " 'Oh!' he yelled." " 'Why?' she whined." Using children's literature from time to time to point out what "real" authors do will be helpful here.

The search for different words and other ways of saying things can be an interesting task for children. "What other words can we use for *sad, happy, fast, silly?*" The introduction of metaphor and simile, without necessarily using those terms, may enter at this point. "How can we say this so that the reader or listener will see, as closely as possible, what we see in our own heads? What is it like—what can it be compared to?" For synonyms, a thesaurus is invaluable. At Halloween time, for instance, one might list other words for *witch, black* and *flew* and then see what the thesaurus has to offer.

Another helpful language activity is one which takes simple, rather barren, sentences and fleshes them out so that they become more vivid. "The noise frightened the boy, and he ran down the stairs," can become, "Bang! The quaking boy flew down the staircase like a Titan rocket." A corollary of this is to examine interesting sentences from trade books and, while retaining the message, make them dull and ordinary.

This is not to say that short, concise sentences cannot be as appropriate as long, involved sentences. Sometimes youngsters begin to think that using large numbers of descriptive words automatically creates good sentences. "Johnnie was a poor, bedraggled, lonely boy who never had any money of his own to spend; so one clear and sunny day, when he saw a crisp, brand-new dollar bill lying on the littered, dirty sidewalk, he jumped with delirious joy," may be better than, "Johnnie was a poor boy. One day he was happy because he found a dollar." However, "What luck! A whole dollar right there on the sidewalk! To Johnnie that was a fortune," is as expressive as the first example and far less ornate.

As in every area, the manner in which the teacher deals with language will affect the amount of creative expression which results. Rejecting comments, boring vocabulary assignments, copying papers over, looking up misspelled words, being told that someone else's work is much better than one's own—these methods discourage rather than foster creative writing and speaking. Usage and spelling are not unimportant; but, if there is too much stress on this, many children will adopt the line of least resistance—short, dull, two- or three-sentence pieces of work which are easy to copy over and use words which can be spelled.

The teacher who encourages each child to improve at his own level, gives worth to every effort, and provides enough time for children to work out their ideas fosters creative expression. The teacher who gives children specific assistance in plot ideas, language development and the processes of putting things together will be the kind of helping person who fosters children's creative expression.

57.

"After All, Mrs. Murphy"

Mauree Applegate

I shall be eternally grateful to the Murphys for furnishing me with an apt answer to those teachers who say, "I just can't get any creative writing from my children!"

The Murphys shared their conversation with their neighbors. From conversation which one could not help overhearing I gathered that Mrs. Murphy was just learning to drive. The vast astonishment felt by Mrs. Murphy upon her introduction to the intricacies of the Machina Deo was exceeded only by that of Mr. Murphy as he contemplated the involvements that arise from the meeting of woman (his woman) and Machine.

One evening I heard Mrs. Murphy's light steps tripping to the garage, and soon after heard her call out to her husband, "But honey, it won't start!" More steps—masculine steps—followed by an outburst of delighted laughter as its owner roared, *"After all, Mrs. Murphy, it isn't magic—you have to turn it on before it starts!"*

And this is the point where my gratitude to Mr. Murphy rises like cream. "After all, Miss Murphy," I always mentally exclaim to those teachers who complain of the lack of creativity of their children, "creative writing isn't magic. You have to turn it on before it starts!"

"Paint a picture!" "Write a poem!" "Create a story!" We glibly ask these things of the children in our rooms from day to day. When children receive such instructions—cold—they are as dismayed as the miller's daughter in the German folktale whose royal husband commanded her to spin straw into gold. They are dismayed and uncreative Creative writing is not magic; except for the most creative children, we must turn it on before it will start. But since a child's creativity is not magic, how can it be turned on or released?

How Do We Turn It On?

Did you ever turn on the faucet at the sink when the water supply was shut off? What happened? No doubt there was first a gurgle of air, then a thin trickle of water, and soon no water at all.

The teacher who asks a whole class to write on the same subject, without first providing experience in that subject common to all, will get only a thin

---

Reprinted from *When Children Write,* Association for Childhood Education International, 23-29, 1955, by permission of publisher.

trickle of creativity at best. For creativity rarely seeks expression unless there is enough experience behind it that the child feels he has something to say. Children who have been on a hike or have taken their first train ride are so full of "talk" that they can easily be guided to write. That's the test of whether a whole class is ready to write—is it full of "talk"? Is interest, like June in the song, "bustin' out all over"? When this is so, *almost any teacher can guide any class to write.*

What are the enriching experiences which a classroom teacher can provide for her children so that they will *want* to write, will be *ready* to write, and will have something to say when they *do* write? The one-dimensional world of one book was exciting to the early twentieth-century child, but it takes the three-dimensional world of many books, visual aids, and radio in the hands of a skilled teacher to catch and hold the interests of today's child.

The stimulating teacher is still the Pied Piper who can call the tunes and the children will follow whether the music comes from a mouth organ or a brass band. The *teacher* is still more important than the *thing*. And to aid his own magic, the modern teacher has more *teaching aids* at his beck and call than Aladdin with his lamp and his ring. He has only to demand them and they will usually appear. Exciting books, for instance, by the dozens—books that can double any day for television and radio. Dozens of books geared to fit the reading ability of every child and as tantilizing to the imagination as the golden promises of a seed catalog. Yet hundreds of schools in America are still geared to one-book classes and the magic carpets often get no higher than the schoolroom ceiling.

Only a dolt could fail to gain enrichment from the exciting "going's on" in today's classrooms: the world of many books, excursions, hikes, radio, television, magazines, wonderful pictures, talks by travelers, exhibits, letters from pen pals, free materials from business houses, maps that do everything but talk, music from every land, folk dances to make one feel other folks through his feet, historical museums alive with dioramas—even the dead past has arisen like Hamlet's ghost to haunt the schoolroom. Dead heroes today are more alive to modern children than live heroes used to be to the children of yesterday. No wonder that the primary child, who had so many exciting books on Lincoln read to her, suggested sending Mr. Lincoln a Christmas card—she "liked that kind man *so* much."

Fullness out of which to write? The modern fifth grader studying South America, for instance, hasn't a chance to escape stimulation and enrichment. And stimulation and enriched experience can be guided into writing as easily as a youngster can be lured by free ice cream.

Almost any child can be stimulated to write if he is first stimulated to *Read*, *Look*, and *Listen* in the modern classroom.

Exchanging Ideas

But will every child write well after stimulation? Of course not. Writing is an acquired skill for most children, as talking is a natural one. Besides, the children in our classrooms fall naturally into three groups: a few who have a real talent for writing; a few who couldn't write more than a few sentences even if they had a gun at their backs; and the largest group—those who are not self-starters at writing but do surprisingly well if stimulated and directed.

We've just discussed methods of stimulation—now about the direction. Most of the stimulation of our three-dimensional classrooms is lost without special direction before the writing starts.

To be specific, let's pretend that the whole class is to write adventure stories of the cowboys, or gauchos on the pampas of Argentina. The stimulation via books, movies, pictures, and exhibits has been provided. The next step is the exchange of ideas. Remember that the large non-self-starting group in your room lacks ideas. You don't want these children to copy a story or sit and do nothing or grow nervous trying to think of stories.

The non-creative *always* get their ideas from the creative. Be realistic and recognize this fact. Share ideas before writing time starts. Ask the children for idea seeds or starters such as for a cowboy adventure story. If the stimulation and the information have been provided, ideas will come faster than you can write them on the blackboard. Some child may suggest that a cowboy was hunting stolen cattle and came upon the rustlers unaware (what matters if that idea is in every Western he has seen at the Saturday movies; his version will be new to him). Another may suggest that a cowboy get caught in a storm with his cattle, another that a baby calf be rescued from wolves (do they have wolves in South America? Direct a bookworm to the encyclopedia). If the class runs out of ideas, add a few of your own (even the teacher gets *stimulated* by his own *stimulation* these days).

Work With Words

By this time, all those children who can be filled with ideas (by anything less than an atomic thought explosion) will be ready and all the teacher needs to do now before writing time actually begins is to work with words. Why stimulate children to write, why let them exchange ideas for stories and then give them no tools of expression—words?

> From the children's study of pictures and books, they may suggest words to describe the great plains of Argentina; the rich stretches of the pampas grass flowing in the wind like a sea; the mahogany faces of the cowboys from long living with the wind and sun; the easy way the gaucho rides his horse and the long, easy lope of his steed, as it covers the flat miles of the pampas; how the sky looks to him as he rides along; what he sees as he goes.

Not a one of these suggested words or phrases may be used by many of the children in their writing, but it is in periods like this that children learn to pick and choose their words, as one chooses an apple from the cellar barrel.

In this mixing of words and phrases, a teacher gets his children interested in the re-creative aspect of creative writing—helping his children first to see and to feel, and then to write. For what is writing but seeing and feeling? This aspect of creative writing is the one most often neglected in the elementary school.

For instance, if you would have your children write about their pets, show them how to study each action of their puppies or cats. How does a puppy act when he rushes to meet his master at night? How does he look as he eats? How does he play? In what attitudes does he sleep? What does he remind one of as he watches a bird? A writer is first of all a see-er; accordingly we must in paint-mixing time teach our children to see.

After seeing time, Mary, a fourth grader, painted this pen portrait of her dog:

> This dog is big and stately. He is the color of a chocolate popsicle after it's been licked. He has big eyes and short perky ears. He looks like a member of Congress. My mother said she thought he should have a cigar. His tail sticks straight up in the air and sprouts out like a fountain.

Notice that these children re-created their pets as well as any adult might:

> I remember when they were pups, little balls of fur. One of the pups was a golden yellow, like when the sun rises on a beautiful morning. The other pup is the color of deep mahogany. I still wonder if the white stripes around their necks aren't an angel's touch. Their noses weren't short and stubby like a common dog's nose, they were just a little black nob. They have eyes like I never saw before. They were dark brown and way big around. They look happy yet sad. They are eager, still they seem to be begging.
>
> —*By a Fifth Grader.*

> A small colt comes out of the barn, into a beautiful world for the first time. He is so gay that he tries to kick up his heels but falls ker-plump. Up he goes to take a few steps, then falls again. Many a time he falls but each time he gets up. With each fall, he gets up. With each fall, he gets more surefooted. Soon he can walk, run, leap, and bound. —*By Karen.*

In the word-study period that precedes a creative writing class, get your children to use picturesque speech or imagery whenever possible. The use of imagery gives one a quick, clear picture and thus is a shortcut to understanding. Show the class how much easier it is to see the basketball player who is described as a "Paul Bunyan of a Fellow" than if he had been said to be merely big. What kind of fellow was this school boy of whom his classmates declared, he could "be trusted like an old paper sack?" Can you see the picture of the boy's dog whose "ears droop like wilted flowers whenever he's sad or scolded and he goes and hides like the sun on a cloudy day?"

Using those picturesque phrases suited to children from the column, "Picturesque Speech," in the *Reader's Digest* will set the children hunting for imagery in the books they read. I don't think I shall ever forget the little girl who suggested that Lincoln's face was as "lined as a relief map"—an apt phrase for which I hunted for years. Picturesque speech is poetry in the egg and it comes naturally to children, if the schools foster its use.

Creative Work Doesn't Just Happen

Remember then that creative work doesn't just happen any more than a garden just happens. If you want more than an occasional good flower, you must prepare the ground, plant the seed, and cultivate the young plants. Two steps for helping children write creatively:

Experience must precede writing. As Natalie Cole says, "Children cannot create out of a vacuum." Enriching experiences may consist of excursions, hikes, school projects or units, observation of things brought into the schoolroom, reading, other school lessons, special days, unexpected happenings, individual experiences shared, hobbies, visitors, radio programs, movies, and television. Oh, almost anything will enrich the experiences of children and start them writing.

The ground must be prepared and ideas scattered before children are ready to write. Stimulate the children so that they will want to write. Read poetry or stories, talk things over, plan for a sharing day or project, put out a school paper, listen to a radio program. Only the literary child will write without outside stimulation.

Gather and give vocabulary help on the board in the form of rich words and phrases. Help with specific observations such as how a cat worries a ball of yarn, how a dog acts toward strangers, how a small child listens, how a skater uses his arms.

Place on the board before writing begins ideas for story plots, poetry seeds, characterizations, and story endings. The intensely original won't use the ideas, but many children are not self-starters at creating. Do not make the ideas complete; just make suggestions to give the children a start.

Rich Dividends from Unassigned Writing

But some of the finest creative writing a teacher will ever receive will come not from mass writing but from individual or unassigned writing—writing by the child who loves the taste and feel of words. One need do no more to set these children writing than strike the match, or just provide the scratcher. Such a one is sixth-grade Ann who wrote "My Tree":

Dear me, Sir! Haven't you got a tree
That is just exactly right for me?
Short, tall, fat, and wide is all I can see,
And that's not what I wanted my tree to be.
This tree must be perfect in height,
But, my! There isn't one in sight!
Its branches must be long in length,
Straight out as though to show its strength.
You see, Sir, this tree is for Him,
The Little Baby Jesus, even to its trim.
And that is why my tree will be,
A perfect tree, just wait and see!

When such a child as Ann comes out with an unusual thought, approach her quietly after class and suggest that she write that thought into a poem or story. Every day give the invitation to write—some days a pictured face on a bulletin board may call out to passers-by, "I have a story written on my face. Can you guess it?" An antique willowware platter on display may bear this caption, "I went across the plains in a covered wagon. Will you be my voice and tell my story?"

Sometimes, just a mere suggestion will start stories "a-borning." What stories do you suppose Paul Revere interrupted that night as he rode through the villages crying out, "The British are coming"?

The creative child needs little groundwork; he needs setting off, as hounds need a rabbit's scent to send them flying. Yet these creative children are stimulated more than any others with playing with words.

But unlike children with special talent, the majority of children must be more than stimulated to write; they must be actually started. Reading aloud to them is one of the best ways to start writing. If you want children to write about "imagi-nageries" or funny animals in a make-believe zoo, read from the incomparable Dr. Seuss—*If I Ran The Zoo, Scrambled Eggs Super*, and *McElligot's Pool*. The children won't copy ideas—they will just dare to be funny. If you want them to write limericks, chuckle with them over Edward Lear's delicious limericks and delightful nonsense.

If your aim is to get children to write true humorous stories, write one yourself or read the account of the fight at school in *Caddie Woodlawn*, or how *Little Britches* licked the bully.

If poems of autumn are what you're after, go for the hike with the children absorbing "October's bright blue weather" through all your five senses. Then come back to the schoolroom and read poetry—"O, world, I cannot hold thee close enough" and "There is something in the autumn that is native to my blood." Then mix paint fast and furiously, describing the sky and the clouds and ways to tell the lilt of the leaves as they ease themselves to the earth.

And don't forget in your reading to include poetry. Children do so need poetry. Not having it is like never having stars to look at or music to listen to. Children, like men, "cannot live by bread alone." Children need poetry to lean on, to laugh at, to learn from, to reach for, and to sing with. Children who grow up with poetry have hidden resources in time of need. If you, the teacher, fail them, they may be poor indeed.

What does poetry reading have to do with poetry writing? Poetry reading leads to poetry writing. It sings the cadences of rhythmic lines into a child's mind and helps him to make his own writing more rhythmic.

Yes, indeed, if you want children to write, read to them. Read to them, and give them every living experience possible in order that their lives be full. For from the fullness comes writing. But you, the teacher, must be the starter, the mover, the prime-er of that fullness.

After all, Miss Murphy, creative writing isn't magic; you have to turn it on before it starts.

58. Is the Display of Creative Writing Wrong?

Wayne L. Herman, Jr.

There are basically two kinds of writing that elementary school children do in school. The first can be labeled practical writing, or that writing which exemplifies correctness in style, grammar, usage, and mechanics. Some examples are compositions and themes, thank-you notes, letters of inquiry and invitation, and lists and reports. The purpose of this writing is to teach skills in written communication.

The other writing that children do is personal, or creative writing. This takes the form of making up a story, completing the ending of an unfinished narrative, writing fables, poetry, or "way-out" episodes. The purpose of this writing, like any other creative activity, is for the enjoyment of the pupil, therapeutic value, the revelation of the child to his teacher and peers so that they can get to know and understand him better, aesthetic development, and the promotion of thinking that is organized and sequential.[9]

To be sure, creativity is concerned with communicating to other persons the ideas and feelings of the creator. But for elementary school children creativity, whether with the media of clay, paints, soap, toothpicks, or written words, has no imposed standards and consequently evaluation is shunned. It is the process of creativity more than the product that is valued.[10] Even though the purposes of the two kinds of writing are antithetical, errors in creative writing can be used—without any reference to the source of the errors—to improve and promote the skills of formal writing.

This article is concerned with the display of creative writing in the classroom or publication and distribution of it to the patrons of the school. The position of the writer is that creative writing at the volition of each pupil is worthy of public display. This is generally an unpopular view, particularly with school principals who must cope with parental complaints about the shabbiness of writing instruction in the grades.

Many teachers, not all of whom fear administrative criticisms, would never think of displaying on the bulletin board a child's creative writing that had misspellings or other blatant errors of English usage and mechanics. They think erroneously that the work is a negative reflection on their teaching competence. It is a reflection, but a positive one. It mirrors a teacher's ability to build the kind of classroom climate that frees children from inhibitions so that they will use words that are part of their vocabulary but which they can't spell . . . so that they will be more enthusiastic in stating ideas than in the style in which they state them . . . so that they will be more inclined to reveal their secretive motives, desires, and insights in writing than in strict attention to paper margins.

Sure, you tell the children that you hope that they will remember some of the things that they have learned in English composition . . . but you also tell them that this is not the most important purpose of their creative writing. Naturally re-writing will improve margins and proofreading will better the finished product . . . but even so some blemishes will remain. For certain children many blemishes will remain.

The "putting the school and its teachers in bad light with the patrons of the school" argument is also backed up by the "putting the child in bad light" rationalization. One venerable national authority wrote the author that "we must protect children from the criticism and downright ridicule they receive when their writing is published in poor form." If we believe this, it follows then that we ought not display any creative product in any media unless it is free of most or all defects . . . and I don't believe this is what we would want to advocate. A pertinent question is whether we protect children from the criticisms they receive from poor products displayed in the visual arts? Or criticism received from peers when a girl expresses her creative ideas in social studies? Or criticism received on the playground from onlookers when a boy strikes out with the bases loaded with his team behind in the score? Good teachers have always admonished those who criticized unreasonably. One could ask if "protecting children from ridicule" is a rationalization used to protect the teacher from possible ridicule and complaint by administrators and parents.

If children are required to put their work in near perfect form, we have prostituted our purposes of creativity to the objectives of the Establishment or to our personal motives. And children, of course, are cognizant of our changing gears. Subsequently creative writing activities will be characterized by inhibitions, the very thing we were trying to free children from. Lost is our philosophy of creativity; what remains is a formal writing period. Proofreading, as was mentioned, can be used but it is doubtful if children would put all of their writing in good form; the teacher would have to proofread and red-mark errors too. And when the teacher tampers with a creative product, it becomes the property of the pupil and the teacher. Even though there are some carpentry mistakes in a piece of furniture that I construct, I would rather have the furniture with the mistakes and know *"it's mine; I made it,"* than to have a carpenter point out and fix the mistakes. *Mine* is then replaced by *ours*, and my intention when I began excluded a team effort.

Another defense of the position of not displaying creative writing is that visual art products must be seen to communicate, but the written word can be heard. While this is undeniable, it must be recognized that the written word has the additional benefit of communicating visually. If the writing is filed away after the oral reading of it, this benefit is lost. Suppose the following creative writings were only read orally and filed away.[11] How many of you reading this page would want the opportunity to reread them again silently?

What A Block

My block is the most terrible block I've ever seen. There are at least 25 or 30 narcartic people in my block. The cops come around there and tries to act bad but I bet inside of them they are as scared as can be. They even had in the papers that this block is the worst block, not in Manhattan but in New York City. In the summer they don't do nothing except shooting, stabing, and fighting. They hang all over the stoops and when you say excuse me to them they hear you but they just don't feel like moving. Some times they make me so mad that I feel like slaping them and stuffing a bag of garbage down their throats. Theres only one policeman who can handle these people and we all call him "Sunny". When he comes around in his cop car the people run around the corners, and he won't let anyone sit on the stoops. If you don't believe this story come around some time you'll find out.

—Grace, age 11

My block is the worse block you saw people getting killed or stabbed men and women in buildin's taking dope. . . . . .

—Mary, age 11

Fables

Once upon a time there was a pig and a cat. The cat kept saying old dirty pig who want to eat you. And the pig replied when I die I'll be made use of, but when you die you'll just rot. The cat always thought he was better than the pig. When the pig died he was used as food for the people to eat. When the cat died he was buried in old dirt.
Moral: Live dirty die clean.

—Barbara, age 11

One a boy was standing on a huge metal flattening machine. The flattener was coming down slowly. Now this boy was a boy who love insects and bugs. The boy could have stopped the machine from coming down but there were two ladiebugs on the button and in order to push the button he would kill the two ladie bugs. The flattener was about a half inch over his head now he made a decision he would have to kill the ladie bugs he quickly pressed the button. The machine stoped he was saved and the ladie bugs were dead.
Moral: Smash or be smashed.

—Kenneth, age 11

It seems incongruous that some educators are willing to display errors in the creative products of the visual arts, e.g., a skinny elephant in a painting, an improperly proportioned clay giraffe, but unwilling to do the same thing with errors in creative writing. The orientation of the artist or sculptor may permit him to display creative writing with its mistakes but not imperfect products in the visual arts. Why should the display of creative writing that contains errors make us any more uncomfortable than exhibited art products that are imperfect?

An inconsistency is noted when principals and teachers are willing and even proud to have nursery and kindergarten children post their inaccurate written work on the bulletin board, but expect primary and intermediate children to have acquired refined and honed skills in their writing before taping it up on the classroom or corridor wall.

There are some recommendations for the school whose philosophy endorses the public display of creative writing. First, after the first initial draft, children ought to be encouraged to try and put their creative writing in the best possible form. This may mean re-writing to get rid of blemishes, smudges, crossed-out words and sentences, misspellings, poor handwriting, run together sentences, and other errors of English usage and mechanics. As in the above selected writings, it is expected and accepted that some culturally deprived children will improve the manuscript little through rewriting.

A written explanation of the school's point of view ought to be distributed to the patrons of the school. A description of the two kinds of writing is needed. It can be stated that errors in creative writing are used as a base for the instructional program in practical writing. Last, when creative writing is exhibited at the school it should be clearly labeled as creative writing. The same holds true when it is duplicated for distribution.

Children are proud of any product that they create. If they wish to exhibit their work, let us not rob them of the personal recognition they receive when they and others view their displayed written products of creativity just because of our inner fears and insecurities or whatever it is.

C.
Basic Writing Skills

Instruction in handwriting must be an integral part of the language arts throughout the elementary school program, for handwriting is the principal tool of written expression. Although there are many advocates of minimizing handwriting instruction in the elementary schools, they offer no alternative to this readily available tool of communication.

Traditionally, handwriting has been taught by and for itself. This factor has contributed to the growing discontent with the handwriting skills of students in institutions of higher education and in industry. The present trend is toward a more functional handwriting program, based on a combination of purposeful writing experiences and systematic instruction. Instruction in handwriting should not be isolated from work in other subjects. It should be emphasized that a child should always have something to write and a reason for writing it. Legibility should be the principal objective of handwriting instruction. The positive attitude of the teacher and the children toward handwriting is fundamental to the success of any handwriting program. Handwriting must be regarded as an important skill and viewed as vitally necessary for effective written expression.

Spelling, like handwriting, is a skill closely allied with composition. The prime objective in teaching spelling is, therefore, to help children learn to spell words which they are most likely to need in their writing activities. Spelling, like all composition skills, is relevant to all areas of the curriculum. Whenever children have the need to write, regardless of what subject they are studying at the time, spelling should be taught.

Spelling instruction has always been a matter of genuine concern for pupils, parents, and classroom teachers. Many educators feel that spelling instruction is the least effective area of the total language arts program. Several different explanations have been offered for the sad state of most spelling programs. The most justifiable explanation seems to be that since few teachers are aware of research findings in the area of spelling, there has been little application of these findings. If such techniques as the spelling pretest and pupil-corrected tests were implemented the overall effectiveness of spelling instruction would be significantly enhanced.

The authors of the following articles have incorporated some of the relevant research data into their presentations. Such problems as when and how handwriting instruction should begin, when children should make the transition to cursive writing, and how we can help the left-handed writer are discussed. Specific suggestions for improving the spelling program are also presented.

59. Those Questions on Handwriting

E. A. Enstrom

Must the schools take time to teach handwriting? Now and then the question is still asked—usually by someone who is not an educator, who knows nothing about education, and who freely expresses opinions in areas of which he knows little.

The questions of critics cannot be allowed to go unanswered, for they can have a detrimental effect on sound educational practice. But answers should be offered for another reason: in the continuing dialogue on education, critics are entitled to answers to sincere questions.

From Whence Cursive Script?

There is a belief that cursive, or joined, handwriting was invented by an evil genie eager to inflict punishment on innocent school children. Nothing could be further from the truth. Joined writing goes back in history as far as records are found. Even the ancient Egyptian hieroglyphics were written in joined forms.[12]

Through the ages man has always had two styles of writing. One is the carefully executed and often highly ornamented formal style used for special documents and handwritten book pages. The other is an everyday, rapidly produced, informal hand.

Cursive, applied to handwriting, means a swift, running or flowing style. It was not invented; it simply evolved over centuries. During the gradual development of cursive writing, many scribes added to or subtracted from each form as they tried to speed the writing task. In so doing they rounded many corners, looped many points, and ceased to lift their writing instrument within words.

Writing began with pictures; hurriedly made; pictures soon degenerated into symbols that stood for the original, carefully made picture. A few of the endless numbers of picture-symbols became characters that stood for sounds rather than things or ideas. These characters, after centuries, finally became the beginnings of the alphabet used by our culture.

The original alphabet, as refined by the Romans, consisted of what we now call *capital letters.* They were quite angular when chiseled on stone. When man began writing on bleached hides and early papers, he curved straight lines and

Reprinted from *Elementary School Journal* 59:44-47 (March 1969), by permission of E. A. Enstrom took short cuts. By 800 A.D. he had produced a double alphabet—the more rapidly written lower-case letters and the highly ornate upper-case letters, or capitals, used for the first word of the page. At this period in history upper- and lower-case letters were designated to serve the needs they serve today. Meantime, the even more swiftly written informal cursive style was modified along with formal writing. Changes in one style affected the other style.

In the evolution of cursive script, man first began sliding through an individual print letter without lifting his writing instrument. Next he began sliding from letter to letter in words where this kind of linking was easily done. Finally, slight changes were made so that it was possible to slide without stopping from letter to letter throughout every word. These early joined print letters, under pressure of speed, became our present-day streamlined cursive script. Fortunately for us this high-speed script advanced further and became more fluent and more rapidly written on this continent than anywhere else in the world.

One advantage of joined script must not be overlooked: in joined script words are attached into units. This is important, since, in hand-produced print, spacing between letters and between words presents a serious problem in legibility. This difficulty may be found in the writing of children in the primary grades as well as in the writing of adults.

After the invention of movable type, the formal print style gradually became (after some two hundred years or more) the product of the printing press; the the informal style became the chief vehicle for handwritten communication. The highly ornamented hand-produced print, known as engrossing, still remains, but this painstaking, beautiful work becomes more rare every year.

What Do Schools Teach?

Throughout history both the formal and the informal styles of handwriting were passed on from adult to adult, frequently by early scribes from father to son, but no attempt was made to instruct young learners.

Many early schools in America were taught by itinerant "writing masters" who held forth in "writing schools," since the ability to write, along with the ability to read (first taught in "reading schools"), distinguished the literate from the illiterate. Only a few older boys attended; later girls and younger children were admitted. Sometimes separate "infant schools" were organized for beginners.

The "writer master," or teacher, taught all pupils the only style of handwriting he knew—cursive script. Older boys and girls learned readily. The younger children, with a few rare exceptions, generally failed to produce skilled work. This practice of teaching only cursive style seemed to prevail wherever schools existed.

In 1913 the difficulties of teaching the adult-developed writing to very young learners caught the attention of Edward Johnson in London, England. In a talk to a gathering of London teachers, he suggested that a simplified Roman print, with lower-case letters in harmony, be used in instructing these children.[13] Teachers experimented with the idea and discovered that beginners could succeed with this style of writing. Unfortunately, because Johnston was pressing for the revival of the ancient and extremely difficult Italic-style script as written with a broad-edged pen on ancient manuscripts, the name *manuscript* became attached to the new simplified print form that showed much promise.

The new style served well for children, because they could make part of a letter, stop, get their bearings, then add another part. There was no long sustained motion from the beginning to the end of a word.

Marjorie Wise was one of the first to bring the new print to America. She was asked to teach the new writing at Columbia University in 1922. It gradually spread into practically universal use during the next twenty to thirty years. Today the term *print handwriting* seems to be replacing the original and meaningless word, *manuscript*.

The new print, then, served the young pupil until he was mature enough to attempt the more adult cursive style. The print-to-cursive pattern remains today.

Why Not Teach Only Print?

The question is sometimes asked, "Why not teach only print?" When educators are speaking, the question probably stems from the troubles many teachers have in making the transition to cursive style, or from problems that arise when teachers slight handwriting in advanced grades. Problems of this kind can be avoided.[14] When individuals who are not in education ask the question, they are concerned with expending less effort in learning to write in an age of typewriters and other machines designed to eliminate the need for hand-produced script.

Early records show that cursive script evolved from angular print. If cursive style is not taught when the child is ready for it, he invents a cursive form of his own. Unfortunately, it is crude and inefficient. It seems far wiser to profit from what has been learned over the centuries and teach the swiftly produced, flowing script that is our heritage.

Cursive style envolved because man discovered that it requires less time and effort to slide from symbol to symbol than to completely stop the writing motion, lift the writing instrument, seek a new, correct beginning point, and then move again, often in an entirely different direction. The very qualities that make print style a desirable form for less mature writers to learn make print style less desirable for the more mature individuals to use as the exclusive tool for recording ideas rapidly. Further, research clearly shows that small, finger-produced print handwriting does not stand up under pressure of use over longer periods of time.[15] There seems to be no good reason for changing our present school practice of following the print-to-cursive pattern in writing by hand.

Is There Much Need for Hand Script?

Some individuals are misled into thinking that handwritten script is on the way out. This is not true at all.[16]

There are echoes here of earlier cries. After the phonograph had been firmly accepted, the radio was invented. The cry was heard: "Throw out the phonograph. The age of radio has arrived." When television came along, the cry went up: "Throw out the radio. This is the age of TV."

Actually phonographs and radios are in greater demand today than ever before. And so it is with handwritten script. With the coming of modern machines, business has expanded tremendously; and, with the expansion, handwriting is used more than ever before.

The daily mail brings orders from homes where business machines are largely unknown. The yearly gross from direct mail promotions runs between thirty and forty billion dollars, and the vast bulk of this business comes in the form of handwritten orders.

Small enterprises must rely on handwritten records, and giant industries have many spots where sophisticated machines have failed to replace the ever convenient pen or pencil.

Businessmen complain bitterly of a yearly loss of millions of dollars, a loss that can be traced to unreadable script; they accuse schools of failure in teaching handwriting.[17] Apparently the business world has not lost interest in the efficient teaching of handwriting.

Does Individuality in Hand-Produced Script Affect Legibility?

There seems to be a misguided impression that cursive script alone is affected by individual laziness and creative efforts. This is not true. Everything done by hand is individualized. Even print often becomes so individualized that it cannot be read. This happened before 800 A.D. Print became so individual that communication was at the point of ceasing. Charlemagne prevailed upon Alcuin of York to open a writing school at Tours to bring greater uniformity and to restore reasonably efficient communication.

The better and more thoroughly the cursive style is taught, the longer it will remain a useful tool. What causes problems today is not the tool, but the long neglect of sound teaching of cursive writing.

Many schools need in-service programs to improve the teaching of handwriting. There is no panacea for this problem. Quality teaching is required for success with this useful tool.

What Are Current In-School Needs?

The larger the classes and the more crowded the curriculums, the greater the need for written communication between children and teacher. No other device can compete with the pen or pencil in carrying out classroom assignments in learning.

Also, in the all-important creative writing, rapid, efficient cursive style facilitates the rapid, efficient recording of ideas.

Some individuals glibly speak of typewriters for every school child. Many schools cannot afford pencils for children! Pupils must buy their own or do without. While dreamers dream, practical educators must face up to reality.

Further, cursive script well learned is no more difficult to read than print. For all problems of readability, efficient teaching, using modern materials, remains the best answer.[18]

One advantage that we dare not omit is the kinesthetic force involved in writing by hand. One tends to remember what one writes. Because more is written when efficient cursive style is used, learning is expanded in most areas of the total program. The gains produced by writing occur at all levels of education whenever the learner gathers, organizes, records, or conveys information.

How Must Handwriting Be Taught?

The answer to this question must be of concern to educators, because quality teaching spells the difference between success and failure in learning this useful tool of communication.

During past decades the problem of a crowded curriculum has often been met by combining various subject areas into one group, such as language arts or social studies. Sometimes the arrangement works fairly well; but because of reduced emphasis on each subject in the combined group and because of variations in teachers' abilities as well as teachers' likes and dislikes, some subject usually suffers; often all subjects combined suffer. Some educators are questioning this entire idea of combining subjects.

In theory, there is some chance for success if the learnings combined are similar. When handwriting, which is a motor skill, is combined with reading, spelling, creative writing efforts, and mechanics of English usage—which are not motor skills—success with handwriting is almost impossible. In more advanced grades, failure is not just likely—it is guaranteed!

The reason for failure is not hard to understand. To generate ideas in creative writing of any type requires great concentration—such great concentration that all mechanics suffer, including spelling, handwriting, sentence structure, and others required in well-prepared papers. Actually, generating thought and developing skill in mechanics work counter to each other.

The only answer to this problem is separate learning sessions to build efficient skill, especially in handwriting. Writing by hand is too complex to be combined with any other area. For efficient learning, handwriting requires the concentrated effort of teacher and pupils on one task and one task only: learning how to handwrite![19]

After the child has learned to write, and indeed while he is learning, some integration can be brought about. Children can practice writing words from reading. They can write sentences from the on-going program. The teacher, however, must set aside short daily learning sessions as he builds a consciousness of the importance of well-written assignments. With sensorimotor skills there must be "separation" as well as "integration" for success. We learn, we build habits, we use the learning in meaningful ways.

Those who do creative writing understand the tremendous distraction brought on by great concentration. Few, if any, turn out a finished product in one sitting. "Write and rewrite" is the rule, and those who do not rewrite many times can seldom take pride in their creative products.

To build automatic skill in handwriting there must be separate, daily learning sessions. To combine lessons on handwriting with lessons in other subjects is not unlike trying to learn to play the violin while learning, at the same time, the history of the invention of the oboe! Educators need to give serious thought to such past errors in judgment and eliminate fruitless subject integration that can only create impossible learning environments.

Are There Other Problems?

Sometimes concern is expressed over children's ability to learn to read cursive script if they have started with, or have been exposed to, print style. This certainly need not be a problem. Printers in second grade can more often than not read cursive with ease. Recent research reports no major problem. The ability to do quite well in reading cursive style is considered a sign of readiness to accept the next challenge.

Also, children want to learn adult-style writing more than many adults realize. A twenty-six-year-old woman recently confided to me: "The happiest day of my school life was the day we began to learn to really write." Teachers sometimes overlook children's strong desires to go on to the next challenge.

In my many talks from coast to coast on solving handwriting problems, many adults who were taught only print in experimental or progressive programs have asked me to recommend a good book so that they could learn efficient cursive script. "I have always felt cheated and inadequate because I was not taught cursive writing," one attender said to me. Surely schools can do better than leave individuals feeling "cheated and inadequate."

Educators who guide the learning programs of children need an understanding of what is being taught and why. A historical background helps increase understanding and can protect us from repeating mistakes. Sound educational programs must not be swayed by the whims of the unknowing few.

Cursive script evolved through the centuries as the most easily produced, the most durable, and the most rapid way of recording thought. It remains our best answer to the need for a swift, streamlined means of handwritten communication. It needs to be taught with a full appreciation of our prodigious heritage.

Print style of handwriting was reintroduced into schools as the best means of meeting the needs of less mature learners. Because the print style is easily produced by hand, it contributes mightily to the scope and quality of early language-learning. As children mature, their agitation to "really write" emerges as a distinct pressure for the education they feel entitled to; wise curriculum-planners move forward with skillfully taught cursive script. This forward pattern resembles closely the development of handwriting through the ages.

There seems to be no doubt about the soundness of present practices. The only problem that merits attention is the weakness in ability to instruct handwriting efficiently. Instead of casting about for a panacea that has the firmness and stability of a will-o'-the-wisp, educators are well advised to strive for in-service programs to improve the instructional ability of those who teach handwriting to children. There is no substitute for quality teaching. Let us expend our efforts in this direction.

60.

Teaching Handwriting: Why and How?

Albert H. Yee and Carl Personke

In today's schools, handwriting instruction has become a poor relation. Teachers appear to neglect it more than any other subject in the elementary curriculum.[20]

In one view, the decline in emphasis on handwriting is due to integrated language arts programs and neglect of the subject in teacher training. Teachers today are much more concerned with *what* children write than *how* they write, and handwriting seems to offer little challenge compared to other issues teachers face. Even those who might be interested find only meager research and many unanswered questions.

Though the subject of handwriting does not appear intellectually challenging or socially important, teachers should not ignore it. Pupils must be competent in basic skills such as handwriting and spelling before they can profit from other concerns of language arts. They cannot deal with the objectives of written expression and communication if they lack these fundamental tools. Yet there need not be either-or choices in planning language arts experiences.

The levels of skill and developmental stages of achieving mature handwriting have never been clearly stated. Like spelling, mature handwriting behavior does not call for conscious deliberation about *how* to write, just *what* to write. Writers are most proficient when they can call on rote behavior, achieving fluent and legible writing with little attention to process.

Our model for handwriting like our analysis of spelling behavior,[21] is based on information theory. Let's see how it helps explain how a person reaches maturity in handwriting.

The **internal input** component includes inner processes which affect writing behavior, such as felt needs to write, motivational patterns, attitudes toward writing, and learned psychomotor responses. This may be viewed as a storehouse of information and responses that can be called upon to meet handwriting needs.

The **external input** includes the elements that provide most of the handwriting instruction to the learner, such as teacher and parent models and handwriting materials.

These lead to the **act of handwriting,** which involves greater conscious effort for beginners than for mature writers. Beginners who copy someone else's writing probably go through the intermediary step of visualizing the letter

Reprinted from *Instructor* 77:126-127 (November 1967), by permission of author and publisher.

form before attempting actually to write. The need for a proper model at this stage requires a professional level of handwriting performance from primary teachers.

The **feedback component** is the point at which the individual evaluates his production in terms of his own standards and the reactions of others. This component is important because it provides the opportunity to affect the other components and improve future handwriting behavior.

The most efficient type of handwriting behavior is produced through the **kinesthetic channel,** proceeding from decision to response without effort or deliberation. A person who follows this channel consistently, with satisfaction to himself and others (especially those in authority over him), has reached an acceptable level of handwriting maturity. What makes this channel feasible is the individual's development of a store of replicable, habitual responses. The mature writer produces an attractive, legible script characteristic of his own kinesthetic channel. Freeman[22] calls this stage of handwriting development "automatization" and "kinesthetic control."

The desideratum for teachers is pupil progress toward utilization of the kinesthetic channel. Since its development depends upon daily learning experiences and upon general language development, students in the lower grades cannot rely on this channel for satisfactory handwriting. They must process their writing through the **learning channel.** However, we believe that handwriting can be fairly well perfected by the fifth grade, with remedial work conducted in the sixth grade.

Initial Handwriting Instruction

Because the first grader is immature in eye-hand coordination and is experiencing his first formal language learning, his handwriting is processed through the learning channel. First-grade teachers are wise to introduce beginners to the combined tasks of writing, spelling, and reading through the simpler requirements of manuscript writing. Copying the teacher's movements, pupils learn to form letters. With further help, they begin to discriminate sounds, words, and meanings from their penciled labors. In time, the typical first grader can write all the letters and some words—such as his first name—through the kinesthetic channel.

It is the first-grade teacher's responsibility to develop the child's handwriting according to acceptable standards. These are revealed to the child by teacher-pupil transactions, by his ability to read and check his own handwriting, and by additional feedback from peers and parents. The first-grade teacher's instruction is crucial in establishing the pupil's learning and kinesthetic channels, a positive attitude toward the use of them, and an understanding of how handwriting skills are related to overall progress in language arts.

In developing these objectives, pupils must conform to the models provided by the teacher. There is little latitude for permissiveness and discovery; unlike concepts in subjects such as social studies and science, handwriting patterns cannot be entirely justified on logical grounds. In these early language learnings, students thus face the constraints of convention. The teacher can help the child realize the worth of such learnings by providing him with the satisfactions of communication and self-expression through interesting and meaningful writings.

Later Handwriting Instruction

If his pupils are typical in readiness and preparation, the second-year teacher guides the transition from manuscript to cursive script. First, however, he should spend about half the year reviewing, reinforcing, and adding to students' training in manuscript writing. In helping develop the complex procedures required by the more advanced script, the teacher should be able to count on the child's ability to follow instruction, to try and to practice responses, and to check them with the teacher and other external sources.

Individual differences will call for special attention to some students. Teachers should respond to obvious handwriting problems the same way they do to grammatical and spelling problems. Since there probably is a positive correlation between handwriting achievement and progress in other language arts areas, grouping for handwriting alone is neither necessary nor desirable. Spelling and writing are highly related in operation, so grouping by these complementary subjects is feasible.

Teachers should require consistent standards for handwriting in all subject areas so pupils will not develop one standard of performance for appearances and one for communication. Handwriting developed by deliberate practice in "penmanship" sessions is likely to be markedly less acceptable when utilized for other areas. This occurs because pupils process their penmanship drill through the learning channel and their "regular" handwriting through the kinesthetic channel. There is little carry-over from the drill, and no teacher-imposed feedback directed consistently toward the pupil's other writings. Handwriting instruction must take effect in the kinesthetic channel, not just the learning channel.

As the student progresses to upper grades, he should continue to maintain natural, legible, neat handwriting in all his writing efforts. Unless the elementary school develops this basic skill, children can be seriously handicapped. Teacher education should not overlook the need to prepare students in this basic language skill.

61. The Left-Handed Child

E. A. Enstrom

Research has long since shown that handedness does not affect learning ability, and the ancient superstition that left-handed people per se are somewhat inferior has almost been forgotten, but the fact remains that this is a right-handed world. Since over 10 percent of the school population is left-handed and the typical class is almost sure to include some left-handed children, teachers need to help such children adjust to living in it.

Manufacturers have solved many of the problems of the left-handed by making special equipment for them. By the simple expedient of providing left-handers with such equipment, the schools can keep left-handedness from being a handicap in most areas.

Handwriting is a different matter, however. As long as a left-hander never has to use a tablet arm chair designed for a right-handed writer, equipment really doesn't enter the picture, but if he is not to be handicapped as a penman, the left-handed child needs to learn special techniques for writing.

To learn these special techniques, left-handed children should all be seated in the front right corner of the room, facing the chalkboard. When they are in this location, the teacher can watch them and individualize the instruction they receive. Other advantages of grouping the left-handers are that it prevents right- and left-handers from confusing each other about proper paper placement and that the left-handers can watch and remind each other about the special tricks of left-handed handwriting. Most important of all, when the left-handers are seated in this part of the room, they see the teacher's writing on the board or the overhead screen from precisely the same angle that they see their own writing when their papers are placed correctly.

To minimize the chance of stigmatizing the left-handers through segregating them, the teacher can help them organize themselves into an ultraexclusive "Leftie Club," open only to left-handers learning to use the correct techniques.

While any child will reverse letters now and then, research shows that left-handers have more tendency to do so. In fact, they often do mirror writing at early stages of learning because of the natural movement of the left hand. Teachers, therefore, need to make sure that left-handed pupils learn not only correct left-to-right direction, but also correct, nonreversing writing habits. They can begin by having the children practice the *rightward* sliding exercise illustrated in Figure 1. The pupils need to practice this, repeating the right-

---

Reprinted from *Today's Education* 58: 43-44 (April 1969), by permission of author and publisher.

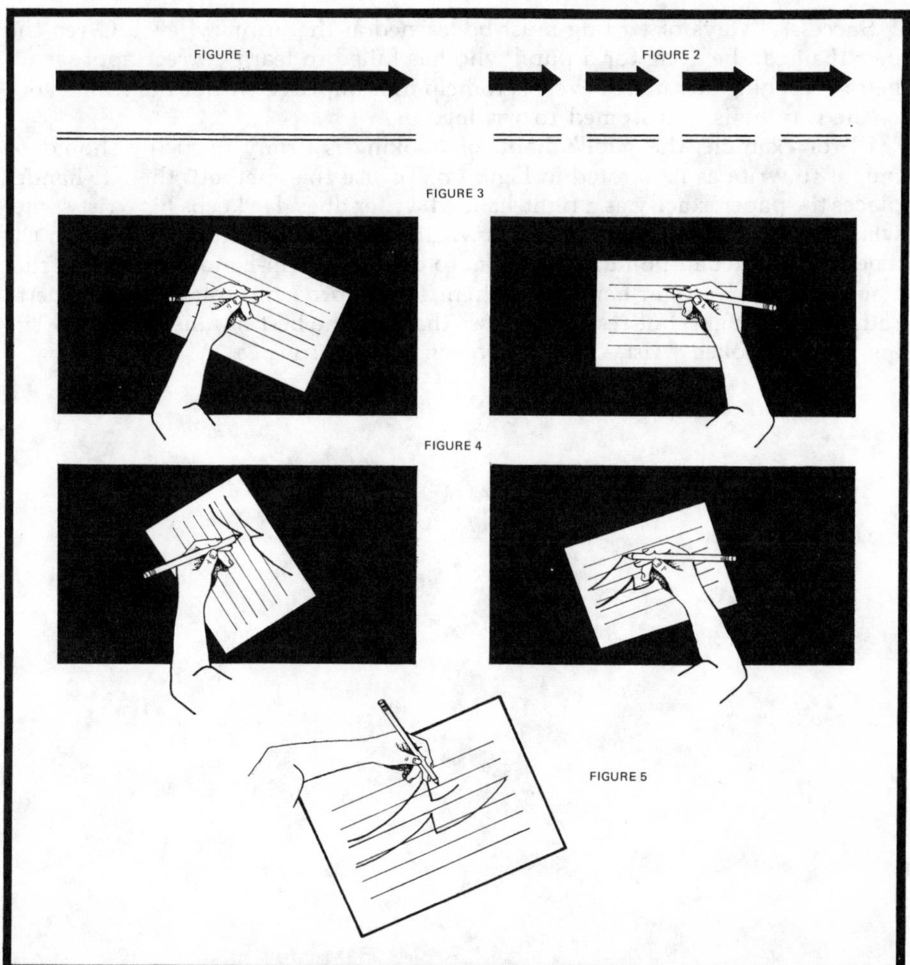
FIGURE 1
FIGURE 2
FIGURE 3
FIGURE 4
FIGURE 5

ward movement many times as they say aloud, "touch, slide, lift" while the teacher watches to make certain that they keep moving in the correct direction.

Next, children should practice the short slides illustrated in Figure 2, while they say, "touch, slide," with each short slide. This movement must be practiced until it becomes an established habit.

As the pupils learn new letters and words, the teacher should be sure that all letters are headed in the correct direction and that the children learn the proper beginning point, direction of movement, and sequence of parts. When he perceives a problem, he must immediately provide the practice necessary to eliminate it.

When first learning to print, the left-hander should always keep the paper turned somewhat clockwise, as is shown in Figure 3. This positioning helps the writer to see what he is writing without "hooking" his wrist. Another help to seeing is sitting at a lower-than-normal desk and holding back slightly farther from the pencil point.

When writing lessons have advanced to slant print and slant cursive, the left-hander turns his paper more clockwise and also slants his writing forward, as illustrated in Figure 4. When he is using cursive script, he *pulls* forward strokes toward himself and *pushes* slant strokes leftward.

Successful ways of writing must be learned at the primary level. Often the best than can be done for a pupil who has failed to learn correct approaches before reaching advanced levels is to help him improve within the framework of the way he is accustomed to writing.

If, for example, the pupil's habit of hooking is firmly fixed, he should be taught to write as illustrated in Figure 5. To use this method, the left-hander places the paper exactly as a right-handed writer does. He keeps his wrist somewhat on edge and flexes it while he is writing. The teacher should have him use a pencil-shaped ball-point and tell him to disregard arm-hand position instructions intended for right-handed children. This approach is tolerated by experts rather than sought, but research shows that it is the best of nine ways of writing with a hooked wrist—the best wrong way, so to speak.

62. Pupils, Teachers, and Sensory Approaches to Spelling

Edna Lue Furness

The first step in teaching spelling is to present common words the pupil must write and use. The second, and perhaps the more important, is to teach the pupil an effective method of *learning* the words he knows and uses. This learning involves perceiving the word, pronouncing it, recognizing its meaning, visualizing the configuration of the word, and stowing away a visual image of it. Learning also involves concentrating on the sequence of letters, writing and checking to be sure the letters are in the proper order, writing the word from memory, writing the word from memory later in the day, then using the word as often as possible in any and all kinds of writing.

Some authorities have emphasized the points that success in spelling is the result of an efficient method of learning to spell and that the method in turn is largely a matter of the individual pupil. Hence the teacher's task becomes that of setting up techniques for those who learn best by the visual, the auditory, the kinesthetic (the feeling of sound or muscular activity), or the multiple sense method. The purpose of this paper is (1) to point up basic principles of the sensory approaches to spelling, (2) to identify distinctive characteristics of each sensory approach, (3) to point out factors affecting a pupil's learning, and (4) to suggest teaching procedures for each sensory approach.

While it is true that children learn to spell in different ways, there are learning principles which every teacher should know and which should be followed by every pupil in his own way. These are:

1. Guide each child to approach the spelling of a word through use and understanding.
2. Guide the child to follow necessary active steps in learning to spell a word. Each should: (a) develop a clear image of the word; (b) recall the spelling of the word; (c) write the word, if possible, from memory; (d) check the correctness of each spelling; (e) master the spelling of each word.
3. Each child should use the word in writing and check its correctness.[23]

Reprinted from *Education* 87: 267-273 (February-March 1968), by permission of author and publisher, The Bobbs-Merrill Company, Inc.

Learning To Spell By Sight

It is maintained that most people employ a visual approach and that people who can recall visual word forms vividly tend to be better spellers. Be that as it may, the researchers who say we learn to spell by sight have some pretty convincing evidence on the predominant role of the eye and on the actual hindrance of the ear. About 1860 a German named Bormann came up with the evidence that deaf and dumb people write only from their visual memory. With the deaf the memory of the word forms is not confused by the auditory memory of sounds.

One of the first to make a really scientific study of spelling by sight was Dr. A. I. Gates of Columbia University. Dr. Gates and a co-worker found that, with reading ability equal, deaf children greatly excel normal children in spelling ability. According to the statistics compiled, the spelling ability of the deaf is about 150 percent of that of the normal child. It is altogether likely that this superiority is a result of the deaf child's more careful visual study of words. That is not all the story.

The superiority of the deaf, when reading ability is rendered constant, increases perceptibly with longer school experience. If these data are reliable and valid—and there seems to be strong evidence they are—the deaf child's ability to distinguish between correct and incorrect spelling increases with extraordinary rapidity, in comparison with normal children, as their reading experience is extended.[24]

Why is this possible? Some experts say that the deaf owe their remarkable spelling ability primarily to a peculiarly effective type of perceiving, of reacting to words. Normal children, despite wider opportunities in reading and writing, do not develop this preciseness and accuracy of word observation. The reason is that they rely mainly on the easier, perhaps more natural phonetic translation. Normal children, enjoying phonic and phonetic experience, learn to depend primarily upon a phonetic translation of the sounds into letters which represent the sounds.

Phonics and Spelling

This discussion about deaf children and their spelling reveals that apparently the more the research workers study the relationship between phonics and spelling the more they learn about the importance of the eye in spelling. However, the evidence does seem to indicate that, except for the deaf, mastery of phonics is related to spelling ability at all levels—from elementary school through high school and college. All this adds up to saying that one-who-knows-his-phonics can become a good speller without too much effort. That raises the question, "What is meant by phonics?"

"Phonetics," the dictionary says, "is the science of dealing with speech sounds." It is a technical subject. Studying phonetics means learning the International Phonetic Alphabet, diacritical marks, syllabication, and pronunciation. It means translating visual (printed or written) words or word elements—letters, syllables, phonograms—into sounds as in reading.

Phonetic spelling is the reverse of the phonetic reading process; it means going from words and their sounds to letters. Phonetics is definitely not a subject you teach to small children. Therefore, about a half century ago, educators who believed in teaching spelling and reading by the phonetic method simplified the system by omitting special symbols and special terminology. They called the new approach "phonics," which, and I quote the dictionary, "is simplified phonetics for teaching reading and spelling."

The pupils who do not visualize words must think of the words in some other terms. They recall visual symbols in auditory or kinesthetic (motor) terms, which are as clear and distinct as the visual. Those who rely on auditory recall require more emphasis on the sound images of the word. That is, they rely on pronunciation, phonetic clues, and "clang" associations. The person who relies upon the kinesthetic sense recalls the words in terms of lip, throat, tongue, hand or eye movements. He actually feels himself saying or writing the word.

Most non-visual individuals rely upon a dual or even multiple sense recall. They get some combination of the two or three forms of recall. Quite often a child will get an auditory image of the word as he says the word to himself, as he thinks the sound, and as he feels the movements the hand makes in writing.

Methods Used In Learning To Spell

An examination of spelling textbooks reveals a variety of activities recommended as a method of learning to spell a word. Frederick S. Breed listed 34 activities, which were suggested by six prominent authorities.[2 5] Breed classified the activities in these general categories: (1) looking at the word, (2) listening to its pronunciation, (3) pronouncing the word, (4) using it in a sentence, (5) visualizing it, (6) saying the letters in sequence, (7) analyzing the hard spots, and (8) writing the word.

It may be observed that the pupil starts with the whole word recognition, meaning, pronunciation; that he then proceeds to the study of parts; and that he finally returns to the whole word in writing. Visualization and actual writing are important parts of the total process.

The teacher's next concern is with specific teaching procedures which will enable the individual learner to realize his spelling potential in terms of his individual sensory approach. In the analysis which follows, the approaches to the learning of spelling are noted in the lefthand column. Factors affecting a pupil's learning are noted in the middle column. Teaching procedures in terms of the visual, the aural, the kinesthetic, and the multiple sense approaches are suggested in the right-hand column. The suggestions undoubtedly will lead the teacher to think of adaptations for his particular classroom situation.

An Analysis of Spelling Method, Factors Affecting Learning, and Suggested Teaching Procedures

Sensory Approaches to Spelling	Factors Affecting Learning	Suggested Teaching Procedures
1. visual	1. perception of position in space 2. perception of a letter or letters 3. perception of spatial relationships 4. meaning vocabulary 5. accurate recognition of visual symbols 6. visual-motor coordination 7. accurate reproduction of visual symbols	1. Post a list of the words the pupils ask for most frequently, such as *should, would, could.* 2. Suggest that the class look at the word closely. 3. Picture *u* or *n*, *b* or *d*, *g* or *q*, *m* or *w*. 4. Write some or all letters on the blackboard. 5. Have pupils find all the words in a column that begin with the same letter or letter combinations.

Sensory Approaches to Spelling	Factors Affecting Learning	Suggested Teaching Procedures
		6. Help the pupil acquire a visual image of the word: a. place several words on a flash card. b. show each card quickly. c. ask the child to write what he sees. d. hold up the card for checking. e. repeat the process for practice.
2. aural	1. auditory acuity 2. phonic intuition 3. syllabication practice 4. acquaintance with the long and short sounds of letters 5. ability to relate the long and short sounds to the spelling of simple words 6. teacher's knowledge of phonics 7. teacher's enunciation and pronunciation	1. Let the pupils listen to the word as someone says it aloud. 2. Say the word aloud; ask the class to pronounce the word. 3. Use the word in a sentence; call for examples from the pupils. 4. Say the letters in sequence. 5. Train pupils to observe likenesses and differences in beginning sounds, in beginning letter and letter combinations. 6. Observe rhyming elements in words. 7. Have pupils group words with similar sound elements: can, man, tan; fun, run, sun. 8. Call attention to pronunciation of long and short vowels in such words as hat, hate;win, wine; cut, cute; bit, bite; not, note. 9. Have the pupils observe that a vowel is long when the word ends in a silent *e* preceded by a single consonant or two consonants, like *th, bathe.* 10. Have the pupils observe also that the vowel is short when the word ends

Sensory Approaches to Spelling	Factors Affecting Learning	Suggested Teaching Procedures
		in a single consonant preceded by a single vowel: not. 11. Assign the memorization of five key words in order to identify the vowels and their sounds. 12. Arrange a phonics quiz: "I'm thinking of a word that sounds like 'that' but it means something I wear on my head." The one who gives the correct answer gives the next statement. Watch lest the pupils confuse spellings of the same sounds as *blue-do*. 13. Give a dictation test using sentences such as: a. The sun is shining. b. The man is robed. 14. Divide long words into syllables and spell syllable after syllable. 15. Check pupil's knowledge of phonics. Does he perceive the difference between *per* and *pre*?
3. kinesthetic	1. muscular control 2. finger dexterity 3. kinesthetic memory	1. Have the child trace over the word after the teacher has pronounced it, pronouncing it as he traces the letter. 2. Request the pupil to turn over the paper and write the word from memory. 3. Check spelling with perfect copy. 4. Ask the pupils to remember the parts that are written as they are pronounced, or ask him to remember the feeling in his hands as he writes the word.
4. dual or multiple sense	1. perceptual constancy (identification of forms, regardless of differences	1. Pronounce the word, pausing between syllables. 2. Point to the word in script

Sensory Approaches to Spelling	Factors Affecting Learning	Suggested Teaching Procedures
	in size, color, texture, position or background)	or print as the child pronounces the word.
	2. eye-hand coordination	3. Look at the word, spell it, pausing between syllables.
	3. curiosity about words	
	4. interest in words and their origin	4. Ask pupil to close his eyes. Have him spell, pausing between syllables.
	5. knowledge of words and their meanings	5. Have the pupil write the word and compare it with the correct form.
	6. writing practice	
	7. resourcefulness in using the dictionary	6. Suggest that he write the word again and compare with the correct form. If the word is correct, have the pupil cover it with his hand and write it again. If the second trial is correct, have the pupil write the word a third time.
	8. desire to maintain high spelling accuracy	
	9. ability to determine when to rely on visual memory, when to rely on phonics only, when to seek help.	
		7. Require the pupil to rewrite each word at intervals during the lesson and at odd times during the day.
		8. Ask the class to study the two most important spelling rules: a. drop the silent *e* before a suffix beginning with a vowel: *hope, hoping*. b. double the final consonant in monosyllabic words preceded by a single vowel: *hopping, robbing*.
		9. Encourage pupils to use the dictionary. Give the class members the first letters of a word like *syllable* or *reciprocity* and ask them to locate the word in the dictionary.

63. The Teaching of Spelling

Paul R., and Jean S. Hanna

A paramount interest of today's generation of parents seems to be concern lest their offspring fail to learn to read. Two generations ago, parents were at least as much concerned about their children's ability to spell. Seldom, however, have parents evidenced much awareness of the close relationship that exists between these two tools of communication, reading and writing (spelling), and of how important it is for each of these subjects to support and enrich the other.

Until a hundred or more years after the invention of printing, communication through print or writing was infrequent, and spelling was therefore a rather unimportant matter. The individual writer or printer used the letters he thought would convey the intended sounds to the reader. The same word was consequently often spelled differently by different writers, and a single writer or printer would often use two different spellings for the same word in a written message or book.

As more and more people learned to read and as more and more books were printed, scholars and printers realized that uniformity in spelling would simplify and speed up the reading process. As a result, a demand arose during the 1600's for word-spellings on which all might agree. This demand culminated in the eighteenth century in the publication of the first authoritative dictionary, a publication that immediately assumed the role of arbiter in the matter of spelling. Ever since then, there has been for most of the words in the English language only one correct spelling. (Words like judgment (judgement), programed (programmed), and gibe (jibe), meaning to mock, are exceptions that allow a choice of one of two correct spellings.)

It was not long after the appearance of that first dictionary that correct spelling became an important criterion of social acceptance. As the common school movement grew and more and more people received at least some formal education, poor spelling was considered increasingly to be a sign of illiteracy or stupidity. People who spelled their words in conformity with the accepted standards were assumed to be intelligent and well educated. The teaching of spelling came to be as important as the teaching of good manners and of accuracy in numbers. So it has continued to the present, with the community at large being almost continuously critical of what it pleases to call the failure of the schools to teach their pupils how to spell.

Spelling and Reading— Different but Related Language Tools

Spelling and reading are both language processes. Spelling is the process of *encoding*, of selecting appropriate letters (graphemes) to represent the sounds (phonemes) in a word and of writing these graphemes in the same order in which the phonemes are articulated. Spelling, therefore, requires a complete job of word analysis. The pupil must respond muscularly to an aural-oral cue. He must decide what letter or letters will convey, suitably, the sounds he thinks or utters, to someone reading what he has written.

Reading, conversely, is a process of *decoding*, of translating the written word into its phonemic or spoken form. Beginning readers use varying methods of unlocking a strange word—of breaking the code. Some depend upon sight patterns plus context (meaning); some must arduously sound out each grapheme orally before "hearing" and thus deciphering a new word. In the evolution of language, the process of encoding necessarily preceded that of decoding, just as with the child, oral communication precedes written communication.

The teaching of the writing and reading tools of communication should begin with and exploit that which the child possesses when he enters school: a large aural-oral vocabulary. We contend that the pupil should be taught the alphabetical structure of the written form of American English by having him first *encode* his own speech. Then logic and psychology both suggest that the decoding of his writing should follow. Such is not the standard practice in most contemporary schools. Too often spelling is given a subordinate position or is submerged in the language arts area where it loses most of its effectiveness as a communication tool. In fact, spelling tends to be a "nuisance" subject in which words are taught pretty much in isolation and with little understanding on the part of the pupil of the interdependence of the encoding and the decoding processes and the importance of the mastery of these two distinctly different but related tools of communication.

Methods of Using the Spelling Tool

The pupil is too often encouraged merely to memorize the spelling of a word by whatever technique appears to be most effective for him. He may learn to spell quite a list of words by repeating orally the alphabetical names of the letters in the words until he has stored the correct orthography in his neurological system and hopefully will be able to retrieve the correct spelling each time the occasion arises for writing the word. Very often the haptical (hand-learning) approach is used: a child writes a word x number of times until the fingers automatically produce the correct recording of the graphemes for that word. Undoubtedly, many pupils master a list of words by employing a visual attack upon them. They use their eyes to fix a mental image of the graphemic representation of the word. Most normal children use various combinations of all three methods.

Some pupils consciously or subconsciously make the spelling process somewhat easier by using various kinds of mnemonic cues and associations. These may vary from the questionable but familiar traditional rhymes (*i* before *e* except after *c* . . .) to rules for adding suffixes (more often than not either incorrectly or inadequately stated) to such trick associations as: *sea* and *tea* (both have water). But such associations are not based upon a sound understanding of the language; they are haphazard crutches which contribute little to the development of real spelling power.

In reading, the pupil may soon learn to identify those graphemic representations that are irregular. Spelling, for most pupils, is a much more complicated process; one that involves the analysis of not only the sounds and their letter representations but the position of the phoneme in the word, the stress of the syllable, and various other factors that influence the choice among options of the particular grapheme to be used.

Written Language—A Code

All written language is a kind of code for the transmission of messages over space and time; messages that might be conveyed in a face-to-face encounter through sign language, but ordinarily are transmitted by means of the spoken word. For communication to take place, both sender and receiver must know the code—must know what each symbol stands for and in what order the symbols are arranged. The code for the written form of most present-day languages is an alphabetic code in which letter symbols are used to represent the units of sound that make up the spoken word.

A *phoneme* is the smallest practical unit of speech sound that can serve in a particular language to distinguish one utterance from another. The first sound, represented by the letter *p*, in the word *pan* is a phoneme because substituting for it the sound that the letter *t* usually represents would create a different word with a different meaning. Similarly, the letter *a* in *pan* represents a middle phoneme which is often called the "short *a* sound." Changing that second sound in *pan* to any other vowel sound would make a crucially different utterance, though not always an accepted and meaningful word. One might, for example, have *pin, pine, pain, pen,* or *pun* as a result of changing the second-position phoneme in *pan*. Likewise, the letter *n* in *pan* stands for a final phoneme that serves to differentiate that word in speech from such words as *pack, pat, patch,* and *pad*.

It is important to note that the word *phoneme* relates only to the sounds of a language. The technical name for a phoneme's representation in written or printed form is *grapheme*.

English—An Alphabetic Language

English is an alphabetic language in spite of the fact that, unlike such languages as Turkish, Finnish, and Spanish, it can hardly be said to have a one-to-one correspondence between phoneme and grapheme. If there were, spelling as a problem would become unimportant if not actually nonexistent. But written American English is made up of words that are comprised of letters or combinations of letters that stand for the sequential phonemes heard in the spoken form. While this is true in the main, there do exist in American English a number of graphemic options for the spelling of a given phoneme and, conversely, a number of phonemic options for many of the graphemes.

Many of the irregularities in the orthography exist because of borrowings from other languages. There has also been a tendency over the generations to alter the pronunciation of a word without bothering to make a corresponding change in its spelling. However, the phonemic nature of the American-English orthography may be illustrated by the fact that we do not hesitate to pronounce such nonsense syllables as *frip* or *glimp* or to spell them from dictation. A sentence containing words incorrectly though phonetically spelled would cause most readers little difficulty as far as getting the message is concerned.

Any good reader would know what is being said in this sentence: *Wee bot sum bate and rented a bote.*

How "Regular" Is American-English Spelling?

Those who insist that the phonemic-graphemic regularity of American English is mythical, or at best highly exaggerated, are fond of citing *ghoti* as a possible spelling of the word *fish,* because (they point out) *gh* represents the sound written *f* in *cough, o* represents the short *i* sound in *women,* and the letters *ti* stand for the *sh* sound in *nation.* This absurd spelling (ghoti) ignores completely the extremely important matter of structural pattern. The letters *gh* represent the sound normally spelled *f* only when that sound comes in final position in a root word, and then only when a preceding vowel sound is spelled *ou* as in *cough* and *tough* or *au* as in *laugh.* The letters *ti* represent the *sh* phoneme only when it is an interior one as in *nation* and *partial,* never when it is the initial or final phoneme. The letter *o* as a representation of the short *i* sound is a rare exception (as in *women*) that must be memorized.

So much stress has at times been laid on the irregularity of American-English spelling that we tend to overlook the very high degree of uniformity with which the phonemes of our language are represented in writing, especially when the important matter of the position of the phoneme is taken into consideration. Most consonants and short-vowel phonemes are nearly always represented *in a specific position* by the same grapheme. The majority of variances are found in the representation of vowel phonemes other than the "short" ones, and even these are ordinarily represented in one of only two or three ways. Many of the assumed irregularities are not genuine irregularities but are governed by rather consistent patterns that the good speller follows, often without even being conscious of doing so. For example, the vowel sound of *cow* is almost invariably represented by the letters *ou* except when it is the *last* sound in a word or is followed by a final *l* or *n* sound as in *owl* or in *crown.* In the latter instances, it is usually represented by the letters *ow,* the principal exceptions being *foul* (homonym of *fowl*) and *noun.*

Stanford Research Project

A research project sponsored by the United States Office of Education was conducted at Stanford University under the direction of the authors and with the participation of Richard E. Hodges, University of Chicago, and E. Hugh Rudorf, University of Delaware. It made a study of the American-English phonemes and the graphemes used to represent them. It was published by the U. S. Government Printing Office for the U. S. Office of Education as Project 1991.

A depth analysis of 17,000 words revealed the fact that relatively few words in this sample of our language have no phonological or morphological cues for spelling. With the aid of modern data processing techniques, it was possible to examine the structure of the orthography to a degree never before attempted or even possible by hand analysis. What kinds of insights into the American-English orthography were developed? This statistical analysis ascertained that the correct graphemic option can be predicted for a given occurrence of a phoneme, in these 17,000 words, approximately 90 per cent of the time when *the main phonological factors of position in syllables, syllable stress, and internal constraints underlying the orthography* are taken into consideration. In addition, this thorough analysis of the relationship between phoneme and grapheme indicates that other linguistic factors are determinates of the ways in which some parts of some words are spelled.

Further, the evidence obtained from Phase I of this investigation made it possible to design a second computer program, Phase II, which takes the findings of the first study and uses them to *predict* the standard spellings of different words. The results of this second computer run were significant. Of the 17,000 words given only as phonemes to the machine to spell, over 8,000 or 49 per cent were spelled correctly on the first computer run. An additional 37.2 per cent were spelled with only one error; 11.4 per cent with two errors; 2.9 per cent with three or more errors. An examination of the error list suggests that many of the misspellings could be obviated with the mastery of simple morphological rules.

Research Project No. 1991 to date suggests that a high degree of regularity does exist in the relationship between phonological elements in the oral language and their graphemic representation in the orthography. A pedagogical method based upon aural-oral cues to spelling (and reinforced with eye and hand-learning) may well prove to be more efficient and powerful than methods that rely primarily upon the visual and/or haptical learning approaches while ignoring the essential alphabetical structure for the encoding or written form of the language.

Phonological Factors That Contribute to Consistency

We have said that the American-English language is not based upon a one-to-one relationship between phoneme and grapheme, but that there are patterns of consistency in the orthography which, based upon linguistic factors, may be said to produce correspondences that are surprisingly consistent. The chief phonological factors contributing to this consistency are 1) position of the phoneme in the syllable or word, 2) syllable stress, and 3) internal constraints or surround.

For example: while one can be sure 74 per cent of the time that the phoneme heard and articulated at the beginning of such words as *face*, *find*, *feet*, and *fact* will be spelled correctly with the letter *f* regardless of the position of this phoneme in a word, it is necessary to remember that this particular phoneme may be spelled differently in a different position in other words. Although this sound is normally written *f*, it is almost never written *f* at the *end* of a word. It may be spelled *ff* as in *off*, *ph* as in *graph*, *gh* as in *cough*, or *lf* as in *half*. Again, when this same phoneme is preceded by a consonant, as in the word *sphere*, the phonome is spelled *ph*. The initial consonant sound, as in words like *sphere* and *sphinx*, acts as a restraint and dictates the choice of a particular graphemic option (*ph*) for the spelling of this phoneme in the word. One must also note that an exception to the spelling of the beginning sound in such words of Greek origin as *photo* and *phonograph* produces the spelling *ph*, rather than the normal or common spelling, *f*.

When the phoneme typically referred to as the long *a* sound occurs at the *end* of a word, here again *position* determines the choice of grapheme to be used to represent the vowel sound in the word. With the exception of a relatively few words, this long *a* sound, when coming last in a word, is usually spelled with the letters *ay*. Two words that are exceptions and should be used to point up the rule are *they* and *obey*.

When this same vowel sound (long *a*) occurs at the *beginning* or in the *middle* of a one-syllable word, it is almost always spelled one of two ways: *ai* as in *aid* and *rain; a-e* as in *ate* and *lake*. A statistically infrequent exception to this rule is found in such words as *eight* and *straight*.

No "Silent Letters" in Spelling

For years, spelling programs have consistently and determinedly identified any grapheme that "doesn't have a sound" (for whatever reason) as a "silent letters." The beginning sound one hears in *night* and *nine* is spelled *n;* the be- there is no such thing as a "silent letter" in spelling. The so-called silent *e,* a diacritical symbol, becomes part of a set of graphemes in spelling, whether it is used as a helping letter in writing the long vowel sounds in such words as *ate* and *made,* or whether it helps spell the final *s* or *z* sound in words like *fence* and *cheese.*

One should also note the unfortunate tendency to refer to such vestigial letters as the *k* at the beginning of *knee* and the *b* at the end of *lamb* as "silent letters." The beginning sound one hears in *night* and *nine* is spelled *n*; the beginning sound one hears in *knight* and *knee* is spelled *kn*; the last sound one hears in *lamb* and *climb* is spelled *mb.*

Consider the word *straight.* This word has five distinguishable phonemes. The first three (str) constitute a consonant cluster. The last phoneme is regularly represented by the letter *t.* What about the next-to-last sound? It is obviously a long vowel sound which in a certain group of words is written with the set of letters *aigh* as in *straight* and occasionally with the set of letters *eigh* as in *weight.*

There are many correspondences that can be analyzed phonologically by the pupils, and they will soon learn to look for variations in spelling which are governed by position as well as by "surround." They should be helped to discover such patterns as represented by a final *k* sound. This sound, when following a short vowel sound in a one-syllable word (*trick*) is almost always written *ck.* This same *k* sound in initial position, when followed by a short *i* or *e* sound, is written *k* (*kitten*); when followed by any other sound, it is usually written *c* (*cat*).

Building spelling power depends to a large extent (but not exclusively) upon a careful, rational, mature examination of all elements of a phonological analysis of words; on an ability to generalize about the effects that position, stress, and constraint have on the choices one makes among alternative graphemes or sets of graphemes to conform to standard American-English spelling.

Morphology Aids Spelling Analyses

Although the phonological analysis of a word is of primary importance in helping one to develop spelling power, there are other factors that can be of great aid. Morphology, the study of word formation, can be a helpful determinate of a choice of spelling options. In spelling, morphology is primarily concerned with compounding, affixation, and word families.

Compounding is a process whereby independent morphemes* join to form compound words. Once a pupil has learned to spell the independent morphemes in words like *playground* (play and ground), *caretaker,* and *lighthouse,* he should have no trouble in mastering the compounded forms.

Affixation and *assimilation* provide rules which, once understood, can be applied by pupils to the spelling of such words as *acute* and *account.* In both words, the phoneme-grapheme correspondences can be accounted for by applying phonological analyses—except for the *k* sound in each word. In *acute,* the *k* sound is spelled with one *c;* in *account,* with two *c*'s. Simple rules of affixation will readily account for the difference in graphemic representation

*A morpheme is a meaningful linguistic unit that may be a free form (child, pray) or a bound form (*hood* in childhood; *un* in unload) that contains no smaller meaningful parts.

of the *k* sound in these two words. In *account*, the letters *ac* represent the prefix *ad* which has been changed to *ac* before being added to the word *count*. This process is called *assimilation* and can be discovered by the pupil with a carefully programed spelling course. And there are reliable rules for adding suffixes to independent morphemes which, when understood, should make the spelling of such groups of words far less burdensome to the average pupil than trying to memorize the spelling of each individual word.

The term *word families*† is a popular bit of nomenclature which has come to be applied to those words that have similar spelling patterns and even partial phoneme similarities (bake, lake, make). Also labeled "families" are groups of words of common etymological origin that have rare graphemic representations for their phonemes. These words are usually spoken of as words of foreign origin, and as the pupil matures in a modern spelling program, he will be able increasingly to recognize the fact that in words like *andante, finale,* and *machete,* the final long *a* sound is spelled *e*, a regular representation in words of Romance origin.

Syntactical Components

A final group of words whose spelling defies phonological and morphological analysis must be explained by syntax. These words are homonyms and homophones. Their correct spelling can be determined only by the contextual surround. In the case of *steak* and *stake*, one simply must remember that when one refers to a pointed stick used for a fence or to mark a spot, the word is spelled *s t a k e* (with the vowel sound spelled *a-e*); that when one is speaking of a cut of meat, the word is spelled *s t e a k* (with the vowel sound *ea*). To master the correct spelling of most homonyms, one ought to use both the visual and haptical approaches in conjunction with the syntactical clues that help to establish the meaning of homonyms. Since consonant phonemes in homonyms are usually written with regular letter representations, phonological clues might be used to establish the way they are written.

The Teacher's Responsibility

The teaching of spelling has proved to be a rather frustrating experience for more than a few teachers and most pupils. Yet the elementary school teacher knows that if pupils are to develop the ability to communicate adequately in written language and if they are to be adjudged worthy of association with or employment by others, he must teach spelling as well as he can. He cannot abdicate his responsibility in this matter; he must plan carefully.

To plan carefully, the teacher needs to know more than that spelling is writing words correctly and that reading is being able to interpret the printed symbols on a page. He must know something of the nature of language in general and of American English in particular. He must understand the relationship that exists between the spoken and the written forms of the language. He must have clearly in mind the essential differences between spelling and reading and must also understand why it is important that all pupils, insofar as possible, be taught to spell correctly the words they use in their writing. He must consider not only the subject matter but the children who are to be taught. He must know their needs and their potentials as well as whatever experiences they have already had that may have helped prepare them for or inhibit them from learning to spell.

†The term is of questionable linguistic respectability and should be replaced by *groups* as soon as practicable.

Listening Vocabularies of First Graders

Before the average child enters upon formal schooling, he has already achieved an extraordinary mastery of the oral language. By listening, he has learned to get meaning from the spoken language of others. He is able to understand complicated and lengthy blends of phonemes in the oral language of his parents, siblings, and friends. By babbling and imitating, he has developed the ability to utter the particular phonemes of his language accurately enough to communicate his own feelings and ideas.

In fact, research indicates that the listening vocabulary of children entering first grade contains between 7,500 and 25,000 different words. Elementary school pupils from the very beginning have a high degree of control over the oral language they will be asked to represent by means of letter symbols in encoding.

Auditory and Visual Discrimination Abilities

Various researches have conclusively demonstrated that the normal first grader has no real difficulty making either auditory or visual discrimination if he is perfectly clear as to what the elements are that he is being asked to consider. If you show him the letters *t*, *f*, and *t* and ask which two are the same and which one is different, he has no difficulty answering correctly. If you say *bad*, *bug*, and *bad* and ask him which word you said twice and which only once, again he has no difficulty (provided, of course, there is no hearing impairment). In fact, if we make perfectly clear what we mean by the beginning sound of a word, most children will have little trouble hearing that *bad* and *bug* begin with the same sound, but that *fish* begins with a different sound.

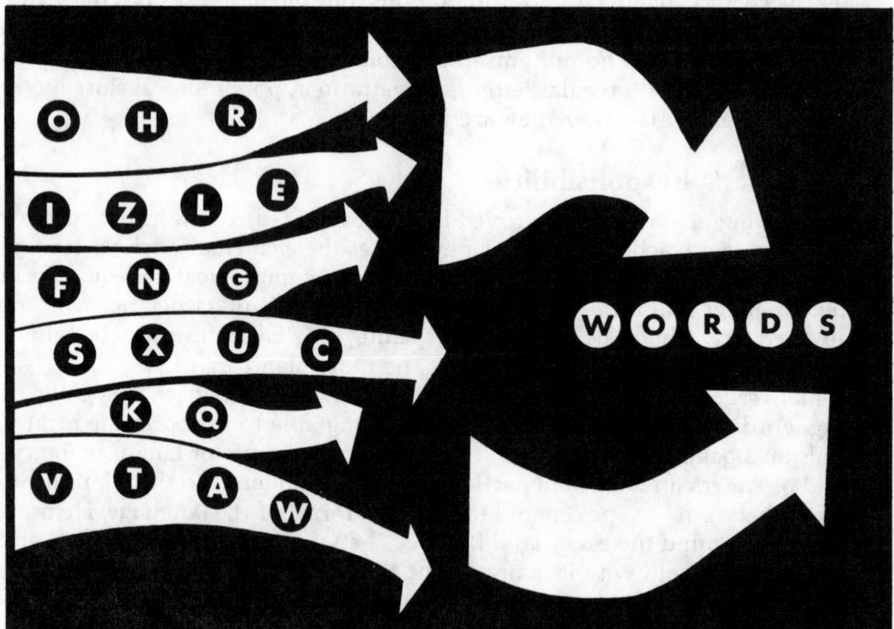

Some pupils whose auditory discrimination is underdeveloped or faulty may have to struggle to recognize any difference between the beginning sounds of *bat* and *pat* or the ending sounds of *can* and *ham*. Until this auditory difficulty is alleviated, such children may be expected to make errors in graphemic representation of such phonemes that are (for them) difficult to distinguish.

Writing Vocabulary Needs of Pupils

The average child enters first grade expecting that within a very short time he will learn both to write and to read. Reading and writing are to him fascinating but somewhat mysterious activities engaged in by parents, older brothers and sisters, and friends. He himself may have felt the need of knowing how to express his thoughts in ways other than speech. But few children entering school have made the effort or even believed they could teach themselves either to write or to read, in spite of the fact that they have taught themselves to communicate orally.

Today, more and more pre-school children are discovering the delight of using letters to write the words they speak and, upon entering first grade, are already in command of a sizable volume of words they can write (spell) correctly.

Suppose the child already knew at the beginning of the first grade how to represent by letters all the words he might want to use in producing written communication. What would be the total number of different words he might wish to write? No research, so far as we know, has yet given us a definite answer to that question. Common sense, however, would suggest that the individual child's writing vocabulary in that imaginary situation would be approximately the same as the vocabulary he himself uses in talking. Let's assume that the child's speaking vocabulary is only half as large as his hearing-understanding vocabulary. The average first grade child would then wish to write at least 3,750 words. Any first grade teacher who has asked pupils in the second half of the year to write independently on some topic, promising to help by writing on the board any word a pupil wants to use, knows how rapidly the available board space will be filled with words that various pupils request.

Much faulty deduction has been derived from the fact that 1,000 different words will account for more than 90 per cent of the running words a first grader will want to use, and that 1,500 different words will account for over 90 per cent of the running words in the writing of sixth graders. The words comprising the slightly less than 10 per cent of running words such pupils need are just as important to them for communication as are the other 90 per cent. To a child who wishes to write to someone about a puppet show he has seen on television, that word *puppet* is just as important as any other, even though the word *puppet* may not appear in a list of the 3,000 words used with highest frequency by elementary school children.

Because of the lack of a one-to-one correspondence between phoneme and grapheme in American English, it would be impossible to teach a first grade child how to spell correctly every word he might want to write once he had mastered the formation of the letters. As we said earlier, certain languages do have almost a one-to-one correspondence and for children in such countries as Turkey and Finland, spelling their own language is not much of a problem. As soon as a child in one of those language areas has learned to write every grapheme, and has also learned the phonemic association for each grapheme, he can write correctly any word he has heard or can pronounce. Unfortunately, the American-English-speaking child is in a less enviable position in this respect and likely will continue so for the foreseeable future. Therefore, there is all the more reason for using every available means to help the American-English-speaking child analyze his language, discover its regularities, notice its unusual spellings, and familiarize himself with certain rules and generalizations which govern the sets of correspondences which comprise the orthography.

Major Aims in a Sensible Teaching Program

It is obvious, to begin with, that a goal of mastery of a specific word list will not answer a pupil's needs, whether that list contain 3,000 or 10,000 words. If we concentrate our efforts on having the child learn to spell a specific list of several thousand words, we are in essence asking the American-English-speaking child to perform the feat required of the *literate* Chinese (a very select minority of the total population) because to read and write the Chinese language requires the memorization of a different symbol for each of thousands of words. This requires a prodigious visual and motor memory and a determination possessed by relatively few pupils. And perhaps more to the point is the fact that with today's escalation of knowledge in every field, there is scarcely time to spend memorizing individually the spelling of thousands of words. The pupil should rather spend his time mastering a technique that will enable him as soon as possible to spell *any* word that he wants to be able to write and to which he has been able to apply that technique.

What is the nature of this technique that will give the pupil independent power in spelling? It is, first of all, developing in the pupil the habit of noticing, whenever he sees a word that he can pronounce, whether or not the spelling of that word deviates from the spelling it would have in a completely consistent one-to-one system. He must be able to analyze the spoken word easily and quickly into its individual phonemes, know what the ordinary, expected graphemic representation of each phoneme is, and be able to think what phonological or morphological influences might cause a *special* graphemic representation of the sounds in that word. If he comes across the word *puppet*, he will know that the word is spelled completely regularly; that the double consonant almost always follows a short vowel sound in a non-final accented syllable.

Teaching pupils the technique of visually noticing and remembering spelling irregularities will reduce considerably the memorization task they face in learning to spell. A pupil who knows the most common letter representation for each phoneme will need to concentrate on observing and remembering the exceptions. In order to learn to spell *bread*, he will concentrate on remembering that the vowel sound in a whole group of words is represented by the letters *ea* rather than just *e*. Once he has mastered the basic sound-to-letter associations, he will be able to spell a great many words without having to memorize anything, since most words that involve only consonant and short vowel sounds are completely regular in their spelling.

Essential Insights and Understandings

If the pupil is to become master of the recommended technique, what are the insights, understandings, and skills he will need?

First of all, the pupil must become aware that written American English is an alphabetic language; that when he writes a word, he is writing letters to stand for the sounds he hears in that word when it is spoken. Secondly, he must learn how to listen for the separate phonemes in a word and to note their positions and the sequence in which they occur. Since the consonantal phonemes of English are not sounded in isolation but always precede or follow a vowel phoneme, it follows that the child must learn to listen for and hear in words a great many phonemes that he never hears separately. Furthermore, because our words are formed of phonemes that usually glide from one to another, he must accomplish the not always easy task of recognizing when one phoneme ends and another begins. This ability to break a spoken word into its component phonemes may not at first be achieved very easily by the average first or second grader, but it is an ability most essential to the development of genuine spelling power.

Since, in the natural spelling situation, the spoken form of a word will be the pupil's own pronunciation as he says it either actually or mentally to himself, it will, of course, be important to give some pupils help in learning to voice the various phonemes correctly. The child, or the adult, in his writing tasks is ordinarily spelling words that he is thinking of rather than words that he is hearing someone else say. Pupils who have developed careless enunciation habits will need to be encouraged to imitate a teacher who says words clearly and accurately so that the phonemes in those words can be correctly identified.

Teaching Sound-to-Letter Associations

As pupils learn to listen for the separate phonemes in words, they should at the same time begin to associate a specific letter or set of letters with each such phoneme. Naturally, the sound-to-letter or phoneme-to-grapheme associations thus presented should be confined in the initial stages to those that are nearly always represented in only one way. This means that the pupil's attention will for some time be directed to the letter representations of the consonant and short vowel phonemes since these are more consistent.

Only after pupils have secured mastery of these sound-to-letter associations should they be introduced to the graphemic representations of vowel sounds other than the short ones or to the few irregular representations involving consonant graphemes, such as the *c* spelling of the *s* sound.

The major variations in graphemic representation occur in connection with the several vowel sounds that are not called short. With these, pupils will often have to learn at least two and sometimes several spellings likely to be used in any one position. Yet, even with these, there are generalizations to which pupils can be led inductively. For example, when the long *a* sound occurs in a word in final position, as we have already pointed out, it is almost always represented by the letters *ay*. Once he has discovered this fact, the pupil will not need to memorize the spelling of *may* and *stray* but will realize that he must remember exceptions like the *eigh* in *weigh* and *sleigh* and the *ey* in *they* and *obey*.

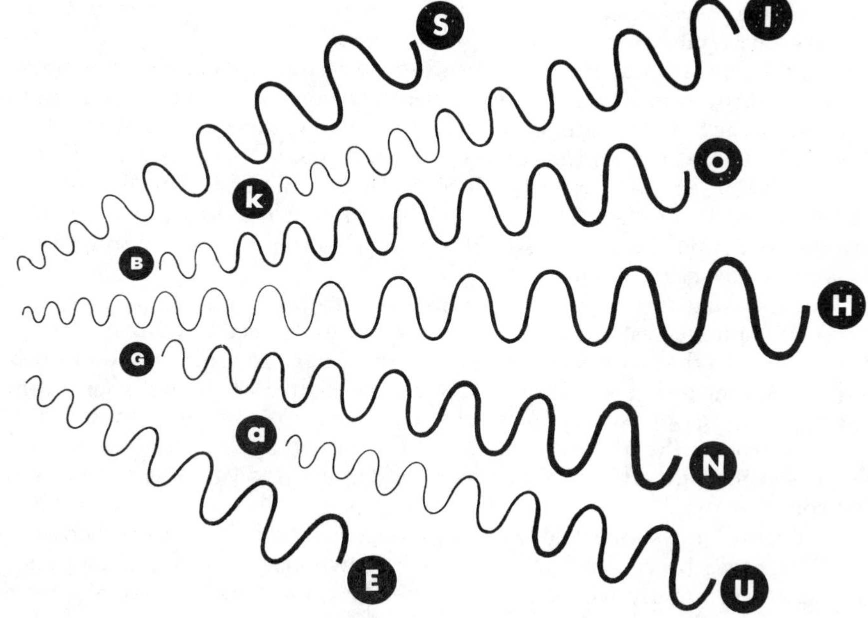

When the teacher finds it necessary to introduce early a high service word like *said* that contains an irregular spelling of a vowel sound, the teaching stress should be placed on bringing out the relationship between the vowel sound and the letters used to represent it in this particular word, rather than on memorizing the spelling of the whole word as if it were a single and distinct symbol unrelated to other words. Thus, in teaching the word *said*, the teacher would point out that the first and last sounds are written just as would be expected and that the pupils should take special pains to remember that in this particular word, the vowel sound is spelled *ai*. Naturally, only as many relationships as a child can reasonably be expected to assimilate without confusion should be taught at any one period.

Once pupils have a firm knowledge of the more regular sound-to-letter associations, the teacher should frequently ask pupils what they will need to remember about a specific word if they want to be able to spell it correctly. As the program develops through the grades, the pupil gradually adds understanding of the effect of position, syllabic stress, constraint, and the cues that come from morphology and syntax.

The acquired knowledge as to possible letter representations of the various phonemes will also provide the pupil with what he needs if he is to make independent use of the dictionary as an aid to correct spelling. If he has learned that a beginning sound may be represented by either *s* or *c*, he may look in both the *c* and *s* parts of the dictionary to locate a word like *citrus*. He can determine its correct spelling if he has heard the word but not seen it, or if he is not certain he remembers how it was spelled when he did see it. Therefore, once a pupil has been taught to use a dictionary properly, he should no longer be told the correct spelling of a word he wishes to use, but should be expected to discover its correct spelling on his own. The only exception to this procedure should be with respect to words or proper names which would not be listed in a school dictionary.

Three Basic Initial Steps

At the very beginning of the spelling program, the following procedure should be carefully observed.

First, the pupils should be led to hear and discriminate among phonemes in different positions in words. For example, they should be made aware of what is meant by the term "beginning sound" and be led to recognize that words like *mop* and *men* begin with the same sound and that a word like *pig* does not begin with that sound. Similarly, they should be encouraged to discover that the second or the next sound after the first sound in *bed* and in *hen* are alike, but different from the second sound in *rug*. This step might be thought of as the auditory discrimination step.

Next, the child should be led to associate with each of the more regularly represented phonemes the grapheme most commonly used to write it. Thus, the pupil will learn that we nearly always use the letter *t* to write the sound heard at the beginning of *top* and at the end of *cat;* no matter where that sound comes in a word. Here, too, he will learn that the letter *s* is commonly used for the sound he hears at the beginning of a one-syllable word like *soap*, but that when it comes at the end, after a short vowel sound, we usually use two *s*'s to write that sound.

Finally, the pupil should be led to an appreciation of the power this knowledge gives him; to see that the learned sound-to-letter associations now make it possible for him to spell many words correctly merely by writing in correct order the letters that stand for the phonemes he hears in those words.

Some Special Cautions

Oral spelling exercises of the old-fashioned "spelling bee" variety should not be used as a teaching-learning technique in spelling. When a teacher is trying to help a pupil hear the phonemes in a spoken word and to translate those phonemes into the correct graphemes for writing purposes, nothing could be more confusing than having those same pupils vocalize the alphabetical *names* of the letters used in spelling the word.

There may be little or no relationship between the sound of the name of the letter and the sound being represented by that letter. Saying "double-you-ay-gee" will hardly help the pupil build a direct response of writing the letters *w*, *a*, and *g* when he hears the very different sounds of the phonemes in the word *wag*. Furthermore, such oral spelling is completely unrealistic. "A spell-down" is acceptable only if it is recognized as a competitive exercise in sheer recall. Ordinarily, we are *writing* something whenever we have occasion to spell.

Because spelling customarily takes place in a writing situation, the teacher should take pains to have most spelling practice consist of writing words in continuing natural context rather than as isolated words in a list. Whenever possible, such practice should be done not directly from dictation of the specific word but in response to a mental stimulus that leads the pupil himself to think of a word to be spelled. In the natural writing situation, the pupil will be spelling words that he is thinking of rather than words he is hearing someone else say.

Haptical and visual reinforcement of the learned spelling will come best from this practice of having the child write the word correctly in a natural situation. His haptical reinforcement results from the combined sensorimotor experiences that are both kinesthetic and tactile. His visual preception of the word will be as it appears in his own handwriting. Having the pupil write the word correctly a number of times in isolation is one way of reinforcing learning, *provided* the pupil takes pains to observe the arrangement of the graphemes within the word he is writing. Repetitive writing is ineffective if allowed to become purely mechanical.

As soon as possible and whenever possible, the teacher should use an inductive approach in developing the recommended sound-to-letter generalizations. This means getting the pupils themselves to notice how a particular phoneme is represented in words of like patterns and to discover a generalization that applies. For example, suppose pupils have learned that a long *o* sound in beginning or second position in a one-syllable word is usually written *oa* or *o-e*. The teacher can call attention to words of the *old* group (sold, told, gold) and lead them to discover and generalize that when the long *o* is followed by the *l* and *d* sounds, we use just the letter *o* to stand for the vowel sound in those words. This *discovery* technique is an essential part of a modern spelling program.

The teacher in such a program will, of course, have to be able to analyze words as to their component phonemes and to know what grapheme stands for each such phoneme. Otherwise, he will not be able to give pupils the help they need if they are to learn to identify and remember the parts of the word that may cause them trouble. The pronunciation symbols used in the phonetic re-spellings in any good dictionary will identify for the teacher the phonemes of our oral language.

Genuine Spelling Power

If the child is taught, beginning with the simplest of sound-to-letter patterns, to relate sound and written symbol and to observe and make mental note of any deviation from the expected pattern, he will be able to spell correctly almost any word that he can pronounce and that he has seen correctly spelled at least once. A knowledge of the most regular representation for each phoneme by position plus the ability to notice and store away for future recall the spelling irregularities of individual words or groups of words is what we call "spelling power." The added power that emerges from discovering the cues from morphology and from syntax rounds out a modern spelling program. The achievement of such spelling power should be the aim of every teacher and every pupil. Whole-word memorization feats should be confined to those few words like *of* and *choir* that are almost completely irregular in their representational patterns.

64.

Paragraph Composition: A Suggested Sequential Outline

Leo M. Schell

The heart of all expository writing and the starting point for narrative composition is the paragraph. It is a truly versatile tool: It can narrate a tale, picture a setting, vivify a character, animate behavior, detail a process—and do myriad other things. It deserves to be a primary focal point in the composition program of the intermediate grades if pupils are to learn to write because the quality of a composition seldom exceeds the quality of its components.

However, a vexing problem for intermediate grade teachers is that pupils are at varied levels of competence in paragraph composition. In reading instruction, a similar problem is typically solved by homogeneously grouping pupils and having them read from varied materials commensurate with their achievement level. But seldom is such a plan feasible in composition instruction. Commonly there is the same text for all pupils. One solution for this problem would be for teachers not to be shackled to the material in the text for that grade level but to have a total picture of the goals in paragraph composition and possible instructional approaches for attaining them. A teacher who knows in general what topics had been introduced previously and which ones would be taught later should be better able to provide the level and amount of instruction needed to care for the varied achievement differences found among the pupils.

Moreover, the textbook need not gather dust; it could be used as a resource and reference tool wherever and whenever appropriate. Steel beams, no matter how long or strong, are not wholly sufficient to build a skyscraper; other materials are needed. And no matter how good a textbook, it is just one of several tools needed to help children learn to compose quality paragraphs.

The activities suggested to achieve the learnings are "functional." They frequently can be studied and implemented in the content fields thus killing two birds with one stone: improving written composition and learning subject-matter content. Additionally, many suggestions are based on the assumption that texts and other children's books can be the best possible model for helping children comprehend a topic by studying many examples and then using these as guides in practice exercises. This assumption, currently widely used in teaching narrative writing, seems equally valid in teaching expository writing.

Reprinted from *Education* 90:158-160 (November-December 1969), by permission of author and publisher, The Bobbs-Merrill Company, Inc.

The outline, while neither complete nor exhaustive, probably includes all of the major items children need to learn in order to construct a thoughtful, well-organized self-contained paragraph. Additionally, the final section leads into the role of several related paragraphs in a longer composition.

Outline

A.

A paragraph should deal with a single topic.

1. Suggested instructional activities:
   a. Detect and discuss extraneous sentences.
   b. Study and discuss "cluttered" paragraphs, e.g.,
      The giant sequoia is the world's largest tree. Some are 100 feet around the trunk. Some grow 300 feet tall. Sometimes they live over 3000 years. They grow only in California.
   c. Study and discuss paragraphs in content field textbooks.
   d. Have the class corporately construct a two-step outline on a topic from content field; write paragraph from outline.
   e. Write from a topic, e.g.,
      Spot "Delivers" the Paper
      Steps in Making Rubber
      At the Planetarium
   f. Expand from a topic sentence, e.g.,
      George Washington Carver helped Southern farmers by finding many uses for the peanut other than eating.

B.

A paragraph typically has a topic sentence.

1. Topic sentences should be general, not specific, e.g.,
   Man communicates in many ways.
   One Japanese holiday is the Feat of Flags.
   In Vermont, skiing is a popular winter sport.
2. Topic sentences often contain a hint or arouse interest.
   "Look out for that ice!" yelled Dad.
   Tony tried hard to be good but usually he was in some kind of trouble.
   Do you know where the moon came from?
3. Suggested instructional activities:
   a. Find, study, and discuss representative paragraphs in books.
   b. Choose the best from more than one, e.g.,
      The gentle, harmless koala lives in Australia.
      The koala has a funny, puzzled expression.
   c. Write on from the rest of the paragraph, e.g.,
      ______________________ . Someone was pounding on the door. "Climb out the window!" Mother shouted. "Some grease caught fire and the kitchen's ablaze. You can't get up the stairs. Hurry before the furnace explodes!"
   d. Create one.
      (1) From a class-constructed outline.
      (2) For a personally-written paragraph.
         Note: The creation of a quality topic sentence may be too difficult to expect a child to do on the initial draft. *Good* beginning sentences are the product of writing-revising rather than initial writing.

C.

A paragraph develops a topic.

1. There are many kinds of paragraph organization, e.g.,
   a. Description (details)
   b. Reasons as proof
   c. Examples
   d. Question-answer
   e. Cause-effect
   f. Time order (sequence)
   g. Space order
      (1) Left-right
      (2) Top-bottom
      (3) Near-far
2. Suggested instructional activities:
   a. Outline exemplary paragraphs.
      Use content-field textbooks or teacher-written material.
   b. Write from outline provided by teacher.
      Discuss outline and then write connected, related sentences on each subtopic and detail.
   c. Find, study, and discuss representative paragraphs in books.
   d. Create own outline.
      Teacher and/or pupils can contribute topic sentences; each pupil choose one and list items that might be included. This could be done for each of the paragraph types listed above. Outlines can be compared, discussed, and turned into paragraphs, either individually or corporately.
   e. Write sample paragraphs.
      Using as models the paragraphs found in 2c, have children write one or more paragraphs of each type. To simplify this, the teacher can suggest a topic or a topic (beginning) sentence. Later, pupils can create a total paragraph on their own.

D.

Sentences in a paragraph are related to each other.

1. "And" and "then" are overused.
2. Suggested instructional activities:
   a. Find, study, and discuss how paragraphs in textbooks avoid these problems.
   b. Find, study, discuss, and use the following transitions:
      Chronological order: first, after, soon, last, finally, next, before, since, when, then, later.
      Cause-effect: therefore, because, as a result of, since, due to, hence.
      Concomitant action: while, during, as, at the same time, simultaneously.
      Other: also, moreover, so, but, however, rather, for example.

E.

A long, self-contained, expository paragraph should be concluded or summarized with a general sentence related to the topic or beginning sentence, e.g.,

Topic sentence: Purifying water is a complicated process.
Concluding sentence: When you drink water, remember all the people who helped make it clean and safe.

1. Suggested instructional activities:
   a. Find, study, and discuss representative paragraphs in books.
   b. Choose the best from more than one, e.g.,
      That's why you should always eat a good breakfast.
      And you should drink some fruit juice, too.
   c. Write one from the rest of a paragraph, e.g.,
      Many people think that all Indians were savage warriors. But this isn't true. Many were gentle and peaceful. The Winnebagos never used weapons to fight with, only to hunt with. And Hopi Indians would rather run than fight.

      ____________________.
   d. Create one.
      (1) From a class-constructed outline
      (2) For a personally-written paragraph.

F.
The last sentence of one paragraph may lead into the next paragraph, e.g.,
   . . . As you can see, precise words make clear pictures, and clear pictures are more interesting than fuzzy, blurred ones.
   What kinds of words help us to make clear pictures? . . .

1. Suggested instructional activities:
   Repeat those listed above in E1, making appropriate modifications.

Concluding Comments

Several comments about this suggested outline seem in order. One, this outline does not imply that paragraph composition needs to be studied as a discrete unit, isolated from other writing skills. In fact, children may better and more easily acquire the major learnings if these are incorporated into a larger unit, report or story writing for example.

Two, numerous skills essential to good paragraph composition were intentionally omitted. Two of these are the use of (1) varied sentence patterns and (2) synonymous subjects. They were omitted, not because they are unimportant, but because they are *general* writing skills and are not unique to *paragraph* writing. These omitted skills should be an integral part of all writing. In fact, they may be important enough to deserve their own separate systematic instruction.

Three, grade level designation has been deliberately omitted. Achievement and ability ranges differ so greatly within and between classrooms that a teacher trying to fit all pupils to the same mold may be unwittingly defeating her real goals. With handy guides like this, the enterprising teacher could dip into it according to the needs and abilities of her pupils and proceed instructionally at an appropriate pace. Thus, these are not standards all pupils are expected to attain but rather guidelines to help the teacher select and plan appropriate goals and learning activities commensurate with the needs and abilities of her pupils. In a sense, this outline is a tool. And just as the knowledge and skill of a surgeon determines how successfully he wields a scalpel—or other tools, so will these same factors determine how successfully teachers use this—and similar—outlines.

65.

Dictionary Skills and Punctuation Habits as Aids to a Child's Writing

LeRoy Barney

For anyone who aspires to set words upon blank paper, be he Nobel laureate or hack, fulltime author or weekender, professional or amateur, adult or child, there is no substitute method for the study of the masters who have already appeared in print. This study, of course, is not intended for an imitation of style. But it is intended to illustrate the turns of phrase, the handling of literary devices, discrimination with word usage, and the practice of punctuation.

Most teachers also know that study of the masters is important for inspiration of a child's writing. And all teachers simply must face the fact that a study of writing samples should be first and foremost, inspiring. But it is often erroneously conceived that only the highest forms of literary endeavor, usually poetry, by the greatest of the adult masters, such as Tennyson, would satisfy the "master writer" criterion or would do justice to true inspiration. Obviously, this is not true when working with children.

Most children do not enjoy, nor do they understand, the subtle nuances of the language used in poetic form by adult masters. The teacher should look, then, toward those undisputed masters of juvenile literature. In addition, it is best to study samples of prose rather than poetry. All children do not love poetry, although most like to read verse (humorous poetry). But few dislike good, fast-paced, action packed stories. Juvenile masters such as Twain and Alcott are enjoyed universally.

The Dictionary Habit

Most teachers try to teach vocabulary by way of a list. They compile a number of obscure words, tabulate them on a piece of paper, and require a child to search for meanings in the dictionary, and memorize the results.

There is little doubt that vocabulary is one of the strongest of all writing tools and that those students with the best vocabulary tend to be the best writers. But effective vocabulary building is not normally accomplished through

Written for this volume by LeRoy Barney, Associate Professor of Education, Northern Illinois University.

direct memorization of lists. It is, however, highly efficient to teach the dictionary habit to check the meanings of words in context when reading the works of the masters.

Pronunciation of Words

When a child encounters an unknown word in his trade literature or "masterwriter" sample, he is first confused as to proper pronunciation. But reference to the dictionary may possibly increase his confusion.

The most important skill of dictionary study is the interpretation of the pronunciation key and its allied concepts of (1) knowledge of diacritical marks and (2) knowledge that diacritical systems are not standard or universal. In other words the diacritical system used in a child's dictionary may not be the same as the one he mastered in his reading text. Moreover, an examination of the respective pronunciation keys of the social studies, science, or health texts may represent a third, fourth, or even a fifth sound-value marking system.

Consequently, when reading a favorite author, the child should understand that symbols noting pronunciations vary from pronunciation key to pronunciation key. This necessitates a careful reading of each key.

Perhaps it should be explained, however, the pronunciation in a dictionary is descriptive, not prescriptive. In other words children should understand that the lexicographers who compiled the dictionary polled various individuals and recorded the ways in which these participants pronounced words. These pronunciations were then recorded by way of diacritical marks under appropriate entries in the dictionary. Therefore, the writers of dictionaries are not stating that words must be pronounced in the way they have recorded them, rather they are merely recording the ways the words were pronounced in the language sample. Should the sample have been collected almost entirely from the east coast of the United States, the words may sound a bit unusual to the ear of the midwestern child from Chicago.

Differences in Spelling

But when reading non-American "masterwriters" such as Fleming, the child may encounter spellings and words which are not only strange to him, but which may not be recorded in the dictionary. The word "color" may be spelled "colour." The familiar word "theater" may be recorded as "theatre," "plow" may be listed as "plough," and misspelled may be written as "mispelt," or "jail" becomes "gaol."

When studying writing samples, these are differences which are significant and which must be explained by the teacher, especially since most of them do not actually appear as entry words in modern American dictionaries.

Differences in mere spelling, however, should not delete some of the best English authors from literary study.

Word Variance

A problem of even more consequence when studying British writers is the difference in word usage. The word "tram," for baby carriage, or "lorry," for truck, does not appear in Americanized vocabulary lists as represented in standard dictionaries. A child may hear his father talk about the "hood" of a car, but in his story, the same device is known as a "bonnet." And "gasoline" or "gas" becomes "petrol."

Word usage is not insurmountable, but it requires special attention from the teacher if the communications barrier is to be broken.

Methods of Vocabulary Study

The presentation of large, unwieldy words, completely unknown to the students has been a favorite among many classroom practitioners. These terms are almost always presented in a list, devoid of explanation. Unfortunately, this method of word study is rarely effective.

Somewhat more efficient means of mastering vocabulary include the etymology approach, semantic technique, word histories, context, and study of words by examining the writings of the masters.

The etymology approach requires the child "to break" a vocabulary word into its component parts. Thus the word "telephone" refers to an instrument as a final referent. But the component parts of the term are "tele" which means "far" and "phone" which signifies "to speak." Thus the word "telephone" is an instrument devised to speak over long distances.

By the same token the word "aqueduct" may be reduced to its component parts. The term "aqua" means "water," and "duct" connotes a tube. Therefore an aqua duct is a tube designed to carry water.

The semantic technique is more interesting than the etymological study, and it contains similar elements. A child may be interested to know that "diaper" once referred to an ornate altar cloth, a "muscle" meant "little mouse," or "rock" denoted a cloud. It is interesting for the child to discover that some words have specialized their meaning while others are more generalized than previously. In addition, some words become elevated in stature and elegance through acceptance and usage, but others are degraded and vulgar.

A study of word histories retains many of the elements of both the etymological approach and the semantic technique, but it is a vast improvement over both of them in utility.

Normally, a term such as "desultory" would be much too difficult for most children to include in their vocabulary study. But if accompanied by a word history, it becomes easy to remember and use. A desultor was a Roman horseman of the circus variety. A team of horses would lope around a tight circle in the arena and the desultor would leap to their backs. Once mounted, he would jump back and forth from the back of one animal to the back of another. Thus "desultory" describes a flitting or changing without any apparent organization or pattern, as in a desultory conversation.

The term "sinister" is also a word which would normally not be taught to children. But the word comes from "sinistral" which means lefthanded. The Romans always taught their troops to use swords in the right hand. A left-handed individual was simply not to be trusted, hence the term "sinister."

Probably one of the most powerful methods of vocabulary study is a combination of word histories, judicious interpretation of context, and study of "masterwriters." When studying writing samples, then, it is important to sensitize children to various literary devices which illuminate word usage as depicted by these experts.

Using the Dictionary for Meaning

Should a child be asked to define "file," he may conjure one of several definitions: (1) an instrument used by a carpenter, (2) an emery board for trimming finger nails, (3) a cabinet to house records, (4) the act of placing data in a file cabinet.

But when the child encounters the word "file" in the writing of one of the authors of juveniles in the following passage, "When George rounded the bush on his rabbit hunt, he spied the rabbit's file in the snow." Obviously, he knows *a* definition for the term "file." But can he understand the meaning intended in this particular passage. When he refers to his dictionary he will be tempted to select the very first definition he comes to as being appropriate. He must be taught to be patient and to explore all of the definitions to determine which makes sense in context. The "file in the snow," for instance, doesn't refer to a carpenter rabbit, a manicurist rabbit, or a secretary rabbit. The meaning intended is a rabbit track.

A term used by older children might be "compose." This word might elicit one of several meanings: (1) create music, (2) write a theme, (3) to "pull oneself together." But if the child should read Somerset Maugham's "Outpost to Progress," he may encounter the phrase "Warburton loved to compose arguments among the tribal chieftans." Should the child apply his immature logic to the context without reference to a dictionary, he may assume the term "compose" to indicate that Warburton loved to create arguments among the tribal chieftans. Actually, Maugham used the word to signify that his hero loved to "settle," not "create," arguments.

Although teachers deplore advising children to make marks in trade books, the following technique has proved successful with a commonsense use of the dictionary when studying the writing of masters. The child should use a soft pencil when reading trade-book literature. Each time he encounters a strange word he should place a light period in the margin. After, and only after, he has completed the story, he should work through the trade-book to find his marks. This assumes the context was not strong enough to unlock the meaning with the first reading. He should try to review the context for clues to unlock the meaning of the word. If the context is too weak to provide positive clues, he should check the definition in the dictionary and record the context and the definition in his word book.

Punctuation

Many teachers are aware of the changes of the meanings of words as they are passed from generation to generation, but they do not realize that punctuation usage also tends to change. True, the comma and period are used today in much the same way that they were used in the classical era dominated by Greek and Roman writers. But some marks have changed in usage (the asterisk); others have changed in function (the single dagger).

To illustrate the drastic changes in punctuation, consider the Declaration of Independence. Of its 47 sentences, 35 terminate with the following marks:

.--	25
,--	1
:--	9

In other words 35 of 47 sentences taken from a "purely" American Document fewer than 200 years old terminate in punctuation which is not used today.

Unfortunately, limited space confines further consideration of punctuation to the comma only.

How Many Rules?

For decades teachers have been drilling their students on the rules governing the use of the comma. For an equal amount of time these same teachers have failed in efficient teaching of punctuation usage. Many have offered cure-alls for the situation, but each, in turn, has proved to be fruitless and has fallen into disuse.

The following procedure is not guaranteed, but normally it works efficiently when conscientiously applied:

Allow students to study punctuation in stories written by masters of juvenile literature. To put it another way, allow the child a great deal of experience of interpreting the commas in his reading before requiring him to use it correctly in his writing.

As it happens, the interpretation of the comma in reading is far simpler than learning to use the mark in writing. To support this view, consider that there are upwards of more than 40 rules for comma placement listed in the majority of elementary-level English texts. Compare those with the basic rules of comma interpretation as applied to reading, of which there are only two.

The first of these two is the single comma used after the manner of the classicists. For an example consider the following sentence:

Mary wore a red dress; Sally, a blue one.

In this statement the comma represents a grammatical concept which must be interpreted by the child if he is to communicate effectively with the author. What is the grammatical function of this comma? Obviously it replaces the verb "wore."

Essentially, then, a single comma used in the classical sense replaces a word or phrase which has been removed from the sentence. This comma announces to the reader that something has been removed from the context and that he, the reader, must replace it.

These commas used in a series are also single commas, as demonstrated by the following sentence:

The tall, angular, tired man slouched through the door.

In this case each comma replaces the word "and." Stylistically, it is smoother to use the commas than a string of redundant coordinating conjunctions.

Some writers, however, use both the comma and the "and" in the terminal phrase of a series. For rationale they declare that both the comma and the conjunction are needed for communication. Other writers delete this last comma with the rationale that the "and" has not been omitted and therefore it is illogical to use punctuation which signifies deletion.

Both positions are correct. The comma is illogical in this position. Yet, if it is needed for communication, best practices requires that it be used.

The second comma rule or situation occurs when a phrase or clause is to be grammatically removed from the rest of the sentence. A historical explanation is necessary.

Maruim occidit Johannes.
Johannes occidit Marium.

Both of these Latin sentences say the same thing. How is that possible? Meaning, in Latin, is declared by the inflectional endings of words, not by word order. Any language which makes meaning by inflectional endings of words is a synthetic language.

English was once a highly synthetic language. But during and immediately after the Scandanavian Wars of King Alfred's time, many of the inflectional endings were lost. Now, when a language requires endings to make meaning and ends up losing those endings, well . . . chaos results. Consequently, printers, such as John Caxton, decided to require word order to make meaning. Any language which makes meaning by word order is an analytic language.

These printers decided that the appropriate order for language was as follows: subject, verb, direct object, and indirect object, each with their respective modifiers. Any phrase or clause which came between the subject and verb, for instance, was set apart as a grammatical intrusion of the sentence. The device used to grammatically set the intruder apart was a pair of commas.

John, come here and help me.
Come here, John, and help me.
Come here and help me, John.

In each of these three instances, the word of direct address, John, was set off from the rest of the sentence by a comma or commas.

The reading of various masters will give many concrete examples of expert use of commas. Moreover, the two interpretation rules make the process far more palatable than basic English drill which requires mastery of more than forty rules. Common practice has shown that when the child has enough successful experience with guided interpretation of punctuation in his reading, he will be able to apply his knowledge to writing with very little extra teaching.

Function of Punctuation

Punctuation of a sentence often reveals the author's intention for meaning. For example, in the sentence, "Buddhism was developed in monasteries, or *viharas*," the good reader would understand several things immediately: (1) "viharas," set off by a comma, is a mere restatement of the more familiar term "monastery." (2) "viharas" is a word adopted from a foreign language and has not yet been anglicized. This is denoted by the term being underlined, the manuscript form of italics.

If the comma had not appeared in the sentence, the context would convey a much different message. In that instance it would signify that Buddhism was developed concurrently in two different institutions; monasteries and *viharas*.

Summary

To aid children in their communications skills, to reduce the quantity and increase the quality of their rewriting, and to add much needed spice to the writing program, the teacher should allow the children to study the publications of masters of the juvenile story. Pronunciation, British spelling, vocabulary study, and punctuation usage should be taught judiciously.

Notes

1. Arthur T. Allen, "Literature for Children: An Engagement with Life," *The Horn Book Magazine* 43 (December 1967): 737.
2. Northrop Frye, *The Educated Imagination* (Bloomington: Indiana University Press, 1964), p. 122.
3. Kornei Chukovsky, *From Two to Five*, Miriam Morton, trans. and ed. (Berkeley: University of California Press, 1963), p. 93.
4. Frye, *op. cit.*, pp. 23, 24.
5. *Ibid.*, p. 22.
6. George Fugita, "Creativity," a taped lecture, University of Hawaii, August 20, 1964.
7. Richard Braddock, Richard Lloyd-Jones and Lowell Schoer, *Research in Written Composition* (Champaign, Ill.: National Council of Teachers of English, 1963), p. 92.
8. Alvina Treut Burrows, Doris C. Jackson and Dorothy O. Saunders, *They All Want To Write* (New York: Holt, Rinehart and Winston, Inc., 1964), pp. 166-174, 207-215.
9. *Ibid.*, pp. 2-3; Miriam E. Wilt, *Creativity in the Elementary School* (New York: Appleton-Century-Crofts, Inc., 1959), pp. 2-3.
10. It is recognized that another school of thought places as much or more emphasis on the product as the process.
11. Herbert R. Kohl, *Teaching the Unteachables* (New York: The New York Review, 1967).
12. Carrol Gard, *Writing: Past and Present* (New York: The A.N. Palmer Company 1937), pp. 31-32.
13. Alfred Fairbanks, *A Book of Scripts* (Hammondsworth, England: The King Penguin Books, 1960), p. 22.
14. E.A. Enstrom, "To Slant or Not To Slant . . . in Print Handwriting," *Grade Teacher* 81 (February 1964): 55, 123, 127; "Ready, Willing, and Able . . . for Cursive Handwriting," *Instructor* 75 (March 1966): 126-127; E.A. Enstrom and Doris C. Enstrom, "Teaching for Greater Legibility," *Elementary English* 41 (December 1964): 859-862; E.A. Enstrom and C.H. Trafford, *The "Common Sense" Approach to Teaching Handwriting* (Greensburg, Pa.: Peterson Handwriting, 1966).
15. E.A. Enstrom, "Research in Handwriting," *Elementary English* 41 (December 1964): 873-876.
16. Leslie J. Nason, *You Can Get Better Grades* (Los Angeles: University of Southern California, 1961), pp. 13-17.
17. Larson D. Farrar, "Dollars and Sense in Handwriting," *Active Advertising* 2 (August 1960): 2; "Poor Penmanship Costs Money," *Nation's Business* 43 (April 1955): 101; Fred R. Zepp, "Please Don't Excuse the Penmanship!" *McCall's* 91 (December 1963): R-7, R-8.; Herman Feldman, "Analyzing the Cost of Illegible Handwriting," *Hospitals, Journal of the American Hospital Association* 37 (February 16, 1963): 70, 74, 77, 80.
18. Peterson Directed Handwriting, *Adventures in Handwriting* (New York: Macmillan Company, 1964); Peterson Directed Handwriting, *Teachers Guides* (all grades), (Greensburg, Pa.: Peterson Handwriting, 1963).
19. C.E. Ragsdale, "How Children Learn the Motor Types of Activities," *Learning and Instruction*, Forty-ninth Yearbook of the National Society for the Study of Education, Part I, Nelson B. Henry, ed. (Chicago: National Society for the Study of Education, 1950), distributed by the University of Chicago Press; Howard L. Kingsley and Ralph Garry, *The Nature and Conditions of Learning*, 2nd ed. (Englewood Cliffs, N.J.: Prentice-Hall, Inc., 1957), Chap. 10; Karl C. Garrison, "Learning the Basic School Subjects," *Educational Psychology*, Charles E. Skinner, ed. (Englewood Cliffs, N.J.: Prentice-Hall, Inc., 1959), pp. 564-567; E.A.

Enstrom and Doris C. Enstrom, "Wanted: Automation in Handwriting," *Catholic School Journal* 66 (November 1966): 51-53.
20. Fred M. King, "Handwriting Practices in Our Schools Today," *Elementary English* 38 (1961): 483-486.
21. Carl Personke and Albert H. Yee, "A Model for the analysis of Spelling Behavior," *Elementary English* 43 (1966): 278-284.
22. Frank N. Freeman, *Teaching Handwriting* (Washington, D.C.: National Education Association, 1954).
23. James A. Fitzgerald, "Spelling: Diagnosis and Remediation," *National Elementary Principal* 38 (May 1959): 27-30.
24. Arthur I. Gates and Esther Hemke Chase, "Methods and Theories of Learning to Spell Tested by Studies of Deaf Children," *Journal of Educational Psychology* 17 (May 1962): 289-300; Edna L. Furness, *Spelling for the Millions* (New York: Appleton-Century, 1964), p. 59.
25. Frederick S. Breed, *How to Teach Spelling* (Dansville, N.Y.: F.A. Owen Publishing Company, 1951).

Selected Bibliography

Ammon, Richard I., Jr. "A Practical Way to Teach Spelling." *Elementary English,* **46** (December 1969): 1033-1035.

Anderson, Dan W. "What Makes Writing Legible?" *Elementary School Journal,* **69** (April 1969): 364-369.

Applegate, Mauree. "As Useful as a Toothbrush." *A Monograph for Elementary Teachers,* No. 75. New York: Harper and Row, 1955.

Arbuthnot, May Hill. "Puss, the Perraults and a Lost Manuscript." *Elementary English,* **46** (October 1969): 715-721.

Ashley, L.F. "Children's Literature Today." *English Quarterly,* **2** (January 1969): 71-76.

Bingham, Alma Irene. "Spelling Should be Functional!" *Instructor,* **78** (February 1969): 77-78.

Ciardi, J. "What is a Dictionary?" *Saturday Review,* **52** (May 24, 1969): 38-39.

Cohen, Dorothy H. "Word Meaning and Literary Experience in Early Childhood." *Elementary English,* **46** (November 1969): 914-925.

Denby, Robert V. "An NCTE/ERIC Report on Creative Writing in Elementary Schools." *Elementary English,* **46** (February 1969): 159-165.

Dimondstein, Geraldine. "What is Meaning in Children's Poetry?" *Elementary School Journal,* **69** (December 1968): 129-136.

Enstrom, E.A. "Handwriting: A Sorry Plight." *Contemporary Education,* **41** (January 1970): 133-136.

Enstrom, E.A. and Doris Enstrom. "In Handwriting It's a Family Affair." *Elementary English,* **45** (February 1968): 236-242.

Groff, Patrick. "A Model for Writing Adventure Stories." *Elementary English,* **46** (March 1969): 364-367.

Groff, Patrick. "The Non-Structured Approach to Children's Literature." *Elementary School Journal,* **70** (March 1970): 308-316.

Groff, Patrick J. "Who Are the Better Writers—the Left-Handed or the Right-Handed?" *Elementary School Journal,* **65** (November 1964): 92-96.

Hodges, Richard E. and E. Hugh Rudorf. "Linguistic Clues in Teaching Spelling." *Elementary English,* **42** (May 1965): 527-533.

Horn, Thomas D. "Spelling." In *Encyclopedia of Functional Research,* 4th edition, edited by Robert L. Ebel, pp. 1282-1299. New York, London: Collier-Macmillan, 1969.

Hunter, Elizabeth. "Fostering Creative Expression." *Childhood Education,* **44** (February 1968): 369-373.

Jacobs, Leland. "Give Children Literature." *Education Today,* Series Bulletin #22. Columbus, Ohio: Charles E. Merrill Books, Inc., 1962.

Kaimann, Sister Marie. "English Composition in the Primary." *Elementary English,* **45** (April 1968): 485-491.

King, Fred M. "Readiness for Handwriting." *Elementary English,* **45** (February 1968): 201-203.

Korbel, Natalie. "How to Encourage Creative Writing." *Elementary English,* **46** (October 1969): 769-771.

Larrick, Nancy. "Life Ain't Been no Crystal Stair." *School Library Journal,* **15** (February 1969): 47-49.

Lasser, Michale. "Literature in the Elementary School: A View From Above." *Elementary English,* 46 (May 1969): 639-644.

May, Frank B. and Robert Tabachnick. "Three Stimuli for Creative Writing." *Elementary School Journal,* **67** (November 1966): 307-313.

Mower, Morris Leon and LeRoy Barney. "Which Are the Most Important Dictionary Skills?" *Elementary English,* **45** (April 1968): 468-471.

Olson, Dorothy C. "A Perfectly Normal Spelling Dilemma." *English Journal,* **58** (November 1969): 1220-1222.

Petty, Walter T. "Handwriting and Spelling Dilemma." *English Journal,* **41** (December 1964): 839-845.

Seaberg, Dorothy I. "Is There a Literature for the Disadvantaged Child?" *Childhood Education,* **45** (May 1969): 508-512.

Shapiro, Phyllis P. "The Language of Poetry." *Elementary School Journal,* **70** (December 1969): 130-134.

Thompson, Phyllis Rose. "The Teacher Bemused: The Use of the Other Arts in the Teaching of Poetry." *Elementary English,* **47** (January 1970): 130-134.

Tiedt, Sidney W. "Self-Involvement in Writing." *Elementary English,* **44** (May 1967): 475-480.

Torrance, E. Paul. "Ten Ways of Helping Young Children Gifted in Creative Writing and Speech." *Gifted Child Quarterly,* **6** (Winter 1962): 121-127.

Wilson, Louis Ada. "Helping Children with Manuscript Writing." *Peabody Journal of Education,* **47** (September 1969): 72-76.

Yee, Albert H. "The Generalization Controversy on Spelling Instruction." *Elementary English,* **43** (February 1966): 154-161, 166.

PART SIX
Evaluation in the Language Arts

A.

Overview

Evaluation is the science of determining the degree to which objectives have been achieved. In education, evaluation should be an ongoing process of assessing outcomes of instruction. Realistically, diagnosis of pupil needs should precede the teaching-learning process. Once the teacher has appraised relevant aspects of his students' individual development and behavior, he may then define his objectives and select the appropriate instructional procedures.

Both objective and subjective criteria are needed to obtain comprehensive data on changes in pupil behavior. For effective learning, evaluation should stress the growth the child makes in terms of his own abilities, interests, and goals, not just how he compares intellectually with his peers. Evaluation techniques may include standardized tests, teacher-made tests, anecdotal records, autobiographical data, logs, inventories, rating scales, recordings, questionnaires, and opinionaires. All of these devices may provide evidence of which goals have been achieved and where there is a need for further instruction.

Standardized tests yield quantitative data which are useful in interpreting how well a child or a class has done when compared with national age or grade norms. Less formal instruments often produce descriptive evidence that reveals students' attitudes, interests, skills, and understandings. Each evaluative device is designed for a specific purpose and should be used accordingly. The selections in this part of the anthology suggest various tests and instruments which may be utilized in evaluating students' growth in the language arts.

The first article surveys briefly some factors which influence language development, reviewing the uses and limitations of standardized tests for assessing the language development of individual children, and then goes on to discuss at length informal classroom procedures for assessing language growth in listening, speaking, oral reading, and composition.

Since evaluation of children's knowledge of elementary school literature does not lend itself to skills development analyses, the author of the second article suggests using three questions as a guide to determining each child's literary interests:

(1) "Is he receptive to literature?"
(2) "To what literature is he receptive?"
(3) "What is his reaction to the literature he receives?"

The third selection stresses further the necessity for analytical testing and the use of appropriate followup materials for remedial instruction in oral and written expression, spelling, and handwriting. Although this article proposes the use of commercial devices for the diagnosis and correction of handwriting weaknesses, the article which follows it entreats the teacher to have students evaluate samples of their handwriting from compositions produced in many subjects over an extended period of time.

Continued self-evaluation is necessary if students are to improve their language skills upon leaving school. In the concluding article, six levels of listening have been modified and adapted as criteria for evaluating compositions. Through healthy self-appraisal of his own writing, each pupil may also improve his self-worth and his self-confidence—qualities that are basic to all worthy pursuits.

66.

Assessing Pupil Growth in Language

John C. Manning

The search for methods of appraising the English language development of pupils has a rich history of continuing experimentation and a somewhat limited heritage of accomplishment. Most successful have been those efforts to measure the quantitative aspects of English language achievement. Studies of the size of the four functional vocabularies, efforts to control the vocabulary content in basal reading systems, and contemporary studies of the effects of redundancy on comprehension skills development merit universal acceptance in our sometimes all too tolerant behavioral science.

Less successful and subject to arbitrary definitions and subjective evaluations have been those efforts to assess the qualitative aspects of English language growth. Factors affecting creativity, development of the higher mental processes, imaginative and elaborative thinking abilities are terms which frequently appear in the professional literature but are seldom defined to the satisfaction of the educational fraternity.

It is generally accepted that many factors of heredity and environment significantly affect the development of a hearing, a speaking, a reading, and a writing vocabulary. Component analysis of those background factors has not shown clear cause-effect relationship on any variable examined with relation to a language outcome.

Cultural deprivation does effect language growth; to what extent is open to conjecture.

Physiological factors do affect achievements in speaking and reading; evidence of the relationship between hyperopia (farsightedness) and reading disability can be established. Legions of excellent readers with this same eye impairment, however, cast doubt on this seemingly logical causal relationship.

Neurological impairments of various types may be diagnosed in pupils who fail in our schools and those students whose language achievements are superior.

The possibilities for investigation of these various sub-strata factors are limitless and will, no doubt, as we move to a more scientifically oriented profession, provide a fertile field for interdisciplinary studies of English language learning.

The effectiveness of standardized testing instruments has done much to

Reprinted from *The Twenty-First Annual Conference and Course on Reading, University of Pittsburgh* 21:103-110, 1965 by permission of the publisher.

advance the possibilities for controlled experimental research in English language development. Many areas of language growth, however, such as reference and research ability, improvement of oral reporting, ability to organize materials, improved quality of written expression, enrichment of concepts and development of pupil interest in language defy the best intentioned efforts of both psychologist and educator.

These opening remarks have been intended to emphasize the complexity of the task which confronts the classroom teacher and to reinforce the thesis that what knowledge exists in our discipline is often contradictory, often not appropriate to practical application and often without a theoretical base, inductively constituted, which cornerstones every profession except our own.

This paper will lightly examine three aspects of the problem of assessing language growth in pupils:

1. Background factors affecting English language development.
2. Normal English language development.
3. Uses and limitations of standardized testing instruments and more pointedly examine selected informal classroom procedures which may be used to improve the teaching of the English language arts.

Background Factors Affecting Language Development

The main argument for intensifying research in this area is that hopefully we will be able to provide a status profile for each pupil on entrance to school that will have immediate practical value for compensatory and intensive instruction in areas of anticipated language deficiency.

Four major tasks must be accomplished if this situation is to eventuate:

1. Specialization of research efforts to determine cause-effect relationships in each sub-strata area through interdisciplinary approaches.
2. The development of needed, and the refinement of existing, measurement instruments.
3. The full utilization of computer systems for analysis of Status Profiles.
4. The use of these same electronic systems for programming educational materials in appropriate intensity to accommodate individual differences among pupils.

Normal Language Development

It would be presumptuous to suppose that valid analysis could be made of the many variables affecting normal language development within the limits of this paper. The complexity of the interrelationships among physiological capacity, environmental conditioning, and intellectual components including psychological-emotional aspects precludes the possibility of a satisfactory treatment here.

I do, however, wish to make brief comment on two significant problems of contemporary importance.

Ample research evidence exists concerning the size of the various functional vocabularies utilized by pupils at various chronological and mental age levels. We speak of normal language development as a sequence of accomplishments in acquiring a hearing vocabulary, a speaking vocabulary, a reading vocabulary and a writing vocabulary appropriate to the satisfaction of our social needs. The extent to which individual pupils utilize these vocabularies varies widely, especially with regard to mental age factors.

It is difficult to find curriculum programs reflecting these language differences. Seemingly, we have not appreciated the fact that elaborative thinking abilities, critical thinking skills and creative thinking attainments can be improved through listening tasks and reflected in the improved speaking accomplishments of pupils. All too many intermediate and secondary school language arts programs revolve around grammar workbooks, written composition assignments and reading comprehension tasks poorly adjusted to the vocabulary abilities of students and ill suited to the full utilization of the communicative media of our time.

The so-called "dropout" problem is aggravated by our reluctance or seeming inability to desire more efficient educational programs in the listening-speaking areas. With automation so emphatically upon us, it is ill advised to concentrate on industrial art or craft programs for terminal pupils in our secondary schools.

A second matter concerns our national commitment, philosophically and economically, to the educational improvement of the culturally deprived. Obviously, language development is of major importance in this endeavor.

A distinction should be made between those vocabularies which are learned somewhat naturally—the hearing and the speaking vocabularies, and those which are learned more formally—the reading and the writing. One difficulty in improving the educational level of the culturally deprived child is that a natural sequential development must be artifically accelerated to overcome language deficiencies and thus insure academic success in the lower primary grades.

The various "Projects Headstart" which I have observed in Texas and in California, and the various local projects courageously started without federal aid, do not, in most instances, regard some basic linguistic principles in language development and thus do not make maximum use of the additional school time which such projects financially afford. Entirely too much effort is expended on experiential activities related to concept development and entirely too little on formal instructional procedures to develop pupil proficiency with English phonology and syntax.

The vocabulary of our English language is not its most difficult component and such concept deficiencies are easily overcome. Those skills learned through oral-aural methods, specifically phonology and syntax, should constitute our major effort in formal language and reading readiness activities designed to overcome language deficiencies caused by socio-economic disadvantage.

Uses and Limitations of Standardized Tests

As a procedure for assessing the language development of individual pupils, the use of standardized tests has obvious advantages in measuring certain reading and writing abilities and glaring limitations in the listening-speaking areas. It would be unfair to criticize standardized testing in the main since a general fault is the use and interpretation of such measures rather than their content or professional intent.

Again, quite realistically, improved methods of correction and diagnostic appraisal must be fashioned before maximum use of such devices will be made. All too often such standardized tests are used solely as achievement measures, and the burden of correction and estimate of grade placement is assigned to the classroom teacher. The dubious motive purports that such correction procedures will result in a more sensitive understanding of the pupils enrolled in any given class. That such understandings *can* and *do* occur is not at question here; that such understanding must come by such debilitating clerical procedures is professionally reprehensible.

Again, I would hope that economical individual school computer systems, impersonal enough to be objective and discriminating enough to hold valuable the unique development of each child, will soon be an integral part of the school facility.

Informal Classroom Procedures for Assessing Language Growth

A distinction is generally made between hearing capacity and listening ability. The former is more frequently defined in physiological terms while the latter refers more specifically to a communication skill. The following remarks relate to this latter classification.

Among the many reasons for assessing the listening abilities of pupils, two are of major significance:

1. A test of listening comprehension will provide suitable evidence of the capacity to read.
2. A test of listening comprehension is useful in determining the functional level for pupil participation in both skills and content subject areas.

In lieu of more formalized procedures, a listening comprehension test is a simple diagnostic measure which may be used to determine the reading capacity of individual pupils with reading disabilities.

Paragraphs, generally narrative or factual in style, may be selected from basal readers of various grade levels. These paragraphs should vary in length from a grade one selection of perhaps twenty-five words to an eighth grade selection of approximately 125 words. Comprehension questions may then be devised appropriate to each paragraph. Four or five questions would be sufficient for the grade one selection to perhaps seven or eight for the grade eight paragraph.

Contrasting the pupil's ability to answer questions following teacher reading of the paragraphs with the pupil's ability to read paragraphs of a similar type but different content will roughly approximate the degree of retardation in reading.

Such information regarding pupil deficiencies should be encouraging for it provides evidence that with properly adjusted educational materials, intensive teaching efforts and teacher dedication to the possibilities of increased achievement, improvement is possible. Further, when such information is professionally presented to parents, it can provide cautioned encouragement and do much to relieve parental anxiety concerning the mental abilities of the academically failing child.

The measurement of listening as a functional ability in various skill and content subject areas may be effected with slightly more elaborate procedures.

The graded paragraph format may again be used, but the content and style of both paragraphs and comprehension questions would change to suit the purposes of the measurement. Graded paragraphs to measure problem solving abilities could be employed, those measuring critical thinking abilities could be used, *while graded paragraphs in the various content areas could be used* as a measure of listening ability for the purposes of following directions, drawing inferences and conclusions, and for ability to determine main idea and logical sequence.

The instructional implications should be obvious; pupils with reading disabilities could benefit from listening skills instruction and classroom activities adjusted to comprehension level.

The matter of attention and persistence in learning is intimately associated with listening abilities. More than likely, pupil inattention in grade one is a major cause of learning disability and also the major symptom of inappropriate instructional procedures. All too often the use of pictures, simple visual directions and routine completion exercises aggravate the inattention problem.

Primary grade teachers could improve the listening abilities of pupils by decreasing the number of demonstrative pronouns used in giving oral directions and by increasing the number of subordinate units and qualifiers used in the assignment of classroom lessons.

At the intermediate and upper grade levels, major improvement in listening ability can be effected through the use of listening study guides which clearly specify the purposes for listening. Oral reporting activities, discussion procedures, and teacher presentation in content areas should be preceded by instructions for improving the efficiency of listening and accompanied by opportunities for pupil-written responses during the conduct of such oral activities.

Assessing Levels of Speaking Ability

The reluctance of many pupils to meaningfully participate in speaking activities in our classrooms no doubt stems from two major causes:

1. A self judgement that what is known by the pupil is not significant enough or pertinent enough to be shared.
2. An attitude of self consciousness or fear having root somewhere in that forest of experiences which affects all human behavior for good or ill.

Both problems are difficult to overcome instructionally and more than likely, each of us suffers in some degree from both.

The classroom teacher may gain some insight into the interests and speaking abilities of individual pupils (and the two are more than casually related) through the use of pictures of various types. Some pupils will readily respond to pictures narratively charged; other pictures more abstractly constituted and stimulus questions such as "What do you think will happen next?" "Why do you think the little girl is so happy?" might yield less enthusiastic results.

Some pupils operate well if the speaking activities are on a rather explicit level; others more imaginative, though not necessarily more intelligent, function well with more implicit motivations.

Following are examples of pictures and appropriate stimulus questions in order of increasing abstraction:

Picture	*Initial Stimulus Question*
1. Children playing	Tell me what the children are doing.
2. Dock or terminal scene	Tell me what is happening here.
3. Family on a picnic	What do you think mother is saying? Father? etc.
4. Boy and his father getting into an auto	What do you think is going to happen?
5. Child gazing out a window	What do you suppose this little girl is thinking?

In a sense, procedures of this kind, rather grossly, measure various thinking abilities as well as speech proficiency. It is difficult, however, to devise clean measures which evaluate one and not, by inference, the other.

Two major instructional adjustments may be made for pupils with limited speaking vocabularies:

1. Adjustment of the speaking task to the demonstrated level of pupil facility.
2. Adjustment of group size to encourage increased pupil participation in oral activities.

Assessing Pupil Growth in Oral Reading

The question of the amount of oral reading proportionate to the amount of silent reading in developmental programs continues to plague the profession and has in past decades provided speaker, orator, and scholar with opportunities to extol the virtues of one and the vices of the other and vice versa.

Aside from certain aesthetic values, the purpose of oral reading is the diagnosis of word recognition errors of individual pupils. As such, certain procedures may be followed to instructional advantage.

When word recognition errors are made during oral reading, two entries should be made by the teacher, the actual error of the pupil and the correct lexical item from the text being read. Errors recorded should be reviewed periodically to determine the "pattern of error" for more effective word recognition instruction in subsequent reading lessons.

Assessment of the individual pupil's "pattern of error" is the important element for effective reteaching and word skills instruction. It is necessary, therefore, that errors be recorded over an extended period of time and that each individual pupil's errors be recorded separately. A tabbed stenographer's notebook is excellent for this purpose.

A symbol system should be devised for accurate recording of the following common error types: mispronunciations, words pronounced for pupils, insertions of words, additions to words, and omissions.

The recording activities should be clearly explained to pupils and the objectives of such recording of error should be demonstrated by sensitive and effective reteaching. I do not support the point of view that such recording methods stir latent feelings of insecurity and failure. Such feelings unfortunately arise when pupils do not understand teacher behavior, do not understand the reasons for their failure, and see no improvement in their subsequent reading attempts.

Similarly, the level of the text being used should come into serious question if too many errors need to be recorded. More than one pupil error in every twenty running words should alert the teacher to a reappraisal of the level of text being used. If no errors are made by pupils, a similar reappraisal would be in order.

It is my contention that parents should be directly and early informed of the specific causes of reading failure. It is of questionable value to chronicle the symptoms of disability such as poor attitude, poor study habits, lack of motivation, daydreaming and the like. The use of such terms, more often than not, gives parents wide latitudes for conjecture and supposition and ultimately may emotionally stretch the deficiency beyond the point of educational remediation.

Most reading disabilities are not complicated beyond the understanding of classroom teachers. Conscientious recording of pupil errors, periodic review of such deficiencies and intensive remedial instruction at the point of word recognition weakness can, and in most cases will, provide failing pupils with a first full measure of success.

The problem we, as educational practitioners, have not confronted is the development of remedial materials in sufficient quantity, largely pupil directed and corrected, which when intensively used will assist the classroom teacher in overcoming reading deficiencies.

Developmental programs of reading instruction as presently constituted are clearly not enough. Instructional materials development, branched to include language-experience instruction, intensive phonics instruction, linguistic instruction and intensive kinesthetic-tactile instruction must be appreciated by the publishers of basal reading materials if we are to be successful in eliminating reading failure from our schools.

Assessing Pupil Growth in Written Language

My final remarks will relate to measurement in spelling and correction for mechanics of language factors.

We are moving as a profession, I think, to a clearer understanding of the contribution which other academic disciplines can provide with regard to subject matter content. The contribution of linguistics to spelling instruction is a case in point.

I am reasonably certain that the number of spelling words introduced per week, the manner of presentation, the type of word presented, and the speller exercises have not changed appreciably in the last three decades. The merit of this contention should be questioned since perhaps at some future time an opportunity to amplify the position will be afforded your speaker.

A major cause of spelling failure is an excess in the number of words presented for individual pupil mastery. It is even more fundamental than that perhaps; it is in the presentation of a spelling list at all.

If a child is failing to learn to read, I see little merit in introducing a spelling list. More appropriate, perhaps, would be the use of the reading vocabulary words as spelling words and instructionally provide visual memory training with those words during the spelling period.

Teachers may justify a modification in the number of spelling words presented to pupils failing in reading using the following simplified classification system:

Words may be classified as:

Content words:	nouns, verbs, adjectives, and adverbs
Function words:	articles, prepositions, conjunctions, word auxiliaries, connectives

Words may be sub-classified as:

Colorful:	words that evoke mental images (grandfather, canoe, dog, etc.)
Abstract:	words which do not evoke mental images (whenever, because, however)
Phonetically regular:	words in which one-to-one correspondence exists between the phonemes and the graphemes (mud, sod, tub)
Phonetically irregular:	words in which an irregular phoneme-grapheme correspondence can be found (most of the words in our language)

A content, colorful, phonetically regular word, therefore, would, in most instances, be more readily mastered in spelling than a function, abstract, phonetically irregular word. Though the point is highly generalized, the classroom implications for instruction should be clear.

A modification in the manner of presenting words in spelling tests might also prove valuable in assessing spelling power.

Spelling words may be presented orally by definition as one phase of a test and then by actual word in another phase. A two columned sheet may be used. Spaces for words not known by definition should be left blank in the first column and then attempted in the second column when the teacher provides the word stimulus.

Rationale for this method rests on the assumption that when we want to write, we have some ideas to communicate, and like Pirandello's "Six Characters" we go searching for the words which best express our thoughts.

And finally, correction procedures for written language.

All too often there is little articulation in the written language program in our schools. The method following is supported by the theory that pupils develop writing skills at various rates of progress and that intensive remedial instruction is necessary to overcome mechanics of language deficiencies. The method is further contingent for success on the preparation of educational materials of sufficient quantity in the specific sub-skills areas of capitalization, punctuation, usage and spelling.

A first problem is to determine the level of corrections; that is, the type of correction mark and the position of that mark relative to the specific error. Obviously, the classroom teacher must begin at a level appropriate to the number of errors made by individual pupils; the greater the total numbers of errors in proportion to total running word count, the lower the level of correction which should be employed.

Level I	Correction at the point of error with the correction item. J to (john sat down too eat.)
Level II	Correction at the point of error by symbol. X X (john sat down too eat.)
Level III	Correction at the line of error. (2X john sat down too eat.)
Level IV	Correcting by indication of the total and type of error. (2p, 2c, 2u, meaning 2 punctuation, 2 capitalization and 2 usages errors)
Level V	Indication by numeral of the total number of mechanical errors without indication as to type.
Level VI	Pupil self-proofreading.

The teacher correction procedures at whatever level conducted should be followed by intensive practice specific to the sub-skills weakness. For this purpose, quantities of practice materials of increasing difficulty should be catalogued by skill, and be readily available for pupil practice and self-correction.

The road to excellence in instructional practice is arduous and professionally demanding.

No developmental language programs thus far outlined will serve all learning needs for all pupils.

No standardized or informal tests thus far designed will assess all language deficiencies.

No teacher education programs thus far operative or envisioned will adequately prepare practitioners for all instructional possibilities.

And certainly no profession has ever undertaken a task so monumental as the development of universal literacy with so optimistic an attitude of eventual and certain success.

67.

Discovering What Children Have Learned about Literature

Norine Odland

What children learn about literature will reflect the process which has been used to teach literature. In curriculum areas for which skill development is the desired outcome, we often *determine*, *define*, and *standardize* what children have learned. Literature in the elementary school usually is not and should not be considered in terms of the skills which can be measured after instruction has taken place. Unfortunately, on the contemporary scene literature may be losing its "time slot" in the elementary school curriculum because the outcomes cannot be measured and graphed. To reverse that trend, ways must be discovered for describing to the child, to his parents, and to the community what he has learned about literature.

Discovery and description of what children have learned about literature can be guided by three questions. In the questions, the word "receptive" is used to refer to the language arts of listening and reading as means of transmitting literature. The singular pronoun is used for reference to the student because literature is personal and individual.

We can ask:

> Is he receptive to literature?
> To what literature is he receptive?
> What is his reaction to the literature he receives?

Is He Receptive to Literature?

Facts about the reading done by the adults in our country are evidence that the teaching of literature has not achieved the goal, "establishing life-long reading habits," or at least the goal has not been achieved for the majority of people. Current studies of the reading, or lack of it, done by individuals retired from full-time work refute the argument, "I would read if I had more time."

Several hundred juniors in a college of education preparing teachers for elementary schools reported reading an average of 4.5 books over a period of one year. The median number of books read by the same group was slightly less than 4, which confirms what you would probably expect about the nature of

---

the distribution. The same students read few magazines regularly and the magazines they did read were predominantly general news, picture, and women's publications. Ten years ago those juniors were in the elementary schools which undoubtedly aimed to teach students the values of personal reading.

Studies also show that reading is rated low among choices of what children would choose to do or have chosen to do with their time outside of school. These findings are exactly what one would expect if the basis for prediction is the importance with which persons who allot school time regard literature and personal reading.

Most elementary schools operate under the assumption that learning to read is absolutely essential to success in school and out of school. This is as it should be! A teacher certainly should be able to answer the question, "Can he read?" with specific as well as with conditional answers. But the same teacher should also be able to answer the question, "Does he read?" The response to the latter question is "What do you mean?"—"in other subjects, in the library, at home? It all depends." It all depends on the teacher and the literature and the child. What about the literature?

To What Literature is He Receptive?

Books and other reading materials are available today in great numbers and in accessible places. The number of libraries in elementary schools has increased, though not necessarily with a proportionate increase in reading by the children in those schools. Children select from the materials available to them and the choices they make show us that *our* choices and *their* choices are not always the same. The Pacific Northwest Library Association Young Readers' Choice Award is an example of an award based on children's choices from books available in libraries.

1940: *Paul Bunyan Swings His Axe* by Dell J. McCormick (Caxton)
1941: *Mr. Popper's Penguins* by Richard & Florence Atwater (Little)
1942: *By the Shores of Silver Lake* by Laura Ingalls Wilder (Harper)
1943: *Lassie Come Home* by Eric Knight (Holt)
1944: *The Black Stallion* by Walter Farley (Random)
1945: *Snow Treasure* by Marie McSwigan (Dutton)
1946: *The Return of Silver Chief* by Jack O'Brien (Holt)
1947: *Homer Price* by Robert McCloskey (Viking)
1948: *The Black Stallion Returns* by Walter Farley (Random)
1949: *Cowboy Boots* by Shannon Garst (Abingdon)
1950: *McElligot's Pool* by Dr. Seuss (Random)
1951: *King of the Wind* by Marguerite Henry (Rand)
1952: *Sea Star* by Marguerite Henry (Rand)
1953: No Award
1954: No Award
1955: No Award
1956: *Miss Pickerell Goes to Mars* by Ellen MacGregor (McGraw)
1957: *Henry and Ribsy* by Beverly Cleary (Morrow)
1958: *Golden Mare* by William Corbin (Coward)
1959: *Old Yeller* by Fred Gipson (Harper)
1960: *Henry and the Paper Route* by Beverly Cleary (Morrow)
1961: *Danny Dunn and the Homework Machine* by Jay Williams (McGraw)
1962: *The Swamp Fox of the Revolution* by Stewart H. Holbrook (Random)
1963: *Danny Dunn and the Ocean Floor* by Jay Williams (McGraw)

1964: *The Incredible Journey* by Sheila Burnford (Little)
1965: *John F. Kennedy and PT-109* by Richard Tregaskis (Random)
1966: *Rascal* by Sterling North (Dutton)
1967: *Chitty-Chitty-Bang-Bang* by Ian Fleming (Random)
1968: *The Mouse and the Motorcycle* by Beverly Cleary (Morrow)

Children also have a chance to help in selecting books for the William Allen White Children's Book Award.

1953: *Amos Fortune: Free Man* by Elizabeth Yates (Dutton)
1954: *Little Vic* by Doris Gates (Viking)
1955: *Cherokee Bill: Oklahoma Pacer* by Jean Bailey (Abingdon)
1956: *Brighty of the Grand Canyon* by Marguerite Henry (Rand)
1957: *Daniel 'Coon* by Phoebe Erickson (Knopf)
1958: *White Falcon* by Elliott Arnold (Knopf)
1959: *Old Yeller* by Fred Gipson (Harper)
1960: *Flaming Arrows* by William O. Steele (Harcourt)
1961: *Henry Reed, Inc.* by Keith Robertson (Viking)
1962: *The Helen Keller Story* by Catherine O. Peare (Crowell)
1963: *Island of the Blue Dolphins* by Scott O'Dell (Houghton)
1964: *The Incredible Journey* by Sheila Burnford (Little)
1965: *Bristle Face* by Zachary Ball (Holiday)
1966: *Rascal* by Sterling North (Dutton)
1967: *The Grizzly* by Annabel & Edgar Johnson (Harper)
1968: *The Mouse and the Motorcycle* by Beverly Cleary (Morrow)

The preceding award winners are not really genuine children's choices because the children can vote only for books on a recommended list.

Results of surveys of reading preferences of 11-12-year-old girls and boys show, somewhere high on the popularity list, the titles *Nancy Drew, Trixie Belden*, the *Hardy Boys.* Choices of younger children, those who depend mostly on oral reception for their literature, are highly influenced by the teacher and by the presentation of the story. They like what they hear and know.

The teacher of a third grade class[1] wanted to know what her students read and how much of what they read was a result of book titles suggested in their basic reading series. Careful records were kept of books read, both from the school library and from the public library. Titles from the basic reader were posted as "Books you might look for when you go to the library." During the period of time the study was conducted, the children made 401 individual book choices and from that total number only fifteen (eight different titles) were suggested by the basic text.

A university junior preparing to be a teacher in the elementary school volunteered her services each afternoon after school in a branch library near an "inner city" school. She wanted to see "What do they read?" After watching for three months, she came to two conclusions, verified by the librarians: First, the most popular shelf in the library was the one which held the textbooks the children were reading in their school, mainly reading textbooks; these books were not only read in the library but they were checked out even though they were neither required reading nor assigned as home-work. Second, displays of books with some special theme close to their lives attracted the children if the books on display were immediately available to be checked out.

What children read is influenced by restrictions and specifications about checking out books. In a library with a rule of "one non-fiction for every two fiction," a teacher studied the reading which sixth grade children did after they took out books according to the rules.[2] Less than 50% of the non-fiction books were read even to the extent of "at least one chapter," while about 90% of the fiction books were considered "read completely" by the children.

There is reason to conclude that children read what they like to read. Whether they have learned to do this from their literature instruction or in spite of it is difficult to determine.

What is His Reaction to the Literature He Hears or Reads?

If we are to discover what the child learns about literature, we need to add to our answers to "Does he read?" and "What does he read?" whatever information we can reasonably accumulate about his reaction to the literature he reads. An obvious circular action exists which indicates that the more we know about the reader's reaction to what he hears or reads, the more we may discover about his being likely to continue to read.

Children's reactions to the literature they hear or read are sometimes immediate, and sometimes slow in coming. The teacher is a powerful factor because of his role in choosing the piece to be read. The teacher is also responsible for deciding how much talk there will be after a selection is read. The teacher observes and listens and so discovers what the children have learned about literature, a discovery which can be recorded on tape or in a diary.

Reactions to literature are not, and should not be, limited to talk. Other creative activities are genuine evidence of the response a youngster makes to a poem, a story, or a play he has heard or read. The picture, the play, the verse he creates tells you that some connection was made between him and the ideas expressed by the creator of the literature.

Reaction to literature can very well lead to some analysis of parts of the selection which has been read or heard. There is strong and convincing evidence that the reverse is not true! Children are usually expected by their teachers to react to the literature they hear or read. It may be that the reaction process is emphasized to the detriment of the learning about literature. An 8-year-old, about to begin third grade, hoped she would have a "nice teacher—one who lets us read books without having to answer questions about every page. And one that will let me keep a book after I finish it, at least a few days. I like to go back and read the good parts." That girl *does* read. She is aware of "good parts." There can be some hope, with her, that her teacher knows there are better ways to get reactions about literature than by asking questions about each page.

The way in which questions about literature are asked influences the responses children make. In Monson's study of children's reactions to humorous situations in literature, selections were considered funny more often by fifth-grade children who could answer objectively "yes" or "no" than by children who were expected to write a few explanatory words if they said it was funny.[3]

In another study, Peterson reported that sixth-grade children reacted differently to characters in excerpts from stories when the variable was the language (dialect) used by the character.[4]

Several years ago the National Council of Teachers of English Research Foundation attempted to encourage research related to literature in the elementary school. Limits seemed to be imposed by lack of any systematic method for comparison. The Research Foundation decided to support an attempt to construct an instrument to be used for research purposes related to literature in the elementary school. The term "test" was provided in all stages of planning. After the instrument had progressed through a series of production stages, it was labeled *A Look At Literature.*[5] It is now available for use with children in grades four, five and six. Any use of *A Look At Literature* will have values only if the study conducted with it is carefully designed and reported. The questions it may help to answer are those related to children's reactions to certain excerpts from literature. Since validation studies were not conducted in the process of the test construction, the information which might be gained from its use should, by all means, be validated in terms of evidence collected about "Does he read?" and "What does he read?"

To discover what children have learned about literature is an exciting challenge and one we must face if literature is to have a place in the elementary school curriculum. The processes we use in our investigation should be characterized by originality, flexibility, and respect for the individual's right to discover literature for himself. "Book Power" was the slogan for National Book Week, 1969, the 50th anniversary of Book Week. The power of the book is latent: the reader must generate the power. The child who has learned literature is the child who knows the power of the book and how to make that power do things for him, whether it be helping him to build a space ship, or to make a complete and joyous escape into an entertaining and inspiring land of make-believe.

68.

Corrective Aspects of Elementary School Language Arts

Paul C. Burns

There are pupils in almost every average classroom who are in need of special corrective and remedial instruction in the language arts; and particularly does this need become apparent in the intermediate school years. Much has been written for such make-up-work in the field of reading. Considerably less attention has been devoted to the related language arts—which is the purpose of this paper.

Analytical Testing

To begin with, provision of materials and procedures for dealing with pupils in need of special instruction is considered a basic part of the regular classroom program of providing for individual differences. And the first major step would be the administration of a survey of language arts test to all pupils in the class. This survey might be the language arts subtest of any standardized test. The survey test should probably not be given until the third or fourth week of school in the fall. The results of the survey test should be examined in detail by the pupils; and, in individual conferences with the teacher, an effort should be made to determine why the overall score may have been low and why individual items on the test may have caused difficulty.

After such a study, the teacher might say, "Perhaps you did not do so well for several reasons. For example, you might have missed something in your earlier study. I have some other tests that may help in locating your difficulties more specifically." The teacher would have a number of such tests dealing with specific topics, as listening skills, capitalization skills, punctuation skills, rhetorical skills, usage, vocabulary, spelling, and handwriting. A sample set of questions from a test dealing with punctuation is provided below. It can be seen that the four uses being tested involve the use of the period (a) at the end of a sentence; (b) after an abbreviation in the title of a person; (c) after an abbreviation such as in an address; and (d) after the initials in a proper name.

From *Elementary English 46:1008-1015 (December 1969)*. *Copyright* © 1969 by the National Council of Teachers of English. Reprinted with the permission of the National Council of Teachers of English and Paul C. Burns.

These are exercises dealing with the period. Each sentence illustrates one usage of the period. Insert the needed period for each sentence.

1. Bill is at his desk
2. Dr Jones is out of his office.
3. The Baker Co is located in Columbus, Ohio.
4. B F Brown is absent today.

Further, the teacher might say, "There are a number of these types of tests. You may start with any one, but since it is likely that you will want to take all or most of them, I suggest you begin with the one dealing with punctuation. Remember, you are taking these to find out what is causing some of your difficulty; so do your best, follow the instructions, and try each item, but do not spend too much time on any one of them." At a later period, items missed on any taken test would be discussed one by one with the pupil until the teacher is reasonably sure the pupil is aware of his deficiency.

Follow-up Materials

For each test there would be a package of follow-up materials and exercises. Again, in introducing them to the children, the teacher might say, "These special worksheets may help you get a better start in punctuation. Look them over and see if you wish to work on some of them instead of the regular work." (Such sets may come from workbooks, other textbooks, the best primary level instructional materials, programmed materials, or teacher-made materials.)

For each of the analytical tests and sets of follow-up material, a procedure similar to that given may be used. The plan need not be used continuously, but can be interspersed with regularly scheduled "special aids periods". But in whatever manner, the effort must be made to create a situation whereby pupils realize their defiencies and are willing to make a serious effort at restudy of some topics. Some of the special study projects are carried out during the regular period and are, of course, used only with the few pupils who volunteer and who are weakest in achievement.

An idea of the type of exercise used on the worksheets may be detected in the sample items presented below.

Corrective Worksheet: Punctuation (The Period)

Doing these exercises may give you a new look at the period and some of its uses. The exercises are not difficult but read each one carefully and think about what is called for before you mark or write.

1. Study each sentence below. Notice each ringed period. Try to figure out why it is used in each case.
   a) John is not at home⊙
   b) Mr⊙ Brown is a busy person⊙
   c) The Book Supply Co⊙ is located in a large city⊙
   d) His name is R. T⊙ Jones⊙
2. Is the period used in 1a at the end of a sentence? Place periods correctly in each of these.
   a) The skaters danced gracefully
   b) Cats like fish
   c) Bill is a good football player
3. Read aloud the sentences in "2". Did your voice drop at the end? Is that where you put a period?

4. Is the period used in 1b after an abbreviation in the title of a person? Place periods correctly in each of these.
   a) Dr Jones is out of town.
   b) Mrs Brooks lives next door to us.
   c) The parade was led by Mr Davis.
5. Is the period used in 1c after an abbreviation of parts of an address? Place periods correctly in each of these.
   a) The Randolph Co makes many toys.
   b) Le Grand, Inc is the name of a large firm.
   c) Jim wrote a letter to Baxter Co for some materials.
6. Is the period used in 1d after initials in proper names? Place periods correctly in each of these.
   a) G L Meers is our class president.
   b) Billy C Stone took a trip to Chicago.
   c) The Book was written by T Robert Smith.
7. Place periods correctly in each sentence below.
   We saw some squirrels in the park The squirrels were eating nuts It was fun to watch them
8. Write four sentences to show the four uses of periods studied on this worksheet.
9. Find examples of the four uses of periods in your reading material.
10. If you like more work with period punctuation, see your language textbook, p.—.

In the package of materials from which the samples as before were taken were a set of seven similar tests and worksheets for punctuation one for each: the period; the comma; the semicolon; the colon; quotation marks to enclose direct address; the apostrophe; the question mark). As suggested, similar sets could be available for other facets of the language arts. Pupils would be encouraged to use as many worksheets as they desire or to repeat any worksheet. The teacher would help the pupils get started with the exercises and show interest in what they are doing in various ways. At times, the teacher may use content from the worksheets in oral exercises for the entire class.

Further Suggestions and Resources

In this section, other aids and materials will be suggested for oral and written expression; spelling; and handwriting. Each will be discussed in turn. As in the earlier part of this paper, attention is focused outside of any intellectual or physical factors which may have limiting effects upon the child's performance.

Oral and Written Expression. At the beginning of the school year, a focus upon oral communication as suggested by Delawter and Eash may be of help in categorizing common class weaknesses which need attention, as well as individual deficiences.[6] Their idea is to analyze prevalent communication deficiencies, contending that fundamental faults need to be identified before they can be the focus of instruction. Through a simple "complete the story" technique, they detected seven pervasive points and offered suggestions for effecting improvement. The seven types of errors were: (a) failure to focus; (b) poor organization of ideas; (c) failure to clarify the question; (d) lack of supporting ideas; (e) inadequate description; (f) lack of subordination; and (g) stereotyped vocabulary. This is a desirable classroom procedure which can be replicated easily. Based upon the findings, the teacher can lessen the deficiencies through use of small group work, media as the tape recorder, and the use of experience records and stories.

Use of check lists (teacher-made or textbook-suggested) of specific oral language skills desired for the various speaking situations can be helpful in further pinpointing a pupil's weaknesses and thus provide clues for instruction. As to usage errors (nonstandard usages), Pooley's list provides a guideline for items to be attacked during the elementary school years and then notes some items which will not be emphasized for the whole class but may be brought to the attention of some pupils.[7] Again, only a few of the most crucial nonstandard usages—and only those found needed by a particular child or group of children—should receive consistent, oral-aural emphasis during the year.

As to speech itself, the teacher should be aware of some common difficulties in articulation, such as the *s* lisp; *t* for *k; d* for *g, th, r, l; w* for *wh;* and *n* for *ing*.[8] And according to Abney, the most frequent errors of enunciation and pronunciation easily detected in speech include:

1. Incorrect vowel sound, as in *get, catch, just*
2. Incorrect consonant quality, *as* in *what, immediately, walking*
3. Misplaced accent, as in *research, discharge*
4. Omission of requisite sounds, as in *recognize, really, February*
5. Sounding silent letters as in *toward, corps*
6. The addition of superfluous sounds, as in *athlete, once, elm*
7. The utterance of sounds in improper order, as in *children, hundred*[9]

Furness has presented in outline form some information concerning possible causes of and teaching procedures for various types of speech disabilities. The list has been found helpful by a number of teachers. For the problem of stuttering, the reader is advised to turn to a basic book on speech-handicapped children.[10]

In the area of listening, a teacher will find it helpful to study Furness' analysis of listening disabilities, their possible causes, and suggested teaching procedures designed to help in overcoming these disabilities. Too, a resourceful teacher will find many uses for the activities included in such a booklet as *Listening Aids Through the Grades.* It goes without saying that appropriate environmental conditions for listening should be provided within the classroom setting; that the subject content should be related to the child's interests and personal experiences; and that desirable purposes should be set for listening.[11]

In addition to observing and recording errors in pupils' composition work, a beginning place for systematic study of written expression might well be the administration of the *Iowa Language Abilities Test* which treats word meaning, language usage, grammatical form recognition, sentence sense, sentence structure, capitalization, punctuation, and paragraph organization. An item analysis of the results of the test will show the specific deficiencies for the class as a whole and for individuals. A useful adjunct to this test would be the subtests on Writing and Essay from the *Sequential Test for Educational Progress.* These two subtests can be quite useful for screening purposes. The first subtest deals with basically the revision of sentences in a passage. The essay test calls for the writing of a composition. Comparison of an individual's score on the writing and the essay may be enlightening. For example, if the writing test score is high but the essay test score is low, it would appear that the pupil may know the specifics of writing, but is unable to apply the skills. If both scores are low, the difficulty likely stems from lack of basic writing skills. Similar comparisons could be useful for class analysis.[12]

For creative writing, the use of scales, such as the ones by Carlson and Yamamato may help objectify the evaluation of strengths and weaknesses for such items as novel ideas, ingenuity, and other qualities of children's narratives. Illustrative samples are included in both scales for the ratings. For poetry writing, Walter's list of ten items should be helpful to the teacher for evaluating and teaching purposes.[13]

For follow-up attention upon the mechanics of written expression, several ideas and sources may be cited. The *Manual for Interpreting the Iowa Language Abilities Test* now out-of-print presents some excellent ideas (for sentence sense, capitalization and punctuation; language usage; and spelling) about possible causes of low scores on the test; evidences of deficiency; and some specific suggestions for remedial treatment. Again, use of checklists for the specific aspects of written language skills can be quite helpful. For example, Greene and Petty present minimal capitalization and punctuation skills by suggested grade level, taking into account the needs of the child in writing and the relative difficulty of the various items. On the basis of findings from such checklists, dictation exercises, both of the studied and of the unstudied type, may prove a beneficial procedure. To explain the unstudied type, one of the better ways to detect the type of mistakes which pupils make in free written work—and thereupon plan a corrective program—is for the teacher at times to prepare short sentences or paragraphs in which the items to be tested are embedded. The teacher can then dictate the sentences and the children write them. An analysis of the written work by the teacher quickly reveals the weak spots in the items tested. This procedure is functional in nature since the conditions approximate those of normal writing. Studied dictation would differ in that pupils would have the opportunity to study the selection—paying particular attention to various aspects of the written form—prior to dictation. Several commercially published workbooks also provide exercises which could be used at this point. Various articles by Furness provide additional suggestions, relative deficiencies, and remedial treatment for punctuation, sentence sense, and verbs.[14]

Informal techniques for diagnosing oral and written expression would continue throughout the year. These would include anecdotal records, free and directed observation of the work habits of pupils, collections of the written work of pupils, teacher-made tests, application of criteria and standards prepared cooperatively by teacher and pupils, informal interviews with learners, and similar procedures. Only through such a comprehensive program of diagnosis can a true and complete analysis of pupil performance be secured upon which continued corrective treatment may be applied.

Spelling. A standardized survey test is a good initial place for critical analysis of a pupil's spelling performance. Such a test as *Morrison-McCall Spelling Scale*, though dated, seems to serve adequately to give a general impression of the child's over-all ability in the field of spelling. For those pupils making the lowest scores, particular attention should be focused upon (a) their pronunciation of words, (b) visual perception, and (c) study methods used in the mastery of a spelling list. A survey of the child's daily written work should give the teacher some clue as to the type of spelling errors being made by the particular child and perhaps some plausible cause for such errors. Two good general references for the teacher's desk would be Gates' list of spelling difficulty and Dolch's list of the most common words for spelling. The first list would alert the teacher to possible misspellings and the second would provide a basic core of common words that should be mastered at the elementary school level. While tentative corrective treatment is being applied, the child may need to be kept motivated through the use of spelling games such as found in the book by Anderson and Groff.[15]

For a rapid method of collecting samples of a pupil's tendencies to spelling errors, Spache's spelling errors tests are recommended.[16] Two separate tests for use in grades 2-4 and 5-6 are offered; each test providing opportunities for the committing of twelve types of common spelling errors, ten words used for each type of spelling error. Easily group-administered, scored, recorded, and interpreted, the tests may be recommended for providing clues for study of poor spellers in the classroom.

For the pupil with more severe spelling retardation, the individual administration of the *Gates-Russell Spelling Diagnostic Test* may reveal more specifically any difficulties—and the manual for the test contains many worthy ideas for remedial instruction. The test is composed of nine subtests:

1. Spelling words orally (power test)
2. Word pronunciation (reading and speech)
3. Giving letters for sounds (oral)
4. Spelling one syllable (oral)
5. Spelling two syllables (oral)
6. Word reversals (oral)
7. Spelling attack (securing evidence as to usual method of study)
8. Auditory discrimination (hearing)
9. Visual, auditory, kinesthetic, and combined study methods (comparison of effectiveness)[17]

The words taught to a pupil with severe spelling retardation should be those of highest frequency—only the most common words. The pupil should be checked—and taught where lacking—against such lists as the first 100 words of Horn's (these account for about 65 per cent of the running words written by adults); the first 254 words of the Rinsland list; Kyte and Neel's list of core vocabulary; and the lists of "demons" by Fitzgerald and Johnson. It is with severe types of spelling disability that an approach such as Fernald's kinesthetic method may be utilized. Further ideas for diagnosis and remediation in spelling may be found in an article by Fitzgerald.[18]

Handwriting. Handwriting quality may be evaluated by means of informal analysis of discrete aspects of handwriting such as form and size; spacing; slant; alignment and line quality. Or commercial scales may be used for measuring handwriting quality. In using the commerical scales—such as Ayres or Freeman, or Newland—the spelling or vocabulary difficulties should be eliminated for the pupils.[19] The sample can be written on the chalkboard several days prior to the testing day where it is read and perhaps written several times. It is preferable that the sample be memorized, but it should appear before the pupil during the writing test. A two minute period for the test has generally been accepted as suitable. The values assigned to papers are determined by comparing the pupil's copy with the scale sample it most nearly matches in appearance. The measurement of rate can be accomplished at the same sitting. The rate is usually expressed in letters per minute—the score being obtained by counting the total number of letters written by the pupil and dividing this number by the number of minutes allowed for the writing.

Instruction following such testing should be based on individual needs. Of course it is helpful to know that researchers have found certain items commonly account for much of the illegibility in handwriting. For example, four common types of errors are: (a) failure to close letters; (b) closing looped strokes; (c) looping unlooped strokes, and (d) straight up strokes, rather than rounded. Certain cursive letters and numerals as *a, e, r t n, o, s, v, 5, 0,* and 2 are common "demons". Other common illegibilities can be pinpointed for instruction—such as making *a* like *u* or *o* or *ci; b* like *li; d* like *cl; e* closed; *i* not dotted; *h* like *li; m* like *w; n* like *u; o* like *a; r* like *i* or *n; t* like *l*. But the most important point to remember is that the pupil needs help with the letters with which he himself has difficulty. Where the pupil has serious difficulty with letter formation, the use of sets of letters made by the teacher or commercial sets can be used for individual analysis and practice.[20] Special attention is deserved by the left-handed writer. Oftentimes it is not single letter formation but combinations of letters which give difficulty—such as *bo, be, bi, br, by, oa, oi, os, va, vi, vo, vu, wa, we, wi, wr.* Slant and spacing are probably next in importance in determining the quality of handwriting and should be given appropriate attention.

If further diagnosis and corrective work seems desirable, the use of specially prepared commercial tools for this purpose is advised—such as the Freeman (Zaner-Blozer) chart and the Noble and Noble chart. These charts give specific ideas for detecting handwriting weaknesses and helpful suggestions for correcting the defects discovered. The directions for the use of these charts should be carefully studied by the teacher. Where follow-up worksheets are required to assist in the elimination of a handwriting fault or faults, such specially prepared materials on numerals, manuscript letters, cursive letters, letter combinations, spacing, slant, and alignment as found in at least one reference source should be provided the pupil. Additional ideas on handwriting diagnosis and remediation may be found in the article by Furness.[21]

Concluding Statement

This paper has dealt with special corrective instruction in the language arts—proposing considerable analytical and diagnostic testing and the use of follow-up materials as a general procedure. Suggestions and resources were offered for oral and written expression; spelling; and handwriting. Finally, for those interested in further study of diagnostic and remedial teaching, with particular emphasis for the area of language arts, four further reference sources are cited.[22]

69.

Evaluating the Quality of Handwriting

Mary Elizabeth Bell

Contests in handwriting, exhibits of handwriting, and certificates in handwriting are disappearing from our educational scene. And this is to be expected and should be desired. Even though we are not concerned with the passing of contests and exhibits of handwriting, it is still desirable that handwriting be evaluated. The point in question is how should it be done. Even though evaluation of students' handwriting is "at the heart" of a sound writing program, it is really nonexistent or very poorly done in our schools because of the lack of teacher preparation and merits immediate attention. Walter T. Petty has included in his list of unsettled issues in the teaching of handwriting the problem of, "How should the evaluation of handwriting be done?"[23]

Children's handwriting cannot be judged on general appearance alone. One must be cognizant of the various essential factors basic to the handwriting skill. Especially now that educators have a greater sensitivity to varying development of children, there should be a recognition of total involvement in considering how well a child writes.

How does one evaluate (judge or grade) handwriting? There is probably no one clear-cut answer. However, the points made and suggestions given in this article may help to determine the progress a child is making in writing.

Use of Handwriting Scales Questioned

Without definite guides, many teachers wonder how to judge (evaluate) and how to grade a pupil's handwriting. Because the physical, emotional, and social developments in children are not the same, a teacher cannot expect every child to meet the same standards of achievement for his particular grade level. This point of view has been emphasized by Lawrence J. Smith. He has pointed out in his article that a teacher who recognizes differences in children's growth patterns will not insist that every child in a given grade meet the same standards of achievement as suggested by handwriting scales.[24]

It would seem to the writer that the use of a handwriting specimen of another student in evaluating or grading a specific student's handwriting achievement (development) is only beclouding a somewhat hazy situation. When a person is learning a new skill he is in the process of clearing his own understanding of the basic factors inherent in the new skill without having his own achievement

Reprinted from *Education* 90:126-129 (November-December 1969), by permission of author and publisher, The Bobbs-Merrill Company, Inc.

level involved with another's level of development. This is what happens when handwriting scales are used.

Handwriting scales are made of representative specimens of children's handwriting in a series of scales that measure a certain number of degrees of quality (what the scale proposes to measure) at each grade level. These specimens are usually selected by people who have been given training in understanding the basic elements of handwriting; however, evidence shows that at best it is difficult to eliminate subjectivity in the choosing of handwriting specimens.[25]

In the last two decades a concern has been shown among some few educators and educational researchers for improvement in handwriting scales and consequently new scales have appeared.[26]

Even though handwriting scales are improved, they can hardly aid the teacher nor the individual student to bring into clear focus the student's own specific development in handwriting. Only by comparing the pupil's present handwriting with his earlier work can this be done.

Selection of Material to Evaluate

Of considerable importance is the selection of type of written material to study. Evaluation should not be based on practice papers or on handwriting lessons alone. All written work—creative writing, social studies papers, science papers, language lessons, spelling lessons, as well as handwriting lessons—should be studied. These are true samples of how a child writes in real functional situations. A pupil's everyday writing is the best example of what he is doing. There is little value in judging a student's writing from a handwriting specimen only. This sample may be an indication of how he *can write*, but it *may not be* an *example* of *how* he *generally writes in* his *daily work*.

When writing was judged for its beauty as was the practice some time ago, a single handwriting specimen may have been sufficient. Since the purpose of most writing is communication, the basis for judging handwriting quality is legibility and speed serviceability. In other words, how quickly and how easily a child's writing can be read should be the basis for judging handwriting. And how well the speed of writing adjusts to serve the various writing situations without decreasing the legibility of the handwriting also enters into the evaluation of handwriting. However, we must take into consideration situations such as taking notes from a speaker when extremely rapid speed is needed that legibility will decrease. But the decrease in legibility in extreme situations should not sacrifice the legibility of handwriting.

Judging Legibility

Legibility is made up of several factors with each one important in its own right. The factors must be added into the evaluation act one at a time with the children until all of them are being used in order to secure the total general quality and legibility. The most important factor which should be considered first for determining legibility is recognition of letters. Each letter should be recognized at sight and not be confused with any other. Because a child may develop individuality in his writing, his teacher should consider a letter legible if it can be easily and quickly read and written.

Other factors which may not only affect legibility, but also will aid the appearance of writing are these:

1. Uniformity of *slant* is of major importance. Some writing may be vertical, and some may have a slight slant from vertical. A forward slant is recog-

nized as faster to write and easier to read. An extreme slant makes writing difficult to read and slower to execute. Uniformity of slant goes hand-in-hand with letter form.

2. *Spacing* between letters and between words should be even and of the desired size. Manuscript letters should be close within the word without touching, and cursive letters should not be crowded. The spaces between words should be equal to the width of the small letter "o," whether it is manuscript or cursive. In cursive the ending of the last letter of each word would also help regulate the spaces between words.
3. The *size* and *heights* of letters should be uniform, varying with each sequential developmental step throughout the elementary grades. Very small writing is difficult to read because letter form, slant, and spacing break down. Not only size, but *proportion* is a necessary factor.
4. *Alignment* enters into legibility. Only as the correct part of each letter rests on the baseline will there be consistent placement of the words.
5. The *quality of line* for easy reading should be a firm, clear-cut line, not too light nor too heavy, written with a medium soft pencil lead.
6. *Position* enters into the legibility of writing (posture of person and position of writing materials). It is important that all students (right- and left-handed) have the best positions suitable for them. Because the placement of the handwriting paper on the desk greatly affects the legibility of handwriting, the correct position of paper should be closely checked.
7. *Speed* that is flexible and meets the various writing situations without decreasing the legibility of the handwriting is necessary. A child needs this skill at a level that will keep up with his thinking. When extremely rapid speed is needed for situations such as taking notes from a speaker, legibility will decrease. But in the extremeness of writing speed the handwriting should remain legible at all times.

It is important that these listed factors should be taken into consideration when evaluating the quality of handwriting rather than some one or two of them.

Goals and Improvement

Children need goals toward which they can work, but every child cannot have the same goal at the same time. Every child can work for improvement, but how much improvement to expect is often a problem. Because we know a child will learn only to the degree that he is involved in the learning act, an ideal solution is for each person to set his own goals for improvement and to work toward attaining these goals. However, not all children are capable of setting their own goals; some pupils may not have the background for selecting them. Lack of background is certainly evident in the carelessly written work of some college and university students. Some of their handwriting is very difficult to read, and some of their work is completely illegible. If children had established and mastered good handwriting skills in the elementary grades they would still have the skills for use in everyday life. So it is the responsibility of every elementary teacher to see that each pupil is given planned systematic as well as "on-the-spot-in-daily-work" guidance in understanding and practicing the basic factors that go into the writing act. Only when a child knows and understands what he is trying to achieve in handwriting can he evaluate. And only through evaluation can he understand how to work toward self-improvement. Evaluation is the link between the child's understanding of the handwriting techniques and the achieving of the handwriting goals in the learning process.

A child can begin to improve writing at the point where he is. By selecting current samples of his writing papers from various writing situations and dating and filing them, he will be able to compare later work with them to note improvement. The filing of sample writing papers that have been dated should continue throughout the year. A teacher's knowledge of a pupil's achievement level in lieu of his ability should help her to judge if the improvement is sufficient when she helps him in the evaluation act.

Thus, each child is working toward his own goals, and he is competing against himself, not against the entire class.

Summary

Evaluation of a pupil's handwriting may be judged by considering:

1. A child's growth pattern (maturation), his achievement level, his ability, and his muscular development.
2. All daily papers; not just handwriting samples.
3. A child's efforts and his improvements over earlier writing, as shown through accumulated dated samples from various writing activities from the beginning of school.
4. The ease and speed with which his writing can be read.
5. The flexibility of his writing in adjusting to the speed needed in the various writing situations throughout his school career. In situations when maximum speed of writing is called for, a good principle to follow is to write as rapidly as possible as long as legibility (reasonable quality) is maintained.

70.

Each Pupil His Own Editor

Charles E. Danowski

Eventually each pupil leaves the confines of the school. This inescapable fact points to an equally inescapable conclusion: The school has the responsibility of helping each pupil develop a way of analyzing his progress and his products to complement evaluations the teacher makes. The need for self-evaluation of written expression is especially acute.

Many techniques have been proposed, and some research has been conducted on appropriate ways for teachers to evaluate pupils' written work. Searles and Carlsen have summarized the results of these endeavors:

> All authorities writing on the subject of evaluation of written English stress the use of multiple techniques rather than depending solely on a single test instrument. Evaluation may be a combination of objective and subjective judgments. It does not have to eventuate necessarily in a numerical rating that may be manipulated statistically.[27]

The literature has much less research on the individual's evaluation of his written work. A survey of the literature turned up only one study of self-evaluation procedures. A report by R. L. Lyman in a 1931 issue of *School Review*[28] was summarized in these words:

> Lyman sought to determine the extent to which pupils in Grades 6-9 could be taught to discover and correct language errors in their own compositions; he attempted to establish a work pattern for writing compositions. This pattern included planning, writing a first draft, proofreading and revision, and writing a final copy. He found that pupils could be taught to discover and correct three-fifths of their own errors.[29]

Even this procedure, however, suggests a work pattern rather than specific phases of evaluation that the pupil could use.

I am proposing a procedure that pupils may find helpful in evaluating their written work. The procedure requires the writer-critic to focus on one aspect

---

Reprinted from *Elementary School Journal* 66:249-253 (February 1966), by permission of Charles E. Danowski and The University of Chicago Press.

(or technique) of writing at a time. The author is not called on to try to fully evaluate his composition each time he reviews it.

The framework of the procedure is a list of six phases of evaluation. The list grew out of "Suggested Levels of Listening" proposed by Leland B. Jacobs in a series of lectures at Teachers College, Columbia University, in 1964. Jacobs' list, in turn, grew out of the article "Levels of Listening—a Theory" by Seth Fessenden, who suggested seven levels of listening. Jacobs revised the levels. His six levels follow:

1. Isolation of sounds, ideas, arguments, facts, organization, and the like
2. Identification of the giving of meaning to aspects already isolated
3. Integration of what is heard with past experience
4. Inspection of the new data, or beginning evaluation
5. Interpretation of what has been heard
6. Introspection as well as listening, noting the effects of what is heard and the effects of knowing that one is being affected[30]

Jacobs' list of suggested levels of listening can be adapted for evaluating written expression.

In any one composition, one or more of the phases may have special importance for the writer. For a complete self-evaluation of a piece of writing, however, all six phases must be considered.

Phase 1: Isolation of Simple, Specific, Discrete Elements

This phase of evaluation is concerned with the technical aspects of writing: letter formation, spelling, punctuation, and grammar. In this phase of evaluation, a pupil would concern himself only with these aspects of his written work.

In the primary grades, pupils would be asked to concentrate on this phase only if attention to mechanics did not have an adverse effect on the children's interest in writing. Overemphasis on mechanics can be detrimental, though by the time a child enters the intermediate grades he should be well aware of the importance of this phase and be skillful in it.

Phase 2: Identification of Descriptive Words, Phrases, and Clauses

In this phase of evaluation, the writer considers his use of descriptive words and his groupings of words. The emphasis is on the accuracy, the precision, the meaningfulness, and the necessity of each descriptive word, phrase, and clause in the composition. Unclear phrases, inaccurate expressions, and inappropriate embellishments are revised or deleted. In this phase even slight revisions can have a significant effect. For a passage can be completely transformed by the change of a single word. Note the effect of changing "whirring lawn mowers" to "clattering lawn mowers."

This phase should be extremely valuable for pupils in the primary and the intermediate grades. Many children at this age delight in learning precise descriptive words to replace overused, ambiguous words like "nice." Children's natural eagerness may be all the motivation needed to pursue this phase of self-evaluation.

Phase 3: Integration of Expressions into Meaningful Ideas

In this phase of evaluation, the focus is on four main aspects of integration. First, the integration of words, phrases, and clauses into meaningful sentences.

Second, the integration of sentences into properly developed paragraphs. Third, the integration of paragraphs into meaningful larger portions of a composition, such as sections, chapters, or other major parts. Fourth, the appropriate use of transitions from sentence to sentence, paragraph to paragraph, and part to part.

Better written work will develop in the elementary school if the focus is on meaningful sentences, well-developed paragraphs, and appropriate transitions, rather than on lengthy compositions. For younger children, short, precise, well-developed paragraphs that make use of colorful phraseology are a more appropriate objective than lengthy works.

Phase 4: Inspection of the Document as a Whole

In this phase of evaluation, the composition is evaluated as a unit. In the first, second, and third phases, the writer considers certain aspects or elements of the composition, but not the work as a whole. In the fourth phase, the writer scrutinizes the choice and the arrangement of words, examples, and ideas; the development of the main theme; and the element of interest. He gets a view of the entire organization of the composition—its form and its style.

In the intermediate grades, this phase becomes increasingly important as the pupils' compositions lengthen from one paragraph to several paragraphs. As the compositions become longer, development and organization become more difficult. Organization will be less burdensome, however, if the pupil has a clear sense of good paragraph form.

Phase 5: Interpretation of the Main Ideas

In this phase, the pupil considers the sincerity of the ideas, the persuasiveness of the presentation, and the relevance of the ideas to the intended audience.

The young writer tends to emphasize the ideas in his composition rather than the organization. Actually, the ideas represent the writer to his audience. These ideas are far more important than the organization, which can be strengthened at a later time. Although the young writer is likely to attach more importance to the relevance, the persuasiveness, and the sincerity of his work, he can come to see that proper organization can lend power to his theme.

Phase 6: Introspection of the Effects of the Document

In the final phase of evaluation, the pupil considers the message and its effect on himself and his readers. This phase can come only after the work has been read by others and the author has had some feedback. The readers' reactions—be they rational, emotional, positive, negative, or bland—are the data the author uses in considering the effect of his composition. The pupil will find these data useful in evaluating his subsequent work.

The data will, of course, include the author's own reactions, though, at this stage, group or peer reaction becomes important to the young author. Evaluations made by his classmates can help him determine appropriate writing techniques.

In using this six-phase plan for self-evaluation of written work, the teacher should discuss each phase with individual pupils in her class. Each phase should be taken up at an appropriate time: the pupil should not be asked to cope with all six phases at once. Nor should the phases be presented at a level beyond the pupil's comprehension. If these phases are to be used meaningfully, the pupil must understand them.

Certainly the six phases should not be taught to the entire class during six consecutive class sessions. It would be more appropriate to help each pupil develop an understanding of a particular phase of self-evaluation as that phase becomes important to his written expression.

A child who has demonstrated proficiency in developing an idea in a paragraph may need to learn to correct his spelling. This child is ready for the first phase—the isolation of simple, specific, discrete elements. He could be taught to read his composition slowly, noting every word. If he is an able reader, he might read each page backward, word by word, to correct his spelling errors.

A pupil may have difficulty in writing colorful phrases. He might well concentrate on the second phase—the identification of descriptive words, phrases, and clauses. The teacher might suggest phrases from books or other sources, or she might ask the pupil to revise sentences. The teacher might give the pupil the sentence, "It was a good movie," and ask him to search for descriptive words to replace the word *good*. The pupil could then write several sentences about the substitutes he suggested.

The teacher might discuss with the class the similarity between these six phases of self-evaluation of written work and the major aspects of the composition process.

In composing, the author generally conceives the effect he wants to produce. (This phase in composition is similar to the introspection phase in self-evaluation.) The author focuses on the main ideas. (This phase is related to the interpretation phase.) The author organizes his theme. (This phase is related to the inspection phase.) The author develops his sentences, paragraphs, and transitions. (This aspect parallels the integration phase.) The author concentrates on descriptive words, phrases, and clauses. (This phase compares with the identification phase.) Finally, the author reviews the mechanics of spelling, punctuation and grammar. (This phase is the counterpart of the isolation phase.)

In composing, as in self-evaluation, it is possible to consider all the phases simultaneously. A beginning writer, however, may want to consider each phase separately. As he does so, he will learn to focus on one aspect of writing at a time. Thus, if he has to search for the proper spelling of a word, he will not lose sight of the main idea of his work while he is correcting his spelling.

As the young writer uses these phases of self-evaluation of written work, it is anticipated that he will gain enough self-confidence to use them to evaluate each composition he writes. It is not easy for children—or adults—to be open to self-appraisal or outside criticism. In developing written expression, the wise teacher will strive to add to each child's self-confidence and sense of worth.

Self-worth and self-confidence are important in language activities, which grow out of the individual's experience and are a part of him. The author's acceptance of his own evaluation and his acceptance of outside evaluation of his written work are related to his acceptance of appraisals of himself. In future years, the ability to make a self-appraisal of written work can help the pupil in his academic career. A sense of self-worth and the ability to make healthy appraisals of self will be of enduring value in all his endeavors.

Notes

1. Helen Cain, "A Study of the Relationship between Independent Library Reading Choices of Third Grade Children and the Reading Selections in their Basal Reader," unpublished master's thesis, University of Minnesota, 1969.
2. Natalie Miller, "Books Selected for Personal Reading," unpublished master's thesis, University of Minnesota, 1963.
3. Dianne L. Monson, "Children's Responses to Humorous Situations in Literature," doctoral dissertation, University of Minnesota, 1966.
4. Sue W. Peterson, "Attitudes of Children Toward Literary Characters Who Speak Regional Dialects of American English," doctoral dissertation, University of Minnesota, 1969.
5. Educational Testing Services, *A Look at Literature* (Princeton, N.J., 1969).
6. Jane Ann Delawter and Maurice J. Eash, "Focus on Oral Communication," *Elementary English* 43 (December 1966): 880-883; Leo J. Brueckner and Guy L. Bond, *The Diagnosis and Treatment of Learning Difficulties* (New York: Appleton-Century-Crofts, Inc., 1955), Chaps. 10-12.
7. Robert C. Pooley, *Teaching English Usage* (New York: D. Appleton Company, 1946), pp. 180-181.
8. Paul McKee, *Language in the Elementary School* (Boston: Houghton-Mifflin Company, 1939), p. 318.
9. Louise Abney, *Teaching Language in the Elementary School*, Forty-third Yearbook Part II, National Society for the Study of Education (Chicago: University of Chicago Press, 1944), p. 186.
10. Edna Lue Furness, "A Remedial and Developmental Speech Program," *Elementary English* 32 (May 1955): 289-295; Wendell Johnson, et. al, *Speech Handicapped School Children*, rev. ed. (New York: Harper and Row, 1956), pp. 272-283.
11. Edna Lue Furness, "A Remedial and Developmental Program in Listening," *Elementary English* 32 (December 1955): 525-531; David Russell and Elizabeth F. Russell, *Listening Aids Through the Grades* (New York: Bureau of Publications, Teachers College, Columbia University, 1952).
12. Harry A. Greene and H. L. Ballenger, *Iowa Language Abilities Test*, (New York: World Book Company, 1948); *Sequential Tests of Educational Progress* (Princeton, N.J.: Cooperative Test Division, Educational Testing Service).
13. Ruth K. Carlson, *An Analytical Scoring Scale for Measuring the Originality of Children's Stories* (Hayward, Calif: California State College, September 1964); Kaoru Yamamato, *Scoring Manual for Evaluating Imaginative Stories* (Minneapolis: Bureau of Educational Research, College of Education, University of Minnesota, January 1961); Nina W. Walters, *Let Them Write Poetry* (New York: Holt, Rinehart and Winston, 1962), pp. 144-145.
14. *Manual for Interpreting Iowa Language Abilities Test* (Yonkers-on-Hudson: World Book Company, 1948); Greene and Petty, *op. cit.*, pp. 212-213, 214-215; Edna Lue Furness, "Pupils, Pedagogues, and Punctuation," *Elementary English* 37 (March 1960): 184-189; Edna Lue Furness, "Pupils, Teachers, and 'Sentence Sense'" *Education* 86 (September 1965): 12-17; Edna Lue Furness, "Pupils, Teachers, and Telltale Verbs," *Education* 87 (October 1966): 111-116.
15. J. C. Morrison and W. A. McCall, *Morrison-McCall Spelling Scale* (New York: World Book Company, 1923); Arthur I. Gates, *A List of Spelling Difficulties in 3876 Words* (New York: Bureau of Publications, Teachers College, Columbia University); E.W. Dolch, *Better Spelling* (Champaign, Ill.: Garrard Press, 1942), pp. 257-270; Paul Anderson and Patrick Groff, *Resources for the Teaching of*

Spelling, 2nd ed. (Minneapolis: Burgess Publishing Company, 1968).

16. George D. Spache, *Spelling Errors Test* (Gainesville, Fla.: University of Florida).
17. Arthur I. Gates and David Russell, *Diagnostic and Remedial Spelling Manual* rev.; (New York: Teachers College, Columbia University, 1940).
18. Ernest A. Horn, *A Basic Writing Vocabulary—10,000 Words Most Commonly Used in Writing,* University of Iowa Monographs in Education, First Series, No. 4 (Iowa City: University of Iowa, 1926); Henry D. Rinsland, *A Basic Vocabulary of Elementary School Children* (New York: The Macmillan Company, 1945); George C. Kyte and Virginia M. Neel, "A Core Vocabulary of Spelling Words," *Elementary School Journal* 54 (September 1953): 29-34; James A. Fitzgerald, "A Crucial Core Vocabulary in Elementary School Language and Spelling," *American School Board Journal* 103 (July 1941): 22-24; Leslie W. Johnson, "One Hundred Words Most Often Misspelled by Children in the Elementary Grades," *Journal of Educational Research* 44 (October 1950): 154-155; Grace Fernald, *Remedial Teaching in Basic School Subjects* (New York: McGraw-Hill Book Company, 1943), Chap. 13; James A. Fitzgerald, "Spelling . . . Diagnosis and Remediation," *National Elementary Principal* 38 (May 1959): 27-30.
19. Leonard P. Ayres, *A Scale for Measuring the Quality of Handwriting of School Children,* Bulletin No. 113 (New York: Division of Education, Russell Sage Foundations, 1912); Frank N. Freeman and Zaner-Bloser staff, *Handwriting Measuring Scales, Grades 1-9* (Columbus, Ohio: Zaner-Bloser Company); Ernest Newland, *Newland Chart for Diagnosis of Illegibility in Written Arabic Numerals* (Bloomington: Illinois Public School Publishing Company).
20. Parker Z. Bloser, *Our Print Letters and How to Make Them* (Columbus, Ohio: Zaner-Bloser Company, 1954). Parker Z. Bloser, *Our ABC's and How to Improve Them* (Columbus, Ohio: Zaner-Bloser Company, 1954).
21. Frank Freeman, *Handwriting Faults and How to Correct Them* (Columbus, Ohio: Zaner-Bloser Company); Noble and Noble, Publishers, Inc., *Self-Checking Handwriting Chart for Correcting The Most Common Errors in Handwriting* (New York, n.d.); Paul C. Burns, *Improving Handwriting Instruction in Elementary Schools,* 2nd ed. (Minneapolis: Burgess Publishing Company, 1968), Chap. 7; Edna Lue Furness, "Diagnosis and Remediation of Handwriting," *Elementary English* 32 (April 1955): 224-228.
22. Glenn Myers Blair, *Diagnostic and Remedial Teaching* (New York: The Macmillan Company, 1956, Chaps. 10-12; Greene and Petty, *op. cit.*, pp. 232-235, 252-253, 315-318, 351-355; Wayne Otto and Richard A. McMenemy, *Corrective and Remedial Teaching* (Boston: Houghton-Mifflin Company, 1966), Chaps. 8, 10-13.
23. Walter T. Petty, "Handwriting and Spelling: Their Current Status in the Language Arts Curriculum" *Research on Handwriting and Spelling,* (Champaign, Ill.: National Council of Teachers of English, 1966), pp. 1-8.
24. Lawrence J. Smith, "Handwriting and Child Development," *Readings In The Language Arts In The Elementary School,* James C. MacCampbell, comp. (Boston: D.C. Heath and Company, 1964), pp. 167-170.
25. Dan W. Anderson, "Handwriting Research: Movement and Quality," *Elementary English* 42 (January 1965): 45-53.
26. Rocky Bezzi, "A Standardized Manuscript Scale for Grades 1, 2, and 3" *The Journal of Educational Research* 55 (April 1962): 339-340; A. Erlebacher, "The Evaluation of Legibility in Handwriting," in *New Horizons for Research in Handwriting,* Virgil E. Herrick, ed. (Madison: The University of Wisconsin Press, 1963), Chap. 8.
27. John R. Searles and G. Robert Carlsen, "English," *Encyclopedia of Educational Research* (New York: The Macmillan Company, 1960), p. 466.
28. R. L. Lyman, "A Co-operative Experiment in Junior High School Composition," *School Review* 39 (December 1931): 748-757.
29. Henry C. Meckel, "Research on Teaching Composition and Literature," *Handbook of Research on Teaching* (Chicago: Rand McNally, 1963), p. 986.
30. Seth A. Fessenden, "Levels of Listening—A Theory," *Education* 15 (January 1955): 288-291.

Selected Bibliography

Anderson, Dan W. "What Makes Writing Legible?" *The Elementary School Journal,* **69** 7 (April 1969): 365-369.

Brown, Carl F. "What Knowledge is of Most Worth in Language Arts?" *High School Journal,* **48** (February 1965): 340-345.

Brown, Don P. "Evaluating Student Performance in Listening." *Education,* **75** (January 1955): 316-321.

Cappa, Dan. "Kindergarten Children's Responses to Storybooks Read by Teachers." *Journal of Educational Research,* **52** (October 1958): 75.

Diederich, Paul. "How to Measure Growth in Writing Ability." *English Journal,* **55** (April 1966): 435-449.

Diederich, Paul. "The Development of a National Assessment Program in English." *Research in the Teaching of English,* **3** (Spring 1969): 5-14.

Ediger, Marlow. "Evaluation for Individualized Differences and Homework for Pupils." *Illinois Schools Journal,* **50** (Spring 1970): 45-50.

Emig, J. "Origins of Rhetoric: A Developmental View." *School Review,* **77** (September 1969): 193-198.

Fitzgerald, James A. "Evaluating Spelling Ability, Progress, and Achievement." *Education,* **77** (March 1957): 404-408.

Glaser, Robert. "Objectives and Evaluation: An Individualized System," *Science Education News.* (June 1967): 1-3.

Groebel, Lillian S. and Richard L. Larson. "Analyzing Curriculum Materials for English." *Elementary English,* **46** 3 (March 1969): 347-350.

Krutch, J.W. "If You Don't Mind My Saying So." *American Scholar,* **38** (Summer 1969): 372+.

Lehrman, S. "What is a Good Children's Book?" *The Reading Teacher,* **23** (October 1969): 9-10.

Lennon, Roger T. "What Can Be Measured?" *The Reading Teacher,* **15** (March 1962): 326-337.

Lundsteen, Sara W. "Teaching and Testing Critical Listening in the Fifth and Sixth Grades." *Elementary English,* **41** (November 1964): 743-747.

McCoy, D. "Individualized Testing Program That Works." *English Journal,* **57** (January 1968): 101-104.

McKey, Eleanor F. "Do Standardized Tests Do What They Claim to Do?" *English Journal,* **50** (December 1961): 607-611.

Norton, M. Scott. "Helping Pupils Help Themselves Through Self-Evaluation." *The Arithmetic Teacher,* **7** (April 1960): 203-204.

O'Connell, Sister Mary Patrick. "An Analysis of Methods and of Textbooks in Teaching Grammar in Elementary School English." Ph.D. dissertation, St. Louis University, 1967.

Odom, R.R. "Capitalization and Punctuation: A Diagnostic Test." *California Journal of Educational Research,* **15** (March 1964): 68-75.

Olson, Helen F. "Evaluating Growth in Language Ability." *Journal of Educational Research,* **39** (December 1945): 241-253.

Reid, Hale C. "Evaluating Five Methods of Teaching Spelling—Second and Third Grades." *Instructor,* **75** (March 1966): 77, 82.

Rudorf, E. Hugh. "Measurement of Spelling Ability." *Elementary English,* **42** **8**, (December 1965): 889-894.

Stanchfield, Jo M. "Boy's Reading Interests as Revealed Through Personal Conferences." *Reading Teacher,* **16** (September 1962): 41-44.

Strickland, Ruth G. "Evaluating Children's Composition." *Elementary English*, **37** (May 1960): 321-330.

Trow, William Clark. "On Marks, Norms, and Proficiency Scores." *Phi Delta Kappan*, **48** (December 1966): 171-173.

Witty, Paul and William Martin. "An Analysis of Children's Compositions Written in Response to a Film." *Elementary English*, **34** (March 1957): 158-163.

Young, Doris. "Evaluation of Children's Responses to Literature." *Library Quarterly*, **37** (January 1967): 100-109.

Index